State/Culture

A volume in the Series

THE WILDER HOUSE SERIES IN POLITICS, HISTORY, AND CULTURE

edited by David Laitin
George Steinmetz

A full list of titles in the series appears at the end of the book.

David Laitin and George Steinmetz, Editors

STATE /CULTURE

State-Formation after the Cultural Turn

Edited by GEORGE STEINMETZ

Cornell University Press   ITHACA AND LONDON

First published 1999 by Cornell University Press
First printing, Cornell Paperbacks, 1999

Printed in the United States of America

Library of Congress Cataloging-in-Publication Data

State/Culture : state-formation after the cultural turn /
  George Steinmetz, editor.
      p.   cm.
    Includes index.
    ISBN 0-8014-8533-9 (pbk. : alk. paper)
    ISBN 0-8014-3673-7 (cloth : alk. paper)—
    1. Nationalism. 2. History, Modern. 3. State, The. 4. Culture.
  5. Ethnicity. 6. Multiculturalism. I. Steinmetz, George, 1957–.
D217.S83 1999   98-30462
306—dc21

Cornell University Press strives to use environmentally responsible
suppliers and materials to the fullest extent possible in the publishing of
its books. Such materials include vegetable-based, low-VOC inks and
acid-free papers that are recycled, totally chlorine-free, or partly
composed of nonwood fibers.

Cloth printing   10 9 8 7 6 5 4 3 2 1

Paperback printing   10 9 8 7 6 5 4 3 2 1

Contents

Contributors

JULIA ADAMS is Associate Professor of Sociology at the University of Michigan, Ann Arbor.

ANDREW APTER is Associate Professor of Anthropology at the University of Chicago.

MABEL BEREZIN is Visiting Associate Professor of Sociology at the University of California, Los Angeles.

PIERRE BOURDIEU is Professor of Sociology at the Collège de France.

PHILIP S. GORSKI is Assistant Professor of Sociology at the University of Wisconsin, Madison.

BOB JESSOP is Professor of Sociology at Lancaster University.

DAVID D. LAITIN is William R. Kenan Jr. Professor of Political Science and Director of the Center for the Study of Politics, History, and Culture at the University of Chicago.

JOHN W. MEYER is Professor of Sociology at Stanford University.

TIMOTHY MITCHELL is Professor of Politics at New York University.

ANN SHOLA ORLOFF is Associate Professor of Sociology at Northwestern University.

STEVEN PINCUS is Assistant Professor of History at the University of Chicago.

NADER SOHRABI is Assistant Professor of Sociology at the University of Iowa.

GEORGE STEINMETZ is Associate Professor of Sociology and German Studies at the University of Michigan, Ann Arbor.

CHARLES TILLY is Joseph L. Buttenweiser Professor of Social Science at Columbia University.

Preface

This book grew out of my ten-year involvement with the community of scholars and students associated with the Center for the Study of Politics, History, and Culture at the University of Chicago and with the series in Politics, History, and Culture. When David Laitin, Leora Auslander, and I wrote the "manifesto" for the Wilder House series in 1989, we pointed to three broad themes as the focus for the future series. It soon became clear that one of these themes, concerning state-formation in relation to cultural systems and processes, was generating the most exciting discussions and the largest number of submissions to the series. A number of scholars working in the state-culture area visited the center in subsequent years, and some ended up publishing their books in the series. These cultural studies of state-formation differ in important ways from the state-centered and structural Marxist perspectives that dominated the field until the end of the 1980s. At the same time, there are significant differences among these cultural approaches to the state. Thus, in addition to showcasing the various sorts of work in this area, and the work promoted by the Politics, History, and Culture project, one of the motivations behind the publication of *State/Culture* was to permit a comparison among the differing perspectives on the culture/state nexus in present-day scholarship.

The conjoining of the terms *state* and *culture* in the title is meant to signal their reciprocal influence and constitution and to break with earlier imageries in which culture was either shaped by state or ignored altogether. It is not indicative of a shared theoretical perspective on the question of state-culture relations, however.

Nor does the present collection exhaust the entire array of theoretical perspectives or empirical focuses that might fall under such a rubric. I decided to emphasize studies of modern Western states and non-Western states that were influenced or directly created by the modern West. Since cultural dynamics have more often been granted importance in interpretations of premodern states, both European and non-Western, it seemed reasonable to exclude these from the collection. Nonetheless, two categories of states on the boundary of this universe are included: early modern European states and non-Western states in the throes of forced or self-induced westernization.

State/Culture also is dominated by social scientists, especially sociologists and political scientists. Scholars mainly associated with departments of literature and cultural studies are absent here, even though some of the most original work on politics and state is now coming from these quarters. But those who study the state have until recently been found primarily in disciplines and subdisciplines where culture (in the anthropological sense) was not taken very seriously as a causal factor or as an object of theoretical reflection. *State/Culture* is intended first of all as an intervention into these latter communities.

In addition to being associated in various ways with the Cornell University Press series in Politics, History, and Culture over the past decade, many of the authors included here attended a miniconference sponsored by the Wilder House at the University of Chicago in September 1995, during which early versions of these papers were discussed. All of the authors provided precious feedback on the overall project. Jean Anderson of the Wilder House provided invaluable assistance with the organization of the conference and with the book manuscript at various stages. I would also like to thank Pat Preston of the Center for Research on Social Organization at the University of Michigan for her extraordinary contribution to the proofreading and indexing of the book. Roger Haydon of Cornell University Press saw the book through from its infancy. Bill Sewell Jr. and Andrew Apter provided crucial encouragement. My coeditor in the Wilder House series, David Laitin, played a significant role in more ways than I can begin to enumerate, from the earliest discussions of the topic of state-culture relations and the initial conceptualization of the book through the 1995 conference and beyond. Above all, I am grateful to Julia Hell for her support throughout the development of this volume. This book is dedicated to her.

GEORGE STEINMETZ

Ann Arbor, Michigan

State/Culture

Introduction: Culture and the State

George Steinmetz

> Mass ritual was not a device to shore up the state, but rather the state . . . was a device for the enactment of mass ritual. Power served pomp, not pomp power.
>
> —CLIFFORD GEERTZ, *Negara*, P. 13

> A state exists chiefly in the hearts and minds of its people; if they do not believe it is there, no logical exercise will bring it to life."
>
> —JOSEPH STRAYER, *On the Medieval Origins of the Modern State*, P. 5

This book examines processes of state formation in light of the ongoing "cultural turn" in the social sciences.[1] The cultural turn encompasses a wide array of new theoretical impulses coming from fields formerly peripheral to the social sciences, as well as submerged traditions within the social sciences themselves.[2]

I want to thank the participants in the 1995 conference for helping me think through the issues raised in this introduction, with special thanks to Bill Sewell Jr. and David Laitin. In addition to commenting generously on this chapter in several settings, both have contributed signally to promoting the cultural turn in U.S. social science. Others who commented on this chapter include Julia Adams, Peggy Somers, Lisa Wedeen, Gary Herrigel, the Wilder House editors and graduate student interns, and the contributors to this book.

[1] The term *social sciences* as I use it here refers not to any analytically or normatively defined unity but simply to the assemblage of existing disciplines clustered into university divisions, arranged together under the purview of specific funding agencies, and also defined by the sharing of certain discursive regularities (including self-understandings). Although my comments implicitly take the academic field of the United States as their main point of reference, many statements apply to other sociolinguistic academic worlds as well. My use of the term *human sciences* signals a more normative understanding—one in which, inter alia, the distance between the humanities and the social sciences recedes.

[2] The former include poststructuralism, narrative theory, and other forms of textual analysis. Submerged social science traditions that have been rediscovered include constructivist epistemology, the sociology of knowledge, and psychoanalytic cultural theory (see Berger and Luckmann 1966; Žižek

Long-standing barriers against the humanities or *Geisteswissenschaften* in the social sciences are eroding. This cultural turn has disrupted entrenched ways of thinking about familiar objects of social research by emphasizing the causal and socially constitutive role of cultural processes and systems of signification.

What exactly do we mean by the cultural turn? It is a more recent phenomenon than the "linguistic turn" in Anglo-American philosophy (Rorty 1967) and is not limited to linguistic approaches. This cultural turn is also more general than the poststructuralist movement of recent decades. Rather than argue for a specific theory of meaning and interpretation, the cultural turn in the social sciences involves a more general assertion of the constitutive role of culture. It is directed against still-powerful social-science paradigms that present meaning and subjectivity as epiphenomenal or causally unimportant. The main divisions within the social sciences revolve increasingly around methodological, epistemological, or ontological issues. "Objectivism" of various stripes is arrayed against perspectives that view human practice as inextricably cultural, as an entanglement of a material "substrate" and its meaning (Taylor 1979: 33; Wittgenstein 1953; Weber 1978: 4–24). Objectivist approaches within the human sciences do not necessarily ignore cultural phenomena, but they treat culture as ultimately determined by material or noncultural factors that are considered more basic. Objectivism in the human sciences also refers by extension to theoretical approaches that project a homogeneous form of human subjectivity across time and place. Within the context of these prevailing conceptual divisions, all theorists who insist on culture's socially constitutive role, who reject assumptions of cultural homogeneity as an analytical starting point,[3] can be seen as part of a common "culturalist" project, regardless of whether they conceptualize culture in linguistic, poststructuralist, psychoanalytic, or hermeneutic terms. From the standpoint of a social-scientific universe still dominated by empiricism and the materialism of "brute facts," the differences between structuralist discourse analysis, *verstehende Soziologie*, and theorists such as Bourdieu, Foucault, Gramsci, and Geertz seem less significant than their similarities.

A more difficult issue involves the relationship between this development in the social sciences and the burgeoning field of "cultural studies." Contemporary cultural studies operates as much within the humanities as the social sciences, even if its professed goal is to break down that disciplinary distinction (see Hall 1994; Grossberg, Nelson, and Treichler 1992; During 1993; Dirks, Eley, and Ortner 1994). Within the humanities, cultural studies stands opposed to deconstruction and a literature-centered curriculum (Berman 1995; Bahti 1997). Yet when these debates are remapped onto the terrain of the social sciences, cultural studies and its deconstructionist opponents end up on the same side of the more

---

1989, 1991). On impulses from the humanities in the social sciences, see Sewell (1992) and other essays in that journal issue; on poststructuralism in sociology, see Lash (1990).

[3] This is not to say that culturalists may not theorize tendencies toward cultural homogenization, perhaps as a result of the growth of the mass media and standardized commodities. But homogenization is an outcome here, not an a priori starting point.

central division between objectivism and culturalism. In this sense it is accurate to describe the cultural turn as more or less synonymous with cultural studies within the field of the social sciences.

Culturalist perspectives are unequally represented across the various social-science disciplines and areas. Cultural theories have made deep inroads into fields such as the sociology of sexuality, gender, popular culture, and social movements and the social and historical study of science.[4] Yet the study of the state has remained relatively aloof from these discussions. If culture has been considered in this context, it has typically been viewed as a product of the state, whereas the strands of causality running from culture to the state have been ignored, marginalized, or declared illegitimate objects of investigation. States might create "concepts" but they were not themselves "concept-dependent" entities (Bhaskar 1979, 1986). Where mainstream social science has allowed culture to play a significant role in the constitution of the state, it has been in the watered-down guise of quantitatively measured "values" (MacIntyre [1967] 1978; Taylor 1979) or as an essentialized national culture. The problems with these approaches are discussed below.

A partial erosion of the barriers to cultural theories and processes is nevertheless visible even in the field of state studies.[5] But until now, research on the culture/state nexus has been scattered across different disciplines and discursive communities. This book brings together some of the pioneers and innovators in this multidisciplinary project. Because the cultural study of the state is still relatively underdeveloped, this book does not focus on a particular theoretical perspective but instead juxtaposes divergent theoretical and methodological approaches in an effort to map the contours of debate. Some of the writers represented in this collection make powerful claims for the shaping of states by culture, whereas others emphasize causal flows running in both directions— and some reject the analytical distinction between culture and nonculture altogether. Some emphasize linguistically mediated culture, and others focus on nonlinguistic forms of subjectivity. Some analyze culture in structuralist terms; others deconstruct the categories and meanings of the state. What all the contributions share is a willingness to take culture seriously, to view it as more than simply a "dependent variable" or product of supposedly more fundamental, acultural phenomena.

[4] On sexuality, see Butler (1993) and Sedgwick (1993); on gender, see Scott (1988); on popular culture, see During (1993); on class formation, see Sewell (1992) and the essays in that issue; on social movements, see Snow and Benford (1988); on science, see Latour (1987).

[5] This essay and volume are more concerned with the effects of this partial erosion than with its causes. The forms of resistance to culture, meaning, and interpretation vary across social-science disciplines and objects of study. In the leftish field of the sociology of social movements, for example, the turn *away* from culture in the 1970s toward a more utilitarian and materialist approach was presented as a rejection of attributions of irrationality to social movements by an earlier generation of theorists. In more conservative fields such as economics or international relations the resistance took a different form, in which culture itself has been associated with leftism. A presenter at a University of Chicago economics seminar in the late 1980s who mentioned the word *culture* provoked a Nobel-prize winning economist to ask his neighbor whether the presenter was a "Marxist" (this story was reported to me by the economist's interlocutor).

Before discussing the relationship between states and culture we need to clarify these two terms, and this is the principal aim of the first two sections of this introduction. The first section, Culture, attempts to delimit the term *culture* while retaining enough openness to accommodate the diverse theoretical perspectives represented in this volume. The second section, The State/State Formation, proposes a working definition of *the state* and also asks whether the state should continue to occupy a privileged position in social analysis during an era that has seen both theoretical challenges to its primacy (Foucault) and practical attacks on its sovereignty (due to economic globalization).

The third section, Culture/State Relations in Earlier Social Theory, reconstructs some of the ways in which culture and the state have been articulated, conceptually and causally, within classical and contemporary theory. Here we find that interest in the cultural underpinnings of states tends to decline as we approach Western modernity and increases as we move away from the West and backwards in time. Classical social theory—including Max Weber's—rarely understood culture as a central determinant or constitutive element of the modern Western state. At the limit, culture was a *product* of the state. Theoretical approaches dominant within more recent discussions of the state—particularly the neo-Marxist and neo-Weberian perspectives—have also tended to marginalize culture or to restrict its purview. This section concludes that cultural themes have emerged *symptomatically* in these recent debates without being discussed explicitly.

Foundationalist Decontextualization in the Study of the State, the fourth section, specifies in greater theoretical detail the differences between contemporary cultural analyses of the state and culturally decontextualized approaches. The most familiar sort of decontextualized social science, rational-choice theory, starts from an assumption of human subjectivity as a universal rational form. Surprisingly, some ostensibly cultural approaches are also decontextualized, though in a different manner, treating culture itself as a foundational essence. Here the argument that cultural factors have typically been granted central importance only in the interpretation of premodern and non-Western states is developed further. Next, Culture as Symptom develops the argument from Culture/State Relations that cultural themes have emerged symptomatically in recent state debates, giving examples of the ways in which discussions of specific states or state forms have reached a theoretical standstill due to the failure to thematize cultural factors explicitly. The Theoretical Terrain of Culture/State Relations maps out the main lines of variation among the culturalist approaches to the state represented in the volume, and the final section provides an overview of the essays in the volume.

Culture

Culture, according to Raymond Williams's celebrated essay, is "one of the two or three most complicated words in the English language" (1983: 87). Kroeber and Kluckhohn's (1952) historical overview of the shifting meanings of the word *culture/Kultur* in German, French, and English estimated that there were more than 160 definitions in use (Brownstein 1995: 313). Cutting through this semantic profusion, Williams identified four main strands during the modern era (1983: 90). The first refers to the "intellectual, spiritual and aesthetic development" of the individual and is derived by metaphor from earlier definitions concerning the cultivation of the land, crops, and animals (Williams 1977: 11). A second, Enlightenment, usage indicates a "general process of social development" or "culture as a universal process"; this usage is close to modern definitions of "civilization" (Bocock 1996: 153). In the third, more recent, definition culture denotes the objects of artistic production (Williams 1983: 90; also Williams 1977: 14).

The fourth sense of culture discussed by Williams, and the one that is closest to the purposes of this volume, emerges from modern anthropological and sociological thought. It begins within late-eighteenth-century German philosophy of history as a view of cultures as *plural*, against the Enlightenment view of a Universal History culminating in a unified civilized state (Williams 1977: 17). As Kroeber and Kluckhohn note (1952: 286), the use of "culture" by Herder and other eighteenth-century German writers such as Adelung has a "modern ring"—even as it continues to draw on the older connotations: "their approach was historical, pluralistic, relativistic, and yet aiming to cover the totality of the known world of custom and ideology." Herder opposes the use of "European culture as a universal standard of human values," insisting that "the culture of *man* is not the culture of the *European*; it manifests itself according to time and place in *every* people."[6] Culture in Herder's view included not just artistic achievements but also language, education, clothing, forms of governance, and general customs (*"die unbestimmte Lebensart"*; quoted in Kroeber and Kluckhohn 1952: 40).

Most commentators trace the more proximate origin of the contemporary anthropological understanding of culture to Tylor's 1877 definition of "Culture or Civilization, taken in its wide enthnographic sense, [as] that complex whole which includes knowledge, belief, art, morals, law, custom, and any other capabilities and habits acquired by man as a member of society" (1).[7] This definition was reproduced in anthropology texts for decades (for example, Lowie 1947: 3). Even Parsons, who insisted on a separation of cultural and social systems, retained Tylor's emphasis on culture as a unified totality which is "transmitted, learned, and shared" (1951: 15); in some of Parsons' writing, culture also included "the artifacts produced" (Kroeber and Parsons 1958: 583). Levi-Strauss led many postwar anthropological theorists to adopt structural linguistics in order to specify the ways in which culture's symbolic matter was created, organized, and transformed. Culture consisted of integrated systems of symbols articulated in artifacts and in public, social practices. These symbolic practices had to be inter-

---

[6] Herder also writes that "The picture of nations (*Völker*) has infinite shades, changing with place and time. But as in all pictures, everthing depends on the point of view or perspective from which we examine it" (first quote, in the text, from *Ideas on the Philosophy of the History of Mankind* [1784–1791], second from *Letters for the Advancement of Mankind* [1793–1797], both in Barnard [1969: 24]).

[7] On the German roots of the modern use of culture, see Elias 1994 [1939].

preted in relationship to more general codes on which they drew and which they helped to reproduce and transform (Geertz 1973a).

More recent versions of this fourth "socioanthropological" strand have seen further shifts in accent. According to Stuart Hall, culture encompasses "*both* the meanings and values which arise amongst distinctive social groups and classes . . . [*and*] the lived traditions and practices through which those 'understandings' are expressed and in which they are embodied" (Hall 1994: 527). Hall's emphasis on "distinctive social groups and classes" signals an important break with earlier views of culture as an integrated whole. Recent approaches to the analysis of symbolic meaning have expanded the older Herderian emphasis on the plurality of cultures, finding such diversity not just *between* one society and the next but also *within* supposedly unified *Völker*. Social units in traditional cultural theory were delimited along geographic lines in a quasinaturalistic fashion, as nation-states, nations, or tribes, and cultural unity was assumed to prevail *within* each spatial unit. Today, by contrast, cultures are seen as divided along lines of class, race, ethnicity, gender, sexuality, age, and so on. Debate concerns the relationship among these multiple cultural systems and with the overarching common culture (if the latter is even assumed to exist; see Laitin 1988). Continuing this line of thought to its logical conclusion, poststructuralists have argued that one should not expect to find stabilized semiotic systems even within these narrower social groups. Any stabilization of meaning is contested, temporary, and contingent (Laclau and Mouffe 1985). Culture here loses any semblance of structural systematicity.

Two other important changes in the anthropological understanding of culture during the past half century have been signalled by Dirks, Eley and Ortner (1994: 3). One has involved increased attention to the ways in which power, inequality, conflict, and systemic logics of domination shape symbolic systems. This theme arose during the first half of the twentieth century in the writing of Marxists such as Lukács (1971), Gramsci (1971), Benjamin (1969), Volosinov (1985), and Horkheimer and Adorno ([1944] 1972) and was carried forward in the postwar period by theorists of "ideology" (see especially Althusser 1971a; Macherey 1978; Barthes [1957] 1972) and by the British school of cultural studies (During 1993). More recently, Pierre Bourdieu (1977, 1984) has detailed the ways in which cultural classification schemes, including apparently disinterested categories of aesthetic judgement, serve to mask and to reproduce inequality. Post-Kuhnian theorists of science have made similar arguments concerning the permeation of scientific discourse by structures of power and conflict (Kuhn [1962] 1970; Bourdieu 1988; Foucault 1970; Latour 1987; Woolgar 1988). Finally, there has been increased attention to fundamental historical transformations of culture—a possibility that was ignored or marginalized in the Herderian "national culture" literature and structuralist worldview (see Sahlins 1981). Increased attention to the historicity of culture was stimulated in different ways by Marxist literature (in addition to the authors cited above, see Thompson 1993 and Postone 1993) and by the writings of Foucault (especially 1970, 1972, 1979).

How do these contemporary views of culture relate to the more substantive arguments about "culturalism"? It is not apparent at first glance that the updated socioanthropological definition takes any stand at all on the question of culture's causal or constitutive role. The definition of culture as "systems of meaning and the practices in which they are embedded" is perfectly compatible with a view of these "meaning systems" as derivative of more fundamental practices or material forces—as in some of the Marxist versions. This definition of culture *does* support the other main tenet of culturalism, however: its opposition to assumptions of universal, equivalent subjectivity (the view that, at bottom, people are all the same).

Many twentieth-century sociologists and anthropologists have rejected the term culture altogether on account of its vagueness and polysemy.[8] Some favor concepts such as ideology, discourse, hegemony, meaning, interpretation, subjectivity, identity, and the unconscious, yet these are no less multivocal.[9] *Culture* seems best able to capture the epistemological, methodological, and substantive distance of these approaches from the hard materialism and cultural homogenization of objectivistic social sciences. Indeed, rejection of the term *culture* itself is sometimes coupled with a strong "naturalist" epistemology, which assimilates the social sciences to the natural sciences. The term *culture* will continue to provoke disagreement as long as basic issues such as the autonomy of the human sciences remain contested.

The field of social theories encompassed by the cultural turn is thus broad, but not impossibly so. They are distinct from much of what is commonly referred to as "cultural sociology" to the extent that the latter explains culture in terms of

[8] The cultural turn in the social sciences should not, of course, be defined by the specific employment of the word *culture*. More important is an understanding of systems of signification and subjectivity as importantly constitutive of social reality. As we will see later, there are at least three widespread uses of the term *culture* within social science studies of the state that do not seem to conform to this definition. Social theory is often forced to rely on semiotically overloaded terms such as *culture* whose meaning is overdetermined by changing historical usage, struggles among discourse communities, and simultaneous existence within lay and academic communities. Anthropologists are most aware of the theoretical pitfalls of the term *culture*, especially *cultural essentialism*, and some have urged me to drop the term altogether. Yet I see no alternative to *culture* as a portmanteau word for the diverse conceptual languages employed in this pandisciplinary discussion.

[9] This is not the place to provide a history of these different terms. For the development of the concept of *ideology*, the reader is referred to Eagleton (1991), McLellan (1995), Larrain (1979), Žižek (1989), and Laclau (1997); on *discourse*, see Thompson (1984), Foucault (1972), Laclau and Mouffe (1985), van Dijk (1985), and Volosinov (1985); on the *culture* concept in anthropology, see Geertz (1973b) and Kroeber and Kluckhohn (1952); on *political culture*, see Almond and Verba (1963, 1980) and Somers (1995); on *subjectivity* and *identity* see Taylor (1989) and Calhoun (1994). Bourdieu's terminological system includes the concepts of doxa/heterodoxy/orthododoxy and cultural capital; when Bourdieu uses *culture* unmodified it usually corresponds to Williams' third semantic field. On *cultural capital*, see Bourdieu (1984, 1986). The psychoanalytic literature on subjectivity and the unconscious is too enormous even to begin referencing, but see Lefort (1986), Žižek (1989, 1991), and Hell (1997) for the relationship to the state. See the essays by Adams and Orloff below for alternative disentanglements of these terms; other efforts to systematize these concepts can be found in Comaroff and Comaroff (1991) and Bourdieu (1977). Some of these terms and vocabularies are mutually incompatible. Poststructuralist theory, for instance, usually rejects "the deep psychological self of the Freudians" (as implied by the "unconscious") in favor of a "culturally mediated . . . self which finds itself in a continuously changing world of meaning" (Rabinow 1977: 6). The theoretical and terminological openness of this volume is justified not only by the objectivism of mainstream social science but also by the unsettled nature of cultural theory itself.

the noncultural or focuses on cultural objects more narrowly (in Williams's third sense of "culture"), rather than analyzing ostensibly noncultural practices in cultural terms. And they also differ from "political culture" models (discussed below) in which culture is allowed to have autonomous effects, but only at the cost of defining it narrowly as values or preferences. But this still leaves room for enormous variation in the exact definition and explanation of culture. The organizing premise of this book retains this terminological and theoretical openness to provide a space for comparing across the alternative culturalist approaches.

The State/State-Formation

Before we begin exploring the relationship between cultural theory and state formation, we also need a general working definition of *the state*. In an influential recent statement, Charles Tilly has defined states as "*coercion* wielding *organizations* that are distinct from households and kinship groups and exercise *clear priority* in some respects over all other organizations within substantial *territories*." Note that this definition includes city-states and does not insist (in contrast to Weber, for instance) on a complete *monopoly* of coercion.[10] This is a baseline definition to which many social scientists would assent.

Does culture come into the definition of the state, or only into theories of state formation? In his contribution to this book, Tilly notes that his definition incorporates "culture—seen as shared understandings and their representations—at each step along the way." Going even further, Timothy Mitchell (1991, this volume) argues that a cultural "state effect"—a perceived distinction between state and society—is produced through various symbolic and ideological techniques. This cultural effect is no less part of the phenomenon "state" than the organizations and agents controlling coercion and exercising jurisdiction within a given territory.[11] A maximal definition of *the state* would thus include not just the reference to "*coercion* wielding *organizations*," but also the claim that the distinctness of the state and its priority over other entities is the result of cultural techniques.

What then is meant by *state formation*? The study of state-formation is inherently historical, because it focuses on the creation of durable states and the transformations of basic structural features of these states.[12] Sometimes

[10] The emphasis on the territorial dimension of states distinguishes them from firms, MNCs, and lineage groups, for example, with their larger, smaller, or more diffuse territorial reach. The focus on the state as coercion-wielding organization distinguishes it from economic power.

[11] Note that including Mitchell's state effect in the definition of the state need not require a reintroduction to the definition of the problematic Weberian criterion of *legitimacy*. Mitchell's argument also helps to clarify why, as Tilly suggests, "kinship groups" should be considered distinct from states (even if they are sometimes coercion-wielding organizations exercising clear priority over other organizations within substantial territories): kinship groups do not necessarily strive to create a sense of their distinctness from society.

[12] Note that "structural features" are defined here to included patterned material practices as well as the intersubjective understandings in which they are embedded.

state-formation is understood as a mythic initial moment in which centralized, coercion-wielding, hegemonic organizations are created within a given territory. All activities that follow this original era are then described as "policymaking" rather than "state-formation." But states are never "formed" once and for all. It is more fruitful to view state-formation as an ongoing process of structural change and not as a one-time event. Structural features of states involve the entire set of rules and institutions that are involved in making and implementing policies: the arrangement of ministries or departments, the set of rules for the allocation of individual positions within these departments, systems for generating revenues, legal codes and constitutions, electoral rules, forms of control over lower bodies of government, the nature and location of boundaries between state and society, and so forth.[13] This suggests that the commonplace contrast between *state-formation* and *policymaking* is often more a matter of "cross-sectional" versus "longitudinal" studies than of a well-grounded distinction between theoretical objects. It is more accurate to say that "policies" that affect the very structure of the state are part of the ongoing process of state-formation. A structure-changing policy is one that alters the state in a way that systematically affects the production of subsequent policies; a structure-reproducing policy expresses and affirms the existing state form. If a state drafts new cohorts of soldiers on an annual basis, for example, each act of conscription does not necessarily represent an episode in the process of state formation; but a shift from the use of conscription to mercenaries or a significant broadening of the social groups that are subject to conscription would be more likely candidates for inclusion.[14] Defined in these terms, all the essays in this book are concerned with dimensions of state-formation.

Before turning to the specific issues at stake in this book, we must respond briefly to two challenges to the basic legitimacy of the study of the state. Following the resurgence of state theory and the state concept in the 1960s and 1970s, various theorists began to raise new challenges to the emphasis on the state in the analysis of modern power. Many heeded Foucault's dictum that power is widely dispersed throughout capillary networks and not "localised in the State apparatus."[15] Writers such as Rose and Miller (1992) and Dean (1994a, 1994b)

---

[13] A more difficult distinction is between an understanding of state-formation in terms of shifts from one major state "form" to the next, as opposed to a more gradual and multilayered process without any clear dividing lines. Many analysts of state-formation focus on key transitions, such as the emergence of the absolutist state or the Keynesian welfare state. Those who focus on less dramatic structural changes are often skeptical of all-encompassing conceptual distinctions between state types.

[14] In practice, of course, it is often exceedingly difficult to distinguish between structure-transforming and structure-reproducing policies. Moreover, one of the only ways of even identifying state "structures" is to study policy formation and implementation. On structure-reproducing versus structure-transforming practices, see Bhaskar (1979); also Giddens (1979).

[15] Foucault, (1980a: 60). Elsewhere Foucault claimed that "we should direct our researches on the nature of power not towards the juridical edifice of sovereignty, the State apparatuses and the ideologies which accompany them, but towards domination and the material operators of power, towards forms of subjection and the inflections and utilisations of their localised systems, and towards strategic apparatuses." Foucault (1980b: 102). See also Deleuze and Guattari (1986).

criticize state theory for underestimating the decentralized and molecular nature of power. In this respect contemporary (post-Foucauldian) theoretical approaches join forces with older systems theory, which has consistently rejected an emphasis on the state (Easton 1953). According to Luhmann (1989: 88), "there is little sense in attributing a special social position to the political system, [something] like a leading role. . . ." Luhmann describes the political system in contemporary, differentiated societies as just one among many "function systems" with no privileges of command or knowledge over the other systems. The notion of an "apex" of power "made sense in the context of stratified differentiation," writes Luhmann, but "these [premodern] conditions . . . have changed" (85).[16] Many network theorists visualize power as a web of shifting ties among a changing set of actors, which leads them to reject the concept of the state as overly unitary (Laumann and Knoke 1987).[17]

A second challenge to state theory focuses not on the entire modern era but on the period since the 1970s. Here the argument is that states are declining in power due to economic globalization, neoliberal hegemony, and the increasing importance of deterritorialized political spaces (see Omae 1990, 1995; Sassen 1996; Ruggie 1993; Brenner 1997). The putative decline of the nation-state is driven and accompanied by systematic "debordering": "the network of systematic and spontaneous trans-border phenomena extending over the system of states has become much denser, and the domain in which the . . . territorial state . . . can still function as itself has become ever smaller" (Brock and Albert 1995: 3; see also Kratochwil 1986). The literature on globalization and post-Fordism suggests that the nation-state is simultaneously too small and too weak to control the increasingly transnational flows of capital, and too large and centralized to coordinate the transition to more flexible forms of production and regulation. The overall result is that nation-states are being downsized, decentralized, or "hollowed out" (Jessop 1994, this volume). Many of the central state's erstwhile functions are being assumed by transnational and nongovernmental organizations (Campbell, Hollingsworth, and Lindberg 1991) or by local and regional governments, or else they are simply lost, as in the dismantling of Keynesian welfare states (Teeple 1995). Nonstate institutions assume the regulation of such diverse areas as law, punishment, education, religion, spatial planning, "welfare," and warmaking. Thatcherism is only the most obvious example of this evisceration of the central state, and similar trends can be seen through-

---

[16] Luhmann is nonetheless in many ways less historical than Foucault. Luhmann's theory equates structural differentiation with modernization, and therefore can understand the reemergence of centralized states only as historical regression. State socialism, for instance, is seen as an example of structural de-differentiation.

[17] One perplexed network theorist even asked me what a course on the "state" and "state theory" might concern. This suspicion of the state concept is clearly justified; as many state theorists, Marxists and poststructuralists alike, have noted, the state-society boundary is traversed by numerous strands of power. Yet what both the Marxists (see the "state derivation" debate of the 1970s; Holloway and Picciotto 1978) and the cultural state theorists (see Mitchell 1991; Abrams 1988; Coronil 1997) recognize is that while the state-society is in some sense fictional, it is nonetheless a very powerful fiction that concentrates certain kinds of power on the "state" side of the equation.

out Western Europe and North America. Even more dramatic is the disappearance or decline in relative importance of socialist states in Eastern Europe and East Asia—states that only a decade ago controlled most of the property and information within their respective territories. Various African states have lost any semblance of a "monopoly of violence" within their borders. A global wave of democratization, from South Korea to Latin America, is also said to have reduced the state's earlier preeminence.

Current perceptions of state decline are also driven by the shifting tides of political culture, especially the increasing hegemony of neoliberalism. American political science in the 1950s had already insisted that the state was a pre-scientific continental European "myth" (see Nettl 1968; Almond 1988). In the context of the Vietnam War, oppositional social movements, and the expansion of the welfare state during the 1960s and early 1970s, the idea of the state was revived in mainstream political culture as well as academic discourse.[18] In a striking reversal of intellectual fashions since the 1980s, academic arguments against the state gained ground again, as antistatism came to dominate mainstream political discourse.[19] The net result of these intellectual and political changes is that reference to "the state" has once again become somewhat suspect in mainstream social science, and anyone writing on it is obligated to defend the topic's legitimacy.[20]

Even if the present-day state has lost some of its erstwhile importance, it can hardly be said to be "withering away." The state may have relinquished some of its earlier capacity to control the movement of capital across its own borders, but it is still the key actor in a number of arenas, including the definition of access to citizenship and its benefits, the control and production of violence, and the metacoordination of the diverse nongovernmental institutions involved in "governance." The strong version of the globalization thesis is also too pessimistic about states' ability to control the movements of capital, confusing a failure of political will with a loss of structural capacity.[21] The state still has crucial advantages over other actors in the effort to construct hegemonic identities and to unify the centripetal identifications within any given territory along nationalist lines. Some contemporary theories allow that the state *may* come to occupy a

[18] By the same token, it is no coincidence that much radical right-wing antistate discourse in the United States today is associated with a militarized mercenary and vigilante culture that can be traced to the Vietnam War. American radical right-wing discourse attributes much more solidity to the central state than does mainstream political folk culture.

[19] Skocpol (1996) traces the rise of pervasive antistatism with respect to the Clinton Health Security bill. Social-democratic parties in Europe have also adopted antistatist rhetoric and monetarist policies (see Kitschelt 1994). See also Rouban (1988: 325), who argues that "the end of the welfare state is also the end of the classical model of political science . . . . [and] undermines the symbolism of the state's . . . power."

[20] The concept of the state was always comparatively weak in the United States anyway, as noted by writers like Badie and Birnbaum (1983). Holloway suggests that this is less true of British political theory, where even today "the state, as a category, is simply assumed" (1994: 52). Perhaps the eagerness of British Foucauldians to denounce the state concept actually confirms this judgment.

[21] See Pierre Bourdieu, interviewed in *Der Spiegel* (1996); Hirst and Thompson (1996); Greider (1996).

central position among various sites of social power, even if this is not a foregone conclusion. In *The Sources of Social Power*, Michael Mann suggests that the state may "crystallize as the center . . . of a number of power networks" (1993: 75). Pierre Bourdieu (this volume) argues that the state is the "culmination of a process of concentration of different species of capital," a process that "constitutes the state as the holder of a sort of metacapital." Foucault himself conceded that the state retained a special status even after the "disciplinary" revolution of the nineteenth century, although some of his followers fail to recognize this.[22] Finally, a deeper historical perspective on the long waves of state expansion and contraction across the centuries should caution us against rashly declaiming "the end of history" and consigning states to the historical waste heap.[23]

Although the more sweeping arguments for the state's irrelevance can be rejected, this book does not attempt to "reinstate" the state or to put it back on the pedestal it has occupied in some of the macrosociological literature. Indeed, one recurrent argument in many of the essays collected here is that states are not "autonomous" from extrastate cultural forces, but are shot through with circuits of meaning that cut across the state-society frontier. Nonetheless, these essays grant the state a central place within complex sociocultural formations and within contemporary social theory.

Culture/State Relations in Earlier Social Theory: Some False Leads

Culture has hardly been ignored in social-scientific writing on the state, but the ways in which culture/state relations have been conceptualized have been quite problematic.[24] This section criticizes three widespread but flawed approaches to this topic. First are various theoretical approaches that deal with culture not as a significant *determinant* of the state but rather as a sort of "dependent variable" or *effect* of the state. Second, where cultural influences on the state *are* acknowledged, they are often framed in restrictive terms as the formally elaborated ideas of academics and other expert elites or as the more generalized features of so-called political culture. Finally, even where culture has been conceptualized more broadly and been allowed to play a central explanatory role, it has been understood in *foundationalist* terms as a universal homogeneous rationality or as timeless national essence.

Social scientists have tended to explain the form and activities of the state with reference to instrumentally rational calculations, such as the official calculus of

[22] See especially Foucault (1980c: 167–168; 1979: 213ff.) and the discussion below.

[23] According to Lefort (1986), even the limit case of state expansion, "totalitarianism," cannot be assumed to be a thing of the past; totalitarian possibilities may even be built into the very structure of liberal democracy.

[24] I have deliberately chosen the formulation "culture/state" rather than "culture and the state" to emphasize the openness of the investigation, an unwillingness to privilege a priori one of the terms in the pair, and also to suggest the interpenetration of the two categories. For this reason I have also consciously varied the order of the two terms.

dominant class interests, party politics, or international security. But they have downplayed the role of what Weber called "substantive rationality," of cultural systems such as nationalism and religion. Tendencies to focus on the more instrumental wellsprings of politics have been further strengthened by the recent expansion of "rational-choice" theory in the social sciences. This latter development, which represents almost a mirror image of the cultural turn, has been especially strong in political science, where research on the state has long been centered.[25]

Theoretical debates on state-formation in recent decades have been dominated by Marxist/neo-Marxist and Weberian/neo-Weberian perspectives.[26] Culture has not been ignored by either of these perspectives but neither has it been analyzed adequately. For Marxists and neo-Marxists, culture has figured primarily as an effect of the state and/or economic forces, and not as a major determinant in its own right. For Weber, cultural factors play a central role in the analysis of non-Western and premodern states but a vastly reduced role in the interpretation of modern Western states. The neo-Weberian "state-centered" perspective, like Marxism, has tended to treat cultural factors as effects of the state or has permitted culture to influence state-formation only in the limited guise of formally organized systems of "ideas."[27]

Marxism and Neo-Marxism: The State's Impact on Culture

The relationship between culture and the state varies in Marx's writings according to the level of abstraction governing a particular analysis. The state emerges in Marx's earlier, neo-Hegelian writing as a key instance governing the production of powerful ideological representations (1964).[28] As in the later

[25] According to one recent estimate, nearly 40 percent of the articles in the *American Political Science Review* now have "a clear rational-choice orientation" (Hedström 1996: 278).

[26] On neo-Marxist state theory, see Gold, Lo, and Wright (1975); Jessop (1982, 1990a); Carnoy (1984); and Barrows (1993); on neo-Weberian perspectives, see Skocpol (1985). Political philosophy will not be considered here, even if a Hegelian tradition on the state (with its origins in Hegel's *Philosophy of Right*) does represent an important strand of "culturalist" thinking on the state. This strand is related only indirectly to current discussions of culture within substantive political theory; Hegel is much more important to discussions of civil society (see Cohen and Arato 1992; Cassirer 1946).

[27] The other tradition within substantive social theory that has explicitly thematized state/culture relations is Durkheimian (see Durkheim 1992; Shils 1972; Eisenstadt 1963). Like traditional Marxism, Durkheimian sociology tends to explain cultural forms in terms of social structure. In *The Elementary Forms of the Religious Life*, Durkheim analyzes religion as the original source of the basic categories of thought; yet at a deeper level, totemism and religious ritual are traced back to more basic social structures and functions. In *Professional Ethics and Civic Morals*, Durkheim argues that the state in modern society represents the ultimate source of authoritative "representations": its "principal function is to think" (1992: 51). More specifically, the state is the supreme "organ of moral discipline," whose purpose is to bring about a "communion of minds and wills" (72, 69). Whereas religion fulfilled certain functions of social cohesion in "simpler" societies, the modern state's function is to combat the anomic tendencies resulting from social differentiation, the division of labor. As in Marxist theory, the cultural forms produced by the state play a central role in social reproduction, but extrastate culture has no independent causal power.

[28] The state for the early Marx represents an "abstract system of political domination which denies the social nature of man and alienates him from genuine involvement in public life" (Jessop 1982: 7; Marx 1964).

work, ideology is described here as contributing to the reproduction of capitalist social relations. At the same time, ideology is itself ultimately determined by
this selfsame capitalist mode of production (see Marx 1970a; Cohen 1978; Elster
1985). Cultural systems thus are on one level causally efficacious, but at a deeper
level they represent an effect, however indirect and mediated, of more fundamental social processes.[29] In his essays on specific political events, Marx attributes more power to cultural factors. Marx evokes the cultural "backwardness"
of the German bourgeoisie, for example, in accounting for the continuing control of the Prussian/German state by the "feudal" Junker class well into the
bourgeois era (Steinmetz 1993), and he traces "The Eighteenth Brumaire of
Louis Bonaparte" partly to the Napoleon cult and the lack of class consciousness
among the French peasantry (Marx 1970b). Cultural arguments do not structure
Marx's theory in a systematic way, however, even if efforts have been made to
reinterpret his theory along these lines (for example, Postone 1993).

Twentieth-century "Western Marxism" has of course been intensely interested in cultural analysis (Anderson 1976: 75–76; Laclau and Mouffe 1987: chap-
ters 1–2). But until recently, even "cultural" Marxists have described culture
as the product of other, more basic structural instances, such as capital, class relations, or modes of production.[30] Two important exceptions, Marxists who
construe culture as an important independent shaper of state-formation, are
Antonio Gramsci and one of Gramsci's most trenchant critics, Perry Anderson
(see Anderson 1977). Gramsci's writings on hegemony are tangled and ambiguous enough to have produced a huge exegetical literature. Yet Gramsci clearly
believed that a prerequisite for the successful assumption of state power by a
revolutionary party was the prior construction of cultural counterhegemony
outside the state, within the "trenches" of civil society. Contrary to the expectations of orthodox Marxism, the success of this counterhegemonic project was,
for Gramsci, far from guaranteed by any objective contradictions between the
forces and relations of production. Nor were the contents of the counterhegemonic cultural project a mere translation of fundamentally economic interests.
According to one commentator on Gramsci, "the subjects of hegemonic practice understood at the level of their discursive constitution will not necessarily
have a class character. . . . to hegemonize *as* a class would simply imply either a
limited or an unsuccessful attempt" (Rosenthal 1988: 47). Successful hegemo-
nizing agents must abandon their "sectional" class interests, organizing ideologies around more general signifiers such as nationalism, religion, or the "people"
(Gramsci 1971; also see Laclau 1977).

Anderson's historical studies of antiquity, feudalism, and absolutism (1978,
1979) are unusual within the Marxist literature for the degree of causal power

[29] For an especially clear expression of this, see Engels's letters to Joseph Bloch and Franz Mehring
in Tucker (1972: 760–67). In other formulations, ideology for Marx is little more than an epiphenomenal reflection of economic foundations and does not even have this "conveyer belt" efficacy.
See Marx (1970a) and discussion in Centre for Contemporary Cultural Studies (1977).

[30] Although the Althusserians saw ideology as playing a key role in the imaginary resolution of real
contradictions, the content of ideology itself was determined—in the "last instance"—by the capitalist mode of production.

they grant to autonomous political and military motives in shaping systems of authority and rule. What often goes unnoticed is the significance Anderson also attaches to cultural determinants of states. One example is his emphasis on the central contribution of Latin civilization to the formation of the imperial Roman state even in the third and fourth centuries, as its center of gravity shifted eastward (1978: 89–90). Another, more familiar argument—but one not often given pride of place in the Marxist literature—concerns the Roman Law tradition, which was a key contributor to the growth of centralized European monarchies (Anderson 1979: 25–27).[31] Unlike some Marxists, Anderson recognizes that the availability of a revived and modernized version of Roman Law in Renaissance Europe was historically contingent and cannot be explained functionally as the effect of a capitalist economy that did not yet exist.[32]

Weber and the Relegation of Culture to Non-Western and Premodern Sites

We might expect a more culturally inflected account of state-formation from Weber, given his advocacy of interpretive social analysis. Weber famously integrated hermeneutic and causal methods in his studies of the relations between religion and economic practices, yet he never completed a full-scale comparative study of state-formation.[33] Weber's many scattered remarks about states do suggest that traditional and non-Western states are profoundly shaped by religious cultural systems. Confucianism was locked into a mutually reinforcing embrace with the Chinese state and acted as a barrier to "political rationalization" (see Weber 1951, 1978: 1049–50).[34] Hindu ethics allowed for the development of an autonomous "Machiavellian" art of politics in India (Weber 1958: p. 123). These "Oriental" states were examples of the *patrimonial* form of domination, which is underwritten by a culture in which "the most fundamental obligation of the subjects is the material maintenance of the ruler" (Weber 1978: 1014). Turning to Europe, Weber notes that early Protestantism similarly "legitimated the state as a divine institution" (1958: 124).

[31] An especially important facet of Roman Law, according to this narrative, was its recognition of private property. But compare Strayer (1970: 26) and Badie (1983: 63), who criticizes Anderson for ignoring the changes in Roman Law over time.

[32] Contrast Poulantzas (1978: 161–67), whose discussion of the absolutist state suggests that the rules of public law "can be dated from the emergence of this power" (163), a state whose character is fundamentally capitalist (p. 166). Because Roman Law was functionally necessary, it would have been invented if it had not already existed.

[33] Johannes Winckelmann notes that Weber's writing during the last three years of his life was concerned with the theme "sociology of the state" and that Weber's penultimate outline for the work that came to be called *Economy and Society* encompassed a final section on "formation of the rational state" and "the modern political powers" (Winckelmann 1956a: 9–13; 1956b: xii). The section on state-formation was to include a discussion of "the rationalism of the modern state and its relationship to the churchly powers." Winckelmann tried to reconstruct this missing section in an edition of *Economy and Society* published in 1956 (Weber 1956a) by combining sections of Weber's *Wirtschaftsgeschichte* and his essays "Politics and Government in a Reconstructed Germany" and "Politics as a Vocation."

[34] For a neo-Weberian argument (via Parsons) about the positive effects of Confucianism and Shintoism on state rationalization in Tokugawa Japan, see Bellah ([1957] 1969).

Cultural factors are thus accorded a central part in Weber's interpretations of premodern and non-Western states. When we turn to the modern Western state, however, a peculiar shift occurs, one that is linked to Weber's overarching conception of rationality (Schluchter 1981, 1989; Kalberg 1980). The most general characteristic of the modern state, according to Weber, is its formal-legal rationality. The ideal-typical modern state has removed itself from the sway of the "substantively rational" cultural systems that pervaded earlier European and non-Western states.[35] Weber's claim that authority strives for legitimation would seem to build culture into the very definition and mode of operation of the state. Weber acknowledges, of course, that actual modern Western states do not always correspond to this ideal type (see his discussion of the English state, with its basis in common law; 1978: 977). One might also counter that formal or instrumental rationality is itself simply another form of culture. Yet in much of Weber's work it functions as a sort of nonculture, a privileged baseline of "pure rationality" against which other action-orientations can be highlighted (6–7). Weber repeatedly describes the modern European style of state as technically superior and rational, with no qualifier (1956a: 17). This Orientalist political teleology complements Weber's larger contrast between capitalism's emergence in Europe and its failure to arise autochthonously in the "East" (Turner 1996: 257–86; 1974; Parsons 1949).

Elsewhere Weber does bring cultural processes into the explanation of modern states, but as in Marx, these arguments do not disturb the central structure of his theoretical system. The most important example may be his discussion of charisma as an alternative basis for the legitimation of domination, even in modern societies. Weber accounts for the rise of charismatic rulership in "cultural" terms, as originating in "collective excitement produced by extraordinary events" (1978: 1121). The "action orientation" of charismatic authority is radically opposed to economic or utilitarian rationality (1113). Calling charisma "the specifically creative revolutionary force in history," Weber recognizes its ability to found a new state, perhaps one based on charismatic kingship (1117, 1121, 1142). Yet the concept of charismatic authority does not undercut Weber's overarching contrast between the modern / Western and the premodern / Oriental. Granting that charisma is "by no means limited to primitive stages of development" (1133), Weber nonetheless argues that it is much more common "the further we go back into history" (1111).[36]

---

[35] Weber does not directly suggest a parallel in the realm of state-formation to his analysis of the way in which the *substantive* rationality of aesthetic Protestantism gave rise to the *formal* rationality of modern capitalism. Rarely does he allude to linkages between specific earlier substantive cultures and the formal rationality of the modern legal state (but see, e.g., Weber 1956a: 18). Such an approach seems completely compatible with Weber's general line of argumentation, however, as Gorski (this volume) and others (e.g., Schilling 1994) have suggested. Of course, Gorski substitutes a vocabulary of "disciplining," avoiding the implication of empty formal rationality as the telos of state formation.

[36] Another place where culture enters the analysis of the modern state is Weber's discussion of the *nation*, which he defines as a subjective sense of belonging, common political memories, and expectations of solidarity (Weber 1978: 922–23). It is significant in this context that Weber did not view national sentiment, at least in Germany, as chiefly a product of the state (Weber 1989).

Neo-Weberian Theory and the Impact of "Ideas" on the State

Weber's "interpretivism" was thus more fully realized in his writing on economic history and the premodern/Oriental than in his work on the modern state. Much post-Weberian research on the state has reinforced this tendency to understand Western states as basically rational and non-Western states as embedded within exotic cultural systems (Edelman 1995). It is perhaps not surprising then that one of the most influential schools of state theory, which arose in the 1970s, the "state-centered" perspective, was able to draw heavily on Weber while explicitly rejecting cultural analysis. The most influential example of this perspective, Theda Skocpol's *States and Social Revolutions*, called on analysts to "rise above" the "viewpoints of the participants" (1979: 18), in direct contrast to Weber's interpretivist starting point in *Economy and Society*.

To understand the state-centered analysts' resistance to cultural arguments we need to recall the way in which their challenge to Marxist theory originally emerged during the 1980s. A key programmatic statement of this perspective was Skocpol's introduction to *Bringing the State Back In* (1985).[37] In response to this book, a generation of doctoral dissertations in the social sciences was structured around arguments for or against the state's autonomy from dominant classes and other "socioeconomic" forces. The neo-Weberian understanding of the state as actor and institution began to supplant the neo-Marxian view of the state as a "collective capitalist." State-centered theory was successful partly because it was able to explain anomalies in orthodox Marxist accounts of the state, particularly those cases in which state structures and policies failed to correspond to dominant class interests. State-centered theorists asserted that states were not just "relatively" autonomous from dominant social classes, but that in some instances they were *fully* autonomous.[38]

The state-centered theorists' efforts to carve out greater space for autonomous state action were thus directed primarily against economistic and class-centered approaches. By reducing the alternatives to the simple binary choice between "state-centered" and "society-centered" explanation, however, state-centered theory was led almost inexorably to reject or to marginalize cultural determinations of the state as well, because most of what we call culture in the anthropological sense is located on the "society" side of the posited boundary. There was some interest in what Skocpol called the "Tocquevillian" problem of the state's "patterning of social conflict" (1985). But here again culture figured primarily as an effect and not a determinant of the state.

[37] Other key works in this "school" were consecrated by Skocpol herself. Of course, there were other writers on the state whose thinking cut obliquely across these lines of debates. Charles Tilly presented an approach to the state which, although associated with the state-centered approach through its inclusion in *Bringing the State Back In* (Tilly 1985) and its emphasis on state predation and warmaking, was equally attentive to social-structural determinants (see Tilly 1990).

[38] The state's "capacities" or "strength" were the central determinant of the realization of the state's potential autonomy (Skocpol 1985). Other factors precipitating the autonomization of the state included economic crises, which were argued to lessen the ability of socioeconomic structures to censor state policies (Block 1988a).

The debate between neo-Marxist and state-centered approaches pointed *symptomatically* to cultural determinants of the state. Questions about the influence of culture on the state were suppressed or raised only indirectly. Below I look briefly at the evolution of two debates on specific state forms to illustrate this symptomatic emergence of the cultural problematic. Several commentators have noted that whereas the state-centered approach elucidates the structural conditions under which state-makers and public officials free themselves from the demands of dominant class actors, it offers only ad hoc explanations of the specific *contents* of the policies these actors seek to implement. In a partial effort to correct this shortcoming, state-centered writers occasionally point to the impact of ideas or intellectuals on state policy. This move gestures toward (official) decision making as an important causal mechanism; and almost inevitably, any attention to decision making opens up the Pandora's box of subjectivity and culture. Any overt emphasis on culture as constitutive of social reality seemed to violate the original strictures of the state-centric approach. Instead, culture played a largely unacknowledged explanatory part in the guise of the subjectivity of state officials (Cammack 1989; Mitchell 1991, this volume). Rather than engaging frontally in a full-scale theorization of the nature and role of cultural determination, state-centered theorists adopted the Whiggish or technocratic language of "political learning" or, as Sewell (1985) pointed out, fell back on a sociologically impoverished conception of ideology as simply ideas, ignoring the role of broader, impersonal cultural systems, including those not organized as formal intellectual bodies of thought.

It is worth noting in this context that the state-centered literature was hardly alone in ignoring broader cultural formations while acknowledging the impact of "ideas" or formally articulated bodies of knowledge on the state. Karl Polanyi (1944: 111–29), for example, argued that the ideas of early political economy accounted for changes in eighteenth and nineteenth century English Poor Law. Linkages of these sorts are often suggested in historical writing: the *Encyclopédistes* incited the French Revolution; the construction of the "well-ordered police state" in early modern Germany and Russia was driven by Cameralist writings (Raeff 1983); Confucian texts undergird the Chinese state; the blueprint for the Nazi state can be found in *Mein Kampf* or in the grumbling of right-wing Weimar academics (Stern 1961).[39]

What is wrong with concentrating on "expert" ideas, formally constituted bodies of thought? First, the mere fact that experts hope that their ideas will influence the state does not mean that these ideas are in fact more powerful than anonymous, impersonal ideologies. Academic analysts who assume that forms of writing that more closely resemble their own are more causally efficacious in the real world seem to be suffering from a sort of professional narcissism. Second, even if one does focus on expert writing and speech, it may be the *formal* aspects

---

[39] For examples of this approach within political research, see Heclo (1974); Haas, Williams, and Babai (1977); Haas (1990); Yee (1996); and Rose and Miller (1992). For related critiques of this work, see Curtis (1995: 585) and Go (1996).

of this discourse rather than its explicit contents that are most significant (Foucault 1972). Finally, it is not obvious that the relevant conceptual or cultural phenomena are necessarily expressed in formal discourse. The "conceptual" aspects of reality that shape the state may also "include tacit conceptual skills and tacitly followed rules . . . unrecognized beliefs and needs, unconscious motives and attitudes, etc." (Collier 1994: 232).

"Political Culture and Political Development": An Excursus

The "political culture" framework of the 1960s and 1970s might seem to resonate with our own present agenda. Following Parsons's injunction to "avoid any appearance of a cognitive bias" (1965: 963) in the study of the "cultural system," political culture was said to encompass "evaluative" and "affective" orientations along with cognitive material (Verba 1965: 516). Nor did the political culture approach ignore non-elite ideas or internal differentiation within a given "culture." Indeed, the political culture approach was committed to using the most "recent advances in the sociological techniques for measuring attitudes" (Pye 1965: 8) and statistical analysis, which led researchers to seek representative samples and to foreground variation (see Almond and Verba 1963; Inkeles 1974).

Alongside these advances over the "elite ideas" approach, however, the political culture approach suffered from a series of assumptions that distinguish it sharply from the current cultural turn.[40] First, it was committed to an essentially "behavioral" form of analysis in which the individual was the privileged unit of analysis, even if individual responses were subsequently aggregated for statistical processing. This individualistic bias was at odds with the point made even by Parsons that culture is not (or not primarily) a property of individuals. The political culture literature misleadingly wrenched "ideas" such as "national pride" from the social conditions in which they were embedded and within which they received their specific meaning (Pateman 1980: 60; Scheuch 1968). As MacIntyre observed in a critique of this approach, "we identify and define attitudes in terms of the objects toward which they are directed," and "no institution or practice is what it is, or does what it does, independently of what anyone whatsoever thinks or feels about it" ([1967] 1978: 262–63).

Another set of drawbacks derived from the interweaving of modernization theory with the political culture approach. Researchers were mainly interested in adherence to a narrow syndrome of attitudes thought to characterize the Anglo-American "civic culture" and deemed relevant to "political development" (Verba 1965: 527; Almond and Verba 1963: vii). While political culture researchers did not fall into the trap of assuming homogeneity *within* cultures, they projected across the globe a common homogeneous scale along which individual respondents were arrayed. Political culture was defined as "orientations toward the political

---

[40] My decision to expand my discussion of the political culture literature, which many now view as little more than a footnote in the history of political research, is due to the urging of Peggy Somers. For a contemporary assessment of the political culture literature from a different perspective, see Somers (1995); for an important earlier critique, see Pateman (1973).

system." This starting point dramatically restricted the range of questions and topics thought to be important. Cultural orientations toward ostensibly "non-political" issues were ignored. Yet these orientations might well influence state-formation. Feminist research, for instance, has traced the ways categories of gender and assumptions about sexuality have shaped the policies and structure of the state (for example, Sylvester 1994; Connell 1990; Peterson 1992; Elshtain 1992; Enloe 1989, 1993; Cohn 1987). Racial classification schemes and racist beliefs played a central causal role, above and beyond calculations of economic interest, in the formation of overseas colonial states (Steinmetz 1997b, forthcoming), the Nazi state (Burleigh and Wippermann 1991), and the antebellum and Jim Crow Southern U.S. polity (Wilson 1980). Even the proponents of the political culture perspective acknowledged that "much of what . . . we have assumed to be the political culture of a society may in fact be the . . . political theory of political scientists"(Verba 1965: 523 n. 11).

The most serious shortcoming of the political culture school in our present context, however, was its failure to unpack the dialectical relations between states and culture. Commentators have noted that this literature frequently asserts a relationship between political culture and political structure without ever investigating or even defining it (Pateman 1980: 75). Political culture was sometimes described as a "connecting link" between "discrete individuals" and the "political systems" (Almond and Verba 1963: 33). Rather than making causal statements about this "link," however, Almond and Verba emphasized the degree of "congruency" between the two terms (21–22). Democratic political culture tends to become part of the very definition of democracy, making it difficult even to pose questions about the connection. In sum, political culture was mobilized to explain "the ways in which people act within these political institutions" (Verba 1965: 514) but not the "institutions" themselves.[41]

Foundationalist Decontextualization in the Study of the State

This section develops in greater detail the earlier argument that Weber granted central importance to cultural factors only in the interpretation of premodern and non-Western states. Such Orientalism in state studies (and its allied "Occidentalism"; see Carrier 1995; Coronil 1997) is not unique to Weber, but can be linked to a broader strategy of *foundationalist decontextualization*. The latter can be defined as a view of human subjectivity as determinable outside its social and historical context.

The linchpin of decontextualized social theory is typically some founding assumption about human nature, such as instrumental rationality, a propensity to violence, or territorialism. Rorty (1979) calls this style of thought "social naturalism." Some privileged institution—the individual, the market, the contract—

---

[41] For a later self-critical discussion of this failure to connect survey data to macropolitical outcomes, see Verba (1980).

is postulated as a presocial foundation. When the assumptions remain implicit, as they do in most contemporary social sciences, they are usually utilitarian. Rational-choice theory consciously embraces this particular version of foundationalism (Wacquant and Calhoun 1989). Within state theory, rational-choice perspectives exaggerate tendencies toward cultural decontextualization that were already present within the state-centered perspective, emphasizing the "state as predator" motif while marginalizing cultural processes to an even greater extent (see Adams this volume).[42]

Sometimes cultural difference is so obvious that it cannot convincingly be subsumed under a decontextualized model. Here other strategies are used to construct foundations. One approach has been to make culture itself into a timeless base by positing the existence of unified and static national (or religious, racial, or ethnic) cultures.[43] As Badie remarks, "political analysts have not always known how to differentiate between a scientific apprehension of the cultural factor and the common-sense discourse on the 'soul of the people' [or] the national character" (1983: 11). National character is thus a *culturalist* version of social naturalism. The proliferation of "national character" arguments in earlier culturalist social science was one reason for the rejection of cultural approaches *tout court*. Yet this view of national culture as timeless tradition, internally coherent and shared equally by all members of the society, is antithetical to the cultural turn (Dirks, Eley, and Ortner 1994: 3).[44]

National culture arguments were rejected for other reasons. Most of these arguments were not truly relativistic, but arranged the various cultures hierarchically along a unilinear developmental scale. Non-Western and colonized cultures were redescribed as earlier stages in a universal teleological path. This allowed cultural theory to preserve a solid foundation in the face of unequivocal cultural otherness and historical change. The notion of a universal historical trajectory is made explicit within social evolutionary and modernization theory, traditional Marxism, and systems theory; it is usually implicit whenever the terms *traditional* and *modern* are used without a specific chronological reference. Past cultural forms that fit poorly with "modern rationality" are lumped together in the category of "tradition"; and where the "traditional" cultures are contemporaneous, space is recoded as time.[45] Even contemporary Western societies sometimes pre-

---

[42] Arguments for the causal importance of human *agency* in rational-choice theory should not be equated with claims for cultural determinism. At the limit, rational-choice theory specifies the workings of a particular cultural system.

[43] Much of the systems-theoretical social science of the 1950s and 1960s took this form, describing national cultures as monolithic and timeless entities. See for example Parsons's own essays on German culture (1993); Inkeles (1961); Doob (1964); and Pye (1962). Recent examples of this style of cultural foundationalism include Huntington (1993; 1996) and Goldhagen (1996).

[44] Contrast, for instance, Sohrabi's account in this volume of the multiple readings of constitutionalism in 1906 Iran with the comments of Verba on the same topic, which imply a singular national culture: "a new constitution . . . will be perceived and evaluated in terms of *the* political culture of a people" (Verba 1965: 517; my emphasis).

[45] The locus classicus in the social sciences of treating contemporary non-Western societies as earlier stages of the modern West is Durkheim ([1915] 1965). This conflation of idealized Western cul-

sent a disruptive otherness that can be countered only by a "self-orientalizing" application of the developmental scheme. The "exceptionalist" literature on the rise of Nazism provides a clear example of this strategy. Germany is said to have deviated from the West due to the peculiar coexistence of "traditional" political elites and cultural forms with modern industrial capitalism before 1933 (see Dahrendorf 1967; Wehler 1985). As has been pointed out, this explanation distracts from Nazism's "modern" character and its roots in developments that were more contemporary with the rise of Nazism (Eley 1986a; Bauman 1989; Prinz and Zitelmann 1991; Dahrendorf 1967).[46] But by drawing a clear line between Germany and the "West," the exceptionalist narrative rescues Western modernity from the taint of barbarism.

State theory has its own variant of this syndrome, a quasi-Orientalist juxtaposition of the rational, modern West with the "cultural" rest, as discussed above with respect to Weber. Frazer's argument ([1900] 1922, [1905] 1920) about the primitive unity of kingship and religion/magic has been reformulated numerous times. On the one hand, the political and cultural spheres in Western societies are seen as functionally differentiated.[47] Within premodern, non-Western, and socialist societies, on the other hand, culture and politics are seen as hopelessly intermingled, even indistinguishable. The unity of culture and polity is a commonplace in the political anthropology of older and non-Western polities (for example, Balandier 1991: 46–47). In Geertz's description of the Balinese Negara, quoted in the epigraph to this chapter, political ritual did not simply exist to legitimate social inequalities: "power served pomp, not pomp power."[48] Additional "theater states" have been discovered in Java (Anderson 1990) and the southern Indian princely state of Pudukkottai (Dirks 1993: 8); Tambiah's Siamese

---

ture with modernity *tout court* is hardly restricted to academic social science. Yang (1994) notes that many contemporary Chinese understand their own country as hampered by "tradition," in contrast to the "modern" West. Badie discusses a similar relationship to the West among intellectuals in "developing" countries (1992: 160ff.).

[46] This argument does not contradict the one made later about the influence of German anti-Semitism, which was a distinctly modern product of electoral politics and mass media since the late nineteenth century. On the uses of the German *Sonderweg* thesis to "normalize" postwar West Germany, see Eley (1986b) and Steinmetz (1997a).

[47] The clearest statement of this thesis is in the work of Luhmann (for example, 1989), whose systems theory occupies a curious position with respect to discussions of the state and culture. On the one hand, Luhmann accords a central place to discourse, or more accurately, communication, in the functioning of the state ("political system"). Communication within any of the "function systems," including the political system, operates according to specific binary codes. At the same time, Luhmann insists on the mutual incommensurability of the various subsystem-specific codes. Subsystems cannot communicate directly with one another; "perturbations" originating in external subsystems must be translated into the local code. Luhmann thus effectively defines the impact of extrastate codes on the state as abnormal, as an indicator of the system's antimodern "de-differentiation." Luhmann (1995) chides theories that assume such interpenetration for their obsolescence.

[48] Similarly, Sahlins (1981: 80) analyzes the "mythical exploits and social disruptions common to . . . successive investitures of divine kings" as symbolic recapitulations of the "initial constitution of social life." Refusing to see such rituals of royal installation as mere mystifications of more fundamental social interests, Sahlins echoes Geertz in insisting that "the rationalization of power is not at issue so much as *the representation of a general scheme of social life*" (81; my emphasis).

"galactic polity" (1976, 1977) is similar. The separation of culture and politics is sometimes argued to be an effect of colonialism (Dirks 1993: 106, 261).

The problem is not that these writers question the separateness of cultural and political systems but that the same doubts are not typically raised when attention is turned to modern Western states. Theorists seem to assume that the subjectivity and motives of officials in modern states are basically the same everywhere. Even Geertz occupies a complex position with respect to this apparently Orientalist division of theoretical labor within state studies. On the one hand, Geertz insists that we must write the "political theology" of twentieth-century states (1983: 143). On the other hand, as some critics have noted, Geertz's reversal of the causal arrows between "pomp" and "power" in *Negara* does not automatically imply that "political action everywhere is a work of symbolic display." Instead, the book's "claim that Balinese political life is theatrical" relies on a "difference between theatrical performance and other kinds of action" (Thomas 1994: 94). As Dirks notes, "The choice of thespian metaphors makes Bali, with all the anthropological romance of the island, seem even more special a case than is perhaps justified" (1993: 402; see also Skalník 1987).

As methodologically diverse as they are in other respects, theorists associated with the cultural turn reject such simplifying assumptions about human subjectivity, the explanatory primacy of utilitarian or material determinants, the directionality of history, and the inexorable differentiation of politics from broader cultural systems in the process of modernization. Social practices and objects such as states or state officials have to be situated in specific historical and cultural settings.

Culture as Symptom: State-Formation and the Need for an Explicit Discussion of Culture

I argued above that one reason for the unsatisfactory condition of state theory has to do with the way in which existing debates have pointed obliquely to the importance of cultural processes while avoiding a direct confrontation with cultural theory. Marxist, state-centric theories and rational-choice theories of the state have seemed congenitally ill-suited to address this problem, although adherents of these perspectives are beginning to pursue cultural themes.

The first example of the symptomatic emergence of the cultural problematic concerns the literature on the formation of the welfare state. Marxist approaches minimized the impact of culture on welfare state formation, tracing ideology to objective economic interests.[49] State-centered theory was primarily interested in demonstrating that welfare policies developed independently of the interests of

---

[49] For a typical class-theoretic account of welfare state formation that ignores cultural processes, see Esping-Andersen (1990). Baldwin (1990) attempted to resuscitate the economic class approach by shifting attention from the working class and capital to the middle classes, but his account is similarly uninterested in cultural factors.

capital, labor, or other "social" forces (for example, Skocpol and Finegold 1982; Skocpol and Ikenberry 1983). Reference was sometimes made to the "political learning" of state managers to explain the kinds of welfare policies adopted, but minimal attention was paid to the sources of the specific contents or form of subjectivity beyond the immediate administrative context.[50] It soon became obvious, however, that features of welfare states such as cross-national differences in the treatment of gender or the overall classification of social problems could not be explained without reference to broader social discourses.

The shifts in Ann Orloff's work illustrate the way in which some state-centered theorists have moved beyond the anticulturalism of the earlier perspective by making cultural discourse a full-fledged determinant of state-formation. In 1984, Orloff and Skocpol argued that differences in the social policy history of Britain and the United States could not be explained in terms of cultural "values." American social policy backwardness was attributed instead to a sort of political memory concerning the corrupting effects of the Civil War pensions. Clearly, this argument was in some sense a "cultural" one. The problem was to clarify the status of cultural determinants within a theoretical perspective that had set out to minimize the space for "social" determinants of the state. Did this mean that the only relevant cultural determinants were those that were "internal" to the state? And if not, what became of the foundational "state-centered" versus "society-centered" polarity? Orloff's more recent work (this volume), along with the work of Nancy Fraser (1987) and others, has emphasized the impact of society-wide gender discourses on the form of welfare policies (see the discussion in the last section of this chapter).

To take another example, my own work on the sources of national and local social policies and state regulation of the social in Germany before 1914 suggests that it is necessary to reconstruct the ideology of state officials and the broader cultural discourses in which they participate before one can make sense of their social-political interventions and reactions (Steinmetz 1993). Bureaucratic elites' understandings of society in Imperial Germany were shaped by historically layered discourses about the nature of social danger and the appropriate methods for regulating the social. Responses to social disturbances associated with the inchoate masses of "the poor" were structured by an older discourse on pauperism which had crystallized in the period before 1848. Official reactions to pressure from organized labor were channeled by more recent class-centered paradigms which emerged during the last third of the century. The key point for our present purposes is that the impact of a given "variable" on policy formation can be understood only by reconstructing what it meant to the relevant actors—in this case, state officials. Failure to culturally embed political or economic factors is a central reason for the proliferation of contradictory findings in multivariate statistical studies of welfare states.

---

[50]Weir and Skocpol (1985), for example, present the adoption of Keynesian ideology by political elites as a process divorced from broader cultural developments.

Interpretations of the Nazi regime provide another example of a debate that became locked into an unfortunate contest between Marxist and state-centric approaches, creating an impasse that could be transcended only through explicit cultural analysis. Orthodox Marxists analyzed the Nazi state as a creature of the monopolies or as the "dictatorship of the most reactionary, the most chauvinistic, the most imperialistic elements of finance capital" (Dimitrov).[51] Those who disagreed with the Marxist approach felt compelled to demonstrate the "primacy of politics" and the Nazi state's autonomy from big business (Bracher 1973; Bracher, Sauer, and Schulz 1979; Kershaw 1993: chap. 3). By limiting debate to these alternatives, however, attention was diverted from the Nazi regime's most distinctive activities, its racial and genocidal politics. The Nazi state's decision to divert limited resources in the middle of the war in order to carry out the "Final Solution" can hardly be explained without reference to ideological processes, since the Holocaust was neither economically nor politically rational (but compare Aly et al. 1987). Both of the main contenders in the recent German historians' debate, Browning (1992) and Goldhagen (1996), agree that a deep culture of modern anti-Semitism was a "necessary condition" in preparing masses of "ordinary men" to perform the killing.[52] It is important to stress that this cultural formation was forged before the Nazis' rise to power, and largely outside the state.

Cultural theory is also necessary to transcend the impasse in state theoretic debates with respect to conceptual issues, including the very definition of *the state*. Several authors have pointed out that state-centered theory, in its attempt to criticize Marxist theory, posited an easily identifiable boundary between state and society. This objectified what is in fact a mobile demarcation, subject to continual construction and deconstruction (see Block 1988b; Jessop 1990b). Marxists have at least recognized that the state-economy border is ambiguous and in some sense illusory (see Jessop 1982; Holloway and Picciotto 1978). The Marxist approach avoided exaggerating the solidity of the state-society boundary, even if it erred in the opposite direction.[53] Clarification had to await the opening of state

---

[51] Dimitrov's 1935 report to the Seventh Congress of the Comintern, quoted in Ayçoberry (1981: 53). Mandel described the Nazi regime as a capitalist state engaged in increasing the rate of surplus value by breaking the back of organized labor (1975: 159–62). Of course, there have been various unorthodox Marxist accounts, starting with those of the Frankfurt School. More sophisticated structural neo-Marxists moved away from simple accounts, granting more autonomy to the (Weimar) political system and focusing on the overall class structure and divisions of interest within the business class (Poulantzas 1974; Abraham 1986). These shifts were not registered in the main lines of theoretical debate, which still tended to move back and forth between capital-analytic and "autonomy of politics" approaches.

[52] The differences between the two revolve partly around whether anti-Semitism was a sufficient and not just a necessary condition. Goldhagen also weakens his argument severely by falling back on the homogenizing "national character" trope discussed above.

[53] Poulantzas (1975), however, was unable to solve the problem of delimiting the state. He locates state power with the dominant class which holds power; and like Althusser, he defines the state in terms of its functions. The functional definition leads to the famous absurdity (see Althusser 1971a; Poulantzas 1978: 36) that the state encompasses institutions such as the family and literature insofar

theory to cultural analysis, which allowed the boundary between the state and the nonstate to be seen as a variable discursive effect (Mitchell 1991, this volume) rather than an ontological constant or a functional requirement of capital.

The Theoretical Terrain of Culture/State Relations

In an overview of the political culture literature, Sidney Verba warned against an "unfortunate tendency in the social sciences to oversell new concepts" (1965: 515). It would indeed be exaggerated to argue that culture, even in the fuller sense described above, has been completely absent from the analysis of state-formation. In addition to the writers represented in this collection, many others have turned to this topic in recent decades.[54] The burgeoning literature on nationalism usually looks at the effects of the state on identities, but sometimes the relations between culture and state are dialectical (for example, Anderson 1983). Lynn Hunt's (1992) proto-Freudian analysis of the French Revolution as a "family romance" argues that key political events, artistic representations, and transformations of the state during the revolution were shaped by a "collective political unconscious" that was itself "structured by narratives of family relationships" (xiii). The most radical aspects of the revolution are explained as a "fraternal" attack on the tyrannical father within both state and family. Claude Lefort (1986) proposes an ambitious Freudian theory of totalitarian regimes and their intimate relationship to democracy. In contrast to historic kingship-based societies, modern democratic regimes are centered around an "empty place of power" and characterized by extreme social heterogeneity. The disappearance of an image of the unified body politic parallels the psychoanalytic account of the "ordeal of the division of the subject" (306).[55] Totalitarianism promises to heal that division, filling the empty center with the image of the leader and the party, radically simplifying social space, and restoring the unity of the community-body.[56]

---

as these institutions are reproductive of capitalist relations. Still, the Althusserian approach had the salutary effect of disrupting commonsense understandings of the state as little more than buildings, men, and machines.

[54] Texts that interpret the modern state as constituted by systems of signification include Geertz (1983); Clastres (1974); Abrams (1988); Badie and Birnbaum (1983); and Corrigan and Sayer (1985). Baudrillard (1983a, 1983b) and Edelman (1964, 1995) connect contemporary politics to the mass media and theatrical representation. Habermas's *Structural Transformation of the Public Sphere* (1989 [1962]) is not primarily concerned with the state in the sense discussed here: his "bourgeois public sphere" is located outside the state. Hobsbawm and Ranger's *Invention of Tradition* (1983) is an important precursor to this volume, but its excellent essays focus principally on the effects of states on culture and less on causality running in the opposite direction.

[55] Lefort historicizes the Freudian concept of the split subject, however cursorily (1986: 306), thus avoiding the universalizing claims found in some Freudian accounts and the critique of foundationalism outlined above.

[56] Julia Hell (1992, 1997) provides a psychoanalytically informed analysis of East German literature and political culture, starting with what she calls the *foundational narratives* of the immediate postwar period and continuing into the 1980s. Combining narrative analysis and pschoanalysis, she traces the unconscious fantasies about the "pure" postfascist body emerging in identification with the iconic

Many other examples of serious cultural analyses of state formation could be given. This book brings together several differing approaches to the problem. It was not designed as a presentation of a single theoretical framework but as an overview of some of the most interesting cultural work on the state. The over-arching goal is to shift the terms of debate by demonstrating how developments in cultural theory can push theoretical and empirical work beyond the stalemate that resulted from the Marxist-Weberian dispute and the rational choice non-solution. This collection has both a dialogic and a critical orientation. The dialogic face involves staging discussion among the various cultural perspectives. The critical face is directed against cultural and historical decontextualization. Within this broad definition, however, each author follows a different path, and no effort was made to enforce a unified theoretical framework or terminology.

Broadly speaking, the essays here can be arrayed along a continuum of increasingly thoroughgoing culturalism. At one end of the continuum is a radical culturalism that rejects the distinction between cultural and noncultural objects altogether, at least within the human sciences. Social objects and practices are inextricably cultural and cannot be understood outside their subjective meaning. Objects like the state or the economy are not just causally determined by cultural systems, but are themselves fully "cultural." Social objects are never just "brute facts" (Taylor 1979, 1985); they cannot even be said to exist in any socially relevant sense outside their discursive or meaningful construction (see Foucault 1980d; Laclau and Mouffe 1985, 1987; Mitchell 1991, this volume; Sismondo 1993).[57] From this perspective, the state could represent "a complex and mobile resultant of the discourses and techniques of rule," "a specific way in which the problem of government is discursively codified, a way of dividing a 'political sphere,' with its particular characteristics of rule, from other 'non-political spheres' to which it must be related" (Rose and Miller 1992: 176–77). In this book, Tim Mitchell's essay is closest to this strong version of cultural constructivism. But an approach that retains the distinction between the discursive and extradiscursive dimensions of social life while insisting on the absolute causal primacy of the former is often indistinguishable in its analysis from the more unadulterated versions of cultural constructivism.

At the other end of our continuum are arguments that combine a view of strategic action reminiscent of the rational-choice perspective with the claim that culture sets the overall context of constitutive rules, the ideological terrain of taken-for-granted assumptions, within which strategic action occurs. At this pole we also find different views of the extent to which strategic action is culturally embedded so that there is really something more than a simple continuum. All theorists at this pole might agree that human action has a certain strategic reasonableness (if not rationality) within an overall context that is determined cul-

---

image of the "antifascist fighter." She argues that the latter functioned as the master signifier of East Germany's legitimatory discourse of antifascism. See also Žižek (1991: 229–77).

[57] There is, of course, a difference between theories that focus on the "discursive" construction of social reality and the less linguistic approaches (hermeneutic or phenomenological).

turally. Cultural systems define the goals of action, the expectations about other actors, and even what it means to be an "actor" (that is, whether the relevant actors in a system are individuals, groups, families, and so on). The difference is that for some analysts, this strategic rationality is unconscious and habitual, involving a "feel for the game" (Bourdieu and Wacquant 1992: 128); for others, strategy involves conscious calculation and choices (for example, Ermakoff 1997). Bourdieu, for example, evokes a quasi-Hobbesian world of struggle for competitive advantage, one that in many ways recalls microeconomic descriptions of rational actors pursuing their material interests. At the same time, however, Bourdieu insists that "strategy" is partly unconscious and habitual and that the crucial conditions for any form of strategic practice—the forms of capital that count as valid and their relative worth, the stakes struggled over, and so on—are utterly "conventional," contextually specific to a given field. Bourdieu's approach can be contrasted in this respect with Laitin's (1986, 1988, this volume). Laitin writes that "culture is Janus-faced: people are both guided by the symbols of their culture and *instrumental* in using culture to gain wealth and power" (1988: 589; my emphasis). For Laitin, hegemonic culture defines relevant actors and the preferences and choices available to them; in a second analytic phase, individual behavior can be modeled using game theory and categories of strategic rationality.

Clearly, this is not a one-dimensional space. In addition to the differing understandings of "strategy" suggested in the preceding paragraph, there are differences in the *dimensions* of culture that count as central. Some theorists conceptualize culture in linguistic terms, while others extend the analysis to nonlinguistic semiosis. Some authors shift the emphasis from ideas to emotions (see the essays in this volume by Berezin and Adams). Some pose the problem as one of drawing out the cultural *subtext* of earlier work on the state that was not ostensibly culturalist (see the essays by Jessop and Tilly in this volume). For some, cultures are relatively unified and coherent, if not unchanging (see Sohrabi and Gorski, this volume), while others describe semiotic systems as inherently unstable and subject to continual rearticulation and disintegration (see Mitchell and Apter, this volume). Yet all the approaches here differ significantly from dominant versions of decontextualized and culturally foundationalist social analysis. And all the authors included here understand culture as more than a conveyor belt for deeper, more fundamental, or more "material" forces.

The selection of cases in this book is meant to illuminate the typically unspoken distinction between the "modern" world and those historical and non-Western societies that are the usual domain of cultural analysis. Above all, this book attempts to demonstrate how taking culture seriously can change the way we understand states that have *not* been stereotyped as "traditional." This set includes, first of all, modern and Western states, along with their colonial and postcolonial extensions. It also seemed crucial to compare state forms at the historical, geographic, and conceptual borders of this modern/Western universe. Deliberately excluded from this collection are the premodern and precolonial (or never-colonized) states, which have long been within the province of cultural analysis according to conventional understandings. Our cases thus fall into three main groups: (1) Western states in their early-modern formative period (Adams,

Gorski, and Pincus); (2) non-Western states at moments of deliberate Western-ization and modernization (Apter, Meyer, and Sohrabi); and (3) states that are part of the supposedly rational and postideological modern world (Berezin, Jessop, Laitin, Mitchell and Orloff).

The Essays in This Volume

None of the essays in this volume are purely theoretical, but those in the first section stake out four differing approaches to the culture-state problematic, drawing on a range of empirical material in developing their arguments.[58]

IN recent writing Pierre Bourdieu has directly confronted the question of the state (Bourdieu 1989), tracing the emergence of what he calls an "autonomous bureaucratic field" in the modern world. The state is analyzed as the universe of a new *noblesse de robe*, one based on scholarly titles rather than pedigrees of noble birth. This scholarly aristocracy works to establish "bureaucratic power positions relatively independent of already established temporal or spiritual powers." The state guarantees this nobility's reproduction by recognizing its credentials and legitimating its claims to dominate the state. In Bourdieu's terminology, the state thus becomes an autonomous "field" with its own indigenous form of "capital." More strikingly, Bourdieu argues that the state actually represents the culmination of a long process of concentrating the diverse types of capital. The state thus emerges over time as the superordinate classifier, underwriting the values of all other fields and transforming their specific forms of capital into legitimate, "symbolic" capital. The state ratifies the value, indeed the very existence, of social relations or events such as marriages, births, accidents, and illnesses, making such events undergo "a veritable ontological promotion, a transmutation, a change of nature or essence." Bourdieu's expansion of the state's importance thus stands in sharp contrast to much current theory, discussed above, which sees the state as declining in significance.

As suggested above, the place of the concept of the *state* within Foucault's writing is problematic. Some commentators (e.g., Rose and Miller 1992, 1995) insist that the state has relinquished any erstwhile sovereignty to the dispersed webs and sites of "disciplinary" power (see also Barry, Osborne, and Rose 1996; Burchell, Gordon, and Miller 1991). Others have called attention to Foucault's continuing use of the term *state*, especially in his writings on "governmentality" (cf. Foucault 1981, 1988, 1991, and 1980: 167; Curtis 1995; Engelstein 1994; Mitchell 1991; Steinmetz 1993).

Timothy Mitchell's essay (Chapter 2) accepts Foucault's imagery of power as capillary and dispersed while acknowledging that these practices also cohere into an apparently independent and abstract structure with practical effects—the

---

[58] One area not represented here in which the cultural turn has made a large impact is the study of international relations and security issues. See Sylvester (1994); Peterson (1992); Enloe (1989, 1993); Der Derian (1994).

state. Michell's goal is to understand how this "state effect"[59] is created. According to Mitchell, "the phenomenon we name the state arises from techniques that enable mundane material practices to take on the appearance of an abstract, non-material form," making an "internal distinction appear as though it were the external boundary between separate objects." Mitchell suggests that the boundary between state and society first emerged as a result of specific tactics of power, which Foucault called *government*, that took "population" as their primary object. Against Foucault, however, Mitchell argues that this object, "population," is not the same as "the economy." The modern idea of the economy as a self-contained and internally dynamic entity emerged only in the twentieth century. The state was imagined as "the most important thing" standing outside of the economy, and was now defined against both the economy and society.

Julia Adams's paper is both a theoretical diagnosis of the missing cultural dimension in rational-choice theories of early modern state-formation and a constructive analysis of the cultural components of this process. Adams argues that rational-choice approaches have successfully identified middle-range causal mechanisms involved in state-formation: the structural factors compelling all rulers, "whatever their preferences or set of values," to pursue economic resources, the strategies rulers tend to embrace in seeking these resources, the social dilemmas that arise among different factions, and the mechanisms evolved to produce "political equilibria, or relatively stable collective outcomes of individual choices." But these approaches ignore the broader "cultural patterns institutionalized in discursive patterns." Culture in this sense does not just determine the ends or "values" that rulers pursue; more important, it shapes the causally prior stage of identifications—who counts as a ruler—and of how rulers classify the social world. Adams draws attention to the *emotional* investment of patrimonial rulers in lineage honor, their own reputations, and a particular form of the family. The explanatory weakness of rational-choice theory emerges most clearly in historical situations in which shifts in "incentives, information, or resources" fail to incite rulers to modify their behavior accordingly. In such situations, Adams suggests that patrimonial elites would instead "struggle to maintain their family footholds" in the state, even where this was irrational from a more narrowly conceived strategic rationality. Moreover, Adams points out that the structuring of these states around familial culture helps explain aspects of popular imagination that emerge in revolutionary situations, such as the symbolic politics of the French revolution analyzed by Lynn Hunt. Adams concludes that the insights of rational-choice theory should be integrated into a broader perspective in which "cultural meaning is a basic analytical starting point on a par with information and resources."

More than a decade ago, Thomas and Meyer insisted that "more work is needed . . . in which the state is viewed as an institution that is essentially cultural in nature" (1984: 461). Political theorists have argued that global cultural

---

[59] Mitchell's notion of "effects" carries definite echoes of Althusser's "knowledge effect," "society effect," and "aesthetic effect" (Althusser 1971b; Althusser and Balibar 1979).

diffusion of political models shapes the formation of states. International culture is sometimes described as *enabling* local state-formation and at other times as applying pressure or constraint. According to Rudolph (1987: 740), processes of institutional *replication* are also characteristic of Asian state-formation (see Southall 1988; Tambiah 1976, 1977). Without ignoring the ways in which international economic structures and direct military and diplomatic pressures contribute to political conformity in peripheral states, Badie's study of the "imported state" (1992) argues that the "universalist and export-oriented pretensions" of the Western state form make it ideally suited for attracting support from various local groups.

John Meyer has assiduously promoted a cultural diffusionist approach to the state, and this paper summarizes his culturalist rereading of world systems theory. Meyer and his colleagues argue that various local institutions, including states, devolve from a global (political) culture (see Meyer 1980, this volume). Peripheral states copy international models, becoming surprisingly isomorphic as a result. Universal religions played the role of world culture in earlier periods; the key factor in the post-1945 era has been the proliferation of international public and private organizations. State isomorphism is strengthened by national elites' self-serving adoption of "world ideologies" (Meyer 1980: 48; see also Badie 1992, part 2). As a result, such fundamental dimensions of state structure as the categories of social problems that they recognize as warranting intervention become increasingly similar (Thomas and Lauterdale 1987).

THE essays in part two concern the formation of the early modern European state in relation to cultural processes. By variously focusing on religion (Gorski) and early nationalism (Pincus), these essays help us understand processes of early modern state-formation in much more complex ways, while leaving open the question of the relative causal importance of these factors.

As noted above, state-centered work on the early modern state has been most interested in refuting Marxian explanations. State-centered theorists concentrated on state-building "entrepreneurs" and their efforts to aggrandize their territory and coffers, the bargaining between monarchs and nobles, and military relations between states. Little attention was paid to the diverse hegemonic strategies used by monarchs to consolidate their power—the processes of civilizing (Elias 1994), disciplining (Oestreich 1982; Schilling 1994), and ordering (Raeff 1983) society—or to the sources of these cultural projects outside the state. Like Adams, Philip Gorski reframes the sociological discussion of early modern state formation by bringing these previously excluded aspects to the fore. Specifically, he extends Weber's Protestant ethic thesis to the realm of state formation, arguing that Calvinism was an essential component in the successful consolidation of the "infrastructural power" (Mann 1986) of the early Dutch and Prussian states over their subjects.

Not religion, but nationalism, Steven Pincus suggests, was the key factor in the rationalization of the English state in the late seventeenth century. Although social scientists have sometimes equated nationalism with state-produced "official nationalism" (see Anderson 1983), recent writing has explored the ways in which nationalist culture and discourse shape states, territorial boundaries, and patterns of inclusion and exclusion among states-in-formation (see Renault 1991; Brubaker 1992). Benedict Anderson (1983) argued that the cultural conditions for the rise of nationalism—and hence for the rise the nationally defined state—included, inter alia, the end of universal religion, and the advent of "print capitalism." Against Anderson, Pincus argues that the English began imagining themselves as a nation before the eighteenth century's "dusk of religious modes of thought"—although nationalism *was* linked to the end of religious universalism in Europe. English nationalism arose in the seventeenth century as part of a vigorous discussion of what was perceived as the grave threat of "universal monarchy"—first associated with the Habsburgs, then the Dutch and the French. This nationalism contributed to the defeat of the "French style of governance" in the English state in 1688–1689 and the subsequent creation of a "new type of state."

THE preceding essays concern the transition to "modern" political forms in Europe; those following look at the modernization of states in non-European settings. More specifically, these essays explore the effect of Western political ideologies and state forms in non-Western, colonial, and postcolonial settings.

Andrew Apter's essay examines the genealogy of the Nigerian Durbar. This state ceremonial has roots in the precolonial period, but as Apter shows, it was reconfigured by the British colonizers. Some components of the Nigerian Durbar were imported from colonial India; these were in turn derived partly from the techniques and imagery of Victorian monarchical rule (Cohn 1983). The colonial-era Nigerian Durbar also put on display the discourse that underpinned British colonial rule. This was particularly evident in the Durbar's organization around displays of Nigerian culture and its ethnic and social divisions. British rule rested culturally on the reinvention of tradition and indirect rule, and the Durbar's form reflected British as well as local culture. In the postcolonial era, finally, the Durbar has been recreated once again, but it has also retained many of the components introduced by the British. Apter's densely textured study throws into clear relief the dialectical relations between culture and state formation: Even as the Nigerian state attempts to invent a precolonial tradition, it is constrained by cultural raw materials that are inherited from the colonial era.

Nader Sohrabi's chapter examines the interplay between Persian sociopolitical discourse and European political models in the unfolding of the 1906 constitutional revolution in Iran. Various writers have focused on the adoption of Western political models by modernizing non-Western countries (see Badie 1992; Meyer this volume).[60] Arjomand (1992), for instance, shows that the contents of each new wave of constitutions reflect the dominant political culture of the

---

[60] See also Bayert (1993) and Davidson (1992), who argue that the Western-style forms of rule prescribed as ideals for postcolonial Africa have been destructive and less appropriate than select precolonial forms.

world-historical era in which they were adopted. Sohrabi's study destabilizes the notion of simple diffusion or emulation by showing in close historical detail how European (specifically French) models of revolution and constitutionalism were articulated with deeply entrenched Iranian political discourses in the new revolutionary setting. Western political ideas were reinterpreted through the conceptual lens of the "Circle of Justice." Sohrabi also demonstrates how the complex interplay between different readings of the constitutionalist model shaped the day-by-day course of revolutionary action and the ongoing transformations of the state. Like Apter, Sohrabi opens up a space for more nuanced approaches to diffusion, cultural modeling, and the reinvention of tradition. In a more general sense this essay illustrates how studies of non-Western state formation can avoid both the Scylla of essentialism found in the Weberian and national culture traditions and the Charybdis of ignoring cultural difference, characteristic of the utilitarian and Marxist traditions.[61]

THE essays in the final section turn their attention to the modern West and its post-Soviet periphery; that is, to the universe of states that are typically seen as "beyond culture."

David Laitin's essay explores the reciprocal relations between states and ethnic or linguistic cultures in the context of the post-Soviet successor states. Laitin's approach combines discourse analysis and rational-choice theory, theorizing the relationship between cultural constraint and strategic choices. Laitin's point of departure is the apparent rise of a diasporic Russian-speaking identity group in states controlled by non-Russian-speaking "titular nationalities." Through a discourse analysis of ordinary language, Laitin is able to demonstrate the unforeseen and counterintuitive emergence of this linguistically delimited "national" group. Laitin argues that the nationality and language policies of the former Soviet Union created the identities of the titular nationalities that dominate post-Soviet states and politics (1995; Kaiser 1994). These inherited identities are in turn shaping the formation of the successor states, especially the processes by which they delimit their citizenry. But the long-term development of these states is shaped not only by these cultural legacies; the cultural *strategies* currently pursued by titular nationals and Russian speakers also make a difference. Laitin explores the microlevel choices made by Russian speakers when confronted with regimes controlled by either culturally nationalist titular elites or those who adopt a more tolerant civic nationalism.

Feminists have written extensively on the impact of ideologies of gender on social policy (Pateman 1988; Connell 1987, 1990). Nelson (1984), Fraser (1987), and Gordon (1988) argue that the division of contemporary social policy systems into male and female "streams" cannot be reduced to economic interests, but expresses culturally specific understandings of appropriate gender roles for women

---

[61] It may not be exaggerated to see Sohrabi's analytical stance as exemplifying what Rabinow (1986: 258; cited in Beal 1995: 301) has called "critical cosmopolitanism," which is "highly attentive to (and respectful of) difference, but is also wary of the tendency to essentialize difference."

and men.[62] In an influential article, Jenson (1986) demonstrated that French and British social policies differed as a function of the "universe of political discourse," especially nationally specific gender ideologies. In an effort to systematize research on gender regimes, Ann Orloff develops a detailed typology for analyzing the different gender-relevant dimensions of welfare states (see Orloff, this volume). Social policies can exhibit contradictory positions with respect to three main gender-relevant dimensions: (1) sameness versus difference; (2) equality versus inequality; and (3) women's autonomy versus their dependency. Her article then provides a densely layered historical comparison of the gender regimes of the Australian, Canadian, British, and American welfare states. This article makes an important contribution to current feminist debates about issues of equality versus difference, redrawing the central question in more complex ways and intervening in the discussion about appropriate political strategies.

Mabel Berezin's essay looks at fascist Italy, the state that pioneered many of the political rituals that we associate with the Nazi state (or contemporary electoral campaigns). Recalling the Geertzian literature on non-Western "theatre states," Berezin argues that twentieth-century states shifted from a textually based "politics of prose," focused on literacy, the rights of man, and the rule of law, to a "politics of theater." The Italian fascists attempted to build a nation through public ritual. Unlike much current writing on nationalism, Berezin focuses not on ideas but on rituals, spaces, actions, and emotions that brought together Italians from different regions. Although political ritual did not achieve its express purpose, the creation of enduring new identities, it was able to communicate to the people and to allow the state to speak *to itself*. Berezin provides a subtle analysis of the ways states both exploit and are constrained by preexisting discourses, such as the Catholic culture of family and motherhood.

Where Adams's paper brings out the "cultural repressed" of the explicitly anticulturalist rational-choice approach, Bob Jessop's piece draws out the culturalist subtext of his own regulation theoretic account of postwar political economy and the state. Jessop points to the "implicit constructivism" of the ostensibly economistic regulationist perspective. Fordism—the dominant postwar mode of regulation, according to regulation theory—involved not only a much greater degree of state involvement in the regulation of financial and labor markets, welfare provision, and production. At the level of political-economic discourse, Fordism was also centered around imagining relatively closed national economies as the natural objects of economic regulation. Fordism was characterized by a strong degree of correspondence between the geographic space of economic regulation and the territory of the nation-state, in ways that reinforced the central state's claim to be the penultimate source of power. By the same token, the emerging post-Fordist regulatory mode represents not only a political-economic shift but also a process of cultural innovation. The most salient aspects of this

[62] Women are especially concentrated in the public assistance sector (Nelson 1984: 210), which assigns them the disempowered role of "client." Men, by contrast, tend to be beneficiaries of the social insurance stream, which grants them the right to social benefits and the relative empowerment that goes with that right.

cultural production are for Jessop discourses of enterprise culture, privatization, and political-economic organization at the subnational level and across national boundaries.

Epilogue

The conclusion is by Charles Tilly, probably the single most important contributor to the literature on state-formation in recent decades. Rather than reviewing the preceding essays, Tilly's intervention is more general and much more ambitious. He argues that the place of culture in political and social analysis can be properly specified only by rejecting individualism and holism as ontological positions and by embracing a position similar to that of contemporary critical realism (see Steinmetz 1998). Tilly then sketches an entire "relational sociology" and its analysis of four central forms of state-culture interaction.

References

Abraham, David. 1986. *The Collapse of the Weimar Republic: Political Economy and Crisis*. Princeton: Princeton University Press.

Abrams, Philip. 1988. "Notes on the Difficulty of Studying the State." *Journal of Historical Sociology* 1 (March): 58–89.

Adams, Julia. 1994. "The Familial State: Elite Family Practices and State-Making in the Early Modern Netherlands." *Theory and Society* 23, no. 4: 505–39.

Almond, Gabriel. 1988. "Return to the State." *American Political Science Review* 82, no. 3: 853–74.

Almond, Gabriel A., and Sidney Verba. 1963. *The Civic Culture: Political Attitudes and Democracy in Five Nations*. Princeton: Princeton University Press.

———, eds. 1980. *The Civic Culture Revistited: An Analytic Study*. Boston: Little, Brown.

Althusser, Louis. 1971a. "Ideology and Ideological State Apparatuses." In *Lenin and Philosophy*, 121–72. London: NLB.

———. 1971b. "A Letter on Art in Reply to André Daspre." In *Lenin and Philosophy*, 221–27. London: NLB.

Althusser, Louis, and Etienne Balibar. 1979. *Reading Capital*. London: Verso.

Aly, Götz et al. 1987. *Sozialpolitik und Judenvernichtung: Gibt es eine Ökonomie der Endlösung?* Berlin: Rotbuch.

Anderson, Benedict. 1983. *Imagined Communities: Reflections on the Origins and Spread of Nationalism*. London: Verso.

———. 1990. *Language and Power: Exploring Political Cultures in Indonesia*. Ithaca: Cornell University Press.

Anderson, Perry. 1976. *Considerations on Western Marxism*. London: Verso.

———. 1977. "The Antinomies of Antonio Gramsci." *New Left Review* no. 100: 5–78.

———. 1978. *Passages from Antiquity to Feudalism*. London: Verso

———. 1979. *Lineages of the Absolutist State*. London: Verso
———. 1976. *Considerations on Western Marxism*. London: Verso.

Arjomand, Said Amir. 1992. "Constitutions and the Struggle for Political Order: A Study in the Modernization of Political Traditions." *Archives of European Sociology* 33: 39–82.

Ayçoberry, Pierre. 1981. *The Nazi Question: An Essay on the Interpretations of National Socialism (1922–1975)*. New York: Pantheon Books.

Badie, Bertrand. 1983. *Culture et politique*. Paris: Economica.

———. 1992. *L'État importé: essai sur l'occidentalisation de l'ordre politique*. Paris: Fayard.

Badie, Bertrand, and Pierre Birnbaum. 1983. *Sociology of the State*. Chicago: University of Chicago Press.

Bahti, Timothy. 1997. "Anacoluthon: On Cultural Studies." *Modern Language Notes* 112, no. 3: 366–84.

Balandier, Georges. 1991. *Anthropologie politique*. 2d ed. Paris: PUF.

Baldwin, Peter. 1990. *The Politics of Social Solidarity: The Class Bases of the European Welfare State 1875–1975*. New York: Cambridge University Press.

Barnard, F. M. 1969. "Introduction." In *J. G. Herder on Social and Political Culture*, edited and translated by F.M. Barnard. Cambridge: Cambridge University Press.

Barrows, Clyde. 1993. *Critical Theories of the State: Marxist, Neo-Marxist, Post-Marxist*. Madison: University of Wisconsin Press.

Barry, Andrew, Thomas Osborne, and Nikolas Rose, eds. 1996. *Foucault and Political Reason*. Chicago: University of Chicago Press.

Barthes, Roland. 1972 [1957]. *Mythologies*. New York: Hill and Wang.

Baudrillard, Jean. 1983a. *In the Shadow of the Silent Majorities*. New York : Semiotext(e).

———. 1983b. *Simulations*. New York: Semiotext(e).

Bauman, Zygmunt. 1989. *Modernity and the Holocaust*. Ithaca: Cornell University Press.

Bayert, Jean-François. 1993. *The State in Africa*. London: Longman.

Beal, E. Anne. 1995. "Reflections on Ethnography in Morocco: A Critical Reading of Three Seminal Texts." *Critique of Anthropology* 15, no. 3: 289–304.

Bellah, Robert Neelly. [1957] 1969. *Tokugawa Religion: The Values of Pre-Industrial Japan*. New York: Free Press.

Benjamin, Walter. 1969. *Illuminations*. New York: Schocken.

Berger, Peter, and Thomas Luckmann. 1966. *The Social Construction of Reality*. New York: Doubleday.

Berman, Russell. 1995. "Global Thinking, Local Teaching: Departments, Curricula, and Culture." *Profession* 95: 89–93.

Bhaskar, Roy. 1979. *The Possibility of Naturalism*. New York: Humanities Press.

———. 1986. *Scientific Realism and Human Emancipation*. London: Verso.

Block, Fred. 1988a. "The Ruling Class Does Not Rule: Notes on the Marxist Theory of the State." In *Revising State Theory*, 51–68. Philadelphia: Temple University Press.

———. 1988b. "State Theory in Context." In *Revising State Theory*, 3–35. Philadelphia: Temple University Press.

Bocock, Robert. 1996. "The Cultural Foundations of Modern Society." In *Modernity: An Introduction to Modern Societies*, edited by David Held, Don Hubert, Stuart Hall, and Kenneth Thompson, 149–83. Cambridge, Mass.: Blackwell.

Bourdieu, Pierre. 1977. *Outline of a Theory of Practice*, translated by Richard Nice. Cambridge: Cambridge University Press.

———. 1984. *Distinction*, translated by Richard Nice. Cambridge: Harvard University Press.

———. 1986. "The Forms of Capital." In *Handbook of Theory and Research for the Sociology of Education*, edited by J. C. Richardson, 241–58. New York: Greenwood Press.

———. 1988. *Homo Academicus*. Stanford: Stanford University Press.

———. 1989. *La noblesse d'état: Grandes écoles et esprit de corps*. Paris: Les Éditions de Minuit.

Bourdieu, Pierre, and Loïc J. D. Wacquant. 1992. *An Invitation to Reflexive Sociology*. Chicago: University of Chicago Press.

Bracher, Karl Dietrich. 1973. *The German Dictatorship: The Origins, Structure, and Effects of National Socialism*. New York: Praeger Publishers.

Bracher, Karl Dietrich, Wolfgang Sauer, and Gerhard Schulz. [1960] 1979. *Die nationalsozialistische Machtergreifung: Studien zur Errichtung des totalitären Herrschaftssystems in Deutschland 1933/34*. Frankfurt am Main: Ullstein.

Brenner, Neil. 1997. "Unthinking State-Centrism: Territoriality, Differentiation, and Spatial Scale in Globalization Studies." Unpublished Essay. University of Chicago.

Brock, Lothar, and Mathias Albert. 1995. "De-Bordering the State: New Spaces in International Relations." Paper presented at annual meeting of the American Political Science Association, Chicago.

Browning, Christopher R. 1992. *Ordinary Men: Reserve Police Battalion 101 and the Final Solution in Poland*. New York: HarperPerennial.

Brownstein, Larry. 1995. "A Reappraisal of the Concept of 'Culture.'" *Social Epistemology* 9, no. 4: 311–51.

Brubaker, Rogers. 1992. *Citizenship and Nationhood in France and Germany*. Cambridge: Harvard University Press.

Burchell, Graham, Colin Gordon, and Peter Miller, eds. 1991. *The Foucault Effect: Studies in Governmentality*. Chicago: University of Chicago Press.

Burleigh, Michael, and Wolfgang Wippermann. 1991. *The Racial State: Germany, 1933–1945*. Cambridge: Cambridge University Press.

Butler, Judith. 1993. "Critically Queer." In *Bodies That Matter: On the Discursive Limits of "Sex"*, 223–42. New York: Routledge.

Calhoun, Craig. 1994. *Social Theory and the Politics of Identity*. Oxford and Cambridge, Mass.: Blackwell.

Cammack, Paul. 1989. "Bringing the State Back In: A Polemic." *British Journal of Political Science* 19, no. 2: 261–90.

Campbell, John L., J. Rogers Hollingsworth, and Leon N. Lindberg, eds. 1991. *Governance of the American Economy*. Cambridge: Cambridge University Press.

Carnoy, Martin. 1984. *The State and Political Theory*. Princeton: Princeton University Press.

Carrier, James G. 1995. *Occidentalism: Images of the West*. Oxford: Oxford University Press.

Cassirer, Ernst. 1946. *The Myth of the State*. New Haven: Yale University Press.

Centre for Contemporary Cultural Studies. 1977. *On Ideology*. Birmingham, England: Centre for Contemporary Cultural Studies.

Clastres, Pierre. 1974. *La société contre l'état*. Paris: Les Éditions de Minuit.

Cohen, G. A. 1978. *Karl Marx's Theory of History: A Defence*. Princeton: Princeton University Press.

Cohen, Jean L., and Andrew Arato. 1992. *Civil Society and Political Theory*. Cambridge: MIT Press.

Cohn, Bernard. 1983. "Representing Authority in Victorian India." In *The Invention of Tradition*, edited by Eric Hobsbawm and Terence Ranger, 165–209. Cambridge: Cambridge University Press.

Cohn, Carol. 1987. "Sex and Death in the Rational World of Defense Intellectuals." *Signs* 12, no. 4: 687–718.

Collier, Andrew. 1994. *Critical Realism: An Introduction to Roy Bhaskar's Philosophy*. New York: Verso.

Comaroff, Jean, and John Comaroff. 1991. *Of Revelation and Revolution: Christianity, Colonialism, and Consciousness in South Africa*. Chicago: University of Chicago Press.

Connell, R. W. 1987. *Gender and Power*. Stanford, Calif.: Stanford University Press.

——. 1990. "The State, Gender, and Sexual Politics." *Theory and Society* 19: 507–44.

Coronil, Fernando. 1997. *The Magical State: Nature, Money and Modernity in Venezuela*. Chicago: University of Chicago Press.

Corrigan, Philip, and Derek Sayer. 1985. *The Great Arch: English State Formation as Cultural Revolution*. Oxford: Basil Blackwell.

Curtis, Bruce. 1995. "Taking the State Back Out: Rose and Miller on Political Power." *British Journal of Sociology* 46, no. 4: 575–97.

Dahrendorf, Ralf. 1967. *Society and Democracy in Germany*. New York: Norton.

Davidson, Basil. 1992. *The Black Man's Burden: Africa and the Curse of the Nation State*. New York: Times Books.

Dean, Mitchell. 1994a. "'A Social Structure of Many Souls': Moral Regulation, Government, and Self-Formation." *Canadian Journal of Sociology* 19, no. 2: 145–68.

——. 1994b. *Critical and Effective Histories: Foucault's Methods and Historical Sociology*. London: Routledge.

Deleuze, Gilles, and Félix Guattari. 1986. *Nomadology: The War Machine*. New York: Semiotext(e).

Der Derian, James. 1994. *Antidiplomacy: Spies, Terror, Speed, and War*. Cambridge: Blackwell.

Dijk, Teun A. van, ed. 1985. *Handbook of Discourse Analysis*. 4 vols. London and Orlando, Fla.: Academic Press.

Dirks, Nicholas. 1993. *The Hollow Core: Ethnohistory of an Indian Kingdom*, 2d ed. Ann Arbor: University of Michigan Press.

Dirks, Nicholas B., Geoff Eley, and Sherry B. Ortner. 1994. "Introduction." In *Culture/Power/History: A Reader in Contemporary Social Theory*, edited by Nicholas B. Dirks, Geoff Eley, and Sherry B. Ortner, 3–45. Princeton: Princeton University Press.

Doob, Leonard W. 1964. *Patriotism and Nationalism: Their Psychological Foundations*. New Haven: Yale University Press.

During, Simon. 1993. "Introduction." In *The Cultural Studies Reader*, edited by Simon During, 1–25. London: Routledge.

Durkheim, Émile. [1915] 1965. *The Elementary Forms of the Religious Life*. New York: Free Press.

———. [1957] 1992. *Professional Ethics and Civic Morals*. London: Routledge.

Eagleton, Terry. 1991. *Ideology: An Introduction*. London: Verso.

Easton, David. 1953. *The Political System: An Inquiry into the State of Political Science*. New York: Knopf.

Edelman, Murray. 1964. *The Symbolic Uses of Politics*. Urbana: University of Illinois Press.

———. 1995. *From Art to Politics: How Artistic Creations Shape Political Conceptions*. Chicago: University of Chicago Press.

Eisenstadt, S. N. 1963. *The Political Systems of Empires*. Glencoe, Ill.: The Free Press of Glencoe.

Eley, Geoff. 1986a. "What Produces Fascism: Pre-Industrial Traditions or a Crisis of the Capitalist State?" In *From Unification to Nazism: Reinterpreting the German Past*, 254–82. Boston: Allen and Unwin.

———. 1986b. *From Unification to Nazism: Reinterpreting the German Past*. Boston: Allen and Unwin.

Elias, Norbert. 1994. *The Civilizing Process*. Oxford: Blackwell.

Elshtain, Jean Bethke. 1992. "Sovereignty, Identity, Sacrifice." In *Gendered States: Feminist (Re)visions of International Relations Theory*, edited by Spike Peterson, 141–54. Boulder, Colo.: Lynne Rienner Publishers.

Elster, Jon. 1985. *Making Sense of Marx*. Cambridge: Cambridge University Press.

Engelstein, Laura. 1994. "Combined Underdevelopment: Discipline and the Law in Imperial and Soviet Russia." In *Foucault and the Writing of History*, edited by Jan Goldstein, 220–36. Cambridge, Mass.: Blackwell.

Enloe, Cynthia. 1989. *Bananas, Beaches, and Bases: Making Feminist Sense of International Politics*. Berkeley: University of California Press.

———. 1993. *The Morning After: Sexual Politics at the End of the Cold War*. Berkeley: University of California Press.

Ermakoff, Ivan. 1997. "Crisis and Abdication: A Comparative Inquiry into the

Process of Republican Breakdowns." Ph.D. diss. Chicago: University of Chicago.

Esping-Andersen, Gøsta. 1990. *The Three Worlds of Welfare Capitalism*. Princeton: Princeton University Press.

Foucault, Michel. 1970. *The Order of Things: An Archaeology of the Human Sciences*. London: Tavistock.

———. 1972. *The Archaeology of Knowledge*. New York: Pantheon.

———. 1979. *Discipline and Punish: The Birth of the Prison*. New York: Vintage Books.

———. 1980a. "Body/Power." In *Power/Knowledge*, edited by Colin Gordon, 55–62. New York: Pantheon Books.

———. 1980b. "Two Lectures." In *Power/Knowledge*, edited by Colin Gordon, 78–108. New York: Pantheon Books.

———. 1980c. "The Politics of Health in the Eighteenth Century." In *Power/Knowledge*, edited by Colin Gordon, 166–93. New York: Pantheon Books.

———. 1980d. *The History of Sexuality: An Introduction*. New York: Vintage.

———. 1981. "Omnes et Singulatim: Towards a Criticism of 'Political Reason.'" In *The Tanner Lectures on Human Values, vol. 2*, edited by Sterling M. MacMurrin, 225–54. New York: Cambridge University Press.

———. 1988. "The Political Technology of Individuals." In *Technologies of the Self: A Seminar with Michel Foucault*, edited by Huck Gutman, Luther H. Martin, and Patrick H. Hutton, 145–62. Amherst: University of Massachusetts Press.

———. 1991. "Governmentality." In *The Foucault Effect: Studies in Governmentality*, edited by Colin Gordon, Graham Burchell, and Peter Miller, 87–104. Chicago: University of Chicago Press.

Fraser, Nancy. 1987. "Women, Welfare, and the Politics of Need Interpretation." *Hypatia: A Journal of Feminist Philosophy* 2, no. 1: 103–21.

Frazer, James George [1900] 1922. *The Golden Bough: A Study in Magic and Religion*. New York: Collier, Macmillan.

———. [1905] 1920. *The Magical Origin of Kings*. London: Macmillan.

Geertz, Clifford. 1973a. "Thick Description: Toward an Interpretive Theory of Culture." In *The Interpretation of Cultures*, 3–30. New York: Basic Books.

———. 1973b. "The Impact of the Concept of Culture on the Concept of Man." In *The Interpretation of Cultures*, 33–54. New York: Basic Books

———. 1980. *Negara: The Theatre State in Nineteenth Century Bali*. Princeton: Princeton University Press.

———. 1983. "Centers, Kings, and Charisma: Symbolics of Power." In *Local Knowledge: Further Essays in Interpretive Anthropology*, 121–46. New York: Basic Books.

Giddens, Anthony. 1979. *Central Problems in Social Theory: Action, Structure and Contradiction in Social Analysis*. Berkeley: University of California Press.

Go, Julian, III. 1996. "Inventing Industrial Accidents and Their Insurance: Discourse and Workers' Compensation in the United States, 1880s–1910s." *Social Science History* 20(Fall): 403–38.

Gold, David A., Clarence Y. H. Lo, and Erik Olin Wright. 1975. "Recent Developments in Marxist Theories of the Capitalist State." *Monthly Review* Oct./Nov.: 29–51.

Goldhagen, Daniel Jonah. 1996. *Hitler's Willing Executioners: Ordinary Germans and the Holocaust*. New York: Knopf.

Gordon, Linda. 1988. "What Does Welfare Regulate?" *Social Research* 55, no. 4: 609–30.

Gramsci, Antonio. 1971. *Selections from the Prison Notebooks*, edited and translated by Quinton Hoare and Geoffrey Nowell Smith. New York: International Publishers.

Greider, William. 1996. *One World, Ready or Not: The Manic Logic of Global Capitalism*. New York: Simon and Schuster.

Grossberg, Lawrence, Cary Nelson, and Paul A. Treichler. 1992. *Cultural Studies*. New York: Routledge.

Haas, Ernst B. 1990. *When Knowledge is Power: Three Models of Change in International Organizations*. Berkeley: University of California Press.

Haas, Ernst B., Mary Pat Williams, and Don Babai. 1977. *Scientists and World Order: The Uses of Technical Knowledge in International Organizations*. Berkeley: University of California Press.

Habermas, Jürgen. [1962] 1989. *The Structural Transformation of the Public Sphere: An Inquiry into a Category of Bourgeois Society*. Cambridge: The MIT Press.

Hall, Stuart. 1993. "Metaphors of Transformation." Introduction to *Carnival, Hysteria and Writing: Collected Essays and Autobiography*, by Allon White. Oxford: Oxford University Press.

——. 1994. "Cultural Studies: Two Paradigms." In *Culture/Power/History: A Reader in Contemporary Social Theory*, edited by Nicholas B. Dirks, Geoff Eley, and Sherry B. Ortner, 520–38. Princeton: Princeton University Press.

Heclo, Hugh. 1974. *Modern Social Politics in Britain and Sweden*. New Haven: Yale University Press.

Hedström, Peter. 1996. "Review of *Pathologies of Rational Choice Theory: A Critique of Applications in Political Science*." *Contemporary Sociology* 25, no. 2: 278–79.

Hell, Julia. 1992. "At the Center an Absence: East German Foundationalist Narratives and the Discourse of Antifascism." *Monatshefte* 84 (Spring).

——. 1997. *Post-Fascist Fantasies: Psychoanalysis, History, and the Literature of East Germany*. Durham: Duke University Press.

Hirst, Paul, and Grahame Thompson. 1996. *Globalization in Question*. Cambridge: Polity Press.

Hobsbawm, Eric, and Terence Ranger, eds. 1983. *The Invention of Tradition*. Cambridge: Cambridge University Press.

Holloway, John. 1994. "Global Capital and the State." *Capital and Class* 52 (Spring): 23–49.

Holloway, John, and Sol Picciotto, eds. 1978. *State and Capital: A Marxist Debate*. London: Edward Arnold.

Horkheimer, Max and Theodor W. Adorno. 1972 [1944]. *Dialectic of Enlighten-ment*. New York: Herder and Herder.

Hunt, Lynn. 1992. *The Family Romance of the French Revolution*. Berkeley: University of California Press.

Huntington, Samuel. 1993. "The Clash of Civilizations?" *Foreign Affairs* 72: 1–22.

———. 1996. *The Clash of Civilizations and the Remaking of World Order*. New York: Simon and Schuster.

Inkeles, Alex. 1961. "National Character and Modern Political Systems." In *Psychological Anthropology*, edited by Francis L. K. Hsu, 172–208. Homewood, Ill.: Dorsey Press.

———. 1974. *Becoming Modern: Individual Change in Six Developing Countries*. Cambridge: Harvard University Press.

Jenson, Jane. 1986. "Gender and Reproduction: Or, Babies and the State." *Studies in Political Economy* 20: 9–46.

Jessop, Bob. 1982. *The Capitalist State*. New York: New York University Press.

———. 1990a. *State Theory: Putting States in Their Place*. University Park: Pennsylvania State University Press.

———. 1990b. "Anti-Marxist Reinstatement and Post-Marxist Deconstruction." In *State Theory: Putting States in Their Place*, 278–306. University Park: Pennsylvania State University Press.

———. 1994. "Post-Fordism and the State." In *Post-Fordism*, edited by Ash Amin, 251–79. Oxford: Blackwell.

Kaiser, Robert J. 1994. *The Geography of Nationalism in Russia and the USSR*. Princeton: Princeton University Press.

Kalberg, Stephen. 1980. "Max Weber's Types of Rationality: Cornerstones for the Analysis of Rationalization Processes in History." *American Journal of Sociology* 85, no. 5: 1145–79.

Kershaw, Ian. 1993. *The Nazi Dictatorship: Problems and Perspectives of Interpretation*, 3d ed. London: Edward Arnold.

Kitschelt, Herbert. 1994. *The Transformation of European Social Democracy*. New York: Cambridge University Press.

Kratochwil, Friedrich. 1986. "Of Systems, Boundaries, and Territoriality." *World Politics* 39, no. 1: 27–52.

Kroeber, A. L., and C. Kluckhohn, eds. 1952. *Culture: A Critical Review of Concepts and Definitions*, vol. 47. Papers of the Peabody Museum of American Archaeology and Ethnology. Cambridge (Harvard University): The Museum.

Kroeber, A. L., and Talcott Parsons. 1958. "The Concepts of Culture and of Social System." *American Sociological Review* 23, no. 5: 582–83.

Kuhn, Thomas. [1962] 1970. *The Structure of Scientific Revolutions*. 2d ed. Chicago: University of Chicago Press.

Laclau, Ernesto. 1977. *Politics and Ideology in Marxist Theory*. London: Verso.

———. 1997. "The Death and Resurrection of the Theory of Ideology." *MLN* 112 (April): 297–321.

Laclau, Ernesto, and Chantal Mouffe. 1985. *Hegemony and Socialist Strategy: Towards a Radical Democratic Politics*. London: Verso.

——. 1987. "Post-Marxism without Apologies." *New Left Review* 166: 79–106.

Laitin, David D. 1986. *Hegemony and Culture: Politics and Religious Change among the Yoruba*. Chicago: University of Chicago Press.

——. 1988. "Political Culture and Political Preferences." *American Political Science Review* 82: 589–93.

——. 1995. "Identity in Formation: The Russian-Speaking Nationality in the Post-Soviet Diaspora." *Archives Européenes de Sociologie* 36: 281–316.

Larrain, Jorge. 1979. *The Concept of Ideology*. London: Hutchinson.

Lash, Scott. 1990. *The Sociology of Postmodernism*. New York: Routledge.

Latour, Bruno. 1987. *Science in Action: How to Follow Scientists and Engineers Through Society*. Cambridge: Harvard University Press.

Laumann, Edward O., and David Knoke. 1987. *The Organizational State*. Madison: University of Wisconsin Press.

Lefort, Claude. 1986. "The Logic of Totalitarianism." In *The Political Forms of Modern Society*, edited by John B. Thompson, 273–91. Cambridge: MIT Press.

Lowie, Robert H. 1947. *An Introduction to Cultural Anthropology*, 2d ed. New York: Rinehart.

Luhmann, Niklas. 1989. *Ecological Communication*. Chicago: University of Chicago Press.

——. 1995. *Social Systems: Writing Science*. Stanford, Calif.: Stanford University Press.

Lukács, Georg. 1971. *History and Class Consciousness*. Cambridge: MIT Press.

Macherey, Pierre. 1978. *Pour une théorie de la production littéraire*. Paris: Maspero.

MacIntyre, Alasdair. [1967] 1978. "Is a Science of Comparative Politics Possible?" In *Against the Self-Images of the Age: Essays on Ideology and Philosophy*, 260–79. Notre Dame: University of Notre Dame.

Mandel, Ernest. 1975. *Late Capitalism*. London: NLB.

Mann, Michael. 1986. *The Sources of Social Power: A History of Power from the Beginning to A.D. 1760, vol. I*. New York: Cambridge University Press.

——. 1993. *The Sources of Social Power: The Rise of Classes and Nation-States, 1760–1914, vol. II*. New York: Cambridge University Press.

Marx, Karl. 1964. *Early Writings*, translated by T. B. Bottomore. New York: McGraw-Hill.

——. 1970a. "The German Ideology (Chapter 1)." In *Marx and Engels, Selected Works, vol. 1*, 16–80. Moscow: Progress.

——. 1970b. "The Eighteenth Brumaire of Louis Bonaparte." In *Marx and Engels, Selected Works, vol. 1*, 394–487. Moscow: Progress.

McLellan, David. 1995. *Ideology*. Minneapolis: University of Minnesota Press.

Meyer, John. 1980. "The World Polity and the Authority of the Nation-State." In *Studies of the Modern World-System*, edited by A. Bergesen. New York: Academic Press.

Miller, Peter, and Nikolas Rose. 1995. "Political Thought and the Limits of Orthodoxy: A Response to Curtis." *British Journal of Sociology* 46, no. 4: 590–97.

Mitchell, Timothy. 1991. "The Limits of the State: Beyond Statist Approaches and Their Critics." *American Political Science Review* 85, no. 1: 77–96.

Nelson, Barbara. 1984. "Women's Poverty and Women's Citizenship: Some Political Consequences of Economic Marginality." *Signs* 10: 209–31.

Nettl, J. P. 1968. "The State as a Conceptual Variable." *World Politics* 20: 559–92.

Oestreich, G. 1982. *Neostoicism and the Early Modern State*. Cambridge: Cambridge University Press.

Omae, Ken'ichi. 1990. *The Borderless World: Power and Strategy in the Interlinked Economy*. New York: Harper Business.

———. 1995. *The End of the Nation-State: The Rise of Regional Economies*. New York: Free Press.

Orloff, Ann Shola, and Theda Skocpol. 1984. "Why Not Equal Protection? Explaining the Politics of Public Social Spending in Britain, 1900–1911, and the United States, 1880s–1920." *American Sociological Review* 49: 726–50.

Parsons, Talcott. 1949. *The Structure of Social Action, vol. 2*. New York: Free Press.

———. 1951. *The Social System*. New York: Free Press.

———. 1965. "Culture and the Social System: Introduction." In *Theories of Society: Foundations of Modern Sociological Theory*, edited by Talcott Parsons, Edward Shils, Kaspar D. Naegele, and Jesse R. Pitts, 963–93. New York: Free Press.

———. 1993. *Talcott Parsons on National Socialism*, edited by Ute Gerhardt. New York: de Gruyter.

Pateman, Carole. 1973. "Political Culture, Political Structure and Political Change." *British Journal of Political Science* 1: 291–305.

———. 1980. "The Civic Culture: A Philosophic Critique." In *The Civic Culture Revisited*, edited by Gabriel A. Almond and Sidney Verba, 57–102. Boston: Little, Brown.

———. 1988. "The Patriarchal Welfare State." In *Democracy and the Welfare State*, edited by Amy Gutmann, 231–60. Princeton: Princeton University Press.

Peterson, Spike, ed. 1992. *Gendered States: Feminist (Re)visions of International Relations Theory*. Boulder, Colo.: Lynne Rienner Publishers.

Polanyi, Karl. 1944. *The Great Transformation*. Boston: Beacon Press.

Postone, Moishe. 1993. *Time, Labor, and Social Domination: A Reinterpretation of Marx's Critical Theory*. New York: Cambridge University Press.

Poulantzas, Nicos. 1974. *Fascism and Dictatorship*. New York: New Left Books.

———. 1975. *Classes in Contemporary Capitalism*. London: New Left Books.

———. 1978. *Political Power and Social Classes*. New York: Verso.

Prinz, Michael, and Rainer Zitelmann. 1991. *Nationalsozialismus und Modernisierung*. Darmstadt: Wissenschaftliche Buchgesellschaft.

Pye, Lucien. 1962. *Politics, Personality, and Nation Building: Burma's Search for Identity*. New Haven: Yale University Press.

———. 1965. "Comparative Political Culture." In *Political Culture and Political Development*, edited by Lucien W. Pye and Sidney Verba, 512–60. Princeton: Princeton University Press.

Rabinow, Paul. 1977. *Reflections on Fieldwork in Morocco*. Berkeley: University of California Press.

———. 1986. "Representations Are Social Facts." In *Writing Culture: The Poetics and Politics of Ethnography*, edited by James Clifford and George E. Marcus, 234–61. Berkeley: University of California Press.

Raeff, Marc. 1983. *The Well-Ordered Police State: Social and Institutional Change Through Law in the Germanies and Russia, 1600–1800*. New Haven: Yale University Press.

Renault, Alain. 1991. "Logiques de la nation." In *Théories du nationalisme; Nation, nationalité, ethnicité*, edited by Gil Delannoi and Pierre-André Taguieff, 29–46. Paris: Editions Kime.

Rorty, Richard M. 1967. *The Linguistic Turn: Essays in Philosophical Method*. Chicago: University of Chicago Press.

———. 1979. *Philosophy and the Mirror of Nature*. Princeton: Princeton University Press.

Rose, N., and P. Miller. 1992. "Political Power Beyond the State: Problematics of Government." *British Journal of Sociology* 43, no. 2: 173–205.

Rosenthal, John. 1988. "Who Practices Hegemony? Class Division and the Subject of Politics." *Cultural Critique*, Spring: 25–52.

Rouban, Luc. 1988. "Innovation, complexité et crise de l'état moderne." *Revue française de science politique* 38, no. 3: 325–47.

Rudolph, Susanne Hoeber. 1987. "Presidential Address: State Formation in Asia—Prolegomenon to a Comparative Study." *Journal of Asian Studies* 46, no. 4: 731–46.

Ruggie, John Gerard. 1993. "Territoriality and Beyond: Problematizing Modernity in International Relations." *International Organization* 47: 139–74.

Sahlins, Marshall. 1981. *Historical Metaphors and Mythical Realities: Structure in the Early History of the Sandwich Islands Kingdom*. Ann Arbor: University of Michigan Press.

Sassen, Saskia. 1996. *Losing Control? Sovereignty in an Age of Globalization*. New York: Columbia University Press.

Scheuch, Erwin K. 1968. "The Cross-Cultural Use of Sample Surveys: Problems of Comparability." In *Comparative Research Across Nations and Cultures*, edited by Stein Rokkan, 176–209. The Hague: Mouton.

Schilling, Heinz. 1994. *Kirchenzucht und Sozialdisziplinerung im frühneuzeitlichen Europa*. Berlin: Duncker and Humblot.

Schluchter, Wolfgang. 1981. *The Rise of Western Rationalism: Max Weber's Developmental History*. Berkeley: University of California Press.

———. 1989. *Rationalism, Religion, and Domination: A Weberian Perspective*. Berkeley: University of California Press.

Scott, Joan Wallach. 1988. "Gender: A Useful Category of Historical Analysis."

In *Gender and the Politics of History*, 28–50. New York: Columbia University Press.

Sedgwick, Eve Kosofsky. 1993. *Tendencies*. Durham: Duke University Press.

Sewell, William Jr. 1985. "Ideologies and Social Revolutions: Reflections on the French Case." *Journal of Modern History* 57: 57–85.

———. 1992. "Introduction: Narratives and Social Identities." *Social Science History* 16, no. 3: 479–88.

Shils, Edward. 1972. "Center and Periphery." In *The Constitution of Society*, 93–109. Chicago: University of Chicago Press.

Sismondo, Sergio. 1993. "Some Social Constructions." *Social Studies of Science* 23: 515–53.

Skalník, Peter. 1987. "On the Inadequacy of the Concept of the 'Traditional State.'" *Journal of Legal Pluralism* 25/26: 301–26.

Skocpol, Theda. 1979. *States and Social Revolutions*. New York: Cambridge University Press.

———. 1985. "Bringing the State Back In: Strategies of Analysis in Current Research." In *Bringing the State Back In*, edited by Dietrich Rueschemeyer, Peter B. Evans, and Theda Skocpol, 3–43. New York: Cambridge University Press.

———. 1996. *Boomerang: Clinton's Health Security Effort and the Turn against Government in U.S. Politics*. New York: W. W. Norton.

Skocpol, Theda, and Kenneth Finegold. 1982. "State Capacity and Economic Intervention in the Early New Deal." *Political Science Quarterly* 97 (Summer): 255–78.

Skocpol, Theda, and John Ikenberry. 1983. "The Political Formation of the American Welfare State in Historical and Comparative Perspective." *Comparative Social Research* 6: 87–147.

Snow, David A., and Robert D. Benford. 1988. "Ideology, Frame Resonance, and Participant Mobilization." *International Social Movement Research* 1: 197–217.

Somers, Margaret R. 1995. "What's Political or Cultural About Political Culture and the Public Sphere? Toward a Historical Sociology of Concept Formation." *Sociological Theory* 13 (July): 113–44.

Southall, Aidan. 1988. "The Segmentary State in Africa and Asia." *Comparative Studies in Society and History* 30, no. 1: 52–88.

Der Spiegel. 1996. "'Wie Maos rotes Buch.' Der französischer Soziologe Pierre Bordieu über die Bundesbank und die neoliberale Wirtschaftspolitik." *Der Spiegel* 50 (December 9): 172–79.

Steinmetz, George. 1993. *Regulating the Social: The Welfare State and Local Politics in Imperial Germany*. Princeton: Princeton University Press.

———. 1997a. "German Exceptionalism and the Origins of Nazism: The Career of a Concept." In *Stalinism and Nazism: Dictatorships in Comparison*, edited by Ian Kershaw and Moshe Lewin, 251–84. Cambridge: Cambridge University Press.

———. 1997b. "Theorizing the Colonial State: The German Overseas Empire,

1880–1914." Unpublished paper presented at the annual meetings of the American Sociological Association, Toronto.

——. 1998. "Critical Realism and Historical Sociology." *Comparative Studies in Society and History* 39, no. 4: 170-186.

——. Forthcoming. *Colonial States, Colonial Minds: The Formation of the German Overseas Empire.*

Stern, Fritz. 1961. *The Politics of Cultural Despair: A Study in the Rise of the Germanic Ideology.* Berkeley: University of California Press.

Strayer, Joseph. 1970. *On the Medieval Origins of the Modern State.* Princeton: Princeton University Press.

Sylvester, Christine. 1994. *Feminist Theory and International Relations in a Postmodern Era.* Cambridge: Cambridge University Press.

Tambiah, Stanley J. 1976. *World Conqueror and World Renouncer.* Cambridge: Cambridge University Press.

——. 1977. "The Galactic Polity: The Structure of Traditional Kingdoms in Southeast Asia." In *Anthropology and the Climate of Opinion,* vol. 293, edited by M. Freed. New York: Annals of the New York Academy of Sciences.

Taylor, Charles. 1979. "Interpretation and the Sciences of Man." In *Interpretive Social Science: A Reader,* edited by Paul Rabinow and William M. Sullivan, 25–71. Berkeley: University of California Press.

——. 1985. "Theories of Meaning." In *Human Agency and Language. Philosophical Papers I,* 248–92. New York: Cambridge University Press.

——. 1989. *Sources of the Self: The Making of Modern Identity.* Cambridge: Harvard University Press.

Teeple, Gary. 1995. *Globalization and the Decline of Social Reform.* Atlantic Highlands, N.J.: Humanities Press.

Thomas, George M., and Pat Lauterdale. 1987. "World Polity Sources of National Welfare and Land Reform." In *Institutional Structure: Constituting State, Society, and the Individual,* edited by George M. Thomas, John W. Meyer, Francisco O. Ramirez, and John Boli, 198–214. Newbury Park, Calif.: Sage Publishers.

Thomas, George M., and John W. Meyer. 1984. "The Expansion of the State." *Annual Review of Sociology* 10: 461–82.

Thomas, Nicholas. 1994. *Colonialism's Cultures. Anthropology, Travel and Government.* Princeton: Princeton University Press, 1994.

Thompson, E. P. 1993. *Customs in Common. Studies in Traditional Popular Culture.* New York: New Press.

Thompson, John B. 1984. *Studies in the Theory of Ideology.* Cambridge: Polity Press.

Tilly, Charles. 1985. "War Making and State Making as Organized Crime." In *Bringing the State Back In,* edited by Dietrich Rueschemeyer, Peter B. Evans, and Theda Skocpol, 167–91. New York: Cambridge University Press.

——. 1990. *Coercion, Capital, and European States, AD 990–1990.* Cambridge, Mass.: Blackwell.

Tucker, Robert C., ed. 1972. *The Marx-Engels Reader*. New York: W. W. Norton.

Turner, Bryan S. 1974. *Weber and Islam: A Critical Study*. London: Routledge and Kegan Paul.

———. 1996. *For Weber: Essays on the Sociology of Fate*. London: Sage Publications.

Tylor, Edward B. [1871] 1877. *Primitive Culture Research into the Development of Mythology, Philosophy, Religion, Language, Art and Custom*, 2d ed. New York: Henry Holt.

Verba, Sidney. 1965. "Introduction: Political Culture and Political Development." In *Political Culture and Political Development*, edited by Lucien W. Pye and Sidney Verba, 3–26. Princeton: Princeton University Press.

———. 1980. "On Revisiting the Civic Culture: A Personal Postscript." In *The Civic Culture Revisited: An Analytic Study*, edited by Gabriel A. Almond and Sidney Verba, 394–410. Boston: Little, Brown.

Volosinov, V. N. 1985. *Marxism and the Philosophy of Language*. Cambridge: Harvard University Press.

Wacquant, Loïc, and Craig Calhoun. 1989. "Intérêt, rationalité et culture dans la sociologie américaine actuelle. A propos d'un récent débat sur la 'théorie de l'action.'" *Actes de la Recherche en Sciences Sociales* 78: 41–60.

Weber, Max. 1951. *The Religion of China: Confucianism and Taoism*, edited and translated by Hans H. Gerth. New York: Free Press.

———. 1956a. *Staatssoziologie*. Berlin: Duncker and Humblot.

———. 1956b. *Wirtschaft und Gesellschaft. Grundriss der verstehenden Soziologie*. Vol. 1, 4th ed. Edited by Johannes Winckelmann. Tübingen: Mohr.

———. 1958. "Politics as a Vocation." In *From Max Weber*, edited and translated by H. H. Gerth and C. Wright Mills. New York: Oxford University Press.

———. 1978. *Economy and Society*. Berkeley: University of California Press.

Wehler, Hans-Ulrich. 1985. *The German Empire 1871–1918*. Leamington Spa, U.K.: Berg.

Weir, Margaret, and Theda Skocpol. 1985. "State Structures and the Possibilities of 'Keynesian' Responses to the Great Depression in Sweden, Britain and the United States." In *Bringing the State Back In*, edited by Dietrich Rueschemeyer, Peter B. Evans, and Theda Skocpol, 107–63. New York: Cambridge University Press.

Williams, Raymond. 1977. *Marxism and Literature*. Oxford: Oxford University Press.

———. 1983. *Keywords*, 2d ed. Oxford: Oxford University Press.

Wilson, William Julius. 1980. *The Declining Significance of Race*, 2d ed. Chicago: University of Chicago Press.

Winckelmann, Johannes. 1956a. Introduction to *Staatssoziologie*, by Max Weber, edited by Johannes Winckelmann. Berlin: Duncker and Humblot.

———. 1956b. Introduction to *Wirtschaft und Gesellschaft. Grundriss der verstehenden Soziolgie*. Vol. 1., 4th ed. by Max Weber, edited by Johannes Winckelmann. Tübingen: Mohr.

Wittgenstein, Ludwig. 1953. *Philosophical Investigations* [*Philosophische Untersuchungen*], translated by G.E.M. Anscombe. Oxford: Blackwell.

Woolgar, Steve. 1988. *Science, the Very Idea*. New York: Tavistock.

Yang, Mayfair Mei-hui. 1994. *Gifts, Favors, and Banquets: The Art of Social Relationships in China*. Ithaca: Cornell University Press.

Yee, Albert S. 1996. "The Causal Effects of Ideas on Politics." *International Organization* 50, no. 1: 69–108.

Žižek Slavoj. 1989. *The Sublime Object of Ideology*. New York: Verso.

——. 1991. *For They Know Not What They Do: Enjoyment as a Political Factor*. London: Verso.

STATE/CULTURE: THEORETICAL APPROACHES

I

Rethinking the State: Genesis and Structure of the Bureaucratic Field

Pierre Bourdieu

TRANSLATED BY LOÏC J. D. WACQUANT AND SAMAR FARAGE

To endeavor to think the state is to take the risk of taking over (or being taken over by) a thought of the state, that is, of applying to the state categories of thought produced and guaranteed by the state and hence to misrecognize its most profound truth.[1] This proposition, which may seem both abstract and preemptory, will be more readily accepted if, at the close of the argument, one agrees to return to this point of departure, but armed this time with the knowledge that one of the major powers of the state is to produce and impose (especially through the school system) categories of thought that we spontaneously apply to all things of the social world—including the state itself.

However, to give a first and more intuitive grasp of this analysis and to expose the danger of always being thought by a state that we believe we are thinking, I would like to cite a passage from *Alte Meister Komödie* by Thomas Bernhard:

> School is the state school where young people are turned into state persons and thus into nothing other than henchmen of the state. Walking to school, I was walking into the state and, since the state destroys people, into the institution for the destruction of people. . . . The state forced me, like everyone else, into myself, and made me compliant towards it, the state, and turned me into a state person, regulated and registered and trained and finished and perverted and dejected, like everyone else. When we see people, we only see state people, the state servants, as we quite rightly say, who serve the state all their lives and thus serve unnature all their lives.[2]

[1] This text is the partial and revised transcription of a lecture delivered in Amsterdam on June 29, 1991.

[2] Bernhard (1989: 27).

53

The idiosyncratic rhetoric of T. Bernhard, one of excess and of hyperbole in anathema, is well suited to my intention, which is to subject the state and the thought of the state to a sort of *hyperbolic doubt*. For, when it comes to the state, one never doubts enough. And, though literary exaggeration always risks self-effacement by de-realizing itself in its very excess, one should take what Thomas Bernhard says seriously: to have any chance of thinking a state that still thinks itself through those who attempt to think it (as in the case of Hegel or Durkheim), one must strive to question all the presuppositions and preconstructions inscribed in the reality under analysis as well as in the very thoughts of the analyst.

To show both the difficulty and the necessity of a rupture with the thought of the state, present in the most intimate of our thoughts, one could analyze the battle recently declared—in the midst of the Gulf War—in France about a seemingly insignificant topic: orthography. Correct spelling, designated and guaranteed as normal by law, i.e., by the state, is a social artifact only imperfectly founded upon logical or even linguistic reason; it is the product of a work of normalization and codification, quite analogous to that which the state effects concurrently in other realms of social life.[3] Now, when, at a particular moment, the state or any of its representatives undertakes a reform of orthography (as was done, with similar effects, a century ago), i.e., to undo by decree what the state had ordered by decree, this immediately triggers the indignant protest of a good number of those whose status depends on "writing," in its most common sense but also in the sense given to it by writers. And remarkably, all those defenders of orthographic orthodoxy mobilize in the name of *natural* spelling and of the satisfaction, experienced as intrinsically aesthetic, given by the perfect agreement between mental structures and objective structures—between the mental forms socially instituted in minds through the teaching of correct spelling and the reality designated by words rightfully spelled. For those who possess spelling to the point where they are possessed by it, the perfectly arbitrary "ph" of the word *nénuphar* has become so evidently inextricable from the flower it designates that they can, in all good faith, invoke nature and the *natural* to denounce an intervention of the state aimed at reducing the arbitrariness of a spelling which itself is, in all evidence, the product of an earlier arbitrary intervention of the same.

One could offer countless similar instances in which the effects of choices made by the state have so completely impressed themselves in reality and in minds that possibilities initially discarded have become totally unthinkable (e.g., a system of domestic production of electricity analogous to that of home heating). Thus, if the mildest attempt to modify school programs, and especially timetables for the different disciplines, almost always and everywhere encounters great resistance, it is not only because powerful occupational interests (such as those of the teaching staff) are attached to the established academic order. It is also because mat-

---

[3] Bourdieu (1991: chap. 2).

ters of culture, and in particular the social divisions and hierarchies associated with them, are constituted as such by the actions of the state which, by instituting them both in things and in minds, confers upon the cultural arbitrary all the appearances of the natural.

A Radical Doubt

To have a chance to really think a state which still thinks itself through those who attempt to think it, then, it is imperative to submit to radical questioning all the presuppositions inscribed in the reality to be thought and in the very thought of the analyst.

It is in the realm of symbolic production that the grip of the state is felt most powerfully. State bureaucracies and their representatives are great producers of "social problems" that social science does little more than ratify whenever it takes them over as "sociological" problems. (It would suffice to demonstrate this, to plot the amount of research varying across countries and periods, devoted to problems of the state, such as poverty, immigration, educational failure, more or less rephrased in scientific language.)

Yet the best proof of the fact that the thought of the bureaucratic thinker *(penseur fonctionnaire)* is pervaded by the official representation of the official, is no doubt the power of seduction wielded by those representations of the state (as in Hegel) that portray bureaucracy as a "universal group" endowed with the intuition of, and a will to, universal interest; or as an "organ of reflection" and a rational instrument in charge of realizing the general interest (as with Durkheim, in spite of his great prudence on the matter).[4]

The specific difficulty that shrouds this question lies in the fact that, behind the appearance of thinking it, most of the writings devoted to the state partake, more or less efficaciously and directly, of the *construction* of the state, i.e., of its very existence. This is particularly true of all juridical writings which, especially during the phase of construction and consolidation, take their full meaning not only as theoretical contributions to the knowledge of the state but also as political strategies aimed at imposing a particular vision of the state, a vision in agreement with the interests and values associated with the particular position of those who produce them in the emerging bureaucratic universe (this is often forgotten by the best historical works, such as those of the Cambridge school).

From its inception, social science itself has been part and parcel of this work of construction of the representation of the state which makes up part of the reality of the state itself. All the issues raised about bureaucracy, such as those of neutrality and disinterestedness, are posed also about sociology itself—only at a higher degree of difficulty since there arises in addition the question of the latter's autonomy from the state. It is therefore the task of the history of the social

---

[4] Durkheim (1922: esp. 84–90).

sciences to uncover all the unconscious ties to the social world that the social sciences owe to the history which has produced them (and which are recorded in their problematics, theories, methods, concepts, etc.). Thus one discovers, in particular, that social science in the modern sense of the term (in opposition to the political philosophy of the counselors of the Prince) is intimately linked to social struggles and socialism, but less as a direct expression of these movements and of their theoretical ramifications than as an answer to the problems that these struggles formulated and brought forth. Social science finds its first advocates among the philanthropists and the reformers, that is, in the enlightened avant-garde of the dominant who expect that "social economics" (as an auxiliary science to political science) will provide them with a solution to "social problems" and particularly to those posed by individuals and groups "with problems."

A comparative survey of the development of the social sciences suggests that a model designed to explain the historical and cross-national variations of these disciplines should take into account two fundamental factors. The first is the form assumed by the social demand for knowledge of the social world, which itself depends, among other things, on the philosophy dominant within state bureaucracies (e.g., liberalism or Keynesianism). Thus a powerful state demand may ensure conditions propitious to the development of a social science relatively independent from economic forces (and of the direct claims of the dominant)—but strongly dependent upon the state. The second factor is the degree of autonomy both of the educational system and of the scientific field from the dominant political and economic forces, an autonomy that no doubt requires both a strong outgrowth of social movements and of the social critique of established powers as well as a high degree of independence of social scientists from these movements.

History attests that the social sciences can increase their independence from the pressures of social demand—which is a major precondition of their progress towards scientificity—only by increasing their reliance upon the state. And thus they run the risk of losing their autonomy *from* the state, unless they are prepared to use *against* the state the (relative) freedom that it grants them.

The Genesis of the State: A Process of Concentration

To sum up the results of the analysis by way of anticipation, I would say, using a variation of Max Weber's famous formula, that the state is an X (to be determined) which successfully claims the monopoly of the legitimate use of physical and *symbolic* violence over a definite territory and over the totality of the corresponding population. If the state is able to exert symbolic violence, it is because it incarnates itself simultaneously in objectivity, in the form of specific organizational structures and mechanisms, and in subjectivity in the form of mental structures and categories of perception and thought. By realizing itself in social structures and in the mental structures adapted to them, the instituted institution makes us forget that it issues out of a long series of acts of *institution* (in the active sense) and hence has all the appearances of the *natural*.

This is why there is no more potent tool for rupture than the reconstruction of genesis: by bringing back into view the conflicts and confrontations of the early beginnings and therefore all the discarded possibles, it retrieves the possibility that things could have been (and still could be) otherwise. And, through such a practical utopia, it questions the "possible" which, among all others, was actualized. Breaking with the temptation of the analysis of essence, but without renouncing for that the intention of uncovering invariants, I would like to outline *a model of the emergence of the state* designed to offer a systematic account of the properly historical logic of the processes which have led to the institution of this "X" we call the state. Such a project is most difficult, impossible indeed, for it demands joining the rigor and coherence of theoretical construction with submission to the almost boundless data accumulated by historical research. To suggest the complexity of such a task, I will simply cite one historian, who, because he stays within the limits of his specialty, evokes it only partially himself:

> The most neglected zones of history have been border zones, as for instance the borders between specialties. Thus, the study of government requires knowledge of the theory of government (i.e., of the history of political thought), knowledge of the practice of government (i.e., of the history of institutions) and finally knowledge of governmental personnel (i.e., of social history). Now, few historians are capable of moving across these specialties with equal ease. . . . There are other border zones of history that would also require study, such as warfare technology at the beginning of the modern period. Without a better knowledge of such problems, it is difficult to measure the importance of the logistical effort undertaken by such government in a given campaign. However, these technical problems should not be investigated solely from the standpoint of the military historian as traditionally defined. The military historian must also be a historian of government. In the history of public finances and taxation, too, many unknowns remain. Here again the specialist must be more than a narrow historian of finances, in the old meaning of the word; he must be a historian of government and an economist. Unfortunately, such a task has not been helped by the fragmentation of history into subfields, each with its monopoly of specialists, and by the feeling that certain aspects of history are fashionable while others are not.[5]

The state is the *culmination of a process of concentration of different species of capital*: capital of physical force or instruments of coercion (army, police), economic capital, cultural or (better) informational capital, and symbolic capital. It is this concentration as such which constitutes the state as the holder of a sort of meta-capital granting power over other species of capital and over their holders. Concentration of the different species of capital (which proceeds hand in hand with the construction of the corresponding fields) leads indeed to the

---

[5] Bonney (1987: 193).

emergence of a specific, properly *statist capital (capital étatique)* which enables the state to exercise power over the different fields and over the different particular species of capital, and especially over the rates of conversion between them (and thereby over the relations of force between their respective holders). It follows that the construction of the state proceeds apace with the construction of *a field of power*, defined as the space of play within which the holders of capital (of different species) struggle *in particular* for power over the state, i.e., over the statist capital granting power over the different species of capital and over their reproduction (particularly through the school system).

Although the different dimensions of this process of concentration (armed forces, taxation, law, etc.) are *interdependent*, for purposes of exposition and analysis I will examine each in turn.

Capital of Physical Force

From the Marxist models which tend to treat the state as a mere organ of coercion to Max Weber's classical definition, or from Norbert Elias's to Charles Tilly's formulations, most models of the genesis of the state have privileged the concentration of the capital of physical force.[6] To say that the forces of coercion (army and police) are becoming concentrated is to say that the institutions mandated to guarantee order are progressively being separated from the ordinary social world; that physical violence can only be applied by a specialized group, centralized and disciplined, especially mandated for such end and clearly identified as such within society; that the professional army progressively causes the disappearance of feudal troops, thereby directly threatening the nobility in its statutory monopoly of the warring function. (One should acknowledge here the merit of Norbert Elias—too often erroneously credited, particularly among historians, for ideas and theories that belong to the broader heritage of sociology—for having drawn out all the implications of Weber's analysis by showing that the state could not have succeeded in progressively establishing its monopoly over violence without dispossessing its domestic competitors of instruments of physical violence and of the right to use them, thereby contributing to the emergence of one of the most essential dimensions of the "civilizing process.")[7]

The emerging state must assert its physical force in two different contexts: first externally, in relation to *other actual or potential states* (foreign princes), in and through war for land (which led to the creation of powerful armies); and second internally, in relation to rival powers (princes and lords) and to resistance from below (dominated classes). The armed forces progressively differentiate themselves with, on the one hand, military forces destined for inter-state competition and, on the other hand, police forces destined for the maintenance of intra-state order.[8]

[6] For example, Tilly (1990: esp. chap. 3).
[7] See Elias (1982, 1978).
[8] In societies without a state, such as ancient Kabylia or the Iceland of the sagas (see Miller 1990), there is no delegation of the exercise of violence to a specialized group, clearly identified as such

Economic Capital

Concentration of the capital of physical force requires the establishment of an efficient fiscal system, which in turn proceeds in tandem with the unification of economic space (creation of a national market). The levies raised by the dynastic state apply equally to all subjects—and not, as with feudal levies, only to dependents who may in turn tax their own men. Appearing in the last decade of the twelfth century, state tax developed in tandem with the growth of *war expenses*. The imperatives of territorial defense, first invoked instance by instance, slowly become the permanent justification of the "obligatory" and "regular" character of the levies perceived "without limitation of time other than that regularly assigned by the king" and directly or indirectly applicable "to all social groups."

Thus was progressively established a specific economic logic, founded on *levies without counterpart* and *redistribution* functioning as the basis for the conversion of economic capital into symbolic capital, concentrated at first in the person of the Prince.[9] The institution of the tax (over and against the resistance of the taxpayers) stands in a relation of *circular causality* with the development of the armed forces necessary for the expansion and defense of the territory under control, and thus for the levying of tributes and taxes as well as for imposing via constraint the payment of that tax. The institution of the tax was the result of a veritable *internal war* waged by the agents of the state against the resistance of the subjects, who discover themselves as such mainly if not exclusively by discovering themselves as taxable, as taxpayers *(contribuables)*. Royal ordinances imposed four degrees of repression in cases of a delay in collection: seizures, arrests for debt *(les contraintes par corps)* including imprisonment, a writ of restraint binding on all parties *(contraintes solidaires)*, and the quartering of soldiers. It follows that the *question of the legitimacy* of the tax cannot but be raised (Norbert Elias correctly remarks that, at its inception, taxation presents itself as a kind of racket). It is only progressively that we come to conceive taxes as a necessary tribute to the needs of a recipient that transcends the king, i.e., this "fictive body" that is the state.

Even today, *tax fraud* bears testimony to the fact that the legitimacy of taxation is not wholly taken for granted. It is well known that in the initial phase

---

within society. It follows that one cannot escape the logic of personal revenge (to take justice into one's hands, *rekba* or vendetta) or of self-defense. Thus the question raised by *The Tragic*—is the act of the justice maker Orestes not a crime just as the initial act of the criminal? This is a question that recognition of the legitimacy of the state causes to vanish and that reappears only in very specific and extreme situations.

[9] One would have to analyze the progressive shift from a "patrimonial" (or feudal) usage of fiscal resources, in which a major part of the public revenue is expended in gifts and in generosities destined to ensure the Prince the recognition of potential competitors (and therefore, among other things, the recognition of the legitimacy of fiscal levies) to a "bureaucratic" usage of such resources as "public expenditures." This shift is one of the most fundamental dimensions of the transformation of the dynastic state into the "impersonal," bureaucratic state.

armed resistance against it was not considered disobedience to royal ordinances but a morally legitimate defense of the rights of the family against a tax system wherein one could not recognize the just and paternal monarch.[10] From the lease *(ferme)* concluded in due and good form with the Royal Treasury, to the last under-lessee *(sous-fermier)* in charge of local levies, a whole hierarchy of leases and subleases was interposed as reminders of the suspicion of alienation of tax and of usurpation of authority, constantly reactivated by a whole chain of small collectors, often badly paid and suspected of corruption both by their victims and by higher ranking officials.[11] The recognition of an entity transcending the agents in charge of its implementation—whether royalty or the state—thus insulated from profane critique, no doubt found a practical grounding of the dissociation of the King from the unjust and corrupt agents who cheated him as much as they cheated the people.[12]

The concentration of armed forces and of the financial resources necessary to maintain them does not go without the concentration of a symbolic capital of recognition (or legitimacy). It matters that the body of agents responsible for collecting taxation without profiting from it and the methods of government and management they use (accounting, filing, sentences of disagreements, procedural acts, oversight of operations, etc.) be in a position to be known and recognized as such, that they be "easily identified with the person, with the dignity of power." Thus "baliffs wear its *livery,* enjoy the authority of its *emblems* and signify their commands in its name." It matters also that the average taxpayer be in a position "to recognize the liveries of the guards, the signs of the sentry boxes" and to distinguish the "keepers of leases," those agents of hated and despised financiers, from the royal guards of the mounted constabulary, from the *Prévôté de l'Hôtel* or the *Gardes du Corps* regarded as inviolable owing to their jackets bearing the royal colors.[13]

All authors agree that the progressive development of the recognition of the legitimacy of official taxation is bound up with the rise of a form of nationalism. And, indeed, the broad-based collection of taxes has likely contributed to the unification of the territory or, to be more precise, to the construction, both in reality and in representation, of the state as a *unitary territory*, as a reality unified by its submission to the same obligations, themselves imposed by the imperatives of defense. It is also probable that this "national" consciousness developed first among the members of the *representative institutions* that emerged alongside the debate over taxation. Indeed, we know that these authorities were more inclined to consent to taxation whenever the latter seemed to them to spring, not from the private interests of the prince, but from the *interests of the country* (and, first among them, from the requirement of territorial *defense*). The

---

[10] See Dubergé (1961) and Schmolders (1973).

[11] Hilton (1987: 167–77, esp. 173–74).

[12] This disjunction of the king or the state from concrete incarnations of power finds its fullest expression in the myth of the "hidden king" (see Bercé 1991).

[13] Bercé (1991: 164).

state progressively inscribes itself in a space that is not yet the national space it will later become but that already presents itself as a *fount of sovereignty*, with, for example, the monopoly to the right to coin money and as the basis of a transcendent symbolic value.[14]

Informational Capital

The concentration of economic capital linked to the establishment of unified taxation is paralleled by a concentration of *informational capital* (of which cultural capital is one dimension) which is itself correlated with the unification of the cultural market. Thus, very early on, public authority carried out surveys of the state of resources (for example, as early as 1194, there were "appraisals of quarter-master sargents" and a census of the carriages *[charrois]* and armed men that eighty-three cities and royal abbeys had to provide when the king convened his *ost*; in 1221, an embryo of budget and a registry of receipts and expenditures appear). The state concentrates, treats, and redistributes information and, most of all, effects a *theoretical unification*. Taking the vantage point of the Whole, of society in its totality, the state claims responsibility for all operations of *totalization* (especially thanks to census taking and statistics or national accounting) and of *objectivation*, through cartography (the unitary representation of space from above) or more simply through writing as an instrument of accumulation of knowledge (e.g., archives), as well as for all operations of *codification* as cognitive unification implying centralization and monopolization in the hands of clerks and men of letters.

Culture[15] is unifying: the state contributes to the unification of the cultural market by unifying all codes, linguistic and juridical, and by effecting a homogenization of all forms of communication, including bureaucratic communication (through forms, official notices, etc.). Through classification systems (especially according to sex and age) inscribed in law, through bureaucratic procedures, educational structures and social rituals (particularly salient in the case of Japan and England), the state molds *mental structures* and imposes common principles of vision and division, forms of thinking that are to the civilized mind what the primitive forms of classification described by Mauss and Durkheim were to the "savage mind." And it thereby contributes to the construction of what is commonly designated as national identity (or, in a more traditional language, national character).[16]

---

[14] The ideal of feudal princes, as well as of the kings of France later, was to allow only the use of their own money within the territories they dominated—an ideal only realized under Louis XIV.

[15] [Translator's note:] "Culture" is capitalized in the French original to mark the appropriation of the emerging bodies of knowledge linked to the state by the dominant, i.e., the emergence of a dominant culture.

[16] It is especially through the school, with the generalization of elementary education through the nineteenth century, that the unifying action of the state is exercised in matters of culture. (This is a fundamental component in the construction of the nation-state.) The creation of national society goes hand in hand with universal educability: the fact that all individuals are equal before the law

By universally imposing and inculcating (within the limits of its authority) a dominant culture thus constituted as *legitimate national* culture, the school system, through the teaching of history (and especially the history of literature), inculcates the foundations of a true "civic religion" and more precisely, the fundamental presuppositions of the national self-image. Derek Sayer and Philip Corrigan show how the English partake very widely—well beyond the boundaries of the dominant class—of the cult of a doubly particular culture, at once bourgeois and national, with for instance the myth of *Englishness*, understood as a set of undefinable and inimitable qualities (for the non-English), "reasonableness," "moderation," "pragmatism," hostility to ideology, "quirkiness," and "eccentricity." [17] This is very visible in the case of England, which has perpetuated with extraordinary continuity a very ancient tradition (as with juridical rituals or the cult of the royal family, for example), or in the case of Japan, where the invention of a national culture is directly tied to the invention of the state. In the case of France, the nationalist dimension of culture is masked under a universalist facade. The propensity to conceive the annexation to one's national culture as a means of acceding to universality is at the basis of both the brutally integrative vision of the republican tradition (nourished by the founding myth of the universal revolution) and very perverse forms of universalist imperialism and of internationalist nationalism. [18]

Cultural and linguistic unification is accompanied by the imposition of the dominant language and culture as legitimate and by the rejection of all other languages into indignity (thus demoted as *patois* or local dialects). By rising to universality, a particular culture or language causes all others to fall into particularity. What is more, given that the universalization of requirements thus officially instituted does not come with a universalization of access to the means needed to fulfill them, this fosters both the monopolization of the universal by the few and the dispossession of all others, who are, in a way, thereby mutilated in their humanity.

Symbolic Capital

Everything points to the concentration of a symbolic capital of recognized authority which, though it has been ignored by all the existing theories of the genesis of the state, appears as the condition or, at minimum, the correlate of all the other forms of concentration, insofar as they endure at all. Symbolic capital is any property (any form of capital whether physical, economic, cultural or social) when it is perceived by social agents endowed with categories of perception which cause them to know it and to recognize it, to give it value. (For example, the concept of honor in Mediterranean societies is a typical form of symbolic

---

gives the state the duty of turning them into citizens, endowed with the cultural means actively to exercise their civic rights.

[17] Corrigan and Sayer (1985: 103).

[18] See Bourdieu (1992: 149–155). Culture is so intimately bound up with patriotic symbols that any critical questioning of its functions and functioning tends to be perceived as treason and sacrilege.

capital which exists only through repute, i.e. through the representation that others have of it to the extent that they share a set of beliefs liable to cause them to perceive and appreciate certain patterns of conduct as honorable or dishonorable.)[19] More precisely, symbolic capital is the form taken by any species of capital whenever it is perceived through categories of perception that are the product of the embodiment of divisions or of oppositions inscribed in the structure of the distribution of this species of capital. It follows that the state, which possesses the means of imposition and inculcation of the durable principles of vision and division that conform to its own structure, is the site par excellence of the concentration and exercise of symbolic power.

The Particular Case of Juridical Capital

The process of concentration of juridical capital, an objectified and codified form of symbolic capital, follows its *own logic,* distinct from that of the concentration of military capital and of financial capital. In the twelfth and thirteenth centuries, several legal systems coexisted in Europe, with, on the one hand, ecclesiastical jurisdictions, as represented by Christian courts, and, on the other, secular jurisdictions, including the justice of the king, the justice of the lords, and the jurisdiction of *municipalités* (cities), of corporations, and of trade.[20] The jurisdiction of the lord as justice was exercised only over his vassals and all those who resided on his lands (i.e., noble vassals, with non-noble free persons and serfs falling under a different set of rules). In the beginning, the king had jurisdiction only over the royal domain and legislated only in trials concerning his direct vassals and the inhabitants of his own fiefdoms. But, as Marc Bloch remarked, royal justice soon slowly "infiltrated" the whole of society.[21] Though it was not the product of an intention, and even less so of a purposeful plan, no more than it was the object of collusion among those who benefited from it (including the king and the jurists), the movement of concentration always followed one and the same trajectory, eventually leading to the creation of a juridical apparatus. This movement started with the provosts-marshals mentioned in the "testament of Philippe Auguste" in 1190 and with the bailiffs, these higher officers of royalty who held solemn assizes and controlled the provosts. It continued under St. Louis with the creation of different bureaucratic entities, the *Conseil d'Etat* (Council of State), the *Cours des Comptes* (Court of Accounts), and the judiciary court *(curias regis)* which took the name of parliament. Thanks to the appeal procedure, the parliament, a sedentary body composed exclusively of lawyers, became one of the major instruments for the concentration of juridical power in the hands of the king.

Royal justice slowly corralled the majority of criminal cases which had previously belonged to the tribunals of lords or of churches. "Royal cases," those in which the rights of royalty are infringed (e.g., crimes of lese-majesty; counter-

---

[19] Bourdieu (1965: 191–241).
[20] See Esmein (1882). See also Berman (1983).
[21] Bloch (1967: 85).

feiting of money, forgery of the seal) came increasingly to be reserved for royal bailiffs. More especially, jurists elaborated a *theory of appeal* which submitted all the jurisdictions of the kingdom to the king. Whereas feudal courts were sovereign, it now became admitted that any judgment delivered by a lord upholder of law could be deferred before the king by the injured party if deemed contrary to the customs of the country. This procedure, called *supplication*, slowly turned into appeal. Self-appointed judges progressively disappeared from feudal courts to be replaced by professional jurists, the officers of justice and the appeal followed the ladder of authority: one appeals from the inferior lord to the lord of higher rank and from the duke or the count to the king (one cannot skip a level and, for instance, appeal directly to the king).

By relying on the *specific interest of the jurists* (a typical example of interest in the universal) who, as we shall see, elaborated all sorts of legitimating theories according to which the king represents the common interest and owes everybody security and justice, the royalty limited the competence of feudal jurisdictions (it proceeded similarly with ecclesiastical jurisdictions, for instance by limiting the church's right of asylum). The process of *concentration* of juridical capital was paralleled by a process of *differentiation* which led to the constitution of an autonomous juridical field.[22] The *judiciary body* grew organized and hierarchized: provosts became the ordinary judges of ordinary cases; bailiffs and seneschals became sedentary; they were assisted more and more by lieutenants who became irrevocable officers of justice and who gradually superseded the bailiffs, thus relegated to purely honorific functions. In the fourteenth century, we witness the appearance of a *public ministry* in charge of official suits. The king now has state prosecutors who act in his name and slowly become functionaries.

The ordinance of 1670 completed the process of concentration which progressively stripped the lordly and ecclesiastical jurisdictions of their powers in favor of royal jurisdictions. It ratified the progressive conquests of jurists: the competence of the place of the crime became the rule; the precedence of royal judges over those of lords was affirmed. The ordinance also enumerated royal cases and annulled ecclesiastical and communal privileges by stipulating that judges of appeal should always be royal judges. In brief, the competence delegated over a certain *ressort* (territory) replaced statutory precedence or authority exercised directly over persons.

Later on the construction of the juridico-bureaucratic structures constitutive of the state proceeded alongside the construction of the body of jurists and of what Sarah Hanley calls "the Family-State Compact," this covenant struck between the state and the corporation of jurists which constituted itself as such by exerting strict control over its own reproduction. "The Family-State Compact provided a formidable family model of socio-economic authority which influenced the state model of political power in the making at the same time."[23]

<hr>

[22] The functioning of this field is sketched in Bourdieu (1987a: 209–48).
[23] Hanley (1989: 4–27).

From Honor to Cursus Honorum

The concentration of juridical capital is one aspect, quite fundamental, of a larger process of concentration of symbolic capital in its different forms. This capital is the basis of the specific authority of the holder of state power and in particular of a very mysterious power, namely his power of nomination. Thus, for example, the king attempts to control the totality of the traffic in *honors* to which "gentlemen" may lay claim. He strives to extend his mastery over the great ecclesiastical prerogatives, the orders of chivalry, the distribution of military and court offices and, last but not least, titles of nobility. Thus is a *central authority of nomination* gradually constituted.

One remembers the nobles of Aragon, mentioned by V. G. Kiernan, who called themselves *"ricoshombres de natura"*: gentlemen by nature or by birth, in contrast to the nobles created by the king. This distinction, which evidently played a role in the struggles within the nobility or between nobility and royal power, is of utmost importance. It opposes two modes of access to nobility: the first, called "natural," is nothing other than heredity and public recognition (by other nobles as well as by "commoners"); the second, "legal nobility," is the result of ennoblement by the king. The two forms of consecration coexist for a long time. Arlette Jouanna clearly shows that, with the concentration of the power of ennoblement in the hands of the king, *statutory honor*, founded on the recognition of peers and of others and affirmed and defended by challenge and prowess, slowly gives way to *honors attributed by the state*.[24] Such honors, like any fiduciary currencies, have currency and value on all the markets controlled by the state.

As the king concentrates greater and greater quantities of symbolic capital (Mousnier called them *fidélités*, "loyalties"),[25] his power to distribute symbolic capital in the form of offices and honors conceived as rewards increases continually. The symbolic capital of the nobility (honor, reputation), which hitherto rested on social esteem tacitly accorded on the basis of a more or less conscious social consensus, now finds a quasi-bureaucratic statutory objectification (in the form of edicts and rulings that do little more than record the new consensus). We find an indication of this in the "grand researches of nobility" undertaken by Louis XIV and Colbert: the decree *(arrêt)* of March 22, 1666, stipulates the creation of a "registry containing the names, surnames, residences and arms of real gentlemen." The intendants scrutinize the titles of nobility and genealogists of the Orders of the King and *juges d'armes* fight over the definition of true nobles. With the nobility of robe, which owes its position to its cultural capital, we come very close to the logic of state nomination and to the *cursus honorum* founded upon educational credentials.

In short, there is a shift from a diffuse symbolic capital, resting solely on collective recognition, to an *objectified symbolic capital*, codified, delegated and

[24] Jouanna (1989).
[25] Mousnier (1980: 94).

guaranteed by the state, in a word *bureaucratized*. One finds a very precise il-
lustration of this process in the sumptuary laws that meant to regulate, in a rig-
orously hierarchized manner, the distribution of symbolic expressions (in terms
of dress, in particular) between noblemen and commoners and especially among
the different ranks of the nobility.[26] Thus the state regulates the use of cloth and
of trimmings of gold, silver, and silk. By doing this, it defends the nobility against
the usurpation of commoners but, at the same time, it expands and reinforces
its own control over hierarchy within the nobility. The decline of the power of
autonomous distribution of the great lords tends to grant the king the monopoly of ennoblement and the *monopoly over nomination* through the progressive
transformation of offices—conceived as rewards—into positions of responsibilities requiring competency and partaking of a *cursus honorum* that foreshadows
a bureaucratic career ladder. Thus that supremely mysterious power that is the
power of *appointing and dismissing the high officers of the state* is slowly instituted. The state is thus constituted as "fountain of honour, of office and privilege," to recall Blackstone's words, and distributes honors. It dubs "knights" and
"baronets," invents new orders of knighthood, confers ceremonial precedence
and nominates peers and all the holders of important public functions.[27]

Nomination is, when we stop to think of it, a very mysterious act which follows a logic quite similar to that of magic as described by Marcel Mauss.[28] Just
as the sorcerer mobilizes the capital of belief accumulated by the functioning of
the magical universe, the President of the Republic who signs a decree of nomination or the physician who signs a certificate (of illness, invalidity, etc.) mobilizes a symbolic capital accumulated in and through the whole network of relations of recognition constitutive of the bureaucratic universe. Who certifies the
validity of the certificate? It is the one who signs the credential giving license to
certify. But who then certifies this? We are carried through an infinite regression
at the end of which "one has to stop" and where one could, following medieval
theologians, choose to give the name of "state" to the last (or to the first) link in
the long chain of official acts of consecration.[29] It is the state, acting in the manner of a bank of symbolic capital, that guarantees all acts of authority—acts at
once arbitrary and misrecognized as such (Austin called them "acts of legitimate
imposture").[30] The President of the country is someone who claims to be the
President but who differs from the madman who claims to be Napoleon by the
fact that he is recognized as authorized to do so.

The nomination or the certificate belongs to the category of *official* acts or discourses, symbolically effective only because they are accomplished in a situation
of authority by authorized characters, "officials" who are acting *ex officio*, as
holders of an *officium (publicum)*, that is, of a function or position assigned by

[26] Fogel (1987: 227–35, esp. 232).
[27] Maitland (1948: 429).
[28] Mauss (1902).
[29] Using Kafka, I have shown how the sociological vision and the theological vision meet in spite
of their apparent opposition (see Bourdieu 1984: 268–270).
[30] Austin (1952).

the state. The sentence handed down by the judge or the grade given by the professor, the procedures of official registration, certified reports or minutes, all the acts meant to carry legal effect, such as certificates of birth, marriage, or death, etc., all manners of public summons as performed with the required formalities by the appropriate agents (judges, notaries, bailiffs, officers of *état civil*) and duly registered in the appropriate office, all these facts invoke the logic of official nomination to institute socially guaranteed identities (as citizen, legal resident, voter, taxpayer, parent, property owner) as well as legitimate unions and groupings (families, associations, trade unions, parties, etc.). By stating with authority what a being (thing or person) is in truth (verdict) according to its socially legitimate definition, that is what he or she is authorized to be, what he has a right (and duty) to be, the social being that he may claim, the State wields a genuinely *creative*, quasi-divine, power. It suffices to think of the kind of immortality that it can grant through acts of consecration such as commemorations or scholarly canonization, to see how, twisting Hegel's famous expression, we may say that: "the judgement of the state is the last judgement." [31]

Minds of State

In order truly to understand the power of the state in its full specificity, i.e., the particular symbolic efficacy it wields, one must, as I suggested long ago in another article,[32] integrate into one and the same explanatory model intellectual traditions customarily perceived as incompatible. It is necessary, first, to overcome the opposition between a physicalist vision of the social world that conceives of social relations as relations of physical force and a "cybernetic" or semiological vision which portrays them as relations of symbolic force, as relations of meaning or relations of communication. The most brutal relations of force are always simultaneously symbolic relations. And assets of submission and obedience are cognitive acts which as such involve cognitive structures, forms and categories of perception, principles of vision and division. Social agents construct the social world through cognitive structures that may be applied to all things of the world and in particular to social structures (Cassirer called these principles of vision of division "symbolic forms" and Durkheim "forms of classification": these are so many ways of saying the same thing in more or less separate theoretical traditions).

These *structuring structures* are historically constituted forms and therefore arbitrary in the Saussurian sense, conventional, *"ex instituto"* as Leibniz said, which means that we can trace their social genesis. Generalizing the Durkheim-

---

[31] Publication, in the sense of a procedure aimed at rendering a state or act public, at bringing it to everybody's knowledge, always holds the potentiality of a usurpation of the right to exercise the symbolic violence which properly belongs to the state (and which is expressed, for example, in the publication of marriage notices or the promulgation of law). Hence, the state always tends to regulate all forms of publication, printing, theatrical representations, public predication, caricature, etc.

[32] "On Symbolic Power," Bourdieu (1991).

ian hypothesis according to which the "forms of classification" that the "primitives" apply to the world are the product of the embodiment of their group structures, we may seek the basis of these cognitive structures in the actions of the state. Indeed, we may posit that, in differentiated societies, the state has the ability to impose and inculcate in a universal manner, within a given territorial expanse, a *nomos* (from *nemo*: to share, divide, constitute separate parts), a shared principle of vision and division, identical or similar cognitive and evaluative structures. The state would then be the foundation of a "logical conformism" and of a "moral conformism" (these are Durkheim's expressions),[33] of a tacit, prereflexive agreement over the meaning of the world which itself lies at the basis of the experience of the world as "commonsense world." (Neither the phenomenologists, who brought this experience to light, nor the ethnomethodologists, who assign themselves the task of describing it, have the means of accounting for this experience because they fail to raise the question of the social construction of the principles of construction of the social reality that they strive to explicate and to question the contribution of the state to the constitution of the principles of constitution that agents apply to the social order.)

In less differentiated societies, the common principles of vision and division— the paradigm of which is the opposition masculine/feminine—are instituted in minds (or in bodies) through the whole spatial and temporal organization of social life, and especially through *rites of institution* that establish definite differences between those who submitted to the rite and those who did not.[34] In our societies, the state makes a decisive contribution to the production and reproduction of the instruments of construction of social reality. As organizational structure and regulator of practices, the state exerts an ongoing action formative of durable dispositions through the whole range of constraints and through the corporeal and mental discipline it uniformly imposes upon all agents. Furthermore, it imposes and inculcates all the fundamental principles of classification, based on sex, age, "skill," etc. And it lies at the basis of the symbolic efficacy of all rites of institution, such as those underlying the family for example, or those that operate through the routine functioning of the school system as the site of *consecration* where lasting and often irrevocable differences are instituted between the chosen and the excluded, in the manner of the medieval ritual of the dubbing of knights.

The construction of the state is accompanied by the construction of a sort of common historical transcendental, immanent to all its "subjects." Through the framing it imposes upon practices, the state establishes and inculcates common forms and categories of perception and appreciation, social frameworks of perceptions, of understanding or of memory, in short *state forms of classification*. It thereby creates the conditions for a kind of immediate orchestration of habituses which is itself the foundation of a consensus over this set of shared evidences constitutive of (national) common sense. Thus, for example, the great rhythms

---

[33] Durkheim (1965).
[34] "Rites of Institution," Bourdieu (1991: 117–26).

of the societal calendar (think of the schedule of school or patriotic vacations that determine the great "seasonal migrations" of many contemporary societies) provide both shared objective referents and compatible subjective principles of division which underlie internal experiences of time sufficiently concordant to make social life possible.[35]

But in order fully to understand the immediate submission that the state order elicits, it is necessary to break with the intellectualism of the neo-Kantian tradition to acknowledge that cognitive structures are not forms of consciousness but *dispositions of the body*, and that the obedience we grant to the injunctions of the state cannot be understood either as mechanical submission to an external force or as conscious consent to an order (in the double sense of the term). The social world is riddled with *calls to order* that function as such only for those who are predisposed to heeding them as they *awaken* deeply buried corporeal dispositions, outside the channels of consciousness and calculation. It is this doxic submission of the dominated to the structures of a social order of which their mental structures are the product that Marxism cannot understand insofar as it remains trapped in the intellectualist tradition of the philosophies of consciousness. In the notion of false consciousness that it invokes to account for effects of symbolic domination, that superfluous term is "consciousness." And to speak of "ideologies" is to locate in the realm of *representations*—liable to be transformed through this intellectual conversion called "awakening of consciousness" *(prise de conscience)*—what in fact belongs to the order of *belief*, i.e., to the level of the most profound corporeal dispositions. Submission to the established order is the product of the agreement between, on the one hand, the cognitive structures inscribed in bodies by both collective history (phylogenesis) and individual history (ontogenesis) and, on the other, the objective structures of the world to which these cognitive structures are applied. State injunctions owe their obviousness, and thus their potency, to the fact that the state has imposed the very cognitive structures through which it is perceived (one should rethink along those lines the conditions that make possible the supreme sacrifice: *pro patria mori*).

But we need to go beyond the neo-Kantian tradition, even in its Durkheimian form, on yet another count. Because it focuses on the *opus operatum*, symbolic structuralism à la Levi-Strauss (or the Foucault of *The Order of Things*) *is* bound to neglect the active dimension of symbolic production (as, for example, with mythologies), the question of the *modus operandi*, of "generative grammar" (in Chomsky's sense). It does have the advantage of seeking to uncover the internal coherence of symbolic systems *qua* systems, that is, one of the major bases of their efficacy—as can be clearly seen in the ease of the law in which coherence is deliberately sought, but also in myth and religion. Symbolic order

---

[35] Another example would be the division of the academic and scientific worlds into disciplines, which is inscribed in the minds in the form of disciplinary habituses generating distorted relations between the representatives of different disciplines as well as limitations and mutilations in the representations and practices of each of them.

rests on the imposition upon all agents of structuring structures that owe part of their consistency and resilience to the fact that they are coherent and systematic (at least in appearance) and that they are objectively in agreement with the objective structures of the social world. It is this immediate and tacit agreement, in every respect opposed to an explicit contract, that founds the relation of *doxic submission* which attaches us to the established order with all the ties of the unconscious. The recognition of legitimacy is not, as Weber believed, a free act of clear conscience. It is rooted in the immediate, prereflexive, agreement between objective structures and embodied structures, now fumed unconscious (such as those that organize temporal rhythms: viz. the quite arbitrary divisions of school schedules into periods).

It is this pre-reflexive agreement that explains the ease, rather stunning when we think of it, with which the dominant impose their domination: "Nothing is as astonishing for those who consider human affairs with a philosophic eye than to see the ease with which the many will be governed by the *few* and to observe the implicit submission with which men revoke their own sentiments and passions in favor of their leaders. When we inquire about the means through which such an astonishing thing is accomplished, we find that force being always on the side of the governed, only opinion can sustain the governors. It is thus solely on opinion that government is founded, and such maxim applies to the most despotic and military government as well as to the freest and most popular." [36]

Hume's astonishment brings forth the fundamental question of all political philosophy, which one occults, paradoxically, by posing a problem that is not really posed as such in ordinary existence: the problem of legitimacy. Indeed, essentially, what is problematic is the fact that the established order is *not* problematic; and that the question of the legitimacy of the state, and of the order it institutes, does not arise except in crisis situations. The state does not necessarily have to give orders or to exercise physical coercion in order to produce an ordered social world, as long as it is capable of producing embodied cognitive structures that accord with objective structures and thus of ensuring the belief of which Hume spoke—namely, doxic submission to the established order.

This being said, it should not be forgotten that such primordial political belief, this doxa, is an orthodoxy, a right, correct, dominant vision which has more often than not been imposed through struggles against competing visions. This means that the "natural attitude" mentioned by the phenomenologists, i.e., the primary experience of the world of common sense, is a politically produced relation, as are the categories of perception that sustain it. What appears to us today as self-evident, as beneath consciousness and choice, has quite often been the stake of struggles and instituted only as the result of dogged confrontations between dominant and dominated groups. The major effect of historical evolution is to abolish history by relegating to the past, i.e., to the unconscious, the lateral possibles that it eliminated. The analysis of the genesis of the state as the foundation of the principles of vision and division operative within its territorial

---

[36] Hume (1758).

expanse enables us to understand at once the doxic adherence to the order established by the state as well as the properly political foundations of such apparently natural adherence. Doxa is a particular point of view, the point of view of the dominant, when it presents and imposes itself as a universal point of view—the point of view of those who dominate by dominating the state and who have constituted their point of view as universal by constituting the state.

Thus, to account fully for the properly symbolic dimension of the power of the state, we may build on Max Weber's decisive contribution (in his writings on religion) to the theory of symbolic systems by reintroducing specialized agents and their specific interests. Indeed, if he shares with Marx an interest in the function—rather than the structure—of symbolic systems, Weber nonetheless has the merit of calling attention to the producers of these particular products (religious agents, in the case that concerns him) and to their *interactions* (conflict, competition, etc.).[37] In opposition to the Marxists, who have overlooked the existence of specialized agents of production (notwithstanding a famous text of Engels which states that to understand law one needs to focus on the corporation of the jurists), Weber reminds us that, to understand religion, it does not suffice to study symbolic forms of the religious type, as Cassirer or Durkheim did, nor even the immanent structure of the religious message or of the mythological corpus, as with the structuralists. Weber focuses specifically on the producers of the religious message, on the specific interests that move them and on the strategies they use in their struggle (e.g., excommunication). In order to grasp these symbolic systems simultaneously in their function, structure, and genesis, it suffices, thence, to apply the structuralist mode of thinking (completely alien to Weber) not solely to the symbolic systems or, better, to the space of *position takings* or stances adopted in a determinate domain of practice (e.g., religious messages), but to the system of agents who produce them as well or, to be more precise, to the space of *positions* they occupy (what I call the religious field) in the competition that opposes them.[38]

The same holds for the state. To understand the symbolic dimension of the effect of the state, and in particular what we may call the *effect of universality*, it is necessary to understand the specific functioning of the bureaucratic microcosm and thus to analyze the genesis and structure of this universe of agents of the state who have constituted themselves into a state nobility by instituting the state,[39] and in particular, by producing the performative discourse on the state which, under the guise of saying what the state is, caused the state to come into being by stating what it should be—i.e., what should be the position of the producers of this discourse in the division of labor of domination. One must focus in particular on the structure of the juridical field and uncover both the generic interests of the holders of that particular form of cultural capital, predisposed to function as symbolic capital, that is, juridical competence, as well as the specific

[37] For a fuller discussion, see Bourdieu (1987b).
[38] For a fuller demonstration of this point, see Bourdieu (1971).
[39] Bourdieu (1989, esp. part V).

interests imposed on each of them by virtue of their position in a still weakly autonomous juridical field (that is, essentially in relation to royal power). And to account for those effects of universality and rationality I just evoked, it is necessary to understand why these agents had an interest in giving a universal form to the expression of their vested interests, to elaborate a theory of public service and of public order, and thus to work to autonomize the *reason of state* from dynastic reason, from the "house of the king," and to invent thereby the *res publica* and later the republic as an instance transcendent to the agents (the King included) who are its temporary incarnations. One must understand how, by virtue and because of their specific capital and particular interests, they were led to produce a discourse of state which, by providing justifications for their own positions, constituted the state—this *fictio juris* which slowly stopped being a mere fiction of jurists to become an autonomous order capable of imposing ever more widely the submission to its functions and to its functioning and the recognition of its principles.

The Monopolization of Monopoly and the State Nobility

The construction of the state monopoly over physical and symbolic violence is inseparable from the construction of the field of struggles for the monopoly over the advantages attached to this monopoly. The relative unification and universalization associated with the emergence of the state has for counterpart the monopolization by the few of the universal resources that it produces and procures (Weber, and Elias after him, ignored the process of constitution of a statist capital and the process of monopolization of this capital by the state nobility which has contributed to its production or, better, which has produced itself as such by producing it). However, this *monopoly of the universal* can only be obtained at the cost of a submission (if only in appearance) to the universal and of a universal recognition of the universalist representation of domination presented as legitimate and disinterested. Those who—like Marx—invert the official image that the bureaucracy likes to give of itself, and describe bureaucrats as usurpers of the universal who act as private proprietors of public resources, ignore the very real effects of the obligatory reference to the values of neutrality and disinterested loyalty to the public good. Such values impose themselves with increasing force upon the functionaries of the state as the history of the long work of symbolic construction unfolds whereby the official representation of the state as the site of universality and of service of the general interest is invented and imposed.

The monopolization of the universal is the result of a work of universalization which is accomplished within the bureaucratic field itself. As would be revealed by the analysis of the functioning of this strange institution called *commission*, i.e., a set of individuals vested with a mission of general interest and invited to transcend their particular interests in order to produce universal propositions, officials constantly have to labor, if not to sacrifice their particular point of view on behalf of the "point of view of society," at least to constitute their point of view into a legitimate one, i.e., as universal, especially through the use of the rhetoric of the official.

The universal is the object of universal recognition and the sacrifice of selfish (especially economic) interests is universally recognized as legitimate. (In the effort to rise from the singular and selfish point of view of the individual to the point of view of the group, collective judgment cannot but perceive, and approve, an expression of recognition of the value of the group and of the group itself as the fount of all value, and thus a passage from "is" to "ought.") This means that all social universes tend to offer, to varying degrees, material or symbolic profits of universalization (those very profits pursued by strategies seeking to "play by the rules"). It also implies that the universes which, like the bureaucratic field, demand with utmost insistence that one submits to the universal, are particularly favorable to obtaining such profits. It is significant that administrative law which, being aimed at establishing a universe of dedication to the general interest and having as its fundamental law the obligation of neutrality, should institute as a practical principle of evaluation the suspicion of generosity: "the government does not make gifts"; any action by a public bureaucracy which individually benefits a private person is suspect if not illegal.

The profit of universalization is no doubt one of the historical engines of the progress of the universal. This is because it favors the creation of universes where universal values (reason, virtue, etc.) are at least verbally recognized and wherein operates a circular process of mutual reinforcement of the strategies of universalization seeking to obtain the profits (if only negative) associated with conformity to universal rules and to the structures of those universes officially devoted to the universal. The sociological vision cannot ignore the discrepancy between the official norm as stipulated in administrative law and the reality of bureaucratic practice, with all its violations of the obligation of disinterestedness, all the cases of "private use of public services" (from the diversion of public goods and functions to graft to corruption). Nor can it ignore the more perverse abuses of law and the administrative tolerances, exemptions, and bartering of favors, that result from the faulty implementation or transgression of the law. Yet sociology cannot for all that remain blind to the effects of this norm which demands that agents sacrifice their private interests for the obligations inscribed in their function ("the agent should devote himself fully to his function"), nor, in the more realistic manner, to the effects of the interest to disinterestedness and of all those forms of "pious hypocrisy" that the paradoxical logic of the bureaucratic field can promote.

References

Austin, John. 1952. *How to Do Things with Words*. Oxford: Oxford University Press.

Bercé, Y. M. 1991. *Le Roi caché*. Paris: Fayard.

Berman, H. J. 1983. *Law and Revolution: The Formation of the Western Legal Tradition*. Cambridge: Harvard University Press.

Bernhard, Thomas. 1989. *The Old Masters*, translated by Ewald Osers. London: Quartet.

Bloch, Marc. 1967. *Seigneurie française et manoir anglais*. Paris: A. Colin.

Bonney, Richard. 1987. "Guerre, fiscalité et activité d'Etat en France (1500–1600): Some Preliminary Remarks on Possibilities of Research." In *Genèse de l'Etat moderne: Prélèvement et redistribution*, edited by P. Genet and M. Le Mené. Paris: Ed. du CNRS.

Bourdieu, Pierre. 1965. "The Sentiment of Honour in Kabyle Society." In *Honour and Shame: The Values of Mediterranean Society*, edited by J. G. Peristiany. London: Weidenfeld and Nicholson.

——. 1971. "Genesis and Structure of the Religious Field," translated in *Comparative Social Research* 13: 1–43.

——. 1984. "La dernière instance." In *Le siècle de Kafka*. Paris: Centre Georges Pompidou.

——. 1987a. "The Force of Law: Towards a Sociology of the Juridical Field." *Hastings Journal of Law* 38: 209–48.

——. 1987b. "Legitimation and Structured Interests in Weber's Sociology of Religion." In *Max Weber, Rationality and Modernity*, edited by Sam Whimster and Scott Lash. London: Allen and Unwin.

——. 1989. *La noblesse d'Etat*. Paris: Ed. du Seuil.

——. 1991. *Language and Symbolic Power*. Cambridge: Polity.

——. 1992. "Deux imperialismes de l'universel." In *L'Amérique des français*, edited by C. Fauré and T. Bishop. Paris: Bourin.

Corrigan, P., and D. Sayer. 1985. *The Great Arch: English State Formation as Cultural Revolution*. Oxford: Basil Blackwell.

Dubergé, J. 1961. *La psychologie sociale de l'impôt*. Paris: PUF.

Durkheim, Emile. [1912] 1965. *The Elementary Forms of the Religious Life*. New York: Free Press.

——. 1922. *Leçons de sociologie*. Paris: PUF.

Elias, Norbert. 1978. *The Civilizing Process*. Oxford: Basil Blackwell.

——. 1982. *State Formation and Civilization*. Oxford: Basil Blackwell.

Esmein, A. [1882] 1969. *Histoire de la procédure criminelle en France et spécialement de la procédure inquisitoire depuis le XIIe siècle jusqu'à nos jours*. Rpt. Frankfurt: Sauer and Auvermann.

Fogel, Michel. 1987. "*Modèle d'État et modèle social de dépense: Les lois somptuaires en France de 1485 à 1560.*" In *Genèse de l'Etat moderne: Prélèvement et redistribution*, edited by P. Genet and M. Le Mené. Paris: Ed. du CNRS.

Hanley, S. 1989. "Engendering the State: Family Formation and State Building in Early Modern France." *French Historical Studies* 16 (Spring): 4–27.

Hilton, Rodney H. 1987. "Resistance to Taxation and Other State Impositions in Medieval England." In *Genèse de l'Etat moderne: Prélèvement et redistribution*, edited by P. Genet and M. Le Mené. Paris: Ed. du CNRS.

Hume, David. 1758. "On the First Principles of Government." In *Essays and Treatises on Several Subjects*. London: Printed for A. Millar, A Kincaid, and A. Donaldson at Edinburgh.

Jouanna, A. 1989. *Le devoir de révolte: La noblesse française et la gestation de l'Etat moderne, 1559–1561*. Paris: Fayard.

Maitland, F. W. 1948. *The Constitutional History of England*. Cambridge: Cambridge University Press.

Mauss, M. [1902] 1975. *A General Theory of Magic*. New York: Norton.

Miller, William Ian. 1990. *Bloodtaking and Peacemaking*. Chicago: University of Chicago Press.

Mousnier, R. 1980. *Les institutions de la France sous la monarchie absolue*. Paris: PUF.

Schmolders, G. 1973. *Psychologie des finances et de l'impôt*. Paris: PUF.

Tilly, Charles. 1990. *Coercion, Capital, and European States, AD 990–1990*. Oxford: Basil Blackwell.

2

Society, Economy, and the State Effect

Timothy Mitchell

The state is an object of analysis that appears to exist simultaneously as material force and as ideological construct. It seems both real and illusory. This paradox presents a particular problem in any attempt to build a theory of the state. The network of institutional arrangement and political practice that forms the material substance of the state is diffuse and ambiguously defined at its edges, whereas the public imagery of the state as an ideological construct is more coherent. The scholarly analysis of the state is liable to reproduce in its own analytical tidiness this imaginary coherence and misrepresent the incoherence of state practice.

Drawing attention to this liability, Philip Abrams (1988) argues that we should distinguish between two objects of analysis, the state-system and the state-idea. The first refers to the state as a system of institutionalized practice, the second refers to the reification of this system that takes on "an overt symbolic identity progressively divorced from practice as an illusory account of practice." We should avoid mistaking the latter for the former, he suggests, by "attending to the senses in which the state does not exist rather than those in which it does" (82).

This seems a sensible suggestion. But if the coherence and definition of the state arise from the state-idea, then subtracting this from the state's existence as a system of power makes the limits of the system difficult to define. Foucault argues that the system of power extends well beyond state: "One cannot confine oneself to analyzing the State apparatus alone if one wants to grasp the mechanisms of power in their detail and complexity . . . ," he suggests. "In reality, power in its exercise goes much further, passes through much finer channels, and is much more ambiguous" (1980a: 72). If so, how does one define the state apparatus (as even Foucault still implies one should) and locate its limits? At what point does power enter channels fine enough and its exercise become ambiguous enough that one recognizes the edge of this apparatus? Where is the exterior that enables one to identify it as an apparatus?

Parts of this essay were previously published in 1991 as "The Limits of the State." *American Political Science Review* 85: 77–96. I am grateful to Philip Corrigan, Bob Jessop, and Bertell Ollman for their detailed criticisms of the earlier article.

The answers cannot be found by trying to separate the material forms of the state from the ideological, or the real from the illusory. The state-idea and the state-system are better seen as two aspects of the same process. To be more precise, the phenomenon we name "the state" arises from techniques that enable mundane material practices to take on the appearance of an abstract, nonmaterial form. Any attempt to distinguish the abstract or ideal appearance of the state from its material reality, in taking for granted this distinction, will fail to understand it. The task of a theory of the state is not to clarify such distinctions but to historicize them.

In American social science of the postwar period, there have been two distinct responses to the difficulty of relating practice and ideology in the concept of the state. The first was to abandon *the state*, as a term too ideological and too narrow to be the basis for theoretical development, replacing it with the idea of *political system*. In rejecting the ideological, however, systems theorists found themselves with no way of defining the limits of the system. Their empiricism had promised precise definitions, but instead they were unable to draw any line distinguishing the political order from the wider society in which it functioned.

The second response, from the later 1970s, was to "bring the state back in" (Evans, Rueschemeyer, and Skocpol 1985). The new literature defined the state in a variety of ways, most of which took it to be not just distinguishable from society but autonomous from it. To reestablish the elusive line between the two, however, the literature made the state-society distinction correspond to a distinction between subjective and objective, or ideal and real. It did so by reducing the state to a subjective system of decision making, a narrow conception that failed to fit even the evidence that the state theorists themselves present.

An alternative approach must begin with the assumption that we must take seriously the elusiveness of the boundary between state and society, not as a problem of conceptual precision but as a clue to the nature of the phenomenon. Rather than hoping we can find a definition that will fix the state-society boundary (as a preliminary to demonstrating how the object on one side of it influences or is autonomous from what lies on the other), we need to examine the political processes through which the uncertain yet powerful distinction between state and society is produced.

A theory of the contemporary state also must examine the parallel distinction constructed between state and economy. In the twentieth century, creating this opposition has become a perhaps more significant method of articulating the power of the state. Yet the boundary between state and economy represents a still more elusive distinction than that between state and society.

We must take such distinctions not as the boundary between two discrete entities but as a line drawn internally, within the network of institutional mechanisms through which a social and political order is maintained. The ability to have an internal distinction appear as though it were the external boundary between separate objects is the distinctive technique of the modern political order. One must examine the technique from a historical perspective (something most literature on the state fails to do), as the consequence of certain novel practices of the technical age. In particular, one can trace it to methods of organization, arrangement, and representation that operate within the social practices they govern, yet create the effect of an enduring structure apparently external to those practices. This approach to the state accounts for the salience of the phenomenon but avoids attributing to it the coherence, unity, and absolute autonomy that result from existing theoretical approaches.

Abandoning the State

When American social scientists eliminated the term *state* from their vocabulary in the 1950s, they claimed that the word suffered from two related weaknesses: its "ideological" use as a political myth, as a "symbol for unity," produced disagreement about exactly what it referred to (Easton 1953: 110–12); and even if agreement might be reached, these symbolic references of the term excluded significant aspects of the modern political process (106–15). These factors do not themselves account for the rejection of the concept of the state, however, for scholars had been disclosing its weaknesses and ambiguities for decades (Sabine 1934). What made the weaknesses suddenly significant was the changed postwar relationship between American political science and American political power. We can see this by rereading what was written at the time. Postwar comparative politics, according to a 1944 APSA report discussing the future "mission" of the discipline, would have to relinquish its narrow concern with the study of the state ("the descriptive analysis of foreign institutions") to become "a conscious instrument of social engineering" (Loewenstein 1944: 541). Scholars would use this intellectual machinery for "imparting our experience to other nations and . . . integrating scientifically their institutions into a universal pattern of government" (547). To achieve these ends, the discipline had to expand its geographical and theoretical territory and become what the report called "a 'total' science" (541). "We can no longer permit the existence of white spots on our map of the world," the report said, employing metaphors reflecting the imperial ambition of postwar American politics. "The frontier posts of comparative government must be moved boldly" (543), both to encompass the globe and, by expanding into the territory of other disciplines (anthropology, psychology, economics, and statistics), to open up each country to far more detailed methods of observation and questioning and thereby "gain access to the true Gestalt of foreign political civilizations" (541).

Political science had to expand its boundaries to match the growth of postwar U.S. power, whose ambitions it would offer to serve. Borrowing concepts and research methods from fields such as anthropology, political science planned not simply to shift its concern from state to society but to open up the workings of the political process to far closer inspection. The field was to become a discipline of detail, pushing its investigation into the meticulous examination of the activities of political groups, the behavior of social actors, even the motivations of individual psyches.

The opening of this new territory to scientific investigation seemed even more urgent by the 1950s, when postwar American optimism had turned into political uncertainty. It was what Easton (1953: 3) gravely called "our present social crisis"—the launching of the cold war and the accompanying domestic campaign against the Left—that made suddenly imperative the elimination of ambiguity from political vocabulary and the construction of general social-scientific laws broad enough to include all significant political phenomena and "pass beyond the experience . . . of any one culture" (319).

The *Suggested Research Strategy in Western European Government and Politics*, proposed in 1955 by the new Comparative Politics Committee of the Social Science Research Council chaired by Gabriel Almond, criticized once again the "too great an emphasis on the formal aspects of institutions and processes," but now spoke of the need for a change in terms of "urgent and practical considerations." In the major western European countries, the committee reported, "large bodies of opinion appear to be alienated from the West, politically apathetic, or actively recruited to Communism." The state was too narrow and formal a focus for research because "the basic problems of civic loyalty and political cohesion lie in large part outside of the formal government framework." Research was needed that would trace the degree of political cohesion and loyalty to the West beyond this formal framework "into the networks of social groupings, and the attitudes of the general population." Such close examination could confirm the committee's expectation that, in cases such as France, "there is at least the possibility of breaking the hold of the Communist party on a large part of its following" (Almond, Cole, and Macridis 1955: 1045).

Responding to the needs of the cold war, the discipline also expanded its geographical territory. In his foreword to *The Appeals of Communism*, Almond claimed that Communism had now begun to spread to non-Western areas, and warned that this was "so menacing a development that it is deserving of special attention" (Almond 1954: vii). These global concerns were the stimulus to the research undertaken in the late 1950s and subsequently published as *The Civic Culture*. The book's introduction addressed itself to the pressing need to export to the colonized areas of the world, now seeking their independence, the principles of the Anglo-American political process. To this end, it sought to codify not just the formal institutional rules of the state but the "subtler components" that formed its "social-psychological preconditions"—that combination of democratic spirit and proper deference toward authority that was celebrated as "the civic culture" (Almond and Verba 1963: 5).

The scientific tone of this literature offered the empiricism of political science an alternative to the concept of the state and its "ideological" (that is, Marxist) connotations. Yet abandoning the traditional focus on the institutions of state created a science whose new object, the political system, had no discernible limit. The ever-expanding empirical and theoretical knowledge that would have to be mastered by the future scientists of comparative politics, Almond warned in 1960, "staggers the imagination and lames the will." Despite the initial tendency "to blink and withdraw in pain," he wrote, there could be no hesitation in the effort to accumulate the knowledge that will "enable us to take our place in the order of the sciences with the dignity which is reserved for those who follow a calling without limit or condition" (Almond and Coleman 1960: 64).

Advocates of the shift from the formal study of the state to the meticulous examination of political systems realized they were embarking on a scientific enterprise "without limit." They assumed, however, that the very notion of political system would somehow solve the question of limits, for, as Almond wrote, it implied the "existence of boundaries"—the points "where other systems end and the political system begins." The boundary required a "sharp definition," otherwise "we will find ourselves including in the political system churches, economies, schools, kinship and lineage groups, age-sets, and the like" (Almond and Coleman 1960: 5, 7–8; see also Easton 1957: 384). Yet this is precisely what happened. The edge of the system turned out to consist of not a sharp line but every conceivable form of collective expression of political demand, from "institutional" groups such as legislatures, churches, and armies, to "associated" groups such as labor or business organizations, "nonassociated" groups such as kinship or ethnic communities, and "anomic" groups such as spontaneous riots and demonstrations (Almond and Coleman 1960: 33).

In attempting to eliminate the ambiguity of a concept whose ideological functions prevented scientific precision, the systems approach substituted an object whose very boundary unfolded into a limitless and undetermined terrain.

The Return of the State

The attempt in the 1950s and 1960s to eliminate the concept of the state was unsuccessful. The notion of political system was too imprecise and unworkable to establish itself as an alternative. But there were several other reasons for the return of the state. First, by the late 1960s it was clear that U.S. influence in the third world could not be built on the creation of "civic cultures." Modernization seemed to require the creation of powerful authoritarian states, as Huntington argued in 1968.

Second, from the late 1960s a more powerful critique of modernization theory was developed by neo-Marxist scholars in Latin America, the Middle East, and Europe. Samir Amin, Cardoso and Faletto, Gunder Frank, and others produced theories of capitalist development in which an important place was given to the nature and role of the third world state. As Paul Cammack (1989, 1990) suggests, this literature obliged U.S. scholars to "return to the state" in an effort to reappropriate the concept by drawing on neo-Marxist scholarship and in most cases denying the significance of the underlying Marxian framework.

Third, in most countries of the West, the language of political debate continued to refer to the institutions of the state and to the role of the state in the economy and society. In 1968, J. P. Nettl pointed out that although the concept was out of fashion in the social sciences, it retained a popular currency that "no amount of conceptual restructuring can dissolve" (1968: 559). The state, he wrote, is "essentially a sociocultural phenomenon" that occurs due to the "cultural disposition" among a population to recognize what he called the state's "conceptual existence" (565–66). Notions of the state "become incorporated in the thinking and actions of individual citizens" (577), he argued, and the extent of this conceptual variable could be shown to correspond to important empirical differences between societies, such as differences in legal structure or party system (579–92).

Clearly, the importance of the state as a common ideological and cultural construct should be grounds not for dismissing the phenomenon but for taking it seriously. Yet Nettl's understanding of this construct as a subjective disposition that could be correlated with more objective phenomena remained thoroughly empiricist. A construct such as the state occurs not merely as a subjective belief, but as a representation reproduced in visible everyday forms, such as the language of legal practice, the architecture of public buildings, the wearing of military uniforms, or the marking and policing of frontiers. The ideological forms of the state are an empirical phenomenon, as solid and discernible as a legal structure or a party system. Or rather, as I contend here, the distinction made between a conceptual realm and an empirical one needs to be placed in question if one is to understand the nature of a phenomenon such as the state.

Mainstream social science did not raise such questions. In fact the conceptual/empirical distinction provided the unexamined conceptual base on which to reintroduce the idea of the state. During the later 1970s, the state reemerged as a central analytic concern of American social science. "The lines between state and society have become blurred," warned Stephen Krasner in *Defending the National Interest* (1978: xi), one of the early contributions to this reemergence. "The basic analytic assumption" of the statist approach it advocated "is that there is a distinction between state and society" (5). The new literature presented this fundamental but problematic distinction, as in Nettl's article, in terms of an underlying distinction between a conceptual realm (the state) and an empirical realm (society). Such an approach appeared to overcome the problem the systems theorists complained about and reencountered, of how to discern the boundary between state and society: it was to be assimilated to the apparently obvious distinction between conceptual and empirical, between a subjective order and an objective one. As I have shown elsewhere, however, this depended on both an enormous narrowing of the phenomenon of the state and an uncritical acceptance of this distinction (Mitchell 1991).

State-centered approaches to political explanation presented the state as an autonomous entity whose actions were not reducible to or determined by forces in society. This approach required not so much a shift in focus, from society back to the state, but some way of reestablishing a clear boundary between the two. How were the porous edges where official practice mixes with the semiofficial and the latter with the unofficial to be turned into lines of separation, so that the state could stand apart as a discrete, self-directing object? The popular Weberian definition of the state, as an organization that claims a monopoly within a fixed territory over the legitimate use of violence, is only a residual characterization. It does not explain how the actual contours of this amorphous organization are to be drawn.

The new theorists of the state did not fill in the organizational contours. They retreated to narrower definitions, which typically grasped the state as a system of decision making. The narrower focus locates the essence of the state not in the monopolistic organization of coercion, nor, for example, in the structures of a legal order, nor in the mechanisms by which social interests find political representation, nor in the arrangements that maintain a given relationship between the producers of capital and its owners, but in the formation and expression of authoritative intentions. Construed as a machinery of intentions—usually termed *rule making, decision making*, or *policymaking*—state becomes essentially a subjective realm of plans, programs, or ideas. This subjective construction maps the problematic state-society distinction on to the seemingly more obvious distinctions we make between the subjective and the objective, between the ideological and the material, or even between meaning and reality. The state appears to stand apart from society in the unproblematic way in which intentions or ideas are thought to stand apart from the external world to which they refer.

Elsewhere I have illustrated these problems in detail through a discussion of some of the leading contributions to the literature (Mitchell 1991). Even those who describe their approach as institutionalist, such as Theda Skocpol (1979, 1981), can demonstrate the alleged autonomy of the state only by appealing to a subjective interest or ideology of the ruler. When the account turns to wider institutional processes, the distinction between state and society fades away.

An Alternative Approach

The state-centered literature begins from the assumption that the state is a distinct entity, opposed to and set apart from a larger entity called society. Arguments are confined to assessing the degree of independence one object enjoys from the other. Yet in fact the line between the two is often uncertain. Like the systems theorists before them, the state theorists are unable to fix the elusive boundary between the political system or state and society. Cammack (1990, 1989) is surely correct to assert that the state theorists fail to refute the argument that modern states enjoy only a relative separation from the interests of dominant social classes and that their policies can be explained adequately only in relation to the structure of class relations. But then the questions remain: how is this relative separation of the state from society produced? And how is the effect created that the separation is an absolute one? These are questions that not even neo-Marxist theories of the state have addressed adequately.

To introduce an answer to these questions, I begin with a case discussed in Stephen Krasner's study of U.S. government policy toward the corporate control of foreign raw materials: the relationship between the U.S. government and the Arabian-American Oil Company (Aramco), the consortium of major U.S. oil corporations that possessed exclusive rights to Saudi Arabian oil (Krasner 1978: 205–12). The case illustrates both the permeability of the state-society boundary and the political significance of maintaining it. After World War II, the Saudis demanded that their royalty payment from Aramco be increased from 12 percent to 50 percent of profits. Unwilling either to cut its profits or to raise the price of oil, Aramco arranged for the increase in royalty to be paid not by the company but in effect by U.S. taxpayers. The Department of State, anxious to subsidize the pro-American Saudi monarchy, helped arrange for Aramco to evade U.S. tax law by treating the royalty as though it were a direct foreign tax, paid not from the company's profits but from the taxes it owed to the U.S. Treasury (Anderson 1981: 179–497). This collusion between government and oil companies, obliging U.S. citizens to contribute unknowingly to the treasury of a repressive Middle Eastern monarchy and to the bank balances of some of the world's largest and most profitable multinational corporations, does not offer much support for the image of a neat distinction between state and society.

Krasner copes with this complexity by arguing that the oil companies were "an institutional mechanism" used by central decision makers to achieve certain foreign policy goals, in this case the secret subsidizing of a conservative Arab regime. Policies that might be opposed by Congress or foreign allies could be pursued through such mechanisms "in part because private firms were outside of the formal political system" (1978: 212–13). This explanation offers only one side of the picture: the firms themselves also used the U.S. government to further corporate goals, as the Aramco case illustrates and as several studies of the oil industry have demonstrated in detail (Anderson 1981; Blair 1976; Miller 1980).

Yet despite its failure to portray the complexity of such state-society relations, Krasner's explanation does inadvertently point to what is crucial about them. The Aramco case illustrates how the "institutional mechanisms" of a modern political order are never confined within the limits of what is called the state (or in this case, curiously enough, the "formal political system"). This is not to say simply that the state is something surrounded by parastatal or corporatist institutions, which buttress and extend its authority. It is to argue that the boundary of the state (or political system) never marks a real exterior. The line between state and society is not the perimeter of an intrinsic entity that can be thought of as a freestanding object or actor. It is a line drawn internally, within the network of institutional mechanisms through which a certain social and political order is maintained. The point that the state's boundary never marks a real exterior suggests why it seems so often elusive and unstable. But this does not mean the line is illusory. On the contrary, as the Aramco case shows, producing and maintaining the distinction between state and society is itself a mechanism that generates resources of power. The fact that Aramco can be said to lie outside the "formal political system," thereby disguising its role in international politics, is essential to its strength as part of a larger political order.

One could explore many similar examples, such as the relationship between state and "private" institutions in the financial sector, in schooling and scientific research, or in health care and medical practice. In each case one could show that the state-society divide is not a simple border between two freestanding objects or domains, but a complex distinction internal to these realms of practice. Take the example of banking: the relations between major corporate banking groups, semipublic central banks or reserve systems, government treasuries, deposit insurance agencies and export-import banks (which subsidize up to 40 percent of exports of industrialized nations), and multinational bodies such as the World Bank (whose head is appointed by the president of the United States) represent interlocking networks of financial power and regulation. No simple line could divide this network into a private realm and a public one or into state and society or state and economy. At the same time, banks are set up and present themselves as private institutions clearly separate from the state. The appearance that state and society or economy are separate things is part of the way a given financial and economic order is maintained. This is equally true of the wider social and political order. The power to regulate and control is not simply a capacity stored within the state, from where it extends out into society. The apparent boundary of the state does not mark the limit of the processes of regulation. It is itself a product of those processes.

Another example is that of law. The legal system, a central component of the modern state when conceived in structural terms, consists of a complex system of rights, statutes, penalties, enforcement agencies, litigants, legal personnel, prisons, rehabilitation systems, psychiatrists, legal scholars, libraries, and law schools, in which the exact dividing line between the legal structure and the "society" it structures is once again very difficult to locate. In practice we tend to simplify the distinction by thinking of the law as an abstract code and society as the realm of its practical application. Yet this fails to correspond to the complexities of what actually occurs, where code and practice tend to be inseparable aspects of one another. The approach to the state advocated here does not imply an image of the state and private organizations as a single totalized structure of power. On the contrary, there are always conflicts between them, as there are between different government agencies, between corporate organizations, and within each of them. It means that we should not be misled into taking for granted the idea of the state as a coherent object clearly separate from "society"—any more than we should be misled by the vagueness and complexity of these phenomena into rejecting the concept of the state altogether.

Conceived in this way, the state is no longer to be taken as essentially an actor, with the coherence, agency, and autonomy this term presumes. The multiple arrangements that produce the apparent separateness of the state create effects of agency and partial autonomy, with concrete consequences. Yet such agency will always be contingent on the production of difference—those practices that create the apparent boundary between state and society. These arrangements may be so effective, however, as to make things appear the reverse of this. The state comes to seem an autonomous starting point, as an actor that intervenes in society. Statist approaches to political analysis take this reversal for reality.

What we need instead is an approach to the state that refuses to take for granted this dualism, yet accounts for why social and political reality appears in this binary form. It is not sufficient simply to criticize the abstract idealist appearance the state assumes in the state-centered literature. Gabriel Almond, for example, complains that the concept of the state employed in much of the new literature "seems to have metaphysical overtones" (1987: 476), and David Easton argues that the state is presented by one writer as an "undefinable essence, a 'ghost in the machine,' knowable only through its variable manifestations" (1981: 316). Such criticisms ignore the fact that this is how the state very often appears in practice. The task of a critique of the state is not just to reject such metaphysics, but to explain how it has been possible to produce this practical effect, so characteristic of the modern political order. What is it about modern society, as a particular form of social and economic order, that has made possible the apparent autonomy of the state as a freestanding entity? Why is this kind of apparatus, with its typical basis in an abstract system of law, its symbiotic relation with the sphere we call the economy, and its almost transcendental association with the "nation" as the fundamental political community, the distinctive political arrangement of the modern age? What particular practices and techniques have continually reproduced the ghost-like abstraction of the state, so that despite the effort to have the term "polished off a quarter of a century ago," as Easton (303) puts it, it has returned "to haunt us once again"?

The new theorists of the state ignore these historical questions. Even works that adopt a historical perspective, such as Skocpol's (1979) comparative study of revolutions, are unable to offer a historical explanation of the appearance of the modern state. Committed to an approach in which the state is an independent cause, Skocpol cannot explain the ability of the state to appear as an entity standing apart from society in terms of factors external to the state. The state must be an independent cause of events, even when those events, as in a case such as revolutionary France, involve the very birth of a modern, apparently autonomous state.

Discipline and Government

To illustrate the kind of explanation that might be possible, one can turn to Skocpol's account of the French state. She describes prerevolutionary France as a "statist" society, meaning a society in which the power and privileges of a landed nobility and the power of the central administration were inextricably bound together. We can now describe this situation another way, as a society in which those modern techniques that make the state appear to be a separate entity that somehow stands outside society had not yet been institutionalized. The revolutionary period represents the consolidation of such novel techniques. Skocpol characterizes the revolutionary transformation of the French state as principally a transformation in the army and the bureaucracy, both of which became permanent professional organizations whose staffs were for the first time set apart from other commercial and social activities and whose size and effectiveness were vastly extended. For Skocpol, such changes are to be understood as the consequence of an autonomous state, whose officials desired to embark on the expansion and consolidation of centralized power. We are therefore given little detail about the techniques on which such revolutionary transformations rested.

How was it now possible to assemble a permanent army of up to three-quarters of a million men, transform an entire economy into production for war, maintain authority and discipline on such a scale, and so "separate" this military machine from society that the traditional problem of desertion was overcome? By what parallel means were the corruptions and leakages of financial administration brought under control? What was the nature of the "mechanical efficiency and articulation," in a phrase quoted from J. F. Bosher (Skocpol 1979: 200), that in every realm would now enable "the virtues of organization to offset the vices of individual men"? What kind of "articulation," in other words, could now seem to separate mechanically an "organization" from the "individual men" who composed it? Rather than attributing such transformations to policies of an autonomous state, it is more accurate to trace in these new techniques of organization and articulation the very possibility of appearing to set apart from society the freestanding apparatus of a state.

An exploration of such questions has to begin by acknowledging the enormous significance of those small-scale polymorphous methods of order that Foucault calls disciplines. The new bureaucratic and military strength of the French state was founded on powers generated from the meticulous organization of space, movement, sequence, and position. The new power of the army, for example, was based on such measures as the construction of barracks as sites of permanent confinement set apart from the social world, the introduction of daily inspection and drill, repetitive training in maneuvers broken down into precisely timed sequences and combinations, and the elaboration of complex hierarchies of command, spatial arrangement, and surveillance. With such techniques, an army could be made into what a contemporary military manual called an "artificial machine," and other armies now seemed like collections of "idle and inactive men" (Fuller 1955: vol. 2: 196).

Disciplinary power has two consequences for understanding the modern state—only the first of which is analyzed by Foucault. In the first place, one moves beyond the image of power as essentially a system of sovereign commands or policies backed by force. This approach is adopted by almost all recent theorists of the state. It conceives of state power in the form of a person (an individual or collective decision maker), whose decisions form a system of orders and prohibitions that direct and constrain social action. Power is thought of as an exterior constraint: its source is a sovereign authority above and outside society, and it operates by setting external limits to behavior, establishing negative prohibitions, and laying down channels of proper conduct.

Discipline, by contrast, works not from the outside but from within, not at the level of an entire society but at the level of detail, and not by constraining individuals and their actions but by producing them. As Foucault puts it, a negative exterior power gives way to an internal productive power. Disciplines work locally, entering social processes, breaking them down into separate functions, rearranging the parts, increasing their efficiency and precision, and reassembling them into more productive and powerful combinations. These methods produce the organized power of armies, schools, bureaucracies, factories, and other distinctive institutions of the technical age. They also produce, within such institutions, the modern individual, constructed as an isolated, disciplined, receptive, and industrious political subject. Power relations do not simply confront this individual as a set of external orders and prohibitions. His or her very individuality, formed within such institutions, is already the product of those relations.

The second consequence of modern political techniques is one that Foucault does not explain. Despite their localized and polyvalent nature, disciplinary powers are somehow consolidated into the territorially based, institutionally structured order of the modern state. Foucault does not dismiss the importance of this larger kind of structure; he simply does not believe that the understanding of power should begin there: "One must rather conduct an ascending analysis of power, starting, that is, from its infinitesimal mechanisms . . . and then see how these mechanisms of power have been—and continue to be—invested, colonised, utilised, involuted, transformed, displaced, extended, etc., by ever more general mechanisms . . ., [how they] came to be colonised and maintained by global mechanisms and the entire state system" (Foucault 1980b: 99–101). Yet Foucault does not explain how disciplinary powers do come to be utilized, stabilized, and reproduced in state structures or other "generalized mechanisms."

An example of the relationship between infinitesimal and general mechanisms can be found in law, an issue already discussed above, where the micropowers of disciplinary normalization are structured into the larger apparatus of the legal code and the juridical system. In discussing this case, Foucault falls back on the notion that the general structure is an ideological screen (that of sovereignty and right) superimposed on the real power of discipline. "[O]nce it became necessary for disciplinary constraints to be exercised through mechanisms of domination and yet at the same time for their effective exercise of power to be disguised, a theory of sovereignty was required to make an appearance at the level of the legal apparatus, and to reemerge in its codes" (Foucault 1980b: 106). The organization of law at the general level "allowed a system of right to be superimposed upon the mechanisms of discipline in such a way as to conceal its actual procedures" (105). Foucault steps away again from the implication that the general level is related to the microlevel as a public realm of ideology opposed to the hidden realm of actual power, by recalling that disciplines, too, contain a public discourse. But his studies of disciplinary methods provide no alternative terms to conceive of the way in which local mechanisms of power are related to the larger structural forms, such as law, in which they become institutionalized and reproduced.

In subsequent lectures, Foucault did turn his attention to the large-scale methods of power and control characteristic of the modern state (Foucault 1991). He analyzed the emergence of these methods not in terms of the development of formal institutions, but in the emergence of a new object on which power relations could operate and of new techniques and tactics of power. He identified the new object as population and referred to the new techniques as the powers of "government." Foucault traces the emergence of the problem of population from the eighteenth century, associating it with increases in agricultural production, demographic changes, and an increasing supply of money. Population, he argues, was an object now seen to have "its own regularities, its own rates of deaths and diseases, its cycles of scarcity, etc.," all susceptible to statistical measurement and political analysis (99). Such analysis produced a whole series of aggregate effects that were not reducible to those of the individual or the household. Politics came to be concerned with the proper management of a population in relation to resources, territory, agriculture, and trade. Population replaced the household as the principal object of politics. The household, or rather the family, was now considered an element internal to population, providing an instrument for obtaining information about and exercising power over the larger, aggregate object (99–100).

To describe this aggregate-level power, Foucault invokes a term that proliferated in the literature of the period, the word "government." For Foucault, the word refers not to the institutions of the state, but to the new tactics of management and methods of security that take population as their object. As with the term *discipline*, government refers to power in terms of its methods rather than its institutional forms. Government draws on the micropowers of discipline; in fact the development of disciplinary methods becomes more acute as they become applied to the problem of population. But government has its own tactics and rationality, expressed in the development of its own field of knowledge, the emerging science of political economy. Foucault also argues that the development of government and of political economy correspond not only to the emergence of population as a new datum and object of power, but also to the separation of the economy as its own sphere. "The word 'economy,' which in the sixteenth century signified a form of government, comes in the eighteenth century to designate a level of reality, a field of intervention" (Foucault 1991: 93). This argument is more problematic.

Conceived in terms of its methods and its object, rather than its institutional forms, government is a broader process than the relatively unified and functionalist entity suggested by the notion of the state. Government is a process "at once internal and external to the state, since it is the tactics of government which make possible the continual definition and redefinition of what is within the competence of the state and what is not, the public versus the private, and so on" (Foucault 1991: 103). For this reason, Foucault suggests, the state probably does not have the unity, individuality, and rigorous functionality attributed to it. Indeed it may be "no more than a composite reality and a mythicized abstraction, whose importance is a lot more limited than many of us think" (103). One can agree with this sentiment, yet still not find in Foucault an answer to the question that is once again raised. If indeed modern governmental power exceeds the limits of the state, if the state lacks the unity and identity it always appears to have, how does this appearance arise? How is the composite reality of the state composed? What tactics and methods in modern forms of power create and recreate this mythicized abstraction? One response to this question is to locate the answer in the phenomenon of the national project. In this view, the state acquires its unity at the level of ideology. Beyond the practical multiplicity of tactics, disciplines, and powers, the state articulates a national project that projects its unity onto society. But such an answer again falls back on the distinction between ideology and practice, instead of placing that distinction in question.

The Appearance of Structure

The relationship between methods of discipline and government and their stabilization in such forms as the state, I argue, lies in the fact that at the same time as power relations become internal, in Foucault's terms; and by the same methods, they now take on the specific appearance of external "structures." The distinctiveness of the modern state, appearing as an apparatus that stands apart from the rest of the social world, is to be found in this novel structural effect. The effect is the counterpart of the production of modern individuality. For example, the new military methods of the late eighteenth century produced the disciplined individual soldier and, simultaneously, the novel effect of an armed unit as an "artificial machine." This military apparatus appeared somehow greater than the sum of its parts, as though it were a structure with an existence independent of the men who composed it. In comparison with other armies, which now looked like amorphous gatherings of "idle and inactive men," the new army seemed something two-dimensional. It appeared to consist on the one hand of individual soldiers and, on the other, of the "machine" they inhabited. Of course this apparatus has no independent existence. It is an effect produced by the organized partitioning of space, the regular distribution of bodies, exact timing, the coordination of movement, the combining of elements, and endless repetition, all of which are particular practices. There was nothing in the new power of the army except this distributing, arranging, and moving. But the order and precision of such processes created the effect of an apparatus apart from the men themselves, whose "structure" orders, contains, and controls them.

A similar two-dimensional effect can be seen at work in other institutions of modern government. The precise specification of space and function that characterize modern institutions, the coordination of these functions into hierarchical arrangements, the organization of supervision and surveillance, the marking out of time into schedules and programs, all contribute to constructing a world that appears to consist not of a complex of social practices but of a binary order: on the one hand individuals and their activities, on the other an inert "structure" that somehow stands apart from individuals, precedes them, and contains and gives a framework to their lives. Indeed the very notion of an institution, as an abstract framework separate from the particular practices it enframes, can be seen as the product of these techniques. Such techniques have given rise to the peculiar, apparently binary world we inhabit, where reality seems to take the two-dimensional form of individual versus apparatus, practice versus institution, social life and its structure—or society versus state (see Mitchell 1988, 1990). We must analyze the state as such a structural effect. That is to say, we should examine it not as an actual structure, but as the powerful, apparently metaphysical effect of practices that make such structures appear to exist. In fact, the nation state is arguably the paramount structural effect of the modern technical era. It includes within itself many of the particular institutions already discussed, such as armies, schools, and bureaucracies. Beyond these, the larger presence of the state in several ways takes the form of a framework that appears to stand apart from the social world and provide an external structure. One characteristic of modern governmentality, for example, is the frontier. By establishing a territorial boundary to enclose a population and exercising absolute control over movement across it, governmental powers define and help constitute a national entity. Setting up and policing a frontier involves a variety of fairly modern social practices—continuous barbed-wire fencing, passports, immigration laws, inspections, currency control, and so on. These mundane arrangements, most of them unknown two hundred or even one hundred years ago, help manufacture an almost transcendental entity, the nation-state. This entity comes to seem something much more than the sum of the everyday powers of government that constitute it, appearing as a structure containing and giving order and meaning to people's lives. An analogous example is the law. Once again, one could analyze how the mundane details of the legal process, all of which are particular social practices, are arranged to produce the effect that the law exists as a formal framework, superimposed above social practice. What we call the state, and think of as an intrinsic object existing apart from society, is the sum of these structural effects.

What is the relationship of this structural effect to the specifically capitalist nature of modernity? The state-centric theorists examined earlier argue that no particular relationship exists. To insist on the autonomy of the state, as they do, means that the programs it follows and the functions it serves should not be explained by reference even to the long-term requirements of the larger capitalist order, but primarily in terms of the independent ideas and interests of those who happen to hold high office. As we saw, however, the evidence they present fails to support this view and provides stronger support for neo-Marxist theories of the state, such as the work of Nicos Poulantzas. The state policies that Krasner describes in relation to the control of foreign raw materials or that Skocpol describes in her work on the New Deal (Skocpol 1981; see Mitchell 1991: 88–89) appear to serve the general requirements of capital. The relative separation of the state enables it to pursue the long-term interests of capital as a whole, sometimes working against the short-term interests of particular capitalists (see Cammack 1990). Yet, as Poulantzas himself recognized in his later work, this functionalist account cannot adequately explain the modern state. It does not account for the particular form taken by the modern state, as an aspect of the regulation of capitalist modernity. It does not explain how state power takes on the form of a seemingly external structure, or its association with an abstract system of law, or its apparent separation from, yet imbrication in, the sphere we call the economy. In other words, it does not tell us how the modern effect of the state is produced.

There are two ways to approach this question of the relationship between capitalism and the state effect. One way is to explain the effect of the state as the consequence of capitalist production. The structural forms of the modern state could be explained by reference to certain distinctive features of the way in which the social relations of production are organized under capitalism (see Ollman 1992). This is the approach taken by Poulantzas in his later work, in which he responded to and was influenced by Foucault. Poulantzas (1978) argues that what Foucault (1977) describes as discipline—processes of individualization, the modern production of knowledge, and the reorganization of space and time—should be explained as aspects of the way capitalism organizes the relations of production. These same processes, he suggests, account for the form taken by the state. The discipline of factory production, for example, introduces the separation of mental labor from manual labor. The state embodies this same separation, representing a distinct mental order of expertise, scientific management, and administrative knowledge. Similarly, in Poulantzas's view, the serial, cellular organization of time and space in modern production processes is reproduced in the new geospatial power of the nation-state and the historical-spatial definition of national identity.

The other approach to the question of the state and capital is the one taken here. Rather than explain the form of the state as the consequence of the disciplinary regime of capitalist production, one can see both the factory regime and the power of the state as aspects of the modern reordering of space, time, and personhood and the production of the new effects of abstraction and subjectivity. It is customary to see the state as an apparatus of power and the factory as one of production. In fact, both are systems of disciplinary power and both are techniques of production. Both produce the effect of an abstraction that stands apart from material reality. In the case of political practice, as we have seen, this abstraction is the effect of the state—a nonmaterial totality that seems to exist apart from the material world of society. In the case of the organization of labor, the abstraction produced is that of capital. What distinguishes capitalist production, after all, is not just the disciplined organization of the labor process but the manufacture of an apparent abstraction—exchange value—that seems to exist apart from the mundane objects and processes from which it is created. The effect of capital is produced out of techniques of discipline, organization, and enframing analogous to those that produce the effect of the state.

Rather than deriving the forms of the state from the logic of capital accumulation and the organization of production relations, both capital and the state can been seen as aspects of a common process of abstraction. This approach to the question of the relation between the state and capital enables one, furthermore, to extend the critique of the concept of the state to include the parallel concept of the economy.

Inventing the Economy

Modern mass armies, bureaucracies, and education systems were creations largely of the late eighteenth and nineteenth centuries. Complex legal codes and institutions and the modern control of frontiers and population movement emerged mostly in the same period. The twentieth century was characterized by a further and different development: the emergence of the modern idea of the economy. Foucault, as we saw, placed the separation of the economy as its own sphere in the eighteenth and nineteenth centuries, as part of the emergence of the new techniques of government centered on the problem of population. This conflation of economy and population as political objects locates the emergence of the economy much earlier than it actually occurred. More important, it overlooks a critical shift that took place in the first half of the twentieth century, when the economy replaced population as the new object of the powers of government and the sciences of politics. This object played a central role in the articulation of the distinctive forms of the twentieth-century state as a set of bureaucratized science-based technologies of planning and social welfare. An adequate theory of the contemporary state must take into account not only the nineteenth-century developments described above but also the new relationship that emerged between state and economy in the twentieth century. The contemporary structural effect of the state is inseparable from the relatively recent creation of "the economy."

The nineteenth-century tactics of power that Foucault describes as government took as their fundamental object, as was noted, the issue of population. Politics was concerned with the security and well-being of a population defined in relation to a given territory and resources, with the pattern of its growth or decline, with associated changes in agriculture and commerce, and with its health, its education, and above all its wealth. The political economy of Smith, Ricardo, and Malthus developed within this general problematic of population and its prosperity. The term *political economy* referred to the proper economy, or management, of the polity, a management whose purpose was to improve the wealth and security of the population. The term *economy* never carried, in the discourse of nineteenth-century political economy, its contemporary meaning referring to a distinct sphere of social reality—understood as the self-contained totality of relations of production, distribution, and consumption within a defined geospatial unit. Nor was there any other term denoting such a separate, self-contained sphere (Mitchell 1995).

Marx followed in the same tradition. "When we consider a given country politico-economically," he wrote, "we begin with its population, its distribution among classes, town, country, the coast, the different branches of production, export and import, annual production and consumption, commodity prices, etc." (1973: 100). He argued that this conventional approach was backward, for population presupposes capital, wage labor, and division into classes. Smith and Ricardo had developed a system that started from these simpler abstractions, but one-sidedly focusing on landed property and on exchange. A proper analysis, Marx argued, should start with capital and material production and then work back toward the totalities of bourgeois society, its concentration in the form of the state, the population, the colonies, and emigration (100–8). The concept of material production has subsequently been misinterpreted as meaning the same thing as the twentieth-century idea of the economy. But Marx had no greater

conception of an economy as a separate social sphere than the political economists whom he criticized.

The economy was invented in the first half of the twentieth century, as part
of the reconstruction of the effect of the state. The nineteenth-century understanding of the production and circulation of wealth and its relation to population growth, territorial expansion, and resources broke down during World
War I and the decade of financial and political crises that followed. The abandoning of gold as the measure of the value of money, unprecedented levels of
debt, unemployment and overproduction, rapid swings from economic boom to
complete collapse, the ending of European territorial expansion and population
growth, the beginning of the disintegration of empire, and the very fear of capitalism's collapse all created a need to reimagine the process of government and
construct new objects and methods of political power. It is in this period that
terms such as "economic system," "economic structure," and finally "the economy" came into political circulation.

Between the 1920s and the 1950s, "the economy" came to refer to the structure or totality of relations of production, circulation, and consumption within
a given geographical space. The emergence of macroeconomics, as the new science of this object was called, coincided with developments in statistics that
made it possible to imagine the enumeration of what came to be known as the
gross national product of an economy and with the invention of econometrics,
the attempt to represent the entire workings of an economy as a single mathematical model (Mitchell 1995). The isolating of production, circulation, and
consumption as distinctively economic processes was nothing new. This had
been done, within the problematic of population, by the classical political economists of the eighteenth and nineteenth centuries. What was new was the notion
that the interrelation of these processes formed a space or object that was self-
contained, subject to its own internal dynamics, and liable to "external" impulses
or interventions that created reverberations throughout the self-contained object. Factors such as population, territory, and even other "economies" were now
considered external to this object. But the most important thing imagined to
stand outside the economy was the one considered most capable of affecting or
altering it—the state.

The idea of an economy as a self-contained and internally dynamic totality,
separate from other economies and subject to intervention, adjustment, and
management by an externally situated state, could not have been imagined within
the terms of nineteenth-century political economy. In the twentieth century, on
the other hand, the contemporary concept of the state has become inseparable
from the fundamental distinction that emerged between state and economy. In
fact, much of the more recent theorizing about state and society is more accurately described as theorizing about the state in terms of its relation to the economy. Curiously, as the new distinction between state and economy emerged
from the 1920s and 1930s onward, so-called economic processes and institutions
became increasingly difficult to distinguish in practice from those of government
or the state. With the collapse of the gold standard and the consolidation of cen-

tral banks and reserve systems, money came to acquire its value as part of a "political" as much as an "economic" process. State bureaucracies gradually became the economy's largest employer, spender, borrower, and saver. The creation of quasipublic corporations such as port authorities; the nationalization of transport, communications, and other services; the state subsidy of agriculture and of military and other manufacturing; even the growth of publicly owned corporations in place of private firms, and especially (as the Aramco case illustrates) the transnational corporations, all blurred the distinction between private and public spheres or state and economy.

As with state and society, so with state and economy, one has to ask why the distinction between these two objects seems so obvious and is taken for granted so routinely, when on close examination their separation is difficult to discern. The answer has to address the same effects of structure already discussed in relation to state and society. One examines the practical arrangements that make the economy appear a concrete, material realm and the state an abstract, institutional structure standing apart from the economy's materiality. Besides the methods of structuring already discussed, two structural effects are especially important to create the distinction between state and economy. First, when twentieth-century political practice invented the economy, the boundaries of this object were understood to coincide with those of the nation-state. Although the new macroeconomics did not theorize the nation-state, it represented the economy in terms of aggregates (employment, savings, investment, production) and synthetic averages (interest rate, price level, real wage, and so on) whose geospatial referent was always the nation-state (Radice 1984: 121). So, without explicit theorization, the state came to stand as the geospatial structure that provided the economy with its external boundary and form. Second, the economy was constructed as an object of knowledge in the twentieth century through an extensive process of statistical representation. Almost all of this process was carried out as part of the new institutional practice of the state. So the relationship between state and economy appeared to take the form of the relation between representor and the object of representation. (Once again, this relationship to the state was not something analyzed by the new science of economics. In fact, economics came to be distinguished among the social sciences by two related features: It was the only major social science with no subdiscipline—"field economics" it could be called—dealing with issues of data collection and questions of representation, and it was a discipline that became dependent on the state for almost all its data. The state thus appears to stand apart from the economy as a network of information, statistical knowledge, and imagery, opposed to the apparently real, material object to which this representational network refers. In practice, once again, this relationship is more complex, not least because the economy itself, in the course of the twentieth century, became more and more a hyperreal or representational object. Its elements came increasingly to consist of forms of finance, services, and so on that exist only as systems of representation; and the dynamics of the economy came to be determined increasingly by factors such as expectations, that are themselves issues of representation. Nevertheless, the appearance of the economy as a real object in opposition to its representation by the state provided a simple means of effecting the seeming separation between state and economy that remains so important to most contemporary theories of the state.

IN conclusion, the argument for a different approach to the question of the state and its relationship to society and economy can be summarized in a list of five propositions:

1. We should abandon the idea of the state as a freestanding entity, whether an agent, instrument, organization, or structure, located apart from and opposed to another entity called economy or society.
2. We must nevertheless take seriously the distinction between state and society or state and economy. It is a defining characteristic of the modern political order. The state cannot be dismissed as an abstraction or ideological construct and passed over in favor of more real, material realities. In fact, we must place this distinction between conceptual and material, between abstract and real, in historical question if we are to grasp how the modern state has appeared.
3. For the same reason, the prevailing view of the state as essentially a phenomenon of decision making or policy is inadequate. Its focus on one disembodied aspect of the state phenomenon assimilates the state-society and state-economy distinction to the same problematic opposition between conceptual and material.
4. We should address the state as an effect of mundane processes of spatial organization, temporal arrangement, functional specification, supervision and surveillance, and representation that create the appearance of a world fundamentally divided into state and society or state and economy. The essence of modern politics is not policies formed on one side of this division being applied to or shaped by the other, but the producing and reproducing of these lines of difference.
5. These processes create the effect of the state not only as an entity set apart from economy or society, but as a distinct dimension of structure, framework, codification, expertise, information, planning, and intentionality. The state appears as an abstraction in relation to the concreteness of the social, a sphere of representation in relation to the reality of the economic, and a subjective ideality in relation to the objectness of the material world. The distinctions between abstract and concrete, ideal and material, representation and reality, and subjective and objective, on which most political theorizing is built, are themselves partly constructed in those mundane social processes we recognize and name as the state.

References

Abrams, Philip. 1988. "Notes on the Difficulty of Studying the State." *Journal of Historical Sociology* 1: 58–89.

Almond, Gabriel A. 1954. *The Appeals of Communism*. Princeton: Princeton University Press.

——. 1987. "The Development of Political Development." In *Understanding Political Development*, edited by Myron Weiner and Samuel Huntington. Boston: Little, Brown.

Almond, Gabriel A., Taylor Cole, and Roy C. Macridis. 1955. "A Suggested Research Strategy in Western European Government and Politics." *American Political Science Review* 49: 1042–44.

Almond, Gabriel A., and James Coleman. 1960. *The Politics of the Developing Areas*. Princeton: Princeton University Press.

Almond, Gabriel A., and Sidney Verba. 1963. *The Civic Culture: Politcal Attitudes and Democracy in Five Nations*. Princeton: Princeton University Press.

Anderson, Irvine H. 1981. *Aramco, the United States, and Saudi Arabia: A Study of the Dynamics of Foreign Oil Policy*. Princeton: Princeton University Press.

Blair, John M. 1976. *The Control of Oil*. New York: Pantheon.

Cammack, Paul. 1989. "Bringing the State Back In? A Polemic." *British Journal of Political Science* 19, no. 2: 261–90.

——. 1990. "Statism, Neo-Institutionalism, and Marxism." In *The Socialist Register 1990*. London: Merlin.

Easton, David. 1953. *The Political System: An Inquiry into the State of Political Science*. New York: Knopf.

——. 1957. "An Approach to the Analysis of Political Systems." *World Politics* 9: 383–400.

——. 1981. "The Political System Besieged by the State." *Political Theory* 9: 303–25.

Evans, Peter, Dietrich Rueschemeyer, and Theda Skocpol, eds. 1985. *Bringing the State Back In*. Cambridge: Cambridge University Press.

Foucault, Michel. 1977. *Discipline and Punish: The Birth of the Prison*. New York: Pantheon.

——. 1980a. "Questions on Geography." In *Power/Knowledge*. New York: Pantheon.

——. 1980b. "Two Lectures." In *Power/Knowledge*. New York: Pantheon.

——. 1991. "Governmentality." In *The Foucault Effect: Studies in Governmentality*, edited by Graham Burchell, Colin Gordon, and Peter Miller, 87–104. Hemel Hempstead, Herts: Harvester Wheatsheaf.

Fuller, J. F. C. 1955. *The Decisive Battles of the Western World and Their Influences upon History*, 3 vols. London: Eyre and Spottiswoode.

Krasner, Stephen D. 1978. *Defending the National Interest: Raw Materials Investments and U. S. Foreign Policy*. Princeton: Princeton University Press.

Loewenstein, Karl. 1944. "Report on the Research Panel on Comparative Government." *American Political Science Review* 38: 540–48.

Marx, Karl. 1973. *Grundrisse: Foundations of the Critique of Political Economy*. Translated by Martin Nicolaus. Harmondsworth, Middlesex: Penguin Books.

Miller, Aaron David. 1980. *Search for Security: Saudi Arabian Oil and American Foreign Policy, 1939–1949*. Chapel Hill: University of North Carolina Press.

Mitchell, Timothy. 1988. *Colonising Egypt*. Cambridge: Cambridge University Press.

———. 1990. "Everyday Metaphors of Power." *Theory and Society* 19: 545–77.

———. 1991. "The Limits of the State: Beyond Statist Approaches and Their Critics." *American Political Science Review* 85, no. 1: 77–96.

———. 1995. "Origins and Limits of the Modern Idea of the Economy." Working Papers Series, no. 12. Advanced Study Center, University of Michigan.

Nettl, J. P. 1968. "The State as a Conceptual Variable." *World Politics* 20: 559–92.

Ollman, Bertell. 1992. "Going Beyond the State? A Comment." *American Political Science Review* 86, no. 4: 1014–17.

Poulantzas, Nicos. 1978. *State, Power, Socialism*. London: Verso.

Radice, Hugo. 1984. "The National Economy: A Keynesian Myth?" *Capital and Class* 22: 111–40.

Sabine, George. 1934. "The State." In *Encyclopedia of the Social Sciences*. New York: Macmillan.

Skocpol, Theda. 1979. *States and Social Revolutions: A Comparative Analysis of France, Russia and China*. Cambridge: Cambridge University Press.

———. 1981. "Political Response to Capitalist Crisis: Neo-Marxist Theories of the State and the Case of the New Deal." *Politics and Society* 10: 155–201.

3

Culture in Rational-Choice Theories of State-Formation

Julia Adams

Certain perennial questions haunt the study of state-formation: What is the root of the stability or instability, rise and decline of states? Why do some states seem to infuse a social system with élan, whereas others parasitically sap social energies? Perhaps most fundamentally, why do we have states at all? Why didn't some other form of organizing power and accumulation come together in that crucible of state-formation, northern Europe? These questions are far too grand and vague to stand as proper historical or social science puzzles. Nevertheless they reappear at intervals and in different disciplinary guises, and the willingness to tackle them is a sure sign of a paradigm's theoretical vitality as well as its hubris. These big questions have surfaced dramatically in rational-choice analyses of state-formation, particularly with respect to feudal and early modern Europe. Douglass North has tried to formulate the basis of "a neoclassical theory of the state" in the context of examining the genesis of institutional structures that explain variable economic performance (1981: chap. 3). Mancur Olson problematizes the role of governance as a key variable in *The Rise and Decline of Nations* (1982). And an explosion of work in sociology and political science has pointed to "rent-seeking," "predation," and other concepts inspired by neoclassical and institutionalist economics as explanatory factors informing the rhythm of European political development.

I begin by summarizing the main lines of rational-choice arguments regarding feudal and early modern European state-formation. This growing body of work has highlighted some important sociological problems—surprisingly,

A draft of this paper was presented at the Tenth International Conference of Europeanists. For their comments and criticisms, I thank the other contributors to this volume, as well as Edgar Kiser, Gary Marks, Art Stinchcombe, Ann Stoler, the participants in the Sociology Department colloquium at the University of Connecticut, the Interdisciplinary Workshop on Social Theory at the University of Chicago, and the Early Modern History Reading Group at the University of Michigan. ISSI, the International Social Sciences Institute of Edinburgh, Scotland, provided facilities and a hospitable atmosphere for work on the final draft.

because historical social arrangements antedating the institutional differentiation of economy, polity, and family on which most key rational-choice concepts
rest seem the hardest terrain to tackle within a rational-choice paradigm. What
rational-choicers have identified, I contend, are mid-range mechanisms, or bits
of "sometimes true theory" to borrow James Coleman's phrase, that clarify certain key political patterns and developmental tendencies characteristic of early
modern Europe.[1] This strikes me as extremely useful, and I hope to convince
those ranged against rational-choice theory that interested outsiders can learn
from it. Yet because the paradigm's assumptions cannot capture the individual
motivations or the institutional and cultural conditions characteristic of patrimonial politics, they impose serious limits on explanation and understanding.
Drawing from my own work on early modern European politics, I maintain
that a culturalist model of familially oriented action generates a more complete
and convincing account of the dynamics of patrimonial state-formation than a
rational-choice approach. Political elites, who as patriarchal family heads became
deeply identified with intergenerational privilege on behalf of their patrilineages,
carried over their emotional investments into genealogies of state office. These
patrimonial political principals had special reasons to participate in intra- or interstate contracts, or to undercut them for family advantage, and were wedded
to historically specific understandings and attachments to other rulers, past, passing, or to come.

   In the context of this volume's overall analytic claim that states and culture belong together, it may seem strange to introduce the rational-choice perspective.
It is, after all, the theoretical approach that has most insistently refused culture
a constitutive role. Nonetheless, signifying practices can be found even there,
lurking in rational-choicers' core concepts and generalizations, which implicitly
incorporate cultural constructs relevant to the actions and outcomes that are
being explained. The goals of rulers, expectations of political principals, and the
regulative institutions that these actors create, are imbued with shared meanings,
including (most troubling for rational-choicers) nonrational desires that impinge
on political structures and state formation. Raising the "cultural repressed" of
these concepts to consciousness invites us to take steps toward explicitly incorporating meaning and affect in the context of our historically grounded generalizations and propels us beyond the limits of the rational-choice paradigm toward a sociocultural approach to state formation and political change.

State-Formation and Rational Choice

   The rational-choice perspective is aptly named. Kiser and Schneider (1994)
summarize its basic premise, the assumption that "all actors are rational, self-
interested wealth maximizers." This assumption actually contains several sepa-

---

[1] I owe this bon mot of Coleman's to Stinchcombe (1991). The original source is Coleman's *In-troduction to Mathematical Sociology* (1964). Deploying it here is a bit of a liberty, perhaps, because my argument is so sharply at odds with Coleman's own work.

rate assertions about social actors: that they apply the standards of means-ends rationality, that they are self-interested, and that they are largely actuated by a desire for maximizing wealth. "Thin" models of rational choice emphasize the first assumption and are agnostic about actors' goals and values, whereas "thicker" versions try to specify actors' desired ends, at least as exogenously given constraints. In either case, variations on these basic conceptual themes characterize the literature on state-formation in the rational-choice tradition, which departs from the methodological individualist standpoint of the individual actor—a deliberately circumscribed construction of that actor—and builds from there.[2] In rational-choice theory of state-formation, the key personnel are rulers—"actors or sets of actors who perform as chief executives of state institutions" (Levi 1988: 2). Rulers are responsible for making political decisions within prevailing rules of the game and, on occasion, spelling out new rules. They are also charged with enforcing those rules, in the last instance with coercive force. If all heads of organizations have a modicum of formal power, by definition the distinctiveness of a ruler is that, in the last resort, he or she lays claim to a superordinate monopoly of coercive force in a given territory.[3]

Rigorous rational-choice theory may be silent on the ultimate ends to which political decisions and the application of force might tend. Or, the argument goes, variations are individual and idiosyncratic, and effectively cancel each other out. But thick and thin have tended to come together on one practical point: whatever any particular ruler's preferences or set of values, economic resources are needed to pursue and realize them. "[Rulers] always try to set terms of trade that maximize their personal objectives," which "require them to maximize state revenues" (Levi 1988: 10). Ultimate ends or goals can still be assumed to be exogenously determined, and random with respect to the general theory, at the same time that they are held to be contingent on a universal means to an end—revenue—that must itself be a goal if any higher-order ends are to be realized.[4] By the same token, wealth is identified as the driving motivation of feudal and early modern rulers, who are therefore, by definition, "predatory."

Wealth-hungry or predatory rulers are also strategic, disposed to match means to ends.[5] Substantively, rulers may deploy an array of tactics, ranging from out-

---

[2] Sometimes the actor's "self-interest" is treated as a bare prerequisite to the satisfaction of any other interest. At other times it is simply assumed to be human nature, or tautologously true, registered by "revealed preferences." For an explicit argument in favor of the strong version of these assumptions, see Coleman, who also insists that the actor is "unconstrained by norms" and that "the theoretical aim of social science must be to conceive of [purposive] action in a way that makes it rational from the point of view of the actor" (1990: 18, 31, 503).

[3] This fundamentally Weberian definition of the state is borrowed by many rational-choicers, whereas others rely on a contractual concept of the state.

[4] An elegant and extended justification of this position can be found in Cohen and Rogers (1983: 66–73).

[5] An emphasis on satisficing rather than maximizing, following Herbert Simon, introduces a number of possible equilibria, a complication that rational-choice analysts of state formation have sought to avoid. For the complexities about means-ends rationality that this tactic introduces, see Green and Shapiro (1994).

right plunder and pillage, to trading property rights for revenue, to constructing full-fledged tax systems, whose attributes are negotiated in a triangular relationship with taxpayers and the rulers' own agents (Kiser 1994; North 1981:
149–50; Levi 1988). One logical and decidedly bleak possibility is that predators
may simply use these strategies to strip the ruled of resources. As Peter Evans
notes, Mobutu's Zaire was "a textbook case of a predatory state in which the
preoccupation of the political class with rent-seeking has turned society into its
prey" (1992: 149). There are plenty of feudal and early modern European examples as well (Lane 1979). In these cases, the state simply becomes the "quintessential protection racket" (Tilly 1985: 169).

Happily for the ruled, their rulers are constrained along a number of dimensions. Rulers may be checked by the presence of rivals who could potentially
substitute for their services (North 1981: 27). Rulers' dependence on the ruled
may be increased by the length of time that a ruler expects to remain at the helm
(rational-choicers call this the ruler's "discount rate"). If that period is long
enough, rulers avid for revenue acquire an interest in reproducing the conditions
that add to their subjects' wealth and expand their productivity, creating more
revenue for appropriation. Thus, a sunnier forecast is that some predatory rulers, however self-interested and idiosyncratic, will discourage rent-seeking, or
"behavior in institutional settings where individual efforts to maximize value
generate social waste rather than social surplus" (Buchanan 1980: 4). Such rulers
also want and need to protect property rights in a more positive sense. They
might even function as tacit agents of the ruled—or, at least, of property holders. Finally, just as they can be enabled by them, rulers are constrained by the
structures of coordination and command that they build to get the job done
(Adams 1996).

Rampant rent-seeking formed the very basis of feudal and early modern European political economies and states-in-formation. Ekelund and Tollison refer to
the early modern "mercantilist" era as one in which "the expenditure of scarce
resources to capture a pure transfer" virtually defined the practices of both rulers
and rent-hungry subjects. Rulers systematically created situations of artificial
scarcity, in the form of state-guaranteed economic privileges, and awarded,
loaned, or sold them to favored individuals or groups. Rents accrued variously
to rulers and those who managed to capture monopoly rights, at the expense of
competing claimants who were excluded and of those at the bottom of the heap,
the consumers or constituents (Ekelund and Tollison 1981: 19–20). The impact
of this modus operandi has generated ongoing debate among rational-choicers. Waste in the form of bribery and lobbying costs is endemic to any system
founded on such principles. Furthermore, property rights are liable to systematic violation. Rulers in feudal and early modern Europe who traded protection
and justice for revenue not only proffered or withdrew favors at will, but also
tended to do so as a matter of expediency, to capture more resources in the short
run. Even the favored recipients of rulers' largesse could never count on its continuing on the agreed-upon terms. The versions of rational-choice theory that
have identified state institutions with expanded rent-seeking and economic in-

efficiency, such as those of Auster and Silver (1979) and Buchanan, Tollison, and Tullock (1980), would be disposed to put forward their case still more strongly with respect to feudal and early modern states, which violated as many contracts as they guaranteed. But more recent versions of rational-choice models have noted that mercantilist practices may be more or less economically efficient in some institutional circumstances. Kiser and Schneider (1994) argue that state revenue collection in nineteenth-century Prussia was well served by personalistic prebureaucratic institutions because they enabled rulers to minimize the costs of monitoring the state's fiscal agents.[6] Root (1994) claims that early modern England evolved a particularly competitive form of rent-seeking, transacted through Parliament, that became a "political market" in which open bidding for property rights facilitated their more efficient use. These are important insights. The fact, however, that the privileges that were delegated also incorporated a range of rights to the exercise of sovereignty posed special challenges beyond considerations of economic efficiency. This does not immediately vitiate the rational-choice paradigm, to be sure, but it raises complications.

Recall that in feudal and early modern Europe, rulers' handout of privilege created interests that then pressed to be maintained and cossetted. These interests were politicoeconomic, representing presumptive claims on resources, backed in the last instance by force, and they were empirically evident in a whole series of political conflicts. In seventeenth-century France, for example, the Bourbon crown found itself face to face with legions of lesser state officers (*officiers*) whom it had created and then unintentionally entrenched by rendering their separate pieces of patrimonial power inheritable. When a predatory crown, in search of still more resources and loyalists, made plans to proliferate additional officers, those already in place feared that the value of their stakes in the state would drop. They took up arms against the crown, inaugurating that great mid-seventeenth-century upheaval, the Fronde. A similar struggle roiled the early modern Netherlands, after the ouster of the Habsburg emperors had lopped off the pinnacle of state patron-client networks in what was becoming the (uneasily) United Provinces. The vacuum at the top of the emerging state was filled by the stadholders (originally a sort of provincial governor) and the many local regent patriciates. As members of each regent elite tried for first pick of coveted patrimonial privileges, and stadholders and regents contended with one another, the situation came to resemble that in France, though it was even further complicated by confrontations among mutually jealous towns within each provincial boundary.

Rulers were handing out shares in state power and claims to economic surplus, and actors were seeking political leverage as well as wealth. Such systems are quintessentially "patrimonial" in Max Weber's sense, involving segmented relations of rule that are simultaneously political and economic (1968 [1922]). They are also unstable. Particularly when extensive rights to sovereignty are delegated

---

[6] See Philip Gorski's (1995) thoughtful critique of Kiser and Schneider's argument.

(even embracing the autonomous capacity to make war against foreign states), power tends to disperse. This tendency engenders a shifting field of strategic political possibility, of both renewed conflict among patrimonial rulers and would-be rulers and of potential deals and agreements (however shaky) among them. Centuries before Weber, Ibn Khaldun (1969) saw these oscillations as parts of a cyclical drama in which some rulers who governed more or less single-handedly would give way to an array of multiple contending candidates, who then vied with one another until a dominant figure reemerged, took charge, and extracted resources from his erstwhile challengers.

These tendencies can be redescribed, with more precision and pessimism, in rational-choice terms. If the capacity to wield autonomous force devolves to agents, they are more likely to capture enough power to turn into principals, and therefore into competitors of their own principals. In iterated interactions, or competitive "games" of indefinite length, notes Bowman, "the equilibrium price generated by the independent behavior of competitors becomes a collective *bad* that they must eliminate in order to survive" (1989: 13). Bowman is studying the collective-action problems generated by intercapitalist competition in the American coal industry, rather than problems besetting patrimonial rulers, but from a rational-choice perspective the point is broadly pertinent. Some feudal and early modern "games" were decades, even centuries, long, and engendered serious "social dilemmas," or situations in which individuals' uninhibited pursuit of gain produces a suboptimal collective outcome (Dawes 1991; Taylor 1987). Extreme cases yield an anarchic, inimical "war of all against all" among patrimonial principals or rulers, but (*pace* Khaldun) with no prospects of even temporary resolution. For assuming that participants recognize an ongoing social dilemma, nothing guarantees that they will join together to address it.

Still, such dilemmas are neither historically nor theoretically intractable, even within rational-choice theory. Social dilemmas can be resolved by swords or covenants, as utilitarians since Hobbes ([1651] 1962) have pointed out: struggles may ultimately give rise to an autocrat's assumption of total power, a multilateral contract among belligerents, or some combination of the two.[7] The role of the absolutist ruler is an easy early modern parallel. Less well-known are the many-sided social struggles among European elites that issued in collective contracts of one sort or another. On occasion these deals were remarkably explicit. The Dutch regents designed what they called Contracts of Correspondence: formal group compacts that rotated offices among various incumbents, targeting a specific town council or other patrimonial organization. These contracts were local, plural, and drawn up among equals. Like other similar compacts, these appear to have furthered, even to have been aimed at, collective rent-seeking. This at least would be the rational-choice interpretation. In general, according to

---

[7] See, among others, Axelrod (1981); Ostrom, Walker, and Gardner (1992); Taylor (1990); Hardin (1990: 358–77); and Heimer (1990: 378–82). I leave aside, for the moment, the conditions that might produce these varied outcomes.

Mancur Olson, cartels that function as distributional coalitions strive to increase their own benefits, whatever the effect on the surrounding society (1982: 41–74). Effective cartels also limit access to the "commons" by blocking entry into the desirable area.[8] The formalization of appropriation of state office accomplished those tasks quite nicely. And as state officers reasserted their corporate prerogatives vis-à-vis rulers, such contracts simultaneously reforged nodal links in patrimonial chains of command and regenerated the state.[9]

Both the predatory and classical contractarian visions of state-formation are enjoying an intellectual renaissance at the moment. Within certain limits—scope conditions that I develop in subsequent sections of this essay—they apply to premodern Europe. Together they reflect inherent tendencies in mechanisms of patrimonial governance and illuminate the process by which workable pacts arose out of conflicts among contending principals, simultaneously shaping and stabilizing relations of rule, whether the contestants are reconstituted as a unitary principal or their clashing interests managed through an overarching structure.[10]

Criticism, Self-Criticism: Culture and Emotion

Let's take a closer look at the structure of politics in early modern Europe, where, as we have seen, rulers held, and often virtually owned and commanded, pieces of the polity, of resource-bearing political privilege. As I have argued elsewhere, this privileged site was also entwined with elite family position (Adams 1994). Politically secured private accumulation promoted a man's reputation, family honor, and the prospects of his descendants, and the prestige of his lineage qualified him to occupy lucrative state offices and to pass them along to his sons, nephews, and grandsons. In other times and places, power holders could have routinely passed on privileges to cross-cousins, younger sons, or women, but in feudal and early modern Europe the typical lines of appropriation and filiation favored primogeniture, patriliny, and patriarchy. This was especially true among the ruling urban patriciates, when the royal or aristocratic family-household was not the dominant symbolic focus and staging-post of rule.

Certainly rational-choicers have acknowledged the role of family practices, especially those undertaken by elite family heads functioning as principals in po-

---

[8] This use of the metaphor of the "commons" derives loosely from Garrett Hardin's classic 1968 article, collected in Hardin and Baden (1977).

[9] I define a hierarchy as a structure embodying relations of authority and subordination, and a contract as an agreement between persons or firms that governs an exchange. Note that patrimonial contracts embrace the exchange of political support as well as economic resources, and patrimonial hierarchies convey economic surplus as well as reflect relationships of fealty.

[10] According to Ekelund and Tollison, the more unified the ruling group (at the limit in the person of a single monarch), the lower the bargaining costs for eager rent-seekers and the more hospitable the state to their activities (1981: chap. 3). See Coleman (1994: 169) for a rational-choice perspective on how one might gain utility by surrendering control.

litical contracts, organizational arrangements, and state-building. Take the work of Eleanor Searle on "predatory kinship" and Norman power. Searle claims that the Norse warleaders who founded the duchy of Normandy chose to recognize each other as kinsmen to unite for the purposes of individual protection and enrichment. They "had a rational assessment of their own interests as well as the capacity for violence that could translate that assessment into profitable feud" (1988: 9). To further this end, the group deployed marriage strategies, intermarrying, recruiting allies, and reallocating scarce resources (including elite women) by marriage. The quasicontractual establishment of a network of kin-allies "was the beginning of centralization and thus the beginning of an effective model of powerbuilding" (24). It was also, according to Searle, the basis of a solution to their particular social dilemma. Here we have a fascinating account of family heads hammering out contracts to advance predation, which in turn advanced state-formation.

Padgett and Ansell (1993) are skeptical about whether ruling patrimonial families really devised grand strategies, and in the context of a magisterial network analysis of the medieval Florentine elite, they contend that family heads engaged in the sorts of "contextual improvisation" favored by localized, heterogeneous, and ambiguous structural situations. Padgett and Ansell also suggest that individual actors calculate within shorter time horizons and coordinate collective action in more modest capacities than Searle claims. Nevertheless, their analysis is framed within the same utilitarian assumptions. One might say that the Florentine lords mastered tactics (defined by the *Oxford English Dictionary* as "handling forces in battle or in the immediate presence of the enemy") rather than strategy: "the art of projecting and directing the larger military movements and operations of a campaign." The bargains and tacit contracts that emerged underwrote political centralization.[11]

These narratives are full of nods to the role of family. What's missing is an explicit theoretical mention of the link between the principles demarcating more- from less-valued families and elite predation—the pursuit of resources and power. It is precisely when explanations are invoked as empirically central but are not registered in theory that the limits of a paradigm emerge. In utilitarian economics, for example, it is sometimes recognized that relations of trust and confidence may bind actors so strongly that they "will not cheat even though it may be 'rational economic behavior' to do so" (Arrow 1984: 104). Comments such as these surface periodically and are quickly sidelined.[12] If elite predation is em-

[11] Mark Granovetter takes much the same position in his influential criticism of economists for ignoring actors' network embeddedness and, more broadly, their rootedness in social structures. "What looks to the analyst like nonrational behavior may be quite sensible when situational constraints, especially those of embeddedness, are fully appreciated" (1985: 506).

[12] See also Stiglitz: ". . . some managers are endowed with a sense of corporate responsibility; they maximize the stock market value of the firm because they believe that this is what a good manager is supposed to do" (Stiglitz 1985: 135). Mark Gould pointed out this example to me in a personal communication.

pirically linked to the value that actors placed on family lineages, then the wealth (and even, if we stretch the point, power) maximizing (or satisficing) assumption of rational-choice theory is incomplete at best.

At minimum, relevant patrimonial resources must be seen as symbolic, involving what rational-choicers would characterize as "tastes" for patriarchal patrilineal honor that are endogenous to the system and that function in tandem with politicomilitary and economic resources. Yet this is still too limiting, for family honor and prestige were clearly more, or less, than what we are wont to think of as resources. For what kind of resource is it that can be gained or lost, but should never be pursued too obviously? "By giving it away, you show that you have it; by striving for it, you imply that you need it"—and therefore lack it (Pitt-Rivers 1968: 508). Stewart hits the nail on the head: "The more closely one looks at honor, the odder it seems" (1994: 145).[13] In fact, what mattered was not whether ruler and family actually were in any real sense honorable or prestigious, but whether they were perceived to be or have something that entitled them to being treated as such. Symbols of gender and generation from which such honor claims were fabricated were only loosely moored in "the biological" and resembled a language as much as a currency.[14] These symbols could be detached from their anchorage and discursively deployed, but their social effectiveness was limited by the normative boundaries imposed by available kin, the acquiescence of other elite families, and the value placed on an unbroken line of honorable, preferably patrilineal, descent. Establishing enduring claims to politicoeconomic privilege meant composing a successful social fiction, one that was based on and assumed a particular collective's evaluative orientation to social life.

Consider how this might have structured the conditions that underlaid individual rulers' political action (the supposed forte of rational-choice theory). Rulers were disposed to present themselves as members and representatives of enduring patriarchal patrilineages as part of the requirements and the very definition of governance in pre-modern Europe: they spoke and wrote from this subject position (Adams 1994). In the Netherlands, for example, the ruling regents kept generations-long family records enumerating the political privileges that were held by ancestors, by themselves, and those that would be held by descendants; these "office genealogies" were passed down from father to son. They commissioned public eulogies that marked a family member's accession to office or marriage into another family of privilege; they left long meditations on political principle meant for their children and children's children, especially the sons who would succeed them. Throughout Europe, office genealogies, as well as correspondence, other written records, and ritual practices evince rulers' self-

[13] In this sense, it partakes of the troubling duality of the larger concept of culture. "Culture is Janus-faced," writes David Laitin, "people are both guided by the symbols of their culture and instrumental in using culture to gain wealth and power" (1988: 589).

[14] One analogy might be to Bourdieu's notion of "cultural capital" (see Bourdieu, this volume). The concept remains a suggestive but anachronistic analogy in this historical context, however, because a rigorous notion of "capital" assumes a circulation of prestige signs that is relatively autonomous from rootedness in money and power—a condition that is not met in the era in question.

understandings as agents of long-dead ancestors and fantasized future descendants. Elite self-representations were bound up with the relatively long time horizons of genealogies of privilege that, though to a lesser degree than some enduring landed estates, became deeply identified with the character and continuity of the proprietor families.[15]

There was certainly variation in how actors mastered the performance of these tropes and how thoroughly they internalized them. Eldest sons could be expected to see things differently from their younger brothers, who were vested with the dual role of supporter and understudy. Women serving as guardians and political representatives of their small sons on behalf of royal lineages could be expected to feel differently about their position as principal, which was hedged with gendered restrictions, than would the prince on attaining his majority. But inasmuch as their lives revolved around the accumulation and inheritance of state office and privilege, all these actors oriented themselves more expansively than with respect to their own tenure in office and privilege. One upshot is that the "self-interest" assumption of rational-choice theory is much too narrow to encompass the actions of patrimonial rulers or to make sense of the views they expressed.

All other things being equal, a principal who sees himself as a bearer of others' interests or (to put it more precisely) as sharing others' discursively defined positions will be more likely to fall in line with the goals of those significant others, be they fellow principals, agents, or the ruled.[16] Thus, principals' actions may be disciplined not only by the three stock rational-choice constraints—competition from other principals, favorable discount rates, and the usual organizational agency problems—but also by mutually shared identifications. Shifting the conceptual lens opens up new ways of thinking about different types or levels of identification that inhere in the structure of patrimonial rule. If patrimonial rulers count themselves as principals because they see themselves as agents of a discursively bounded collective of ancestors and descendants, then "representative of elite lineage" is one crucial cultural ground on which rest assessments of the identity of fellow political principals as well as perceptions of political selfhood. How do the distinctions that principals draw within this category, and the different levels of identification with each subgroup, structure principals' political actions, solidarities, and antagonisms? Under what circumstances are these categories of identification enlarged to embrace something beyond the familial, such as a "nation"? Such crucial questions can be adapted to

---

[15] Regarding the blurred boundaries between elite families and landed estates in England, see, for example, Stone and Stone ([1984] 1986).

[16] Elite family heads who were also rulers might fail to adopt collectively approved positions, and face negative sanctions—from relatives or from other family heads in powerful political and legal capacities—but this does not mean that norms are analytically reducible to the threat of sanctions. What rational-choice models portray as manipulation of sanctions is often attempted manipulation of normative commitments and values that impel agents to take actions that are not in their self-interest (see Gould 1992). In multivocal patrimonial systems, values were also, and as a matter of course, family values, anchored in patriarchal patrilineal structures of rule.

the quirks of each historical case while remaining generally applicable in patrimonial contexts.

To understand early modern politics, we must grapple not only with these kinds of culturally specific cognitive expectations and cognitively informed practices, but also with actors' expressed feelings about ancestors and descendants, political privilege, and family line. This is a particularly troublesome area for rational-choicers. The issue of emotion/affect/feeling/passion/sentiment/cathexis (there are many names, hailing from many theoretical provenances) touches the heart of the theory because it threatens to undermine, or at least radically condition and complicate, the bedrock maxim of actors' "rationality"—the last of the three foundational assumptions left standing, now that I have, I hope, persuaded readers that the core utilitarian principles of wealth-maximization and self-interest do not generate a conceptual space in which we can comfortably account for the actions of patrimonial rulers.[17]

We know that emotions infuse the moments of extraordinary mass politics in which political institutions and cultural patterns are dramatically reformulated. William Sewell Jr. (1995, 1996) offers an excellent example from the early days of the French Revolution, when the representatives of the Third Estate recast themselves as the National Assembly in 1789. After a good deal of interpretive struggle, they approved the taking of the Bastille and went on to remake the fundamental laws and political arrangements of France. En route, they helped transform the meaning of revolution itself, by redefining the Parisian crowd's action as an instance of legitimate popular sovereignty. This process certainly incorporated elements of strategic action on the part of the Assembly and therefore invites examination by rational-choice theory, but a full explanation, Sewell notes, would also include an analysis of the link between discursive innovation and the rousing emotional response elicited by contact with a charismatic collective upsurge "that touched ultimate sources of order" (1995: 16). Certainly Sewell is right to underline the role of symbolically focused emotion in the revolutionary semiotic transformations that rang down the curtain on Old Regime France. I want to argue for its constitutive role in everyday life—in this case, the politico-familial lives of patrimonial rulers.

Family heads sacrificed *for* their children, actual and hoped-for, insofar as they represented the continuity of the patrilineage, which also—and this is a key point—organized the continuity of the pinnacle of the corporate state (Adams 1994). By the same token they also sacrificed them. As Giesey (1977) has shown for the early modern French elite, living family members were expected to advance the familial-political vision, and though the burden fell more heavily on some (such as women and younger sons) than on others, family heads and eldest sons generally sustained their part. One exemplary practice was office venality: buying state-sponsored privileges that would come to fruition for families, not

---

[17] Cognitive assessments are also conditioned by imperfections in reasoning, of course, including memory lapses, perceptual distortions, and other sources of miscalculation. See Kahneman and Tversky (1986) for a discussion of cognitive limits on individual rationality.

individuals, and even then only after several generations. Affectual attachment animated those actors' family strategies, and insofar as progeny composed part of a collectively held image of a glorious destiny for the family's name and descendants, adults' instrumental manipulation of children might be entirely compatible with warm feelings for them. This particular version of intergenerational emotional identification, both forged and invested in a patrimonial family form, should not be confused with present-day Euro-American understandings of either altruism or love.[18]

But surely families are always crucibles of emotion, strong negative as well as positive affect, and are generally ambivalent domains par excellence, in which the layered histories of childhood—of gender identifications, desire, refusals, and repressions—constitute sexed subjects (Butler 1995; Freud 1961 [1909]: 51). The definition of normative masculinity (with respect both to ideas of femininity and to alternative nonnormative masculinities); the instability and unease inherent in the dominant organization of masculine power; the ways that family figures serve as powerful fetish objects, as precipitates of contradictory expectations and desires: do not these processes potentially contribute to the cross-cultural formation of subjectivities activated in any and all macropolitics? True, but the specific historical connection of interest here, in the patrimonial systems of early modern Europe, is the path (or paths) by which forms of elite masculinity come to be linked to ideologies of rule through emotionally charged symbols of fatherhood.[19] This specific connection provides the missing theoretical link that rational-choice theorists need, whether they are attempting to invoke European elites' responses to their kings' family position as a factor in royal legitimacy (Root 1994: 217–18) or are fleshing out the "relative closeness" of ties between rulers and their heirs as a variable in rulers' capacity to make credible commitments (Kiser and Barzel 1991: 400).

It is interesting that rational-choicers themselves seem increasingly unwilling to consign all things apparently nonrational, including culture, emotion, and even habit, to a residuum, the category of exogenous input, background noise, or the "tosh" that Oliver Williamson decrees should "remain in its place" (1994: 98). Least successful so far are efforts to endogenize emotion. One increasingly common approach forswears sociological analysis altogether and asserts that emotion is a biologically wired reinforcer (see, for example, Frank 1988). Others have tried to redefine emotion as somehow "rational" and treat it accordingly.

---

[18] Given the stark empirical division that rational-choicers tend to draw between "family" and "world," and their tendency to assign emotions to the former and calculative orientations to the latter, my point is likely to prove a difficult historical dish for rational-choicers to digest. For a more sympathetic perspective than mine, see Green and Shapiro's (1994) summary of the literature on altruism and rational-choice theory.

[19] Feminist theorists have been helpful in this context. They have underlined the patriarchal nature of ideologies of early modern European monarchical power, mainly by means of rereading classical commentaries by theorists of state power and political authority, to draw out the limits of political discourse. See, among others, Landes on Rousseau (1988), Pateman on the English contract theorists and their opponents (1988), and Hunt (1992), who focuses on popular propaganda surrounding the French royal family.

This is a logical conceptual gambit, given the constraints of the paradigm, but it is doubly unsatisfactory. "By clothing the null hypothesis in the garb of selective incentives," as Green and Shapiro (1994: 87) point out, this analytical move erodes the very distinction that calls for explanation and integration.[20] Furthermore, the stark conceptual divide between reason and emotion is itself a cultural construction, with a historical lineage that is causally implicated in our object of analysis, European familial politics. The very idea of rational discourse emerged as a clarion call in the waning years of Europe's Old Regimes and became a weapon raised against the nepotistic closure of patrimonial power (see, for example, Maza 1993). "Instrumental rationality" then figured as a revolutionary maxim and prescribed rule of conduct for state agents, purged of their family entanglements, and, as Max Weber's ([1922] 1968) work shows, a discourse of legitimation and justification as well as a valued property of political organization after the great bourgeois revolutions. By the nineteenth century, European states were assumed to be the special province of reason, however much their rational-legal discourse was actually imbued with unacknowledged emotion. "The rational" led a triply complicated life in Old Regime Europe, as symbol, prescriptive institutional principle, and analytical tool, and I am not convinced that it was readily available as a ideal-typical template for rulers' agency at the historical juncture at which rational-choicers invoke it. The sociohistorical process by which "rational choice" emerged as a paradigm for political action needs more analysis, but that is another project.[21]

Rational-choice work on incorporating "cultural beliefs" into models of political institutional change has been more successful, but has not advanced very far. North's (1981) work on pre-modern Europe is a well-known example that raises hackles among more orthodox practitioners (see Nee and Ingram 1998). Avner Greif also argues that so-called cultural factors impelled feudal and early modern societies to develop along distinctive social trajectories (1994: 914). Greif defines cultural beliefs as "ideas and thoughts common to several individuals that govern interaction . . . and differ from knowledge in that they are not empirically discovered or analytically proved" (915). In particular, actors hold beliefs about the courses of action that other actors are likely to take when confronted with contingencies, and those beliefs influence ensuing social arrangements. North similarly suggests that rational-choicers need an approach "that

---

[20] The difficulty of making empirical distinctions between the rational and emotional is underlined by Lynn Smith-Lovin, who wonders: "Is a 'rational choice' made unconsciously on the basis of affective associations and available interaction partners still a calculated, self-interested endeavor?" (1993: 291). Nonetheless, I want to be able to capture the separate analytical dimensions, perhaps especially when they are empirically indistinguishable. See Smith-Lovin's contribution and other papers in the special issue of *Rationality and Society* (1993).

[21] An excellent starting point for those interested in this latter problem is Hirschman's (1977) analysis of the development of separate discourses designating passions and interests, and the assignment of the latter to matters economic. Steven Pincus's essay in this book includes a fascinating discussion of the emergence of the language of political interest from the "obsolete" (and, Pincus indicates, highly gendered) "language of confessional strife" in early modern England. For a contrasting argument emphasizing the affective character of colonial states, see Stoler (forthcoming).

explains how different perceptions of reality affect the reaction of individuals to the changing 'objective' situation" (1981: 7–8). In this view, culture is a bundle of cognitive expectations and cognitively ordered practices. Its contribution to the institutionalization of organizations, including states, is understood as "fundamentally a cognitive process" (Zucker 1983: 25).

To the extent that expectations and beliefs are seen as separate from "reality" (or as North puts it, the "objective situation"), they could be treated as relatively plastic and discursively manipulable, in which case the theory would take on a pronounced culturalist tinge. This has been a direction that most rational-choicers have been loath to take, since it threatens to give meaning an analytically constitutive role in social action and social structure. Most prefer to argue that culture is active in situations of objective indeterminacy, that is, in interactions off the equilibrium path, so to speak. Thus, Greif (1994) tries to show that divergent cultural beliefs crystallized with special force in overseas ventures, which posed inherent principal/agent problems in the feudal and early modern eras, heightening the uncertainty that always attends exploratory transactions. When uncertainty is high, it is argued, culture has special causal power. This is still a minimalist's notion of culture and of the explanatory work that culture might do.

A more expansive reevaluation of beliefs qua values can be found in the work of some theorists—whether, like North, they say that shared ideologies and moral codes constitute the real cement of society (1981: chap. 5) or, like Jon Elster, insist that "The chain of norms must have an unmoved mover, to which the rationalist reduction does not apply" (1990: 47). These views, as yet tentatively expressed, jar with a "thin" theory of rational choice unless it is assumed, following Hechter, that whereas actors may be motivated by immanent and not merely instrumental values, the distribution of those values across the population remains random (1994: 320, 323). Whatever its validity with respect to the actions of capitalist employers or managers, however, this assumption would not hold up for patrimonial principals.

(Discursive) Formation of Familial States

If I am correct about the structuring effect of ideologies of paternal power and family identity on actors, and more generally emotionally charged meanings in patrimonial politics, then we may expect both the severity of social dilemmas and the motivation for solutions to be heightened. For if it were deemed essential to their families, one would expect rulers and aspiring rulers to try that much harder to grab a piece of state power, and to struggle to squeeze sons and other relatives into office, at the risk of depriving similarly situated patriarchs of perquisites. Family cliques did at times manage to monopolize local state apparatuses and corporate bodies at the expense of rival groupings, as we saw earlier. They were vulnerable to being toppled by competing factions, who were then toppled in their turn, and so forth. But by the same token, the impetus toward and effectiveness of solutions, whether propelled by covenants or swords, would increase commensurately. When family heads are committed to preserving family position in and through a patrimonial state, they are wedded to maintaining the organization as an elite commons of patriarchal patrimonial privilege. Not only would any single elite patriarch be unlikely to act in ways that would obviously dilute or sacrifice his or his children's (particularly his sons') position, but when the resources and prestige that it offered were accessible only by entering into a group accord, each family head's motivation to do so would increase. Once party to such a collective corporate pact, each participant would try to hold others to their end of the bargain. The exit of any participant threatened the position of all others, and rulers could be expected to negatively sanction those that tried to secede. By the same token, however, the collective deals would have made exit less likely. They created a basis for socioemotional bonds among rulers, the male family heads encamped inside the centralizing state apparatus. The autocratic solution would also become more compelling. Influential ideologists of absolutism argued that a *pater patriae* representing, or rather incarnating, a single royal or crypto-royal lineage could provide a key symbolic focus and first among equals to whom warring elite family interests would, and should, subject themselves.[22] The twin solutions of covenant and sword were not mutually exclusive, a fact that the defamilized language of rational choice conceals: they were ideologically and organizationally interdependent.

As distributional coalitions, groups of patrimonial families differed from Bowman's capitalist cartels or Olson's nation-states. A cartel constituted by families-in-relationship can draw on deeper reservoirs of loyalty and trust than other, more elective and less affective groupings. These "family regimes" (as the Dutch called them) could be a force for elite political cohesion and stability. In the Netherlands, for example, they reinforced and elaborated the localism of patrician authority. In France, this arrangement strengthened the fiscal and political interdependence of crown and elite. By dangling the prospect of intergenerational family privileges in front of potential investors, the crown lured them into putting resources into areas that would supply funds (corporate monopolies) and committing political support to an absolutist organization of which they were increasingly a corporate component. In both these and other cases, family regimes ratified the shift in class character from merchant capitalists into state *rentiers*. Elite family bases of organization and identity were not automatically superseded in modernization projects, but incorporated into the constitutive foundations of each patrimonial state.

Precisely when—that is, at what historical conjuncture—elites implanted their families in the state was also potentially important for political development. Krasner's (1984) model of "punctuated equilibrium" in politics, derived from the work of Stephen Jay Gould and Niles Eldredge, holds that the stable social

---

[22] See, among others, Jean Bodin (1992) and Sir Robert Filmer (1991), early modern political theorists of French and English politics, respectively. Pateman's (1988: 77–115) discussion of Filmer is of particular interest in this context.

arrangements that structure politics-as-usual are periodically disrupted by crises that undermine these arrangements, opening up the possibility of abrupt institutional transformation and thus for heated conflicts over the shape of change. In patrimonial contexts, the family coalitions that control the state during these periods of institutional fluidity have a decisive say over future institutional arrangements and policy. They can be expected to forward the discursively defined goals of particular lineages and kin groups, as well as to stake claims to the state on behalf of family members and clients. If patrimonial state-formation can be seen as a process of tying together nodes in a single cartel or network, in mutable arrangements that are variably centralized and contingently and culturally integrated, then elite family settlements in moments of political crisis are likely to freeze those arrangements in place.[23]

This is not to say that political conflict was absent in patrimonial states. Far from it. Medieval and early modern political history is rife with epochal dynastic struggles. But at certain key junctures, interfamily alliances stabilized distributional coalitions that closed ranks against newcomers, forming the basis for a more thoroughgoing equilibrium by organizing against changes in political procedures and fixing "traditional" mechanisms of governance in place. Like the Dutch regents' Contracts of Correspondence, and the deals among French *officiers*, these sorts of compacts envisioned family, gender relations, and the regulation of sexuality in a way that supplied a long-run dynastic basis embedding fractious elite factions into a single stable body. I refer to these organizations as "familial states" to convey that we are dealing with not just another variable, but patterned properties and forms of organization pervaded by gendered family ideologies and relationships. Patriarchal family ties directly constitute relations of corporate rule, recruitment to top political offices is restricted to certain men on the basis of their family ties and position, and claims to political authority are made on the basis of gender-specific familial criteria, with aspirants asserting their claims to rule on the basis of patriarchal power and hereditary qualification, or "blood," rather than on, say, competence. In early modern European patrimonial polities—republican/estatist as well as monarchical/absolutist—discourses of dynasty and paternity were necessarily foregrounded because heritable offices and privileges descended through the male line, and developing state institutions were mobilized around the political symbolism of ruling fatherhood.

It may seem that by bypassing rational-choice theory to explore the institutionalization of ideologies of paternal power and family identity, and more generally emotionally charged meanings in patrimonial politics, we may find ourselves trading parsimony for texture, universality for historical variability. But why, after all, as Margaret Somers (1998) asks, should we prefer one set of qualities over another? The only convincing reason, she adds, would be if we believed

---

[23] The literature on early modern European "elite settlements" (for example, Lachmann 1989; Higley and Burton 1989) lacks a systematically theorized familial dimension, but it captures and elaborates important aspects of the mechanism of competitive monopoly.

that these qualities actually captured the reality of the world being theorized—if, "that is, the world really *is* 'parsimonious' and 'invariant.'" Somers takes issue with this picture of the social world on a number of grounds, including the general objection that it is implausibly "comprised of agents with essential and unchanging properties that operate independently of the very relationships by which they are constituted." In these terms, my argument diverges from that of rational-choice theorists, for although it doesn't stand or fall on embracing any particular twentieth-century conception of subjectivity, it insists on the socially malleable boundaries of self, originally formed in the family, the cultural component of identity, and the historically specific role of affect for early modern elite political actors.[24] That it is also able to generate a more complete understanding of the repertoire of social dilemmas and solutions is a strength of my approach, which stresses the conditions and limits of strategic action rather than denying its existence.

There are also major points at which my more culturalist model generates an account of political development and transformation that departs from the rational-choice story of state-building. Familial states were inserted in an evolving global structure that they were simultaneously creating. Maintaining a hegemonic or even workable position as a corporate actor, including as a mercantilist "going concern" operating in the chaotic early modern world, was a continuing achievement, as Arthur Stinchcombe points out in his work on monopolistic competition as a general social mechanism. Desirable structural sites or opportunities were vulnerable to the particular advantages of certain corporate groups, competing with one another to exploit those network niches from which flowed the possibility of continuing advantage (1998). In the early modern world, as we have seen, these corporate actors were a motley assemblage, including sovereign states, urban leagues, chartered companies, pirates, mercenary organizations, and empires, and the fact that their shifting relationships were not organized along territorially exclusive lines created distinctive political pressures for individual units in an increasingly economically competitive and militarized interstate system (see Spruyt 1994; Thomson 1994).

In this unstable situation, the same family and lineage privilege that promoted creative elite relationships to the state and its fruits also made it less likely that a shift in incentives, information, or resources would spur changes in individual or corporate behavior. Affective bonds that motivate special effort on behalf of the group impose commensurate limits on organizational flexibility and responsiveness, even when the existing political structure serves rulers inefficiently and when they have the resources and capacity to dismantle it. In these institutional conditions, under which, in North's (1981) utilitarian nightmare, "maximizing behavior" by actors fails to produce increased output, rational-choice theorists

---

[24] Many readers will be wary of more sustained exploration of what seems like psychoanalytical territory, even when nuanced with fillips of historical cultural studies. This rich psychosexual vein has yet to be much worked with sociohistorical tools, and here I merely point to it, rather than excavate it deeply. For two intriguing efforts to integrate psychodynamics with studies of aspects of the political and social landscapes of early modern Europe, see Marvick (1986) and Roper (1994).

expect actors to attempt to modify their behavior accordingly. And they may, under certain historical circumstances, but probably not in patrimonial politics. Precisely at this point, my expectations diverge most sharply from those of the rational-choice model, for I expect patrimonial elites to struggle to maintain family footholds, even if alternative, more resource-rich opportunities presented themselves.

An unlikely path of structural change for patrimonial states, therefore, would be a top-down revolution that involved calculated elite participation in over-throwing the familial state. Along with the special form of their privileges, patrimonial elites would have to surrender the keystone of their and their families' identities. We should expect to find extraordinary conditions before the bulk of elite political actors in any particular political field could make such a radical break.[25] It is more probable that quotidian pressures for change would come either from "below" or from "way above," and based on what we know of patrimonial politics, we can say something of the retrospective form those pressures might have assumed. First, the features of rule that evoke elite and popular allegiance also channel hostility upward toward rulers in their guise as family authority figures. During the French Revolution, for example, the popular imagination was fired by rage at a weak father-king allegedly under the sway of a hypersexual, unmotherly queen (Hunt 1992; Maza 1993). These tropes were applied to elites as well as royalty in the lead-up to early modern political upheavals, and they were not confined to French politics. Their effectiveness in mobilizing opposition rested on subterranean relationships between perceptions of the ruler as incapable of governing his family and therefore, symbolically, his kingdom. Thus, perceptions of normative political authority in patrimonialism also described the gendered familial lines on which that authority would be challenged (Adams 1994). A ruler's cultural charisma, as well as bargaining capacity, was not simply secured, but also sharply limited by the symbolic and institutional logic of family politics.

Another potential source of pressure lay in the emerging suprastate system. It is not simply that we should include the "international strategic factor as an explanatory variable," as Aristide Zolberg (1980) has emphasized, although that task is still important. We also need to recognize that suprastate niches were actually restructured as functional alternatives to aristocratic dynastic ideologies and connections reorganized the drift of interstate relations, transforming the character of culturally appropriate claims to sovereignty. This shift might take as subtle a discursive form as it did during the repeated wars of Louis XIV's reign, when his opponents' propaganda began to condemn the principle that the state was in any way "possessed" by the ruler "who could dispose of it according to his whim," as Carlos II of Spain was to do in 1700: "Everyone knows," proclaimed one of the Allies' most prominent pamphlets, "that kingship is an office, an ad-

[25] Sewell's (1995, 1996) account of the reaction to the taking of the Bastille at the outset of the French Revolution captures just such a rare and transformative political moment, experienced by the representatives of the Third Estate as they became the National Assembly. For the range of radical elite as well as popular demands addressed to France's Old Regime rulers, see Weitman (1968).

ministration, giving kings no proprietary possession" (Rowen, quoted in Bonney 1991: 530). That familial states had begun to be portrayed as internationally outdated and outdistanced is part of the story of their increasing ineffectiveness in the international strategic arena, as they gave way to, or were abolished in favor of, nimbler forms of doing politics.

Putting Rational Choice in its Place

I have shown that the basic assumptions of rational-choice theory do not credibly model the principles of action that animated feudal and early modern European rulers. How, then, has rational-choice theory generated reasonable expositions of certain political equilibria, or relatively stable collective outcomes of collective strategies? In particular, rational-choicers have helped us understand how elites in a variety of patrimonial political settings forged contracts that enabled them to overcome social dilemmas and claim the state as the fount of benefits for their distributional coalitions. In some cases, these contracts gave rise to conditions for political centralization and other ruling-group modernization projects. The puzzle is: how do flawed assumptions about key causal attributes produce, or seem to produce, even partially adequate accounts? [26]

The answer in this case is, I think, twofold. First, rational choice contains the seeds of its own transcendence, in the latent, historically and systemically specific meanings smuggled into key concepts like "predation" and "rulers' goals." I have shown that these concepts are doing unacknowledged cultural work in rational-choice narratives. The "personal objectives" that Levi sees predatory rulers as maximizing (1988: 10); the "credibility" of the intergenerational commitments that Kiser and Barzel's rulers make (1991: 400)—once these and the other conceptual repressions discussed earlier have been raised to consciousness, historians and social scientists can do a better job of sorting out the dimensions of culture—including its neglected affective elements—and using them in theory and explanation. Conversely, as we recast basic utilitarian assumptions and survey the wider analytical landscape that is revealed, we can see that it will be a challenge for culturalists to hang onto the advances that have taken place within rational-choice research and to incorporate the "culture concept" in the context of historically grounded generalizations about patrimonial politics and familial state-formation, dissolution, and revolution. [27] It should already be clear, however, that in addressing the big (intractable yet inevitable) questions surround-

[26] There are, of course, a number of reasons why this might be so (see King, Keohane, and Verba 1994: chap. 3). I argue that the theoretical leverage that rational choice has over core historical problems is less than its practitioners have imagined.

[27] Tacit rational-strategic tropes can be found in avowedly culturalist narratives of macropolitical change. In Landes's tale of the French Revolution, for example, Jacobin authorities bent on doing away with the Society of Revolutionary Republican Women and reestablishing male dominance succeed partly by appealing to less-privileged men and women for support (1988: 142–46). They appear to have authored a political pact or bargain that crossed class and gender lines in service of joint interests in repression; all the more reason, therefore, for culturalists and rational-choicers working on overlapping empirical problems to confront one another's work.

ing the rise and decline, stability and instability of states, cultural meaning is a basic analytical starting point on a par with information and resources.

The second point revolves around the role of mid-range mechanisms in feudal and early modern European politics. By describing elements of these mechanisms, rational-choicers have improved on standard sociological tales of state-formation that invoke couplets such as centralization/decentralization, differentiation/dedifferentiation, or development/decline as if they were un-problematic structural features or processes. Still, meso-level mechanisms do not a grand theory make. Competitive struggles among elite families in early modern Europe effectively mimic, and may even adumbrate, broader social mechanisms of monopoly competition, but only at certain historical junctures, when the parameters of patrimonialism are fixed and the familial and symboli-cally invested character of paternal power is basically a social given. The differ-ences between my arguments and the utilitarians' highlight the crucial impor-tance of spelling out the systemic scope conditions of theoretical and empirical generalization.

Neil Smelser (1992: 404) calls on us to treat an actor's disposition to act ra-tionally as a variable rather than a postulate and to organize our research around "the question of the contextual conditions—motivational, informational, and institutional—under which maximization and rational calculation manifest themselves in 'pure' form, under which they assume different forms, and under which they break down." One possible response stresses the cultural, histori-cal, or institutional specificity of notions of rationality (Wacquant and Calhoun 1989); another, the variability of rationality itself (Stinchcombe 1986); other im-pulses, deriving from feminist theory, portray the contextual conditions favoring calculative outlooks as rooted in socially masculinist institutional environments (McCloskey 1993) or advance the position that modern European concepts of rationality have been developed in inherently androcentric ways (Bordo 1986).

These are intriguing paths to explore, but I have tried to answer Smelser's call and the Weberian intellectual legacy that it evokes somewhat differently, retain-ing some of the insights generated from within the rational-choice perspective while contesting its basic theoretical underpinnings and beginning to embed it in a higher-order explanation of historical persistence and change. Specifically, this essay identifies the points at which a sociocultural story undercuts, or alter-natively enfolds and enriches, the utilitarian portrait of the mechanisms under-lying patrimonial political equilibria. For example, I have argued that political elites, who as male family heads became lineally identified with intergenerational privilege, invested those sentiments in particular political arrangements. On that basis, patrimonial political principals organized or undermined collective politi-cal deals among early modern male elites. Thus, peculiarly familial concerns and discourses structured those negotiations and struggles.[28] My argument further diverges from rational-choice theory when patrimonial elites face a choice be-

---

[28] The ideologies centered around the shah in early twentieth-century Iran, analyzed in Nader Sohrabi's paper in this book, also had familial dimensions and can be read as presenting some fasci-nating parallels with early modern Europe.

tween family state privilege and other means of acquiring politicoeconomic resources. I expect their identities, buttressed by their emotional attachments, to
be resistant to change, even apparently advantageous change.

This new optic enables us to raise further productive questions about state
formation and collapse. I am particularly interested in how and why dynastic
attachments were supplanted by identification with generalized notions of fellow ruling principals, state agents, and of course the ruled. To approach such
questions, which are essentially about an argument's scope conditions and which
are central to understanding changing forms of sovereignty and legitimation, we
need to integrate theories of historical cultural meaning into our arguments
about economic and political advantage. Along the way, it is important to heed
Olson's methodological dictum, even as we are refusing his rational-choice perspective. "What we should demand of a theory or a hypothesis," he cautions, "is
that it be clear about what observations would increase the probability that it
was false and what observations would tend to increase the probability that there
was some truth in it" (1982: 15).

So one general sociological problem to be addressed concerns the place of
emotionally charged symbols—including, ironically, "rationality" itself—in
various political formations and in the relationships among states. This is obviously an enormous issue, of which this essay has examined only one part. Nevertheless I hope we have made a start.

References

Adams, Julia. 1994. "The Familial State: Elite Family Practices and State-making
in the Early Modern Netherlands." *Theory and Society* 23: 505–39.
———. 1996. "Principals and Agents, Colonialists and Company Men: The Decay
of Colonial Control in the Dutch East Indies." *American Sociological Review*
61, no. 1: 12–28.
Arrow, Kenneth J. 1984. *Collected Papers of Kenneth J. Arrow: vol. 4: The Eco-
nomics of Information*. Cambridge: Harvard University Press.
Auster, Richard, and Morris Silver. 1979. *The State as a Firm: Economic Forces in
Political Development*. Boston: Martinus Nijhoff.
Axelrod, Robert. 1981. "The Emergence of Cooperation among Egoists."
American Political Science Review (June): 306–18.
Bodin, Jean. 1992. *On Sovereignty*. New York: Cambridge University Press.
Bonney, Richard. 1991. *The European Dynastic States, 1494–1660*. New York: Ox-
ford University Press.
Bordo, Susan. 1986. "The Cartesian Masculinization of Thought." *Signs* 11:
439–56.
Bowman, John R. 1989. *Capitalist Collective Action*. New York: Cambridge Uni-
versity Press.
Buchanan, James M. 1980. "Rent Seeking and Profit Seeking." In *Toward a The-
ory of the Rent-Seeking Society*, edited by J. M. Buchanan, R. D. Tollison, and
G. Tullock. College Station: Texas A & M University Press.

Buchanan, James M., Robert D. Tollison, and Gordon Tullock, eds. 1980. *Toward a Theory of the Rent-Seeking Society*. College Station: Texas A & M University Press.

Butler, Judith. 1995. "Melancholy Gender/Refused Identification." In *Constructing Masculinity*, edited by M. Berger, B. Wallis, and S. Watson. New York: Routledge.

Cohen, Joshua, and Joel Rogers. 1983. *On Democracy: Toward a Transformation of American Society*. New York: Penguin.

Coleman, James. 1964. *Introduction to Mathematical Sociology*. New York: Free Press.

———. 1990. *Foundations of Social Theory*. Boston: Harvard University Press.

———. 1994. "A Rational Choice Perspective on Economic Sociology." In *The Handbook of Economic Sociology*, edited by Neil J. Smelser and Richard Swedberg, 166–80. New York: Russell Sage.

Dawes, Robyn M. 1991. "Social Dilemmas, Economic Self-Interest and Evolutionary Theory." In *Frontiers of Mathematical Psychology: Essays in Honor of Clyde Coombs*, edited D. R. Brown and J. E. Keith Smith. New York: Springer–Verlag.

Ekelund, Robert B., and Robert D. Tollison. 1981. *Mercantilism as a Rent-Seeking Society: Economic Regulation in Historical Perspective*. College Station: Texas A & M University Press.

Elster, Jon. 1990. "When Rationality Fails." In *The Limits of Rationality*, edited by K. S. Cook and M. Levi, 19–50. Chicago: University of Chicago Press.

Evans, Peter. 1992. "The State as Problem and Solution: Predation, Embedded Autonomy, and Structural Change." In *The Politics of Economic Adjustment*, edited by S. Haggard and R. Kaufman, 139–81. Princeton: Princeton University Press.

Filmer, Sir Robert. 1991. *Patriarcha and Other Writings*. New York: Cambridge University Press.

Frank, Robert H. 1988. *Passions within Reason: The Strategic Role of the Emotions*. New York: Norton.

Freud, Sigmund. 1961 [1909]. *Five Lectures on Psycho-Analysis*, translated and edited by James Strachey. New York: W. W. Norton.

Giesey, Ralph E. 1977. "Rules of Inheritance and Strategies of Mobility in Pre-revolutionary France." *American Historical Review* 82 (April): 271–89.

Gorski, Philip. 1995. "The Protestant Ethic and the Spirit of Bureaucracy." *American Sociological Review* 60, no. 5: 783–86.

Gould, Mark. 1992. "Law and Sociology: Some Consequences for the Law of Employment Discrimination Deriving from the Sociological Reconstruction of Economic Theory." *Cardozo Law Review* 13: 1517–78.

Granovetter, Mark. 1985. "Economic Action and Social Structure: The Problem of Embeddedness." *American Journal of Sociology* 91, no. 3 (November): 481–510.

Green, Donald P., and Ian Shapiro. 1994. *Pathologies of Rational Choice Theory: A Critique of Applications in Political Science*. New Haven: Yale University Press.

Greif, Avner. 1994. "Cultural Beliefs and the Organization of Society: A Historical and Theoretical Reflection on Collectivist and Individualist Societies."
Journal of Political Economy 102, no. 5: 912–50.

Hardin, Garrett, and John Baden. 1977. *Managing the Commons*. San Francisco:
W. H. Freeman.

Hardin, Russell. 1990. "The Social Evolution of Cooperation." In *The Limits of
Rationality*, edited by K. S. Cook and M. Levi, 358–78. Chicago: University
of Chicago Press.

Hechter, Michael. 1994. "The Role of Values in Rational Choice Theory." *Rationality and Society* 6 (July): 318–33.

Heimer, Carol. 1990. "Comment: On Russell Hardin's 'The Social Evolution
of Cooperation.'" In *The Limits of Rationality*, edited by K. S. Cook and
M. Levi, 378–82. Chicago: University of Chicago Press.

Higley, John, and Michael G. Burton. 1989. "The Elite Variable in Democratic
Transitions and Breakdowns." *American Sociological Review* 54 (February):
17–32.

Hirschman, Albert O. 1977. *The Passions and the Interests*. Princeton: Princeton
University Press.

Hobbes, Thomas. [1651] 1962. *Leviathan*. New York: Macmillan.

Hunt, Lynn. 1992. *The Family Romance of the French Revolution*. Berkeley: University of California Press.

Kahneman, Daniel, and Amos Tversky. 1986. "Rational Choice and the Framing
of Decisions." *Journal of Business* 59: S251–78.

Khaldun, Ibn. 1969. *The Muqaddimah: An Introduction to History*, translated by
Frank Rosenthal. Princeton: Princeton University Press.

King, Gary, Robert O. Keohane, and Sidney Verba. 1994. *Designing Social Inquiry: Scientific Inference in Qualitative Research*. Princeton: Princeton University Press.

Kiser, Edgar. 1994. "Markets and Hierarchies in Early Modern Tax Systems: A
Principal Agent Analysis." *Politics and Society* 22: 284–315.

Kiser, Edgar, and Yoram Barzel. 1991. "The Origins of Democracy in England."
Rationality and Society 3, no. 4 (October): 396–422.

Kiser, Edgar, and Joachim Schneider. 1994. "Bureaucracy and Efficiency: An
Analysis of Taxation in Early Modern Prussia." *American Sociological Review*
59: 187–204.

Krasner, Steven D. 1984. "Approaches to the State: Alternative Conceptions and
Historical Dynamics." *Comparative Politics* 16, no. 2: 223–46.

Lachmann, Richard. 1989. "Elite Conflict and State Formation in 16th- and
17th-Century England and France." *American Sociological Review* 54 (April):
141–62.

Laitin, David. 1988. "Political Culture and Political Preferences." *American Political Science Review* 82, no. 2: 589–93.

Landes, Joan B. 1988. *Women and the Public Sphere in the Age of the French Revolution*. Ithaca: Cornell University Press.

Lane, Frederic. 1979. *Profits from Power: Readings in Protection Rent and
Violence-Controlling Enterprises*. Albany: SUNY Press.

Levi, Margaret. 1988. *Of Rule and Revenue*. Berkeley: University of California Press.

Marvick, Elizabeth Wirth. 1986. *Louis XIII and the Making of a King*. New Haven: Yale University Press.

Maza, Sarah C. 1993. *Private Lives and Public Affairs: The Causes Célèbres of Prerevolutionary France*. Berkeley: University of California Press.

McCloskey, Donald N. 1993. "Some Consequences of a Conjective Economics." In *Beyond Economic Man: Feminist Theory and Economics*, edited by Marianne A. Ferber and Julie A. Nelson, 69–93. Chicago: University of Chicago Press.

Nee, Victor, and Paul Ingram. 1998. "Embeddedness and Beyond: Institutions, Exchange, and Social Structure." In *The New Institutionalism in Sociology*, edited by M. C. Brinton and V. Nee. New York: Russell Sage.

North, Douglass. 1981. *Structure and Change in Economic History*. New York: Norton.

Olson, Mancur. 1982. *The Rise and Decline of Nations*. New Haven: Yale University Press.

Ostrom, Elinor, James Walker, and Roy Gardner. 1992. "Covenants with and without a Sword: Self-Governance is Possible." *American Political Science Review* 86: 404–17.

Padgett, John F., and Christopher K. Ansell. 1993. "Robust Action and the Rise of the Medici, 1400–1434." *American Journal of Sociology* 98: 1259–1319.

Pateman, Carole. 1988. *The Sexual Contract*. Stanford: Stanford University Press.

Pitt-Rivers, Julian. 1968. "Honor." In *International Encyclopedia of the Social Sciences*, vol. 6, edited by D. Sills, 503–11. New York: Macmillan.

Rationality and Society. 1993. 5, no. 2 (April) (Special Issue on emotions and rational choice).

Root, Hilton. 1994. *The Fountain of Privilege: Political Foundations of Markets in Old Regime France and England*. Berkeley: University of California Press.

Roper, Lyndal. 1994. *Oedipus and the Devil: Witchcraft, Sexuality, and Religion in Early Modern Europe*. New York: Routledge.

Searle, Eleanor. 1988. *Predatory Kinship and the Creation of Norman Power, 840–1066*. Berkeley: University of California Press.

Sewell, William H. Jr. 1995. "Calculation, Culture, and Revolution" (unpublished manuscript).

———. 1996. "Historical Events as Transformations of Structures: Inventing Revolution after the Bastille." *Theory and Society* 25: 841–81.

Smelser, Neil J. 1992. "The Rational Choice Perspective." *Rationality and Society* 4 (October): 381–410.

Smith-Lovin, Lynn. 1993. "Can Emotionality and Rationality Be Reconciled? A Comment on Collins, Frank, Hirshleifer, and Jasso." *Rationality and Society* 5, no. 2 (April): 283–93.

Somers, Margaret. 1998. "'We're No Angels': Realism, Rational Choice, and Relationality in Social Science." *American Journal of Sociology*, 104, no. 3: 722–84.

Spruyt, Hendrik. 1994. *The Sovereign State and its Competitors*. Princeton: Princeton University Press.

Stewart, Frank Henderson. 1994. *Honor*. Chicago: University of Chicago Press.

Stiglitz, Joseph. 1985. "Credit Markets and the Control of Capital." *Journal of Money, Credit, and Banking* 17: 133–52.

Stinchcombe, Arthur. 1986. "Rationality and Social Structure: An Introduction." In *Stratification and Organization: Selected Papers*, 1–29. New York: Cambridge University Press.

———. 1991. "The Conditions of Fruitfulness of Theorizing about Mechanisms in Social Science." *Philosophy of the Social Sciences* 21, no. 3 (September): 367–87.

———. 1998. "Monopolistic Competition as a Mechanism: Corporations, Universities, and Nation States in Competitive Fields." In *Social Mechanisms: An Analytical Approach to Social Theory*, edited by Peter Hedström and Richard Swedberg, 265–305. Cambridge: Cambridge University Press.

Stoler, Ann Laura. Forthcoming. "Affective States." In *Culture Work in the Colonial Archives*. Princeton: Princeton University Press.

Stone, Lawrence, and Jeanne C. Fawtier Stone. 1986 [1984]. *An Open Elite? England 1540–1880*. New York: Oxford University Press.

Taylor, Michael. 1987. *The Possibility of Cooperation*. New York: Cambridge University Press.

———. 1990. "Cooperation and Rationality: Notes on the Collective Action Problem and Its Solutions." In *The Limits of Rationality*, edited by K. S. Cook and M. Levi, 222–40. Chicago: University of Chicago Press.

Thomson, Janice E. 1994. *Mercenaries, Pirates, and Sovereigns*. Princeton: Princeton University Press.

Tilly, Charles. 1985. "Warmaking and State Making as Organized Crime." In *Bringing the State Back In*, edited by P. Evans, D. Rueschemeyer, and T. Skocpol, 169–91. New York: Cambridge University Press.

Wacquant, Loïc J. D., and Craig Jackson Calhoun. 1989. "Intérêt, rationalité et culture dans la sociologie américaine: A propos d'un récent débat sur la 'théorie de l'action.'" *Actes de la Recherche en Sciences Sociales* 78: 41–60.

Weber, Max. 1968 [1922]. *Economy and Society*, 2 vols. Berkeley: University of California Press.

Weitman, Sasha Reinhard. 1968. "Bureaucracy, Democracy, and the French Revolution," 2 vols. Ph.D. diss. Washington University.

Williamson, Oliver E. 1994. "Transaction Cost Economics and Organization Theory." In *The Handbook of Economic Sociology*, edited by N. J. Smelser and R. Swedberg, 77–107. New York: Russell Sage.

Zolberg, Aristide R. 1980. "Strategic Interactions and the Formation of Modern States." *International Social Science Journal* 32, no. 4: 687–716.

Zucker, Lynne. 1983. "Organizations as Institutions." In *Research in the Sociology of Organizations*, edited by S. Bachrach. Greenwich: JAI Press.

4

The Changing Cultural Content
of the Nation-State:
A World Society Perspective

John W. Meyer

In reaction to lines of thought analyzing the nation-state on its own terms as a bounded actor, institutional conceptions are now becoming more prominent. In these views, the nation-state is seen as highly embedded in wider or prior structures of power and meaning. In this essay, I pursue lines of argument following from one particular institutionalist conception: the idea that the nation-state, as an "actor," is embedded in and constructed by an exogenous, and more or less worldwide, rationalistic culture. Culture in this sense is less a set of values and norms, and more a set of cognitive models defining the nature, purpose, resources, technologies, controls, and sovereignty of the proper nation-state. In contemporary, rather stateless, world society, exogenous controls of this cultural kind are highly expanded and play important roles in constituting nation-states and their activities. The nation-state is prominently an imagined community (Anderson 1991; see also Adams, this volume, on the cultural base of the identity of state actors), and the cultural imagination involved is substantially constructed in the wider world environment. Arguments of the sort put forward here can help explain a number of features of contemporary nation-states: the rather standardized character of these entities around the world; the tendencies to isomorphic change in their constitutive and organizational structures, and in the activities they pursue; the decoupled character of the links between

Lines of argument here derive from Thomas, Meyer, Ramirez, and Boli (1987), Jepperson and Meyer (1991), Meyer (1994), Meyer, Boli, Thomas, and Ramirez (1997), and current collaborative projects with colleagues and students (as noted below). I emphasize these linkages, rather than review the literature in general, in the references. Useful specific suggestions came from written comments by George Steinmetz, Deborah Barrett, John Boli, and Francisco Ramirez and from extended comments and discussions by Stanford's Comparative Workshop and by the Workshop in Comparative Politics and Historical Sociology at the University of Chicago.

structure and policy, on the one hand, and practical activity and reality on the other—especially notable, perhaps, in the peripheries of world society; and the very rapid expansion over time of nation-state structures and policy domains, even in these peripheries. I discuss general theoretical issues, features of modern world society that make up a world institutional system, and empirical studies and research designs on the impact of world institutional arrangements on the nation-state.

Theoretical Background

Modern culture emphasizes a social world made up of bounded, purposive, and rational actors and gives preference to entities conceived and constructed in this way—particularly individuals, nation-states, and formal organizations. This deemphasizes other sorts of social units (tribes, clans, families, ethnic groups, communities, and the like). Many useful social scientific theories take this cultural world at face value (Bourdieu, this volume) and produce analyses of social activity as the product of such actors and their interaction. One line of reductionist criticism, especially in analyzing organizations and nation-states, sees actorhood as a kind of fiction masking the power of real subgroup actors (for example, resource dependency models). But many other lines of criticism see actors as deeply embedded in, and constructed and controlled by, wider forces—institutions, conceptualized in widely varying ways.

The term *institution*, in this very broad sense, has little meaning: anything exogenous to a putative actor can be seen as an institution (Jepperson 1991). From the point of view of an organized work group, the personality quirks of the boss, the habits of other members, or the general cultural rules of interaction or worker-safety laws can be seen as an institution. The idea simply designates embeddedness: conceptions of some sort of environmental patterning arise as critical social scientific notions wherever culture and analysis postulates actors. Distinct ideas about environmental institutions do not much arise in analyses of families and tribes and communities, where almost all lines of culture and analysis emphasize embeddedness (and are thus more casually institutionalist). Environmental (or in the broadest sense, institutionalist) models fall into three classes. Some retain the realism of actor-centered models, but see actors as embedded in larger structures, often themselves seen as actors or as regimes constructed by actors (Krasner 1983). Others emphasize the level of analysis of the actor, but see this actor as phenomenologically embedded in its own history, culture, and interpretive system. Still others—those addressed in this essay—incorporate both lines of thought simultaneously, becoming more phenomenological and also more macrosociological. We briefly review the other forms first: these different versions are captured well in the various papers in this book (see also the introduction by Steinmetz in this volume).

Realist macroinstitutionalism: Useful lines of thought see the nation-state as highly embedded in and constrained and constructed by larger interests, operating as actors. Wallerstein (1974) sees them as constructions of world economic forces of capital accumulation and exchange domination and as differentially organized by these forces. Tilly (1984) sees them as constructions of competing military/ political elites (see also Krasner 1983). Similar lines of thought (external resource dependency arguments) interpret modern organizations as constructed and constrained by states and economic dominance. And it is conventional in sociology to see individuals as heavily constrained by roles organized by wider forces. In all these cases, macro-level institutions are invoked, but in a way that is essentially realist: culture, aside from a bit of derivative false consciousness, is little involved. For the most part, culture may be conceived in this tradition as expressive material providing actors with identities and goals; the more rationalistic and cognitive culture I emphasize below (for example, scientific analysis) is conceived in the realist tradition as hard-wired social reality, not culture.

Phenomenological microinstitutionalism: Many contemporary lines of thought see actors as interpreting themselves as much as acting from a fixed and prior identity. Extreme lines of thought here—stressing individual personality, organizational culture (Smircich 1983), or political culture as prior and causal—are in some disrepute but continue to be employed (see Mitchell and Adams, this volume, for alternative evaluations). Weaker arguments, emphasizing the interpretive problematics arising from rationality failure, are common (for example, March 1988); ignorant actors are thought, for instance, to copy mechanically their accidental successes in future actions. In between, much modern sociological thinking stresses the ways in which individuals and organizations (less often, nation-states) are simultaneously interpreting and acting that are highly indeterminate. In all these lines of argument, actors are seen as embedded in some sort of institutionalized culture of their own making (Bourdieu, this volume). This culture may be conceived as expressive, as in the realist tradition, or may include the cognitive and rationalistic (for example, professional) material I stress below.

Phenomenological macroinstitutionalism: I employ in this essay a narrower conception of institutions and a broader conception of culture than those outlined above. In this view, modern actors are embedded in—and constructed, empowered, and constrained by—wider cultural forces (Adams, this volume). Modern individuals occupy the constructed identities of person, citizen, and now human, and derive many properties (for example, rights and responsibilities) from these rather standardized notions (Meyer 1987; Jepperson 1992). Modern organizations, similarly, are creatures of standardized social theories written into law and science (Meyer and Rowan 1977; DiMaggio and Powell 1983; Meyer and Scott 1992; Powell and DiMaggio 1991; Guillen 1994; Jepperson and Meyer 1991). In the same way, throughout its history the rationalized nation-state has been a theorized society and imagined community (Anderson 1991; Hall 1986; Mann 1986; see also Robertson 1992). Its sovereignty and boundaries are given exogenous cultural legitimacy (originally religious and legal, later more scientific and legal). Its proper goals (for example, progress, now roughly the gross national product per capita, and justice, now described in terms of individual equality) are defined and measured by the rules of the wider cultural system: they have clear religious roots in the sanctified individual soul and collective sacralized community, and are now scientized in logics such as those of psychology and economics. Appropriate means/ends technologies for the pursuit of these goals are defined in exogenous culture and science (for example, proper strategies, currently including educational improvement and structural deregulation, for economic development; or proper mechanisms, such as state redistribution, educational expansion, and legal protection, to accomplish equality and justice). Appropriate resources and costs are defined (human and physical capital, natural resources, and now environmental constraints). Standard mechanisms for integration and control (rationalized formal organization, democratic political participation) are promulgated exogenously (Guillen 1994).

Thus, the nation-state as an actor (a purposive, rational, bounded, integrated, and functional system) is laid out in scientific, legal, cultural, and religious theory. (Mitchell, this volume, takes the same view, but considers only internal social forces as constructing the theory involved.) Naturally, the evolving codification of all this cultural theory has had enormous impact. All sorts of unlikely populations and areas are now at least nominally organized as nation-states. In so organizing, standard legitimated forms are employed. New nation-states copy them and gain strength and legitimacy by doing so; older ones adapt to the supply and constraints provided by highly legitimated exogenous rules (Meyer 1980; Jackson and Rosberg 1982).

World Polity as Culture

Phenomenological macroinstitutionalist models are especially useful in analyses of the modern nation-state and its continuing development because of the nature of modern world society. Two properties of this society are relevant, with the first more commonly noted than the second. First, there is little by way of a sovereign world state, a point emphasized dramatically by Wallerstein (1974) and many others. If there were such a state, with nation-states as subordinated subunits under direct organizational control, macrorealist models of the system would obviously be appropriate. In the absence of a central state, much of the world social control system takes forms that can usefully be called cultural: cognitive and normative models and rules. Second, the system is far from an anarchy of genuinely autonomous and self-defining entities. Nation-states claim their sovereignty in terms of general and universalistic rules. They present these claims both internally (as justifications for their authority and as claims on the loyalty of internal participants) and externally (as justifications for their autonomy and as claims on the support of external bodies including each other). There is great interdependence in terms of reciprocal legitimation and in terms of dependence on common organizations (for example, the United Nations system, see McNeely 1995) and rules (for example, doctrines about how to produce economic growth). Thus, the whole system is something of a cultural construction.

But culture in this usage is far from the expressive material conceived in more realist models of world society. It is made up of the elaborate cognitive (scientific and professional, in good part) rationalistic analysis of the functioning of the modern society, state, organization, and individual (see Steinmetz, this volume, for a parallel analysis). The whole edifice of modernity is seen, in other words, as centrally cultural in character: the cultural specification of modern "actor" identities and the elaborate functional analysis of how these actors work. A partial analogue here is the prehegemonic American polity. Seeing its statelessness,

European observers anticipated anarchy and have always been surprised by its coherence. Skowronek (1982) discusses it as a state of courts and parties. Tocqueville (1945) had a broader view, noting the conformity produced by its dependence on common cultural material: law, science, association, opinion, and a sort of religious nationalism. The open polity of empowered (and formally isomorphic) individual actors generates a great deal of collective culture.

This situation describes well the modern world polity, made up of strong nation-state actors built up around a common identity as nation-states. This system has generated a great deal of cultural theorizing—much of it about the nation-state and its properties—throughout its history. In recent decades, this discourse has been consolidated in several different ways. There are thousands of international nongovernmental associations, speaking for various collective goods, the vast majority of which have been formed in recent decades (Union of International Associations, various years; Feld 1972; Thomas, Boli, and Kim 1993; Boli and Thomas 1999). There are hundreds of international intergovernmental organizations, the vast majority founded in recent decades (Union of International Associations, various years); and central ones have grown substantially in scale. Scientific communities (and communications) at the international level have greatly expanded, as have the associated numbers of international scientific bodies. This whole system, and its rise, gets less social scientific attention than it deserves. This happens because the world polity involved is not organized as a set of proper bounded actors, the exclusive source of activity defined in much modern social theory and ideology. By both world cultural and social scientific accounts, the actors involved—the units that have the authority and power to produce purposeful action—are the nation-states conceived to make up world society.

The structures of the world polity are mostly, in this sense, not actors. They produce talk (Brunsson 1989)—scientific talk, legal talk, nonbinding legislation, normative talk, talk about social problems, suggestions, advice, consulting talk, and so on—not binding authoritative action. Even the European Community—the nearest thing to a trans-state actor—mostly operates in this way (Soysal 1994). Sometimes, world organizations move a bit to action through incentives and constraints (as with the World Bank and its criteria for loans), but mostly their products are talk. This position is strikingly true of the world's scientific communities, which produce a great deal of powerful talk—about the ozone layer, about failures and requirements in national development policy, about the natural human needs of persons, and so on—but often do not assume the authority to act (see Bourdieu, this volume). As befits a cultural system postulating strong actors, most of the talk involved is addressed to these actors: in the modern world, the nation-states, which are supposed to put into decision and action the policies proposed in the talk (for example, to control the chemicals creating problems for the ozone layer). And most of the talk addresses the nation-states in terms of their own putative interests and goals—advising them how to be better and more effective actors in pursuit of such goals as economic development, social justice, and environmental regulation. The world polity is not principally addressed to a world sovereign concerning collective world goods; it is addressed to the constituent nation-state actors in terms of their own proper goals and requirements. When world talk instructs a country on appropriate educational or economic policy, it is in terms of the nation-state's supposed interest, not mainly or only the world's interest.

A Theoretical Aside

The world polity, at the collective level, is organized as a set of consultants more than a set of actors. We lack language for this sort of situation. One cannot usefully call the world collectivity a set of agents, since this term now supposes that there some actors as principals. World political/cultural discourse speaks in terms of higher goods than that—scientific truths about nature, the environment, national economic development, and technology; basic moral laws about human and group justice; and so on. I suggest we go back to Mead (1934), who said that the social world is made up of actors but also of Others who advise actors what to do. In the modern world, actors are rationalized and so are the Others, who speak for the rationalized ideals of the universal scientized truth, law, and moral order and apply these considerations to the proper interests and needs of the actors.

The point is that systems that construct and legitimate standardized, rationalized, universalized actors create a great deal of social space for Rationalized Others to produce talk about what these actors should be like and should do. Actors depend on these Others to become better and more effective actors (Strang and Meyer 1993). We thus live in a world thick with consultants: economists who wander to the South and East to advise on the universal truths about the market economy; educators who propose to the world the universal validity of American (or now Japanese) educational models; scientists who tell about the problems of the ecosystem; legal and moral inspectors advancing principles of the equality of the races, ethnic groups, and genders; organization theorists who unravel the true principles of effective political and economic structures (Guillen 1994; Jepperson and Meyer 1991); and so on. Others tend to be structured differently from rationalized actors. Actors are to be interested, Others to be disinterested (the economic consultant who stands to gain too much from the implementation of advice loses credibility). Actors require the myth of boundedness; Others can be members of a poorly specified community (for example, the economics profession). Actors should have definite resources (for example, property); Others may not. Actors must have some organization doing means-ends work and organizational control structures; Others may not. Actors are figures; Others may merge with the cultural ground.

A final theoretical point is of importance. In the modern stateless world polity, comprising highly legitimated nation-state actors, many normal constraints over the expansion of Rationalized Otherhood (both organizationally and in terms of substantive jurisdiction) are missing. This is true because Others do not bear many costs for the expanding proposals they make: actors bear the costs. Thus, if an economist creates new dimensions of economic life (human capital) that must be regulated by rational actors, the authority of economics expands but the actors bear the costs. If a scientist discovers a new environmental problem, scientific authority expands but the actors bear the costs. If organizational theorists discover expanded principles of effective organization (Japanified work teams, Americanized personnel training), the actors involved bear the costs. So too if world legal professionals develop new human rights, or social scientists new forms of injustice and inequality that must be regulated. A true world state, which had to bear the costs involved in the constant expansion of modernity by Rationalized Others, would be inclined to suppress a good deal of this activity. A world sovereign might be disinclined to support expensive discoveries about the ozone layer or about new human rights (for example, associated with gender) or about new requirements (for example, educational) for economic progress. Our world society, in the absence of a central actor, is one in which the rapid invention of collective goods by a variety of Others is relatively unfettered; Tocqueville noted the same process as one for which American society is well known.

Specific structures of Otherhood: I note some specific forms taken by the world polity as a cultural system (Meyer 1994; Robertson 1992). First, there are obvious organizational forms—intergovernmental organizations and nongovernmental associations—that define expanding models for nation-state action. These cover the domains of rationalized life—the economy, the polity, education, health, the environment, and so on—providing recipes for proper nation-state activity in these domains (McNeely 1995; Boli and Thomas 1999).

Second, there are the communities of the sciences and professions, sometimes only partly organized (see Bourdieu, this volume, on credentialism). These generate more or less consensual definitions of problems and solutions in a wide variety of domains. Third, nation-state actors themselves, in a world stratification system, provide models for each other. This process is especially powerful because nation-states are formed and legitimated under myths of ultimate similarity of identity (Strang and Meyer 1993). The same circumstances mean that copying is likely to be mediated by scientists and professionals providing theoretical interpretation, rather than to be direct and mechanical (mimesis, in the terms of DiMaggio and Powell 1983). It thus becomes rational rather than treasonous to propose copying policies and structures that appear to be successful in a virtuous or dominant competitor (Dobbin 1994). Nation-states obviously try to influence each other in their own interest through mechanisms of exchange and dominance. Here I call attention to another process by which they present themselves or are presented by intermediaries as models for each other. Thus, Japanese success leads to a wave of copying throughout the system—of Japanese policy, organization, education, and so on (Cole 1989). In the same way, the hegemonic United States has provided many models for other countries throughout the century. This process can occur through a country's own efforts (for example, foreign aid), since a nation-state gains both internal and external legitimacy if it can successfully portray itself as a model; the search for proper models by potential recipients; and the selection of models by intermediary professionals and international organizations. The last of these processes seems especially important in the contemporary period, in which world organization is so highly developed; countries are unlikely to be able to copy successes directly and effectively. They copy these successes as institutionalized and interpreted (often to the point of unrecognizability) in scientific and international communities. Such theorized entities as modern nation-states are especially susceptible to well-theorized models (Strang and Meyer 1993).

Research Areas

The general proposition here is that the rise and institutionalization in the world polity of models of the nation-state greatly affect the presence of, and change toward, such models in particular nation-states. Every rationalized aspect of the modern nation-state is in part driven by such processes. More complete analyses require explanations of the development of the world polity itself and of the models that become institutionalized in it; in this essay, I focus principally on its impact.

Existence

Strang (1990) shows that with the consolidation of the nation-state system in the last two centuries, dependent and external territories move at increasing rates into sovereign status. Once in this status, departures are extremely rare. Rates of transition increased notably after World War II and the increased international privileging of nation-state status. McNeely (1995) shows that independent states joined the international system (with formal application for UN membership) increasingly rapidly over time and that doing this required clear evidence of conformity to the basic nation-state model.

Form

Boli (1979, 1987) shows that national constitutions clearly reflect standard world models of the state and its proper powers (Sohrabi, this volume). These models become more elaborated over time, and new countries entering the system do so with constitutions reflecting the models current at that time (Sohrabi). Boli and others (Meyer, Boli-Bennett, and Chase-Dunn 1975) also show worldwide increases in nation-state organizational size. A number of studies also show systemwide changes, reflecting changed world standards, in the functions built into the centers of states, for example, lists of cabinet-level offices expand and seem to become increasingly isomorphic. Following the creation of the United Nations Environment Programme in 1972, for instance, countries form a Ministry concerned with the environment at increasing rates (Meyer, Frank, Hironaka, Schofer, and Tuma 1997). Overall impacts here may be especially strong in the third world. The old core often shows some capacity to adapt to changing requirements while retaining or even intensifying older forms (Huntington 1968; Guillen 1994; Dobbin 1994; Jepperson and Meyer 1991; see also Apter, this volume).

New models of the nation-state tend, of course, to arise from the core countries and their organizations and intellectuals. This follows from every aspect of their resources and centrality in the system. But these new models are by no means simple enactments of the interests or characteristics of core states as powers in the system. Perceptions and analyses of crucial matters such as economic development or human rights arise out of core experience and analysis, but may be weakly codified in formal structures there. As they are formulated and flow through the system, they become much more highly structured (Sohrabi, this volume). Thus, economic planning principles, arising in the core but only modestly employed there, become central organizational structures in peripheral societies. As another example, implicit British constitutionalism becomes highly explicit and elaborate on those former colonies most influenced by Britain. And the weak American constitution, translated into peripheral areas most under American influence, depicts a much stronger and more centralized state. It is true that the political culture of the core is dominant, but it is a mistake to imagine that this means that peripheral structures simply copy core ones. Cultural hegemony works through processes other than simple power dominance. The formation of nation-state identity is one of them (Adams, this volume).

Data Systems and Self-Conceptions

Nation-states depict themselves in their data systems in expanded and standardized ways, which tend to be strongly affected by world standards. Ventresca (1995) shows that with the rise of international statistical standards about the proper depiction of the nation-state, countries adopt the institution of the census at increasing rates, and censuses increasingly collect the data prescribed by the world order (and apparently decreasingly collect other types of data). McNeely (1995) shows that world rules strongly affect national economic data systems—countries increasingly develop these, do so along standard lines, and conform to an increasingly elaborate set of standards in doing so (the international system suggested a simple accounting system with eight items of information in 1948, expanding to eighty-four items by the late 1980s). In many other sectors (for example, education or health) the same process has been dramatic.

Education

Since the early nineteenth century, scientific and ideological doctrines holding that mass education is a crucial element of the modern nation-state (both in the interests of collective progress and in the interests of equality and justice for individuals) have been central in world society (Ramirez and Ventresca 1992). These doctrines became increasingly dominant over time and, after World War II, were celebrated in many UN and UNESCO pronouncements and in the highly developed scientific ideologies about education as a direct ingredient in national economic and political development, as with human capital theory

(Huefner, Naumann, and Meyer 1987; Fiala and Gordon-Lanford 1987). Several studies show that rather standardized systems of mass education arose around the world, in all sorts of countries, at increasing rates over time. Countries became susceptible on entering world society (with claims of sovereignty and recognition), and the rates at which they adopted mass educational systems increased— most dramatically, after World War II (Meyer, Ramirez, and Soysal 1992). Rates of enrollment expansion followed a similar pattern, and again increased in all sorts of countries after World War II (Meyer, Kamens, and Benavot, with Cha and Wong 1992). Independently, the custom of creating national rules of compulsory mass education (little related empirically to actual enrollments) spread and became almost universal (Ramirez and Ventresca 1992). Mass educational curricula, throughout the modern 'period, show pronounced isomorphism around the world and tend to change in remarkably isomorphic ways; in both cases, changing world standards are clearly involved (Meyer, Kamens et al. 1992). For instance, the originally American notion of replacing history and geography instruction with an integrated social studies subject spread widely under some direct encouragement from UNESCO (Wong 1991).

Even some idiosyncratic educational changes tend to spread isomorphically, for instance, the UNESCO data system classifying mass education in a 6–3–3 pattern from primary to senior secondary school has influenced the actual educational organization of many countries, which shift their entire structures to the 6–3–3 model. But central educational issues show the same pattern—for instance, a worldwide shift to greatly expanded enrollment of females in both mass and higher education (Ramirez 1987; Bradley and Ramirez 1996)—appearing in every country for which there are data. The same effects appear in higher education: the Western university model spreads at increasing rates throughout the entire world, so that almost all nation-states organize universities (Riddle 1993)—and they follow clearly isomorphic models. An unlikely field such as sociology, for instance, is now to be found almost everywhere, and in remarkably similar forms.

Science

The principle that science, and its management, is to be incorporated in the nation-state was developed in the seventeenth century (Wuthnow 1987), and central scientific academies spread among the European countries. The theorized linkage between science and national goals became progressively tighter in the nineteenth and early twentieth centuries. After World War II, models of national development (built around economic theories, in particular) built a still tighter linkage. In OECD and UNESCO models, science moved from being seen as a general world good to a specific instrument of national development (Finnemore 1993, 1996; Schofer 1999), associated with specific preferred forms of national organizational control. After this development, all sorts of countries rapidly established national science policy structures, and these appear in a great many countries (Finnemore 1993). Similar patterns of diffusion describe increases in national scientific activity, which spreads around the world in increasingly standardized ways, sponsored by nation-states and the university systems they control (Drori 1989). Thus, the range of countries producing authorships cited in the science citation indices greatly expands over time, and countries increasingly produce scientific work in the fully expanded range of approved scientific fields. Predictive factors here probably have much more to do with linkages to the evolving international system than with any domestic factors.

Welfare, Population, and Health

Collier and Messick (1975) noted that the spread of welfare models among nation-states followed diffusion lines rather than the functional ones (for example, associated with national development) conventionally predicted. Strang and Chang (1993; see also Chang and Strang 1990) show the effects of world patterning as organized by the ILO, which set out a constantly expanding set of preferred welfare models over time. National patterns are more predicted by national linkage to the ILO, and to the expansion of the standard ILO models, than by internal functional factors. Health regulation and provision have followed similar patterns, highly structured by international organization, and most recently by internationally standardized systems of diagnostic categories (Thornton 1992). The international system has contained discussion of the virtues of population control (as opposed to an earlier pronatalism, justified on military grounds) since the turn of the century (Barrett 1995; Barrett and Frank 1999). This had little impact, as the collective goods imagined had to do with the human race generally (in a generalized Malthusianism). After World War I, but only loosely associated with the League of Nations, ideas about national interests as calling for eugenic control developed in the system and in some measure spread among nation-states. This line of theorizing fell into disrepute with World War II and was replaced in the 1950s with the model of population control as a crucial mechanism for national development. Major world institutions, and the sciences associated with development theories, then took up the call (Barrett 1995; Barrett and Frank 1999). After this development, which produced a very elaborate international organizational system, national policies for population control spread very rapidly and widely throughout the third world; linkages to this wider system seem to be more important predictive factors than any internal characteristic of these countries.

Human Rights and the Individual

Since the French Revolution, the model of the nation-state as ultimately rooted in individuals as citizens has been dominant, reinforced by long traditions of the sacralization of the individual in Western religious history. There are obvious variations in the conception of citizenship (Bendix 1964; Marshall 1948), running from liberal to communitarian and from emphasis on participation to emphasis on entitlements, but one or another version is celebrated in every vision of modern rationalization. Boli (1979, 1987) shows the extent to which such doctrines are to be found in ever-expanding ways in national constitutions over the last century, with expanding definitions of citizen rights and responsibilities entering the constitutions of both old and new countries throughout the period. The League of Nations was founded as an international security organization, with little emphasis on expanding human rights. But the UN system, founded in reaction to World War II, incorporated such conceptions from the outset. These have expanded greatly and have bound organizational bases in many intergovernmental and nongovernmental associations.

The impact of this wider system on particular nation-states has been enormous (for the European case, see Soysal 1994). Berkovitch (1999) shows the rise, for instance, in international emphasis on women's rights over the twentieth century and the shift in this emphasis, after World War II, from corporatist to liberal equalitarian terms. She also shows the enormous expansion in national law and policy devoted to the question. Practical effects, running from female participation in the labor force (Charles 1992; Ramirez and Weiss 1979) and government and education, to changed family laws, are widespread throughout the world (and often poorly related to internal national culture and development levels). The same changes describe world models of ethnic and racial incorporation and consequent national-level principles of the incorporation and legitimation of such properties of individuals (Ramirez and Meyer 1992).

The Environment

Meyer, Frank et al. (1997) and Frank (1994; Frank et al. 1999) show the rise in international discourse about the environment and the shift in this discourse from narrow issues (about resources) to generalized ones (about ecosystems). This produces a flood of treaties, and ultimately intergovernmental organizations, providing standard prescriptions and models in the area (Frank et al. 1999). A worldwide wave of national environmental policies and structures follows; many countries construct cabinet ministries to properly deal with the environment. The impact of international change, and linkages to the international system, is obvious.

Economy

Hall (1989) discusses international flows in specific economic policies and ideas. More generally, it is obvious that preferred basic economic structures tend to flow around the world (Mitchell's discussion, this volume, considers the "economy" as a constructed model, but not as a model organized by and in world discourse). At odds with neoclassical and dependency theories predicting international differentiation, economic structures tend to change worldwide in similar directions (for example, Meyer, Boli-Bennett, and Chase-Dunn 1975). This is true of the general expansion of industrial and service sectors, and it is also true of labor force composition. The preferred forms of the modern economy, if not the wealth supposed to be associated with them, tend to find at least symbolic implementation in a very widespread way (see Jessop, this volume). In this area, cultural diffusion sometimes occurs despite the explicit policies of such international organizations as the World Bank, which tends to encourage more differentiated developments.

Research Issues

The sorts of studies noted earlier tend to be extremely convincing in showing that nation-state forms, in many specific areas, reflect world models, change along with these models, and change in similar directions despite obvious international diversities in local culture and resources. There is a decreasing tendency to question the power of such effects. The empirical studies have been less successful, however, in isolating the particular world structures and the particular mechanisms involved in the effects in question. We can show clearly, for instance, that national educational systems have tended to develop and change in isomorphic ways and that this process intensified after World War II. It is harder, however, to show exactly which factors and processes are involved: (1) the hegemony of the general liberal model of the nation-state in such arrangements as the UN system, which rendered the actors so created susceptible to preferred nation-state models; (2) the hegemony of the specific educational arrangements particular to this model; (3) the specific doctrines and activities associated with the main international organizations; (4) generalized American hegemony in the world; (5) the rise of high professionalized and scientized consensus on the virtues of education and of particular educational models; and so on. Future research can usefully investigate such questions by measuring more carefully the particular links of countries to particular parts of world society, by mapping the structure of this society more precisely in particular domains, and by incorporating longer time periods in research designs so as better to capture multiple changes in world society itself as independent variation.

Studies that find substantial variation in the direction of world influence over time, and consequent variations in structural change in particular countries, are especially useful. Examples include Frank's (1994) observation of change in world environmental emphasis toward more generalized ecological models, Barrett's (1995) findings of similar change in the population area from eugenics models to national development ones, and Berkovitch's (1999) discussion of shifts in world discourse about women's rights from corporatist to more liberal models. In all these cases, World War II seems to have been an important break point. Future research might well discover that 1989 presaged a similar break point: for instance, with the end of the cold war and the ideological contest involved, the rapid world creation of new generalized human rights, for example, for women, children, the aged, the handicapped, racial and ethnic minorities (Ramirez and Meyer 1992), may be expected to decline.

Other directions for future work include more careful analyses of the flow of practices, in comparison to policies. Effective studies of the flows of structures around the world require data on many countries over time (as well as on the system itself, as discussed immediately above). This means that much of the research reviewed above employs rather superficial data on each case, such as the presence of a few rules or structures, and data that cover policies rather than the real penetration of changed practice. Obviously, world cultural effects can be especially strong on symbolic policies that are easily brought into line with exogenous standards of rational organization—equally obviously, a great deal of decoupling is likely to be involved so that policies and practices are inconsistent (Meyer and Rowan 1977; DiMaggio and Powell 1983; Weick 1976; Orton and Weick 1990). A system in which national communities are principally imagined or theorized is likely to create decoupled inconsistency with practice as a stable outcome. In some areas—education is conspicuous here—studies can examine effects on patterns of actual enrollment, and thus examine practice as well as policy. In other areas (for example, science policy structures, some types of human rights), ritualized policy or structural change may be the main outcome.

In most areas, we need analyses with data on a wider array of practice-related dependent variables. There is no reason, however, to suppose that the processes involved function only in a top-down hierarchical way, with states ritualistically adopting exogenous policies and structures and with only occasional implementation. It is clear that world pressures affect not only nation-state centers, but also social groups in national society. Interest groups, organizations, professions, and social movements within nation-states tend to be highly sensitive to changes in models provided and legitimated by the exogenous world polity; empowered by such changes, they more easily mobilize to create not only policy change but practical adaptation as well. Local groups, for instance, use evolving world environmental ideology to mobilize against their own systems and to demand changes, and so do local groups concerned with the expanded rights of women or ethnic minorities or citizens in general. In the same way, historically, professional educators within a country use world-legitimated policies as the basis for claiming the need for change and expansion in the domestic educational system. World changes, in other words, change the internal structure of the nation-state actor, empowering some forces and weakening others. Thus simple proposals that world polity arrangements produce only rhetorical national change are likely to be naive. Empirical research—ideally with more detailed dependent variables—is needed to discuss the conditions under which this may be true.

The Resultant Fragmented Nation-State

Nation-state "actors" operating in the current world polity thick with Rationalized Otherhood tend to take on somewhat changed forms. An older nation-state form, built around more autonomous sovereignty, often generated the simple limited bureaucratic state organized around international competition. The little-controlled flood of cultural Others, operating at the world level in an expanded and fragmented way, changes the organizational situation. Nation-states come under pressure to assume expanded responsibilities for the widest array of social domains (Meyer 1994). These pressures are little integrated with each other and penetrate the nation-state in different ways (for example, through different structures in both state and society). World educational arrangements come in through one set of channels and strike one set of state and society structures, and world economic ideologies come in through different mechanisms and influence different structures. The one thing all the pressures of world Otherhood tend to produce in common is demand that the nation-state expand its responsibilities as actor.

Thus nation-states, even in the periphery, have tended to expand very rapidly in the current period. But this expansion has not been characterized by tight bureaucratic integration—rather, it has been characterized by organizational fragmentation (Meyer 1994; Meyer and Scott 1992; contrast the first and last parts of Skocpol 1985), with components of the state responding to fragmented exogenous pressures and standards. All this occurs under the continuing myth of nation-state sovereignty and responsibility, claimed both by states and by the Others of world society. Everyone agrees that nation-states are the core actors and should carry the burden of the world-defined responsibilities. I contend that the consensus on this myth may make the myth exceptionally untrue in terms of real policy and outcomes. Actors so structured in a dense world of fragmented exogenous consultants and advisers may be fairly rational. But they are by no means really actors. They are enactors of multiple dramas whose texts are written elsewhere. Thus the modern world situation produces systematic changes in the contemporary nation-state—sprawling, weakly integrated, expanded organizational forms. The results are strikingly clear in Europe—the area in which nation-states are most strongly influenced by an exogenous fragmented rationalizing polity.

MODERN nation-states are constituted and constructed as ultimately similar actors under exogenous universalistic and rationalized cultural models. This produces a good deal of isomorphism and isomorphic change among them and high rates of diffusion between them and between centers of world discourse and particular nation-states. In a wide range of social sectors, nation-state change is driven by opportunities and pressures from, and changes in, these exogenous models. The rapid development and change in the models involved is produced by the enormous expansion in world-level social roles played by Others rather than actors, itself reflecting the fundamental structure of a system with a stateless center but strongly legitimated nation-state actors, all rationalized in a common frame. Arguments along these lines may be especially relevant to the interpretation of the modern stateless world system. They add appreciably to other arguments about the modern world system: centrist or leftist models of the differentiated world economy, functional models of national societies, or political models of raw interstate competition under conditions of anarchy. These other arguments are better at explaining differentiation than structural similarity and isomorphic change among nation-states. They have trouble explaining, for instance, why the world's educational systems might show such drive to similarity. Institutional models, in the present world context, are especially valuable for this purpose.

More realist lines of thought see dominant or hegemonic states (in the recent period, the United States) as playing much of the part of the missing world state in the present system and attribute the phenomena we discuss as arising somehow from American dominance. It is certainly true that modern world cultural models of the proper nation-state and national society tend to arise in core countries, given the resources and capacities (organizationally, intellectually, and in terms of communication centrality) located there. It is unconvincing that this simply reflects the organizational power and interests of the American national state, which has little at stake in spreading particular models of education, health, scientific activity, or even economic organization around the periphery of the world. It is more realistic to see the modern world core as the source of much cultural (for example, scientific, professional, and associational) mobilization—this sometimes may work in core interests, often works in opposition to core interests (as with the rapid spread of "world systems theory" or doctrines of "new international economic orders"), and often seems utterly orthogonal to the particular interests of core states.

It is important to emphasize the special, and tendentious, use of the concept of culture in the present argument. In modern social science usage, and in modern rationalistic culture, the term *culture* tends to be reserved for the primordial, the expressive, and the particular—in short, for all those things that are not the core rules of modern rationality. This pattern reflects a fundamental myth of the modern system—the beliefs that its structures and systems and "actors" and transactions are real entities that have transcended embeddedness and culture (Meyer 1988). I maintain that precisely this set of myths is the grounding culture of the modern system. Their mythological (or imagined, or theorized) status helps explain why they flow so rapidly around the world and why they penetrate so easily into the rationalized "actors" constituted to receive them.

The blind spot in the modern system—the systematic denial of the secularized protoreligious or cultural base of the system—is a prominent feature of contemporary social science. Even the current "cultural turn" emphasizes the irrational, arational, or expressive aspects of culture (see the parallel discussion in Steinmetz, this volume). We social scientists share with the participants in the modern system an Enlightenment base emphasizing that social reality is defined and produced by the empowered actors seen as exclusively walking the earth (variously individuals, organizations, and national states). These actors are real structures with clear prior purposes, sovereignty, and a good deal of technical capacity: Rome is celebrated here. The actors also have (presumably from Greece) great internal (and potentially irrational) subjectivity. Both these qualities somehow derive from Nature. Jerusalem, and the systemic authority of the God of Christendom, disappears from the analysis, so the instrumental culture of the modern system is mistakenly taken as real.

Thus, in each social arena where cultural authority should be emphasized, our analyses are weak and evasive. On science, we have good research on scientific organizations and careers and careful critical research on the arbitrariness of scientific work, thought, and activity. We have almost no good analyses of scientific authority—of why the world is listening. On religion, we have career and organizational analyses, and surveys of individual beliefs, but almost no analyses of why this cultural frame has authority. So also with the law—elaborate analyses of legal and judicial organizations and careers, and considerable work on legal thought and analyses, but almost nothing on why the law, seen as quite a universal instrument, has such magical status and authority in the modern world. The same points could be made of the sociology of culture and of knowledge.

To understand better the nature of the modern system, we need to parallel our analyses of organizational and actor structure and of subunit subjective agency with similar analyses of the patterns of cultural authority that are central elements in modern world society. The authority involved is highly collective, is extraordinarily globalized, and has the most widespread roots in analyses of nature and the ultimate moral order. It is about science, the ultimate moral authority, and conceptions of human (and nation-state) actorhood derived from these sources.

References

Anderson, Benedict. 1991. *Imagined Communities*, 2d ed. London: Verso.

Barrett, Deborah. 1995. "Reproducing Persons as a Global Concern: The Making of an Institution." Ph.D. diss., Stanford University.

Barrett, Deborah, and David Frank. 1999. "Population Control for National Development: From World Discourse to National Policies." In *Constructing World Culture: International Nongovernmental Organizations Since 1875*, edited by J. Boli and G. Thomas. Stanford: Stanford University Press.

Bendix, Reinhard. 1964. *Nation-Building and Citizenship*. New York: Wiley.

Berkovitch, Nitza. 1999. "The International Women's Movement: Transformations of Citizenship." In *Constructing World Culture: International Nongovernmental Organizations Since 1875*, edited by J. Boli and G. Thomas. Stanford: Stanford University Press.

Boli, John. 1979. "The Ideology of Expanding State Authority in National Constitutions, 1870–1970." In *National Development and the World System*, edited by J. Meyer and M. Hannan, 222–237. Chicago: University of Chicago Press.

———. 1987. "World Polity Sources of Expanding State Authority and Organizations, 1870–1970." In *Institutional Structure*, edited by G. Thomas, et al., 71–91. Beverly Hills: Sage.

Boli, John, and George Thomas, eds. 1999. *Constructing World Culture: International Nongovernmental Organizations Since 1875*, Stanford: Stanford University Press.

Bradley, Karen, and Francisco Ramirez. 1996. "World Polity and Gender Parity: Women's Share of Higher Education, 1965–1985." In *Research in Sociology of Education and Socialization* 15. Greenwich, Conn.: JAI Press.

Brunsson, Nils. 1989. *The Organization of Hypocrisy: Talk, Decisions and Action in Organizations.* New York: Wiley.

Chang, Patricia, and David Strang. 1990. "Internal and External Sources of the Welfare State: A Cross-National Analysis, 1950–1980." Paper presented at the annual meeting of the American Sociological Association, Cincinnati.

Charles, Maria. 1992. "Cross-National Variation in Occupational Sex Segregation." *American Sociological Review* 57, no. 4: 483–502.

Cole, Robert. 1989. *Strategies for Learning: Small-Group Activities in American, Japanese and Swedish Industry.* Berkeley: University of California Press.

Collier, David, and Richard Messick. 1975. "Prerequisites versus Diffusion: Testing Alternative Explanations of Social Security Adoption." *American Political Science Review* 69: 1299–315.

DiMaggio, Paul, and Walter Powell. 1983. "The Iron Cage Revisited." *American Sociological Review* 48, no. 2: 147–60.

Dobbin, Frank. 1994. *Forging Industrial Policy: The United States, Britain, and France in the Railway Age.* New York: Cambridge University Press.

Drori, Gili. 1989. "On the Effect of Science on the Economy of Less Developed Countries." Ph.D. diss. Tel Aviv University.

Feld, Werner. 1972. *Nongovernmental Forces and World Politics.* New York: Praeger.

Fiala, Robert, and Audri Gordon-Lanford. 1987. "Educational Ideology and the World Educational Revolution, 1950–1970." *Comparative Education Review* 31, no. 3: 315–32.

Finnemore, Martha. 1993. "International Organizations as Teachers of Norms: United Nations Educational, Scientific, and Cultural Organization and Science Policy." *International Organization* 47, no. 4: 565–597.

——. 1996. *National Interests in International Society.* Ithaca: Cornell University Press.

Frank, David. 1994. "Global Environmentalism: International Treaties in World Society." Ph.D. diss. Stanford University.

Frank, David, Ann Hironaka, John Meyer, Evan Schofer, and Nancy Tuma. 1999. "The Rationalization and Organization of Nature in World Culture." In *Constructing World Culture: International Nongovernmental Organizations Since 1875,* edited by J. Boli and G. Thomas. Stanford: Stanford University Press.

Guillen, Mauro. 1994. *Models of Management: Work, Authority, and Organization in a Comparative Perspective.* Chicago: University of Chicago Press.

Hall, John. 1986. *Powers and Liberties.* New York: Penguin.

Hall, Peter, ed. 1989. *The Political Power of Economic Ideas.* Princeton: Princeton University Press.

Huefner, Klaus, Jens Naumann, and John Meyer. 1987. "Comparative Education Policy Research: A World Society Perspective." In *Comparative Policy Re-*

search, edited by M. Dierkes, H. Weiler, and A. Antal, 188–243. Aldershot: Gower.

Huntington, Samuel. 1968. *Political Order in Changing Societies*. New Haven: Yale University Press.

Jackson, Robert, and Carl Rosberg. 1982. "Why Africa's Weak States Persist: The Empirical and the Juridical in Statehood." *World Politics* 35, no. 1: 1–24.

Jepperson, Ronald. 1991. "Institutions, Institutional Effects, and Institutionalism." In *The New Institutionalism in Organizational Analysis*, edited by W. Powell and P. DiMaggio, 143–63. Chicago: University of Chicago Press.

———. 1992. "National Scripts: The Varying Construction of Individualism and Opinion across the Modern Nation-States." Ph.D. diss. Yale University.

Jepperson, Ronald, and John Meyer. 1991. "The Public Order and the Construction of Formal Organizations." In *The New Institutionalism in Organizational Analysis*, edited by W. Powell and P. DiMaggio, 204–31. Chicago: University of Chicago Press.

Krasner, Stephen. 1983. *International Regimes*. Ithaca: Cornell University Press.

Mann, Michael. 1986. *The Sources of Social Power*. Cambridge: Cambridge University Press.

March, James. 1988. *Decisions and Organizations*. Oxford: Blackwell.

Marshall, T. H. 1948. *Class, Citizenship, and Social Development*. Garden City: Doubleday.

McNeely, Connie. 1995. *Constructing the Nation-State: International Organization and Prescriptive Action*. Westport: Greenwood.

Mead, George Herbert. 1934. *Mind, Self, and Society*. Chicago: University of Chicago Press.

Meyer, John. 1980. "The World Polity and the Authority of the Nation-State." In *Studies of the Modern World-System*, edited by A. Bergesen, 109–37. New York: Academic Press.

———. 1987. "Self and Life Course: Institutionalization and Its Effects." In *Institutional Structure*, edited by G. Thomas, et al., 242–60. Newbury Park: Sage.

———. 1988. "Society without Culture: A Nineteenth-Century Legacy." In *Rethinking the Nineteenth Century*, edited by F. Ramirez, 193–201. New York: Greenwood.

———. 1994. "Rationalized Environments." In *Institutional Environments and Organizations*, edited by W. Scott and J. Meyer, 28–54. Newbury Park: Sage.

Meyer, John, John Boli, George Thomas, and Francisco Ramirez. 1997. "World Society and the Nation-State." *American Journal of Sociology* 103, no. 1: 144–81.

Meyer, John, John Boli-Bennett, and Christopher Chase-Dunn. 1975. "Convergence and Divergence in Development." *Annual Review of Sociology* 1: 223–46.

Meyer, John, David Frank, Ann Hironaka, Evan Schofer, and Nancy Tuma. 1997. "The Structuring of a World Environmental Regime, 1870–1990." *International Organization* 51, no. 4: 623–51.

Meyer, John, David Kamens, and Aaron Benavot, with Yun-Kyung Cha and

Suk-Ying Wong. 1992. *School Knowledge for the Masses: World Models and National Primary Curricular Categories in the Twentieth Century*. London: Falmer Press.

Meyer, John, Francisco Ramirez, and Yasemin Soysal. 1992. "World Expansion of Mass Education, 1870–1980." *Sociology of Education* 65, no. 2: 128–49.

Meyer, John, and Brian Rowan. 1977. "Institutionalized Organizations: Formal Structure as Myth and Ceremony." *American Journal of Sociology* 83, no. 2: 340–63.

Meyer, John, and W. Richard Scott. 1992. *Organizational Environments: Ritual and Rationality*. 2d ed. Beverly Hills: Sage.

Orton, J. Douglas, and Karl Weick. 1990. "Loosely Coupled Systems: A Reconceptualization." *Academy of Management Review* 15: 203–23.

Powell, Walter, and Paul DiMaggio. 1991. *The New Institutionalism in Organizational Analysis*. Chicago: University of Chicago Press.

Ramirez, Francisco. 1987. "Global Changes, World Myths, and the Demise of Cultural Gender." In *America's Changing Role in the World-System*, edited by T. Boswell and A. Bergesen, 257–73. New York: Praeger.

Ramirez, Francisco, and John Meyer. 1992. "The Institutionalization of Citizenship Principles and the National Incorporation of Women and Children, 1870–1990." Unpublished paper, Stanford University.

Ramirez, Francisco, and Marc Ventresca. 1992. "Building the Institutions of Mass Schooling." In *The Political Construction of Education*, edited by B. Fuller and R. Rubinson, 47–59. New York: Praeger.

Ramirez, Francisco, and Jane Weiss. 1979. "The Political Incorporation of Women." In *National Development and the World System*, edited by J. Meyer and M. Hannan, 238–49. Chicago: University of Chicago Press.

Riddle, Phyllis. 1993. "Political Authority and University Formation in Europe, 1200–1800." *Sociological Perspectives* 36, no. 1: 45–62.

Robertson, Roland. 1992. *Globalization*. London: Sage.

Schofer, Evan. 1999. "Science Associations in the International Sphere, 1860–1994: Rationalization of Science and the Scientization of Society." In *Constructing World Culture: International Nongovernmental Organizations Since 1875*, edited by J. Boli and G. Thomas. Stanford: Stanford University Press.

Skocpol, Theda. 1985. "Bringing the State Back In." In *Bringing the State Back In*, edited by P. Evans, D. Rueschemeyer, and T. Skocpol, 3–43. Cambridge: Cambridge University Press.

Skowronek, Stephen. 1982. *Building a New American State*. New York: Cambridge University Press.

Smircich, Linda. 1983. "Organizations as Shared Meanings." In *Organizational Symbolism*, edited by L. Pondy, et al. Greenwich: JAI Press.

Soysal, Yasemin. 1994. *Limits of Citizenship: Migrants and Postnational Membership in Europe*. Chicago: University of Chicago Press.

Strang, David. 1990. "From Dependency to Sovereignty: An Event History Analysis of Decolonization, 1870–1987." *American Sociological Review* 55: 846–60.

Strang, David, and Patricia Chang. 1993. "The International Labor Organization and the Welfare State: Institutional Effects on National Welfare Spending, 1960–1980." *International Organization* 47: 235–62.

Strang, David, and John Meyer. 1993. "Institutional Conditions for Diffusion." *Theory and Society* 22: 487–511.

Thomas, George, John Boli, and Young Kim. 1993. "World Culture and International Nongovernmental Organization." Paper presented at the annual meeting of the American Sociological Association, Miami.

Thomas, George, John Meyer, Francisco Ramirez, and John Boli. 1987. *Institutional Structure: Constituting State, Society and the Individual*. Beverly Hills: Sage.

Thornton, Patricia. 1992. "Psychiatric Diagnosis as Sign and Symbol: Nomenclature as an Organizing and Legitimating Strategy." In *Perspectives on Social Problems*, edited by G. Miller and J. Holstein. Greenwich: JAI Press.

Tilly, Charles. 1984. *Big Structures, Large Processes, Huge Comparisons*. New York: Russell Sage.

Tocqueville, Alexis de. 1945. *Democracy in America*. New York: Vintage.

Union of International Associations (UIA). Various years. *Yearbook of International Organizations*. Munich: K. G. Sauer.

Ventresca, Marc. 1995. "Counting People When People Count: Global Establishment of the Modern Population Census, 1820–1980." Ph.D. diss. Stanford University.

Wallerstein, Immanuel. 1974. *The Modern World System*, vol. 1. New York: Academic Press.

Weick, Karl. 1976. "Educational Organizations as Loosely Coupled Systems." *Administrative Science Quarterly* 21, no. 1: 1–19.

Wong, Suk-Ying. 1991. "The Evolution of Social Science Instruction, 1900–86." *Sociology of Education* 64, no. 1: 33–47.

Wuthnow, Robert. 1987. *Meaning and Moral Order*. Berkeley: University of California Press.

PART TWO

CULTURE AND EARLY
MODERN STATE-FORMATION

5

Calvinism and State-Formation in Early Modern Europe

Philip S. Gorski

> The flourishing and decaying of all civil societies, all the move-
> ments and turnings of human occasions are moved to and fro
> upon the axle of discipline.
>
> —JOHN MILTON

In his epic novel, *Joseph und seine Brüder*, Thomas Mann cautions that "treating religion and politics as fundamentally different things is to oversee the unity of the world."[1] Mann was speaking of Ancient Egypt, but his caveat applies equally to early modern Europe. For at perhaps no other time in European history were religion and politics more tightly intertwined than in the two centuries following the Reformation.

Most historical sociologists have ignored Mann's dictum. They have sought to explain early modern political development solely as the consequence of two processes: capitalist development and military competition.[2] By contrast, the central thesis of this essay is that the structure and strength of early modern states was also shaped by another factor: the processes of confessionalization (*Konfessionalisierung*)[3] and social disciplining (*Sozialdisziplinierung*) unleashed by the Reformation.

---

[1] Mann, 1960–75: 1377, quoted in Schilling (1991a).
[2] The most important Marxist accounts are Anderson (1979) and Wallerstein (1974–87). On the institutionalist perspective see especially Tilly (1975, 1990) Poggi (1979), and Downing (1992).
[3] In German usage a distinction is made between *Bekenntnis* and *Konfession*. The former refers to the written doctrines espoused by a particular faith and is equivalent to the English "confession" (for example, "Augsburg Confession," "Heidelberg Confession," and so on). The latter refers chiefly to the bodies of organized Christians who accept a certain interpretation of Christian doctrine and has no simple English equivalent. "Confessionalization" thus refers to the emergence of churches organized around a particular understanding of Christianity, usually encoded in a written confession.

I present three arguments. First, confessionalization stimulated the creation of a new infrastructure of social and moral control that allowed states and state rulers effectively to regulate the everyday conduct of ordinary people for the first time in history, and new forms of collective identity emerged that were at once socially inclusive and territorially exclusive, which laid the foundations for modern forms of national identity. Second, the effects of the confessionalization process were particularly pronounced in Calvinist countries because of the particular emphasis that Reformed Protestantism placed on religious and social discipline. Third, previous work on the social disciplining process has paid far too little attention to religious ideologies, elites, and institutions.

Confessionalism, Calvinism, and Social Disciplining

The Reformation fractured Latin Christendom into a multitude of amorphous and overlapping religious tendencies. By the middle of the sixteenth century, however, there coalesced three distinct and opposed "confessions"—Catholicism, Lutheranism, and Calvinist or Reformed Protestantism. The stage was set for one hundred and fifty years of intense and often violent conflict, in which the three confessions and their political allies vied with one another for the control of souls and territory. The result was a progressive sharpening of boundaries, both doctrinal and geographical, between the confessions, as well as a gradual extension of control, both religious and social, within them. Europe thus came to be divided into three great confessional blocs, which differed from one another not only religiously but, to an increasing degree, culturally and institutionally, as well.[4]

Of course, the transformation of Latin Christendom into a system of competing territorial states was already well under way by the onset of the Reformation. But it was dramatically accelerated by confessionalization in two ways. First, confessional mobilization and countermobilization contributed to the emergence of powerful new identities.[5] Though neither wholly universal nor strictly local, these confessional allegiances were not strictly speaking "national" either. Nonetheless, like the idea of the nation, confession was an "imagined community," which constituted bonds of solidarity among individuals who never experienced face-to-face contact, bonds which could be—and were—mobilized by political elites.[6] Confessionalization thus generated a set of protonational or territorial identities, a sort of nationalism *avant la lettre*. The second way in which confessionalization contributed to state formation was through the ef-

---

[4] There is a burgeoning literature on confessionalization within Reformation historiography. The seminal works on this subject are Zeeden (1964) and Schilling (1988a). In English, see Schilling (1992).

[5] To my knowledge, the only systematic treatment of this development is Schilling (1991b).

[6] On this topic, see Anderson (1982). In the burgeoning sociological literature on nationalism, see especially Brubaker (1992); Hobsbawm and Ranger (1992); and Smith (1984).

forts of religious reformers to regulate individual behavior.[7] Although the post-Reformation churches differed greatly in their understandings of Christianity, they all agreed about the need to impose "right" doctrine and practice on their followers, to effect a more thoroughgoing Christianization of society. In this, they often cooperated closely with state-building elites, who, quite apart from their personal religious convictions, tended to see a strong church as the best guarantor of the social and political order. Throughout Europe, church and state worked together in an effort to regulate all aspects of everyday life—sexuality, education, work, even consumption and amusement. To this end, they constructed new mechanisms of moral regulation (for example, inquisitions, visitations, consistories) and social control (for example, schools, poorhouses, hospitals). Neither purely religious nor strictly political, these institutions were rather *res mixtae* in which church and state interpenetrated one another to varying degrees. Nonetheless, these institutions could be and eventually were absorbed and appropriated by the state.[8] Confessionalization thus forged a new "infrastructure of power" (Michael Mann 1984–1993), by which the state began to effectively penetrate social life for the first time.

These processes of confessional mobilization and social disciplining were endemic to post-Reformation Europe. But, as I have argued elsewhere, they were particularly pronounced in those areas where Calvinism became the dominant confession (Gorski 1993a, 1993b). This had to do, first of all, with the revolutionary character of the Calvinist movement, itself.[9] Unlike the Lutherans, the Calvinists faced strong resistance from Catholic reformers (for example, the Jesuits) and from conservative monarchs (especially the Habsburgs). Where this resistance was strong and sustained, as in Scotland, France, the Netherlands, England, and Bohemia, the Calvinist movement developed in a revolutionary direction.[10] In those cases where the militant Calvinists won the day (Scotland, the Netherlands, and England), they proceeded to implement a radical and far-reaching reform of social life. Unlike the Catholics and Lutherans, who were mainly interested in enforcing doctrinal and liturgical conformity, the Calvinists

[7] There is an extensive literature on the relationship between religious reform and social disciplining. For an overview, see Ronnie Po-Chia Hsia (1991).

[8] I owe this as well as many other insights to Heinz Schilling, who first raised this point in a seminar on "Confessional Europe," sponsored by the Center for German and European Studies, University of California, Berkeley, in the fall of 1994.

[9] It has become customary among historians and sociologists to contrast Calvinist activism with Lutheran passivity and to locate the origins of this difference in doctrine. Calvinism, it is argued, promoted individualism and resistance to authority whereas Lutheranism instilled corporatism and obedience to authority (see Weber [1920] 1988; Hintze n.d.; Baron 1939; Walzer 1965). This contrast, in my view, is somewhat overdrawn. To begin with, Lutherans were certainly not "passive"—witness the Revolution of 1525, the Revolt of the Imperial Knights, and the Schmalkaldian League. In fact, as Quentin Skinner has clearly shown, the first coherent doctrine of political resistance was actually set forth by Lutheran theologians. Calvinist thinkers such as the Monarchomachs merely took up and elaborated these ideas.

[10] A broad overview of most of these conflicts can be found in Prestwich (1985). The various national literatures are cited in greater detail in the conclusion.

laid particular emphasis on *disciplinas*, the outward conformity of the Christian community with biblical law. The Calvinists instituted a voluntary system of "Christian discipline," in which each congregation policed the morals of its members. Acting in concert with "godly magistrates," they also worked to impose discipline on those outside the church, by establishing new mechanisms of moral regulation and social control. Thus, where Calvinism became the official or dominant confession, it unleashed a veritable *disciplinary revolution* that profoundly transformed state, society, and the relationship between them.

This revolution occurred in three stages. Its origins, of course, lay in Switzerland and, more specifically, in Calvin's Geneva, where religious reform was implemented by urban magistrates in a relatively bloodless—if not altogether peaceful—fashion. From there, Calvinism spread to the territories of northwestern and south-central Europe. Here, Catholic opposition catalyzed violent revolutionary struggles, in which the Calvinist movement sometimes proved victorious (Scotland, the Netherlands, England) and sometimes did not (France, Bohemia, Hungary). Finally, impressed by the political successes of Calvinism, a number of German territorial princes, most notably the Electors of Brandenburg and the Palatinate, introduced Reformed Protestantism against the opposition of the Lutheran clergy and nobility.

The effects of this process were not limited to the Calvinist countries. On the contrary, the disciplinary revolution sent shock waves throughout Europe. It contributed to the emergence of ascetic reform movements within the Lutheran and Catholic churches (for example, Pietism and Jansenism) and stimulated the diffusion of various strategies and techniques of social and moral control, such as the workhouse. More than that, it helped to crystallize a new understanding of politics as "police," that is, as the maintenance of social stability and order. The disciplinary revolution, in short, catalyzed the emergence of both a new "ideal" of the state as well as the institutions through which it could be partially achieved.

Before examining the course of this revolution in greater detail, however, I first review existing work on state-formation, confessionalization, and social disciplining.

Marxist Models: Class Relations or Exchange Relations?

Over the last two decades, sociological analysis of the state has been dominated by two principal perspectives: neo-Marxism and institutionalism. In this section, I begin by briefly reviewing two important neo-Marxist works on early modern state-formation—Perry Anderson's (1979) *Lineages of the Absolutist State* and Immanuel Wallerstein's (1976) *The Modern World System*.

In Anderson's view, the early modern period was an "age of absolutism." The origins of absolutism, he argues, lie in the "crisis of feudalism" that overtook western Europe in the fourteenth century, as oversettlement and overpopulation began to weaken the grip of the nobility over the land. At the same time, the re-vival of commerce gave rise to a new class of urban merchants, which challenged the nobility's monopoly on political power (1979). The twin threats of peasant unrest in the countryside and merchant dominance in the cities drove the west-ern European nobility into the arms of the crown. In Spain, France, England, and Austria, a series of "new monarchs" enhanced their power by entering into an alliance with the nobility against the peasants and merchants. It was this al-liance, Anderson argues, that provided the social foundation of absolutism. The absolutist state was, in his phrase, "a redeployed and recharged apparatus of feu-dal domination."[11] In eastern Europe, socioeconomic conditions were quite different: unsettled areas remained plentiful, the population sparse, the towns weak. It was not an indigenous crisis that toppled the feudal order, but an exog-enous threat—the military threat posed by west European absolutism. To meet this threat, eastern rulers were compelled to construct standing armies and cen-tralized extractive apparatuses to finance them. But because the peasantry and merchant classes were weaker and less able to resist the absolutist onslaught, absolutism took a particularly "harsh" and "despotic" form in eastern Europe. Whereas in western Europe, absolutism merely compensated the nobility for its declining social power, in eastern Europe, it actually strengthened the social position of the nobility, through the imposition of the second serfdom. Thus, despite the mediating role he ascribes to international military competition, Anderson explains early modern state-formation in primarily socioeconomic terms. "In the last instance," he insists, state structure is determined by the mode of production and the patterns of class relations that result from it.

For Immanuel Wallerstein, exchange relations rather than class relations are primary. A state's structure, he argues, corresponds to its location within the global ecology of production, the "capitalist world system" that first emerges in the early modern period. This system of exchange relations is divided into three major zones: core, periphery, and semiperiphery. In the economically advanced "core," which controls the "terms of trade," there arise "strong states," possess-ing "a strong state machinery coupled with a national culture" and serving the interests of the dominant merchant classes (1974: 349). In the economically back-ward "periphery," which serves as a source of raw materials and corvée labor for the "core," states are "weak," that is, lacking in organization and autonomy, and even the dominant classes are subordinated to their imperial overlords. Between the core and the periphery lies the "semiperiphery," a liminal area inhabited by rising and falling states and controlled by social classes in decline or state-building elites on the make. Wallerstein explains state development in terms of the following causal chain: varying roles in the world economy "le[a]d to differ-ent class structures which le[a]d to different polities" (157).

---

[11] Anderson (1979: 18) thus rejects the traditional Marxist interpretation of absolutism, first set forth by Engels, as a balancing act between the bourgeoisie and the aristocracy.

Institutionalist Explanations: The "Fiscal-Military Model"

In contrast to the Marxists, the institutionalists view international military competition as the main driving force behind state-formation. Institutionalists take Marxists to task on two counts. First, they object that Marxist stage theories, in which economic development and state development move together in lockstep, ignore that "many different kinds of states were viable at different stages of European history," a charge to which Anderson seems particularly susceptible.[12] Second, they argue that a monadic emphasis on socioeconomic development within states overlooks the significance of military competition between states, an omission that is particularly glaring in Wallerstein's work.[13] Recent formulations of the institutionalist approach thus have tried to account for the full range of variation in early modern "state structure and strength" and to incorporate both socioeconomic and geopolitical "variables" in their explanatory accounts by focusing on the interaction between economic development and military mobilization, an approach that one scholar has aptly dubbed the "fiscal-military model" (Ertman 1997). In this section, I review two versions of this model, Charles Tilly's (1990) *Coercion, Capital, and European States* and Brian Downing's (1992) *The Military Revolution and Political Change*.

Tilly explicitly sets out to synthesize institutionalist and Marxist models of state development. He begins by reaffirming the institutionalist tenet that "war drives state-formation and transformation," but he argues that levels of economic development crucially affect strategies of military mobilization (1990: 20). Variations in state structure, he contends, thus are best explained by the *interaction* between military competition and economic development. Where resources are scarce—that is, in economically backward areas—they must be extracted directly from the population through centralized, extractive and administrative apparatuses. Where resources are plentiful—that is, in economically advanced areas—rulers can obtain resources by making "compacts with capitalists" (30). Some states—the strongest ones—succeed in combining the advantages of economic development (plentiful resources) with those of administra-

[12] Tilly (1990: 7). Anderson simply ignores that some early modern states, such as Switzerland, the Netherlands, Scotland, England, and Poland, did not develop into absolute monarchies in the first place. In all these countries, monarchical authority was supplanted or strongly limited by the power of representative institutions. Anderson's efforts to explain—or rather explain away—these cases are ad hoc and unsatisfactory. For example, Anderson argues that in England absolutism was stillborn due to an "early bourgeois revolution" and "brought on aristocratic particularism and clannic desperation on its periphery" (1974: 142). He suspends judgment on the Polish case until better scholarship is available and simply excludes the other constitutional regimes from consideration.

[13] In fairness to Wallerstein, it should be emphasized that he does not advance an explanation of state formation per se. He merely offers a general model of capitalist development that purports, among other things, to account for basic variations in state structure. To suggest therefore that his entire theory of the world system is invalidated by its failures on this particular front is therefore logically fallacious. At most, the institutionalist critiques of world systems theory merely point up the limitations of Wallerstein's model. See especially Skocpol (1976).

tive centralization (effective extraction). Tilly therefore sees three main paths to state-formation: "coercion-intensive," "capital-intensive," and "capitalized-co-ercion," which correspond historically to three different types of states: "tribute-taking empires," "territorially fragmented" states, and "national-states." In the end, he argues, only the latter was able to withstand the heat of military competition. Thus, Tilly aims to set forth a general explanation for the rise of the modern nation-state.

Brian Downing pursues a somewhat different (if no less ambitious) explanatory end. Following in Barrington Moore's footsteps, he seeks to locate the "origins of dictatorship and democracy." He traces the roots of "modern liberal democracy" to "medieval constitutionalism," the tradition of "local government . . . , parliamentary bodies, and the rule of law" common to most of Europe (1992: 27). In some countries, constitutionalism survived, providing the foundation for democratization. In others, it perished, clearing the path to autocracy. The key turning point, Downing argues, was the "military revolution" of the sixteenth century, which led to the creation of standing mercenary armies. Raising and supporting these armies placed enormous fiscal pressures on early modern rulers. Where they sought to mobilize the necessary resources domestically, as in France and Brandenburg–Prussia, the representative institutions of the *Ständestaat* were destroyed and replaced with a centralized bureaucracy under royal control. The result was "military-bureaucratic absolutism." Where rulers were sheltered from the military revolution by geography, as in England, or found other means for mobilizing resources (for example, capital markets or military conquest), constitutional arrangements were left intact, providing the institutional base for democratization in the nineteenth century. States such as Poland, which simply ignored the imperatives of international military competition, were conquered and destroyed. Thus, concludes Downing, the origins of "dictatorship and democracy" were not so much social as political. They lay in varying national responses to the military revolution.

The fiscal-military model thus distinguishes two basic outcomes: "coercion-intensive" versus "capital-intensive" (Tilly) or "military-bureaucratic" versus "constitutionalist" (Downing) or, more simply, absolutist and nonabsolutist. The problem with this typology is that it is historically and theoretically underspecified. In Tilly's analysis, for instance, a wide variety of nonabsolutist political formations—city-states (Venice), urban leagues (the Hansa), and confederal states (the Dutch republic)—are all lumped together under the rubric "capital intensive." Similarly, Downing groups together all those states in which the basic elements of "medieval constitutionalism"—representative assemblies, local government, and rule of law—withstood the assaults of centralizing monarchs. This category includes states that differed substantially in both structure and strength—for example, Poland's neofeudal "Republic of Nobles," Sweden's conquest-driven military empire, and the republican regime of the northern Netherlands. Hence, although Tilly and Downing do a good job of explaining absolutist versus nonabsolutist outcomes, they do not discriminate between, much less explain, the various types of nonabsolutist ("capital-intensive," "constitutionalist") states. The fiscal military model leaves a great deal of "unexplained variance."

Marxist and Institutionalist Models: Some Historical "Anomalies"

It would be unfair—and even methodologically suspect—to reject the Marxist and institutionalist models based on the criticisms outlined above.[14] Most explanations in the social sciences omit certain causally relevant factors and/or fail to explain some cases fully. Simply because a model is incomplete does not mean that it is false. The only fair test of a model's empirical adequacy is whether it fully explains those outcomes that it regards, for whatever reasons, as most important.[15] In this section, I subject the Marxist and institutionalist models of early modern state-formation to just such a test. I try to show that even the most fully developed and clearly specified versions of these models (that is, Wallerstein's and Downing's) are inadequate on their own terms, that they fail to account fully or convincingly for just those cases they claim to explain best.

For Wallerstein, the key cases are the "strong core states" of the early modern world—the Netherlands and England. These are precisely the cases that presented the greatest challenge to earlier Marxist models, such as Anderson's, and it is to Wallerstein's credit that he squarely addressed this "anomaly" in his work. He insists, quite correctly, that these states were "strong," that is, they were able to maintain order internally and project power externally. At the same time though, he acknowledges that they were relatively "liberal," that is, they lacked the centralized administrative apparatus typical of absolutist monarchies. Clearly, there is something of a riddle here, but Wallerstein simply tries to finesse it. He asserts, somewhat confusingly, that these states possessed a "strong state machinery" and a "unified national culture" without telling us what this "machinery" consisted of or where this "national culture" came from. In short, Wallerstein does not tell us how state strength was related to state structure. Given that the "core states" were quite decentralized and possessed relatively feeble administrative apparatuses, what was it that made them so strong?

The key case for Downing—and perhaps the paradigmatic one for the fiscal-military model in general—is Brandenburg–Prussia.[16] Nowhere else in early modern Europe was constitutionalism so completely dismantled and royal administration so thoroughly bureaucratized (Gorski 1995). Following earlier institutionalist accounts of Prussian state-building,[17] Downing emphasizes the reign

---

[14] For a critique of falsificationist methodology in social science, see Gorski (1994a).

[15] For a more extensive statement of the method of "fair causal comparison" employed here, see Miller (1987, esp. chap. 5).

[16] The institutionalist tradition originated in the work of Otto Hintze and the historians of the "Prussian School," and the case of Brandenburg-Prussia continues to be central to institutionalist work on state-formation. Tilly, for example, argues that "the later history of Prussia illustrates the process by which national states are formed" (1990: 22). Downing, too, opens the empirical segment of his book with a case study of Prussian absolutism (1992: chap. 3).

[17] The classic statements of this thesis are Carsten (1954) and Rosenberg (1966).

of Frederick William (1640–1688), a period during which Prussia was involved in a series of intense and protracted military conflicts. And indeed it was the "Great Elector," as he is known to posterity, who established Prussia's first standing army and founded the General War Commissary (*General Kriegskommissariat*), the organizational node around which the Prussian central administration later crystallized.[18]

Yet as most historians agree, the decisive phase of Prussian state-building actually came later, during the reign of Frederick William I (1713–1740), Frederick William's grandson.[19] It was the "soldier-king" (*Soldatenkönig*) who transformed Prussia's ramshackle mercenary force into one of the largest and most disciplined armies in Europe.[20] And he engineered the expansion of the Prussian civil service centralization into a single fiscal and administrative agency, the General Superior Finance War and Domains Commissary (*General Ober-Finanz-Kriegs und Domänenrat*). By the end of Frederick William I's reign, Prussia had the largest standing army in Europe, relative to its population, and arguably the most centralized and efficient administrative system (Gorski 1993a: 295–99). Yet there is an unmistakable irony here, for this unprecedented mobilization for war occurred during a period of relative peace. In fact, Frederick William I never led his much-vaunted regiments into battle. Thus, although his policies were clearly oriented toward preparation for war, they were not directly driven by participation in war. Of course, one might still argue that Frederick William I's reforms were driven by the *threat* of war. But this does not explain why he, unlike many other rulers, was so quick to respond to this threat. The timing of Prussian state-building, then, remains something of a conundrum for the institutionalist model.[21] For if bureaucratization was not directly stimulated by war, then what was the proximate cause?

Thus, both world systems theory and the fiscal-military model fail to explain fully those cases they purport to explain best. Important as capitalist development and military mobilization were in determining the "structure" and

[18] Structuralists have tended to exaggerate the historical significance of these events. The army was still small (5000 men) at this time, and the "bureaucracy" tiny (at one point, it had only one member). As Gawthrop convincingly argued (1993), there was as yet little difference between Prussia and other German principalities. See also Gorski (1994b).

[19] A clear and compact overview of the subject can be found in Neugebauer (1981). The classic studies of Prussian political development during the eighteenth century are Hintze (1901) and Bornhak (1884–1886). On administrative reforms under Frederick William I, see especially Breysig (1892).

[20] The seminal work on the development of the Prussian army is Büsch (1962).

[21] Eighteenth century Prussia might nonetheless seem to offer powerful confirmation for another central tenet of institutionalism: that state strength derived, above all, from administrative and political centralization, from the creation of a strong central bureaucracy and the destruction of representative institutions. But if we look further east, this thesis too appears questionable. Petrine Russia exhibited a degree of administrative centralization similar to that in Prussia; indeed, its administrative system was modeled after Prussia's. Moreover, Russia was even more politically centralized than Prussia, lacking as it did any tradition of representative government above the village level. Yet no one would argue that Peter the Great's Russia was as strong as Frederick the Great's Prussia. On the contrary, Peter's administration was as notorious for its corruption and inefficiency as Frederick's was legendary for its probity and diligence.

"strength" of early modern states—and their importance is not at issue here—they evidently do not by themselves suffice to explain certain basic features of the cases in question. The missing factor in these accounts, in my view, is religion and, more specifically, confessionalization. But before spelling out in greater detail how confessionalization affected early modern state-formation, I first specify more clearly just what it is that the Marxist and institutionalist alternatives leave unexplained—and indeed untheorized.

State Power: Extensive Versus Intensive

The various models reviewed here differ substantially in *how* they explain early modern state-formation, that is, which causal factors they see as decisive. But they differ relatively little in *what* they are trying to explain, that is, in their understanding of the state as a theoretical object. This is evident in the fact that both Marxists and institutionalists categorize outcomes in terms of the same criteria: regime structure, that is, which social groups control the state, and administrative structure, that is, the centralized organizational means by which control is exercised. Of course, Marxists tend to stress the former, institutionalists the latter. But the difference is mainly one of emphasis. For example, administrative centralization figures prominently in both Anderson's and Wallerstein's partition of outcomes—more versus less "despotic" forms of absolutism and "stronger" versus "weaker" states. By the same token, regime structure is implicit in Tilly's distinction between coercion-intensive (noble) states and capital-intensive (bourgeois) ones, and even to some degree in Downing's contrast between absolutist and constitutionalist states. This is not to deny that there are significant differences between the two approaches. Marxists and institutionalists disagree sharply as to who "really" controls the state—social classes or administrative elites[22]—as the ongoing debate over state "autonomy" makes quite clear. But behind this vocal dispute over where state power is located lies a tacit consensus about what this power consists of, for both Marxists and institutionalists understand state power primarily as control over territory and resources. Accordingly, they conceptualize state-formation in similar terms, as the monopolization and centralization of political control or, to use Michael Mann's terminology, the growth of "extensive power."

This understanding of state-formation is not "false," but it is one-sided, for it ignores—indeed, is blind to—the development of *intensive* state power, the growing capacity of states to mobilize human resources and regulate populations.[23] To put it differently, Marxist and institutionalist approaches fail to consider—or even theorize—two critical determinants of state strength: (1) *ide-*

---

[22] For a penetrating analysis and comparison of the various theories of the state, see Alford and Friedland (1985).

[23] On extensive versus intensive forms of state power, see Mann (1984–93: esp. vol. 1, 7–10, and more generally vol. 2, chap. 3).

ological infrastructure, that is, the availability of symbols and identities through which rulers can mobilize the energies and harness the loyalties of their staffs and subjects and (2) *administrative infrastructure*, that is, the existence of networks and organizations through which state administrators can penetrate into everyday life and regulate individual conduct.

This omission is all the more serious, since it is precisely the combination of extensive and intensive power that distinguishes the modern nation-state from earlier forms of state organization. Tribute-taking empires, for example, controlled enormous amounts of territory and resources, but they generally lacked the capacity to mobilize human resources and regulate populations. Conversely, city-states possessed the capacity to mobilize human resources and regulate populations, but as a rule they controlled relatively small amounts of territory and resources.[24] It was the nation-state, as it developed in western Europe, that first fused the extensive power of empires with the intensive power of cities.

Of course, neither the Dutch republic nor Hohenzollern Prussia was a modern nation-state. But both possessed infrastructures that were unusually strong for their day and that exerted strong "demonstration effects" in both the old and new worlds. Indeed, they gave birth to organizational technologies without which the modern nation-state would be unthinkable. It was in the Dutch republic that modern techniques of social and military discipline were invented, and it was in Brandenburg–Prussia that a fully bureaucratic system of state administration first made its appearance. Moreover, it was in the Dutch republic and Brandenburg–Prussia that two elements of the modern political ethos— nationalism and statism—first arose, albeit in highly nascent forms. Thus, more than mere "anomalies" or "outliers," the Dutch republic and Brandenburg– Prussia were actually pivotal cases in the development of the modern nation-state.

I now turn to a more general discussion of the confessionalization paradigm and its significance for early modern historiography.

Rethinking the Reformation: Religion and Politics in the "Confessional Age"

Over the last several decades, Reformation historiography has undergone a major transformation. Traditionally, accounts of the Reformation began with Luther's Ninety-five Theses (1517) and concluded with the Peace of Augsburg (1555).[25] Recent accounts have adopted a very different periodization, however,

---

[24] Of course, the most successful empires sometimes built up substantial infrastructural powers by co-opting indigenous elites and "colonizing" the institutions of conquered peoples. By the same token, the most successful city-states sometimes attained control over fairly large amounts of the surrounding hinterlands. (Thus, during the sixteenth century, the city-state of Bern controlled more territory than some of the smaller German principalities.)

[25] This periodization was first set forth in von Ranke (1852).

dividing the Reformation into three overlapping segments: (1) a diffuse "evangelical movement" (ca. 1517–1525), which advocated religious reform based on the Gospels, often with strong social and political overtones; (2) a "reformation from above" (*obrigkeitliche Reformation*) (ca. 1520–1545), in which the "civil authorities" effected various liturgical and ecclesiastical reforms; and (3) a "confessional age" (ca. 1540–1648), in which the construction of "national" or territorial churches and "wars of belief" reinforced and drove one another forward.[26] Behind the new periodization lies a revised understanding of the dynamics of the Reformation. Traditional accounts tended to see the Reformation in strictly religious or even theological terms, tracing its origins to the corruption of the Catholic Church and its outbreak to the mass appeal of Luther's teachings. By contrast, recent scholarship, strongly influenced by social history and historical sociology, has attempted to set the Reformation within a wider context, emphasizing the importance of social factors in its reception and of political factors in its propagation. In short, they have tried to understand how the Reformation stimulated and interacted with other historical processes, such as the expansion of commercial capitalism and the formation of the early modern state. It is this latter connection that is of particular interest here.

Confessionalization, Social Disciplining, and State-Formation

In recent years, the relationship between confessionalization and state-formation in early modern Europe has been explicitly taken up by an increasing number of Reformation historians.[27] Church-building, they point out, required state support. The clergy lacked the power to suppress sectarian movements or discipline recalcitrant clergy by themselves. Only with strong backing from state elites could they impose a uniform set of religious beliefs and practices on the populace. The civil authorities, for their part, were generally happy to cooperate in this endeavor. They were invariably alarmed by the appearance of "heretics" and "sectarians." From their perspective, religious uniformity provided the best foundation for political stability. In the phrase of the age, "religion is the bond which holds society together" (*religio vincula societatis*).

The creation of territorial churches also enhanced state power. It did so, most obviously, by greatly increasing the authority of the state over the church. In Lutheran territories, the church came under the de facto control of the ruler in his capacity as "emergency bishop." In Calvinist territories, the church had greater autonomy, but representatives of the magistrate generally sat in the "consistories," the boards of church "elders" that governed each congregation. And even in Catholic territories, where the authority of Rome was maintained, rulers expanded their control over clerical appointments and often established royal

[26] On recent developments in Reformation historiography, see Klueting (1989) and Goertz (1987). On issues of periodization, see Zeeden (1977, 1983) and especially Schilling (1988b).

[27] The most important figure here is Schilling (1981).

agencies to oversee the church administration. Finally, the seizure of church property in Protestant territories filled state coffers.

The church also played a critical mediating role in the project of "social disciplining," the ambitious attempts of the state to control everyday life (Monter 1987). The early modern period witnessed a veritable flood of legislation regulating everything from the rations allowed the poor to the clothing permitted the rich (Raeff 1983). But rulers lacked the administrative capacities to enforce these rules. It was here that the church proved crucial. As Heinz Schilling has aptly put it: "Driven by confessional zeal, the Lutheran pastors, the spiritual counselors of the Tridentine clergy, and Calvinist elders and ministers became . . . the most important mediators of the new moral-ethical and political-legal system of norms. Through domestic counseling (*Hausbesuche*), church visitations, ecclesiastical discipline, church discipline and episcopal justice (*Episkopalgerichtsbarkeit*), they monitored and disciplined everyday life-conduct, penetrating into the last house in the most isolated little village" (1988a: 369, my translation).

Moreover, religious reform broke down barriers to social reform. Attempts to rationalize and centralize urban poor relief had long been opposed by the Catholic Church and especially by the various mendicant orders for over a century. By desanctifying the poor and dissolving the monasteries, the Reformation cleared the way for a thoroughgoing reorganization of inequitable and inefficient systems of poor relief. Beginning in the 1520s, cities throughout Europe issued new poor-relief ordinances, which gave urban magistrates greater control over the dispensation of alms and discriminated between the "truly deserving poor"—the young, the old, the infirm—and "the able-bodied poor," providing aid to the former and setting the latter to work.[28] Another area of reform was education. In Protestant regions, elementary schools were created for the poor and the popular classes to enable them to read the Bible. In Catholic regions, special academies were founded, especially by the Jesuits, to educate members of the upper classes. And throughout Europe, university education was expanded to improve the quality of the clergy. Finally, Catholic and Protestant churches alike sought to tighten and enforce rules governing sexuality and marriage. Marriage ordinances were promulgated publicly, and for the first time baptisms and marriages were recorded in church and parish registers.[29] In all these areas—poor relief, education, and the regulation of sexuality and marriage—cooperation between the religious and civil authorities was generally tight. In fact, in most early modern polities, it would have been difficult to draw a clear line between "church" and "state." And in a world where princes served as bishops, bishops as princes, magistrates as elders, and elders as magistrates, such a distinction would only have been anachronistic. Not only had the medieval symbiosis between the "two swords" persisted, it had grown tighter. But instead of

[28] A recent survey of the literature on this subject is Jütte (1994).
[29] Important recent research in this area includes Ingram (1987) and Roper (1989).

having two centers—the papacy and the empire—it now had many. In the long run, however, this symbiosis proved more beneficial to one party than the other: ultimately, it was the state that monopolized control over the new infrastructures of power—the prisons and workhouses, the schools and universities, the law and the courts.

Calvinism and Social Disciplining

Processes of social disciplining such as those just described occurred throughout "confessional Europe." But they were especially intense in Reformed polities. This is because of the peculiar emphasis that Reformed Protestantism placed on *disciplinas*, the outward conformity of the Christian community with biblical law. Of course, *self*-discipline was a central element of the "Protestant ethic." Calvin viewed the growth of "voluntary" and "inward" obedience to the law as a key sign of spiritual election. And his followers invented a variety of techniques for internalizing and maintaining self-discipline, for example, keeping moral logbooks in which they dutifully charted their spiritual progress or adhering to rigid daily schedules that minimized opportunities for sinning.[30] But when Calvin and other Reformed theologians spoke of "discipline," they meant ecclesiastical discipline, not individual discipline. The ideal of *disciplinas*, to be sure, was not unique to Calvinism. The Lutheran and Catholic churches espoused it as well, particularly with regard to dogma. But the Reformed system of discipline was unusual, both because it focused mainly on conduct, especially social conduct, and because it established a set of formal rules and mechanisms for enforcing congregational discipline at the congregational level. The Calvinist disciplinary project was not, however, limited solely to the church proper. On the contrary, Calvin and his followers aimed at nothing less than the creation of a *respublica christiana*, in which church and state would work hand in hand to impose godly law on the political community as a whole. To this end, they extended the disciplinary strategies pioneered in the Reformed church to a wide range of public institutions—to schools, orphanages, poorhouses, and even the army. The result was a thoroughgoing disciplinization of social life, a veritable disciplinary revolution that gave rise to powerful new forms of social control and political domination.

Social Disciplining and State-Formation

Of course, the thesis that social discipline was critical to state-formation is not entirely novel. It has been advanced, most notably, by Gerhard Oestreich, Michel Foucault, and Norbert Elias. It was in fact Oestreich, an Austrian historian, who first coined the term "social disciplining" (*Sozialdisziplinierung*).[31] He under-

---

[30] See Hill (1967) and Cohen (1986).

[31] Unfortunately, Oestreich's work remains little known in the Anglo-American world, except among Reformation scholars, despite the translation of his most important essays into English.

stood it as a top-down process, in which the state—that is, the absolutist state—"molded, directed and regimented the attitudes and actions of individuals, even of the simplest subjects" (Oestreich 1968: 168, my translation). Discipline, in this account, was something that the ruling classes imposed on the common people as part of an overarching political project. Foucault (1980, 1990), by contrast, understood disciplining as a diffuse, decentralized process in which certain basic "strategies" (for example, panopticism) are replicated and applied within a widening variety of institutional fields. By creating polymorphous mechanisms of social control that subsequently could be appropriated by dominant elites, argues Foucault, the diffusion of disciplinary techniques laid the "micropolitical" foundations for the "grand strategy" of the modern state. Elias (1976) takes another approach and views disciplining as a social-psychological process in which the regulation of drives and affects becomes internalized in the individual. Historically, he argues, "civility" spread from the aristocracy to the middle classes and helped create "pacified populations" more susceptible to control by a centralized administrative apparatus (Elias 1969; see also Giddens 1987).

All of these analyses are, in my view, too unidimensional. Oestreich tends to see disciplining in solely instrumental terms, as a form of domination. Elias, on the other hand, rightly underlines the normative component of social disciplining, but he reduces it to the individual level, to self-discipline. Foucault, meanwhile, rightly perceives the connection between self-discipline and political domination, but ignores the normative bases of discipline and overlooks how "ideal interests" play in its propagation. And all three theorists fail to recognize the critical role that religious ideals, elites, and institutions played in the disciplining process.

A general theory of social disciplining, I believe, must take account of both the normative and strategic dimensions of social disciplining as well as its individual, institutional, and societal levels. Discipline is embodied in individual practices, which are constituted by disciplinary ethics and techniques. Disciplinary ethics prescribe the control of drives and affects and the systematic channeling of psychic energies toward the realization of ideal interests. Disciplinary techniques consist of the psychological strategies and physical operations through which discipline is maintained. These practices are instilled and reproduced within definite institutional fields, constituted by disciplinary codes and strategies.[32] The codes specify, usually in written form, a general set of behavioral norms and standards, and the strategies are ways of organizing physical space and social positions so as to facilitate monitoring and surveillance. These fields are imposed and legitimated within institutional regimes, which are constituted by disciplinary ideologies and carrier groups. The ideologies posit a link between institutionalized discipline and various moral or social goods—for example, order and efficiency. The carriers are social groups whose claims to status and strategies of domination are based on social discipline. These three levels of discipline

---

[32] I use these terms in much the same sense as does Bourdieu.

may also be understood as three phases in the process of disciplining: the disciplining of the self, the institutionalization of discipline, and the imposition of a disciplinary regime.

This is how the disciplinary revolution unfolded in theory. But how did it occur in practice?

The Disciplinary Revolution: From Geneva to Berlin and Beyond

The Calvinist disciplinary revolution occurred in three phases. It began in the city-states of Switzerland and Lower Germany (ca. 1520–1560)—for example, Zürich, Bern, Strasbourg, and Geneva. It then spread, mainly through Geneva, to the *Ständestaaten* of western and south-central Europe (ca. 1550–1590). And from western Europe, it penetrated, finally, into the heartland of the Lutheran Reformation, Germany itself (ca. 1580–1615).

Reformed confessionalization assumed a somewhat different form in each of these contexts, imparting a distinctive dynamic to the disciplining process. In the Swiss and lower German city-states, where the Reformed church had a broad popular base and strong elite support, social discipline was imposed by the local churches in close cooperation with the urban magistrates.[33] The most important example of this pattern was Geneva.[34] By the time of Calvin's (first) arrival in 1536, the process of religious reform in Geneva was already well under way. But Calvin and several other more zealous members of the clergy were dissatisfied with the discipline of the church. They called for the creation of an independent church consistory that would have full authority over ecclesiastical discipline. This proposal met with considerable resistance from the Genevan magistrate, protective of its newly won powers over the church, and Calvin eventually was forced to leave the city. But Calvin was not without his supporters, and his departure sparked considerable unrest. In 1540, a purged and chastened magistrate voted to reinstate him. Calvin agreed to return to Geneva (he had since taken up residence in Strasbourg), but only on the condition he be allowed to draft a new set of church ordinances. The magistrate consented, albeit reluctantly, and in 1541, Calvin's *Ordonnances ecclésiastiques* became law.[35] In them, Calvin outlined the system of ecclesiastical discipline that became the hallmark of the Genevan church and eventually served as a blueprint for Reformed churches throughout Europe. The heart of this system—an elaboration of the earlier reform proposal—was the consistory, a special church body composed of the pastorate together with a body of lay "elders" chosen from the ranks of the magistrate. The principal task of the consistory was to enforce congregational discipline—

---

[33] On Zürich, see Locher (1982). On Basel, see Durr (1921–1950). On Konstanz, see Dobras (1993).

[34] Literature and an overview can be found in Lewis in Prestwich (1985: 39–70) and Naphy (1994).

[35] The ordinances of 1541 are translated and reprinted in Calvin (1971: 229–44).

by interviewing prospective church members, visiting parishioners in their homes, and, most important, reprimanding notorious sinners.[36] A summons before the consistory was a serious matter in Geneva. Even a mild offense usually resulted in a stern tongue-lashing, and serious offenses could lead to public exclusion from communion or even to complete excommunication from the church. Individuals who ran afoul of the consistory were also likely to face other sanctions. If the offense were civil in nature—and in this age of "good police," most "sins" were also "crimes"—they could be tried before the Genevan magistrate. Even if the offense were purely religious, it could result in social sanctions of various kinds—diminished marriage prospects, the loss of business connections, exclusion from a trade, even social ostracism and physical violence. The Genevan consistory, then, was tightly intertwined with traditional mechanisms of social control and was merely the hub of an extensive web of moral surveillance that penetrated deeply into all aspects of life. Some observers even compared it to the Catholic Inquisition. Suggestive as it is, however, this juxtaposition is highly misleading. For the primary purpose of religious discipline, as Calvin understood it and the Genevan church practiced it, was neither to enforce the uniformity of religious belief nor to punish individuals for their sins, but rather to safeguard the moral purity of the church as a whole. Indeed, Calvin and his followers drew a sharp distinction between "private" and "public" sins, between sins known only to a few people and sins known to the general public. Only the latter were objects of ecclesiastical discipline *stricto sensu*, for only they were seen as threats to the collective morality and public standing of the church. The attention of the Genevan consistory accordingly tended to focus not simply on moral misconduct per se but on social misconduct, on offenses that endangered the social order in one way or another—on drunkenness and fighting, wife-beating and adultery, theft and financial impropriety. In Calvin's Geneva, then, religious discipline was first and foremost social discipline. Given this fact, however, the process of social disciplining had surprisingly little effect on the basic structure of social institutions in Geneva. To be sure, Calvin and his followers did undertake a number of important reforms, particularly in the areas of public education and poor relief.[37] They established a more rigorous course of religious instruction in the public schools, and they set stricter standards for the dispensation of public aid. But they did not break new ground in this area—in fact, the Genevan reforms were actually similar to ones introduced elsewhere, particularly in the Lutheran city-states of southern Germany.[38] Reversing the earlier formulation, then, one might also say that social discipline in Calvin's Geneva was first and foremost religious discipline.

[36] Much has been written on the organization and operation of the Genevan consistory. The definitive account, which places Geneva within a wider context, is Köhler (1932–1942). The best short treatment is still Kingdon (1972a).

[37] On this subject, see particularly Kingdon (1972b).

[38] On the south German reforms, see especially Winckelmann (1914–1915).

It was in the *Ständestaaten* of northwestern and south-central Europe that techniques of religious discipline were first used as a basis for social institutions.[39] As in the Swiss city-states, social discipline was imposed primarily by the church consistories in close cooperation with the local governments, but on a territorial basis rather than a civic one.

The Netherlands provides a particularly clear example of this pattern.[40] Here, as elsewhere, the spread of Reformed Protantism was closely intertwined with resistance to monarchical authority. Strapped for cash to finance their military exploits in southern Europe, the Habsburgs demanded ever-larger financial contributions from the Netherlands and repeatedly sought to seize control of the purse strings from the States General in Brussels. The simmering conflict between crown and estates was brought to a boil during the 1550s by the efforts of Philipp II to suppress Dutch Protestantism, and it erupted into open revolt during the 1560s after Calvinist radicals embarked on a spree of image-breaking, the so-called iconoclastic fury.[41] Following William the Silent's "liberation" of the northern Netherlands from Habsburg control during the 1570s, Reformed Protestantism was declared the official faith of the Dutch republic. Initially, membership in the Reformed Church remained quite low—perhaps around 20 percent in the cities and probably no more than 10 percent.[42] By the 1620s, however, Calvinists were clearly in the majority in most parts of the Netherlands and overwhelmingly so in some areas of the north and east. And while the Reformed church never achieved a complete monopoly over religious life in the Netherlands, it did subject the majority of the population to a Genevan-style system of ecclesiastical discipline.[43] Of course, only church members were subject to ecclesiastical discipline. And relations between the church consistories and the local magistrates were not always harmonious, especially in the provinces of Holland and Utrecht.[44]

But if the impact of Reformed discipline on social life was more superficial in the Netherlands than in Geneva, its impact on social institutions was considerably more profound. For it was in the Dutch republic—and in northwestern Europe more generally—that Reformed techniques of mutual surveillance were first transformed into generalized strategies of social control. Although there are many illustrations of this transformation in the Netherlands, one of the most striking—and certainly the most famous—is the Amsterdam *Tuchthuis* or "House of Discipline."[45] Located, appropriately enough, in a former cloister, the *Tuchthuis* was a sort of all-purpose correctional institution, whose purpose

---

[39] For brief case studies and additional literature, see Prestwich (1985).

[40] The best survey in English is Israel (1995). In Dutch, see Groenveld et al. (1991).

[41] The best survey of the Dutch Revolt in any language is Parker (1988).

[42] On the "protestantization" of the Dutch populace, see especially Rogier (1945–1946) and, from a quantitative point of view, de Kok (1964).

[43] On ecclesiastical discipline in the Dutch Reformed Church, see especially Van Deursen ([1979] 1991) and Roodenburg (1990).

[44] On the "religious quarrels," see especially Kaplan (1995) and Nobbs (1938).

[45] The best study of the Amsterdam *Tuchthuis* is Sellen (1944).

was to reform layabouts and ne'er-do-wells of all stripes, from the petty vagrant to the dissolute burgher, through a regime of hard physical labor and unremitting moral supervision. Those who resisted this regimen were punished—not arbitrarily or aimlessly, but systematically and with a clear pedagogical intent. Runaways, for example, were forced to wear a ball and chain, whereas ruffians were put in stocks and the foulmouthed were fitted with gags. The harshest punishment of all, however, was reputedly reserved for the indolent.[46] They were given a hand pump and placed in the "drowning tank," a special cell that gradually filled with water. In this way, even the most stubborn inmates quickly learned the value of work. The influence of the Amsterdam *Tuchthuis* was immense. It was a "must see" for all visitors to the city and served as a model for correctional institutions in the Netherlands and throughout Europe.[47] Indeed, it would be no great exaggeration to say that the foundation of the Amsterdam *Tuchthuis* marks the birth of the modern prison.

The Dutch also applied techniques of mutual surveillance to the field of military organization.[48] The key figures in this process were Maurice of Orange, the stadholder and captain-general of the Netherlands, and Simon Stevin, a Dutch mathematician and engineer. Drawing their inspiration from the Ancient Romans, they introduced a series of radical and innovative military reforms, including, most notably: (1) a new form of encampment, in which each soldier was assigned a specific bunk, an officer was assigned to each tent, and the command post was situated in the center (rather than at the head) of the camp, thus allowing for top-down surveillance; and (2) the use of drills, in which the soldiers were taught to march in lines and to load and fire their weapons in strict sequence, thus making it possible for Dutch regiments to deliver an uninterrupted volley of gunfire—the so-called countermarch. The contribution these reforms made to Dutch military successes against the Spanish was probably minimal—the Eighty Years' War was primarily a war of sieges. But their influence on European military history can hardly be overstated. Tours of duty in the Dutch army were avidly sought after, and noblemen and officers from all over Europe came to watch the Orangist regiments perform their drills near the Hague, among them, Frederick William of Hohenzollern, future ruler of Brandenburg–Prussia.[49] The Dutch were widely acknowledged as the leaders in military strategy and organization during the seventeenth century, and, in fact, it would not be entirely farfetched to call Maurice of Orange and Simon Stevin the fathers of modern military discipline.

The Dutch were not the only ones to use mutual surveillance as a tool of social control, however. Similar developments in disciplinary organization may be

[46] Several historians have argued that the drowning cell was a myth. See, for example, Spierenburg (1991). If so, it reflects the intense fear and anxiety that the *Tuchthuis* invoked among the respectable.

[47] On the diffusion of the *Tuchthuis* system throughout the Netherlands, see Hallema (1958) and the numerous articles by Hallema cited therein.

[48] The most comprehensive discussion of the Moritizian reforms is Wijn (1934).

[49] On the influence of the Dutch military reforms, see especially Oestreich (1969).

observed in other Calvinist countries, such as England. In fact, the English developed their own version of the *Tuchthuis*, the so-called Bridewells, quite independently of (and a bit earlier than) the Dutch.[50] And it was Oliver Cromwell who picked up where Maurice and Stevin left off, creating a yet more disciplined military force, the "New Model Army."[51] On the whole, however, the impact of social disciplining on state-formation in these cases was mainly indirect: it forged stable and orderly societies that could be ruled effectively by decentralized and "democratic" states.

It was in the Reformed principalities of Germany that the disciplinary energies of the Calvinist movement were first fully absorbed by the absolutist state.[52] There, social discipline was imposed mainly from the top down by the monarch and his administrative staff with the assistance of the clergy. The most important example of this pattern was Brandenburg–Prussia.[53] Here, as elsewhere in Germany, Reformed Protestantism was introduced from above under the guise of a "Second Reformation." By the early sixteenth century, Reformed Protestantism had won a number of influential converts at the Electoral Court. And in 1613, the Hohenzollern elector, Johann Sigismund, and his closest advisers received communion from a Reformed minister. The Second Reformation was only partially successful in Brandenburg, however. All attempts to impose Reformed Protestantism on a territorial basis met with stiff and determined opposition from the Lutheran clergy and provincial estates.[54] Consequently, the Reformed Church never developed a significant popular following except in the Rhineland provinces. Still, it would be wrong to describe the Second Reformation in Brandenburg as a failure. For if its influence on the general populace was slight, its impact on the ruling house and the royal bureaucracy was considerable. Externally, the confessional switch laid the foundations for an aggressive stance toward the Habsburg Empire and the Catholic Church, which soon made it one of the leading powers in the Protestant world. And internally, it stimulated the development of a loyal and disciplined civil service, whose ethos and "life conduct" were distinctly bourgeois in character—no accident, to be sure, given the predilection of the Hohenzollerns for bourgeois officials. But it was not until the reign of Frederick William I that the seeds planted by Johann Sigismund a century earlier finally came to full fruition.[55] A deeply religious man whom one historian has described as a "Puritan in purple robes," the new king immediately set about reforming the state apparatus from top to bottom. First, he subjected the bureaucracy to a quasimonastic discipline, founded on rigid rules, strict supervision, and promotion by merit. Then, he turned his attention to the army,

[50] On the history of the London Bridewell, see O'Donoghue (1923). On the diffusion of the Bridewell system, see Innes (1987).

[51] On the significance of Puritanism for the Cromwellian reforms, see Firth (1967 [1902]) and, more recently, Gentles (1992: chap. 4). For a skeptical view, see Kishlansky (1979).

[52] On the "second" or Calvinist reformation in Germany, see Press (1970), Verein für Reformationsgeschichte (1985), and Schaab (1993).

[53] On the Second Reformation in Brandenburg-Prussia, see especially Nischan (1994).

[54] On these conflicts, see Gorski (1996a: chap. 3); Landwehr (1894), and Lackner (1973).

[55] On the importance of religion for Frederick William I's administrative, military, and social reforms, see Gorski (1996a: chap. 4), Gawthrop (1993), and Hinrichs (1971).

treating it to an endless barrage of physical blows and moral harangues, often delivered personally. Finally, with the aid of the Pietists, an ascetic reform movement within German Lutheranism, he undertook a sweeping reform of public education, which combined practical training with moral supervision in an effort to produce useful and obedient subjects. The administrative, military, and educational reforms of Frederick William I transformed Brandenburg–Prussia from a backward outpost of the Holy Roman Empire into one of the most powerful states in Europe and the very paradigm of absolutist rule. The secret of this success—or at least one of them—was the application of disciplinary strategies first pioneered within the Reformed church to all areas of social life, a fact that prompted some observers to describe Prussia as the "Sparta of the North." But it was a French diplomat who put it most astutely, when he compared the Prussian state, perhaps unwittingly, to Bentham's panopticon, characterizing it as "a vast prison in the center of which appears the great keeper, occupied in the care of his captives" (cited in Rosenberg 1966: 41). Not everyone reacted so negatively however. In fact, absolutist Prussia provided a model for military and administrative reforms in France, Russia, and even Japan. Indeed, to a considerable extent, the roots of the modern "state idea" may be traced back to nineteenth-century Prussia, to Hegel, von Stein, Schmoller, Hintze, and Weber—all good Prussians. It is in Prussia, then, that the Calvinist disciplinary revolution first broke free of its religious moorings, loosing upon the world a formidable new strategy of political domination now shorn of its moral fetters.

The reverberations of this revolution were felt within the Lutheran and Catholic worlds too, where religious and social reformers raced to impose a discipline of their own.[56] Within the Lutheran countries of northern Europe, the chief instruments of religious discipline were marriage courts (sometimes also called consistories), which prosecuted sexual misconduct of all kinds; church visitations, which punished wayward clerics and laymen; and, somewhat later, Pietist "conventicles," private devotional circles that sought to promote piety and charity among their members.[57] Lutheran princes and magistrates were also quick to adopt the workhouse and other social technologies pioneered by the Calvinists. But they were much slower to copy the strategies of bureaucratic control and military discipline elaborated by the Hohenzollerns—one reason, no doubt, for the eclipse of the Lutheran principalities in the struggle for central European hegemony.[58] Like their Lutheran counterparts, the Catholic countries of the Mediterranean lacked a single, congregational-level mechanism of ecclesiastical discipline such as the consistory. But they developed a variety of "functional equivalents," such as the Inquisition, which gradually shifted its focus from Protestant heretics to unreformed Catholics; the sacrament of confession, which was

---

[56] Instructive overviews can be found in Verein für Reformationsgeschichte (1992), Schilling (1994), and Reinhard and Schilling (1995).

[57] The best works on social disciplining in the Lutheran context are regional and local studies such as Abray (1985), Franz (1971), and Brecht (1967). On Luther's views and practices, see Götze (1959).

[58] For studies of state-formation in Lutheran principalities, see, for example, Vann (1984), and on Hessia, see Hollenberg (1986, 1988) Demandt (1965). Alas, there is no comparable study or series of essays for Saxony.

increasingly used as a means of monitoring and controlling the behavior of the laity; and diocesan synods, regular meetings of the parish clergy that allowed reformist bishops to keep a close eye on the conduct and outlook of their underlings.[59] Many Catholic cities also sought to centralize, rationalize, and secularize their systems of social welfare, so as to deliver more relief to the "deserving" and deny it to the "undeserving."[60] Some even established workhouses. A particularly important role in this process was played by devotional confraternities, many of which dedicated themselves to charity work and the "reform" of the poor.[61] The new ethos of discipline even touched the Catholic ruling strata to a certain degree, as manifested by the proliferation of various upper-class ascetic and devotional movements, such as the Marian congregations.[62] But it does not seem to have had a genuinely transformative effect on administrative elites and state institutions, such as occurred in Prussia.[63]

Of course, it would be wrong to suggest that social disciplining in Lutheran and Catholic countries was a mere by-product of the Calvinist disciplinary revolution. In fact, social disciplining was, to a considerable degree, the result of interconfessional competition, that is, of the confessionalization process as a whole. Nonetheless, it seems clear—at least to me—that the Calvinists were always at the forefront of this competition; that they went further and faster in every regard; and, in short, that they served both as the catalyst and as the "avant-garde" of Europe's disciplinary revolution.

WHILE a great deal of work has been done on confessionalization and social disciplining in early modern Europe, considerably less has been written on confessionalization and collective identity.[64] The following excursus, then, is a somewhat speculative attempt to sketch out the broader connections and to suggest how one might set about studying them in greater detail.

Excursus: Confessionalism and Identity

If we were to look at a political map of pre-Reformation Europe, we would see much that is familiar. Of course, the central north-south axis of the continent

[59] On religious discipline in the Catholic context, see especially the various studies of French dioceses that have appeared over the last three decades: Ferté (1962), Soulet (1974), Châtellier (1981), Sauzet (1979), Pérouas (1964), Luria (1991), and Venard (1993).

[60] The best work on this subject has been done by Italian historians. See especially Pullan (1971), Calori (1972), and the case studies collected in *Timore e carità* (1980). For overviews of the literature, see Pullan (1988: 177–207) and Pastore (1986). On France, the best studies are Gutton (1970) and Dinges (1988).

[61] The Italian confraternities have been particularly well studied. A fine overview can be found in Black (1989). On lay initiatives in France, see especially Rapley (1990).

[62] On this, see especially Châtellier (1989).

[63] The best recent work on state-formation in France is Collins (1995).

[64] To my knowledge, the only systematic discussions of this topic are Armstrong (1982) and Schilling (1991b). There is also some work on the connection between Calvinism and "nationalism" in England and the Netherlands, cited below.

running from the Italian peninsula through Germany to the Rhine delta is still a bewildering patchwork of city-states and principalities (and would remain so until the nineteenth century). But the borders of some countries, such as England, France, and Switzerland, already look quite familiar, whereas the outlines of several others, such as Poland, Hungary, and Denmark, are a good deal larger but not altogether unrecognizable. All that remains to be done is to create a few larger political units in the west and pare down the empires of the east and the north.

Yet reading the map in this way would be to impute a significance to borders that they did not yet have. Pre-Reformation Europe was not a system of nation-states, in which political, linguistic, and cultural boundaries were congruous to any meaningful degree. In fact, the sociocultural structure of Latin Christendom strongly resembles Ernst Gellner's (1983) model of the "agroliterate polity."[65] Like the agrarian empires of antiquity, Latin Christendom was riven by a deep split between the encompassing universalistic culture of the elites and the segmented localistic culture of the popular classes. The elites—the upper strata of the clergy, nobility, and urban patriciate—participated in a truly pan-European culture. They were linked together by complex ties—language (Latin), kinship, and commerce—that spanned political boundaries. Some made peregrinations that would daunt even the most experienced modern traveler. By contrast, the popular classes—the peasantry and the urban laborers—were still deeply embedded in segmented cultures that bore little relationship to political divisions. Not only were the common people excluded from the "high" culture of the elites, they were divided from one another by variations in language, dialect, belief, and custom. Most, in fact, never traveled more than a few miles from their home communities. To be sure, one should not exaggerate the differences between the high- and the low-born in this era. There were members of the privileged classes and even of the clergy who possessed little high culture, just as there were social outcasts—vagrants, bandits, and soldiers-for-hire—who were more mobile than most lords. Still, the culture of Latin Christendom was divided both horizontally (by class) and vertically (by segment). At the apex of the social pyramid was a small body of individuals unified by their access to high culture; at the bottom was the large mass of the populace who lived in the segmented cultures of the peasant village.

The Reformation did not transform Latin Christendom into a system of national states, nor did it give birth to the idea of nationalism, as has sometimes been asserted. It did not even close the gap between high and low culture. But it did shatter the cultural unity of the elites and wear down the localism of popular culture. It drove a wedge between the various segments of the privileged classes, and it injected high culture into the lives of the common people. More than that, it established new organizational and ideological bonds between the elites and the populace. This was particularly the case when confessional conflict escalated into armed struggle and civil war, as it did in most areas of Europe sometime during the sixteenth and seventeenth centuries. For as members of

[65] Gellner (1983).

the privileged classes squared off against one another—prince against prince, class against class, brother against brother—a spiral of confessional mobilization and countermobilization was set in motion, which inevitably drew the popular classes into the fray and dramatically increased the stakes of the game. The result of these conflicts was a gradual—though imperfect—alignment of political and religious boundaries.

Thus, if confessional Europe was not a system of nation-states, it resembled one in certain respects, for confessionalism, like nationalism, constituted a form of "social closure," which threw up ideological, political, and legal obstacles to social interaction. Gone were the days when a north German cleric could absolve his studies in Rome and Paris. Gone the days when an English king could reap advantages from marrying a French princess. Gone, finally, the days when a trader from Venice could ply his wares in Bremen without concern for his physical safety. At the same time, however, confessional Europe was also markedly less segmented and localistic than Latin Christendom had been. Like nationalism, confessionalism forged new "horizontal" bonds of social solidarity. In 1600, a Huguenot *hobereau* from the Languedoc would have been met with a warm welcome in Edinburgh, London, Amsterdam, Heidelberg, Geneva, Prague, Budapest, or Cracow, as, for that matter, would a Calvinist peasant from the Cevènnes. Their Calvinist beliefs would have served them as a passport to all of Reformed Europe. More important, confessionalism broke down—or at least lowered—many of the barriers between high and low culture. A combination of closely interrelated developments—the invention of movable type, the triumph of the vernacular, and the growth of popular literacy—gave the common people access to symbolic resources, most notably the Bible, which had long been the monopoly of elites.[66] These same developments also made the common people into targets of ideological mobilization in elite struggles, as demonstrated by the explosive growth in religious and political pamphleteering during the sixteenth century.

When did confessional identities first emerge? What symbols and discourses did they draw on? And how "national" were they? It is not possible to provide any firm answers to these questions at the present time: not enough research has been done. Based on my own work on the Netherlands and Brandenburg–Prussia, however, I can suggest some tentative answers for the Calvinist case.

Toward the "New Israel": Calvinism and Collective Identity in the Dutch Republic and Brandenburg–Prussia

With its sharp, almost Manichean division between the saved and the damned, between those who were "elected" and those who were not, the Calvinist doctrine of predestination provided a particularly favorable foundation for the construction of strong and exclusive forms of group identity, which Calvinist ministers and rulers were able to exploit in their struggle for religious liberty and

[66] See Eisenstein (1981) and Wuthnow (1987).

political hegemony. The specific shape that Calvinist identity took, however, was strongly influenced by the social and political context in which the Calvinist movement first emerged. Broadly speaking, it is possible to distinguish two basic types of Calvinist identity—populist and elitist—that correspond to the two patterns of confessional mobilization, "from below" and "from above," which were discussed earlier. The former was typical of western and south-central Europe, where the Calvinist movement had a broad social base and crystallized around opposition to a Catholic (or crypto-Catholic) monarch.

A clear example of this pattern may be found in the Netherlands, where Calvinist propagandists used biblical analogies to mobilize their followers and demonize their opponents.[67] In the popular ballads of the Dutch rebels, the so-called "Beggars Songs," the leading personalities in the revolt repeatedly were compared to figures from the Old Testament, with the princes of Orange cast as Moses or David and Philipp II as Pharaoh or Goliath. Calvinist historians later elaborated the Israelite analogy further, drawing intricate parallels between the events of the revolt and the saga of the Ancient Jews. And by the mid-seventeenth century, some orthodox ministers even went so far as to proclaim the Dutch republic a "New Israel" and the Netherlanders a "chosen people," thereby abandoning the realm of analogy altogether. Of course, there were many, even within the Reformed church, who rejected this view. But the Israelite analogy was a common motif in representations of the Netherlands, and not only in orthodox Calvinist circles. The Catholic poet and playwright Joost Van Vondel, for instance, appended a foreword to his dramatic rendering of the Passover story in which he explicitly drew the readers' attention to the "numerous parallels" between Dutch and Jewish history. Rembrandt, too, showed a particular predilection for Old Testament themes, despite his rocky relationship to the Reformed church (his common-law marriage had brought repeated reprimands from the Amsterdam consistory). In fact, the Israelite analogy was a veritable touchstone of Golden Age culture. It was also a powerful tool for popular political mobilization, particularly in the hands of the Dutch stadholders, who skillfully used the Israelite analogy to bring the Calvinist bloc behind them in their struggles against the regents during the late seventeenth century.

The political salience of confessional identity was hardly unique to the Dutch case. On the contrary, similar developments can also be observed in other Calvinist polities. In Scotland, for example, it was the metaphor of the "covenant," first popularized by John Knox, that provided the shibboleth of Calvinist identity and anti-episcopal sentiment.[68] In England, on the other hand, it was the ideal of the "elect nation" that served as the rallying call for Puritan militants.[69] That western European Calvinists were so fond of the Exodus saga and the Book of Judges is surely no coincidence. With their undertones of collective redemption and popular sovereignty, these episodes in Old Testament history provided

---

[67] On the connection between Reformed Protestantism and "national" identity in the Dutch republic, see especially Schama (1988). The following is based primarily on Gorski (1996b).
[68] See Morrill (1990).
[69] See Haller (1963).

a metaphorical prism for transforming the conviction of personal salvation into a basis of group solidarity.[70]

It was precisely this solidarity in the face of animosity that so impressed the princes of central Europe when faced with Catholic resurgence in Empire. But a very different sort of confessional identity arose in the Reformed principalities of Germany, where the Calvinist movement had a narrow social base and coalesced around opposition to the Catholic resurgence within the empire and the perceived unwillingness of the Lutheran princes to halt it. Brandenburg–Prussia represents a particularly important—and extreme—example of this pattern. There, as we have seen, confessional conflict produced a sharp and lasting split between a Calvinist elite centered in the royal court and a Lutheran populace led by the provincial estates.[71] The Calvinists, for their part, despised the particularism and pacifism of the Lutheran estates. They regarded themselves as the "purer sort of Protestant," and openly proclaimed themselves the "buttress of the throne." Confessional tensions were eased somewhat during the early eighteenth century by the rise of Prussian Pietism, an ascetic reform movement within the Lutheran church, whose activist ethos of discipline and charity bore clear affinities to Calvinism. But the Reformed church remained the confessional foundation of the Prussian bureaucracy and the Hohenzollern monarchy even under Frederick the Great, whose personal indifference to things religious is well known. Indeed, the Calvinist ethos continued to shape the self-understanding of the Prussian elite until well into the nineteenth century. Even so enlightened an observer as Hegel did not hesitate to extol the moral virtues of the Prussian bureaucracy, which he regarded as the "heart and mind" of the Prussian state. But it was the Prussophile literatus, Theodor Fontane, himself a scion of Huguenot refugees, who expressed this secularized version of the Protestant ethic most succinctly: "In Prussia," proclaims the protagonist of *Der Stechlin*, "the smaller number is, of course, always the greater." Given the obvious affinity between Calvinism and elitism, one might expect to find similar developments elsewhere. But for historical reasons, this is not the case. Most of the Reformed kingdoms in Germany were too small to withstand the terrible heat of military competition during the seventeenth century (Sayn-Wittgenstein). And the one Reformed principality comparable in size and status to Prussia, the Palatinate, died on the muddy slopes of White Mountain in the first great battle of the Thirty Years' War. Thus, Prussia once again stands as a challenging "exception" to the dominant trends of early modern political development.

It has not been possible, in the present context, to examine the formation of confessional identity in a comprehensive way, only the shape it took in the Calvinist context and, more specifically, in the cases of Holland and Prussia. But these cases clearly illustrate the role that confessional identity played in the formation of territorial states and, conversely, the role that political context played

---

[70] On this, see especially Walzer (1985).
[71] On Calvinism and elite identity in Brandenburg-Prussia, see especially von Thadden (1959).

in shaping confessional identity. At the present stage, however, they are little more than that—bold illustrations. The argument developed in this section should thus be understood as a set of tentative hypotheses that might serve as a basis for further research into the historical genesis of national identity rather than as a set of empirically validated conclusions grounded in a large and well-established literature. In closing, then, it may be useful to restate the foregoing analysis in somewhat bolder and more theoretical and schematic terms, that is, as a set of theses or provocations that could serve as a point of departure for future discussion.

Theses Toward a General Theory of "Religious Nationalism"

Confessional identity is the product of confessional conflict and tends to develop in four stages, each of which corresponds to a particular level of confessional mobilization. In the first stage, confessional tensions remain latent, confessional identities diffuse. Organizational and doctrinal boundaries between the confessions are poorly defined, and individual believers circulate freely from one movement to another or even participate in several simultaneously. In the second stage, clear doctrinal and organizational boundaries develop between the confessions. Formal mechanisms of confessional closure are instituted (for example, statements of faith, membership rolls), and boundaries between various religious movements become less permeable. In the third stage, confession becomes a basis for political mobilization (and vice versa), resulting in the formation of organized "religious parties," which espouse distinct and opposed views of church and polity. In the fourth stage, the entire polity becomes polarized along confessional lines, as religious violence breaks out and confessional polemics heat up. It should be emphasized that these processes occurred at different times and in various areas of Europe and that they were strongly influenced by the political context. Generally speaking, they occurred earlier in the west than in the east, and were more intense where they became intertwined with intra-elite conflicts.

Confessional identity was a harbinger—indeed, a precursor—of national identity and contributed to the territorialization of political identity in three ways: (1) by weakening cross-"national" ties between religious, political, and economic elites (ministers, nobles, and merchants); (2) by strengthening cross-communal ties between the common people (for example, peasants and artisans); and (3) by creating new ideological and institutional links between the elites and the common people. It is important, however, to underline that confessional identity was still more universalistic than national identity, insofar as the three major confessions were all "international."

Confessional identity was a vital state-building tool deployed by centralizing rulers in three different ways: (1) to mobilize popular opposition to local and regional power holders, who sought to preserve their autonomy and privileges vis-à-vis the territorial state; (2) to harness elite loyalty to dynastic rulers, who sought to concentrate fiscal and administrative power in their own hands; and (3) to strengthen or supplement centrally controlled mechanisms of mobilization and control, where these were weak or absent. While most early modern state-builders drew on one or more of these strategies, they did not always combine them in precisely the same way.

THE central thesis of this essay is that the confessional age witnessed a profound intensification of state power. It has been argued that confessionalization unleashed processes of social disciplining and identity-formation that dramatically increased the capacities of states and state actors to regulate and mobilize subject populations. Confessionalization thus contributed to state-formation in two ways: (1) it forged institutionalized networks of popular socialization and moral control that were gradually absorbed by the state, and (2) it created new forms of territorial identity that could be instrumentalized by state-building elites. In short, it laid the micropolitical and religiocultural foundations of the national state.

Nonetheless, the early modern state differed from the national state in at least two important respects. First, it did not possess a monopoly over the means of popular socialization and moral control (for example, schools, prisons, workhouses). The power networks of church and state remained tightly intertwined during the confessional age and were not disentangled until after the French Revolution—and then only partially. Second, it was not a fully integrated political community: cultural and territorial boundaries still crosscut each other in various ways and would only be brought into (nearly) complete alignment by the nationalist movements of the nineteenth and twentieth centuries. In sum, the secularization of political power and the territorialization of cultural identity were still far from complete.

The early modern state should be seen not merely as a general transitional form, however—as a not-yet-national state—but also as a specific historical formation—as a confessional state distinguished by a complex intertwining of religious and political institutions at all levels of rule and a deep interpenetration of confessional and political identities at all levels of society. The confessional state, in other words, was a form of polity whose power derived largely from the capacity to colonize church institutions and mobilize religious sentiment.

Of course, early modern rulers did not see their kingdoms as "confessional states." But they did see them as having a confessional foundation—whence their concern with religious uniformity. And they saw the maintenance of social order or "good police" as one of the constituents of "stateness" and one of the central tasks of the "good prince"—whence their sudden and determined interventions into the daily lives of the common people and their mania for institutionalized mechanisms of moral and social control. Like the modern world, early modern Europe had its own distinctive "culture of the state" (see Meyer, this volume), a normatively grounded understanding of what made a state a state and of what made a good ruler good. And at the center of this understanding was "discipline," both as a religious ideal and as a social practice.

Naturally, it might be argued that the imposition of social discipline was merely a strategy of political domination, pursued by rational and self-interested rulers. And yet, as in the case of "family strategies," such as those examined by Julia Adams, this would be a highly one-sided and grossly oversimplified reading of the historical record. For how "rational" were consistories, workhouses, and bureaucracies? Certainly, the most astute observers were well aware of their limitations. They understood that legalism could suffocate piety; that enclosure could harden the vagrant; that bureaucracy could stifle individual initiative—complaints that are still heard today. But despite their evident "irrationality" and "inefficiency," the disciplinary mechanisms and strategies put in place during the sixteenth century could not be so easily removed—and are still with us today, in slightly altered form. Why? Because challenging them means challenging some of the most deeply held "values" within modern Western culture—individual "moral responsibility," the "Protestant work ethic," and the impersonal "rule of law"—and the elite groups whose domination is premised on them—the clergy and the "helping professions," the managerial class, and the state bureaucrats. Once it has become crystallized in a particular set of institutions and monopolized by a particular set of elites, it seems that a set of cultural "values" or "ideals" becomes highly resistant to change, even when change would be in the individual self-interest of the rulers or the collective self-interest of the ruled. If this is true, a second question arises: how do such sociocultural configurations—Weber called them "historical individuals"—emerge in the first place? The answer suggested by the foregoing analysis—and it is a highly specific and strongly delimited one—is that cultural crystallizations tend to become fluid only in the heat of revolution, when cross-class coalitions mobilize around an alternative vision of the social and moral order—an "ideology." This is not to suggest that cosmic upheavals of this sort are the *only* source of social change. In "calmer" periods, the "meso-level" mechanisms identified by rational-choice theory are probably more important. But for those who wish to study "macro-level" change, involving the reconstitution of orders and "interests," the nexus between culture and politics, and thus between culture and the state, must be paramount.

References

Abray, Lorna Jane. 1985. *The People's Reformation: Magistrates, Clergy and Commons in Strasbourg, 1550–1598*. Ithaca: Cornell University Press.

Alford, Robert R., and Roger Friedland. 1985. *Powers of Theory*. Cambridge: Cambridge University Press.

Anderson, Benedict. 1982. *Imagined Communities*. London: Verso.

Anderson, Perry. 1974. *Passages from Antiquity to Feudalism*. London: Verso.

———. 1979. *Lineages of the Absolutist State*. London: Verso.

Armstrong, John A. 1982. *Nations before Nationalism*. Chapel Hill: University of North Carolina Press.

Baron, Hans. 1939. *Calvinist Republicanism and Its Historical Roots*. Chicago: Private edition.

Black, Christopher. 1989. *Italian Confraternities in the Sixteenth Century*. Cambridge: Cambridge University Press.

Bornhak, Conrad. 1884–86. *Geschichte des preußischen Verwaltungsrechts*. 3 vols. Berlin: Julius Springer.

Brecht, Martin. 1967. *Kirchenzucht in Württemberg vom 16. bis zum 18. Jahrhundert*. Stuttgart: Calwer Verlag.

Breysig, Kurt. 1892. "Die Organisation der brandenburgischen Kommissariate in der Zeit von 1660–1697." *Forschungen zur brandenburgischen und preußischen Geschichte* 5: 135–56.

Brubaker, Rogers. 1992. *Citizenship and Nationhood in France and Germany*. Cambridge: Harvard University Press.

Büsch, Otto. 1962. *Militärsystem und Sozialleben im Alten Preußen*. Berlin: De Gruyter.

Calori, Gianfranco. 1972. *Una iniziative sociale nella Bologna del '500: L'Opera dei Mendicanti*. Bologna: Azzoguidi.

Calvin, John. 1971. *Selections from his Writings*, edited by John Dillenberger. Missoula, Mont.: Scholars Press.

Carsten, Frederick. 1954. *The Origins of Prussia*. Oxford: Clarendon.

Châtellier, Louis. 1981. *Tradition chrétienne et renouveau catholique dans le cadre de l'ancien diocèse de Strasbourg (1650–1770)*. Paris: Ophrys.

———. 1989. *The Europe of the Devout*, translated by Jean Birrel. Cambridge: Cambridge University Press.

Cohen, Charles L. 1986. *God's Caress*. New York: Oxford University Press.

Collins, James B. 1995. *The State in Early Modern France*. Cambridge: Cambridge University Press.

Demandt, K. E. 1965. "Die hessischen Landstände im Zeitalter des Frühabsolutismus." *Hessisches Jahrbuch für Landesgeschichte* 15: 38–108.

Deursen, A. Th. Van. [1979] 1991. *Bavianen en slijkgeuzen*. Franeker: Van Wijnen.

Dinges, Martin. 1988. *Stadtarmut in Bordeaux, 1525–1675*. Bonn: Bouvier.

Dobras, Wolfgang. 1993. *Ratsregiment, Sittenpolizei und Kirchenzucht in der Reichsstadt Konstanz, 1531–1548*. Gütersloh: G. Mohn.

Downing, Brian. 1992. *The Military Revolution and Political Change*. Princeton: Princeton University Press.

Durr, Emil. 1921–50. *Aktensammlung zur Geschichte der Basler Reformation in den Jahren 1519 bis Anfang 1534*. 6 vols. Basel: Verlag der historischen und antiquarischen Gesellschaft.

Eisenstein, Elizabeth. 1981. *Revolution in Print*. Cambridge: Cambridge University Press.

Elias, Norbert. 1969. *Die höfische Gesellschaft*. Neuwied: Luchterhand.

———. 1976. *Über den Prozeß der Zivilisation*. Frankfurt am Main: Suhrkamp.

Ertman, Thomas. 1997. *Birth of the Leviathan: Building States and Regimes in Medieval and Early Modern Europe*. Cambridge: Cambridge University Press.

Ferté, Jeanne. 1962. *La vie religieuse dans les campagnes parisiennes (1622–1695)*. Paris: Librairie philosophique J. Vrin.

Firth, C. H. 1967 [1902]. *Cromwell's Army*. London: Methuen.

Foucault, Michel. 1980. *Power/Knowledge*, edited by Colin Gordon. New York: Pantheon.

———. 1990. *Politics, Philosophy, Culture*, edited by Lawrence D. Kritzman and translated by Alan Sheridan, et al. New York: Routledge.

Franz, Gunther. 1971. *Die Kirchenleitung in Hohenlohe in den Jahrzehnten nach der Reformation: Visitation, Konsistorium, Kirchenzucht und die Festigung des landesherrlichen Kirchenregiments, 1556–1586*. Stuttgart: Calwer Verlag.

Gawthrop, Richard. 1993. *Pietism and the Making of Eighteenth-Century Prussia*. Cambridge: Cambridge University Press.

Gellner, Ernst. 1983. *Nations and Nationalism*. Ithaca: Cornell University Press.

Gentles, Ian. 1992. *The New Model Army*. Oxford: Blackwell.

Giddens, Anthony. 1987. *The Nation-State and Violence*. Berkeley: University of California Press.

Goertz, H. J. 1987. *Pfaffenhaß und groß' Geschrei*. Munich: C. H. Beck.

Gorski, Philip S. 1993a. "The Protestant Ethic Revisited: Disciplinary Revolution in Holland and Prussia." *American Journal of Sociology* 99, no. 2 (September): 255–316.

———. 1993b. "Revolutionary Calvinism and the Rise of Parliamentary Regimes." Paper presented at the annual meeting of the American Sociological Association. Miami.

———. 1994a. "The Poverty of Deductivism: A Constructive-Realist Model of Sociological Explanation." Paper presented at the annual meeting of the American Sociological Association. Los Angeles.

———. 1994b. "Review of Richard L. Gawthrop, *Pietism and the Making of Eighteenth-Century Prussia*." *German Politics and Society* 32, Summer: 171–76.

———. 1995. "The Protestant Ethic and the Spirit of Bureaucracy." *American Sociological Review* 60, no. 5 (October): 783–6.

———. 1996a. "Disciplinary Revolution: Calvinism and State Formation in Early Modern Europe." Ph.D. diss. University of California, Berkeley.

———. 1996b. "Towards the New Jerusalem: Calvinism, Collective Identity and Political Mobilization in the Dutch Republic, 1517–1672." Paper presented at the annual meeting of the Social Science History Association. New Orleans.

Götze, Ruth. 1959. *Wie Luther Kirchenzucht übte*. Göttingen: Vandenhoeck and Ruprecht.

Groenveld, S., H. L. Ph. Leeuwenberg, M. E. H. N. Mout, and W. M. Zappey. 1991. *De Tachtigjarige oorlog*. 3d rev. Zutphen: De Walburg Pers.

Gutton, Jean-Pierre. 1970. *La société et les pauvres: L'exemple de la généralité de Lyon, 1534–1789*. Paris: Société d'édition, "Les belles lettres."

Hallema, A. 1958. *Geschiedenis van het gevangeniswezen, hoofdzakelijk in Nederland*. The Hague: Staatsdrukkerij-en Uitgeverijsbedrijf.

Haller, William. 1963. *The Elect Nation: The Meaning and Relevance of Foxe's Book of Martyrs*. New York: Harper and Row.

Hill, Christopher. 1967. *Society and Puritanism in Pre-Revolutionary England*. New York: Schocken.

Hinrichs, Carl. 1971. *Preußentum und Pietismus*. Göttingen: Vandenhoek and Ruprecht.

Hintze, Otto. n.d. "Kalvinismus und Staatsräson in Brandenburg zu Beginn des 17. Jahrhunderts." In *Geist und Epochen der preußischen Geschichte*, edited by Fritz Hartung, 289–346. Leipzig: Koehler and Amelang.

———. 1901. *Die Behördenorganisation und die allgemeine Verwaltung in Preußen um 1740. Acta Borussica, Behördenorganisation*, vol. 6. Berlin: Paul Parey.

Hobsbawm, Eric, and Terence Ranger, eds. 1992. *The Invention of Tradition*. Cambridge: Cambridge University Press.

Hollenberg, Günther. 1986. "Landgraf Philipp von Hessen und die hessischen Landstände im Bauernkrieg." *Zeitschrift des Vereins für hessische Geschichte und Landeskunde* 91: 123–29.

———. 1988. "Die hessen-kasselischen Landstände im 18. Jahrhundert." *Hessisches Jahrbuch für Landesgeschichte* 38: 1–20.

Hsia, Ronnie Po-Chia. 1991. *Social Discipline in the Reformation*. Cambridge: Cambridge University Press.

Ingram, Martin. 1987. *Church Courts, Sex and Marriage in England, 1570–1640*. Cambridge: Cambridge University Press.

Innes, Joanna. 1987. "Prisons for the Poor: English Bridewells, 1555–1800." In *Labour, Law, and Crime*, edited by Francis Snyder and Douglas Hay, 42–122. London: Tavistock.

Israel, Jonathan I. 1995. *The Dutch Republic: Its Rise, Greatness and Fall, 1477–1806*. Oxford: Oxford University Press.

Jütte, Robert. 1994. *Poverty and Deviance in Early Modern Europe*. Cambridge: Cambridge University Press.

Kaplan, Benjamin. 1995. *Calvinists and Libertines: Confession and Community in Utrecht, 1578–1620*. Oxford: Clarendon.

Kingdon, Robert M. 1972a. "The Control of Morals in Calvin's Geneva." In Lawrence P. Buck and Jonathan W. Zophy, eds., *The Social History of the Reformation*, 3–16 (Columbus, OH: Ohio State University Press).

———. 1972b. "Social Welfare in Calvin's Geneva." *American Historical Review* 76: 50–69.

Kishlansky, Mark. 1979. *The Rise of the New Model Army*. Cambridge: Cambridge University Press.

Klueting, Harm. 1989. *Das Konfessionelle Zeitalter*. Stuttgart: Ulmer.

Köhler, Walther. 1932–1942. *Zürcher Ehegericht und Genfer Konsistorium*. 2 vols. Leipzig: Heinsius.

Kok, J. A. de. 1964. *Nederland op de breuklijn Rome-reformatie*. Assen: Van Gorcum.

Lackner, Martin. 1973. *Die Kirchenpolitik des Großen Kurfürsten*. Witten: Luther Verlag.

Landwehr, Hugo. 1894. *Die Kirchenpolitik Friedrich Wilhelms, des Großen Kurfürsten*. Berlin: Ernst Hoffman.

Locher, Gottfried. 1982. *Zwingli und die schweizerische Reformation*. Göttingen: Vandenhoeck and Ruprecht.

Luria, Keith P. 1991. *Territories of Grace: Cultural Change in the Seventeenth Century Diocese of Grenoble*. Berkeley: University of California Press.

Mann, Michael. 1984–1993. *The Sources of Social Power*. 2 vols. Cambridge: Cambridge University Press.

Miller, Richard L. 1987. *Fact and Method*. Princeton: Princeton University Press.

Monter, E. William. 1987. *Enforcing Morality in Early Modern Europe*. London: Variorum.

Morril, John, ed. 1990. *The Scottish National Covenant in Its British Context*. Edinburgh: Edinburgh University Press.

Naphy, William G. 1994. *Calvin and the Consolidation of the Genevan Reformation*. Manchester: Manchester University Press.

Neugebauer, Wolfgang. 1981. "Zur neueren Deutung der preußischen Verwaltung im 17. und 18. Jahrhundert in vergleichender Sicht." In *Moderne preußische Geschichte*, edited by Otto Büsch and Wolfgang Neugebauer, 541–97. Berlin: De Gruyter.

Nischan, Bodo. 1994. *Prince, People, and Confession: The Second Reformation in Brandenburg*. Philadelphia: University of Pennsylvania Press.

Nobbs, Douglas. 1938. *Theocracy and Toleration: A Study of the Disputes in Dutch Calvinism from 1600 to 1650*. Cambridge: Cambridge University Press.

O'Donoghue, Edward G. 1923. *Bridewell Hospital: Palace, Prison, Schools, from the Earliest Times to the End of the Reign of Elizabeth*. London: Lane.

Oestreich, Gerhard. 1968. *Strukturprobleme der frühen Neuzeit*. Berlin: Duncker and Humblot.

——. 1969. *Geist und Gestalt des frühmodernen Staates*. Berlin: Duncker and Humblot.

Parker, Geoffrey. 1988. *The Dutch Revolt*. London: Peregrine.

Pastore, Alessandro. 1986. "Strutture assistenziali fra Chiesa e Stati nell'Italian della Controriforma." In *Storia d'Italia, Annali*, vol. 9, *La Chiesa e il potere politico*, edited by Giorgio Chittolini and Giovanni Miccoli, 433–65. Turin: Einaudi.

Pérouas, Louis. 1964. *Le diocèse de la Rochelle de 1648–1724*. Paris: SEVPEN.

Poggi, G. 1979. *The Development of the Modern State*. Stanford: Stanford University Press.

Press, Volker. 1970. *Calvinismus und Territorialstaat*. Stuttgart: Ernst Klett.

Prestwich, Menna, ed. 1985. *International Calvinism, 1541–1715*. Oxford: Oxford University Press.

Pullan, Brian. 1971. *Rich and Poor in Renaissance Venice*. Oxford: Basil Blackwell.

——. 1988. "Support and Redeem: Charity and Poor Relief in Italian Cities from the Fourteenth to the Seventeenth Century." *Continuity and Change* 3: 177–207.

Raeff, Marc. 1983. *The Well-Ordered Police State*. New Haven: Yale University Press.

Ranke, Leopold von. 1852. *Deutsche Geschichte im Zeitalter der Reformation*. 3d ed. Berlin: Duncker and Humblot.

Rapley, Elizabeth. 1990. *The Dévotes: Women and the Church in Seventeenth Century France*. Montreal and Kingston: McGill-Queen's University Press.

Reinhard, Wolfgang, and Heinz Schilling, eds. 1995. *Die katholische Konfessionalisierung*. Münster: Aschendorff.

Rogier, L. J. 1945–46. *Geschiedenis van het katholicisme in Noord-Nederland in de 16e en 17e eeuw*. 2 vols. Amsterdam: Urbi et Orbi.

Roodenburg, Hermann. 1990. *Onder censuur. De kerkelijke tucht in de gereformeerde gemeente van Amsterdam, 1578–1700*. Hilversum: Verloren.

Roper, Lyndal. 1989. *The Holy Household: Women and Morals in Reformation Augsburg*. New Brunswick, N. J.: Rutgers University Press.

Rosenberg, Hans. 1966. *Bureaucracy, Aristocracy, and Autocracy: The Prussian Experience*. Boston: Beacon.

Sauzet, Robert. 1979. *Contre-réforme et réforme catholique en bas Languedoc*. Louvain: Nauwelaerts.

Schaab, Meinrad, ed. 1993. *Territorialstaat und Calvinismus*. Stuttgart: Kohlhammer.

Schama, Simon. 1988. *The Embarrassment of Riches*. Berkeley: University of California Press.

Schilling, Heinz. 1981. *Konfessionkonflikt und Staatsbildung*. Gütersloh: G. Mohn.

——. 1988a. *Aufbruch und Krise, Deutschland 1517–1648*. Berlin: Siedler.

——. 1988b. "Die Konfessionalisierung im Reich." *Historische Zeitschrift* 146: 1–45.

——. 1991a. "Luther, Loyola, Calvin und die europäische Neuzeit." Inaugural Lecture. Humboldt University, Berlin.

——. 1991b. "Nationale Identität und Konfession in der europäischen Neuzeit." In *Nationale Identität und kulturelle Identität*, edited by Bernhard Giesen, 192–252. Frankfurt am Main: Suhrkamp.

——. 1992. "Confessionalization in the Empire: Religious and Societal Change in Germany between 1555 and 1620." In *Religion, Political Culture and the Emergence of Early Modern Society*, translated by Thomas Brady Jr. Leiden: E. J. Brill.

——, ed. 1994. *Kirchenzucht und Sozialdisziplinierung im frühneuzeitlichen Europa*. Berlin: Duncker and Humblot.

Sellen, Thorsten. 1944. *Pioneering in Penology*. Philadelphia: University of Philadelphia Press.

Skocpol, Theda. 1976. "Wallerstein's World Capitalist System: A Theoretical and Historical Critique." *American Journal of Sociology* 82, no. 5: 1075–90.

Smith, Anthony. 1984. *The Ethnic Origins of Nations*. Oxford: Basil Blackwell.

Soulet, Jean-François. 1974. *Traditions et réformes religieuses dans les Pyrénées centrales au XVIIe siècle*. Pau: Marrimpouey Jeune.

Spierenburg, Petrus C. 1991. *The Prison Experience: Disciplinary Institutions and Their Inmates*. New Brunswick: Rutgers University Press.

Thadden, Rodolf von. 1959. *Die brandenburgisch-preußischen Hofprediger im 17. und 18. Jahrhundert*. Berlin: De Gruyter.

Tilly, Charles, ed. 1975. *The Formation of National States in Western Europe*. Princeton: Princeton University Press.

———. 1990. *Coercion, Capital, and European States*. Oxford: Basil Blackwell.

Timore e carità. 1980. Cremona: Biblioteca statale e libreria civica di Cremona.

Vann, James Allen. 1984. *The Making of a State: Württemberg, 1593–1793*. Ithaca: Cornell University Press.

Venard, Marc. 1993. *Réforme protestante, Réforme catholique dans la province d'Avignon–XVI siècle*. Paris: CERF.

Verein für Reformationsgeschichte. 1992. *Die lutherische Konfessionalisierung in Deutschland*. Gütersloh: G. Mohn.

Verein für Reformationsgeschichte. 1985. *Die reformierte Konfessionalisierung in Deutschland: das Problem der "Zweiten Reformation."* Gütersloh: G. Mohn.

Wallerstein, Immanuel. 1974–87. *The Modern World-System*. 3 vols. New York: Academic Press.

Walzer, Michael. 1965. *The Revolution of the Saints*. Cambridge: Harvard University Press.

———. 1985. *Exodus and Revolution*. New York: Basic Books.

Weber, Max. [1920] 1988. "Theorie der Stufen und Richtungen religiöser Weltablehnung." In *Gesammelte Aufsätze zur Religionssoziologie*, vol. 1, 550. Tübingen: Mohr.

Wijn, Jan Willem. 1934. *Het krijgswezen in den tijd van Prins Maurits*. Utrecht: Joeijenbos.

Winckelmann, Otto. 1914–15. "Über die ältesten Armenordnungen der Reformationszeit (1522–1525)." *Historische Vierteljahrschrift* 17: 187–228, 361–400.

Wuthnow, Robert. 1987. *Communities of Discourse*. Cambridge: Harvard University Press.

Zeeden, Ernst Walter. 1964. *Die Entstehung der Konfessionen*. Munich: R. Oldenbourg.

———. 1977. "Gegenreformation als Modernisierung." *Archiv für Reformationsgeschichte* 68: 226–52.

———. 1983. "Zwang zur Konfessionalisierung? Prologomena zu einer Theorie des konfessionellen Zeitalters." *Zeitschrift für historische Forschung* 10: 257–77.

6

Nationalism, Universal Monarchy, and the Glorious Revolution

Steven Pincus

"The welfare of England," one polemicist observed shortly after the Glorious Revolution, "is involved in the common fate of Europe." Although living on an island, the English knew that they were not self-sufficient. The need to trade, thought another pamphleteer, made the English "citizens of the world," necessarily interested in political and cultural developments beyond the English Channel (*Nero* 1690: 29; *The Cities Great Concern* 1674: sig. A1v).

This cosmopolitan, nationalist, and commercially driven English self-conception of the later seventeenth century sits in uneasy tension with traditional accounts of the origins of nationalism. These accounts, although differing in emphasis and implications, generally agree that no nationalist consciousness was possible before the advent of industrial capitalism. Apparently it was only with the mobilization of an industrial labor force that the political nation could be created (Suny 1993: 7; Alter 1989: 77–78; Gellner 1983: chap. 2).[1] Others who are more willing to entertain the possibility of early modern nationalism insist that the conditions in England were not conducive to the evolution of nationalist ideologies. English gradualism and universalism and the absence of a foreign

I am grateful to Sharon Achinstein, Bernard Bailyn, Toby Barnard, Tom Cogswell, Mark Goldie, Tim Harris, Meg Jacobs, Wallace MacCaffrey, Peter Miller, Bill Novak, Jenny Paxton, Jennifer Poulos, John Robertson, and Blair Worden for their comments and criticisms of this essay in its draft forms. I have profited a great deal from the comments and suggestions of the participants in the Wilder House Culture/State conference in Chicago, September 1995. In particular, I am grateful for the suggestions of George Steinmetz. The research for this essay was made possible in part by a grant from the English-Speaking Union.

[1] I concur with Anthony Smith that "the movement to a market economy," which occurred much earlier, was a sufficient economic precondition for nationalism (1991: 60). An extremely important exception to this line of argument is that advanced by Finn (1993: 14–22). The present essay can be read as an early modernist's attempt to enrich and delineate the process she describes. Naturally, Benedict Anderson also dissents from accounts that insist on industrialization as a prerequisite for nationalism. My differences with Anderson are set out below.

presence, according to John Breuilly, "explain the absence of any distinctive English nationalist ideology". (Breuilly 1993: 87).[2] For Jonathan Clark, the tradi-
tionalism, agrarianism, and religiosity of early modern English society made it a
poor candidate for the early enunciation of nationalism. "Nationalism," he has
insisted, was "impossible without the nation state whose secular and republican
framework demanded and was eventually given a different rationale" (1994: 47).[3]
Because the English had no notion of popular sovereignty, Clark suggests, the
English people could express no politically efficacious national sentiment.

English historians who have discussed the development of an English national
self-consciousness have done so in insular terms that make no reference to constructive cultural engagement with continental European developments. They,
like so many other students of nationalism, have seen the phenomenon developing either through an internal political logic or as a result of colonies developing a self-conception that justified their independent political existence. Historians of England have traditionally denied the essential Europeanness of their
subject, preferring instead to explain the causes and consequences of English political and cultural transformations without reference to developments across the
channel or the North Sea. They have insisted on both a British exceptionalism
and a British isolationism. British culture, John Pocock contends, was "autonomous, insular, and oceanic rather than Continental or European, self-directed by
a national and (more ambiguously) imperial political sovereignty which was . . .
the connecting theme along which English and Anglo-British history have been
conducted and written" (1992: 362). "Britons defined themselves in terms of
their common Protestantism as contrasted with the Catholicism of continental
Europe," Linda Colley has recently claimed, "they defined themselves . . . in
conscious opposition to the Other beyond their shores" (1992a: 316; see also
Colley 1992b). I contend that by denying the cosmopolitan nature of English
political culture, these historians are reinscribing the nationalist inclination to
describe the nation as natural rather than constructed. In so doing, they make it
impossible to develop an account of the origins of English nationalism.

British insularity has been explained in two different ways. One group of historians has maintained that the English were far more interested in local affairs
than in European developments. Members of Parliament might be "men of con-

---

[2] This view fits into a broader tradition in the social sciences—fully aided and abetted by the revisionist tradition in English historiography—to deny that there was a meaningful revolution in England in the seventeenth century. Theda Skocpol, for example, although she concedes that there was
a "political revolution" in seventeenth-century England, denies that there was a social revolution
"because it reinforced and sealed the direct political control of a dominant class . . . fundamentally
a landed upper class" (1979: 140–42). I argue here, and elsewhere, that the events of 1688–1689 were
a nationalist revolution in which the arguments of those who thought property was created by
human endeavor rather than by God came to dominate the English ideological landscape. In 1688–
1689, a broad-based social movement overthrew the old order, paving the way for a nationalist state.
The evidence for this is developed in greater detail in Pincus (1998).

[3] Here, ironically, Clark agrees almost completely with Eric Hobsbawm, who also dates the origins of modern nationalism to the nineteenth century. "Nations do not make states and nationalisms," Hobsbawm insists, "but the other way round" (1990: 10).

siderable local standing and influence" but they had "often limited their mental and political horizons" (Jones 1980: 12). The British monarchy restored in 1660, Ronald Hutton argues, aimed to promote a "lack of interest in public affairs," and it largely succeeded (1985: 157 and passim). By the accession of James II in 1685, it is claimed, "politics in a popular sense no longer existed" (Jones 1987: 6). Consequently, when the Dutch stadholder William III looked to England for support in his European crusade against Louis XIV in 1688, he received little sympathy. Even those who invited William to intervene in English politics in the summer of 1688 looked "at matters from a strictly insular point of view," Jonathan Israel asserts, hoping that the Dutch stadholder would tilt the domestic political situation in their favor but knowing little and caring less about the European situation (1989: 32).[4] "Popular participation in politics" before the 1750s, the sociologist Charles Tilly has therefore reasonably concluded, was "relatively parochial, particular and bifurcated" (1995: 107, 346–47).[5]

Recently, however, a group of historians has argued that Restoration Englishmen and women were deeply concerned with, and implicated in, European developments. But, the Europe in which England participated was not a Europe of nations. Rather, it was a Europe divided by one single issue: the issue of religion. Jonathan Scott—the most eloquent proponent of this interpretation—insists that the seventeenth century "was the century of the victories of the Counter-Reformation. It was a century of disaster for European protestantism" (1991: 8; see also Clark 1986; Condren 1989; and Bosher 1994). In this context, seventeenth-century English history should be read as a continuous struggle against the menacing tide of the Counter-Reformation. "It was concern about religion, not about politics or economics," Scott proclaims, that "drove seventeenth century English people to compromise their political allegiances and mire themselves in one another's blood" (1988b: 458–62; 1990: 110).

Against these views, I maintain that the English in the Restoration period (1660–1689)—from a wide variety of social classes and geographical milieus—participated actively in a European debate and that European debate was about universal monarchy, not about the true religion, and about the right ordering of political power, not about the discovery of religious truth. While religious concerns often played a vital role in English political discourse, a narrowly confes-

---

[4] It should be pointed out that Jonathan Israel has been in the vanguard of those calling for an English history that is not "treated apart from that of continental Europe." Indeed, my essay merely argues that many in England, like the States of Holland and the States General, hoped that the events of 1688 would "turn England round against France" and that "English involvement in the Nine Years War, against France . . . was not incidental to but inherent in the Glorious Revolution" (Israel 1991: 11, 23).

[5] Whereas I think this is a fair summary of the revisionist position—a position from which I strongly dissent—it is remarkable that Tilly cites Tim Harris in support of his claim. Harris, as I read him, is making exactly the opposite argument (1987: 14–35). There is much evidence in *London Crowds* to suggest that the politicization of which Harris speaks is national, not parochial. But Harris makes this point abundantly clear (1993: 235). For other recent arguments that later-seventeenth-century English popular politics was national, cosmopolitan, and autonomous, see Knights (1994: esp. 356–63); and Pincus (1996a).

sional focus is unable to explain why parts of the English political nation demanded war against the Protestant Dutch in the 1660s and an attack on France in the later seventeenth century. An examination of the arguments about European affairs over the entire course of the Restoration reveals that, far from being an anachronistic imposition of Whig historians, the definition of national interest and integrity and their assertion in the face of an aspiring universal monarch was at the center of English political polemic. In this examination, I develop the argument through the use of narrative, and heavy deployment of primary materials, in the firm belief that analytical discussions of early modern activities dehistoricize and naturalize the motivations of early modern actors.

Here, I contribute to the rich interdisciplinary discussion of nationalism. By nationalism I mean a broad-based, though not all-inclusive, social movement of people for whom the single most important political touchstone is the nation and the national interest rather than dynastic, confessional, or localist interests. While a nationalist might prioritize other elements of her identity, she is someone who privileges the nation among her political commitments. A nationalist, distinguished from a universalist, recognizes the legitimacy and existence of nations other than her own; a nationalist must posit the existence of more than one nation.

I argue, then, that the origins of European nationalism lie in the early modern period. I claim that the English imagined themselves to be a nation in the late seventeenth century because "the dawn of the age of nationalism" did not require, as Benedict Anderson has insisted, "the dusk of religious modes of thought" and "the rise of rationalist secularism," but only the advent of a skepticism about the immediate possibility of human knowledge of divine truth and the consequent rejection of universalist religious and political beliefs (1991: 11; Alter 1989: 10).[6] Nationalism was one ideological solution to the problem posed by the vicious and bloody wars of religion—wars in defense of universalist principles—fought in the sixteenth and seventeenth centuries. The late-seventeenth-century struggle against universal monarchy was an attempt to establish the nation—a social and political grouping that was intrinsically particularist—as an acceptable basis for coexistence in a Europe comprising many cultures, religions, and types of polity.[7]

[6] I find Hans Kohn's more equivocal formulation of the relationship between nationalism and religion more congenial (1946: 14–15, esp. 23–24). Significantly, Kohn also sees the Glorious Revolution as nationalist, with Locke as its defender (180).

[7] I am very sympathetic to the claim of G. M. Tamas that "post-republican or ethno-cultural nationalism"—which he identifies as "the main East European version"—is closely allied with "the new-fangled theories of multiculturalism and post-modernism." And I am willing to entertain Tamas's claim that there is structural similarity between the arguments of Derrida, Heidegger, and Rorty on the one hand and contemporary Eastern European nationalists on the other. It is my contention that Tamas ignores the central skeptical strain in early modern nationalist polemic. Early modern nationalists, at least, found a third way between that position and "universalist discourse." They were willing to posit the possibility of universal truth, and insist that it should be sought out, but to accept that in this world politics should be governed by some national principles. They were skeptics, not relativists (Tamas 1994: 129–39, and passim.)

By attempting to recover and analyze the complex Restoration discussion of universal monarchy, I hope to cast the Glorious Revolution in a fresh light, a light that goes beyond the old Whig and Tory historiographical traditions, and to suggest that the strong Augustan state of the eighteenth century was not forced on the English by an outsider but was essential to achieve the European and nationalist ends to which most of the English political nation was committed. The English state did not invent English nationalism. However, the state that began to emerge in the mid-seventeenth century did create the cultural and structural preconditions for its development. Once the English had developed a heightened sense of political self-awareness, and the social institutions for the circulation and discussion of political information, the monarchy was no longer able to determine the contours of public opinion. The English public increasingly defined the terms of political discussion. Because the perceived primary function of early modern states was to maintain peace at home and prestige abroad, the English political nation was extremely vigilant in demands for maintenance of the national interest. That interest was determined through a complex discussion based on English traditions and contemporary international developments. English nationalism developed out of a sense that the later Stuart monarchy (1660–1688) failed to play its proper domestic and international role. Charles II and James II had exchanged an English governmental style for a French one. Instead of defending the English and other European nations against French universal dominion, they had become the toadies of France. The English people demanded instead a nationalist state, a state that resisted French universalist aspirations and rejected French modes of governance.

Anglican Royalist Fears of Dutch Universalism

By 1660, most members of the political nation knew that England had spent the better part of the past century trying to prevent the Habsburgs from achieving their goal of universal monarchy—initially in the Elizabethan wars against Philip II and then in the early Stuarts' halting interventions in the Thirty Years' War (1618–1648).[8] The works of Traiano Boccalini, Henri Duc de Rohan, and Tomasso Campanella—all of which outlined the Spanish pretensions to "the Universal Monarchy, which only the Romans arrived unto"—were very familiar to English audiences (Boccalini 1669: 327, 333; Campanella 1660: sig. A4v; Rohan 1641: sig. A8, 25–27, 74–75). These classics were assiduously read, commented on, and cited throughout the later seventeenth century. Their arguments appeared in learned discourses, in popular ballads, in plays, and in doggerel verse; in short they became part of the stock of popular knowledge (*Europae* 1665: 104–05; Everard 1679: 5; Temple 1680: 19–20).

[8]There is a vast literature about the Thirty Years' War. Almost all, whether seeing it as a religious, geopolitical, or socioecomically driven conflict, interpret the struggle in part as about Habsburg hegemony. Most English people thought the Spanish and Austrian Habsburgs were seeking universal monarchy. For the most recent survey of the literature, see Parker (1984).

The widespread public discussion of national and international issues was a relatively recent phenomenon in early modern England. The massive cost of the English Civil Wars (1642–1649) and the ensuing naval conflict with the Dutch (1652–1654) had forced England for the first time to build up a military and naval bureaucracy, and to tap in a regular manner the quickly growing reserves of mobile wealth. England's new taxpayers, the people who underwrote the wars, demanded to know why they were fighting and paying (Pincus, forthcoming). The English taste for news quickly became a habit, and this habit demanded new social institutions. From the 1650s, coffeehouses exploded on the English scene, simultaneously providing the English with a fashionable new drink and allowing a wide range of people from every social strata and every geographical milieu to sample the latest newspapers, poems, pamphlets, and plays. The coffeehouses provided a social setting for the newly emerging English public sphere, called into being in large part by the new demands of the state (Pincus 1995).

The English, in their coffeehouses, taverns, and alehouses, frequently discussed England's place in world affairs. They might have disagreed about the relative merits of Elizabethan and early Stuart foreign policy, but they all concurred that the Habsburgs had "for a long time aspired after an Universal Monarchy" and that their forefathers had done all they could to prevent the Spanish and Austrians from achieving this aim (*French Intrigues* 1685: 3). After 1660, however, Spanish power was clearly on the wane. Although English commentators fiercely debated the origin of Spain's decline, the reality was undeniable. "The Spanish Monarchy, and the House of Austria (whose great accessions of territory gave rise to those observations on which the policy of the last age was founded)," noted the author of *Europae Modernae Speculum* uncontroversially, "are concluded to be consumptive and to stand merely on the defensive part" (*Europae* 1665: 4, 103; Everard 1679: 37; *French Intrigues* 1685: 8). The problem now was to identify and deter the next aspirant.

The most enthusiastic supporters of the restored monarchy, the Anglican Royalists, quickly became convinced that the Dutch republic was seeking universal dominion (Pincus 1996a: 195–268). Although no one can doubt the cultural and economic vitality of the Dutch polity, some might question the imperial potential of a small cluster of watery provinces, so recently emancipated from the clutches of the Habsburg monarchy. Why did this Protestant trading republic evoke so much fear and loathing from the now triumphantly restored English monarchy?

Much of the answer lies in the later-seventeenth-century conviction that trade was the key to power and dominion. Seventeenth-century Europeans felt certain that the most lucrative commercial endeavors were the new long-distance maritime trades. Control of the sea became the key to the universal monarchy. After all, Columbus's discovery of the New World, and the resultant Spanish claims to the monopoly of the South American silver mines, had led the Habsburgs to think "of no less than an Universal Monarchy" (Molloy 1676: sig. A6r; *French Intrigues* 1681: 23; Aglionby 1669: 154). "Whosoever commands the sea, commands the trade," Sir Walter Raleigh had noted long before, "whosoever commands the trade of the world commands the riches of the world and conse-quently the world itself" (Raleigh 1667: 20; Evelyn 1674: 15–17). By the 1670s, it was "a maxim as true as common, that he who is the master of the sea, carries the keys of the world in his hand" ("A Letter" 1677: f. 11r; Temple 1814: vol. 2, 210; *The Character* 1686: 13). Clearly, control of the sea was widely felt to be the first and essential step toward the universal monarchy.

The Dutch, it was argued by enthusiastic Royalists, were not merely eager and aggressive merchants seeking to trade in new territories, they were grasping for a monopoly of all the world's trade. Like the king of Spain in the sixteenth cen-tury, the Dutch "stretched their power to the East and West Indies; in many places whereof they are Lords of the sea-coasts, and have likewise fortified on the main, where king and people are subject to their devotion, and our countrymen the English, lying open to all the outrages a cruel and insulting tyrant can inflict upon them," explained one Restoration pamphleteer (*A Discourse* 1672: 44–45). Anglican Royalist opinion at court, on the London exchange, in the provinces, and even in Persia was unanimous in this interpretation of Dutch economic strategy. The court poet John Dryden expressed the sentiment most eloquently: "Trade, which like blood should circularly flow, / Stop'd in their Channels, found its freedom lost: / Thither the wealth of all the world did go, / And seems but shipwreck'd on so base a coast" (Dryden 1956: 59–60; *Hogan-Moganides* 1674; *The Dutch Design* 1688: 18).

Anglican Royalists were convinced that once the Dutch had control of the seas, they would have all but established the universal monarchy. "The world is now at that pass, that he who is Lord of the Sea, is also of the shore," averred the loyalist and future poet laureate James Howell in his elaborate political al-legory *Dodona's Grove*, "nor, I dare avouch did the Roman Republic, though as well swaddled in her infancy as any ever that was, come near to [the Dutch re-public] in so short a time" (1645: 22; Appelbome 1665: f. 251). It had become commonplace that the Dutch "thought to grasp a pow'r great as old Rome, / Striving to carry all commerce away, / And make the universe their only prey" (Wild 1673: 3; Waller 1963: 25; Crouch 1665: 7; Ogilby 1672: 1–2). When a Dutch-man in a tavern asked why the English insisted on calling his compatriots "butter-boxes," he was reputedly told because "you are so apt to spread everywhere, and for your sauciness must be melted down" (*The Complaisant Companion* 1674: Part 2, 32). Although "no nation can be rich that abounds not in some part of his dominions in shipping, or who neglects trade," the moderate Anglican Royalist Sir Philip Warwick insisted, "yet it is no policy to think to engross it, or be monarchs of it, as Holland hath for a time affected, & pursued that Sea-Monarchy as eagerly as Charles the Fifth or Francis the First did the Land Mon-archy" (1956: 182).[9]

For Anglican Royalists—whether at the Council table, in trade company com-mittee rooms, or in country taverns—the Dutch needed to be fought not be-

---

[9] Warwick did not believe, in 1679, that the Dutch were still pursuing that policy. I owe this ref-erence to the kindness and generosity of Dr. Blair Worden (1978).

cause they were England's greatest economic competitors—although they were that—but because their unconstrained materialism threatened to subvert the entire nexus of ideas on which Restoration England was based. Their commercial republicanism was a cancer that ate away at monarchy. Their religious pluralism and nominal Calvinism threatened to replace morality with atheism and grasping ambition. It was the amoral materialism of the Dutch that generated the political and economic threat to England. The Anglican Royalists complained not that the Dutch were making use of vastly superior economic resources, but that "they treacherously burnt our stores, and murdered our men, committing outrages that the world cannot parallel" (*A Prophecie* 1672: 3; Hyde 1664: f. 377). "We are now chastising" the Dutch, one pamphleteer explained during the third Anglo-Dutch War, "not for their industry . . . but for their ingratitude, incivility, and rag-manners" (*A Discourse* 1672: 50). Anglican Royalist merchants wanted to fight the Dutch not because they thought that they would be able to seize new trade routes, not to pursue their short-term economic self-interest— indeed many of them knew that an Anglo-Dutch war would be disastrous for their particular trades—but because they thought their long-term economic survival was at stake.

Redefinition of Universalist Fears

The Anglo-Dutch War of 1672–1674 was nevertheless a turning point. Immediately after the Restoration, while memories of the anarchy and confusion of the later 1650s were still fresh in the minds of most Englishmen and women, the Anglican Royalist case had seemed particularly strong. A broad range of moderate opinion, including many who had opposed the king in the 1640s or who had accommodated themselves to the protectorate, had been convinced that the threats from the radical sects and from the republicans demanded a foreign policy directed against their European allies, the Dutch. Louis XIV's invasion of the United Provinces in the Dutch Year of Wonders of 1672, however, changed their thinking. The image of the Dutch forced to slit the dikes in a desperate attempt to prevent French armies from overrunning the country made claims that the Dutch were seeking universal monarchy seem incredible.[10] More important, the demise of the Dutch republican regime and William III's consequent assumption of the offices of captain general and stadholder alleviated English fears of the ideological threat posed by the United Provinces. Once again led in arms by the Prince of Orange against a power that sought to dominate Europe, the Dutch now sparked memories of Elizabeth's virtuous comrades in arms.

[10] "After the States of the United Provinces had by their powerful arms constrained Spain to acknowledge them a free state . . . they were for a time the object of their neighbor's admiration and envy, every one endeavoring to court and make alliances with this growing state, which began to be looked upon as the umpire of Europe," recalled one observer from the perspective of the 1680s, "but this high reputation of theirs has suffered notable eclipse since the war of 1672, when France . . . brought them to the very brink of destruction" (*The Designs* 1686: 7).

English moderates had supported war against the Dutch in the 1660s and early 1670s because the Dutch republican party, led by John De Witt, appeared to be ideologically committed to the overthrow of the English monarchy. It was this republican faction, not their domestic enemies the Orangists, who had fallen from Protestant virtue, replacing godly worship with a base materialism. All of the Dutch infringements on the English fishing trade, the atrocities perpetrated in the East Indies, the casuistical application of treaties, even the ideological justification for Dutch mercantile policy—Grotius's *Mare Liberum*—indeed "all the mischief which hath befallen this nation," wrote Stubbe (1673a: sig. C1) "hath ever been occasioned, or fomented by that [republican] party." Consequently, the moderates had never wanted to destroy the Dutch, but only the republican faction. "We may hope for a better neighborhood when persons of honor and integrity shall rule their Councils, and the Government be reduced into some rational form," argued Henry Stubbe, who was working as a government propagandist at the time, "but certain it is that most of the mischiefs which have befallen Europe during the last century have had their origin from this perfidious faction of Oldenbarnevelt" (Stubbe 1673a: sigs. C3–C4). English moderates, then, were fighting the Dutch on behalf of the Prince of Orange and rational government. "Be just to him, and us, the quarrel ends," one poet simply put it (Crouch 1665: 8; Wild 1673: 4–5).

The sensational demise of the republican party in the United Provinces coming, as it did, in the wake of the spectacular successes of the French armies, made the Nonconformist and radical claim—a claim made persistently and with increasing frequency throughout the 1660s—that the French had been seeking universal monarchy all along seem all the more credible. This grouping in the English political nation had always denied that the Dutch were seeking universal monarchy. Instead the success of Dutch commerce, the republican Slingsby Bethel insisted, could result only from "industry and ingenuity" (1671: 30–31). In this view, the wars against the Dutch made no economic sense. The Nonconformist divine and former parliamentarian Joseph Hill derided "the senseless clamor of men" for war, crying, "We are competitors for trade! It's our interest! Our interest! Down with the Dutch!" because it was manifestly clear that "the world is wide enough, and the sea large enough for both nations to exercise their skill and industry" (Hill 1673: sig. G2). The only explanation for the Anglo-Dutch wars, Nonconformists and their ideological fellow travelers had claimed, was that they were part of the French grand strategy, a strategy designed to achieve the universal monarchy. The massive French naval buildup, Colbert's mercantilist policies, and the duplicitous French mediation between the English and the Dutch were all of a piece. No one could now doubt that they were "setting up an Universal Monarchy of commerce" (*The French Intrigues* 1681: 5).

In the 1670s, as French armies seemed poised to overrun all Europe, the English began to ask themselves how they had been duped into fighting wars so manifestly against their interest. The answer was omnipresent in Restoration England: the French had successfully implemented a policy of cultural subversion. The French, cognizant that it would be "a hard matter" to conquer England, had discovered "finer ways to victory than by force of arms, and their gold has done them better service than their iron" (Bethel 1677: 24–25; 1680: sigs. A4v–A5r). Indeed, French inducements had been so successful that the English court was overflowing with French agents. It was precisely these "French counsels," these men who "applied themselves to France," these men who scrutinized "all over the kingdom to find out men of arbitrary principles, that will bow the knee to Baal, in order to their promotion to all public commissions and employments," these men who have "undertaken and do make it their business, under so legal and perfect a government, to introduce a French slavery, and instead of so pure a religion, to establish the Roman idolatry," whom the parliamentarian poet Andrew Marvell blamed in his classic *Account of the Growth of Popery and Arbitrary Government* for England's failure to prevent the growing power of France and for attempting to make the English monarchy "absolute" (1677: 14, 16, 100, 151, 154). While the Dutch had posed a real threat to invade England, French conquest would necessarily be more subtle. This realization led to a politicization of culture.

The powerful and cunning Louis XIV had a wide variety of means to infiltrate the English political nation. French women were well known to be "engines of state," who brought with them "corresponding colonies of that restless, ambitious and intriguing nation, to make the interest of that court where they go bend to that of their native country" (*The Politician* 1681: 24–25). Charles II's well-publicized affairs with French women, principally Louise de Kerouaille, Duchess of Portsmouth, led at least one member of Parliament to exclaim that "he cannot repose any confidence in the King, if he puts his counsel into 'strange women'" (Grey 1763: vol. 4, 367; Reresby 1875: 191).[11]

More subtle, yet perhaps more dangerous than French embraces, were French dresses and French manners. French romances, French dances, French plays— alas, even French fruit—were all the rage. "A Curse on these French cheats," swore one of the Trimmer playwright Thomas Shadwell's stage creations, "they begin to be as rife amongst us as their country disease, and do almost as much mischief too: No corner, without French tailors, weavers, milliners, strong watermen, perfumers, and surgeons" (1671: 2). "We must have all French about us," seethed another pamphleteer in mock disbelief, "their behavior, their fashions, their garb in wearing them, their mean way of house-keeping (to the utter extinguishment of the noble way of Old English Hospitality), their needy men for servants, their mere dietary leeches or scholastic methodists (no better than

---

[11] Speech of Michael Mallet, May 23, 1677 (cited in Grey 1763: vol. 4, 367). Mallet was drawing an explicit parallel to Solomon's loving many foreign women and the consequent demise of Israel detailed in 1 Kings 11. One popular poem of 1679, "The Dissolution," made a similar point: "When French runs through the Prince's veins / And he by theirs not our law reigns / When French creeps into the Royal bed / First charming codpiece then the head / And Monarchs swives on good behaviour / But as he'll show dear Monsieur favor / When female buttocks dictate thus / Good Lord what will become of us? / Is there no end of monarch's itch / who lolls upon a fulsome bitch / Who ranker as the adder grows / Ferreting her belly with his nose / And swears upon her bawdy skin / He'll let the mass & French troops in / Assign his crown & regal power / To be disposed of by a whore" (British Library, Add. MSS 34362, f. 49r).

most of our own) for physicians; their cast tooth-drawers and barbers that had not worth enough to earn bread at home, to become our admired surgeons; French music, French dancing-masters, French air in our very countenances, French legs, French hats, French compliments, French grimaces" (Nedham 1678a: 37–38). "Such is the witchcraft also upon the other nations of Europe," another author warned, "that having made the French language and humors universal, I cannot but look on it as a sad omen of Universal Slavery" because "a nation's taking of language from another nation, and preferring it before their own, hath usually been a fore-runner of, and prepared the way for, its conquest" (*Nero* 1690: 13).

When, in the early 1670s the English attempted to emancipate themselves from French fashion and reassert the native style of wearing vests, the French were furious and sent Charles's sister, the Duchess of Orleans, to "laugh us out of these vests" (Savile 1689: Vol. 1, 227). The French placed a high value on this minor incident, the Marquis of Halifax recalled, because they knew well "that it is a natural introduction first to make the world their apes, that they may be afterwards their slaves" (*Nero* 1690: 67).[12] Although English attempts "to ape the French" had only rendered them "ridiculous," it brought "great pride" to the French because they realized it allowed them "to preside over our genius, and to guide it into all the fashions which their rambling fancies take" (*Remarques* 1673: 97–98).

Along with French fashions came French principles. "That same legereté, on which the French so value themselves," and that had so recently become the fashion in London as well as Paris, "is but in plain English, a lightness of humor, by the which they are easily piped into a new mode of government" (*A Prospect* 1681: 66–67). "Who is so blind not to see what farther steps have been taken by the conspirators," Robert Ferguson asked, "not only to be in love with the French mode and manners, but also with the very French yoke of slavery put about the necks of their own natives, longing for that day to come, when the same yoke of tyranny and slavery, shall be fitted upon the Englishmen's shoulders, as now upon the French asses" (1682: 159–60; see also De Hay 1681: 1–2; *The Catholick Ballad* 1674).

After the Dutch revolution of 1672, large numbers of Presbyterian Royalists and moderate Anglicans, those who had loathed and feared the aggressive republicanism of the De Witt faction, could now join their more radical Protestant brethren in denouncing the political machinations of the King of France. They felt free to call for a new Dutch alliance, an alliance that they very much hoped would bring as much glory as had the old Elizabethan Anglo-Dutch alliance, because their quarrel had been with a corrupt political party and not with Dutch political or religious culture.

The Presbyterian Royalist Anthony Ashley Cooper, Earl of Shaftesbury, was merely the most flamboyant of those who shifted from an anti-Dutch to an anti-

---

[12] For discussions of the emergence of the vest, and its resubmergence under the weight of French style, see De Beer (1938–1939), De Marly (1974), and Kuchta (1990).

French alignment in the early 1670s. As lord chancellor, and member of the infamous Cabal, the Earl of Shaftesbury delivered the single most celebrated piece of Restoration oratory. Comparing England to Rome, the United Provinces to Carthage and himself to Cato, he exclaimed "*Delenda est Carthago*" (Grey 1763: vol. 2, 2). "Let this be remembered," Shaftesbury thundered, "the States of Holland are England's eternal enemy both by interest and inclination." This, he explained, was because they were "the common enemies to all monarchies, and I may say especially to ours, their only competitors for trade and power at sea, and who only stand in their way to an universal empire, as great as Rome" (*Journal of the House* 1672: Vol. 12, 525–26). Although this speech has usually been interpreted as a spectacular piece of Hollandophobic rhetoric, Shaftesbury was at pains to make clear that he attributed Dutch policy not to the nation as a whole but to the republican faction. England declared war against the Dutch republic, Shaftesbury elucidated in autumn 1673, because "the king was obliged for the security of a lasting peace, as also by the laws of gratitude and relation, to see the House of Orange settled, and the Loevestein, that Carthaginian party brought down" (*Journal of the House* 1673: vol. 12, 589).[13]

Shaftesbury was not being inconsistent and not displaying pique for having been dismissed from the Privy Council in 1675 when he warned that the King of France "is grown the most potent of us all at sea." "'Tis incredible the money he hath, and is bestowing in making harbors, he makes nature itself give way to the vastness of his expense," marveled Shaftesbury, and after all this, shall a Prince so wise, so intent upon his affairs, be thought to make all these preparations to sail over land and fall on the back of Hungary, and batter the walls of Kaminitz, or is it possible he should oversee his interest in seizing Ireland, a thing so feasible to him, if he be master of the seas, as he certainly now is; and which when attained gives him all the Southern Mediterranean, East and West India trade and renders him both by situation and excellent harbors, perpetual Master of the Seas without dispute." The only hope for "disengagement from the French interest," Shaftesbury insisted, lay in the "two Houses differing from the sense and opinion of Whitehall" (*Two Speeches* 1675: 8–9).

Who were these men who prevented England from going to war against France? This pernicious "French interest" and "opinion of Whitehall," Shaftesbury identified as "some of the Episcopal clergy of our British isles" as well as the "High Episcopal Man and the Old Cavalier." These men wanted "to fight the old quarrel all over again" in defense of the principle that "monarchy is of divine right." "Our statesmen and bishops," insisted Shaftesbury, drawing the most frightening of parallels, are "now as well agreed as in old Laud's time, on the same principles with the same passion to attain their end" (*Two Speeches* 1675: 10–11; Ashley Cooper 1675: 1, 7, 34).[14]

---

[13] The Dutch republican party were known as the Loevesteiners because the supporters of Jan van Oldenbarnevelt, including John de Witt's father and Hugo Grotius, had been imprisoned in Loevestein castle by Prince Maurice.

[14] Henry Stubbe undertook a similar ideological odyssey to that of Shaftesbury (Jacob, 1983: 117–18, 131–32; Stubbe 1672, 1673a, 1673b).

John Milton's godson and nephew John Phillips, who catered to more popular audiences than Shaftesbury, also shifted in the 1670s from castigating Dutch designs on universal dominion to excoriating the French pretensions on universal monarchy. In his almanac for 1672, Phillips claimed that the Dutch sought to "establish the fifth monarchy in an Universal Commonwealth" (1672: 6). A decade later, Phillips published a popular dialogue between the devil and his servants, delineating the French strategy for achieving the universal monarchy. Louis XIV "no more dreaming of mortality, than you of dying," Belsagor explained to Pluto, "is resolved to make himself the Universal Monarch . . . to which purpose he goes daily on, vexing, tormenting and encroaching upon his neighbors, that nobody can live in quiet for him. No leagues will hold him, no faith will bind him up." Phillips's Frenchman, "Monsieur François," neatly summarized the inevitable consequence: "my master will have all or none; for though he may be constrained to use the Turk, you may be sure he'll give him Polyphemus's Law, devour him last, for he hates competitors" (1682: 2, 28–29, 38).

French economic policies, French military victories, and manifest French perfidy convinced all but the hottest Cavalier, all but the most extreme Tory, in short all but the Duke of York and his immediate supporters, that England needed to join the European struggle against the intended French universal monarchy (Reresby 1875: 115–16, 118; Coventry 1677: ff. 16v–17r; "The Duke of York's Farewell" 1679–1680; "Hodge's Vision" n.d.). Throughout the 1670s, anti-French sentiment was building in a powerful crescendo of vituperation. "If his Majesty will give up all such as speak with freedom of the French," the English envoy John Doddington reported as early as 1670, "for anything I know he must part with most of his subjects" (June 20 and June 27, 1670). William Garroway informed Parliament that "our fears of ruin from the French are in everybody's mouth" (Grey 1763: vol. 3, 8). "There are ninety in a hundred against France, all England over," chimed in Colonel Birch (vol. 3, 127). The London weavers were said to be "in a mutiny against the French" ("A Letter" 1677: f. 15r). Sir John Reresby was certain that "the nation did much desire a war with France" (Reresby 1875: 118). "There is no discourse here but of war," the Earl of Huntingdon reported from London in the Winter of 1678 (Hastings, 1678b). As Colonel Birch returned to London for the parliamentary session, people everywhere cried, "God bless you, you are going to fight against the French" (Grey 1763: vol. 5, 238–39). The Earl of Danby, who was in a position to know, wrote to the Earl of Essex that "truly things appear to me more like a war with France than otherwise" (Osborne 1944: 62). The English were not unaware of the costs involved in fighting the world's greatest power, nor were they unwilling to augment the state machinery to fight a war on which their existence as a nation depended. "They of the country seem not to be afraid of war, nor what is the necessary concomitant of it, taxes," Thomas Thynne informed Halifax, "so universal is their dread of the growth of France" (Thynne n.d.). Indeed, so certain was one English army officer that there would be war with France that he prepared and published an inspirational speech for his troops (*Advice* 1680). In this context, it does not seem that Marchamont Nedham was exaggerating by much when he claimed "that if it were put to the vote of the people, whether a war or no war with France, I believe not one in a thousand, but would be for a war" (Nedham 1678b: 6).

The Reign of James II

While Charles II never did begin the much-desired war against France, he at least promised to do so as soon as the country was again united. James II (1685–1688), however, never felt it necessary to make even a rhetorical concession to public opinion. To the contrary, he made every effort to suppress public discussion of European affairs.

The Tory reaction of the 1680s had provided James II with a remarkably loyal and united political nation. The ease with which he suppressed the Duke of Monmouth's religiously inspired rebellion (1685) convinced all who cared to comment that the time was right for James to take on the great European menace, Louis XIV. Instead of opposing French tyranny, however, James appeared to adopt the French style of government. Rather than send English redcoats to resurrect the glories of Crecy, Poitiers, and Agincourt, James II burdened his own people with a standing army, violated parliamentary prohibitions against employment of papists in the army and in the government, and made every effort to make Parliament itself subservient to his will. Consequently, the English people throughout the country welcomed William III's intervention. Far from expressing a traditional xenophobia, the English were well aware that in autumn 1688, the battle for the mastery of Europe was being fought in England. In Yorkshire "neither the gentry nor common people seemed much afraid or concerned," marveled the loyalist Sir John Reresby (1875: 408). The Earl of Dorset, a political moderate, was heard to say "that if they come it may be called the Merry Invasion" (Westby n.d.: f. 40). A pamphleteer friendly to James II could not but admit that the people "are running headlong into a slavery to the Dutch" (*Dutch Design* 1688: 32). When discussing the intended Dutch invasion, the "people yet speak of it smilingly," reported the Londoner William Westby (n.d.: f. 37r). Reflecting on the events of 1688 more than a decade later, Charles Davenant explained William III's popular support in the simplest of terms: he had achieved the desired ends. "The Late Revolution, and the war that happened upon it," Davenant recalled, "were both carried on upon the same foot of opposing the growth of the French Monarchy" (1701: 28).

A Struggle between Competing Universalisms?

Was the Restoration debate about foreign policy, then, a debate over competing universalist religions? Was Louis XIV opposed exclusively because he was a Roman Catholic? Did Englishmen and women desert James II in 1688 because he was a Catholic pursuing a Catholic foreign policy? In short, were the events of 1688 merely a rerun of those of 1588 with Louis XIV replacing Philip II as the universalist Catholic archvillain? Or, as Lawrence Stone has recently asked, "was British nationalism fueled by fear of France or hatred of popery, or were the two indistinguishable?" (1994: 2).

A close examination of the language of political discussion makes one doubt the absolute continuity of political argument from the late sixteenth through the late seventeenth century. Although it is true that both those in favor of war against the Dutch and those insistent on doing battle with the French thought that their policies would reduce the risk from popery, popery no longer had a predominantly theological meaning. A term so flexible as to embrace the predominantly Calvinist Dutch and the largely Roman Catholic French commented on more than just religious proclivities. Indeed, it is clear that in Restoration England the competing definitions of *popery* turned on political and cultural as well as religious associations. The Dutch, the Anglican Royalists pointed out, were Papists because they endorsed king-killing, something that no good Protestant could stomach. In the view of the Nonconformists and their allies, the French monarchy was papist, despite its celebrated Gallicanism and spectacular squabbles with the pope, because it was willing to use the power of priestcraft to promote absolute power and arbitrary government. Indeed, even those who saw popery in the policies of the Restoration government did not believe that the Stuart brothers—more celebrated for their sexual exploits than for their personal piety—were religious enthusiasts. Instead, it was claimed, Charles II and James II derived their religious principles from their politics. The two brothers in exile "suffered their heads to be intoxicated with a necessity of absolute power, looking upon it as the only remedy to prevent the frequent revolutions in England," maintained one pamphleteer, and they soon realized "that the only means to bring about their ends upon the English, and to free the Crown from depending upon Parliaments, was to introduce Popery by degrees into the island; for that under pretense of those insensible changes which religion would suffer, it would be easy to alter the laws and form of government." In short, they determined that "of all the Christian sects, the Roman is that which best agrees with arbitrary dominion, and is most proper to blind obedience" (*Happy Union* 1689: 1, 13–14).

Seventeenth-century European politics, in the eyes of Restoration Englishmen and women, then, was a struggle to maintain national integrities against aspiring universal monarchs and not an unending series of religious wars.[15] Protestant England had a special role to play in this international power game, but it was not a confessional role. England should maintain a Protestant foreign policy only in that it should protect Protestantism where it was established by national laws; very few still called for crusades against Rome. During the Thirty Years' War a wide variety of European princes united "against the aspiring House

[15] The rhetoric of balance of power is necessarily incompatible with a confessional foreign policy. An eschatological struggle between the forces of the Reformation and Counter-Reformation, between the forces of good and evil, can brook no compromise. It had to be a fight to the death.

of Austria for the general good and liberty of all Europe. . . . Some ascribe all this to controversies in religion," the republican Algernon Sidney admitted, "but besides many reasons that persuade me to believe that even Urban VIII, then Pope, did at first favor the design of Gustavus; no man can continue in that opinion who considers that France, Venice, and Savoy three Popish states were the contrivers and advancers of it" (1666: 153–54).[16] Supporters of the restored monarchy understood international conflicts in the same terms. "Wars for religion," maintained one 1660s polemicist, are "but a speculation, an imaginary thing or as some problems in the metaphysic, astrology, or chimie, which wise or rather cunning men make use of to abuse fools, and that in truth there never was nor ever will be any" (Clifford 1665: 5). It was the historical role of maintaining the European balance, of preventing the growth of a universal monarchy, that, their critics claimed, the restored Stuarts had abdicated. "That equality between the two monarchies which we might forever have preserved," mourned the moderate Royalist Marquis of Halifax, "hath been chiefly broken by us, whose interest it was above all others to maintain" (Savile 1689: 224).

Not only did the English deny that their own role in European politics was primarily confessional, but also they insisted that Louis XIV's drive toward the universal monarchy had precious little to do with religion. It was true that Louis XIV mercilessly persecuted his Protestant subjects, but the former Royalist Sir William Coventry was quick to point out, "the rigors in religion, in states, arise from interest rather than religion; formerly Spain was more rigorous in religion, and now France" (Grey 1763, vol. 2, 203). The implication could not have been clearer. Religious persecution was a means to appear holy, while actually following the precepts of Machiavelli. The totality of Louis XIV's actions made a mockery of his claim to be *dévot*. Since the French king was not above weakening the Catholic Church "especially in secular advantages of wealth and power," argued the government propagandist Marchamont Nedham in the 1670s, "it almost equally concerns both Papist and Protestant, in reference to religion, to adventure their distinct powers and interests in one common bottom and resolution, to war with him, and to hinder the obstinate pursuit of an Universal Monarchy" (1678a: 72).[17] Neither Protestant nor Catholic polemicists believed that they were engaged in the last phases of the great struggle between the Reformation and the Counter-Reformation.

Philip II of Spain might have seen himself as the secular arm of the papacy, but it was pure anachronism to describe Louis XIV in those terms. "Nobody thinks that France in its intentions of conquering us, ever thought of the Church," scoffed one Orangist, "or that the Emperor troubled his head about religion, when he designed our assistance; this was frequent pretense about a hundred

---

[16] Clearly Algernon Sidney understood foreign policy in terms of opposition to universal monarchy, not in terms of "uniting the Protestant cause in Europe," as Jonathan Scott claims. Apparently Dr. Scott has based his analysis on the same pages from the "Court Maxims" (Scott 1988a: 204–06). My reading of this document is much closer to that offered by Houston (1991).

[17] Roman Catholic pamphleteers made the same point (*The Present Policies* 1689: 19–20).

years ago; but time and experience has taught us all wit" (*Two Letters* 1673: 9). "The question now on foot is a communion of state, not of faith" argued the author of a print distributed in 1688 (*A Learned Discourse* 1685: 4–5). Clearly "the main business is not now either about Calvinists or Catholics" but rather about "the restitution to everyone of that which belongs to him; and to prevent the further usurpation of Lewis XIV" (*Present French King* 1691: 18–19; see also *Nero* 1690: 4; Yalden 1681; sig. B3; *A New Discovery* 1691: 4; Lawrence 1961: 38–39; *A Learned Discourse* 1685: 130–31; *A View* 1689: 58).

In this context, it is hardly surprising to discover that the alliance against France was multiconfessional, and indeed multinational. Though it is true, of course, that the Dutch and the English were particularly concerned with protecting the Protestant religion, this was only because it was the religion established by law in their dominions. Freedom of Protestant worship was but one of the plethora of liberties threatened by the French. "For though the preservation of the Protestant religion be most the concernment of England and Holland," elaborated one observer of the European scene, "yet the special and immediate end of the preservation of Flanders, and the general end of holding the balance of Europe is Universal" (*Discourses upon the Modern Affairs of Europe* 1680: 9–10). Such a multiconfessional alliance was possible because England and its Protestant allies, unlike the French, were firmly committed to national self-determination in matters of religion. As early as the 1660s, Sir Richard Temple, the country M.P., had argued that "foreign alliances" are to be secured "with respect to the balance of monarchy & obviating that design [for universal monarchy]." Therefore, Temple concluded, "not only the Protestants but all who are on a distinct foot as the Portugal, the Catholic Princes of Germany, Dutch Italian Princes not dependent on Spain, nay the Pope himself, *qua* Prince are to be united in this common bottom" (1667: f. 13r).

Religion formed but one part of the national identities threatened by France. Consequently a war against France was a war to protect national integrities, not a war of religion. One particularly eloquent polemicist explained:

> The grand concern is now to support the right of nations, which is common to all and to prevent the introducing of maxims into the world which destroy all commerce among men, and will certainly render humane society no less dangerous and insupportable than that of lions and tigers . . . to stop the inundation of a rapid torrent against the impetuosity of which neither leagues nor marriages, neither oaths nor ties of blood and parentage, neither amity nor condescensions, are mounds or dams sufficient to defend the common bulwark of Christendom against a vast design, which has no other ground but the insatiable thirst of conquest, no other end than despotic domination by clout of arms and slight of intrigue, nor any limits but such as fortune shall prescribe. In short, England is now to decide the fate of Europe, and to pronounce the sentence of her liberty or bondage (*Nero* 1690: 63–64).

This language was not a "Xerox copy" of early-seventeenth-century religious enthusiasm that one historian claimed to discover.[18]

---

[18] The phrase is Jonathan Scott's (1991: 6).

The European experience in the Thirty Years' War and the English experience during the Interregnum had taught them all the impossibility of ever concluding a war of religion. The Treaty of Westphalia ending the Thirty Years' War and the resignation of the Barebones Parliament (1653)—which ended England's brief flirtation with a theocracy—marked a fundamental turning point in European history. The bloody experiences of wars, both within countries and among different European polities, had convinced most in Europe that governments could not promote the salvation of their subjects. Competing religious universalist claims could never be resolved. Therefore, when contemplating the impending war against France, the English moderate Sir Thomas Lee warned Parliament that "if you make this a war of religion, you will never have done" (Grey 1763: vol. 5, 242).

In the later seventeenth century the defense of national identities, and not the propagation of the true religion, had become the organizing principle of English political discourse. Although English society remained profoundly religious, as the reformation of manners movement amply demonstrates, English political debate was taking place in increasingly Erastian terms. The Protestant religion now made up but one element of the national interest.[19] Interest had replaced religious enthusiasm and ideas of English liberty had displaced conceptions of apocalyptic Protestant internationalism as the dominant themes of Restoration political discourse. "The genius and disposition of the times," the courtier Samuel Fortrey found soon after the Restoration, was "to study more the interest and improvement of the nation than usually heretofore" (1907: 9). Slingsby Bethel, who was more likely to speak a popular than a courtly language, agreed that "the prosperity or adversity, if not the life and death of a State, is bound up in the observing or neglecting of its interest" (1671: sig. A2r). The Tory lord keeper Sir Heneage Finch, who agreed with Bethel about little else, emphasized that "joint interests have often secured the peace of differing religions, but agreeing professions hath no example of preserving the peace of different interests. Religion never united those whose interests were divided" (1673). It was to this language of interest, not to the obsolete language of confessional strife, that polemicists appealed when they suggested that war against the Dutch or the French would protect England's trade (De Ronquillo 1681: 2).

The nation, not Scripture, determined the proper interest of the government. Indeed, though government itself existed by divine right, the form was necessarily a national creation.[20] "But where this high power and sovereignty rests, in

---

[19] Let me emphasize that I am not arguing that religion was unimportant or that religious proclivities had nothing to do with political alignments. Indeed, I am convinced that Nonconformists were far more likely to be Whigs, and High Churchmen tended to be Tories. Rather, I am trying to highlight an important phase in the *process* of secularization. Private devotion remained very profound; public politics, however, were discussed in terms of interest rather than religious truth. For other comments on secularization of political language, see Zwicker (1988), Slack (1985: chap. 9), and Worden (1978: 5–16, 51–55). Alan Houston has shown that for Algernon Sidney "separating religion and politics . . . made it possible to preserve the integrity of each" (Houston 1991: 125).

[20] The idea of unique national interests was central to later-seventeenth-century defenses of monarchy (Houston 1991: 81).

whom 'tis lodged, this is a point not so obvious: nor can the [saints] or holy Fathers any way help us in the discovery," observed one commentator; "the customs and particular laws of every nation, are only capable to direct us in that scrutiny" (*A Prospect* 1681: 6; Sidney 1990: 99, 502–10).[21] "There can be no universal rule," agreed Daniel Defoe in his justly famous *Reflections on the Late Great Revolution*, "because that the laws vary according to the differing constitution of government that is in several nations" (1689: 56–57). Because governments existed to serve the nation, even though they were not necessarily created by the people, it was absolutely incumbent on them to adopt a foreign policy that was in the best interest of the nation. In the English case, this precept necessarily elevated the importance of Parliament, the national assembly. "Now since interest will not lie, how is it morally possible, that the major part of the nation so qualified should act contrary to the true and proper interest of their country?" asked one controversialist, "for tho' particular men may be imposed upon by artifice, or deluded with pretenses, or biased by private advantages, yet 'tis not imaginable, that the whole body should be so infatuated as not to see or so stupidly tame as not to oppose, as far as lawfully they may, what tends their universal ruin" (*Vox Patriae* 1681: sig. A1v). The application to England's role in European affairs was obvious. "This House has many years now advised the King to suppress the growing greatness of France, and the ministers would not," complained Sir Thomas Meres, whose principles were sufficiently moderate to receive approbation from both Whigs and Tories, "the interest of the nation is in this House, and the ministers are of another interest" (Grey 1763: vol. 5, 357).

The center of later seventeenth-century political discussion was captured by those who understood the world in national rather than religious terms. Naturally, extremists on either end of the political spectrum persisted in describing domestic politics in exclusively religious terms and demanded an international crusade against the anti-Christ.[22] But these men and women were already marginal to a debate conducted fundamentally about interest. Halifax's Trimmer, an imaginary Restoration moderate,[23] came very close to expressing the typical worldview. "Our Trimmer is far from idolatry in other things, in one thing only he cometh near it, his country is in some degree his idol," elaborated the Marquis of Halifax, "he doth not worship the Sun, because it is not peculiar to us, it rambleth about the world and is less kind to us than it is to other countries; but for the earth of England, though perhaps inferior to that of many places abroad, to him there is divinity in it, and he had rather die than see a spire of English grass trampled upon by a foreign trespasser." The conclusion was clear: "before the French blood can be let into our bodies, every drop of our own must be drawn out" (Savile 1689: 237).

---

[21] I find it difficult to accept Jonathan Scott's claim that Sidney had an "exceedingly incomplete" notion of "where the boundaries between nation states lay" (Scott 1991: 87). The notion of nation and national interest is central to Sidney's critique of absolute monarchy.

[22] Both non-Jurors and extreme Dissenters, such as William Penn, continued to place religion first on their lists of political objectives. Unsurprisingly, both groups became Jacobites.

[23] I discuss Trimmer or moderate ideology in greater depth in Pincus (1996b).

The Advent of Later Seventeenth-Century Nationalism

After decades of debate and discussion in coffeehouses, playhouses, country taverns, Anglican churches, and Dissenting meeting houses, the English knew what was at stake in their struggle with France. " 'Tis true this war must needs be prodigiously expensive," admitted the author of one pamphlet distributed soon after William of Orange had arrived in London, but "in cases of this quality, people must do as in a storm at sea, rather throw part of the lading overboard, than founder the vessel" (*A Short Discourse* 1688: 16). "France does endeavor by certain emissaries that are never wanting to her, cunningly to persuade everyone, that the war, besides the blood of part of their best soldiers, will cost them vast sums of money," sneered another defender of the Revolution, but "one must needs have a mean opinion of that generous people, to think that they are either so covetous as to be thus wrought upon, or so simple, as for the saving their money and sparing the blood of some few, to do that which would most certainly be the cause of both their lives and fortunes, or plunge them at least into a constant misery" (*Fate of France* 1690: sig. A2v). The English people did indeed prove willing—if not always cheerfully—to spend their money in wars against the French aspirant to universal monarchy. The establishment of the Bank of England (1694) was only the first of a series of institutions that amounted to "a peculiarly British version of the fiscal-military state, complete with huge armies and navies, industrious administrators, high taxes and huge debts." I claim that Englishmen and women were willing to suffer through the infringements on their personal liberty implicit in the Augustan state because they knew the alternative was subjugation to a universal monarch. Although the full extent of the newly created state might have been unanticipated and unintended by the revolutionaries of 1688, they were well aware of the potential costs (Brewer 1989: 250).[24] The socially diverse nationalist revolutionaries of 1688–1689 created the English Augustan state.

It is not quite right, however, to say that a nationalist culture in and of itself created the Augustan state. The process was more complicated. The religiously charged universalist culture of late-sixteenth- and early-seventeenth-century Europe had created the preconditions for the European Thirty Years' War (1618–1648) and the English Civil Wars. Even though Charles I ultimately was able to avoid participating fully in the European struggle, his policies drew him into the domestic conflict. These civil wars, in turn, created fiscal demands that required the development of a massively expanded state apparatus. It was this expansion

[24] Charles Tilly might be right to claim that "the eighteenth-century wars so greatly accelerated the expansion [of the state] that from the perspective of century's end the beginning looks puny" (1995: 124). But in stating the issue this way, he minimizes the revolution in attitudes instantiated in 1688–1689. The state was not created Minerva-like. In 1688–1689, people all over England, from a wide variety of milieus, declared that a state defined in national terms was necessary. By insisting on the insularity and localism of seventeenth-century English political sensibilities—by failing to read deeply in the primary materials of early modern England—Tilly doesn't grasp this point.

of the state that helped to create the cultural demand and social institutions for a new national political culture. Once created, however, that national political culture drew on traditions and information that allowed for criticism as well as support of state action. When James II chose to ignore this potent national public opinion, he sparked a nationalist revolution. The emerging embryonic state created the conditions necessary for the emergence of a nationalist culture, which in turn demanded a new nationalist state.

The purveyors and participants in the new national political culture naturally took a new and abiding interest in political economy. Discussions of universal monarchy increasingly turned on the economic as well as the narrowly defined martial resources of the various European states. However, the shift in English national sentiment from an anti-Dutch to an anti-French orientation had little to do with any change in the relative economic status of those two powers. Instead, that shift involved a shift in the national political economic thinking—from an agrarian zero-sum game model to a more commercial model of expanding economic horizons. That move in public sentiment, in turn, was related to a larger ideological shift in favor of a politics of liberty, a politics of national liberty understood in juxtaposition to the politics of universal monarchy. In this case, to use George Steinmetz's formulation, the new "social 'variable'" was the widespread realization that Louis XIV's overrunning of the Spanish Netherlands made it a more serious threat. This new data could be understood only "within the meaning systems"—the discussion of universal monarchy—of the English political nation (Steinmetz, introduction to this volume.)

Finally, the newly enlarged and politically charged English nation had come to a nationalist/particularist, rather than a religious/universalist, understanding of domestic and international politics. James II, it becomes clear, lost his crown not because of his religious belief, but because he had forsaken the national interest. Englishmen and women rallied around James, despite his known Catholicism, in the Exclusion Crisis of 1681 and during Monmouth's religiously inspired rebellion of 1685, because they hoped he, as the rightful heir to the throne, would maintain the ancient political and cultural constitution and protect England against the aspiring universal monarch. "I am not of opinion that the King being a Papist, has made himself incapable of the Crown," argued the Whig jurist Serjeant Maynard (Grey 1763: vol. 9, 17). A polemicist friendly to James II also knew that "it is not Roman Catholic or Protestant religion is the quarrel" (*Dutch Design* 1688: 21). Instead the Stuart brothers' crime was they have "forsaken their true interest, blindly to follow that of France." " 'Tis an untruth that the new King of England is an usurper under the pretense of religion," insisted one of William's supporters, "James II, seduced by the crafty and violent counsels of the French, together with his own haughty and capricious humor, had violated the laws of which he was the Protector and not the sovereign" (*Present French King* 1691: 19).[25] "If this King had followed his true interest," concluded one postrevolutionary pamphleteer, "it is certain, as great a Catholic as he was, he

[25] Algernon Sidney predicted that James II would "rather be a tributary to France than a lawful king of England" (1990: 265).

might have peaceably enjoyed his three kingdoms; might have been the arbitrator of all Christendom, might have maintained peace and tranquility throughout Europe, might have openly professed his religion, favored his Catholic subjects, and might even have placed some of them in public employments, especially military, without much offending his Protestant subjects" (*A View* 1689: 37, 43).

But James II chose instead to mimic Louis XIV at home and appease him abroad. In so doing, he united Whigs, Trimmers, and moderate Tories in a fragile, yet potent nationalist alliance. The events of 1688–1689, then, should not be seen as yet another in a long string of religious wars, but as a permanent redefinition of English political culture and society, a final rejection of the French style of governance.[26] Arguments against French universalist aspirations enunciated by the newly important commercial sectors, by common lawyers, and by Anglican ministers and Dissenting preachers all demanded a war against Louis XIV. When James II refused to fight that war, in part because it implied a theory of politics that he abhorred, the English rejected him and forged a new government and state apparatus that would combat the French. This account of the origins of England's Glorious Revolution calls into question the "decisive causal import" that Philip Gorski attributed to "Calvinism and ascetic Protestantism" in early modern national state-formation. Only after a retreat from the universalist claims of Calvinism could the English imagine a particularist nation and consequently create a national state (Gorski 1993: 305).[27] Late-seventeenth-century English nationalism, then, was not merely a cultural construction of a few disenchanted intellectuals. It was a popular social movement created as a response to a historically specific set of material and political circumstances. After two centuries of struggle among universalist principles—an age in which the only means to combat one universalism was to set up another against it—the English and a wide variety of other Europeans discovered that defining political goals in nationalist terms provided the only hope of escaping from insoluble conflict. Studying the international context provides a rich and nuanced account of the genesis of nationalism as political ideology, and only in going beyond the nation in question can one transcend a nationalist account of the nation as natural and imminent. Nationalism, I contend, arises out of the nexus of international politics.

Later-seventeenth-century England, then, did not witness the dawn of the age of secularism, but the advent of a new skepticism about the possibility of attaining religious truth in this world.[28] The English situated their resistance to James II not in the traditional accents of universalist religious discourse, but in a new

[26] This was the point the Earl of Danby made to the Earl of Chesterfield in September 1688: "I confess as to my own part I had rather lose my life in the field than live under an arbitrary power, and see our laws and religion changed, which is now visibly the King's intention" (Osborne 1944: 135).

[27] Although Gorski is right to highlight problems with the accounts of Anderson, Corrigan, and Sayer—England did not remain an absolutist state throughout the seventeenth century—he is surely wrong to assert that administrative centralization was "undone during the political upheavals of the 17th century" (1993: 267). The Glorious Revolution, as Brewer (1989) has shown, created a huge new state apparatus.

[28] The centrality of the retreat from universalism, in this case religious universalism, to the advent of nationalism was noticed by Polin (1981). But his dating of this phenomenon to the late eighteenth century reflects his Francocentric focus.

ideology of nationalism.[29] This ideology—made possible but not inevitable by the advent of print capitalism—became plausible and persuasive in the context of a pan-European struggle against an aspiring universal monarch. The English drew on a national identity that had long existed and, in the crucible of political resistance, forged a nationalism, a political "loyalty" as Ronald Suny has put it, "which overrides all other loyalties" (Suny 1993: 13; Breuilly 1993: 2).[30] A Glorious Revolution indeed.

References

Advice to a Soldier. 1680. London: John Shadd.

Aglionby, William. 1669. *The Present State of the United Provinces of the Low Countries.* London: John Starkey.

Alter, Peter. 1989. *Nationalism.* Translated by Stuart McKinnon-Evans. London: Edward Arnold.

Anderson, Benedict. 1991. *Imagined Communities: Reflections on the Origins and Spread of Nationalism.* Rev. ed. New York: Verso.

Appelbome, M. 1665. Letter to Chancellor of Sweden, 6/16 October 1665. Bodleian Library, Oxford, Clarendon MSS, vol. 83.

Ashley Cooper, Anthony. 1675. *A Letter from a Person of Quality to His Friend in the Country.* London.

Bethel, Slingsby. 1671. *The Present Interest of England Stated.* London: D. B.

——. 1677. *The Present State of Christendome and the Interest of England with Regard to France.* London: J. B.

——. 1680. *The Interest of Princes and States.* London: John Wickins.

Boccalini, Traiano. 1669. *I Ragguagli di Parnasso: Or, Advertisements from Parnassus,* 2d ed. Translated by Henry Earl of Monmouth. London: T. Dring, J. Starkey, T. Basset.

---

[29] I both acknowledge the importance of Greenfeld and record my areas of disagreement. Greenfeld has demonstrated, with a wealth of learning and subtlety, the ways in which nationalism could be formed in preindustrial societies. She has delineated effectively many of the ways in which English nationalism evolved. However, I dissent from her view that "the great importance of Henry [VIII]'s break from Rome consisted in that it opened the doors to Protestantism, perhaps the most significant among the factors that furthered the development of the English national consciousness" (1992: 51). The arguments generated by her position were, on the whole, universalist arguments. John Aylmer's claim that "God is English" (cited in Greenfeld 1992: 60), for example, was not an admission that there might be a French God, a Dutch God, or a German God, but a powerful claim that as England had become the bastion of Protestantism, it was only England's soldiers who fought "in defense of hys true religion." An identity that can be imagined as universal is not a nationalism. The retreat from universalism, which I think happened in Catholic as well as Protestant lands in the later seventeenth century, was essential to transform the ideological materials that Greenfeld has described into a nationalism, an ideology that took as its starting point that there must exist a multiplicity of nations.

[30] In accepting this definition of nationalism—though without the conviction that nationalism requires a commitment to indivisible sovereignty—I reject Roland Mousnier's definition of nationalism as a phenomenon that ineluctably culminates in "chauvinism, jingoism, Nazism" (1981: 30).

Bosher, J. F. 1994. "The Franco-Catholic Danger, 1660–1715." *History* 79, no. 255: 5–30.

Breuilly, John. 1993. *Nationalism and the State*, 2d ed. Chicago: University of Chicago Press.

Brewer, John. 1989. *The Sinews of Power: War, Money and the English State 1688–1783*. London: Unwin Hyman.

Campanella, Tomasso. 1660. *Thomas Campanella, an Italian Friar and Second Machiavel, his Advice to the King of Spain for Attaining the Universal Monarchy of the World*. Translated by Edmund Chilmead. London: Philamon Stephens.

The Catholick Ballad. 1674. London: Henry Brome.

The Character and Qualifications of an Honest Loyal Merchant. 1686. London: Robert Roberts.

The Cities Great Concern. 1674. London: William Godbid.

Clark, J. C. D. 1986. *Revolution and Rebellion*. Cambridge: Cambridge University Press.

———. 1994. *The Language of Liberty 1660–1832*. Cambridge: Cambridge University Press.

Clifford, Sir Thomas. 1665. Pamphlet. National Maritime Museum, Greenwich. Clifford MSS, vol. 3, Dw 100.

Colley, Linda. 1992a. "Britishness and Otherness: An Argument." *Journal of British Studies* 31, no. 4: 309–29.

———. 1992b. *Britons*. New Haven: Yale University Press.

The Complaisant Companion. 1674. London: H. B.

Condren, Conal. 1989. *George Lawson's* Politica *and the English Revolution*. Cambridge: Cambridge University Press.

Coventry, Sir William. 1677. Letter to Marquis of Halifax, 27 May 1677. British Library, Althorp House MSS, vol. C18.

Crouch, John. 1665. *The Dutch Imbergo upon the State Fleet*. London: Edward Crowch.

Davenant, Charles. 1701. *Essays upon I the Ballance of Power II the Right of Making War Peace and Alliances III Universal Monarchy*. London: James Knapton.

De Beer, Esmond S. 1938–1939. "King Charles II's Own Fashion: An Episode in Anglo-French Relations 1660–1670." *Journal of the Warburg Institute* 2: 105–15.

Defoe, Daniel. 1689. *Reflections on the Late Great Revolution*. London: Richard Chisniell.

De Hay, T. 1681. *A Letter from Paris*. London.

De Marly, Diana. 1974. "King Charles II's Own Fashion: The Theatrical Origins of the English Vest." *Journal of the Courtauld and Warburg Institutes* 37: 378–82.

De Ronquillo, Pedro. 1681. *The Last Memorial of the Spanish Ambassador Faithfully Translated into English*. London: Francis Smith.

The Designs of France against England and Holland. 1686.

A Discourse Written by Sir George Downing. 1672. London: John Littone.

Discourses Upon the Modern Affairs of Europe. 1680

Dryden, John. 1956. *Works*, vol. 1: *Poems: 1649–1689*. Edited by Edward Niles Hooker and H. T. Swedenberg Jr. Berkeley: University of California Press.

"The Duke of York's Farewell Speech to his Friends." ca. 1679–80. Folger Shakespeare Library, Washington, D. C., MSS, G.c. 2.

The Dutch Design Anatomized. 1688. London: Randal Taylor.

Europae Modernae Speculum. 1665. London: T. Leach.

Evelyn, Sir John. 1674. *Navigation and Commerce, their Original and Progress*. London: Benjamin Tooke.

Everard, Edmund. 1679. *Discourses of the Present State of the Protestant Princes of Europe*. London: Dorman Newman.

The Fate of France. 1690. London: Richard Baldwin.

Ferguson, Robert. 1682. *The Second Part of the Growth of Popery and Arbitrary Government*. Cologne: Philliotus.

Finch, Sir Heneage. 1673. "Speech for Supply," 33. 31 October 1673. Leicestershire Record Office, Leicester. Finch MSS, vol. D. G. 7/ Box 4957.

Finn, Margot. 1993. *After Chartism: Class and Nation in English Radical Politics, 1848–1874*. Cambridge: Cambridge University Press.

Fortrey, Samuel. 1907. *England's Interest and Improvement 1663*. Edited by Jacob H. Hollander. Baltimore: Johns Hopkins University Press.

The French Intrigues Discovered. 1681. London: R. Baldwin.

French Intrigues: Or, The History of Their Delusory Promises Since the Pyrenean Treaty. 1685. London: W. Hensman.

Gellner, Ernest. 1983. *Nations and Nationalism*. Ithaca: Cornell University Press.

Gorski, Philip S. 1993. "The Protestant Ethic Revisited: Disciplinary Revolution and State Formation in Holland and Prussia." *American Journal of Sociology* 9, no. 2: 265–316.

Greenfeld, Liah. 1992. *Nationalism: Five Roads to Modernity*. Cambridge: Harvard University Press.

Grey, Anchitell. 1763. *Debates of the House of Commons from the Year 1667 to the Year 1694*. 10 vols. London: D. Henry and R. Cave.

The Happy Union of England and Holland. 1689. London: Richard Baldwin.

Harris, Tim. 1987. *London Crowds in the Age of Charles II*. Cambridge: Cambridge University Press.

——. 1993. *Politics under the Later Stuarts*. London: Longman.

Hastings, Theophilus, Earl of Huntingdon. 1678a. Letter to John Geary, 10 January 1678. Huntington Library, San Marino, Calif. Hastings MSS, no. 5942.

——. 1678b. Letter to John Geary, 24 January 1678. Huntington Library, San Marino, Calif. Hastings MSS, no. 5943.

Hill, Joseph. 1673. *The Interest of these United Provinces*. Amsterdam: Thomas Berry.

Hobsbawm, E. J. 1990. *Nations and Nationalism Since 1780*. Cambridge: Cambridge University Press.

"Hodge's Vision." n.d. Huntington Library, San Marino, Calif., Temple Stowe MSS, vol. Lit (7).

Hogan-Moganides: Or, The Dutch Hudibras. 1674. London: William Cademan.

Houston, Alan. 1991. *Algernon Sidney and the Republican Heritage in England and America*. Princeton: Princeton University Press.

Howell, James. 1645. *Dodona's Grove, or, The Vocall Forest*, 3d ed. Cambridge: R. D.

Hutton, Ronald. 1985. *The Restoration: A Political and Religious History of England and Wales 1658–1667*. Oxford: Clarendon Press.

Hyde, Edward, Earl of Clarendon. 1664. "A Brief Narrative of Lte Passages." Bodleian Library, Oxford. Clarendon MSS, vol. 83.

Israel, Jonathan. 1989. "The Dutch Republic and the 'Glorious Revolution' of 1688/89 in England." In *1688: The Seaborne Alliance and Diplomatric Revolution*, edited by Charles Wilson and David Proctor, 32–44. London: National Maritime Museum.

———. 1991. General Introduction. In *The Anglo-Dutch Moment*, edited by Jonathan Israel, 1–43. Cambridge: Cambridge University Press.

Jacob, James. 1983. *Henry Stubbe, Radical Protestantism and the Early Enlightenment*. Cambridge: Cambridge University Press.

Jones, J. R. 1980. *Britain and the World 1649–1815*. Glasgow: Fontana Paperbacks.

———. 1987. *Charles II: Royal Politician*. London: Allen and Unwin.

Journal of the House of Lords. 1672–1674. Vol. 12.

Knights, Mark. 1994. *Politics and Opinion in Crisis, 1678–81*. Cambridge: Cambridge University Press.

Kohn, Hans. 1946. *The Idea of Nationalism: A Study in its Origins and Background*. New York: Macmillan.

Kuchta, David M. 1990. "Graceful, Virile, and Useful: The Origins of the Three Piece Suit." *Dress* 17: 118–26.

Lawrence, William. 1961. *Diary*, edited by Gerald Aylmer. Beaminster: J. Stevens Cox.

A Learned Discourse on Various Subjects. 1685. London: H. Sawbridge.

"A Letter from a Gentleman in Holland to a Worthy Member of the House of Commons," 13/23 December 1677, British Library, Additional MSS, 28092.

Marvell, Andrew. 1677. *An Account of the Growth of Popery and Arbitrary Government in England*. Amsterdam.

Miller, John. 1991. *Charles II*. London: Weidenfeld and Nicolson.

Molloy, Charles. 1676. *De Jure Maritimo et Navali*. London: John Bellinger.

Mousnier, Roland. 1981. "La naissance des nationalismes en Europe." In Université de Paris IV: Sorbonne, ed., *Nationalisme et universalisme: colloque*, 30–37. Paris: Université de Paris, Sorbonne.

Nedham, Marchamont. 1678a. *Christianissimus Christianandus: Or, the Reason for the Reduction of France to a More Christian State in Europe*. London: Henry Huills.

———. 1678b. *The Pacquet-Boat Advice*. London: Jonathan Edwin.

Nero Gallicanus: Or, the True Pourtraicture of Louis XIV. 1690. London: R. Taylor.

A New Discovery of the Private Methods of France. 1691. London: J. Weld.

Ogilby, John. 1672. *The Frog, or the Low-Country Nightingale, Sweet Singer of Amsterdam*.

Osborne, Thomas Earl of Danby. 1944. *Thomas Osborne, Earl of Danby and Duke of Leeds 1632–1712*, vol. II, *Letters*, edited by Andrew Browning. Glasgow: Jackson.

Parker, Geoffrey. 1984. *The Thirty Years War*. London: Routledge and Kegan Paul.

Phillips, John. 1672. *Montelions Predictions, or the Hogen Mogen Fortune Teller*. London: S. and B. Griffin.

——. 1682. *A Pleasant Conference upon the Observator and Heraclitus*. London: H. Jones.

Pincus, Steven. 1995. "'Coffee Politicians Does Create': Coffeehouses and Restoration Political Culture." *Journal of Modern History* 67, no. 4: 807–34.

——. 1996a. *Protestantism and Patriotism: Ideologies and the Making of English Foreign Policy 1650–1668*. Cambridge: Cambridge University Press.

——. 1996b. "Shadwell's Dramatic Trimming." In *Religion, Literature and Politics in Post-Reformation England, 1540–1688*, edited by Donna B. Hamilton and Richard Strier, 253–74. Cambridge: Cambridge University Press.

——. 1998. "'To Protect English Liberties': The English Nationalist Revolution of 1688–89." In *Chosen Peoples: Protestantism and National Identity in Britain and Ireland*, edited by A. M. Claydon and I. McBride. Cambridge: Cambridge University Press.

——. forthcoming. "From Holy Cause to Economic Interest: The Rise of the English State in English Political Thought." In *A Nation Transformed*, edited by Steven Pincus and Alan Houston. Cambridge: Cambridge University Press.

Pocock, J. G. A. 1992. "History and Sovereignty: The Historiographical Response to Europeanization in two British Cultures." *Journal of British Studies* 31, no. 4: 357–89.

Polin, Raymond. 1981. "Nationalisme et universalisme: etude conceptuelle." In Université de Paris IV: Sorbonne, ed., *Nationalisme et universalisme: colloque*, 5–17. Paris: Université de Paris, Sorbonne.

The Politician Discovered. 1681. London: Langley Curtis.

The Present French King Demonstrated an Enemy to the Catholick as well as Protestant Religion. 1691. London: Tom Goodwin.

The Present Policies of France and the Maxims of Lewis XIV Plainly Laid Open. 1689, London.

A Prophecie Lately Transcribed from an Old Manuscript of Dr. Barnaby Googe. 1672. London: J. C.

A Prospect of Government in Europe. 1681. London: Daniel Brown.

Raleigh, Sir Walter. 1667. *Judicious and Select Essays and Observations*. London: A. M.

Remarques on the Humours and Conversation of the Town. 1673. London: Allen Banks.

Reresby, Sir John. 1875. *Memoirs*, edited by James J. Cartwright. London: Longmans, Green.

Rohan, Henri Duc de. 1641. *A Treatise of the Interest of the Princes and States of Christendom*, translated by Henry Hunt. London: Ric. Hodgkinsonne.

Savile, George, Marquis of Halifax. 1689. *Works*, edited by M. B. Brown. Oxford: Clarendon Press.

Scott, Jonathan. 1988a. *Algernon Sidney and the English Republic, 1623–77*. Cambridge: Cambridge University Press.

——. 1988b. "Radicalism and Restoration: The Shape of the Stuart Experience." *Historical Journal* 31, no. 2: 452–67.

——. 1990. "England's Troubles: Exhuming the Popish Plot." In *The Politics of Religion in Restoration England*, edited by Tim Harris, Mark Goldie, and Paul Seaward, 107–31. Oxford: Basil Blackwell.

——. 1991. *Algernon Sidney and the Restoration Crisis, 1677–1683*. Cambridge: Cambridge University Press.

Shadwell, Thomas. 1671. *The Humorists*. London: Henry Herringman.

A Short Discourse upon the Designs, Practices, and Counsels of France. 1688. London: Randal Taylor.

Sidney, Algernon. 1666. "Court Maxims." Warwicksire Record Office, Coventry.

——. 1990. *Discourses Concerning Government*, edited by Thomas G. West. Indianapolis: Liberty Press.

Skocpol, Theda. 1979. *States and Social Revolutions*. Cambridge: Cambridge University Press.

Slack, Paul. 1985. *The Impact of Plague in Tudor and Stuart England*. Oxford: Clarendon Press.

Smith, Anthony D. 1991. *National Identity*. Reno: University of Nevada Press.

Stone, Lawrence. 1994. "Introduction." In *An Imperial State at War: Britain from 1689 to 1815*, edited by Lawrence Stone, 1–32. New York: Routledge.

Stubbe, Henry. 1672. *A Justification of the Present War against the United Netherlands*. London: Henry Hills and John Starkey.

——. 1673a. *A Further Justification of the Present War against the United Netherlands*. London: Henry Hills and John Starkey.

——. 1673b. *The History of the United Provinces of Achaia*. London: Andrew Clark.

Suny, Ronald Grigor. 1993. *The Revenge of the Past: Nationalism, Revolution, and the Collapse of the Soviet Union*. Stanford: Stanford University Press.

Tamas, G. M. 1994. "Old Enemies and New: A Philosophic Postscript to Nationalism." *Studies in East European Thought* 46: 129–48.

Temple, Sir Richard. 1667. "An Essay upon Government." Bodleian Library, Oxford. English History MSS, vol. c. 201.

Temple, Sir William. 1680. *Miscellanea*. London: A. M. and R. R.

——. 1814. *Works*. London: F. C. and J. Rivington.

Thynne, Thomas. n.d. Letter to Marquis of Halifax. British Library. Althorp House MSS, vol. C5.

Tilly, Charles. 1995. *Popular Contention in Great Britain 1758–1834*. Cambridge, MA: Harvard University Press.

Two Letters. 1673.

Two Speeches. 1675. Amsterdam.

A View of the True Interest of the Several States of Europe. 1689. London: Thomas Newborough.

Vox Patriae. 1681. London: Francis Peters.

Waller, Edmund. 1963. "Instructions to a Painter." In *Poems on Affairs of State*, vol. 1, edited by George deF. Lord. New Haven: Yale University Press.

Warwick, Sir Philip. 1679. "Of Government," 28 August 1679. Huntington Library, San Marino, Calif. Huntington MSS, 41956.

Westby, William. n.d. "Memorandum Book." Folger Shakespeare Library, Washington, D.C. MSS, vol. V.a. 469.

Wild, Robert. 1673. *A Panegyricke Humbly Addresst to the King's Most Excellent Majesty*. London: A. P.

Worden, A. B. 1978. Introduction. In *Edmund Ludlow: A Voyce from the Watch Tower*, edited by A. B. Worden, 1–80. London: Royal Historical Society.

Yalden, John. 1681. *Machiavil Redivivus*. London: Will, Cademan.

Zwicker, Steven N. 1988. "England, Israel, and the Triumph of Roman Virtue." In *Millenarianism and Messianism in English Literature and Thought 1650–1800*, edited by Richard H. Popkin, 37–64. Leiden: E. J. Brill.

PART THREE

CULTURE AND THE MODERNIZATION / WESTERNIZATION OF NON-EUROPEAN STATES

7

The Subvention of Tradition:
A Genealogy of the Nigerian Durbar

Andrew Apter

"The processes of cultural objectification are as much a part
of national culture as the cultural 'stuff' that is objectified."
—RICHARD HANDLER, *Nationalism and the Politics
of Culture in Quebec*, 1988

It has become a commonplace, if not a banality, to acknowledge that traditions are invented. Since the publication of Hobsbawm and Ranger's important collection of essays, "the invention of tradition" has come to mean more than the domain of staged rituals and symbolic practices originally specified (Hobsbawm 1983: 1) and to encompass a general critical perspective, shared by many anthropologists and historians, of all cultural representations of the past. Hobsbawm's initial distinction between invented traditions on the one hand, and "old," "genuine," or "evolved" traditions on the other, has been overshadowed by a new episteme in which, for example, if all traditions are invented, so too all communities are imagined and all ethnicities constructed. Benedict Anderson's (1983) critique of the primordial foundations of nationalism is perhaps the best-known turning point in this direction. Another is Corrigan and Sayer's *The Great Arch* (1985), which identifies the cultural foundations of the English state and examines state-formation as cultural revolution. In this and similar approaches, cultural forms and practices move from a secondary explanatory status—as mere symbols or window dressing for the political and material relations they represent—to the more fundamental position of necessary conditions. Cohn (1983) makes a similar argument for Victorian India, as do Ranger

For Barney Cohn

(1980) for northern Rhodesia and Callaway (1987) for colonial Nigeria. The "thin white line" of imperial power in the colonies rested not on British force and fortitude alone, but on the foundations of colonial culture.

This groundwork is useful, especially for the sociocultural anthropologist whose domain of expertise can fruitfully extend to the very cultural conditions within which traditions are invented, communities imagined, ethnicities constructed, states formed, and empires built. But within this constructivist episteme, new developments are pulling the cultural rug from beneath our feet. This later shift is signaled by Pemberton's critical ethnography of "traditional" Javanese culture, which, he argues, developed as a "culture effect" first under Dutch colonialism and then under Soeharto's New Order regime. Javanese culture, much like the anthropologist's, emerges under specific historical conditions not only as an object of knowledge and reflection but of production and reification as well. Thus, culture too is invented.[1]

How can culture serve both as a condition of state formation and as its consequence? How do we distinguish the prior "cultural foundation" from the consequent "culture effect"? Clearly such questions invite a closer look at the complex relations between culture and power and the ways in which they are dialectically and historically informed. Hence the more general goal of this essay, which returns to Hobsbawm's initial distinction between older and more "genuine" versus invented traditions to sketch a genealogy of the Nigerian durbar as it developed under British colonialism and came to represent the Nigerian nation in a state-financed festival of African arts and culture known as FESTAC '77.

In a sense, the durbar is an invented tradition par excellence. It was devised by the British with specific political objectives in mind, first in Victorian India and then in West Africa. There it initially signaled the Royal Niger Company's transition to Imperial Protectorate—a portentous event held on January 1, 1900, literally at the dawn of the new century—whereafter it naturalized the policy of indirect rule in choreographed public spectacles, honoring emirs, governors, district officers, and even such distinguished guests as the Prince of Wales (1925) and Queen Elizabeth II (1956). By 1977, however, the durbar's colonial content was mysteriously phased out. Staged in FESTAC to recuperate indigenous culture, the state memorialized a "precolonial" durbar—explicitly associated with Islamic Sallah celebrations—with which the new Nigeria, enriched by oil, could celebrate its national development. Like the oil industry that financed FESTAC, the durbar was seen as a natural resource in the fertile fields of cultural production and was nationalized. It is this process of objectification and indigenization which I mean by the *subvention* of tradition, an underwriting by the oil-rich state that, in the context of Nigeria's political history, reconsolidated Hausa-Fulani

---

[1] Pemberton (1994) provides a brilliant historical and ethnographic analysis of cultural objectification as it occurred under Dutch colonialism and became manifest in routine appeals to tradition in a number of marked and everyday practices. He is concerned "less with official policies of the Indonesian Department of Education and Culture than with the Javanese culture that this department would find most recognizable as an object for preservationsist attention" (10).

hegemony by projecting a northern regional identity over the nation at large. In short, the genealogy of the durbar reveals how the cultural foundations of colonial authority were transformed into the culture effect of an emergent nation-state.

In terms of the broader themes addressed by this book, the case of the Nigerian durbar carries the arguments and perspectives of Mitchell and Bourdieu into postcolonial situations of third world nation-states. Following Mitchell's lead both here and in earlier works (1988), in which he discusses the emergence of the state and the economy not as functional domains of institutional differentiation but as representational "effects" of modern political practices, we consider the domain of "culture" in a similar light. The point here is not merely synthetic, adding a new domain-variable to Mitchell's analysis of the state, but follows his radical shift in perspective on the very processes of institutional differentiation and objectification. In brief, this refers historically to the practical and technical demarcation of internal distinctions—"methods of organization, arrangement and representation"—that come to be seen as external boundaries between the state and civil society, the state and a "free" market, or in the case of the Nigerian durbar, the state and its national "culture." It was in fact through Nigeria's cultural events and national festivals that the domain of "culture" was rendered visible and autonomous and was distinguished from, if underwritten by, the state and its booming oil economy. From this perspective, Nigeria's postcolonial "culture effect" should not be seen in isolation, but as concomitant with the distinctive political and economic spheres that emerged under oil capitalism.

The historical development of an autonomous sphere of culture in Nigeria addresses central issues in Bourdieu's critical sociology of the state as well; most specifically, what he has called "the field of cultural production" (1993) in modern Europe and its implicit economies of symbolic and cultural capital. Like Mitchell's, Bourdieu's contribution to this volume shows how internal distinctions generated by the state become universalized and objectified into rational forms and functions—of administration, adjudication, even thinking and knowing—that extend into the organization of the natural world according to the model of the imprimatur. Unlike Mitchell, however, Bourdieu relates the genesis of these structuring domains to positional fields of interest within which agents compete for different forms of capital. Bourdieu thereby introduces issues of agency and value into the cultural constitution of modern political orders, specifying the hidden strategies as well as technical mechanisms of the bureaucratic field and its distinctive domains. As we shall see, such strategic concerns and forms of "capital" accumulation and exchange were central to the various agents and actors who participated in durbars and operated behind the scenes.

Dubious Origins

Featured as "the greatest and biggest event to be staged by Nigeria," the "Grand Durbar" was the finale of FESTAC '77, and as such acquired regional, national, and international dimensions.[2] As a regional festival, it brought together emirs, chiefs, and district heads from Nigeria's ten northern states under the traditional jurisdiction of the Sultan of Sokoto, still recognized as "Commander of the Faithful."[3] As a national event, organized by the federally appointed National Participation Committee through various ministries and secretariats, it epitomized the grandeur of Nigeria's cultural heritage. But in its global dimensions the durbar best captured the spirit of FESTAC, connecting the black world to the world system, by flying in dignitaries and heads of state as guests of the multimillion-naira Durbar Hotel, built specifically for distinguished visitors, and by broadcasting the durbar via satellite to worldwide television audiences. And at least temporarily, the durbar shifted the exemplary center of FESTAC's black and African world from Lagos, Nigeria's congested and bustling port city on the Atlantic coast, to the northern city of Kaduna, the administrative headquarters of the former Northern Region, where spacious vistas and savanna winds offered temporary relief from the steamy south. In a concerted logistical initiative, the federal military government commandeered buses, trains, and the national airline to transport many of the estimated two hundred thousand spectators from Lagos to Kaduna, and back again.[4]

On February 8, 1977, in Kaduna's Murtala Mohammed Square, Lt. General Olusegeun Obasanjo, Nigeria's head of state and FESTAC's "Grand Patron," addressed the black and African world. He spoke from a dais that included America's U.N. ambassador Andrew Young, Prime Minister R. C. Bradshaw of St. Kitts, and seven African heads of state, together with Kaduna's state governor and other top brass from the Supreme Military Council.[5] Praising the horsemanship, drumming, dancing, and acrobatics of the participating emirs and their colorful retinues, Obasanjo also discussed the durbar's broader significance as a genealogical charter for FESTAC itself and explained how "the FESTAC was in a sense, one Grand Durbar in which African people with their kith and kin were in one event trying to recapture their common identity and pride which was a beginning of a new independent and collective future."[6] It was in terms of this ideological project—building a postcolonial black and African world on precolonial cultural foundations—that the durbar's historical pedigree was defined. The durbar was portrayed as a precolonial tradition of a great indigenous civilization, with horsemen, warriors, standard bearers, musicians, camels, dancers, bodyguards, and jesters representing their leaders and expressing their loyalty in the climactic charge of the *jahi* (or *jinjina*) salute. As Obasanjo made abundantly clear, "In witnessing the Durbar and savouring its splendid spectacle

[2] "FESTAC's Triumphant End," *West Africa* no. 3110, 14 February 1977: 311.

[3] The former northern region was reorganized into first six, and then ten states. The ten states represented at the FESTAC durbar were Borno, Sokoto, Kano, Kaduna, Gongola, Bauchi, Plateau, Benue, Niger, and Kwara.

[4] Estimates varied from 200,000 to 100,000 in the Nigerian press, while the *New York Times* (Darnton 1977) offered the more conservative figure of 40,000.

[5] The African leaders were Presidents Ahmadu Ahidjo of Cameroon, Aghostino Neto of Angola, Mouktar Ould Daddah of Mauritania, Seyni Kountche of Niger, Mobutu Sese Seko of Zaire, Gnassingbé Eyadema of Togo, and Sangoule Lamizana of (then) Upper Volta.

[6] "Durbar Recaptures our Identity." *The Nigerian Chronicle*, 10 February 1977: 15.

we are symbolically paying our respect to a civilization that existed here in this country, as well as in many other parts of Africa, at various times in our continental history before the advent of imperialists from Europe." As a specific institution, he maintained, the durbar derived from the emirate system of the north, where it served as a mechanism to unite different African peoples within an overarching state. In this respect, the durbar was portrayed as a constitutional expression of good governance and political accountability, in which "the opinions of the governed counted greatly in influencing the conduct of policies and popularity of Emirs." Obasanjo continued: "to my mind the Durbar is a device whereby the Emir can judge the popularity of his rule as well as an indication of loyalty of those governed to his rule."[7] Thus, the durbar provided a fitting parable for a general who would soon return his country to civilian rule, with the northerners in power.

On a more militant note, the federal commissioner for information, Major-General I. B. M. Haruna (who also served as chairman of Nigeria's National Participation Committee for FESTAC) warned against the imperialist propaganda surrounding the durbar. In his opening speech, he disassociated the Grand Durbar from its colonial history in India and Nigeria, where durbars had been staged to incorporate local rulers into British administrative structures: "Those of you who have read and absorbed the imperialist literature would have concluded that the word 'Durbar' is used in English to describe the receptions which used to be held for 'Native Princes' at the courts of the British viceroys of India. You might also have read that first British Viceroy of Nigeria (as Lord Frederick Lugard pictured himself), aping the practices of his more distinguished colleagues, held the first durbar for the chiefs of Northern Nigeria in Zaria in 1911, and that thereafter this became a regular practice of the imperialist rulers of this country, designed to remind the people whom they had conquered of their enforced allegiance to the British king" (Haruna 1977: 18). Instead, the major-general assured his audience, the Grand Durbar of FESTAC '77 boasted an older, nobler lineage from precolonial times: "This great gathering of emirs and their officers and horsemen that you are going to see bears only some very superficial resemblance to the assembly of chiefs that were ordered by the British in 1911. In fact, this is something quite different. It is perhaps something akin to those great gatherings of nawabs and rajas which were held at the court of the great Moghul Sultans of India which were called 'Durbar' long before the British stole the Urdu tongue of the rulers of that country" (18). The Nigerian durbar is thus akin to its Indian counterpart in that both belonged to civilizations that predated British conquest, upheld indigenous empires and states, and were appropriated, transformed, and disfigured by the British. The Nigerian durbar, moreover, is older than its Indian cousin; hence its pedigree is even more distinguished. Haruna explained:

I can also assure you further that what you are about to see is still not an old Moghul custom that by some strange act of cultural subservience we have adopted here, for

[7] Quoted in "FESTAC's Triumphant End," *West Africa* no. 3110, 14 February 1977: 311.

we had been practising this custom long before the rise of the Moghul Empire. . . .
What you are about to see in ceremonial form is variably called Wa'rigo Pucci, or
Kawuske, or Hawan Dawaki, [which] means 'the mounting of the horses'. This
is something which has been done year after year for more than half a millennium
in one part or the other of this country; and the memory of it and of what it has
stood for over the centuries, are basic elements of our cultural heritage: something
which has not been wiped out by the impact of foreign imperial rule, but which remains strong and active in the hearts and minds of our people to this day. (Haruna
1977: 18)

In the spirit of FESTAC's recuperation of cultural origins, and translated into
Fulani, Kanuri, and Hausa terms, the Grand Durbar would purge its colonial ac-
cretions and resurrect its traditional political and spiritual values to rebuild the
black and African world.

In genealogical terms, two lines of "descent" were thus articulated by Nigeria's head of state, serving as FESTAC's Grand Patron, and by the federal commissioner for information, who chaired FESTAC's National Participation Committee. One, the imperial-colonial tradition that Britain imposed on Nigeria
via India, represented the exogenous lineage of a cunning stepfather, an alien
monarch whose superficial imprint could be erased and finally transcended. The
other, an equestrian tradition of well-staged statecraft reflecting the glorious histories of the Sokoto Caliphate and the Borno empire, represented the indigenous lineage of the African motherland, something of a submerged matriline
under colonialism that FESTAC would restore. According to Haruna, this latter
line extended "as far back as the twelfth century . . . when the Mai Dunama Hu-
maimi [the forerunner of the Shehu of Borno] could put 100,000 horsemen
and 20,000 infantry and an impressive personnel guard into the field" (1977).
According to this history, then, the "original" durbar existed among the Habe
ruling dynasties and their surrounding kingdoms—such as Jukun, Gwari, and
Nupe—before the nineteenth-century Islamic *jihad* of the Fulani invaders and
the rise of the Muslim emirates.

It is easy to dismiss this indigenous lineage as speculative history motivated by
politics, as indeed it was. The pre-Islamic durbar grounds an originary ancestry
for all Africans of whatever religion or denomination, whereas once Islamicized,
it glorifies northern Nigeria and Muslim Africa at large. Haruna was quick to
point out the Islamic virtues of Hawan Dawaki, as he preferred to call the durbar. It mobilized society for defense of the community, it fostered loyalty
to leaders and fulfillment of political obligations, and it embodied the Islamic
spirit of a nation in arms. Quoting a passage of the Holy Qur'an from which, he
claimed, "the principles and practice of the hawan dawaki derive" (1977: 18),
Haruna recast the black and African world in an Islamic idiom, a world that
should keep a vigilant watch for enemies from within and neocolonial racists
from without, as both are enemies of God.[8] The three official sources of the durbar are thus unstable. If the British source, via India, is "false," appropriating a

---

[8] The passage reads: "And hold in readiness against them all your strength, and of horses tether
as many as you can, that the enemies of God and your enemies may be put in fear" (VIII, 62).

prior Mughal tradition, the African source, which is "true," is pre-Islamic (older even than the Moghul empire) and yet derives from the Qur'an. These inconsistencies are hardly surprising, because we know (from the celebrated Tiv case) that all genealogical charters are manipulated according to whose interests and claims are at stake.[9] Rather than dismiss this genealogical charter, however, as yet another invented history of the present, I take its claims seriously, not to authenticate a particular pedigree, but to better understand the historical conditions within which such pedigrees are constructed. With due respect for the sins of anachronism, I briefly review some available evidence of the Nigerian durbar's mysterious ancestry.

The pre-Islamic evidence of an indigenous durbar is perhaps the most difficult to establish with any certainty, given the impact of Islam in the region and the predation the so-called pagan tribes suffered at the hands of the slave-raiding emirs. Generally associated with equestrian cultures, this early durbar was presumably connected with local kingship and performed during funerals, installation rites, and agricultural festivals. Kirk-Greene (1959: 18) quotes the earliest written account (c. 1829) from the explorer Denham, who encountered the people of Bornu and described how "three separate small bodies kept charging rapidly towards us, to within a few feet of our hourses heads, whithout checking the speed of their own until the very moment of their halt." A partial glimpse of such practices is provided by Meek's classic monograph on the Jukun-speaking peoples of Nigeria (1931), whose kingdom was heralded as "the only remaining example of the type of state which was characteristic of the Western Sudan before the advent of the Muhammadan religion and culture."[10] Discussing the Jukun institution of divine kingship, Meek describes a festival of Puje (lit. "booths of menstruation" [144]) associated with the harvesting of corn, beans, and millet, during which the king proceeded on horseback, was attended by a royal drummer and fiddler, and was surrounded by Ba-tovi grooms in rank and file who "support him in the saddle when necessary, shout his praises, and draw attention to any impediments on the road" (149). Behind these grooms followed senior officials from vassal communities, each "surrounded by his own courtiers and attendants" (150). After performing sacrifices and ablutions within the Puje booths or pavilions, the Jukun king returned in state, this time following rather than leading the procession back to the palace. Each group of attendants was preceded by "Akie," men with peeled sticks who drove away spectators to clear the king's path. At this point, Meek (152) describes what may well have been the precursor of the Islamic durbar's *jahi* salute:

> Then follows the Abô Achuwo who rides in at a gallop with the other senior officials. All turn their horses swiftly and gallop back again to meet the king as he enters the eastern gate amidst loud shouts of welcome from his people. . . . The procession

[9] See Bohannan (1952) for the clearest statement of how politics structures genealogical reckoning.

[10] Quoted from the dust jacket of the first edition. We should note that C. K. Meek, the Anthropological Officer of the Administrative Service in Nigeria, placed the Jukun "tribe" within another dubious genealogy of Hamites coming from Egypt. I thank Richard Fardon for this information (personal communication).

Plate 1. Private, infantry, in review order, Nigeria Regiment. *Nigeria Handbook: Containing Statistical and General Information Respecting the Colony and Protectorate.* [Fifth ed.]. Lagos: Chief Secretary's Office, 1924, p. 184.

then moves forward in a swaying mass, and at intervals the king pulls up his horse in order to survey the people and receive their acclamations. It is noteworthy that whereas during the day the king and his officials are all dressed in the typical Jukun fashion, i.e., with a cloth rolled at the waist and extending to the feet, the upper part of the body being left bare, these garments are changed for the triumphal return to the capital. All the officials wear gowns, and the king dons the coat known as *nyikpo*, which is decorated with red and white representations of birds and scorpions. He also wears a decorated fez. . . . After visiting the north and south gates the king returns to the palace and there dismisses the people, saying: "I thank you all. I have performed the custom of our forefathers."

Now if this custom of the forefathers represents a pre-Islamic practice that—like the Jukun kingdom—may have been characteristic of the western Sudanic states more generally, can we assume, genealogically, that it preceded the Islamic "durbar" which (as we shall see) came to be associated with Sallah, the high holidays of Id el Fitr and Id el Kebir in the emirates? The answer is complicated by the fact that some of the subordinate chiefdoms ruled by the Jukun king were already Islamicized in the nineteenth century and may have influenced Jukun rituals in the reciprocal exchange of gifts and tributes built into their political relationship. For example, the decorated fez mentioned by Meek may well be an Islamic innovation, incorporated into the iconography of Jukun kingship. Or perhaps it was adopted from the uniforms of Africans serving in the colonial administration, as illustrated by the fezes worn by soldiers and policemen in northern Nigeria (Plate 1). This does not confirm or deny the historical priority of a pre-Islamic "durbar," but indicates that the "pagan," Islamic, and even colonial traditions had most likely been mixing for some time.[11]

Three ethnographic snapshots from colonial Nigeria illustrate this composite character of the Islamic durbar, or Sallah.[12] Analyzing Hausa praise-singing (*roko*), M. G. Smith (1957: 29) describes the political relationship between a district head and his king in Zaria as dramatized by salutations and the distribution of gifts:

> At Sallah, when the District head has to attend the king at his capital, the band of *maroka* accompanies him on horseback, and plays him into the city with bugle and drum. After the Sallah rite on the prayer ground outside the city (*masallacin Idi*), the District head, together with his subordinate village chiefs and administrative staff, declares allegiance to the king by a cavalry charge with drawn swords outside the palace, while the *maroka* [praise-singers] who take part in this gallop, drum, pipe, and blow their master's title-praise (*kirari*) on horseback. During the distribution of largesse which marks Sallah, the *maroka* are rewarded by their lord with meat, kola nuts, clothes, money, occasionally a horse, and titular promotions.

Here we glimpse the administrative relations between king, district head, and his subordinate village chiefs mobilized by the performance of Sallah, legitimated by the district head's "cavalry charge" and negotiated by gift-giving. Already the critical components of the Muslim durbar can be distinguished: the state, the salute, and the circulation of symbolic capital. The state structure of the emirate is clearly made manifest, even if it is already mediated by the administrative framework of indirect rule, whereas the cavalry salute—in this case, with drawn swords—appears to be a potentially rebellious act, ritually framing the latent possibilities of armed resurrection against the king. Finally, the "distribution of largesse" sets up the "durbar" as a political arena in which hierarchical relations are ritually sanctified and, in cases of promotion, reorganized.

Nadel (1942) provides a more elaborate description of a Sallah festival in the Nupe kingdom, ruled by an emir bearing the title of *Etsu* from the capital city of Bida. The basic components of the "durbar" can be discerned within a more complex description of sociopolitical relations:

> The *Sallah* feast is like a Friday celebration on an immensely enlarged scale. On the first day the king on horseback under the state umbrella and surrounded by his noblemen and state officials, leads the vast procession to the praying-ground outside the town, where the *Liman* holds the service. After the service the procession returns to the royal residence. Here a great display of horsemanship takes place, at which the bodyguard of the king, his police, and officers of state parade before him and his guests of honour—the foremost among whom are the District Officer and all the Europeans living in Bida Emirate. On the second day of the *Sallah* the *Etsu* holds the great *nko* of the year, a reception at which everyone who holds rank and

---

[11] For an Indian parallel to this ironic inversion, wherein an indigenous native symbol derives from a colonial source, see Cohn's treatment of the Sikh turban (Cohn 1989: 305).

[12] See also Madauchi 1968: 38–39.

Plate 2. "The *Jahi* Salute during *Sallah*." From Nadel (1942: opp. p. 144).

title and every person of consequence comes to salute his sovereign, to offer gifts of loyalty and to receive counter-gifts expressing the king's favour. For two days tens of thousands of people crowd the streets of Bida and assemble in front of the royal residence—Bida people as well as peasants from the villages who flock to the capital to see the *Sallah*. There they watch their rulers ride past in all their splendour, equipped with their paraphernalia of rank; they listen to music, drum signals, and songs of praise; they join in the general rejoicing, made more joyful by the largesse and gifts of food and kola-nuts which a gracious sovereign causes to be distributed among his loyal subjects. (144)

Like the Puje ceremony among the Jukun, the Nupe king rode with his body-guard and retinue to a sacred place outside the town and returned to the palace for a great display of horsemanship (Plate 2).[13] And like the Sallah at Zaria, the Nupe state turned out in its hierarchical glory, with all social groups and categories in their proper place, from exalted nobles—including the district officer and resident Europeans—to lowly peasants and strangers. We can also discern additional reciprocities within the ritual economy of distributed largesse, in that the *Etsu*'s loyal clients and chiefs brought him gifts and received counter-gifts, thereby exchanging fealty for protection while representing, and in some cases negotiating, status distinctions and political relations. Presents from the king ranged from a small bowl of kola nuts (on which the king held a royal monop-

---

[13] Although Nadel makes no specific mention of a "cavalry charge" as such, we can see a subordinate chief galloping with his retinue, with one footman and one rider brandishing a sword and a lance as they approach Nadel's camera, in the lower plate opposite, p. 144.

oly) to a silk gown or a horse. As Nadel explained, not only was rank indicated by the type of gift received from the king, but it could also be stripped or restored: "At the great Mohammedan festival of the year, the *Sallah* as it is called in Nigeria, every one of the hundreds of people who by the right of birth or status are entitled to the king's attention are honoured with a smaller or larger gift. To be left out means disgrace; and the sending of a present to a man with whom the *Etsu* was known to be on bad terms expresses conspicuously reconciliation and new favour" (1942: 91). Indeed, the emir's gift economy exchanged personal power and religious authority. If personal loyalty to the sovereign could be demonstrated with gifts, it could be rewarded with a title, which was conferred by the presentation of a turban and a sword—insignia of clientship, office (143), and conversion or submission to Islam.[14]

If the Nupe Sallah described by Nadel reveals a growing British presence, this was not limited to administration and personnel. The presence of the district officer and other Europeans as guests of honor raises interesting questions about who was ultimately in charge and control and whose loyalty was tested and expressed. Clearly the agents and representatives of the colonial government legitimized the emir's authority in the Sallah, even as they were drawn into its orbit of obligations and its economy of signs. But here is precisely where the currencies of symbolic capital—the mutual investments of gifts and counter-gifts—become blurred. For if the Sallah operated at the intersection of the colonial state "above" and the native emirate "below," expressing in its cavalry charge a potential rebellion against the colonial order, it also harnessed colonial forms of power and value. This can be understood abstractly as an appropriation of colonial charisma and seen concretely in the adoption of European commodities and in the reversal of ritual roles.

Two final examples illustrate the point. The first involves a subsequent Sallah that Nadel observed, noting the "corrosive" influence of market forces on traditional craft-guilds:

> The Great *Sallah*, once the occasion for numerous orders from the court, which kept the workshops of Bida busy for weeks, is now an occasion for making purchases at the stores that trade in European goods. At the *Sallah* of 1935, the first *Sallah* of the newly installed *Etsu*, the traditional royal gifts of kola-nuts were sent out, not in ornamental brass bowls of native make, but in newly bought enamelled teapots; the king's bodyguard, newly equipped, wore, not Bida gowns and turbans or native-made straw hats, but red blankets and Trilby hats; and many notables who would have appeared formerly on horses with costly trappings and gorgeous saddle-cloths, rode in on new, shining bicycles (1942: 292).

Here we see how major shifts in the political economy of colonial rule, such as breaking the king's monopoly on certain commodities and liberalizing the market for labor and goods, were realized through the ritual substitution of prestige

---

[14] Not all gifts were political. Distinguishing collective gifts such as a brass tray sent by the brass-smiths from personal gifts sent by individuals, Nadel (1942: 273–74) shows how the former marked occupational status and the latter was an investment to attract the king's custom.

symbols and wares. The new Sallah introduced imported commodities into its ritual economy of icons and gifts, commodities that carried with them changing relations of production and consumption. To a significant if limited extent, blankets replaced gowns, Trilby hats replaced turbans, and bicycles replaced horses. Clearly key symbols of Nigerian Islam were making way for British industry. In the language of genealogy, foreign blood was thereby introduced into the Islamic Sallah and its body politic.

A second example, from the Yoruba emirate of Ilorin, illustrates another colonial variation on the Sallah theme. Describing the festival in 1960, just months before Nigeria's formal independence, P. C. Lloyd distinguished pre-Islamic ingredients of Yoruba sacred kingship absorbed by the Sallah from more recent adaptations to the colonial situation. Of special note in his account is how the Islamic "church" and British "state" were ritually separated and combined. As the emir with his retinue left the palace for the prayer ground, where his war chiefs (*Balogun*) were waiting, the Resident of the province, with his senior administrative officers and their wives, assembled on the tower of the palace gateway to watch a different set of ceremonies. Here the police band marched back and forth, "playing everything from highlifes to Scottish laments" (Lloyd 1961: 278). As the colonials gazed from on high, the emir returned, following an attendant bearing his official staff of office, which was "presented to him on his accession by the Governor or his agent," and flanked by bodyguards, sword bearers, war chiefs, musicians, and even the Native Authority police—all in a spectacle of color and a "cacophony of sound" (268). In this manner, with the customary cavalry charge, the emir was reintegrated with the secular state and greeted by the Resident and his subordinates at the palace. And in what amounted to a reversal of ritual roles the following day, the emir and his chiefs rode in procession to the Residency, where they were entertained, "just as the Emir had earlier entertained his Baloguns" (268). The Ilorin Sallah was thus ritually encapsulated within the political framework of indirect rule, and the British took final control over the distribution of largesse.

These ethnographic vignettes of the precolonial and Islamic "durbar" pose the usual problems of inferring earlier ritual practices from contemporary performances. From the available evidence, my examples are already mediated by the colonial situation and reflect this mediation in interesting ways. My intent in sketching the "matriline" of the durbar's genealogy is not to demonstrate its ideological impurity, which would be easy, but to affirm, despite the methodological challenges, that it exists, which is much more difficult. What these vignettes illustrate is not a pure ritual blood line polluted by foreigners—FESTAC's vision, more or less—but that the indigenous ceremonies associated with "durbars" were active sites of political negotiation and mediation during which local and regional identities and authority relations were reshaped and remade. To a greater or lesser degree, Habe, Nupe, and Yoruba practices were surely incorporated into Fulani Sallahs, and these in turn were reconditioned by the changing colonial order. But in the meantime, at the dawn of a new century, a different kind of durbar had made its royal entry, giving birth to the protectorate of northern Nigeria. And it is here that we turn to the role of the imperial durbar in the making of colonial authority.

Colonial Authority

The first colonial durbar performed in Nigeria was an imperial rite of passage, marking critical transitions for a number of key actors and conjunctural relations. For Sir George Goldie, it marked the surrender of the Royal Niger Company, Chartered and Limited, to the administration of the British Crown. If the Royal Niger Company had consolidated a monopoly on the Niger's riverine trade, it suffered, as Lugard ([1922] 1965: 19) had put it, "the inherent defect of all chartered government, where dividends to shareholders must inevitably compete with administrative expenditure." General Lugard (soon to become Sir Frederick and later, Lord) took charge of the takeover, staging it rather dramatically at the Niger-Benue confluence on January 1, 1900. Through this first official durbar, the protectorate of northern Nigeria came into being at Lakoja, bringing with the new century a new government and high commissioner. As reported by Perham (1960: 24–25) and described by Callaway (1987: 58):

> At 7 a.m. General Lugard . . . walked on to the parade ground to read the Queen's Proclamation to the assembled units of the Royal Niger Constabulary and the West African Frontier Force. The flag of the now defunct Royal Niger Company was drawn down, and the Union Jack raised as the visible sign of British authority. Guns fired in noisy salute and then the military band struck up the chords of the national anthem. Next, the Nigerian troops gave three hearty cheers for their new sovereign, Queen Victoria. After Lugard had been sworn in as High Commissioner, the troops executed a march past and were praised for their excellent appearance. Both during this event and the two days of sports which followed, the Nigerian troops and the watching crowds showed intense enthusiasm. This impressive celebration served at once to display mystical authority and to incorporate the Nigerian military units and local populace into British Empire.

No clearer statement of symbolism and purpose could identify this durbar with colonial authority. Later elaborations, as Callaway (58) notes, would incorporate the galloping *jahi* and *jinjina* cavalry salutes of Fulani horse and camel divisions, but the durbar's exogenous, colonial line came directly from British India, where it had fulfilled a number of ceremonial functions.

One such function was the proclamation of Queen Victoria's accession to the imperial title of kaiser-i-hind, a neologism designating empress of India (Cohn 1983: 201), during viceroy Lord Lytton's extravagant imperial assemblage. As Cohn (1983) has illuminated so clearly, the elaborate planning, staging, and choreography of this event, with its feudal pageantry and *feux-de-joie*, brought the art of the imperial durbar to new heights. On a scale rivaling Hollywood stagecraft, with elephants, coaches, and trumpeters "attired in medieval costume" (204), Lytton mounted his "throne" before thousands of spectators, in-

cluding princes and troops in precise formations, declaring that it was to "unite
the British Crown and its feudatories and allies that Her Majesty had been gra-
ciously pleased to assume the Imperial Title" (206; Plate 3). Calculated "to satisfy native sentiment" (Trevithick 1990: 563), one wonders whether British sensibilities were equally at stake. Certainly the organization of ceremonial space
placed the crown at the center of a grand imperial cosmology, but historical timing was equally significant.[15] The imperial assemblage took place on January 1,
1877, not only marking the dawn of new majesty but also commemorating the
anniversary date of Queen Victoria's 1858 proclamation extending royal authority to India (Nuckolls 1990: 535). It was this inaugural moment—when the
crown took over from the East India Company—that Lord Lytton recalled in
Delhi and that Lugard clearly recuperated on the banks of the Niger at Lakoja.

More generally, the colonial durbars of British India were held when the viceroy went on tour or by governors or lieutenant governors to represent the status of their regional princes and chiefs (Plate 4). In a process that Nuckolls (1990:
531) calls "feudalization," loyal Indian princes were ritually incorporated into a
rigid administrative order established by Indian titles that were ultimately con-
firmed and granted by the viceroy. Durbars served as the ceremonial contexts in
which these titles were conferred, thereby adapting and transforming a Mughul
ritual of kingship to serve Britain's civilizing mission. Cohn (1983: 174–80) describes how in the early days, the governor-general would hold durbars for one
Indian ruler at a time to bring him under crown command, but by 1876, these
rulers convened at larger durbars where they were ritually, indeed *ordinally*,
ranked by clothes, weapons, gun salutes, retainers, and their proximity to the
viceroy receiving them. Through this organization of traditional titles, and by
establishing an order of Indian knights to reward loyal service, India's political present came to embody Britain's feudal past. This fundamental precept of
the British empire—that lower races could be helped along their evolutionary
path—rationalized both the colonial presence and the population they governed. As Cohn (1983: 184) summarizes the imperial imperative: "India was diversity—it had no coherent communality except that given by the British rule
under the integrating system of the imperial crown."

The colonial and imperial durbars of India did not exist in ceremonial isolation, but belonged to an elaborate cosmology and culture of rule expressed as
much by the rational techniques of governmentality—mapping populations,
codifying laws, collecting taxes, or training troops—as by political ritual and
everyday routines. If the colonial order was visible, even spectacular, its habitus
was hidden in the details and disciplines of new forms of etiquette and knowledge. The durbar does stand out, however, in this total ideological context as
a powerful mechanism of its production, whereby indigenous ceremonial and
social orders were both underwritten and reorganized by the colonial adminis-

---

[15] As Cohn (1983: 169) explains, "In durbars there were well-established rules for the relative
placement of people and objects. The spatial order of a durbar fixed, created and represented relationships with the ruler."

Plate 3. "Imperial Assemblage, Delhi, 1887." From Pal and Dehejia (1986: 86). Photo credit anon., Walter Collection.

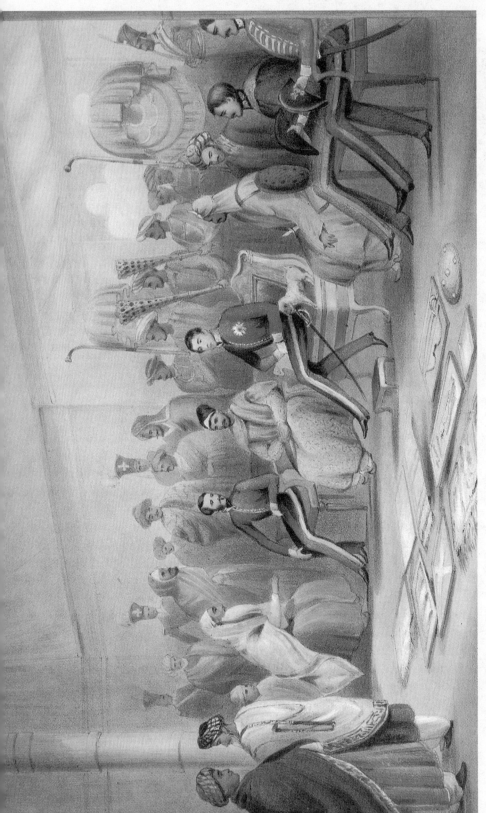

Plate 4. "Lord Aukland Receiving the Raja of Nahun in Durbar, 1844." Watercolor by Emily Eden. Walter Collection. From Pal and Dehejia (1986: opp. p. 105).

tration and naturalized by the colonial sciences of native races and their evolutionary paths. I am in no position to examine this dense historiography, but I suggest that the colonial cosmology and administrative logic exemplified by the imperial durbar in India were brought by Lugard to Nigeria, where they took root and developed in similar ways.

As in India, for example, the first colonial durbars in Nigeria served as rituals of virtual enfeoffment.[16] From 1900 to 1903, Lugard undertook a series of military operations that forced the northern emirs and the sultan of Sokoto to recognize the higher sovereignty of the British crown. In 1900, he deposed the ruling *Etsu* of Nupe and replaced him with a new emir over a more limited jurisdiction, who "having accepted British conditions, was formally installed at Bida, before a full parade of British troops and a great assemblage of his own people, in February of 1901" (Lady Lugard [1906] 1964: 428). He then pacified the Kontagora, Yola, and Bauchi emirates, installing new rulers under ceremonial oath before taking over Kano and finally Sokoto. With this latter victory, the former Sokoto caliphate and its theocratic domain were incorporated into the colonial administration, a framework that preserved the form of the emirate system while transforming its political and procedural content (Smith 1960). In more symbolic and ideological terms, the locus of politicotheocratic authority shifted profoundly. Although the emirates could remain Islamic, the Sultan was subject to the sanctity of the crown, and it is with respect to this new political cosmology that we can reexamine the colonial durbar.

On March 22, 1903, the installation of the new sultan of Sokoto transformed the terms of ceremonial exchange. The symbolic idiom was to some extent "traditional," following customary patterns of Fulani investiture, but the logic was in key ways reversed. As described by Lady Lugard ([1906] 1964: 453): "The details of the ceremony were determined in consultation with the proper Mohammedan authorities, and it was arranged that, in sign of the acceptance of the sovereignty of Great Britain by Sokoto, the Sultan, who had never hitherto received a gift of investiture, should, like the lesser emirs, receive a gown and turban from the hands of the representative of the king of England. These were to represent the insignia of office, which up to the present day it had been the custom for Sokoto alone to present on installation to his subordinate emirs." An Islamic ceremony was thus reinscribed within a British imperial cosmology, wherein the symbols of theocratic rule—the turban and the gown—traced back metonymically to the English monarch. As the giver of gifts became the recipient, the investor became the invested. Moreover, the sultan of Sokoto was politically displaced from the center of the Fulani empire to the periphery of British empire, receiving his insignia of office from the hands of an infidel. And if such arrangements were deemed unacceptable to the locals, new stage props brought the firepower of the foreigners into full view:

> The installation ceremony was performed with some pomp. The troops, with guns and Maxims mounted, were drawn up on three sides of a hollow square. An im-

[16] In 1948, for example, the Emir Lamido of Yola (Adamawa) was still installed with "the Lugard Sword" as his staff of office in an elaborate durbar, replete with "jinjina" salute (Duckworth 1948).

mense crowd of natives were assembled. On the arrival of the High Commissioner on the spot he was received with a royal salute. A carpet was spread for the emir and for his principal officers of state. The High Commissioner then made a speech. . . . On the conclusion of the speech the High Commissioner called upon the Sultan to say if he fully understood the conditions of his installation. The Sultan replied that he understood and that he accepted. The High Commissioner then proclaimed him Sarikin Muslimin and Sultan of Sokoto, and the gown and turban were presented to him as the insignia of office. The High Commissioner shook hands publically with the Sultan, and gave permission for the royal trumpets, which can only be sounded for a duly appointed and accepted emir, to be blown. A prayer was recited aloud by the criers, and the crowd dispersed amid discordant sounds of rejoicing and expressions of mutual goodwill. (453–54)

Similar if less momentous installations at Kano, Katsina, and Zaria followed. The protectorate of northern Nigeria was thus formalized and gowns, turbans, staves of office, and letters of appointment were accorded to every recognized emir and district head.

It was through such installation durbars that the Nigerian protectorate was both ritualized and rationalized. Emirs and chiefs who had been loosely federated under the sultan of Sokoto by ties of ceremonial tribute were now clearly ranked and ordered into four grades, represented by the appropriate staves and certificates of office. Staves of the first order, reserved for the Shehu and the great Fulani emirs, were surmounted by silver headpieces; those of the second order were decorated with brass, and the third and fourth graded staves were "short and of plainer design" (Lady Lugard [1906] 1964: 437). And as Lord Lugard ([1922] 1965: 212) pointed out, they signified not only differences of rank, but also British overlordship and protection: "These staves of office, which are greatly prized, symbolise to the peasantry the fact that the Emir derives his power from the Government, and will be supported by its exercise." In addition to their staves, chiefs of each grade were received by political officers according to elaborate protocols that marked privileges and status differentials down to the smallest details. In his *Instructions to Political and Other Officers on Subjects Chiefly Political and Administrative*, Lugard (1906: 193) laid down the following rules: "When a Resident interviews a Chief of the first grade, he should shake hands with him, and offer him a chair to sit upon. He will never be summoned to an officer's quarters. . . . Chiefs of the second grade should not be given a chair, but should be provided with a raised seat (such as a box covered by a carpet). . . . Chiefs of the third . . . [and fourth] grades should be seated on a mat. . . . A Government official should in no circumstances sit on the ground in the presence of a Native Chief. While himself taking off hat in the house of a Chief, he should insist on a corresponding observation in the case of Chiefs visiting him. A Mohammedan should remove his shoes, and cover his head in the house of a European. . . ."

As in British India, such formalized structures of political authority and protocol were part and parcel of a developing colonial regime as well as of a general ideology that naturalized indirect rule. The Fulani emirs were seen as "natural" rulers over the less advanced and racially darker "pagans" whom they had conquered.17 Closer to the British in racial and evolutionary terms, deemed "Hamito-Semitic" in their heritage, they served as appropriate mediators of the civilizing mission. In the early days of this colonial encounter, the Fulani were likened to Indian castes who could be similarly domesticated. Speaking of the Fulani warriors, Mockler-Ferryman (1902: 170) opined that "eventually, when they get a better understanding of our methods, their greed for gain will induce them to follow in the footsteps of some of the old 'fighting castes' of India, and become peaceful citizens and loyal subjects of the Great White King." The colonial durbar and its associated protocols provided an appropriate mechanism for colonizing Nigeria, bringing many of the ideas and methods of British India to the African territories.18 As in India, Nigerian durbars moved from dyadic salutations between more independent emirs and political officers to collective events, in which the emirs, entourages and native troops of an entire province turned out. As early as 1908, Martin Kisch, an assistant resident in Sokoto, witnessed and photographed a durbar held for Lugard, who was touring on inspection. The emirs of Argungu and Gando and the sarikin mussulmi (sultan) of Sokoto turned out for the event, fully robed and turbanned with contingents of horsemen and camels totaling fifteen thousand. In what he described as "a very grand sight," with twenty-five thousand mounted infantry and "natives" assembled to watch, the emirs and sarikis were received "in turn," providing sixteen ponies for Lugard as "dash" and prostrating before him on the ground (Plate 5).19 What is so remarkable about this illustrated description is, first, that Lugard actually accepted the rather substantial tribute, as would befit the former sultan and, second, that even the sarikin mussulmi prostrated in an expression of fealty and respect. Cohn (1989: 329) describes how in colonial India, it was not

17 For a marvelous elaboration of this colonial philosophy, see Temple [1918] 1968, particularly chapter 2, "On the Relations Between Dominant and Dependent Races." See also Lugard ([1922] 1965: 198): "The Fulani of Northern Nigeria are, as I have said, more capable of rule than the indigenous races, but in proportion as we consider them an alien race, we are denying self-government to the people over whom they rule, and supporting an alien caste—albeit closer and more akin to the native races than a European can be," and again (210): "Their traditions of rule, their monotheistic religion, and their intelligence enable them to appreciate more readily than the Negro population the wider objects of British policy."

18 As Lugard (1902: 84) wrote in the early days of the Protectorate, "in my view the tradition of British rule has ever been to arrest disintegration, to retain and build up again what is best in the social and political organisation of the conquered dynasties, and to develop on the lines of its own individuality each separate race of which our great Empire consists. That has been our policy in India; and Northern Nigeria, though but a third the size, and many centuries behind the great Eastern dependency, still presents to my imagination many parallel conditions. I believe myself that the future of the virile races of this Protectorate lies largely in the regeneration of the Fulani."

19 Although Lugard served as high commissioner of the protectorate of northern Nigeria from 1900 to 1905, a title that changed to governor in 1907, it is not clear that he was the man Kisch referred to simply as "H.E." (His Excellency) in this account. According to the The Nigeria Handbook 1924 (1924: 221), Sir E. P. C. Girouard was governor, while Sir W. Wallace served as acting governor, in 1908. It is possible that either of these men, rather than Lugard himself, received the sarikin in Kisch's photograph.

Plate 5. "The Sarikin Mussulmi Being Received by H. E. [His Excellency]." From Kisch (1910: opp. p. 110). Photo credit M. Kisch.

until the imperial durbar of 1911 that the leading princes were told to prostrate in what was dubbed "the homage pavilion." In Kisch's account we find an African precedent for this innovation, in which the colonizer interpolated himself into the ritual of the colonized, appropriating its center of command.

As Callaway (1987: 58–59) points out, the durbar was employed "as a regular feature for imperial celebrations," including one marking Lugard's appointment as governor-general of Nigeria in 1913.[20] As such, it belonged to the more general theater of empire that punctuated daily life in the colonies, where social distinctions of the metropole were refined and elaborated, differing only to the degree that Africans were explicitly included *in their place*. But if durbars formalized local authority relations, they did so within a general imperial cosmology of truly global proportions. Much has been written both for and about the coronation durbar of George V, held in Delhi in December 1911. The *Coronation Durbar, Delhi, 1911: Official Directory with Maps* (1911) lays out the entire schedule of events with an inventory of camps and important personages; there is also a special souvenir edition of *The King Emperor and His Dominions* (1911), replete with scientific appendices, not to mention recent historical and anthropological analyses. But precious little has been written about the coronation durbar held in Zaria, admittedly less elaborate than its Indian counterpart and

[20] This was what Haruna undoubtedly referred to as the "first" colonial durbar in Nigeria, in his speech quoted above.

lacking the dramatic person of the king himself (represented instead by His Excellency) but for that very reason particularly significant, because its very performance brought northern Nigeria into the global imperial order. In the coronation durbar at Zaria, the political structure of the northern protectorate was sanctified by the ultimate investiture of King George V, participating in an imperial spectacle that reflected the providential plan of Britain's national destiny throughout the world.

A contemporary description (*Blackwood's* 1912) of the durbar at Zaria dwells on grand themes in purple prose, interpreting the ceremony as a local expression of a higher moral purpose. Of interest is not the imperial ideology writ large, but the way the "chaos" of Africa was reduced and informed by colonial spectacle. First, there is the organization of the African forces, a "seething mass of colour presented by the brightly caparisoned throng—reds and blues and greens and masses of dazzling white," which forms into a line and "comes tearing down the avenue of soldiery, gathers way momentarily, and comes to a halt in front of his Excellency" (356). Line after line of horsemen follow, "all jingle and glitter and flashing color . . . like wave following wave," charging their "wild eyed" horses toward none other than Lord Lugard himself, halting a few yards in front of His Excellency in the "Jafi" salute of a mock attack. Much can be read into this ritual confrontation between the master and his subjects, incorporated from the Islamic Sallah into the colonial durbar proper. There is the threat of armed rebellion against the colonial order, as well as the reciprocal demonstration of imperial authority and domination. Clearly portrayed by the organization of riders and the sequence of their salutes to the "King," however, is the hierarchy of races in northern Nigeria, ranked according to their natural abilities and propensities to rule and be ruled. First, among the native races come the Fulani aristocrats, born to ride and rule; beneath them the Nupe and Yoruba traders, followed by diminutive swarms of pagans: "Men of Kano, followers of the Emir of Katsina, gallant in red and white robes; Zaria men in Cossack-like caps of black goat-skin; Bornu riders with white shields and curious Crusader helmets. . . . There are Filanis [sic] from Muri and from Yola too. Warriors all these—well mounted—the aristocracy of the many races that go to make up the people of the Protectorate. After the warrior, the man of trade. And now we see, lolloping gently up the ground, portly, panting envoys of Ilorin and Bida, Yorubas and Nupes, excellent worthy fellows all, moneyed men, fathers of the coming race of trousered Negro lawyers, but they don't sit a horse well, these trader men, not as do the Kano and Muri and Yola and Bornu people" (356). Thus the durbar choreographed the native races of Nigeria, "feudalized" into a castelike order that was clarified by colonial administration. We see how the Fulani aristocrats were identified by place as well as position, the different emirs serving as sole native authorities within their respective administrations, and how these in turn were stratified into lower racial orders with associated occupations. If the Fulani represented landed aristocrats, the Yoruba and Nupe possessed the virtues and limitations of a nascent bourgeoisie, "moneyed men" destined for business and the professions, perhaps more educated than the Fulani but less refined. But it is the third category, the brutish pagans, occupying the lowest position in the colonial pecking order, that best capture the moral imagination of the coronation durbar:

> Last of all comes a very wondrous sight indeed. You are to imagine, if you please, a swarm of bees represented by men: smallish, black men, *very* scantily clothed, armed all of them, some with spears, others with knives, or clubs, or swords, or axes; others again with nothing more deadly than a drum, or a horn. . . . Arrived in the presence, the swarm breaks, and the swarmers engage in a dance, abating in no wise their musical (!) activities, and there is a halt in the morning's proceedings what time the Political responsible for these pagans walks amongst them, trying to reduce them to some sort of order and consciousness. . . . His excellency is an old hand in Northern Nigeria, and knows the pagan, none better, so receives them in a fashion that delights their primitive souls, and send them off perfectly, not to say frantically, happy. (356–57)

Naked, black, swarming like stinging insects, the pagans are "reduced to some kind of order and consciousness" by the civilizing mission and its rational administration. They are, moreover, included in the durbar, protected by the British from Fulani slave raids and encouraged to come down from their hilltops and out of their caves to engage in peaceful agriculture (Lugard [1922] 1965: 581). The hill pagan, as he was called, represented primitive savagery and arrested evolutionary development. Hunted and persecuted by his superiors until the British *Pax*, he could now assume his natural place within the imperial order of things.

The administrative order of the northern protectorate was ceremonially mobilized through such durbars, as moral in inspiration as they were rational in plan. A regional coherence was ritually sanctified, drawing together emirs, chiefs, and pagans and putting them in their proper places. It served, I maintain, as one of the key expressions of indirect rule, designed by Lugard in the north and eventually extending throughout Nigeria after the northern and southern protectorates were amalgamated in 1914. But my argument is less about causality, because surely durbars were part of a general political transformation of the colony, and more about a form of cultural recuperation and production that was implicated in the process, an inventing of traditions that, as Ranger (1983) has sketched out for colonial Africa more generally, involved the codification of customs and tribes into administrative schedules and categories. Nonetheless, drawing on indigenous durbars and Sallahs in what has been called—in another context—"the central institution of ceremonial interaction" (E. Haynes 1990: 461), the colonial administration forged a northern regional unity that acquired a distinctive political culture vis-à-vis the south. As Coleman (1958: 353–68) has pointed out, the northern region was the last to develop a nationalist movement in Nigeria, and when it did, it remained cautious and parochial. Its dominant political party, the Northern People's Congress (NPC), was controlled by the traditional ruling class of emirs, mallams, and hereditary officials whose privileged position and sense of natural entitlement had been upheld by colonial authority.[21] I mention this here to illustrate the extent to which the formal hierarchies of native administration in the north, partly racialized in the coronation durbar, were naturalized within an emergent regional culture that, by the 1950s, had become explicitly antinationalist and hostile toward the south. In the more refined terms of colonial distinction, the northern emirs held more common cause with the nobility of Britain than with the invasive southern barbarians.[22] And what better occasions to affirm such common cause than the imperial durbars of 1925, held in Kano for the Prince of Wales, and of 1956, staged in Kaduna for none other than the queen herself.

The durbar for Edward, then Prince of Wales, was part of his general tour of West Africa—in the battle cruiser *Repulse*—which included stops in the Gambia, Sierra Leone, and the Gold Coast before reaching Nigeria. In each of these colonies the heir apparent received the appropriate traditional authorities, some bearing gifts, others kissing his hand (Adock n.d.). In the Gold Coast, a grand palaver was held in the polo ground, where the prince met chiefs of the Ashanti Confederacy as well as representatives of the northern territories, seated under umbrellas and arranged into fifty-four groups. But it was the durbar in Kano—the commercial capital of the northern region—which the royal souvenir book describes as "the most gorgeous and impressive that had yet been staged for the Prince in Africa" (Adock n.d.). Surely great prestige accrued to the emir of Kano, who played host not only to the future king-emperor, but also to the sultan of Sokoto, the emir of Bauchi and the sheik of Dikwa from the Cameroons. In addition to the Nigerian durbar's signature "salute of the desert," in which fierce-looking warriors in helmets and chain armour or cloaks and turbans . . . gallop[ed] furiously almost up to the Royal stand before they abruptly reined in their flying steeds and wheeled aside," the "Emirs and Chiefs were conducted to the dais and presented in order of precedence by the Resident . . . [where] the Prince addressed them and the assembly at large."[23] An official photograph of the emirs "making their obeisance to the Prince at the Durbar" reveals the vertical dimensions of colonial authority. The prince, leaning down from his throne on the dais, shakes the hand of the sultan, which stretches up as he prostrates with two emirs behind him on the ground—fealty with a personal touch (Adock n.d., Plate 6). This helping hand of colonial overrule had growing horizontal implications too, because it was through the durbar itself that greater regional integration and awareness was achieved. As Nigeria's Colonial Reports—Annual

---

[21] For example, the sultan of Sokoto became the patron of the Northern People's Congress in 1954.

[22] Thus in a Nigerian Legislative Council session of 1948, the Mallam and future Prime Minister Abubakar Tafawa Balewa went on record as saying: "The Southern tribes who are now pouring into the North in ever increasing numbers, and are more or less domiciled here do not mix with the Northern People . . . and we in the North look upon them as invaders." Quoted in Coleman (1958: 361).

[23] See the unpaginated section of Adock (n.d.) called "Nigeria, and Crossing the Line."

Plate 6. "Emirs of the Northern Province Making Their Obeisance to the Prince at the Durbar, Kano, Nigeria." Photo credit anon., From Adock, St. John. n.d. [1925?]. *The Prince of Wales' African Book*. London: Hodder & Stoughton, Ltd.

for 1925 recorded: "A Durbar was held in Kano which was attended by practically all the chiefs of the Northern Provinces. Not only were the chiefs impressed by the magnificence of the spectacle, but they met people and tribes many of whom were but names to them or in some cases traditional enemies, and found they were all at one in their allegiance to the king, whose son's personality so . . . impressed their imagination."

Thirty-one years later, Nigeria was preparing for independence. The Richards Constitution of 1945 had sought to reconcile the native authority system as the primary unit of self-government with more representative parliamentary institutions advocated by the nationalists. The resulting compromise was intensified regionalism, with three new regional houses of assembly to be established at Kaduna, Ibadan, and Enugu, each with its own budget. Although regionalism was criticized by more southern nationalists as separatist and divisive, "to all northerners it was the single most attractive feature of the constitution" (Coleman 1958: 277), which gained the overwhelming support of the traditional emirs who formed the Northern House of Chiefs. In the developing political climate, the native authority system became increasingly antiprogressive, allied with the forces of conservation rather than the tides of change. The NCNC protest campaign (1945–1947) notwithstanding, regionalism emerged as the primary focus of Nigerian nationalist development (ibid., 319), articulated in increasingly politicocultural terms. The dominant northern party, the NPC, was led by the Alhaji Ahmadu Bello, the sardauna of Sokoto, who became premier of the northern region, while his kinsman, the sultan of Sokoto, became official patron of the party.

Within this political tug-of-war between conservatives favoring regional autonomy and more militant nationalists pushing for enlightened self-government, the royal tour of Nigeria in 1956 and its "crowning" event, the Kaduna durbar, took place. And it was in this context, in the administrative capital, that the last imperial durbar in Nigeria expressed a cultural unity for the northern region, representing its distinctive position vis-à-vis its southern and eastern counterparts within the emerging nation-state. The selection of participating representatives from all twelve provinces extended to the lowest administrative levels though a series of associated grassroots competitions. David Williams, then editor of *West Africa*, described his impressions of this extensive preparation to the Royal African Society: "I remember, for example, being present last December at an agricultural show in far off Adamawa where a dancing competition was held to choose a team to go to Kaduna. This competition was itself the result of organisation in remote villages, and was typical of what was happening all over" (Williams 1956: 113). In the end, contingents from the region's twelve provinces arrived "by canoe, road, horse and rail" from as far as seven hundred miles, spending up to five weeks in the saddle, to settle in the durbar camp in preparation for the spectacle. For the provincial emirs, the event boosted their senior status and perhaps their political clout. As Letchworth (1956: 29–30), the senior resident of Bornu Province, reported: "At Kaduna the Shehu of Bornu, now over eighty-two, insisted on taking his place on horseback at the head of his contingent in spite of the fact that he had not ridden since 1948 and the Emir of Fika, aged sixty, accompanied by the Emir of Biu, took a leading part in the traditional gallop to the foot of the Royal stand. As one Fika trader said with great satisfaction on hearing of his Emir's part in the proceedings, 'Ah ha, that will lengthen Mai Fika's beard.'"

Similarly, Cooke (1956: 11), the acting resident of Bauchi Province, quoted the leading emir's annual report, that "The memory of the Royal Visit, which has put the Northern Region on the map, will never be forgotten in the history of the Region." Of more immediate interest to Cooke, however, were the durbar's political consequences for Bauchi Province, because it was through their cooperative efforts at the regional celebration that the five native authorities of Kaltungo, West Tangale, Waja, Dadiya, and Cham saw that they could get along and agreed to federate (11). For the most part, however, local voices and perspectives are difficult to discern from available sources. Internecine political struggles were surely simmering beneath the surface, as indicated by the politically motivated Kano riots of 1953.[24] The media tended to focus on the bigger picture, and there was plenty to see.

The queen and the Duke of Edinburgh arrived in an open Rolls Royce, circling the racecourse twice before taking their seats on the dais of the durbar pavilion, where they were joined by the governor of the region, Sir Bryan E. Sharwood-Smith, and his wife, Lady Sharwood-Smith, by the premier, the sardauna of Sokoto, and by the sultan of Sokoto and the Shehu of Borno, who left their seats only to lead their contingents on horseback. The region's twelve provincial contingents were grouped into blocks within the durbar arena, with a *jahi* group comprising representatives from each contingent in front. During the inspection, the marching bands reflected the regional government, with the military band of the Nigeria Regiment followed by separate police bands of the native authorities.[25] After the orderly "march past" of the provincial contingents, including horsewomen from Bauchi, jesters from Jos, and pagan dancers from Numan wielding agricultural tools, the culminating *jahi* charge took place. As featured by the *West African Review* (1956: 274): "A solid phalanx of screaming warriors, on horseback and clad in chain mail, thundered across the ground in an awe-inspiring gallop. With a great shout, they halted, seemingly inches from Her Majesty, dipped their standards and lances and wheeled proudly away—an unforgettable sight." Here is one of the final and finest expressions of colonial ambivalence in Nigeria, a charge that carried all the contradictions of indirect rule to the sacred center of colonial authority. The northern emirs no longer prostrated before the Crown, but they still acknowledged fealty. Later in the

[24] The riots were sparked by the proposed Action Group tour headed by Akintola. See the *Report on the Kano Disturbances, 16th, 17th, 18th, and 19th, May 1953*. Northern Regional Government: Government Printer, Nigeria, 1953. Many northern newspaper editorials blamed the riots on resident southerners, while even the *Report* cites fundamental cultural differences between northerners and southerners as a general cause.

[25] Actually, there were only eight police bands from Sokoto, Bornu, Gwandu, Kano, Bauchi, Katsina, Ilorin, and Katagum native authorities.

evening, the queen invested the sultan of Sokoto with the Knight Grand Cross of the Order of the British Empire and bestowed other honors on local chieftains and notables (Plates 7 and 8).[26]

In sketching the imperial paternity of the durbar as a tradition of colonial incorporation, I have highlighted the descent line that FESTAC suppressed. What began as the cultural foundation of indirect rule under Lugard, and what Haruna called "imperialist propaganda" in his FESTAC speech, developed into something else. If in 1925, the imperial durbar upheld expanding colonial interests in Nigeria, promoted by the Prince of Wales' visit to the commercial capital of the northern provinces, by 1956 it consolidated the northern region's political identity and autonomy vis-à-vis the imminent nation-state. In this latter capacity, the official durbar was no longer a regular feature of state ceremonials, since colonial authority was on the wane. The naturalization of authority relations that the earlier durbars expressed gave way to a different if related project— the making of a regional culture. This was not to deny ethnic difference, as the Kaduna durbar testified, but to redefine it in the more lateral terms of regional unity, *contra* the south and east. As Kirk-Greene (1959: 16) proclaimed on the eve of independence: "[the Durbar] is something we in the North should be proud of—both the splendour of the event and the national characteristics so clearly discernible in that representation of the long history and colour of the Northern Region. . . . The thesis developed in this article is that of the durbar as the 'Heart of the North'; as a ceremony symbolizing not only the quintessential North but also springing from the very inspiration of the Northern peoples."

In the twilight of British colonialism, we can thus grasp the beginnings of a fundamental shift in the cultural politics of the Nigerian state, whereby the invented traditions of the colonial order were indigenized by Nigerian political elites. It was a process, which FESTAC later clarified, whereby the cultural foundations of the colonial order became "quintessential" expressions of the new nation-state.

National Culture

By February 5, 1977, when FESTAC's Grand Durbar took the nation's center stage, the Nigerian state had changed dramatically. After achieving independence in 1960, six years of federalism under the First Republic broke down in the first of a series of military coups. Immediately, a tendency away from regionalism and toward unification accentuated the role of the state in national affairs.[27] In 1967, Nigeria's federated regions were reorganized into twelve states, and again

---

[26] *The Queen's Tour of Nigeria* (1956: 13).

[27] One of the major goals of Ironsi's coup of 1966 was to break up the regions and consolidate the central military government, as proposed by his Unification Decree of May 1966, to which the northerners were bitterly opposed (Joseph 1987: 77).

Plate 7. "150 Tribesmen Charge at Royal Dais." From *The Queen's Tour of Nigeria: Commemorating the Visit of H. M. Queen Elizabeth II and H. R. H. the Duke of Edinburgh.* 1956. London: Pitkin Pictorials, p. 12.

Plate 8. "The Sultan of Sokoto Knighted by Queen Elizabeth II, 1956." From *The Queen's Tour of Nigeria: Commemorating the Visit of H. M. Queen Elizabeth II and H. R. H. the Duke of Edinburgh.* 1956. London: Pitkin Pictorials, 13.

into nineteen by 1969. The bloody tragedy of the secessionist Biafran war (1967–1970), in which an estimated two million people were killed or starved to death, brought home the need for a strong national center. But the greatest single factor in fueling the growth and centralization of the state was the oil boom of the 1970s, combining military rule and economic statism (Joseph 1987: 69–90) in what Watts (1992: 36) has dubbed "the bureaucratic petrostate." From 1970 to 1977, the revenues accruing to the federal budget increased by 1000 percent, with oil exports and rents accounting for over 80 percent of the returns. The consequences of this oil bonanza were legion, but three very general trends can be discerned that consolidated a state-capitalist sector fraught with contradictions. First, a new pattern of capital accumulation developed that relied less on the peasant producer surplus formerly controlled by the regional elites through marketing boards—cocoa in the west, palm oil in the east, groundnuts and cotton in the north—and more on direct oil revenues allocated by the center. As described by Joseph (1987: 74), "the national purse to be distributed became increasingly filled with funds gained from the pumping of crude oil from the Nigerian subsoil and offshore areas and its transshipment abroad, a process which involved minimal input of Nigerian labor." Second, the state itself expanded, through public-sector institutions such as schools, hospitals, highways, and electrification projects—all on the public payroll—as well as parastatal industries including auto assembly, iron and steel, and petrochemicals (Watts 1992: 36). And finally, enriched by a highly internationalized commodity, the state itself was internationalized and hooked into circuits of global capital. Nigeria's growing role in world affairs was signaled by its participation and leadership in OPEC, the OAU, the Economic Community of West African States (ECOWAS), and the UN committee on the New International Economic Order, established to improve the terms of trade between the industrial north and the developing south. It was during this sudden rise and consolidation of state wealth and power, and in celebration of such fortune and fame, that Nigeria hosted and financed FESTAC '77.

The planning and execution of FESTAC belonged with the national development schemes, afforded by the oil boom, that would rebuild the country after the Biafran war and launch it fully into the modern era. These included programs for universal primary education, building national infrastructures, conducting a national census, setting up oil refineries in Enugu and Kaduna, and preparing for a return to civilian rule through democratic elections. FESTAC's contributions to the new Nigeria included the construction of a National Theatre, a FESTAC Village, and a National Council of Arts and Culture that used the latest communications technologies to promote national integration. As Nigeria's Constitutional Drafting Committee resolved, "The State shall foster a feeling of belonging and of involvement among the various sections of the country, to the end that loyalty to the nation shall override sectional loyalties."[28] Toward this end, Nigeria would celebrate its national culture at the center of FESTAC's black and African world. Drawing on the glorious traditions of its precolonial past, Nigeria would lead the way into an even more glorious future. Breaking free from its colonial heritage, decolonizing its collective mind, the African world would "recapture the origins and authenticity of [its] heritage."[29] In this pan-African idiom, the production of a Nigerian national culture developed as an explicit state project. Funded by oil, it mirrored the very regional, national, and international dynamics of Nigeria's oil economy as local tradition and national heritage embraced the wealth of all black nations. Rationalized by the state and commodified by the economy, Nigeria's national culture was produced as an object of knowledge and value. As such, it was separated from the conditions of its production as an autonomous entity, to become a thing, a fetish. Through various federal ministries, councils, and agencies, Nigeria's national culture became visibly distinct.

It was through the state's subvention of FESTAC '77 that the invented traditions of colonial authority were nationalized, erasing the very colonial history in which they developed and took shape. If the Grand Durbar was lauded as a representation of indigenous tradition, it resembled in scale, organization, and execution the imperial durbars that it explicitly disavowed. To be sure, basic allegiances had shifted. Ties with Britain were strained over the British Museum's refusal to return the original Benin ivory that served as FESTAC's trademark. The absence of any high-ranking British representatives at the Kaduna durbar was offset by the presence of Andrew Young, Jimmy Carter's ambassador to the United Nations, who saw Nigeria as America's strongest African ally in promoting business on the continent and fighting apartheid in South Africa.[30] More to the delight of the Nigerian media, however, was Young's deference to the sultan of Sokoto, for whom the ambassador knelt in showing his respect. Here was the

---

[28] Cited in Joseph (1987: 43).

[29] The quote comes from General Olusegun Obasanjo, Nigeria's head of state and FESTAC's grand patron, during the official opening ceremony (quoted in *West Africa* no. 3107, 24 January 1977: 172).

[30] "We Should Participate." *Washington Star*, December 26, 1976.

incarnation of historical justice, as a black representative of the world's leading superpower paid homage to traditional African authority. Young was amused—and slightly annoyed—by the excessive attention that his gesture received.[31] In terms of the politics of the imperial durbar, it made perfect sense, revoking the helping hand of Britain's Prince of Wales that had extended to the kneeling Sultan half a century earlier. But if Andrew Young and the sultan of Sokoto were prominently seated in the first row of the reviewing stand, they were joined by a select group of very important persons who watched the horsemen and dancers from the ten northern states, followed by the collective *jahi* salute.[32]

Bearing the national flag, Nigerian police mounted on horseback stood by, as contingents from the states and their emirates marched past, each with its own banner and retinue, including hunters, warriors, dancers, acrobats, and mounted guards. The Wasan Burtu dancers from Borno state, dressed in animal skins with bird heads to lure game, were joined by the Shehu's standard bearers, Kanuri "Kazagama" dispatch riders, and Waziri Dumas dancers. Tambari mounted musicians heralded the emir of Kano, flanked by his Dogorai bodyguards and Yan Lafida heavy cavalry unit riding horses protected by quilted armors. Camels from Katsina and Bori dancers from Zaria added local variation to Kaduna state. If subordinate leaders and district heads commingled in the festive confusion of music, dance, and dust, seniority was sorted out by the seats allocated to emirs and chiefs in the State Box, where the paramount traditional rulers from each state retired from the saddle.[33] Thus was the traditional culture of the northern emirates displayed, celebrating precolonial ceremonies and values through the very administrative forms and categories that the colonial durbars innovated, but that somehow got lost in the spectacular fanfare. For example, the Borno state contingent, comprising the Borno, Dikwa, Fika, Biu, and Bade emirates, represented a heterogeneous population whose unity was imparted by what had been Borno province under the British, now reorganized as a state. To indicate this political unity, the Borno contingent invented an appropriate uniform. The minutes of Borno state's durbar planning committee reported: "For purposes of distinction, uniformity and some kind of identity for the Borno contingent in costume was discussed. It was finally agreed that this identity should be in the 'Aji' cap and the turban Akkal which all Borno horsemen should be wearing."[34] Thus was the colonial order displaced into the past, by the very innovations that commemorated a timeless tradition. Even the venue at Kaduna Racecourse, now re-

[31] Personal communication, interview May 19, 1993, Quadrangle Club, University of Chicago.

[32] The state contingents proceeded in the following order: Bauchi, Borno, Gongola, Kaduna, Kano, Kwara, Niger, Plateau, and Sokoto, with dancers representing Benue state. The Tor Tiv was supposed to represent Benue, but it is not clear that he arrived.

[33] The rank order was (1) Sultan of Sokoto, (2) Shehu of Borno, (3) Emir of Kano, (4) Emir of Katsina, (5) Lamido of Adamawa, (6) Emir of Bauchi, (7) Etsu of Nupe, (8) Emir of Ilorin, (9) Tor Tiv, and (10) Chief of Jos. From "Proposed Program for the Durbar at Kaduna, 8th February, 1977." NPS Folder 19, vol. 2: 40.

[34] "Minutes of Meeting of Emirs and Chiefs in Borno State held in the Council Chambers of the Borno Local Authority." NPS Folder 19, vol. 2: 65 (National Participation Secretary, Lagos, Nigeria).

Plate 9. "Andrew Young (U.S. Ambassador to the United Nations) at the Festac Durbar, 1977." From Lahey (n.d.). Photo credit Richard Saunders.

modeled into Murtala Mohammed Square, maintained the same location where the Queen of England and the Duke of Edinburgh surveyed equivalent contingents from the northern provinces in 1956.

The new players at FESTAC's durbar were not on the field, but could be seen on the viewing stand (Plates 9 and 10). In addition to Andrew Young, Sir Abubakar (sultan of Sokoto) and Nigeria's head of state, General Obasanjo, they included members of the younger and more educated northern military elite,

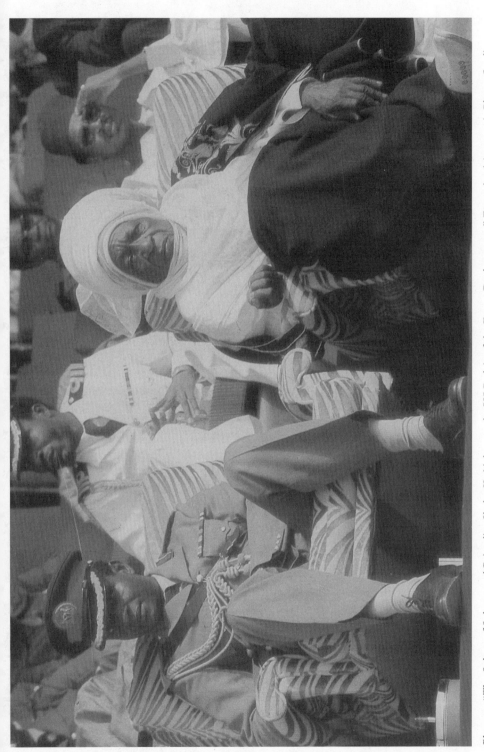

Plate 10. "The Sultan of Sokoto and Brigadier Shehu Yar'Adua on the V.I.P. dais of the Festac Durbar, 1977." From Augi (1978: 22). Photo Credit: G. O. Nwaobi, M. O. Omole, and A. Francis.

whose alliance with the old aristocratic order would ensure northern control over the country and its petroleum resources. Seated next to Young, Joseph Garba, who was Nigerian commissioner for external affairs, and Brigadier Shehu Yar'Adua, chief of staff Supreme Headquarters, had engineered the coup against Gowon to place Murtala Mouhammed—"scion of the traditional establishment of Kano" (Joseph 1987: 130)—in power and represented the real military muscle of the Obasanjo regime. Yar'Adua in fact belonged to the Fulani establishment in Katsina, in northern Kaduna state. Among other prominent northerners were the Kaduna state governor, Group Captain Usman Jibrin, and chief of army staff, Lt.-General Danjuma, also rumored to be an architect of the previous coup. Present also was Ibrahim Buhari, who would soon become oil minister in the Second Republic before bringing back the military in his New Year's coup d'état. At the time, with elections for the Second Republic in the planning stages, this consolidation of northern hegemony, linking the authority of the old elites with the power of the military's inner circle (and the money of its civilian hand, the "Kaduna Mafia"), would prove to be portentous.[35] But even before the 1979 elections, Obasanjo knew how to play his cards. As Joseph (130) explains, "General Obasanjo, the second non-northern leader of Nigeria since the brief rule of General Ironsi in 1966, knew that the stability of his regime depended on his retention of support from the traditional and modern elites of the North and he was assiduous in ensuring that this support never wavered." I suggest that FESTAC's Grand Durbar in Kaduna was a cultural concession to such northern hegemony. Not only were large sums allocated to its northern planners, with finances for the expensive Durbar Hotel included, but cultural capital was invested as well.[36] Framed in the idiom of precolonial northern culture, a regional culture that—we have seen—came into focus under colonialism and nationalized as an allegory of Nigerian culture and as a template for African civilization and governance, the durbar further consolidated the political hegemony of the north. Planned and produced by Nigeria's National Participation Secretariat, the durbar signaled a time-honored tradition that disguised not only the historical conditions of its colonial development but also the political agenda behind its successful execution. When a correspondent from the *New York Times* reported, after witnessing the durbar, that "it seemed that the North was trying to outdo its Southern rival in a single spectacular afternoon" (Darnton 1977), he could not have summarized its politics more concisely.

IN tracing the genealogy of the Nigerian durbar, I have "excavated" its history as a composite tradition stemming from two dubious sources, one indigenous, with its own complex layerings of sacred kingship and equestrian culture (in some sense represented by the Jukun ethnography) that was assimilated to the

[35] For a variety of perspectives on the so-called Kaduna mafia, see Takaya and Tyoden (1987).

[36] Official allocations for the durbar event and its commemorative hotel totaled nearly 20 million naira, which at the time equaled $32 million. From NPS 19, EC 75 (National Participation Secretariat, Lagos, Nigeria).

Islamic religious calendar, and the other exogenous, as an instrument of imperial ideology and colonial authority imported from Victorian India. This model of "double descent" is not unproblematic, since the exogeneous "patriline" and the indigenous "matriline" can never be established as ethnohistorically "pure." We have seen, for example, how the pre-Islamic Jukun "durbar" showed signs of Islamic and colonial influence and perhaps is better historicized in parallel rather than prior terms. We also saw how the Nupe Sallah incorporated relations of colonial authority and commodity value into its ritual economy. But these influences in no way undermine the lineage model; rather, they illuminate the changing political fields in which the indigenous durbar developed.

Like all genealogies, the pedigree that I have sketched for the Nigerian durbar is structurally selective and inevitably incomplete. I have overlooked some of the durbars recorded in colonial memoranda and early press reports, as well as the northern region's independence durbar of 1959 and the Hailie Selassie Durbar of 1972.[37] These latter durbars undoubtedly prepared important ground for the Grand Durbar of FESTAC '77. My more analytical aim, however, was to explore the distinction between the historicity of the durbar, which, as professed by FESTAC's genealogy, recuperated a precolonial African purity, and the durbar's "actual" history as an important colonial tradition. I am not suggesting that because the durbar was colonial, with roots in British India, it was therefore not African. The organizers of FESTAC may have rejected the colonial patriline on ideological grounds, but my goal has not been to deconstruct, in turn, the precolonial matriline. Rather I am interested in the process whereby the colonial durbar in northern Nigeria became regionalized, nationalized, and Africanized as its imperial pedigree was erased. This process divides into three general phases.

The first phase, spanning 1900–1925, involves the constitution of colonial authority through imperial rituals such as the durbar itself. Here the colonial durbar was directly associated with indirect rule, ranking native races in administrative categories and transforming "tradition" through its codification and preservation. As the central institution of ceremonial interaction between colonial and native authorities in the north, the durbar served as the cultural foundation of an administrative system that was generalized throughout Nigeria. The colonial durbar made no claims of cultural authenticity. If it respected native emirs and their bureaucratic institutions while rearranging them into the colonial order, its officers innovated without customary constraint. In this capacity, the durbar belonged to the political machinery of the colonial state. The past that it recuperated and projected onto Africa was not an African past; rather, it came from feudal England and the feudatories of Victorian India.[38]

---

[37] For a vivid description of the 1913 durbar in Kano, taken from Lugard's own dispatch to London, see Kirk-Greene (1959: 19). For descriptive fragments of independence durbars held in honor of Princess Alexandra in 1960, see "The Princess and the Premier." *West Africa*, October 22, 1960, no. 2264: 1187.

[38] Richard Rathbone (personal communication) has suggested that the colonial durbars of India and Nigeria played into the contemporaneous remaking of the British monarchy as well, adding an extremely important dimension of domestic politics and iconography at the metropole, which I have not addressed.

The second phase of the Nigerian durbar belongs to the liberalization and decline of colonial power, from after the war until 1956, culminating in Queen Elizabeth's triumphal return. During this time the durbar came to represent a conservative northern regional culture in the context of growing militant nationalisms in the south and east. In the imperial durbar of 1956, the northern region distinguished itself in two ways. First, unlike its regional counterparts, its ruling aristocracy allied with the British Crown, postponing the transition to self-rule while requesting continued colonial custodianship. Second, it defined itself in explicitly cultural terms invoked and made visible through ceremonial display. In this capacity, the durbar provided the ritual idiom and cultural framework for consolidating northern political hegemony over an imminently self-governing Nigeria. The significant development that should be foregrounded here is one of separation and objectification, in that a regional culture forged under colonialism emerged as an explicit and autonomous domain—a natural feature, as it were, of Nigeria's national landscape rather than a political instrument of the state. Thus the very administrative hierarchies and categories that the first colonial durbars naturalized in racial terms became nationalized in the language of regional culture. As culture emerged in the spotlight of spectacle, taking on an independent life of its own, the postcolonial state took shape behind the scenes. And in the political context of Nigerian federalism, the north remained "on top."

After independence, the durbar entered its final phase as a national charter for an oil-rich Nigeria that could afford to celebrate a new pan-Africanism. If the state was centralized and internationalized by its access to global capital, it was controlled by an inner circle of established emirs and new elites, represented by younger military officers and the so-called Kaduna mafia. In this context of state expansion and rapid national development, traditional culture was not just objectified, but was commodified and fetishized by state-sponsored festivals.[39] Further disassociated from the conditions of its production, the durbar was universalized as Nigerian national culture and globalized as black and African culture (Apter 1996). FESTAC's official genealogy of the Nigerian durbar could thus explicitly disavow its colonial heritage while maintaining it in political terms as continuous northern domination. In this capacity, the durbar emerged as a culture effect of the swollen bureaucratic petrostate. Produced and financed by the state, the durbar came to stand outside of it, as historically prior to Nigeria's colonial past and indicative of its future.

If the genealogy of the Nigerian durbar illustrates how the cultural foundations of colonial authority became the culture effect of an oil-rich state, it stands as a variation on the more general dialectics of national culture in the postcolony. In crude terms, the problem is how to naturalize a sovereign territory based on arbitrary boundaries, such as those drawn up for Africa at the Berlin Conference.

---

[39] For a useful background to Nigeria's state and national councils of art and culture, and the festivals they organized, see Fasuyi (1973).

Politically, it concerns the transition from colonialism to self-government, in-volving, whether consciously or not, a negation of the former metropole and a recuperation of indigenous tradition. Intellectually, it produces varieties of am-bivalence ranging from *négritude* in French and consciensism in English to a principled return to indigenous languages as a way of decolonizing the mind.[40] The predicament of national culture in the postcolony is thus one of national identity politics, growing out of anticolonial struggle, to some extent sustained by neocolonial struggle but leading in no clear direction. Forged by the colonial categories that are negated and transcended at independence, the postcolony remains caught in apparent ideological contradiction. And the contradiction will remain as long as the terms of struggle remain categorically opposed: Afri-can versus European, indigenous versus colonial, traditional versus modern, even black versus white. What the genealogy of the Nigerian durbar really reveals is not, as FESTAC proclaimed, a decolonization of cultural tradition based on the rejection of imperialism, but rather the nationalization of colonial tradition by the postcolonial state. Explicitly erased, such traditions were indigenized through the very festivals and ministries that objectified culture for citizens and tourists.

Similar trends have been noted before.[41] Following the colonial durbar in India until the eve of independence, Douglas Haynes (1990: 527) concludes that the adoption of imperial ritual idioms by the Indian National Congress shows only too clearly that "liberating a society from the mental models of authority provided by imperialism can be an even more difficult task than bringing about the formal end of colonial power." I argue from the Nigerian case that it is time to abandon this binary logic and its political rejection of colonialism's culture. The imprint of imperial pasts can be transformed into national tradition but never fully erased. In FESTAC '77, the conversion of the colonial durbar into an exalted expression of Nigeria's national heritage was not the intention of the re-gime's cultural renaissance, but its effect.

References

Adock, St. John. n.d. [1925?]. *The Prince of Wales' African Book*. London: Hod-der and Stoughton, Ltd.

Anderson, Benedict. 1983. *Imagined Communities: Reflections on the Origin and Spread of Nationalism*. London: Verso.

Apter, Andrew. 1996. "The Pan-African Nation: Oil-Capitalism and the Spec-tacle of Culture in Nigeria." *Public Culture* 8, no. 3: 441–66.

---

[40] See, for example, Nkrumah (1970), Ngugi (1986), and Senghor (1964).

[41] See Austen (1992) for an interesting francophone African variation on this theme, in which the Ngondo Assembly among the Duala of Cameroon, an institution that was largely "invented" under colonialism, was commemorated as a venerable precolonial festival, and even incorporated aspects of "canoe races held on colonial and national holidays" (305).

Augi, Abdullahi Rafi. 1978. *The History and Performance of the Durbar in Northern Nigeria*. Lagos: Nigeria Magazine, Cultural Division, Federal Ministry of Information.

Austen, Ralph. 1992. "Tradition, Invention and History: The Case of the Ngondo (Cameroon)." *Cahiers d'études africaines* 126, XXXII-2: 285–309.

Blackwood's Magazine. 1912. "The Durbar at Zaria." 91 (1956): 352–58.

Bohannan, Laura. 1952. "A Genealogical Charter." *Africa* 22, no. 4: 301–15.

Bourdieu, Pierre. 1993. *The Field of Cultural Production: Essays on Art and Literature*. New York: Columbia University Press.

Callaway, Helen. 1987. *Gender, Culture, and Empire: European Women in Colonial Nigeria*. Urbana: University of Illinois Press.

Cohn, Bernard. 1983. "Representing Authority in Victorian India." In E. Hobsbawm and T. Ranger, eds., *The Invention of Tradition*, 165–209. Cambridge: Cambridge University Press.

———. 1989. "Cloth, Clothes, and Colonialism: India in the Nineteenth Century." In Annette Weiner and Jane Schneider, eds., *Cloth and Human Experience*, 303–53. Washington: Smithsonian Institution Press.

Coleman, James S. 1958. *Nigeria: Background to Nationalism*. Berkeley: University of California Press.

Cooke, N. F. 1956. "Bauchi Province." In *Provincial Annual Reports 1956*, Northern Region of Nigeria, 11. Kadura: Government Printer.

Coronation Durbar, Delhi, 1911: Official Directory with Maps. 1911. Calcutta: Superintendent Government Printing, India.

Corrigan, P., and Sayer, D. 1985. *The Great Arch: English State Formation as Cultural Revolution*. Oxford: Basil Blackwell.

Darnton, John. 1977. "Young Attends a Vast Pageant in Virginia." *New York Times* (February 9).

Duckworth, E. H. 1948. "Over the Hills to Yola." *Nigeria* no. 29: 181–222.

Fasuyi, T. A. 1973. *Cultural Policy in Nigeria*. Paris: UNESCO.

Handler, Richard. 1988. *Nationalism and the Politics of Culture in Quebec*. Madison: University of Wisconsin Press.

Haruna, I. B. M. 1977. "Meaning and Significance of Durbar." *New Nigerian* (February 7): 18.

Haynes, Douglas. 1990. "Imperial Ritual in a Local Setting: The Ceremonial Order in Surat, 1890–1939." *Modern Asian Studies* 24, no. 3: 493–527.

Haynes, Edward S. 1990. "Rajput Ceremonial Interactions as a Mirror of a Dying Indian State System, 1820–1947." *Modern Asian Studies* 24, no. 3: 459–92.

Hobsbawm, Eric. 1983. "Introduction: Inventing Traditions." In E. Hobsbawm and T. Ranger, eds., *The Invention of Tradition*, 1–14. Cambridge: Cambridge University Press.

Joseph, Richard. 1987. *Democracy and Prebendal Politics in Nigeria: The Rise and Fall of the Second Republic*. Cambridge: Cambridge University Press.

The King Emperor and His Dominions: Souvenir of the Coronation Durbar of H. I. M. George V, Delhi, December, 1911. 1911. London: Burroughs Wellcome.

Kirk-Greene, Anthony. 1959. "Breath-Taking Durbars." In *Advancing in Good Order*, 15–20. Kadura: Government Press.

Kisch, Martin. 1910. *Lettres and Sketches from Northern Nigeria*. London: Chatto and Windus.

Lahey, John. n.d. *Celebration: The Second World Black and African Festival of Arts and Culture*. Washington, D.C.: United States Information Service.

Letchworth, T. E. 1956. "Bornu Province." In *Provincial Annual Reports 1956, Northern Region of Nigeria*, 29–30. Kadura: Government Printer.

Lloyd, P. C. 1961. "Sallah at Ilorin." *Nigeria Magazine* 70: 266–78.

Lugard, Flora Shaw. [1906] 1964. *A Tropical Dependency: An Outline of the Ancient History of the Western Sudan with an Account of the Modern Settlement of Northern Nigeria*. London: Frank Cass.

Lugard, Frederick D. 1902. "Colonial Reports—Annual, No. 409." *Northern Nigeria, 1902*. In Annual Reports. Northern Nigeria, 1900–1911.

———. 1906. *Instructions to Political and Other Officers on Subjects Chiefly Political and Administrative*. London: Waterlow and Sons.

———. [1922] 1965. *The Dual Mandate in British Tropical Africa*. London: Frank Cass.

Madauchi, Ibrahim. 1968. *Hausa Customs*. Zaria: Northern Nigeria Publishing.

Meek, C. K. 1931. *A Sudanese Kingdom: An Ethnological Study of the Jukun-Speaking Peoples of Nigeria*. London: Kegan Paul, Trench, Trubner.

Mitchell, Timothy. 1988. *Colonising Egypt*. Cambridge: Cambridge University Press.

Mockler-Ferryman, A. F. 1902. "British Nigeria." *Journal of the Royal African Society* 1, no. 2: 151–73.

Nadel, S. F. 1942. *A Black Byzantium: The Kingdom of Nupe in Nigeria*. London: Oxford University Press for the International African Institute.

Ngugi wa Thiongo. 1986. *Decolonising the Mind: The Politics of Language in African Literature*. Portsmouth, N.H.: Heinemann.

Nigerian Handbook: Containing Statistical and General Information Respecting the Colony and Protectorate, 5th ed. 1924. Lagos: Chief Secretary's Office.

Nkrumah, Kwame. 1970. *Consciencism: Philosophy and Ideology for Decolonization*. New York: Monthly Review Press.

Northern Regional Government. 1953. *Report on the Kano Disturbances: 16th, 17th, 18th, and 19th May, 1953*. Kadura: Government Printer.

Nuckolls, Charles W. 1990. "The Durbar Incident." *Modern Asian Studies* 24, no. 3: 529–59.

Pal, Pratapaditya, and Vidya Dehejia. 1986. *From Merchants to Emperors: British Artists and India, 1757–1930*. Ithaca: Cornell University Press.

Pemberton, John. 1994. *On the Subject of "Java."* Ithaca: Cornell University Press.

Perham, Margery. 1960. *Lugard: The Years of Authority 1898–1945* London: Collins.

The Queen's Tour of Nigeria: Commemorating the Visit of H. M. Queen Elizabeth II and H. R. H. the Duke of Edinburgh. 1956. London: Pitkin Pictorials.

Ranger, Terence O. 1980. "Making Northern Rhodesia Imperial: Variations on a Royal Theme, 1924–1938." *African Affairs* 79, no. 316: 349–73.

——. 1983. "The Invention of Tradition in Colonial Africa." In E. Hobsbawm and T. Ranger, eds., *The Invention of Tradition*, 211–62. Cambridge: Cambridge University Press.

Senghor, Léopold S. 1964. *Liberté I: Négritude et Humanisme*. Paris: Editions de Seuil.

Smith, M. G. 1957. "The Social Function and Meaning of Hausa Praise-Singing." *Africa* 27: 26–45.

——. 1960. *Government in Zazzau, 1800–1950*. London: Oxford University Press for the International African Institute.

Takaya, Bala, and S. G. Tyoden, eds. 1987. *The Kaduna Mafia: A Study of the Rise, Development and Consolidation of a Nigerian Power Elite*. Jos: Jos University Press.

Temple, C. L. [1918] 1968. *Native Races and their Rulers: Sketches and Studies of Official Life and Administrative Problems in Nigeria*. London: Frank Cass.

Trevithick, Alan. 1990. "Some Structural and Sequential Aspects of the British Imperial Assemblages at Delhi: 1877–1911." *Modern Asian Studies* 24, no. 3: 561–78.

Watts, Michael. 1992. "The Shock of Modernity: Petroleum, Protest, and Fast Capitalism in an Industrializing Society." In A. Pred and M. Watts, eds., *Reworking Modernity: Capitalisms and Symbolic Discontent*, 21–63. New Brunswick: Rutgers University Press.

West Africa. 1960. "The Princess and the Premier." No. 2264 (October 22): 1187.

West African Review. 1956. Vol. 28, no. 343.

Williams, David. 1956. "Nigeria Today." *African Affairs* 55, no. 218: 109–19.

8

Revolution and State Culture: The Circle of Justice and Constitutionalism in 1906 Iran

Nader Sohrabi

Early in August 1906, after a series of protests, the shah of Iran issued a decree that, despite its ambiguous wording, came to be widely interpreted as the order for the establishment of a constitutional assembly. The protests were spearheaded by clerics and joined by westernist intelligentsia, some statesmen, and a significant number of guildsmen. The following two years witnessed a contentious fight over the functions, responsibilities, and powers of the new constitutional regime and its assembly. The confrontation culminated in a royalist counterrevolution in 1908 that ended with the shah's defeat and overthrow in 1909.

In this essay I explore two paradoxical developments. First, I investigate why the crowds participated in the constitutional revolution and lent avid support to an assembly, when the majority had scant, if any, knowledge of constitutional states. Second, I ask, when the newspapers and the assembly representatives showered the state administrators with the most malignant remarks, why did they couple such abuse with the most exaggeratedly naive expressions of loyalty toward the shah? Was not the shah, a patrimonial ruler, considered in close and personal contact with his administrators and would not an attack on his state also constitute an attack on his person?

Answers to both questions may be found only after noting that not one but two cultures of politics were at work during the revolution and that each pointed to a widely varying conception of state. The majority appeared to follow a Western constitutional script and demanded a parliament, but on closer inspection it becomes clear that most actors diverged from this script and acted according to another discourse of kingship, justice, and rule embodied in the local paradigm of the Circle of Justice.

The westernist elite demanded a constitution and a parliament, and the guilds and clerics rallied alongside with supposedly the same goals. But the latter groups had minimal, if any, understanding of such Western concepts. For them, participating in this antistate social movement meant reviving an institution that attended to public grievances according to the local ideals of kingship and justice. This mindset was evinced by their initial set of independent demands, which included a call for the establishment of a "House of Justice" rather than a Western parliament.

The peculiarities of the local discourse of state and kingship provided the public with the opportunity to manipulate it and legitimize antistate revolt in the guise of loyalty to the shah. It was clear to many that the shah opposed the constitutional system. Yet the public and the assembly, rather than denouncing him, praised him with intensely "naive" expressions of loyalty (Field 1989) and portrayed him as an innocent victim of his ministers and associates, as they continued to fight his government.

On a theoretical level, this position takes a strong stance against the assumption that the ordinary public simply followed the prewritten script of politics. Instead, it demonstrates that the public, as active agents, manipulated culture to achieve its own ends (Scott 1985, 1990). It is essential, however, to note that the public manipulation was confined only to certain aspects of political culture; conniving actions did not amount to a wholehearted rejection of the larger discursive framework of the indigenous politics (Bourdieu 1976).

Nonetheless, because of the presence of new elements in the culture of politics, this manipulation placed the traditional categories at risk, and attempts at reproducing the ideology of kingship ended in its transformation. A novel culture of politics emerged that was not imagined or intended by any of the participants. Agency initiated the transformation but did not determine the final outcome. What emerged was an unwitting product that was both in continuity with and departed from the local culture of politics (Sahlins 1981, 1985).

This line of argument does not contradict the conclusion that the constitutional revolution in Iran was influenced by the French Revolution (Sohrabi 1995) and is sympathetic to Meyer's (this volume) argument concerning diffusion of "successful" state models across national boundaries. Yet, here I consider the complexities of diffusion of a Western state model in a non-Western, noncolonial setting and demonstrate that diffusion did not make its way in one stroke but gradually and in unexpected ways. This is not the story of imposing a Western state form on a tabula rasa, but of a far more intricate process of interaction that led to the creation of a novel synthesis.

The Local Language of State and Kingship

The Circle of Justice

The Iranian conception of kingship was laid out in a body of "mirrors for princes" that traced its lineage to pre-Islamic Iranian kingship. After conversion to Islam in the seventh century, this genre of advice literature reached new heights late in the eleventh century. Modeling itself most prominently after the pre-Islamic mirrors, the Iranian-Islamic mirrors attended to themes such as order and justice, methods of enforcing them, the shah as their guardian and upholder, the shah's relation to his vizier, and the shah's sacredness, and they incorporated the religious and political teachings of Islam into these pre-Islamic political doctrines (Lambton 1956, 1962, 1974; Frye 1963: 224–44; Dankoff 1983: 1–35; Kuhrt 1987: 52–55).

The theory of Iranian kingship can be summarized in the metaphor of the Circle of Justice, according to which the population was divided into four estates. Mirrors vary in the occupations they name and in those they group together under each estate, yet they have in common a hierarchical ordering of estates, moving from the powerful to ordinary subjects. For example, a third-century mirror, believed to have been written by the shah for his son, divided the four estates into (1) military leaders, (2) men of religion, (3) teachers, astronomers, and doctors, and (4) agriculturalists, artisans, and merchants ('Abbas 1969: 78–79, 24n.2). The contemporary *Letter of Tansar* divided the estates into (1) clergy, (2) military, (3) scribes, and (4) artisans, with the last estate comprising merchants, those who till the land, those who herd cattle, and all those who live by trade.[1] One of the most famous classifications was found in *Nasirean Ethics*, which identified each estate with one of the four natural elements: (1) men of pen (water), (2) men of sword (fire), (3) men of negotiation, such as merchants, tradesmen, masters of crafts, and tax collectors (air), and (4) men of husbandry, such as sowers, farmers, ploughmen, and agriculturalists (earth) (Tusi 1964: 230).

In the pre-Islamic mirrors, the shah stood at the apex of the circle and accorded everyone his station in life ('Abbas 1969: 79n.1; Boyce 1968: 39). From among the subjects, states the *Letter of Tansar*, God chose one to be the king and with his grace endowed him with kingship (Boyce 1968: 54–63).[2] Religion and state were put on a par in the pre-Islamic mirrors; each was considered necessary for the survival of the other. The *Letter of Tansar* recounts a saying from the king: "Do not marvel at my zeal and ardour for promoting order in the world, that the foundations of the laws of Faith may be made firm. For Church and State were born from one womb, joined together and never to be sundered. Virtue and corruption, health and sickness are of the same nature for both" (Boyce 1968: 33–34). Overall, however, religion was given a subservient role to that of the state.[3]

Striking is the degree of continuity between the pre-Islamic and Islamic mirrors, both of which considered the shah sacred and placed kingship and religion,

[1] "Know that according to our religion, men are divided into four estates. This is set down in many places in the holy book and established beyond controversy and interpretation, contradiction and speculation. They are known as estates, and at their head is the king" (Boyce 1968: 37).

[2] The king would accept the covenant by saying, "Please God I shall be given grace to secure the welfare of my people" (Boyce 1968: 63).

[3] *'Ahd Ardashir* is even quite explicit about the dangers of religion and religious leaders and warns the shahs against the great harm that may come from the ease with which men of religion find wide following among the ordinary subjects ('Abbas 1969: 70–71).

and thus the shahs and prophets, on the same rank. In the Islamic mirrors, the shah still stood at the apex of the circle, accorded everyone their stations in life, and derived his aura or charisma from association with divinity. From among the subjects, the mirrors relate, God chose one to be the shah and with His grace endowed him with divine light (*farr-i Izadi*); as such he was considered the Shadow of God upon Earth (Nizam al–Mulk 1993: 1–2, 36–37, 44, 72; Ghazzali 1938: 39–41; Tusi 1964: 230). The Islamic mirrors, in continuity with the pre-Islamic tradition, also regarded religion and kingship as brothers and dependent on one another. Furthermore, both the shah and prophet were considered to have been chosen by God—the prophets were to direct people toward God and the shahs were to protect them from one another (Ghazzali 1938: 39–41, 53–57; Nizam al–Mulk 1993: 71). Although there is greater attention to religion in the Islamic mirrors, a sense of priority of politics over religion is shared with pre-Islamic mirrors. As *Siyasatnamah* counsels the shah, "Kingship survives with irreligion but not with injustice" (Nizam al-Mulk 1993: 6).

Analogous to the Western theory of kingship, where the king was held to be the "Fountain of Justice" (Kantorowicz 1957: 5),[4] the Iranian mirrors considered the shah to be the source of justice. It was his duty to maintain balance among the estates and the preservation of balance was equated with justice. "The emperor is obliged to consider the state of his subjects, and to devote himself to maintaining the laws of justice," relates Tusi, "for in justice lies the order of the realm" (Tusi 1964: 230). Also, prosperity and flourishing (*abadani*), a recurrent theme in the mirrors, were deemed to depend directly on justice. As the mirrors recounted, religion is dependent on kingship, kingship on army, army on wealth, wealth on flourishing, and flourishing on justice; conversely, injustice led to ruin, and it was the shah's duty to bring about prosperity (Ghazzali 1938: 47–48; Nizam al-Mulk 1993: 3). Long lists of just shahs, their secure subjects, and their orderly and prosperous domains, juxtaposed against examples of tyrannical ones and the rampant chaos and destitution in their realms, helped the authors explicate the benefits of justice and dangers of tyranny (Ghazzali 1938: 39–41, 47–48, 53–57). In particular, the methods of disseminating justice and the links between justice, order, and prosperity, or their converse—injustice, disorder, and destitution—were central to the dynamics of constitutional revolution.

The shah was required to preserve balance and ensure order in his realm in two ways. First, he was to do his utmost to prevent the occupants of each estate from moving into another. Such movement, the rulers were warned, shook the foundation of rule and could lead to the shah's overthrow, for movement from one's position, whether upward or downward, always provoked aspiration to a higher estate ('Abbas 1969: 78–79; Boyce 1968: 37–39, 45). Second, and more

---

[4] One should of course be wary of the differences. Kantorowicz, citing Blackstone, relates, "His majesty in the eyes of the law is always present in all his courts, though he cannot personally distribute justice" (1957: 5). By contrast, distribution of justice by the person of the shah was a central tenet of Iranian kingship. In fact, establishing contact with the shah in search of justice was at the center of controversy during the constitutional movement.

important, the shahs were to prevent the powerful estates from extorting and mistreating the estates at the lower rungs, for that also led to the breakdown of balance in the circle. In the same way that the four natural elements were in equilibrium in natural compounds, no one dominating the others, so should the estates be held; for just as natural compounds that deviate from equilibrium dissolve, so would social order (Tusi 1964: 230).

A central theme during the constitutional revolution was the method of disseminating justice. To be able to protect his subjects and disseminate justice effectively, the mirrors consistently repeat, the shah should hear grievances as they are told personally by the subjects and without intermediation of others. This advice is consistent with one of the central postulates of the mirrors: the shah's mistrust of all, but especially of those in his immediate surrounding.[5]

Some of the best-known methods for establishing direct contact between the shah and his subjects are to be found in the parables of *Siyasatnamah* where the shah was advised to allot two days of the week to meet personally with the aggrieved. To guard against interested parties and tyrants from deterring the aggrieved to reach the shah, it was recommended that the shah hold audience in an open field rather than in enclosed quarters. The mirrors further advised the shah to mount an elephant or a horse standing on a platform, and those desiring to meet him were advised to wear red clothes for better visibility (Nizam al-Mulk 1993: 9–10; Ghazzali 1938: 16). Another suggestion, apparently the practice of the just shah Anushirvan (A.D. 531–579), was to suspend a belled chain at the palace's entrance to allow the aggrieved to notify him personally and relieve them from relying on a messenger, a potential collaborator with interested parties (Nizam al-Mulk 1993: 35–47).

Thus, a prosperous and just government functioned only when the balance among the various estates was preserved by the shah and the shah could perform his proper function only when he was in direct unmediated contact with his subjects. That the reverse was also held to be true had important implications for explaining a crisis or unpopular policies. A crisis occurred when balance among the estates broke down. Ultimately the responsibility for breakdown rested with the shah, yet the mirrors consistently elaborated on a scheme that allowed the shah to devolve responsibility to others, especially those closest to him. The pretext used on such occasions was that those in high ranks, the grand viziers in particular, had surrounded and isolated the shah; he thus was unaware of subjects' grievances and innocent of hardships inflicted by powerful estates.

This line of reasoning was illustrated by means of various examples in the *Siyasatnamah*, in which the patrimonial character of Iranian kingship was captured in the familiar Near Eastern imagery of the shah as the shepherd to the flock of sheep (subjects) who was betrayed by his grand vizier and co-conspirators (Nizam al-Mulk 1993: 23–34; Ghazzali 1938: 82–84). Throughout history it was

[5] For the mistrust and suspicion between the ruler and the ruled, see 'Abbas (1969: 47, 69–71, 76–77). For the necessity of independent reporters to the king and spies, see Nizam al-Mulk (1993: 75–76, 90). See also Lambton (1956, 1962, 1974).

common for the shahs to blame a crisis or unpopular policies on their viziers, a practice that occasionally led to the viziers' dismissal and sometimes cost them their lives. Max Weber, though not aware of the official ideology of kingship, was conscious of this practice and regarded dissociation from their grand viziers as a necessary ingredient for preserving the charismatic legitimation of the Iranian shahs and the Ottoman sultans (Weber 1978: 1147).

Yet, it is one thing to demonstrate the intricacies of the theory of kingship in early mirrors, and it is quite another to argue that the same vision of kingship dominated the political thought of the nineteenth and early twentieth centuries. I maintain that this state ideology was intact during the nineteenth and early twentieth centuries, the state deployed it in practice, and it was used to preserve, in Weber's words, the charismatic legitimacy of the Iranian shahs at time of crisis. A valuable study of the unpublished mirrors of the nineteenth century demonstrates that such continuity was indeed striking (Adamiyat and Natiq 1977). Almost every representative theme enumerated in the early mirrors was repeated, sometimes word for word, in the mirrors of the nineteenth century. Whether this was the portrayal of the ruler as the shepherd and subjects as his sheep, the central role of justice, the ruler as the source of justice and upholder of balance among the four estates, the affinity and dependence of state and religion on one another, the charismatic legitimation of the king as the Shadow of God upon Earth, or the reference to pre-Islamic shahs such as Anushirvan as exemplars of just rulers, these mirrors dramatically resemble the classical ones.

After referring extensively to pre-Islamic shahs to evidence the benefits of justice to the reigning Qajar monarch, a mid-nineteenth century mirror placed the four estates in correspondence with the four natural elements: (1) men of the pen (water), (2) men of the sword (fire), (3) men of trade (air), (4) men of agriculture (earth). It described the just government as one that created balance among these estates and placed individuals in the right professions according to their abilities (Adamiyat and Natiq 1977: 17–19). Another mid-century mirror described the affinity between state and religion as follows: "Sultanate and Prophethood are two gems on one ring; Imamate and Kingship are twins born of one womb" adding that "the sayings of the prophet and those of the sultan are the same" and "without doubt, the just ruler should be obeyed, for he is the Shadow of God upon Earth." After recounting the equal footing of religion and state, however, like many other mirrors before, it quickly privileged kingship over religion: whereas the shah, like religious leaders, had the right to infer religious opinions, the religious leaders were unable to rule as the shah did (Adamiyat and Natiq 1977: 13–14). Others approved of such privileging by repeating the old dictum that a "Sultanate, however irreligious, lasts with justice, but it would not last with injustice, however religious[ly upright] it may be" (33). With respect to just rulers, expectedly, Anushirvan was upheld as the exemplary shah, and shahs in general were considered to be the source of justice and shepherds to the flocks of sheep entrusted to them by God (12). To obtain justice, explained an author, people should take refuge in the shah, for he is the one responsible for justice and the intermediary between his subjects and God (13–14).

There were mirrors, more critical ones, that combined their reliance on the general lessons of classics with specific advice on contemporary problems, intending to halt the alarming and rapid decline the authors were witnessing. One such mirror, written immediately after the 1827 defeat by Russia, encouraged learning from Europe, and another insisted on a more rational administration in which a single individual was not appointed to several jobs, depriving capable people of the opportunity to serve in appropriate positions. Still, other solutions for preventing Iran's decline were found in traditional methods such as the dissemination of justice by the shah and in consultation (*mashwarat*) with the viziers and the sages (27–40).[6]

I refer to the ideology of kingship as the "official" or "public transcript" of the center—the state ideology according to which the center defined and presented itself to the broader audience of subjects (Scott 1990).[7] The above survey of the nineteenth-century mirrors demonstrated that the official ideology of the classics was still fully alive down to its most intricate details. Mirrors of the nineteenth century, however, lost their novelty and seemed to repeat, in a formulaic fashion, the teachings of the classics. As I explore here, the manner in which the statesmen at the center used these classical teachings in their writings to preserve the charismatic legitimacy of the shah at a time of rapid decline and crisis was more interesting and creative than the mirrors.

The Official Ideology: The Shah Is Innocent

Other works, written by statesmen close to the shah, drew out one of the central implications of the lessons of mirrors. The decline during the Qajar period, whatever its real origins, was first and foremost discussed, imagined, and written about as precipitated by individual personalities. Yet, in keeping with the tradition of preserving the charismatic legitimacy of the king, the decline was blamed on the high-ranking government officials and those close to the shah whose greed for wealth and status had jeopardized the survival of an ancient monarchy. The shah was considered to be entirely unaware of harm inflicted on his subjects and innocent of doings that had led to social breakdown.

---

[6] The combination of two disparate discourses on government, one based on European rational administration and the art of "government," and the other based on Irano-Islamic theories of rule, was characteristic of the period of change, a theme that repeated itself throughout the nineteenth and early twentieth centuries. Foucault addresses a somewhat similar pattern of mixing of two discourses of state during the period of transition to modernity: "from the middle of the sixteenth century to the end of the eighteenth, there develops and flourishes a notable series of political treatises that are no longer exactly 'advice to the prince', and not yet treatises of political science, but are instead presented as works on the 'art of government'." See Foucault (1991: 87). Here I do not claim that these developments were parallel, but merely point out that changes in the discourse of state were also reflected in the traditional Iranian mirrors when they began to combine local and Western theories of government.

[7] Scott has discussed public and hidden transcripts predominantly from the point of view of the dominated. Less emphasized is that the powerful may just as well be acting on the basis of hidden and public transcripts. I maintain that ideology of kingship was the public transcript of the center, on the basis of which it acted and expected others to act toward it in like manner.

These are the dominant themes in the narrative of one of the shah's viziers, Majd al-Mulk (Muhammad Khan Sinaki). His book, *Rislah–'i Majdiyah*, written in 1870 during the reign of Nasir al-Din shah (1848–1896), presents a gloomy picture of a monarchy in rapid decline. The shah is portrayed as an uninterested ruler overcome by pessimism who, instead of being occupied with state business, spends the greater part of his time in hunting expeditions surrounded by a group of "beastly hunters." These close associates, we are told, distract the shah from governing and manipulate him for their own ends. They "have so repulsed the royal temperament from the kingdom's capital—the place where governmental affairs are attended to—that the imperial retinue's departure is with ultimate joy and speed, and its return, with utmost languidness and reluctance" (Majd al-Mulk 1979: 19). The greater part of the blame, however, was placed on the minister of finance and his staff, the "tax robbers." Whenever they decide the shah has stayed in the capital too long, the author relates, the tax robbers conspire with the beastly hunters to send him on another hunting excursion and postpone the affairs of the realm so that chaos may reign and profiteers prevail (18–21).

Though the readers were warned of an imminent uprising and the real possibility that the subjects may begin to hate the shah and blame him for others' deeds, the subjects are depicted as loyal, confident of the shah's justice, and aware of his innocence. Various assertions admit but also explain away the shah's abeyance such as the one that attributed his quiescence to supernatural causes: "Because the shah's resignation and silence has surpassed its limits, people are afraid that the shah, God forbid, is bewitched and bound by a spell" (Majd al-Mulk 1979: 19–20). Another likened him to the inheritor of an ancestral house now reduced to a tenant who considered repairs beyond his responsibilities, adding: "All the inhabitants of Iran are either oppressors or oppressed, and the most oppressed of all is the shah of Iran who has acquiesced to being a tenant in his own house while all the strong-fisted tyrants under a special pact collaborate to evict him before the end of his [lease]" (96).

I address how credible this scenario was for the public more fully in my discussion of the movement for constitution. Apparent, however, was the use of doctrine of kingship to deny the shah's complicity with corrupt officials and to absolve him of the blame for social disintegration. Typically, the entire blame was placed on the shoulders of the shah's ministers:

None of the Sultans of the age have exerted so much effort for the progress of the state and cultivation of subjects as the [present] shah of Iran. But out of his exertions and efforts not even the smallest bit of desired progress has come about, and in fact strength and power have declined, bearing opposite results. The reason is that the above-mentioned viziers would never want to allow their status, income, and independence be jeopardized by the enactment of law. Even when they obeyed the law according to the shah's insistence and wish, they never adapted the principles of law [which consist of] separating the legislative from the executive. Instead they focused all their attention on mimicking particulars, ignoring the principles, and confusing the two so that they may prove to the shah that the nation of Iran is by nature incapable of accepting laws and unable to enforce them. (Majd al-Mulk 1979: 90)

The viziers were then warned that in the near future the shah will enact just laws, jail the traitor ministers, and prove that the Iranians were not by nature incapable of accepting laws (98).

True to the author's claims, Nasir al-Din shah was in fact spending the greater part of his time in hunting excursions outside the capital. This is borne out by the detailed memoirs of another of his viziers, I'timad al–Saltanah, who was by his side on an almost daily basis. In one of his critical semifictional works written at the end of the nineteenth century, I'timad al-Saltanah angrily asked, "Who is responsible for this ruin and destruction? What are the reasons for this hardship and distress? Who has committed such obscenities?" (I'timad al-Saltanah 1966: 125). Expectedly, the entire blame for the decline during the reign of Nasir al-Din shah was placed on the shoulders of his "traitor" Grand Vizier Atabak, whose intrigues and trickeries in collaboration with other courtiers and powerful individuals against the shah captured center stage (I'timad al-Saltanah 1969: 125–250).

Parallels to the story of the just shah Bahram—centerpiece of *Siyasatnamah*—who spent inordinate time in hunting grounds while his domain fell into ruin, are clearly evident here. Yet, whereas parallels such as hunting habits may be purely coincidental, other similarities such as the shah's innocence and unawareness of the conditions in his domain, being the source of justice, his betrayal by high-ranking trustees (especially the viziers) who cut him off from ordinary subjects, the exploitation of his subjects for personal gain by those very individuals, and finally the state of ruin because of his unawareness, do not appear by mere chance. Far from mere rhetoric, the logic and explanatory power of statements in the shah's support become apparent when placed within the cultural context of the mirrors' doctrine of politics.

The later mirrors and the paradigmatic employment of their teachings in statesmen's accounts reveal the forceful presence of traditional theories of rule late in the nineteenth century, yet it was not in writing alone that the traditional theory revealed itself. As a remedy to the crisis that gripped the nineteenth century, the state initiated various institutional means for bringing the shah and subjects into unmediated contact.

Before moving on, I should note Majd al-Mulk's expressed desire for modern laws and separation of the legislative and executive. This line of thinking clearly placed him in the modernist camp of officials, a group that attempted to create a Western legal and administrative framework through reforms inspired by European state models. Typical of the many preconstitutional Western-influenced tracts written in the second half of the nineteenth and early twentieth centuries, this book incorporated European political and administrative ideals within the framework of the traditional culture of politics. This synthesis was not always smooth and gave rise to many inconsistencies, ambiguities, and confusions. The westernist inclinations within the bureaucracy and the state's attempt to synthe-size these two traditions were crucial for the history of constitutionalism.

Institutional Means for Realizing the Ideal of Kingship in the Nineteenth Century

The idea that all subjects may have direct access to the shah at all places and all times may sound impractical. Yet, the state, to uphold its "public rela-tions stunt," did establish a few practical means to provide the subjects with a chance to air their grievances to the shah through the office of ombudsman under the Safavids, Zand, and even the later Qajar dynasties (Perry 1978: 203). More conspicuous than this minor office during the Qajar period were two in-stitutional innovations to put in practice a central tenet of kingship and bring the shah into direct contact with his aggrieved subjects: the Box of Justice and later the Council for the Investigation of Grievances, known as the Council of Grievances.

Before the establishment of these two institutions, an 1860 decree announced that the shah had set aside Sundays exclusively to give audience to the aggrieved. On that day, all state business ceased and officials were banned from meeting the shah, save those whose presence was required, such as the minister of justice and his deputy. Subjects in the provinces who could not readily travel to the capital were instructed to hand sealed letters to the postmaster to be delivered to the shah in special sealed bags (Mustawfi 1945: vol. 1, 126).

Holding audience for the aggrieved on a weekly or even a regular basis must not have lasted very long. Other institutional arrangements, such as the Box of Justice, seemed to have been more practical devices implemented in its place and in the same spirit. In March 1874, the official announcement for the establish-ment of the Box of Justice stated that the shah of Iran, the Shadow of God upon Earth, considered it his duty to provide comfort to his subjects and to dissemi-nate justice. The shah was to carry out this noble deed by dealing with subjects directly, rather than risk relying on messengers. This was again based on the rea-soning that if a message was transmitted verbally, essential details might be left out, or worse, it could suffer outright distortion if delivered through interested intermediaries. The shah ordered that a guarded, locked, and sealed wooden box be placed in a busy city square with only a narrow opening for the insertion of petitions. The public could drop their petitions in the Box of Justice with utmost comfort and trust, and without the need to entrust them to an inter-mediary or to pay bribes for their delivery. The guard was punishable by death if he prevented anyone from depositing petitions or if he was covetous toward the petitioners. Twice each week, the shah's trustee delivered the petitions in a sealed bag to the shah, who then responded in person (Damghani 1978: 99–101; Adamiyat 1972: 414–15n.34). Sometime in the same year, the governors were ordered to follow Tehran's example and place similar boxes in the provinces (Mustawfi 1945: vol. 1, 185–88; Damghani 1978: 103–06; Adamiyat and Natiq 1977: 451).

Apparently, the public responded enthusiastically, stuffing the box with every-thing from genuine requests, to satire, to obscenities aimed at officials (Hidayat 1982: 75; Damghani 1978: 101; Adamiyat 1972: 414–15; Nashat 1982: 52). A gov-ernment announcement one month after the Box of Justice was established urged the public to confine their petitions to relevant issues (Damghani 1978: 101–03). Within a few years, for not entirely clear reasons, the Box of Justice was discontinued (Hidayat 1982: 75; Damghani 1978: 107–08; Adamiyat 1972: 414–15; Nashat 1982: 52).

The Council of Grievances (ca. 1882) was more successful in bringing the shah and subjects into direct, unmediated contact. The public again responded to it eagerly and petitioned from all around the country. The shah did respond to these, yet his orders, as acknowledged by some petitioners, seemed to have been without consequence and not binding (Adamiyat and Natiq 1977: 375–413; Ettehadieh 1989).

These institutional innovations, disappointing as they were, served as crucial precedents for the constitutional assembly. The revolution began with the de-mand for the establishment of a House of Justice and not a parliament. This choice was significant because it demonstrated that the revolutionary outbreak, at least for the ordinary public, aimed to revive an institution that brought the subjects and the shah into unmediated contact. Previously, attempts to create in-stitutions for realizing the ideal of kingship had originated from the state but now the initiative had come from below. The nineteenth-century institutional innovations, such as the Council of Grievances, formed the theoretical under-pinning for the actors who demanded the creation of the House of Justice in 1905 (Ettehadieh 1989: 52).

The survival of the doctrine of kingship was not evinced only in the outdated and little-acclaimed nineteenth-century mirrors but, more important, in the statesmen's consciousness as indicated by their political tracts and the institu-tions they created. Together, they demonstrate that the lessons of the mirrors were taken for granted in late-nineteenth-century politics.

Between Old and New:
Constitutional Ideology and the Circle of Justice

By the end of the first constitutional period (1906–1908), Western constitu-tional concepts were winning popularity, but more popular was a new synthesis of the local and Western concepts. The mixing of two political cultures gave a confusing picture to political discourse and practice at first glance. Political lan-guage was expressed in different forms in the hands of four broadly defined groups.

On the one hand, a small group of westernist radicals spoke exclusively in the language of Western constitutionalism and challenged the shah and the govern-ment by invoking concepts such as accountability, responsibility, separation of powers, dominance of the legislative over the executive, and the sovereignty of the nation. They progressively brought into question the right of the uncooperative shah to rule. But their more significant challenge, one that made them revolutionaries rather than mere rebels, was that they sought to transform the kingship with its traditional meaning and functions. More than challenging the "person" of the shah, to use Gluckman's (1963) structural distinction, their language contested the "position" of the shah, or to use a similar distinction drawn by Kantorowicz (1957) between the king's two bodies, they sought to transform the immortal King, not merely the mortal king, that is, the office rather than the person.[8] A second group, moderate constitutionalists, spoke in a mixed, eclectic, and often confusing language, drawing on both Western and local concepts as needed.

Two other groups, the conservatives and the radical "traditionalists," which constituted the majority, had an entirely "folk" (Scott 1985: 319) conception of constitutionalism and despite their invocation of constitutional concepts, spoke for the most part in the local language of politics and acted according to its prescriptions. The conservative constitutionalists—the more prominent clerics and some guilds—drew on the traditional ideology of kingship and expressed unconditional loyalty toward the position and the person of the shah.

The radical traditionalists—the guilds and their radical committees—also used the language of the Circle. But unlike the conservatives, they opposed the person of the shah and consciously manipulated certain aspects of the language of kingship to defy authority and legitimate their revolt. Far from following the cultural guidelines unquestioningly, they deliberately manipulated aspects of traditional state culture to advance their own goals. Their folk constitutionalism shared with conservatives the local framework of politics and as such did not challenge the shah's position. Yet, because of two new developments in the course of revolution—introduction of the assembly into politics as a competing source of authority and the assassination of the grand vizier with its immense symbolic impact—the committees' traditional practice took on a slightly new form and their practice unwittingly threatened the kingship.

The synthesis that emerged out of this interaction was more than an arbitrary mixture of concepts; cultural change, though unpredictable, had a logic. Once the two cultures of politics clashed, the actors' attempt to reproduce the culture according to traditional guidelines within the new circumstances led to cultural transformation. After the clash, the actors who appeared to follow the traditional script of politics and reproduce the ideology of kingship, surprisingly and unintentionally threatened the shah's sovereignty.

During the revolution, unlike Weber's observation of earlier times, it was not the apologists at the center who invoked the ideology of the Circle of Justice at a time of crisis to preserve the charismatic legitimacy of the shah. In contrast to

---

[8] One should, however, be careful in extending Kantorowicz's distinction between "body natural" and "body politic" to Islamic-Iranian kingship. For a discussion of some of the differences between Western and Islamic theories of politics, see Lewis (1988).

the usual practice, and this is significant, the center's official ideology was invoked from below by the ordinary participants. By manipulating the metaphor of the Circle, the actors expressed exaggerated loyalty toward the shah at a time of revolt against authority. Although it was clear to all that the shah stubbornly opposed both the constitution and the assembly, even the most radical of the revolutionaries refrained from implicating the shah for quite some time. Instead, they resorted to a variety of euphemisms and confined their harshest criticism to high-ranking officials and courtiers, leaving the institution of kingship and the person of the shah relatively immune from direct attacks. They explained away the young shah's apparent animosity by invoking central tenets of kingship. The rhetoric of loyalty continued until the assassination of the grand vizier brought the shah into direct confrontation with the assembly.

The National Assembly or the House of Justice

There is reason to believe that the majority of participants in the revolution were following the local script of politics rather than a constitutional one. The overwhelming demand throughout the revolution, but particularly at the beginning, was a cry for justice and not creation of a parliament. In their first official declaration of demands, the actors, under the leadership of the Islamic clerics, requested the creation of the House of Justice in every province "to attend to subjects' petitions and grievances and to treat them with justice and equity" (Kirmani 1983: vol. 1, 358). The institution, despite its novel name, bore many similarities to the state institutions created previously to bring the subjects in contact with the shah. The House of Justice, in particular, bore strong resemblances to the late-nineteenth-century Council of Grievances and even the earlier ombudsman councils.

That the public overwhelmingly attacked the grand vizier rather than the shah to express its dissatisfaction with the state indicated again the presence of the traditional script. The first official list of demands in December 1905 did not mention the grand vizier, and instead targeted Tehran's governor. Yet, the grand vizier was a primary target from the beginning; not only did he become the target of protestors eventually, but also his transition to center stage happened so naturally that it hardly generated any commentary by the contemporaries (Kirmani 1983: 334, 357–58). This desire was expressed in a sermon before the large-scale protests in mid-April 1905, when a clerical leader bluntly declared that the protestors' only goal was to dismiss the "traitor" grand vizier and another official, adding that "this Grand Vizier stands as an obstacle between the shah and his subjects and does not allow our petitions to reach the shah" (Kirmani 1983: 293), and after the escalation of movement in early July 1906, when the principal clerical leader, Tabataba'i, stated explicitly in his sermon before a vast audience in the language of Circle of Justice, "The shah may remain shah by means of his treasury, and the treasury would not be filled except by the country's flourishing and the country would not flourish except by justice. . . . Here I proclaim . . . there is a single person who is responsible for the injustice and that is the Grand Vizier. Seek the cure in him. The shah is kind and compassionate and ill, disinclined to oppression and injustice. He is unaware of the conditions in the land. . . . We do not talk of constitution or republic, we [demand] the Assembly of House of Justice based on religion (*majlis-i mashru'ah-'i 'adalat-khanah*)" (Kirmani 1983: 446, 447, 453). The statesmen were cognizant of the clerics' stance. In an internal communication, a high-ranking statesman wrote that the clerics had made it abundantly clear that as the shah's loyal subjects they demanded neither a constitutional government nor a republic, but protested against the grand vizier who isolated the shah and prevented the "nation's" petitions from reaching him (Safa'i 1973: doc. 2, 29–30).

When the grand vizier was dismissed on July 31, 1906, as a concession to the agitators, interestingly enough it became a cause of concern among the constitutionalists who had pressured the crowds to forfeit their demand for the grand vizier's dismissal and to consider instead the grant of a parliament as their primary goal. The westernist elites' actions indicated their awareness of the cultural significance of this "traditional" demand and expressed their concern that, with the grand vizier's dismissal, the protestors might conclude the movement had attained its goal and dissipate the protests prematurely (Kirmani 1983: 534, 541).

Despite a temporary lapse that was about to prove the westernists' worst fears, the large-scale protests continued until the granting of an assembly. Yet, the crowds' actions and the assembly proceedings amply demonstrated that the National Assembly was regarded as a parliament by only a few and as a House of Justice by the majority. The mixture of the House of Justice with a constitutional assembly created a great deal of confusion for those who perceived the assembly with lenses borrowed from the local culture of politics, those who acted in this new circumstance according to the accepted categories, or those who "reproduced" the assembly according to what had been hitherto familiar to them (Sahlins 1981: 8, 33, 67–68).[9]

The traditionalists' primary form of action was to petition the assembly to come into direct contact with the "source of justice," and from the very first days they flooded the assembly with petitions. In response to this deluge, the westernized constitutionalists delivered speeches to dislodge the assembly's image as a mere House of Justice and substitute the idea of a modern European parliament. A modernist representative discouraged the public from sending their trivial petitions, for they wasted the assembly's precious time; the assembly had vital tasks to address, such as organizing the finances, specifying the borders, and holding discussions with the minister of foreign affairs, and could not listen to complaints of some teacher against a certain principal. He urged the public to refer their complaints to the Ministry of Justice, the institution established to deal with public grievances (*Majlisi*, February 3, 1907, 73). He solicited a radical

---

[9] Here "reproduction" has a meaning slightly different than that usually encountered in the literature and is not equivalent to "function."

representative to help dissipate the confusion in the newspapers and tell the public that "the meaning of Assembly is not what you have understood it to be" for as he stated explicitly later, "this Assembly is not a House of Justice" (*Majlisi*, February 3, 1907, 73. *Majlisi*, April 2, 1907, 124). Baffled and frustrated, another deputy complained, "every day at this place we are encumbered by someone's grievances—one day [we hear from] the people of Kirmanshah, another from the inhabitants of Tunikabun and the like. What should we do about these?" (*Majlisi*, September 11, 1907, 286). Another deputy lamented that after six months they had discussed and dealt only with petitions, a matter that was not the assembly's duty, and suggested addressing petitions to a special assembly council created for this purpose (*Majlisi*, March 23, 1907, 115). The council, after reviewing petitions, forwarded them to relevant ministries for proper response and informed the assembly of only the most important ones for consideration in its public sessions.[10]

Establishing a separate Council for the Investigation of Grievances was the constitutionalists' solution to the problem of dissociating the Assembly from a House of Justice both symbolically and practically. It was significant that the appellation of the assembly-established council was virtually identical to the nineteenth-century Council for the Investigation of Grievances.[11] A compromise was, of course, still apparent as representatives agreed to read certain important petitions during assembly sessions. In practice, the compromise was more than superficial and entire sessions were devoted to petitions.

Both radical and conservative "traditionalists" opposed the modernists' intention to relieve the assembly of the duty to deal with grievances, and they resisted relegation of this task to a special council. One constitutionalist deputy who had argued that answering petitions was trivial, a waste of time, and outside the responsibility of the assembly was confronted with the objection of the deputy of the guild of perfumers and spice traders (*'atar*), druggists, tea sellers, and wholesale spice dealers (*saqat furush*): "For years the public have set their hopes on this Assembly, but now you intend to suspend it. How then will the public's petitions be attended to?" (*Majlisi*, January 3, 1907, 41). When other modernist deputies retorted that the commission forwarded the petitions to various ministries and requested answers, that the assembly was a place to enact laws for the nation and should not waste its time reading petitions, and that only one day of the week would be allocated for reading the most important of them, they were met with angry protest from the deputy of the guild of coppersmiths, gun-

---

[10] In response to the large number of petitions reaching the assembly, such a council was established quite early as attested by clause 59 of the Internal Regulations of the Assembly. See *Majlisi*, December 26, 1906, 33. At least on one occasion, the council claimed to have addressed 2800 letters to various ministries and received answers for 1500. *Majlisi*, April 17, 1907, 142.

[11] The nineteenth-century Council for the Investigation of Grievances, in reference to petitions or grievances, used the word *mazalim*. The assembly used the interchangeable and identical term *'ara'iz* in the title of the newly formed council. With this minor exception, the councils bore identical titles. In the assembly debates, the terms *'ara'iz, tazallum*, and *mazalim* were used interchangeably to refer to petitions.

smiths, coach builders, glaivesmiths, founders, and whitesmiths: "What then is this Assembly established for? Is it in vain?" In support, the deputy of the grocer, wholesale dealer, dried nuts seller, fruit seller, corn chandler, and rice seller guilds added that a mere one day of grievance reading would not satisfy the public, which had long awaited the assembly (*Majlis1*, January 3, 1907, 42). In the same spirit, a deputy urged the assembly to attend to petitions to prevent the public from losing faith in it (*Majlis1*, February 28, 1907, 97). The symbolic similarity to the shah's practice of allocating days for attending to grievances is worthy of notice here.

Tabataba'i, the liberal cleric who sided with the assembly and together with a few other clerics lent it a semblance of religious legitimacy against the onslaught of counterrevolutionary clerics, also agreed with the guild representatives. In his view, the assembly had confused the public and failed to assign a proper place for addressing petitions (*Majlis1*, March 26, 1907, 117). In April 1907, in a more frustrated mood, he interrupted the "all important" proceedings of the Administrative Protocol of the Municipality, "Before everything, you should think of something for the petitioners so that I may be relieved. If attending to the public's grievances is not the Assembly's duty, then inform the public so that they may leave me alone. Otherwise think of something so that I may attend [the Assembly], for the present situation is intolerable. Every time I come to the Assembly, from the entrance [of the compounds][12] to [the building] ten to twenty people hinder and annoy me. This place is not for drafting laws only. You should finally think of a measure for the petitioners. Now a petitioner downstairs claims his son was murdered. Investigate, see if it is true and take action" (*Majlis1*, April 17, 1907, 142).

The constitutionalists, in one of their oft-repeated responses on such occasions, answered that they could not interfere in the affairs of the executive branch and that in any event attending to petitions was the responsibility of the already-established Council for the Investigation of Grievances. In response, Tabataba'i agreed that the assembly could not interfere with the executive, yet added that the public was unaware and took refuge at the assembly because the government did not respond to their requests. He thus suggested that the Council for the Investigation of Grievances meet separately but in the same hours as the assembly (*Majlis1*, April 17, 1907, 142).

The most prevalent form of protest around the country attested to the public's belief in the assembly as a House of Justice, a place for addressing petitions. First the bazaars and places of trade shut down, then protestors took sanctuary at the telegraph offices and the militia engaged in symbolic military drills as a show of force. The crowds occupied the telegraph offices to petition the source of justice directly and they sent telegrams to both the assembly and the shah and left only after they heard a positive reply, a matter that would sometimes take weeks. The following report, dated May 16, 1907, from the city of Anzali was quintessential of this form of protest.

---

[12] The assembly compounds were a common place for the sanctuary of aggrieved.

[The province of] Gilan shut down for three days. In Rasht and Anzali the bazaars and shops were closed and most people of Anzali and its environs came to the city, took sanctuary at the telegraph office, and raised the cry of Hail Constitution, Hail Laws, Hail Ratification, Hail Implementation to the heavens. The factions of Mujahidin and Fada'iyan, whose numbers were many, put on military attire, paraded in the city and performed martial drills in the compound of the telegraph office. The locals entered the compound in companies carrying red banners. The students paced the compound with red banners and delivered lengthy speeches. The notables, the clergy, and the rest also came to the telegraph office and sent telegrams to Tehran, to the Assembly, and to His Majesty, demanding the completion and ratification of the constitutional law, other laws, and their implementation. Until yesterday afternoon, there was a marvelous commotion. On the 20th of the month an answer came from Tehran, indicating that within one week all matters would be rectified and [the Supplement to the constitution] ratified. However, the Fada'iyan were not content with this answer. They left the telegraph office with their military uniforms and headed for Rasht to join the Fada'iyan there so that they might devise a plan for the ratification and the implementation of laws. They were not convinced by the courtiers' promises. . . . (*Habl al-Matin*, no. 16, May 16, 1907, 3–4; See also *Anjuman*, no. 90, June 1, 1907, 1–4; *Anjuman*, no. 91, June 2, 1907, 1–4; *Anjuman*, no. 92, June 3, 1907, 1–4)

Throughout the movement, public ceremonies and declarations elicited a strong sense of loyalty toward the shah. On the day of the assembly's commencement, the crowds carried a portrait of the bedridden Muzaffar al-Din shah at the front of a large procession heading for the representatives' temporary meeting place. Once the assembly found its permanent compounds, as a gesture of loyalty its entrance was adorned with the words *'adl-i Muzaffar* (Muzaffar's justice). Similarly, in its commencement ceremonies, a clerical leader sanctioned the shah's claim that the National Assembly was granted by the shah's free will and was a manifestation of the sacred shah's wishes and the Iranian people (*Majlis1*, n.d.: 10).

After the death of the ailing shah, the assembly continued to express loyalty toward the heir apparent. The shah's young and ambitious son, Muhammad Ali, was quick to formalize his accession to the throne in a controversial coronation ceremony that, despite including a few deputies, had not included those deputies in their official capacity as representatives of the "nation." The disgruntled representatives and committees considered this exclusion a clear sign of animosity toward the constitution. Yet, they refused to denounce the shah's action severely or to hold him personally responsible (*Majlis1*, January 19, 1907, 53; *Anjuman*, no. 43, February 13, 1907, 2; Browne 1910: 134).[13]

If the ministers were branded as traitors and enemies, the shah's implicitly acknowledged animosity toward them was explained away by arguing that he was surrounded by malicious ministers who led him astray. The ministers who be-

---

[13] The assembly later retaliated in article 39 of the supplement which required, before coronation, an oath of allegiance to the constitution administered by the assembly for the shah and the entire cabinet. *Musavvabat* 23–24.

trayed the shah were blamed for separating the "nation" from the "state," the "body" from the "head," or the "children" from the "father." By surrounding the shah, the ministers were accused of preventing subjects' petitions (*tazallumat* or *'ara'iz*) from reaching him and cutting off the "nation" from direct contact with the shah. The solution was to bypass them.

Mi'marbashi, representative of the guilds of well diggers, builders, brick bakers, kiln men, tilers, potters, and pot sellers, blamed the ministers for the government's uncooperative stance and the country's destitute and pathetic circumstances. "None of the Qajar shahs acted unjustly toward us. Whatever was done, was done by the [ministers]. These ministers are all traitors and the nation is prepared to prove their treason" (*Majlisi*, January 22, 1907, 60). They were disloyal thieves who mischievously surrounded the young shah and deceived him, a matter that was corroborated through personal information from a reliable source: "The compassionate and affectionate shah is always busy reading and answering petitions and letters. Other than time spent on eating or drinking tea, his time is entirely spent on work and toil. But these traitors and cheats who . . . have surrounded him and distract his blessed attention do not allow matters to be accomplished" (*Majlisi*, January 22, 1907, 60). Many others, including a clerical leader, agreed that the shah intended to cooperate but the ministers and those in high ranks isolated the shah and did not allow it (*Majlisi*, January 22, 1907, 59–60; *Majlisi*, August 26, 1907, 262). The two principal clerical leaders, Bihbahani and Tabataba'i, also agreed that the shah was on the assembly's side but surrounded by those who provoked him against the assembly (*Majlisi*, January 29, 1907; *Majlisi*, April 13, 1907, 132).[14] A representative of Azarbaijan added, "The [ministers] do not pity the country or the nation. Only the shah does," yet the ministers so consistently feign loyalty to the shah and nation that the shah is led into error. Someone should advise the shah to "distance yourself from these traitors and allow our petitions to reach you without an intermediary so that they may be presented to His Majesty without a mediator" (*Majlisi*, January 22, 1907, 60). Thus, a representative of notables and landowners of Tehran proposed a direct telephone line between the shah and the assembly (*Majlisi*, January 22, 1907, 60) and another suggested a permanent assembly delegate for regular meetings with the shah (*Majlisi*, April 13, 1907, 132).

For the great majority of participants and many assembly representatives, the culture of politics was the same as that laid out in the "mirrors." The public took sanctuary at the telegraph offices in the provinces and at the assembly compound in Tehran to come in direct contact with the source of justice. Much to the dismay and disapprobation of the constitutionalists, the public ceaselessly petitioned and turned assembly sessions into displays of grievance reading.

[14]Tabataba'i was, however, more critical of the shah than was Bihbahani. In later sessions of the assembly, even though still defending the shah and blaming the ministers, he was nonetheless forced to explicitly acknowledge the shah's opposition to constitutional principles and question the counterrevolutionaries' connection to the shah (*Majlisi*, July 6, 1907, 206–7; *Majlisi*, August 16, 1907, 246).

The Circle of Justice as an Ideology of Revolt and the Limits of Loyalty

The public expression of loyalty to the shah, however, was not unconditional and had limits. Two trends were particularly salient. Public forums, such as the assembly and the newspapers, withheld direct attacks on the person of the shah. This was true even when he was manifestly cooperating with the counterrevolutionaries. Although contradictory, and even schizoid, statements betrayed antagonism toward the shah, the public forums preserved at least their pretense of loyalty for a long time. The later we move in time fainter are such public expressions of loyalty, and the occasional denouncements grow stronger in tone. Similarly, the farther we move from the public forums to places where anonymity could be preserved, the harsher the posture toward the shah. In these more anonymous domains, along with strong expressions of loyalty to the shah we also observe devastating attacks on him even from the early days.

How do we resolve these contradictory assessments by the public? For now let's resolve this anomaly by relying on the useful but limited concepts provided by James Scott who, with his keen awareness of the distorted nature of the open communication between the dominant and subordinates, has talked about the subordinates' true and pretended beliefs. The "hidden transcript," the discourse of the powerless in the absence of the powerful and among the subordinates in "backstage" is radically at odds with the "public transcript," the discourse of the dominated in presence of the dominant (Scott 1990: 2–4). Here, I contend that the official declarations of loyalty to the shah and adherence to the idiom of the Circle of Justice were part of the public transcript of the rebelling crowds. The public manipulated this idiom mainly as a shield against the harsh reprisal of the authorities. As I demonstrate, this argument does not support the claim that backstage the public rejected wholesale the tenets of the traditional idiom. The public may have strongly believed in the injustice of the shah, but its answer to this dilemma remained solidly within the realm of the idiom; if the shah was unjust, he was to be replaced with a just one. This situation did not call for a radical reorganization of the functions and responsibilities of the shah. As I argued at the beginning of this section, the ordinary public, in contrast to the constitutionalists, initially questioned the "person" rather than the "position" of the shah.

Examples from protests of Russian peasantry and its invocation of the doctrine of Tsar the Deliverer demonstrate the manipulative tactics at work with an ideology of revolt that had implications strikingly similar to those of the doctrine of the Circle of Justice. According to Field, the myth of the Tsar-Deliverer allowed the Russian peasantry to profess loyalty to the tsar at times of revolt and to legitimate its rebellion through this manipulative strategy. A nineteenth-century Russian reformer described an extant version of this myth from the peasants' view as: "The nobility has separated the common people from the tsar.

Standing as an obstacle between them, it conceals the common people from the tsar and does not permit the people's complaints and hopes to reach him. It hides from the people the bright image of the tsar, so that the tsar's word does not get to simple people, or does so in distorted form. But the common people love the tsar and yearn for him and the tsar, for his part, looks fondly upon the common people, whom he has long intended to deliver from their woes. And some day, reaching over the head of the nobles, the tsar and the people will respond to one another" (Field 1989: 1). Other versions of the same myth held that the true tsar had miraculously escaped the courtiers' plot to kill him and was now in hiding among the ordinary folk, awaiting restoration of his throne with their help. At times of revolt, peasants drew on one or the other version of this myth to argue that their rebellion was directed at restoring the just and true tsar to his throne, who was either held back by the courtiers at the capital or was in actual residence among them. In either case, the uprising became an expression of loyalty toward the tsar. The prevalence of this myth among the peasants was interpreted by many radicals and conservatives alike as "naive monarchism" as they took the peasants at their words. In contrast, Field has masterfully argued that the invocation of the myth was part of peasant strategy to defy authority, revolt, resist taxes, divide the land, delay the official response, create division between skeptics and officials who believed them, and, often by proving their "misguided" loyalty and "naivete," reduce their punishment considerably (Field 1989: 199–202, 210, 214).

Drawing on Field's work, Scott places the notion of Tsar the Deliverer and the paradox of naive monarchism within the realm of public transcript: the language and actions of the powerless that are invoked and acted out in the presence of authorities to advance their unspoken desires and goals (Scott 1990: 96–101). Similarly, we may argue that the revolutionaries used the language of the Circle of Justice as their public transcript. Yet there are even stronger reasons to believe that the idiom of Circle of Justice was used more effectively than that of Tsar the Deliverer. The Circle of Justice was not an invention from below, a myth created by the powerless, but an ideology of the center, the official myth. In Russia, the peasants were obliged to spend a great deal of time communicating their "naive" belief to the authorities and to risk selling their story, hoping that it would be believed but also fearing that it might fall on deaf ears, however well known it had become over the centuries. In Iran, however, when the actors invoked this ideology from below, all parties were immediately aware of its meaning; its truth was never disputed, and it was more binding because its rejection by the center in the name of falsehood and invention went against the ideology the state itself had propagated for many centuries. Thus, the image projected from those at the center became a political resource in the hands of those at the periphery of politics as the shah and his statesmen were "called upon . . . to live up to their own ideological presentation of themselves to their subordinates" (Scott 1990: 54).

With the invocation of the ideology of the Circle the rules of the political game were immediately apparent to the dominated and the dominant. Using this knowledge, the rebels turned the tables and held the shah accountable for his promise. They manipulated an aspect of the official ideology to advance their own cause and to deflect the officials' harsh response or to delay it and make further room for their obviously defiant activities. Thus, the actors responded to the political culture by consciously manipulating various elements of the official ideology to their own advantage. The tacit knowledge of this political culture, what Bourdieu calls the "community of unconscious," made this communication between the two sides possible (1976: 80).

Closer to the revolutionary situation in Iran was the Young Turk constitutionalist movement in the neighboring Ottoman Empire, a context that shared a similar cultural heritage in both religion and kingship. The Young Turks at this time resided predominantly in Europe and, like their Iranian counterparts, were strategizing about ways to transform the sultan's absolutist government into a constitutional one. A rare debate between a sympathetic critic and the editorial board of the most influential Young Turk newspaper published abroad was one of the most explicit indications that the Circle of Justice had been used before as a public transcript for the explicit motive for manipulation. The exchange, though published, took place "backstage" under conditions of relative anonymity of authors and away from the reach of the sultan and his agents. In his letter, the author criticized harshly the editors' revolutionary rhetoric which blamed Sultan Abdulhamid II for all the problems in the declining empire. The author polemicized the Young Turks' criticisms, "Today the Ottoman government is about to disintegrate. The reason for this is the malicious desire and intentional maladministration of Abdulhamid who, after ruining the country and destroying it, jumps like an owl on top of the ruin and screams a nerve-wrecking laughter" (Şura-yi Ümmet, no. 26, April 13, 1903, 1). The author strongly disapproved of the Young Turks' style of criticism, which blamed the sultan personally as the source of all problems and the principal reason for the decline of the empire. Even though their allegations may be principally correct, the author held, this attitude demonstrated the Young Turks' insensitivity to the popular sensibilities and their inadequate understanding of the rich history of uprisings in the Ottoman Empire, the first lesson of which was that "almost always, the uprisings begin with targeting the Sultans' Grand Viziers, the ministers, or in short, the high ranking government members. The Sultan is considered unaware of maladministration and innocent at all times" (Şura-yi Ümmet, no. 26, April 13, 1903, 1).

Although agreeing with the Young Turks that the sultan should be deposed, he thought the sultan should not be openly attacked. This absolute requirement was because of the Ottomans' extraordinary ignorance and slavish attitude toward the sultan, a mixed product of the Byzantine and Iranian traditions of kingship, the Islamic Caliphate, and the Turkish custom of obedience to authority. Under these influences, the sultan occupied a grotesque position in the public mind between man and God and was considered the Shadow of God upon Earth, and it thus was impossible for ordinary Turks or the Empire's other Muslims to rise against the sultan, about whom there existed a thousand legends (Şura-yi Ümmet, April 13, 1903, no. 26, 2).

How then should we change the present regime, the author asked. His suggestion was to look back to the empire's history of uprisings, especially the immediately preceding Young Ottoman movement of 1876. The Young Ottomans, like the Young Turks, strove to establish a constitutional system, but unlike the Young Turks they portrayed the sultan as an innocent ruler and directed their criticisms toward the ministers and grand viziers or, in a Western rendition, toward the "government" (*hukumet*). They even depicted the sultan as a sort of captive to the people surrounding him and portrayed him as worthy of pity. The movement thus found widespread acceptance because the people could freely criticize the government officials who, like themselves, lacked divine qualities (*Şura-yi Ümmet*, no. 26, April 13, 1903, 2).[15]

Interestingly enough, the author added that the Young Turks could also discern important lessons from the contemporary upheavals in Russia. The Russian peasants exhibited the same sense of loyalty and slavishness toward the tsar and attributed to him a divine status complete with numerous bizarre titles, such as the "White Emperor" who sat on his golden throne and accorded everyone their station in life. Aware of the public's attitude, the Russian revolutionaries knew it was useless to incite the peasants against the tsar and thus resorted to a tactic almost identical to that of the Young Ottomans: they depicted the officials as the cause of all maladministration, the peasants' poverty and destitution, famine, and unjust land distribution; they absolved the tsar of all responsibility and portrayed him as an innocent ruler who unsuccessfully struggled to rescue himself from the detestable officials. Consequently, the Russian revolutionaries argued that the tsar was hoping the faithful peasants would rise up against the officials and punish the traitors. Using such a revolutionary tactic, the author claimed, the Russian radicals had been able to incite important rebellions in the past few years (*Şura-yi Ümmet*, April 13, 1907, no. 26, 2).

The Young Turks disagreed adamantly and defended their unrelenting attacks that portrayed Abdulhamid as the chief culprit. They argued that contrary to the author's claim, it was blasphemous for the Turkish public to worship anyone but God and accused the author of having confused the Perso-Arabic (and hence non-Turkish) title of Shadow of God upon Earth, a title given the sultans by authors of decrees and court historians seeking favor, with the real beliefs of ordinary Turks (*Şura-yi Ümmet*, no. 26, April 13, 1903, 2–4).[16]

The debate explicitly established that the "official transcript" of the Circle of Justice had been manipulated as an ideology of revolt to depose the reigning sultans and that the actors were consciously aware of this tactical dissimulation. The debate was also important for placing in sharp focus the various discourses of the constitutional movement: the local kingship ideology, the Western constitutional ideology, and their mixture. The Young Turks' angry response in the same issue, as much as it enunciated the modernist attitude of the new generation of Ottoman constitutionalists (that is, the Young Turks), was just as telling for

---

[15] For the centrality of the Circle of Justice to the Young Ottoman movement, see Mardin (1962).
[16] Significantly, the westernist Young Turks neglected commentary on Byzantine kingship.

the constitutional movement in Iran for it explicated what the radical Iranian constitutionalists also desired to verbalize but could not, at least not publicly. It also revealed that the belief in the Circle of Justice should be intermixed with the constitutional ideology to accomplish the goals of a constitutional movement. Throughout the nineteenth and early twentieth centuries, the constitutionalists had done precisely that in Iran. A faction of the constitutionalist opposition still clung to the mixed political language, but another faction avidly sought to separate the two at the expense of the tradition. Other participants, such as guild members, held on to the Circle of Justice, but being more conniving than the naive subjects portrayed by the Ottoman author, they actively manipulated the traditional metaphor in a "symbolic jujitsu" against the center (Scott 1985: 333). Their ultimate aim, however, was not to question the entirety of the traditional structures of rule to replace it with a constitutional system, but to restore justice.

The Limits of Loyalty Revealed: Attacks on the Shah

That the revolutionaries went to such extremes to demonstrate their loyalty to the shah during the early days and to argue that the establishment of the assembly was the manifestation of the "shah's justice" was not without good reason. To revolt in the name of the shah portrayed the uprising against the state as its opposite—as an act of loyalty toward the shah. By manipulating the metaphor of the Circle of Justice, the revolutionaries distanced the shah from the state officials, against whom the revolt was putatively directed, and by labeling the assembly "Muzaffar's Justice" they claimed to be restoring the just monarchy by means of an assembly that brought the subjects into direct contact with their shah. A second dimension of such ideological manipulation was that the actors, by invoking this ideology from below, bought time. Thus, they continued to attack the government symbolically and physically around the country, and they gave the shah time and maneuvering room to side with the assembly and dissociate himself from the policies for which he was responsible, but without the embarrassment of accepting defeat and losing face. The constitutionalists hoped that once the shah realized his lack of support, he would also resort to this explanation and end his severe animosity toward the assembly.

There had certainly been instances when, if not the "position" of shah, then the "person" of the shah had been devastatingly attacked in the open. It was only in 1896 that a commoner assassinated Nasir al-Din shah, the father of Muzaffar al-Din, in a public space. At trial, the assassin recounted the hardship suffered at the hands of a ruthless high official and justified his decision to kill the shah in place of the official by his resolve to strike at the source of injustice rather than its extension: "One had to cut off the foundation tree of injustice rather than its branches and leaves" (*Sur-i Israfil*, no. 9, August 8, 1907, 8). The trial transcripts appeared for the first time in 1907 in the radical constitutionalist newspaper

Sur-i Israfil some eleven years after the incident and in the midst of struggles with the state. The editors described its publication as a gesture of unconditional loyalty toward the present shah and a warning to the high-ranking officials surrounding him. For them the testimony illustrated that the subjects' hatred of the previous shah was caused by the very same officials who now surrounded the present shah and continued their machinations, favoritism, and nepotism (*Sur-i Israfil*, no. 9, August 8, 1907, 1–8). Contrary to the editors' claims, however, the text sounded like a condemnation of the previous shah and a warning to the present one, rather than a condemnation of the officials who were described, after all, as the shah's extension.

In the early days of the 1905 public protests, the shah and his son were openly attacked on several occasions. Less than a year before the death of Muzaffar al-Din shah, a high official writing to the grand vizier reported on a scandalous Tehran crowd that paraded a large dog embellished with a corn silk mustache sitting on a small carriage dragged by an ass. The crowds that ran with the dog swung their sticks and clubs at the public in royal guard style, forcing them to open the way for the "crown prince" on the move (Safa'i 1973: 77). During the same days, an anonymous leaflet called the shah an idiot who followed the advice of his associates and believed in their loyalty and went on to speculate about the shah's response to a large-scale insurrection: "Will he kill everyone at once? He cannot! In case of a mass uprising and disturbance, it is his life and those of his government's ministers that will be in peril." The letter, signed by the "Nation's Awakened" thus made tacit reference to the possibility of an uprising that spared not even the shah (Sharif Kashani 1983: 22).

At the major gathering of protestors in the British Legation in 1906, numbering the highest concentration of westernist constitutionalists, a leaflet was read aloud to the crowd of protestors ridiculing the sanctity of the shah and mentioning that because the shah was an otherworldly, nonhuman entity, he was not interested in justice and prosperity for his worldly subjects. It was also stated that the shah's riches and sums spent on his and his associates' frivolous pleasures were not the taxes of his twelve million subjects, but riches delivered from heavens by angels (Sharif Kashani 1983: 77–81). Around the same time, two daring notes disguised as petitions were personally handed to the shah by a man and a woman, addressing the shah in the name of the public—those who had bequeathed him with the kingship regalia—and warning him of the hazardous fate that would befall him after the public stripped him of his scepter and crown (Kirmani 1983: vol. 1, 360–61). In contrast to traditionalist attacks, the constitutionalists questioned not only the shah but also the prerogatives and pretensions of kingship.

The unstable language of those who systematically mixed constitutionalism with traditional theories was even more interesting. On the one hand, they portrayed the monarch as a blameless, innocent ruler manipulated by the strong-willed grand vizier and other officials, with subjects confident of his innocence. At other times, however, the purity of the shah's character and his good intentions were seriously doubted. On at least one occasion, a representative of this group acknowledged, albeit in his typically roundabout way, that the shah was indeed hated by his subjects (Kirmani 1968: 96). In a stronger condemnation of the shah, a poem desacralized the shah by asserting that if the shah killed the innocent, he should be punished by death, for God's laws were without exception and considered shah and subjects as one and the same (367).[17]

More typical, however, were leaflets that at most called the shah a simpleton in the hands of his viziers (Sharif Kashani 1983: 40–45) or an innocent ruler captive to his officials: "Today, the shah believes that he is the shah, when all the royal dignities have been usurped by the traitor ministers. In fact, today the shah is a face whose spirit has been robbed by treason and a skin whose brain has been eaten by trickery" (63). In addition to blaming the viziers, other leaflets displayed an overwhelming concern with justice and called on the shah to act according to his God-given duties (93–95, 99–101).

Newspapers and many representatives repeatedly wavered in their stance toward the shah, indicating their disbelief that ministers and courtiers acted in isolation from the innocent shah. A vivid example of lies cum ideological manipulation, in which the hidden transcript ruptured the surface of the public one, was the set of contradictory statements the committee in Tabriz issued within a short time span, both in support and in condemnation of the shah during protests sparked by the shah's opposition to the drafting of the supplement to the constitution, a document far more radical than the constitution itself. The inhabitants of Tabriz already had firsthand experience with the uncooperative shah and his court during his governorship as crown prince. During one of their recurrent public protests, the particularly active revolutionary committee of Tabriz condemned the appointment of the well-known "tyrants," "despots," and "betrayers of the nation and state" to high official posts; the traitors who were driven from Tabriz had once again surrounded the shah and ascended to high positions, and they criticized the assembly for allowing it and expressed surprise at such occurrences under a constitutional government (*Anjuman*, no. 42, February 11, 1907, 1; *Anjuman*, no. 43, February 13, 1907, 2). The committee newspaper reported on a constitutionalist who urged the excited crowds to calm down, but in a significant reference to the shah's character, he had added that all matters should come under the control of the National Assembly because the affairs of twenty million inhabitants could not be managed by a single conceited person who was raised, trained, and surrounded by tyrants, and thus one of them. The same issue reported the content of radical Azarbaijan deputies' dispatches, which revealed their belief in the shah's opposition to the constitutional regime and exposed an opinion that the representatives had not yet dared to voice openly in the assembly (*Anjuman*, no. 43, February 13, 1907, 3). Contradicting

---

[17] For attacks on Muzaffar al-Din shah's character describing him as weak, cowardly, oblivious to affairs, gullible, and superstitious, among other qualities, see Kirmani 1968: 277. It is difficult to determine whether the author wrote these words before the death of the ailing monarch Muzaffar al-Din shah and the flare-up between the assembly and the new shah. If they were written before his death, as the author claims, then the contradictory assertions acquire even greater significance for what they reveal about the hidden transcript.

itself, the newspaper still did not hesitate to publish a letter from a prominent cleric who praised the shah for his support of the constitution and blamed the conflict on the short-sighted thieves surrounding him (*Anjuman*, no. 43, February 13, 1907, 4).

The letters from Tehran caused a furor and prompted the public to gather in the telegraph office in protest. The following describes the events on the fifth day of protest:

> On Monday the 27th, the swarming of the crowd was greater than on other days and impossible to control. The thread of events was about to break loose from the hands of the prudent. The crowd wanted to confiscate the armory and distribute arms and weapons among the people and to free prisoners from jail. The Mujahidin [the militia] went to the prison, took count of the prisoners and identified their names, gave them bread and water, and returned. It was decided that the next day, after investigation, any one of them who was innocent would be freed. A great insurrection was in the making at the courtyard of the telegraph office and the French and American nations' songs of liberty were heard. At that time, the students of Adabiyah school entered the telegraph office with red banners, singing rhythmical songs with words that added to the people's excitement. They delivered a speech in Turkish about the oppression of tyrants and putting an end to them and incitement of the will to freedom and equality for all. The crowd became excited, their voices rose and uproar ensued. . . . Then the students of [two schools] came to the telegraph office while carrying red banners adorned with "long live the constitution," "long live the committee," and "long live Liberty." Because of lack of space they went to the rooftops, lined in orderly rows, affixed the banners, and began singing the following. . . . (*Anjuman*, no. 44, February 14, 1907, 4)

The extent of the commotion in Tabriz prompted the shah to address the protestors directly and pronounce his loyalty to the constitution. The shah's letter, significantly, was not sent to the protesting crowd but was delivered instead to the National Assembly and from there relayed to the scene of gathering. The protestors, however, refused to leave and open shops. They disputed the authenticity of the telegram, adding that their protest would continue until certain viziers were dismissed.[18]

Divergence between the public and hidden transcripts was indicated by the wide discrepancy between the committees' actions and their language of loyalty. Engaging in serious antigovernmental acts with arms did not stop them from expressing profuse loyalty toward the head of the government. This rather odd context prompted the revolting crowd to explain their actions, lest they be "misinterpreted." One of the gatherings demonstrated this clearly:

> [The Mujahidin's] uniforms were frocks and white pants with green stripes, made of domestically manufactured fabric, and their hats were nicely made from white sheepskin. When marching in beat, they yelled in unison "Long live the commit-

[18] They were convinced to disperse the next day only after assurances about the telegram's authenticity by their leaders who claimed the telegram contained the secret code of the Azarbaijan deputies. *Anjuman*, no 45, February 16, 1907, 1–2.

tee." Truly, [the sight of] the Mujahidin's drill, march, and discipline and their posture, uniforms, and zeal were laudable, arousing passion and excitement among the
spectators. From the depths of their hearts they yelled, "O God, make His Majesty,
the monarch of we Iranians, kind and compassionate toward his subjects so that with
his regal instruction he may elevate this gentle and talented nation to high ranks in
a brief time. Make the treasonous ministers who impede Iran's progress wretched
and miserable, for Iran can no longer endure the weight of their tyranny and injustice. . . . Let it not occur to the traitors and tyrants that this movement is mere
mockery and whimsy or that [these people] who wear military uniforms and learn
the science of martyrdom (*jihad*) are, God forbid, rebelling against the state and nation (*dawlat va millat*). Far from it! Rather, they are all guildsmen, bazaar tradesmen, and our humble folks who diligently strive for the motherland (*vatan*), for the
glory of His Majesty Muhammad Ali shah who is the king of Islam, and for the
progress of the country and the advancement of the constitution." (*Anjuman*,
no. 75, May 6, 1907, 1–2)

Characteristic of the unstable discourse of revolutionary times, however, by
the end of the declaration the protestors had twice asked for God's help in bringing the monarch to his subjects' side, and thus indirectly acknowledged, even in
this context, that the monarch was not on their side. Within a few days they made
apparent their complete disbelief in the public transcript invoked and defended
earlier when the committee claimed that from inception, the shah had not been
on the constitutionalists' side and, in fact, every day he had attempted to de-
range this divine endeavor (*Anjuman*, no. 80, May 14, 1907, 3).

It is hard to uncover hidden transcripts, evidence the actors would rather conceal. And the difficulties compound the farther we move from the event. Yet accepting the alternative would amount to accepting a standpoint that is incapable
of dealing with the logical and prevalent expressions of systematic euphemism,
dissimulation, lying, double-talk, hypocrisy, exaggeration, understatement, de-
ceit, falsification, misrepresentation, and all communicative actions that are
aimed at distortion in the face of power, distortions that are intentionally acted
out by those whose stake in the game is often not less than their lives.

Once the lessons of the above scenario are understood, it becomes compre-
hensible why Grand Vizier Atabak, a reputed anticonstitutionalist who turned
out to be far more moderate than imagined, was assassinated by the committees,
and why his assassination was a significant symbolic act with immense impact on
the conflict. At a time when counterrevolutionary activities were reaching their
peak, the official ideology, now an ideology of revolt, singled out the grand vizier
as the prime target. His assassination on August 30, 1907, within the paradigm
of the Circle of Justice, amounted to the removal of the "traitor" grand vizier by
the subjects, an act that within this context could be interpreted as a gesture of
loyalty toward the shah. Had not the shahs proven their loyalty to subjects by re-
moving "traitor" grand viziers before? On a symbolic level, this was the shah's
chance to back away from this serious confrontation and claim that he had been
on his subjects' side all along.

After the assassination, the shah was quick to introduce his handpicked cabinet, only to have it ousted quickly by the disgruntled assembly. In October 1907,

the first proconstitutional grand vizier and a largely sympathetic cabinet were introduced, but by mid-December, after tolerating the new cabinet for a brief period, the shah arrested, threatened to execute, and finally banished the grand vizier and two ministers. The shah's actions coincided with a major counterrevolutionary outburst in Tehran in which the shah clearly was implicated. From this moment, the pretense of loyalty to the shah at the time of revolt against the state was no longer a viable strategy and the confrontation could no longer be mediated through the grand vizier. When the shah blatantly rejected the subjects' choice for grand vizier, no longer could committees use grand viziers as the target of their dissimulatory tactic. No longer could he be blamed for having cut off the shah from his flock, for it was the shah himself who firmly rejected a pro-assembly grand vizier after his subjects had removed a supposedly anticonstitutional one.

The assembly, the newspapers, and the committees continued to vacillate even after the assassination, sometimes blaming the courtiers and high-ranking officials, and sometimes implicating the shah personally. Yet, with the assassination, matters took a clear turn, and the voices that argued the shah's simple innocence became fainter and less heard.[19] The removal of the buffer between the shah and his subjects pitted them against one another. A traditionalist constitutionalist commented on the symbolic significance of the grand vizier's assassination by stating that until then, all counterrevolutionary activities, disorders, and general chaos, both internal and at the borders, were attributed to him. With the continuation of disorders after his death, the public implicated the shah as the main instigator and turned against the shah, especially after the mid-December incidents when he came face to face with the assembly (Kirmani 1983: vol. 1, 277–78). Thus, the language of newspapers, the public, and the assembly representatives took a dramatic turn and began to target the shah directly. Telegrams sent by the committees from around the country immediately after the mid-December incident displayed the public's loss of confidence in the monarch and openly threatened the shah with the overthrow of the Qajar dynasty (Sharif Kashani 1983: 147–51). The hidden transcript could no longer be kept backstage, prompting the committees to carry out an assassination attempt against the shah himself in February 1908. The assassination ended in failure, but the committees, through public display of force, were able to gain the release of detainees with the help of the assembly (*Habl al-Matin*, no. 273, April 15, 1908; *Habl al-Matin*, no. 274, April 16, 1908, 3). It was surprising but understandable that this event did not attract as much attention as the assassination of the grand vizier because it was only the logical culmination of forces the latter had unleashed.

In the wake of the grand vizier's assassination, the stance of the Western constitutionalists, who from the beginning had not expressed the same sense of loyalty to the shah, was winning out. Within the assembly, the defenders of the idea that the shah did not cooperate with the assembly because of the people sur-

[19] For the continued yet infrequent use of the language of the Circle in newspapers, see *Habl al-Matin*, no. 182, December 8, 1907, 1–4; *Habl al-Matin*, no. 189, December 24, 1907, 7.

rounding him became less visible.[20] With the election of the first proconstitutional cabinet, the radical leader Taqizadah no longer blamed the ministers for
the lack of progress and disorder, but actually defended them. Instead, he eu-
phemistically pointed to the palace, the courtiers, and the bureaucrats as barriers in the path of the legislature and prescribed the removal of such obstacles;
the people surrounding the shah were no longer portrayed as traitors who led
him astray, but as collaborators (*Majlisı*, November 25, 1907, 397).

The Synthesis

The actors' attempt to manipulate some aspects of the Circle of Justice did
not amount to their absolute disbelief in the traditional ideals of kingship and
justice, or the position of the shah, as a radical dichotomous distinction between
the public and the hidden transcript may imply.[21] The crowds' actions attested
to their belief in large portions of the traditional culture of politics. In this context, rather than speaking of official ideology in terms of a popularly known,
rejected, yet publicly adhered-to ideology, it is more useful to think of political
culture as an arena where actors are members of a community of unconscious
(Bourdieu 1976: 80). Within this arena, large areas remain taken for granted and
unquestioned, *doxa* in Bourdieu's terminology, yet a subfield remains open to
debate, dispute, and ultimately manipulation (165–68). If the effect of doxa is
that the "established cosmological and political order is perceived not as arbitrary, i.e. as one possible order which goes without saying and therefore goes unquestioned" (166), then the counterhegemonic discourse of modernist constitutionalists constantly attempted to expose the limits of doxa and reveal the
arbitrariness of the traditional political culture, but only to replace it with their
own, and in their minds superior, political culture. This resulted in the clash of
two cultures of politics. The new culture that emerged, as Sahlins has shown in
another context, was unexpected, yet it was by no means an arbitrary system
(1981, 1985).

A conflict of opinion divided the "westernists" and the "traditionalists." The
westernist constitutionalists questioned the entire realm of traditional politics.
In contrast, the traditionalist constitutionalists, even when they attacked the
shah, did not question the position of the shah or the traditional structure of
monarchy. If the shah was unjust, he was to be replaced with a just shah. If, as
Kantorowicz noted, the Puritans' cry was "We fight the king to defend the King"
(1957: 18), the same could be said more or less about the greater number of traditionalist constitutionalists at the height of their radicalism. This attitude was

---

[20] For one of the last defenders of recommending that an Assembly delegate enter negotiations
with the shah, see *Majlisı*, April 14, 1908, 508.

[21] It should also be noted that Scott's conclusions are more outlandish than Field's. Field, quite
correctly in my view, wavers between peasants' "strategic" and "true" beliefs. As such, he does not
agree with Scott's radical distinction between hidden and public transcripts. For a review of Scott
(1990), see Field (1994).

rather different from the modernists' view, which questioned not only the present shah but the entire structure of traditional kingship. They had no desire to save the King from the king and if they had a war cry, it would perhaps be "We fight the king to change the King." From the beginning, as the debates on the question of sovereignty demonstrated, the modernists questioned unconditional loyalty to the institution of kingship. In an early assembly session many modernist representatives challenged the eleventh clause of the constitution, which required them to take an oath of loyalty to the pillars of monarchy. In its place they demanded a new clause that required the representatives to remain loyal to the monarch as long as the government and the monarch acted according to the principles laid out by the constitution and the monarch acted in a manner that strengthened the pillars of constitutionalism (*Majlisı*, December 27, 1906, 36).

For the traditionalists, the institution of kingship and its meaning was within the realm of doxa, taken for granted and unquestioned.[22] Questioned was the particular shah in power, not the institution of kingship. Yet, surprisingly, the traditionalists' practice of reproduction according to existing ideological notions ended in transformation of the old ideology. The traditionalists' quest to come into direct contact with the shah ended with the elevation of the assembly to the level of the source of justice, thus replacing the shah with the assembly. In place of petitioning the shah directly, or petitioning him through the assembly, the population was now content to petition the assembly only. Thus, they challenged the shah's sovereignty, for their manner of petitioning implied that they no longer considered him the source of justice.

Despite the constitutionalists' repeated attempts to dissociate the assembly from a House of Justice or Council of Grievances, their efforts were not entirely successful. But their efforts were not entirely in vain either, opening the way for the assembly to become a mixture of the House of Justice and a Western parliament. In practice, the assembly remained until the very end of the first period, at least partially, a Council of Grievances where complaints and grievances from all around were read aloud and discussed. Yet, with all their failures, the radical newspapers and the assembly debates enabled the modernists to gradually cast aside the assembly's image as a mere intermediary institution connecting the subjects to the shah and subordinated to the latter.

Establishing the assembly as a parliament required a new definition of statecraft and government. Regular interpellation of ministers, insistence on responsibility and accountability, and separation of powers was part of the representatives' effort to "construct" a modern state. Another effort was to dissociate the shah from the state (*dawlat*), a distinction that the traditional theory of kingship failed to make. As Sa'd al-Dawlah, a modernist representative, complained,

---

[22] In his discussion of doxa, Bourdieu makes the following remark: ". . .the established cosmological and political order is perceived not as arbitrary, i.e. as one possible order among others, but as a self-evident and natural order which goes without saying and therefore goes unquestioned, the agents' aspirations have the same limits as the objective conditions of which they are the product" (1976: 166).

"we still do not know the meaning of state (*dawlat*). We imagine that state is the sacred person of the shah. This is not the meaning of state. The meaning of state is the committee of ministers called the cabinet which works in unison with its leader, the Grand Vizier" (*Majlis*, January 22, 1907, 60). The representatives' initial attempts to dissociate themselves from the shah were fully realized with the assassination of the grand vizier and the flare-up of counterrevolutionary activities.

It was fortuitous, however, that the radical constitutionalists could not fully dissociate the assembly from its image as a House of Justice. The public sent their petitions either to both the assembly and the shah or to the assembly alone. Contrary to the crowd's expectations, the assembly did not communicate their grievances to the shah, and it did not expect redress from him, but instead sent their petitions to various ministries such as the Ministry of Justice. Furthermore, the assembly expected the executive to carry out the judiciary's order independently from the shah. It is not hard to imagine the confusion the constitutionalists must have created in the public mind. What was the source of justice: the assembly or the shah? Yet the public continued to petition the assembly, and this became a serious challenge to the shah's sovereignty; the assembly was no longer considered a transition point between the public and the shah but rather a location to which the public addressed its petitions and sought redress without the shah's intervention.

By petitioning the assembly, the public placed the traditional practice of petitioning the source of justice at risk. According to tradition, their petitioning made sense by demanding redress from the source of justice, presumably the shah. Yet, no such assembly had existed before, and no matter how insistently the public interpreted it within the confines of the traditional categories, the assembly refused to be a mere transition point between the monarch and his loyal subjects. Petitioning continued and preserved its meaning as an expression of loyalty toward the institution—but in the new circumstance the institution was no longer the person or position of the monarch, but the assembly. If the public, acting previously within the confines of the traditional theories of rule, had challenged the person but not the position of the shah, in this new circumstance its practice of petitioning the assembly challenged the position of the shah as well. "Everything that was done . . . was appropriately done, according to their own determinations of social persons, their interests and intentions. Yet the effect of thus putting culture into practice was to give some significance to the actors and actions that had not been traditionally envisioned" (Sahlins 1981: 35).

With continued petitioning, the assembly assumed the shah's position at the apex of the Circle of Justice, taking with it the position of dispenser of justice and threatening sovereignty. In light of this practice, we can appreciate the serious implications of the radicals' attempt to dissociate the assembly from the shah. More important than their success in creating a Western parliament, this attempt violated an entire sense of traditional political culture and substituted, unwittingly, the assembly for the shah as the "source of justice." To refer back to Sahlins, "Nothing guarantees that the situations encountered in practice will stereotypically follow from the cultural categories by which the circumstances are interpreted and acted upon. Practice, rather, has its own dynamics—a "structure of the conjuncture"—which meaningfully defines the persons and the objects that are parties to it. And these contextual values, if unlike the definitions culturally presupposed, have the capacity then of working back on the conventional values" (1981: 35).

That the shah understood the public petitioning of the assembly to be a challenge to his sovereignty may be detected from his symbolic maneuvering in the mid-December counterrevolutionary gathering. To mobilize negative popular sentiment against the assembly's financial reforms and in competition with the assembly, he ordered a telegraph established in a major city square so that the public could contact the palace and communicate their grievances to the shah directly. The parallels to the nineteenth-century Box of Justice were unmistakable. Those harmed by the assembly's financial measures raised tents around the telegraph and took sanctuary there against the assembly and the representatives. Even though the gathering grew to be large scale, we do not hear of other attempts to establish independent telegraphs in competition with the assembly. Yet, this event highlighted the symbolic significance of petitioning and the challenge the assembly posed to the institution of kingship (Dawlatabadi 1983: vol. 2, 114).

Much like the outcome of the clash of two cultural systems, what emerged from the clash between the constitutionalists' and the traditionalists' languages of politics was something both familiar and unexpected. It was familiar because it was in continuity with the structure of traditional politics—the public did not demand representation but justice—and used the method of direct petitioning. Yet what emerged was unfamiliar and unexpected because now the crowds did not solicit the shah for justice, but expected it from an institution that was independent of him and with supposed power over him. This situation was just as novel for the constitutionalists. Even though they succeeded in replacing the shah with the assembly in the public mind, they were still far from establishing a representative assembly with constitutional functions.

What started as reproduction ended in cultural transformation. The resulting synthesis, by being both continuous with and divergent from the two political cultures, was "at once conservative and innovative" (Sahlins 1981: 67–68). Practice led to cultural transformation. The new discourse of politics, by inserting an assembly with independent powers into the structure of traditional political culture, transformed the "tradition." Yet, although altering the old conceptions of state, the new synthesis was in many ways still within the bounds of tradition.

The far-reaching consequences of such transformation cannot be underestimated. It amounted to replacing the person of the shah with an institution composed of a group of individuals. Though not engaged in the duty of representation, the exercise of authority by such an institution and its popular acceptance was without precedent and served as a potential building block for a future full-fledged representative parliament. Furthermore, the altered traditional conception of state sounded the death knell of monarchy.

Yet not all aspects of the synthesis were as consistent as the consequence of re-placement of the shah with the assembly. The cultural clash also resulted in much inconsistent and confused political discourse, characteristic of periods of social change. The uneasy mix of two conceptions may be sensed in the two central clauses of the Supplement to the Fundamental Laws on the issue of sovereignty. One clause clearly relegated sovereignty to the nation by asserting that the state[23] (*mamlakat*) was empowered by the nation, and the constitution stipulated the exercise of such power (*Musavvabat, I–II*, article 26, 19–20). Yet, the constitu-tionalists, regardless of their desire to break away from the traditional notions of kingship and state, could not do so as they pleased. In contrast to the Young Turks, they balked at resolutely denouncing the divine pretensions of the king as the Shadow of God upon Earth. Instead, in a second article of the supple-ment they confounded this sensitive issue by stating that "kingship is a pledge entrusted from the nation upon the person of the shah with the grace of God," a statement that sounded as confusing in its Persian original as it does in its En-glish translation.[24]

THIS article began by considering two paradoxes: (1) why did the crowds participate in the constitutional revolution and (2) why was their antistate rev-olutionary rhetoric infused with such naive expressions of loyalty toward the shah? Here I argued that answering these questions would require us to take account of two radically different political cultures that were simultaneously present during the 1906 revolution in Iran: the Circle of Justice and Western constitutionalism.

The Irano-Islamic and Western discourses of politics were each rooted in a dif-ferent conception of state. The mixture of the traditional ideology with consti-tutionalism allowed the modernist revolutionaries to successfully mobilize the crowds behind the constitutional assembly. Furthermore, the traditional ideol-ogy provided the crowds with the opportunity to manipulate it as an ideology of revolt. Yet, because of the presence of a new culture of politics, the crowds' attempt at reproduction of the local culture ended by transforming and replac-ing it with a new synthesis. The new emergent culture of politics was not the re-sult of a linear serial diffusion of Western constitutionalism, but a synthesis that emerged from the clash of two cultures of state. Despite the ultimate victory of the Western constitutionalists, the Iranian state, in the eyes of its ordinary sup-

---

[23]The decision to translate *mamlakat* as *state* was an obvious one. The addendum divided the power of *mamlakat* (that is, the state) into legislative, judiciary, and executive. *Musavvabat, I–II*, article 27, 20

[24]*Grace of God* is the translation for *muhibat-i ilahi*. See *Musavvabat, I–II*, article 35, 21. In the earlier handwritten drafts of the supplement, this ambiguous article did not exist, whereas it did con-tain the more explicit article 26. This indicated that the latest article was the result of a political compromise. See Afshar 1989: 91–100. For a blatant attack on kingship and the shah's sanctity dur-ing the short triumph of the counterrevolution, see the famous article "Tabi'at-i Saltanat Chist," in the Switzerland edition of *Sur-i Israfil* January 23, 1909, no. 1: 2–5.

porters at least, was still far from a constitutional one. In place of a Western parliament, the assembly supplanted the shah as the source of justice and was expected to disseminate justice in response to petitions.

Here I make no strong claims about the long-term consequences of this transformation in the culture of politics. But I like to point to some possibilities. Was it due to the transformation between 1906 and 1909 that the Qajar monarchy could not regain its legitimacy, which finally led to its overthrow in 1925? More significant, was it due to this transformation that the successors to the Qajars, the Pahlavi monarchs, could never truly establish themselves as shahs, and instead lingered in a perpetual crisis of legitimacy? It is always assumed that something about the Pahlavis made them particularly illegitimate—and perhaps it is time to begin to investigate whether it was kingship that was in crisis, a crisis that began in 1906.

Bibliography

Newspapers and Official Publications

Anjuman (Tabriz)
Habl al-Matin (Tehran)
Majmu'ah-'i Musavvabat-i Advar-i Avval va Duvvum-i Qanun-Guzari-i Majlis-i Shawra-yi Milli (Tehran: Idarah-'i Qavanin va Matbu'at-i Majlis-i Shawra-yi Milli, abbreviated as *Musavvabat, I–II*)
Musavat (Tehran, Tabriz)
Ruznamah-'i Majlis (Tehran, Parliamentary debates during the first constitutional period, abbreviated as *Majlis1*)
Sur-i Israfil (Tehran, Yverdon)
Şura-yi Ümmet (Cairo, Paris)

References

'Abbas, Ihsan, ed. 1969. *'Ahd Ardashir*, translated by Muhammad 'Ali Shushtari. Tehran: Silsilah-'i Intisharat-i Anjuman-i Asar-i Milli.
Adamiyat, Faridun. 1972. *Andishah-'i Taraqqi va Hukumat-i Qanun: 'Asr-i Sipahsalar*. Tehran: Khvarazmi.
Adamiyat, Faridun, and Huma Natiq. 1977. *Afkar-i Ijtima'i va Siyasi va Iqtisadi dar Asar-i Muntashir'nashudah-'i Dawran-i Qajar*. Tehran: Intisharat-i Agah.
Afshar, Iraj. 1989. *Qabalah-'i Tarikh*. Tehran: Talayah.
Bourdieu, Pierre. 1976. *Outline of a Theory of Practice*, translated by Richard Nice. Cambridge: Cambridge University Press.
Boyce, M., ed. 1968. *The Letter Of Tansar*, translated by M. Boyce. Rome: Instituto Italiano per Il Medio Ed Estremo Oriente.

Damghani, Muhammad Taqi, ed. 1978. *Avvalin Qavanin-i Iran Qabl az Mashrutiyat*. Tehran: Markaz-i Pakhsh-i Intisharat-i Bihzad.

Dankoff, Robert. 1983. "Introduction." In *Wisdom of Royal Glory (Kutadgu Bilig): A Turko-Islamic Mirror for Princes*, by Yusuf Khass Hajib, translated by Robert Dankoff, 1–35. Chicago: University of Chicago Press.

Dawlatabadi, Yahya. 1983. *Hayat-i Yahya*, vol. 2. Tehran: Intisharat-i 'Attar, Intisharat-i Firdawsi.

Ettehadieh (Nezam-Mafi), Mansoureh. 1989. "The Council for the Investigation of Grievances: A Case Study of Nineteenth Century Iranian Social History." *Iranian Studies* 22, no. 1: 51–61.

Field, Daniel. 1989. *Rebels in the Name of the Tsar*. Boston: Unwin Hyman.

——. 1994. "Review of *Domination and the Arts of Resistance: Hidden Transcripts*." *American Historical Review* 99, no. 1 (February): 195–96.

Foucault, Michel. 1991. "Governmentality." In *The Foucault Effect: Studies in Governmentality*, edited by G. Burchell, C. Gordon, and P. Miller, 87–104. Chicago: University of Chicago Press.

Frye, Richard N. 1963. *The Heritage of Persia*. Cleveland: World.

Ghazzali Tusi, Muhummad. 1938. *Nasihat al-Muluk*, edited by Jalal Huma'i. Tehran: Chapkhanah-'i Majlis.

Gluckman, Max. 1963. "Rituals of Rebellion in South-East Africa." In *Order and Rebellion in Tribal Africa*. London: Cohen and West.

Hidayat, Mahdi Quli (Mukhbir al-Saltanah). 1982. *Khatirat va Khatarat*, 3d ed. Tehran: Kitabfurushi-i Zuvvar.

I'timad al-Saltanah, Muhammad Hasan Khan. 1966. *Ruznamah-'i Khatirat-i I'timad al-Saltanah*, edited by Iraj Afshar. Tehran: Intisharat-i Amir Kabir.

——. 1969. *Khalsah*, edited by Mahmud Katira'i. Tehran: Intisharat-i Tuka.

Kantorowicz, Ernst H. 1957. *The King's Two Bodies: A Study in Medieval Political Theology*. Princeton: Princeton University Press.

Kirmani, Ahmad Majd al-Islam. 1968. *Tarikh-i Inqilab-i Mashrutiyat-i Iran: Safarnamah-'i Kalat*, edited by Mahmud Khalilpur. Isfahan: Intisharat-i Danishgah-i Isfahan.

Kirmani, Muhammad Nazim al-Islam. 1983. *Tarikh-i Bidari-i Iraniyan*, 2 vols., edited by 'Ali Akbar Saidi Sirjani. Tehran: Intisharat-i Agah, Intisharat-i Nuvin.

Kuhrt, Amelie. 1987. "Usurpation, Conquest, and Ceremonial: From Babylon to Persia." In *Rituals of Royalty: Power and Ceremonial in Traditional Societies*, edited by David Cannadine and Simon Price, 20–55. Cambridge: Cambridge University Press.

Lambton, A. K. S. 1956. "Quis custodiet custodes: Some Reflections on the Persian Theory of Government." *Studia Islamica* 5.

——. 1962. "Justice in the Medieval Persian Theory of Kingship." *Studia Islamica* 17.

——. 1974. "Islamic Political Thought." In *The Legacy of Islam*, 2d ed., edited by Joseph Schact and C. E. Bosworth. Oxford: Oxford University Press.

Lewis, Bernard. 1988. *The Political Language of Islam*. Chicago: University of Chicago Press.

Majd al-Mulk (Sinaki), Muhammad Khan. 1979. *Rislah-'i Majdiyah*, edited by Fazl Allah Gurkani. Tehran: Iqbal.

Mardin, Şerif. 1962. *The Genesis of Young Ottoman Thought: A Study in the Modernization of Turkish Political Ideas*. Princeton: Princeton University Press.

Mustawfi, 'Abdullah. 1945. *Sharh-i Zindagani-i Man ya Tarikh-i Ijtima'i va Idari-i Dawrah-'i Qajariyah*, vol. 1. n.p.: 'Ilmi.

Nashat, Guity. 1982. *The Origins of Modern Reform in Iran, 1870–1880*. Urbana: University of Illinois Press.

Nizam al-Mulk. 1993. *Siyasatnamah*, edited by 'Abbas Iqbal. Tehran: Intisharat-i Asatir.

Perry, John. 1978. "Justice for the Underprivileged: The Ombudsman Tradition of Iran." *Journal of Near Eastern Studies* 37, no. 3: 203–15.

Safa'i, Ibrahim. 1973. *Asnad-i Mashrutah*. Tehran: Rushdiyah.

Sahlins, Marshall. 1981. *Historical Metaphors and Mythical Realities: Structure in the Early History of the Sandwich Island Kingdom*. Ann Arbor: University of Michigan Press.

——. 1985. *Islands of History*. Chicago: University of Chicago Press.

Scott, James. C. 1985. *Weapons of the Weak: Everyday Forms of Peasant Resistance*. New Haven: Yale University Press.

——. 1990. *Domination and the Arts of Resistance: Hidden Transcripts*. New Haven: Yale University Press.

Sharif Kashani, Muhammad Mahdi. 1983. *Vaqi'at-i Ittifaqiyah dar Ruzgar*, edited by M. Ettehadieh (Nezam-Mafi), and S. Sa'dvandiyan. Tehran: Nashr-i Tarikh-i Iran.

Sohrabi, Nader. 1995. "Historicizing Revolutions: Constitutional Revolutions in the Ottoman Empire, Iran, and Russia, 1905–1908." *American Journal of Sociology* 100, no. 6: 1383–1447.

Tusi, Nasir al-Din. 1964. *The Nasirean Ethics*, translated by G. M. Wickens. London: Allen and Unwin.

Weber, Max. 1978. *Economy and Society*, vol. II, edited by Guenther Roth and Claus Wittich. Berkeley: University of California Press.

PART FOUR

CULTURE AND THE MODERN WESTERN STATE

9

The Cultural Elements of Ethnically Mixed States: Nationality Re-formation in the Soviet Successor States

David D. Laitin

This paper examines the evolving cultural framework in four of the former Soviet "union republics." It shows how a dialectic between discourse in society and nationalizing policies of the new states fashions the cultural boundaries of the populations living within those states. The construction of new cultural identities is the object of analysis. As a contributor to *Bringing the State Back In* (Evans, Rueschemeyer, and Skocpol, 1985), the intellectual foil for this book, I might be accused of having hunted with the statists and now trying to run with the culturalists. But my overall project excerpted in *Bringing the State Back In*, as Steinmetz points out in the Introduction to this volume, proposed a "Janus-faced" approach to culture (Laitin 1986). This approach recognizes that states, at least at foundational moments, have the capacity to fashion the cultural framework of the society over which they govern. Yet it insists that those very cultural frames have an independent impact on political life, outside the purview of the state. *Bringing the State Back In* included a summary of the state-fashioning effect; readers of *Hegemony and Culture* saw the two faces of culture in dialectical relationship.

In this essay, I abstract again from my current research, where both faces of the cultural dialectic are portrayed (Laitin 1998). But here, the focus is on discourse within society that gives meaning and boundaries to the cultural groups

The research for this paper has been supported by the National Science Foundation, Grant No. POLS/SES92125768, David Laitin and Jerry Hough, principal investigators. Dominique Arel, Bhavna Davé, and Vello Pettai performed fieldwork that was essential for the results herein. Pål Kolstø helped provide the data. Elise Guiliano and Matthew Light provided research assistance.

that are beginning to influence the newly independent states of the postsoviet world. Although I include some material on the "state effect" in fashioning the cultural framework within society, my principal contribution in this essay is the mirror image of what was abstracted in *Bringing the State Back In*.

The important lesson is not to make the "cultural turn" blind to the insights of state theory—or rational-choice theory, for that matter. To say all politics is discourse, or culture, is to relegate these concepts to an explanatory void. States have only limited capacities—and not in all periods—to reframe culture.[1] On the other side of the dialectic, discourse strategies only rarely naturalize new cultural formations. New nationalities do not appear with each new narrative proposing one. Cultural symbols shape action, but these symbolic frames can be crushed by the state. Or they can be made irrelevant by the maximizing strategies of individuals who subvert the intentions of their self-appointed cultural entrepreneurs seeking to stake out a cultural realm in which they would be *virtuosi*.

Seeking a delimited but not dismissive notion of culture, this essay shows that in extraordinary times, the groupness of culture cannot be taken for granted. People take advantage of their multiple cultural repertoires and refashion their identities to make them relevant to the crises they face. Similarly, state actors seek to frame cultural groups better to assure themselves the possibility of meeting the demands these groups will make on the state. Out of this dialectic, and here the focus is on the postsoviet space, a new cultural identity—a "Russian-speaking population"—is in formation. This new identity is quite different from what was consciously sought by those in society who now classify themselves in terms of a Russian-speaking identity and by the state elites as well. Yet this new identity category sets limits and gives focus to the claims that can be made on the postsoviet states. To be sure, the long-term trends are not clear. Russian-speaking identity groups may make only an epiphenomenal appearance on the postsoviet stage. Yet this identity marker might in some republics naturalize into a new ethnic category, perhaps even a national one. It is too early to know. But the research presented herein shows—consistent with the ethos of this book— that it would be a terrible error to examine the strategies of the new nationalizing states or the individuals within them without careful attention to the changing cultural frame within which state actors and ordinary people act.

Cultural identities, it is now well-established, are not merely genetically inherited but socially constructed. Yet the tools used for these constructions have not been well-identified. In an attempt to elucidate the mechanisms by which cultural identities are constructed, this paper presents new data on nationality re-formation in four of the Soviet successor states (Estonia, Latvia, Ukraine, and Kazakhstan) and will demonstrate the early emergence of a conglomerate identity group—called the "Russian-speaking population." This new identity—

---

[1] My claim about state capacities to define culture is far less encompassing than that of Bourdieu, in this book.

with distinct parameters in the different republics—is reconfiguring ethnic politics in the postsoviet states.[2]

As shall be shown, the parameters of a Russian-speaking population depend on the degree to which titulars, in postsoviet space, can establish titular hegemony. Differential capacity to establish such hegemony has historical roots.[3] To be sure, all titular nationalities, as Kaiser (1994) points out, were given sufficient institutionalized resources to make a claim for postsoviet hegemony. They all (save the RFSFR—that is, Russia itself—which dominated the Soviet institutions) had their own Academies of Science charged with the recording of national histories and their own Ministries of Education charged with writing texts in the national language. Those nationalities that had their own union republic, Anderson and Silver (1990) show, had instruction in the indigenous language reaching to a much higher grade level than those nationalities that had lower institutional status. When in 1991 the Soviet Union collapsed, the union republics alone had the resources and power to take advantage of Russian president Boris Yeltsin's admonition to take all the sovereignty they could get. In large part because of Soviet rule, the identities of all the titular nationalities did not, in the wake of Soviet collapse, need to be constructed.

But not all titular groups had the same degree of power in their societies. The Baltic states that were incorporated into the union only after World War II had the interwar experience of sovereignty. Furthermore, the capitalist world never formally recognized the Soviet occupation of these states. Their nationalist leaders therefore had the option in 1991 to declare their states as having legal continuity with the interwar republics. This ultralegalistic move enabled nationalists from Estonia and Latvia to exclude all Soviet-era migrants from automatic citizenship rights in their restored republics. Because the great majority of voters would then be titulars, political parties that sought to define a non-ethnic basis for nationality had little chance for success.

Meanwhile, in Ukraine and Kazakhstan, there was no way to exclude Russians from the vote. The titulars and Russians had equal claims to receive citizenship in these two postsoviet republics. Also in Ukraine and Kazakhstan, in part due to the longer period of Soviet rule, there were many titulars by nationality who spoke Russian more regularly and freely than they spoke the titular language. These Russified titulars were less enthusiastic about a resolute nationalist program than were their counterparts in the Baltics, and they presented a barrier to the potential success of radical nationalists at the polls. It is in this context of na-

---

[2]In Laitin (1995) I took two "most different" cases—Estonia and Bashkortostan—and assumed that if the notion of a "Russian-speaking population" was evolving in both of these places, it was likely to be developing in all the other republics as well. There, I left open the issue of the possible differences in makeup of this formation in the different republics. Here, I address this issue by showing that the potential membership of a Russian-speaking population in Estonia and Latvia is quite different from that of one in Ukraine and Kazakhstan.

[3]The best accounting of the link between the historical roots of titular consciousness and the growth of nationalism in the late Soviet period is that of Suny (1993).

tional elites having inherited the institutions of the Soviet state within their republics that nontitulars have had to represent themselves politically and culturally, not fitting the new national myths. They have had to define themselves to make collective representations to the state; and titulars have had to define them to administer culturally plural states. The search to understand nontitulars in terms of their cultural identities—by both titulars and nontitulars—provides the empirical foundation of this paper.

The paper is organized as follows. The first section presents data on the discourses of nationality politics among members of the so-called Russians in diaspora. It shows that the consolidation of a Russian identity is by no means inevitable; it is, in fact, improbable. In all four republics, despite their historical differences, the discourse analysis will show that the notion of a Russian-speaking population has become an obvious, taken-for-granted cultural category in the postsoviet world. The second section elaborates on the implications of these data for understanding the ethnic cleavages that are emerging in each of the four republics. Here the historical differences are taken into account, as they help to explain why the boundaries separating cultural groups in the different republics have different shapes. Although the primary attention in this section is on the shape of the cultural cleavages, I make some suggestions of the mechanisms by which those cleavages might drive ethnic conflict in the Soviet successor states. The essay concludes with general comments on the relationship between ethnically mixed states and the cultural elements whose populations live within the boundaries of those states. This relationship is a key part of the "state/culture" nexus that is the focus of this book.

Discourses on Nationality in the Soviet Successor States

Russian-speakers in the former union republics experienced a double cataclysm: the first was in 1988–1989 when republican language laws raising the official status of titular languages undermined their privilege to remain monolingual; the second was in 1991, when the union republics achieved sovereignty. The cataclysm of 1991 created a "beached" diaspora in the Soviet successor states. People who were not members of the titular nationality, but secure in their assumptions that they were living in "their" country, the Soviet Union, suddenly found themselves "occupants" of nationalizing states. The leaders considered these states the organizational tool for the historical fulfillment of their titular nationalities (Brubaker 1995).

Those members of the diaspora who had "Russian" stamped on their passports were shell-shocked. For most of them, in Russia and in the union republics, there was hardly a difference between a Russian and a Soviet nationality (Solchanyk 1982: 34). Suddenly, however, there was no longer a territory to correspond with half of their identity. Would they "return" to their "homeland" Russia, even if they never lived there? Would they organize for special protection as "Russians" in their new states? Would they organize for secession? Or would they assimilate into the national cultures that were beginning to establish their hegemony? This is the question that Kaiser (1994) addressed in the final chapter of his book on the geography of Soviet and postsoviet identities, and one that has dominated discussion among analysts of postsoviet politics.

My answer to these questions is based on my finding that most analysts have missed a crucial alternative. The Russians in the Soviet successor states, I have found, were impelled by the uncertainties of the transition period to explore new identities, those that made sense to them in a new political context. One such identity—that of a Russian-speaking population—has already begun to have strong rhetorical appeal. Here, after reviewing the choice set available to actors on the postsoviet stage, I focus on this invention of a new identity. It emphasizes the everyday use of the term *Russian-speaking population* as if it were already a cliché.[4]

The Choice Set of Identity Categories

Before 1989, it was rare to see any public identification of Russians living in the union republics outside the Russian Federation. The Soviet Union, in the official line of thinking, had solved its nationality problem, and it was a "family" of nations. To be sure, Russians were sometimes described as the "elder brothers" of this family, but Lenin's excoriation of "Great Russian chauvinism" made it politically incorrect to rely on this appellation. Among the titular populations, many of whom resented the presence of outsiders in "their" republics, the diverse set of postwar migrants and soldiers were called "Russians," and these Russians would face all sorts of epithets by angry titulars urging them to return to their homeland (Karklins 1986: 29, 52). Nationality "talk," to the extent that it was permissible, existed within the confines of the vocabulary on the fifth line of the Soviet passport.

During the period of publicity (*glasnost'*), nationality talk mushroomed, although most of it had to do with titular rights, in which the Stalinesque categorization of identity categories was completely accepted. But with the Soviet collapse, a new form of discourse arose, which tried to categorize—or stigmatize—the Soviet diaspora. Simply calling the diaspora "Russians" had great appeal, especially for the titulars. From the point of view of nationalist-minded Estonians, Latvians, and Kazakhs, the subtle differences between Russians, Ukrainians, Belarusans, and Jews were not very important—all were Soviet agents and the Soviet Union was—in their minds—a euphemism for the

---

[4]The data for this section are from newspaper articles from Russia and the four republics. Nearly all the articles are from the Russian-language press, although a small number are translated from the republican language. The goal is to capture the way nontitulars categorize themselves and are categorized by state authorities, and this goal can be achieved by looking for everyday speech and writing by people who are not self-consciously trying to be sociological. In the full elaboration of these data, presented in Laitin (1998), I analyze frequencies. In that book, I also suggest reasons why the newly constructed identity categories might take on cultural meaning beyond a label. Space does not permit an elaboration of this theme here.

second Russian empire. Of all the terms that referred to the diaspora, only "Russian" (*russkie*) could serve as an adjective modifying "nationality" (*natsiia* or *natsional'nost'*).

But "Russian" (and especially *Great Russian velikorossy*) was an uncomfortable label for many interlocutors who participated in nationalist discourse in the wake of the double cataclysm. In a discourse analysis of the Russian language press, from both Russia and the republics, the terms used to describe the diaspora as an identity category were diverse. In coding these terms, I broke them down into the following categories:

1. Russian-speaking population (*russkoiazychnoe naselenie*). There are many variations on this theme. At first, it was common to use *the Russian-tongued* part *of the population*. Later, the word *part* was dropped in most uses of the term. Before *Russian-tongued population* became the clichéd phrase, there were other circumlocutions, as in "those for whom Russian is their native language" (*tekh, dlia kotorykh russkii iazyk iavliaetsia rodnym*), or "the population whose native language is the language of inter-nationality communication" (*naselenie, rodnym iazykom kotorogo iavliaetsia iazyk mezhnatsional'nogo obshcheniia*), or "those who think in Russian" (*te, kto dumaet na russkom iazyke*). *Tongued* indeed became the preferred usage, but often still "Russian-speaking" is used (*russkogovoriashchie*) as a synonym. The Russian-speakers are never referred to as a nation, and very rarely as a people (*narod*), but not always as a population. Instead, they are often referred to as persons (*liudi*) or as a community (*obshchestvo*).

2. Negations. After the double cataclysm, the characteristic most widely shared among the diaspora was that they were not titulars. They were categorized in a variety of ways in terms of what they were not. They were called "the unrooted" (*nekorennye*), "people without a country" (*apatridy*), "foreigners" (*inorodtsy* or *inostrantsy*), "foreign speakers" (*inoiazychni*), "the denationalized groups" (*denatsionalizirovannye gruppy*), "noncitizens" (*negrazhdane* or *nepoddanstvo*), "people with undefined citizenship" (*neopredelivshiesia c grazhdanstvom*), illegals (*nelegal'nye emigranty*), "residents of other nationalities" (*zhiteli drugikh natsional'nostei*), "nonspeakers of the titular language" (for example, *grazhdane Estonii, ne vladeiushchie Estonskim iazykom*), "non-natives" (*inozemtsy*), "unwanted residents" (*nezhelatelnye zhiteli*), "those without rights" (*bezpravnye*), and "voiceless" (*bezgolosie*). An interesting negative neologism in Latvia, which has already been offered as a legal category, is "self-made foreigners" (*vol'nostrantsy*).

3. Slavs. To the extent that the diaspora could be differentiated from Asians (in Kazakhstan) or Europeans (in the Baltics), a unifying aspect of the diasporic population was that they were "Slavs."

4. Members of the Russian state (*Rossiiskii* or *Rossiiane*). In Russian, there is a clear differentiation between Russian as an ethnic category (*russkie*) and Russian as a political category (*rossiiskii* or *rossiiane*). It was perfectly understandable in the context of postsoviet politics to refer to a range of nationality groups of the diaspora as "Rossiiskii" or "Rossiane" to demonstrate their political identification with the Russian Federation. This is especially the case in reference to members of the Russian army or veterans, and they were referred to as *Rossiiskie voennye*, indicating loyalty to Russia rather than ethnic identification as Russians.

5. Colonists or occupants. Referring to the diaspora as either colonial settlers (*kolonisty*) or the occupying forces of the Soviet state (*okkupanty*) became so com-

mon in the early nationalist rebirth of the 1980s that Russians would commonly self-refer in this manner, with bitter sarcasm in their tone.

6. Cofatherlanders (*sootechestvenniki*). This term leaves ambiguous the identity of the fatherland, whether it is Russia or the Soviet Union. In either case, identification as a cofatherlander suggests a close identity link between the diaspora and the dominant identity group of the Russian Federation, however that is defined. A reference to *Kazakhstanskie soplemenniki* (fellow countryman in this context of Russians in Kazakhstan) is analogous to cofatherlanders.

7. Soviets. "Soviet" became a protonationality in Soviet official discourse by the 1950s, with the hope that the nationalities would merge. Designating a population as "Soviet" referred to this identity project. Sometimes it was used in a more neutral way, as in *citizens of the former Soviet Union* (*grazhdane byvshego SSSR*), or the humorous *eks-grazhdan SSSR* (ex-Soviet citizens). In Crimea, Soviets are referred to as those who carry "sickled" (*serpastye*) passports.

8. Migrants. There is a range of distinctions for migrants. *Migranti* is used most commonly, but *movers* (*pereselentsy*) and *leavers* (*vykhodtsi*) are synonyms. Sometimes *fresh* (*svezhie*), *fresh migrant* (*svezhii migrant*), or *newcomers* (*priezzhie*) is used to differentiate Soviet era newcomers from the presoviet Russians (*staro-russkie*). Those who came under stress, especially after the war, are sometimes referred to as "refugees" (*bezhentsy*) or "postwar people" (*poslevoennye*). Those who came to the titular republics under state supervision are called "transfers" (*peremeshennye litsa*). Finally, those who are preparing to return or who have already returned are called "re-patriots" (*repatrianty*).

9. Residents. The diaspora is often thought of as "residing" in the republic without really belonging to it. Calling them "permanent residents" (*postoiannye zhiteli*) is a way of describing the social fact of the group's existence without legitimating them as members of the emerging national society in the titular republic.

10. Minorities. The diaspora (or particular national subsets of it) are often referred to as a "national minority" (*natsional'noe men'shistvo*).

11. Cossacks. Cossacks were historically an ethnically and racially mixed set of frontiersmen who entered state service in defense of the Russian borderlands. They have taken on a kind of separate nationality, and President Yeltsin formally recognized them as a *kul'turno-etnicheskaia obshchnost'* ("cultural-ethnic social formation"). In fact, one of the leaders of the Cossack Union declared, "We are the only national group in Russia that does not want to break off from Russia. We stand strongly for the territorial integrity of Russia" (Skinner 1994). In the near abroad, *Cossack* now refers to a subset of the population that are descendants of the Cossack armies, which in Ukraine includes titulars but in Kazakhstan tends to exclude them. In the Baltics, there was no Cossack tradition at all. But *Cossack* has taken on added semantic baggage after the double cataclysm and often refers to those who have an interest in the restoration of the former Soviet Union.

12. Epithets. A range of expressions that are less than cordial pepper nationalists' discourse in the near abroad. In Ukraine, Russians are often called "moskali" (Muscovites), but in a sense of being from the filthy political center. There is an occasional reference to the hibernating foreign force that will one day arise to confront the new titular nation, the "Bear" (*medved'*). In Estonia, these foreigners were referred to as "envoys" of Russia, Belarus, Ukraine, and other Soviet republics (*poslantsev Rossii*, and so on). One Estonian correspondent referred to those envoys ironically as the "guardians of the peace" (*strazhi mira*).

Occasionally they were referred to merely as "enemies" (*vragi*). In the Baltics, nontitulars sometimes ironically describe themselves—making gallows humor out of the state classifications of nontitulars—as the "citizens of the second sort" (*grazhdane vtorogo sorta*), or up to the tenth sort. The Russian term *chuzhaki* (aliens) is a typical epithet. Less typical is the phrase *Ivan i Petr* to refer to Russians as imperialists all. In Latvia, a bitter joke in the editorial office of *SM— Segodnia* shortened "noncitizen" (*negrazhdanin*) to *negr* (which the English-speaking staff pronounced as "nigger"). This term caught on as a popular epithet. Russians used the term sardonically, as in *belye negry*, calling themselves the "white niggers" of the near abroad.[5] Newspapers now use street expressions such as "damned Russians" (*prokliatye russkie*) and "Russian shit" (*Russkoe govno*).

13. Mixed categories. Interlocutors in nationalist discourse were not imprisoned by these categories and often mixed them up within a single paragraph. Previously unknown combinations took on new meaning. One common expression was *etnicheskie rossiiane* (*ethnic state-Russians*), which is a contradiction in terms but easily understood. Often, there were interesting mixes with one category serving as adjective, the other as noun. Already mentioned are *illegal immigrant* (a negation and a migrant) and *nezhelatelnye zhiteli* ("unwanted residents"). But there were others: *nekorennye russkie* ("unrooted Russian"), *russkoiazychnye negrazhdane* ("Russian-tongued noncitizen"), *inostrantsy negrazhdane* ("foreign noncitizen"), and *moskal' velikoross* ("Muscovite Great Russian"). The choice set for describing the beached diaspora had almost no boundaries.

In the content analysis reported elsewhere (Laitin 1998: chap. 10) of 318 newspaper articles, and 2197 terms referring to these still-to-be-hegemonically identified populations, 17 percent of the references were variations on *Russian-speaking population*. This is in third place behind Russian as an ethnic category (40 percent) and a congeries of negations (20 percent). Since negations do not make for a permanent name, *Russian-speaking population* is the principal competitor to simply *Russian*. After *Russian-speaking, Russian* as a political category got 5 percent of uses, and *migrants* and *Slavs* each got 3 percent. All other terms in the choice set were used less than 3 percent of the time. In the discussion that follows, I contextualize the use of *Russian-speaking population* inasmuch as it is the principal positive alternative to *Russian*—and by so doing, delineate the parameters of an identity in formation.

Estonia

In the 1989 census, Estonians made up 62 percent of the population of the Estonian Soviet Socialist Republic. Russians constituted 30 percent, Ukrainians 3 percent, Belarusans 2 percent, and others, including Poles, Jews, and Finns, were 3 percent. Most of the Western press reports saw the ethnic divide as both obvious and ominous: the titular nationality of Estonians against the representatives of the defunct empire, the Russians. This matchup does not accurately name one of the "teams." In Estonia, the Belarusans, Ukrainians, Poles, and Jews—all

---

[5] Dominique Arel, an authority on Ukrainian nationalism but with a deep knowledge of Quebec, informs me that this rhetorical move has antecedents in Canada. See Pierre Vallières (1968).

speaking Russian as their primary language—found themselves in 1989 and again in 1991 to be "in the same boat" with the Russians. The Russians found themselves forming both a diasporic (now living outside their "Soviet" home-land) and conglomerate (now suffering equally with other Russian speakers) identity at one and the same time. Estonians found themselves accepting and re-ifying these new cultural boundaries. And by sort of a rhetorical consensus, a "Russian-speaking" social identity is in formation in postsoviet Estonia.

Despite a free rhetorical market in postsoviet Estonia, Russian nationalist sym-bology is not being liberally produced. Residents in Estonia tracing their roots to Russia almost never rely on symbols of Russia's historical past. To be sure, vet-erans and schoolteachers refer regularly to the "Great Fatherland War" (World War II), but the fatherland is Soviet, rather than Russian, in imagery. In a sys-tematic review of the Russian language press in Estonia (but mostly Narva) from 1988 to 1994, I came across practically no examples of Russian chauvinism. When the Estonian government passed the "law on foreigners," L. Shlimonov, a cor-respondent for the *Narvskaia gazeta* (January 14, 1993), wrote a philosophical essay on the "greatness" of "the Russian people" who were "humbled" to be called "foreigners." But this symbolism is mixed, as Shlimonov refers to Russians inhabiting a variety of republics in "the common *Soviet* [my emphasis] home." A second example also has ambiguities. After the October 1993 armed insurrec-tion in Moscow, the *Narvskaia gazeta* (October 5, 1993) invited local dignitaries to comment on the "cataclysm." Nikolai Kulikov, a city councilman, wrote: "Russia—my historical homeland although I wasn't born there and have not lived there. But my father . . . I have a brother, sister, aunt, uncle there . . . My soul hurts for them." Here, Kulikov both identifies himself with (*my* historical homeland) and separates himself from (hurts *for them*) Russia. One school-teacher emphasized to me in an interview (May 11, 1994) the depth and richness of her Russian culture. This, however, was more a wistful memory of teaching great literature during the Soviet era than a category of present national mem-bership. But even vague references like this to a period of Russian cultural great-ness are rare among Estonian Russians.

The route toward a clear alternative to "Russian" to encompass the not-quite-Russian identity has not been smooth, however, and nontitulars from Estonia have experimented with a variety of terms. An early formulation was in response to the draft of the Estonian republic's language law in late 1988 and what this would mean for the Russian-speaking part of the population (*russkoiazychnoi chasti naseleniia*) (Y. Mishin, *Narvskaia gazeta*, November 17, 1988). As men-tioned, many other terms were used simultaneously, for example, the *unrooted population* (*nekorennoe naselenie*), as was the case when the Narva City Council resolved to advise a revision of the Law on Foreigners (minutes, Narva City Council, April 20, 1994). Rhetorical groping, rather than a universal acceptance of *Russian-speaking population*, marks identity exploration among non-Estoni-ans living in Estonia.

Furthermore, the rhetorical value of referring to the Soviet diaspora as Rus-sians remains high, especially for Estonian politicians seeking to link this popu-lation to Soviet totalitarian rule. Here, "Russian" is often a synonym for *occu-*

pant, foreigner, and *KGB*. Peter Olesk, then serving as Minister of Nationalities (but Russian speakers, in a pun, *vyselennia* for *natseleniai*, called him "Minister for Deportation"), said in an interview with *Narvskaia gazeta* (February 19, 1994), "I never said Russians presented a danger to Estonia. The danger will come with a much greater quantity of Russian citizens. Let it be one third who live in Estonia, not more." In an ironic statement to the Estonian Parliament on the ambiguities of the Law on Foreigners, and how the Russians had misinformed the world of its contents, one deputy mused: "We, Estonians, don't know how to write laws, but they, the Russians, don't know how to read them" (*Den' za dnem*, July 1, 1993).

Despite the variety of "namings" of this new identity, and attempts to stigmatize all noncitizens as Russians (not completely abjured by Russian-speaking politicians themselves), the prevalence of *russkoiazychnogo naseleniia* (Russian-speaking population) among every sector of Estonian political life cannot be denied. This is because the category serves the interests of actors from all points on the Estonian political spectrum. Russian politicians in the former Soviet republics may be the only remaining fervent Soviet internationalists in the world. They see themselves as historically beyond attachment to nationality (*natsional'nost'*). Many therefore bristle at the idea of organizing themselves as Russians. But there is no doubt among the internationalist Russian speakers, even if they are not a nationality but merely a population, that they have a grievance in Estonia. Organizing their aggrieved members (as a conglomerate Russian-speaking population) to stand against the policies of what they see as a linguistically discriminatory state has no chauvinistic overtones. Meanwhile, Estonian leaders, who face international criticism for policies that look too nationalistic, have an interest in showing that they have nothing against Russians *qua* Russians. Their laws, they insist, put pressures only on illegal immigrants and those Russian speakers who have not yet adjusted to the language requirements of the state. For Estonian nationalists, then, using the term *Russian-speaking population* allows them to set national criteria for membership in the society without naming a particular nation.

In regard to the non-Russian minorities, there are cross-pressures. For Estonian authorities, there is an interest in dividing the Russian-speaking population into its constituent parts, so that there will be no unified minority of non-Estonians. Thus with its Law on Cultural Minorities, the state finances the development of these small nationality groups. As for these minority groups themselves—the Ukrainians, Belarusans, Poles, and Jews, all of them minuscule in number and all Russian-speaking—their members have an interest in uniting with Russians to further their language and citizenship goals. Their cross-pressured interest in developing organizations representing their own ethnic groups, due to their small numbers and their full integration into the world of the Russians, has not yet been translated into serious political action. Thus their leaders, for the most part, claim to be representing parts of the Russian-speaking population, which includes them along with Russians.

In light of a confluence of interests in using *Russian-speaking* as if it were a social category, it has become almost a cliché in Estonian popular speech and writing. I have recorded its use by the Estonian State Minister in Charge of Negotiations with the Russian Federation, J. Luik (protocol, Narva City Council, June 30, 1993: 2); a leading politician of Isaama coalition, I. Hallaste (protocol, Narva City Council, April 14, 1992); the leader of Estonia's first Popular Front Government, E. Savisaar (*Narvskii rabochii*, June 30, 1990); the Secretary of the Estonian Community party, M. Titma (*Narvskii rabochii*, June 6, 1989); the leader of the Center Coalition and two-time prime minister of Estonia, T. Vähi (*Narvskaia gazeta*, September 14, 1991); and many others. There is even a reference by then-Prime Minister Mart Laar to his electoral tactics in regard to the Russian-speaking voters (interview in *Molodezh' Estonii*, November 4, 1993).

Of vital importance on this issue is the creation of an assembly of those noncitizens who were not represented in the Estonian parliament. The leaders of the various organizations that met to form such an assembly recognized that the term "Russians" was too exclusionary, as there were many non-Russians who were sinking politically in the same boat. An assembly of noncitizens would not do either. This label implicitly accepted as a fact a status category that many of the leaders sought to contest—they believed that they were rightfully citizens of the Estonian Republic as they had been citizens of the Estonian Soviet Socialist Republic. Eventually, leaders agreed on calling themselves the "Representative Assembly of the Russian Speaking Population of Estonia."

Legally, this is a social organization called merely the "Representative Assembly." It was formally registered with state authorities on July 6, 1993. It could not be registered as a party, because noncitizens are not legally permitted to join political parties in Estonia. And the addition of "Russian Speaking Population" was unacceptable as well, as it is doubtful whether the Estonian government would have permitted a legal organization naming itself after an aggrieved, and potentially revolutionary, segment of the population.

Despite legal niceties, this organization is connected in the public mind with an inchoate group called the "Russian-speaking population." In the Estonian press, in its Russian-language and Estonian-language variants (see *Estoniia*, September 18, 1993, with translations from the Estonian press), as well as in everyday references to the organization, the Representative Assembly is seen as representing the Russian-speaking population of Estonia. For example, A. Semionov, a leading figure in the Representative Assembly, gave an interview to the Estonian-language press (reported in *Narvskaia gazeta*, April 23, 1994) in which he spoke movingly about the psychological problems faced by the Russians, as independence came unexpectedly and they were not fully prepared. He emphasized that mobilizing politically based on national criteria was alien for this Russian-speaking population. He therefore claimed that his leadership in the Representative Assembly is to allay some of the fears faced by Russian speakers and to try to keep politics off the streets.

To be sure, the validity of this term occasionally is questioned. L. Vahtre, a deputy of the Estonian State Assembly, presented an address to a scientific seminar where he referred to non-Estonians as members of the "Russian-speaking nationality." A leader of the Jewish Society of Estonia questioned him on this term, and Vahtre, a bit defensive, said the term went back to "Soviet times" and that they use that term themselves, so it is not a term reflecting any prejudice (Friedrich-Naumann-Stiftung, "Kodanikud ja Mittekodanikud-Õiguslikud ja Sotsioloogiliset Probleemid Taastuvas Eesti Rahvusriigis," May 31, 1994). Earlier, I had asked my principal collaborator in Estonia about the citizenship situation for the Russian-speaking population. Livid, he responded that this isn't a "scientific" category and there cannot be official figures on it. This questioning is normal, because the term is so clearly "invented." However, because the term has become so widely accepted, from such a wide range of ideological and institutional positions, the invention is becoming a tradition (Hobsbawm and Ranger 1983). In Estonia, then, the identity of a Russian-speaking nationality has become, in Durkheim's phrase, a "social fact."

Latvia

Non-Latvians in independent Latvia are referred to with a variety of euphemisms and unflattering terms. In fact, the content analysis reveals that negations are used more regularly in the Latvian context than in any of the other three republics. Among the negations, they are the *unrooted population*, the *noncitizens*, the *stateless population*, and the *population of the second sort* (up to the "tenth sort" depending on context, but *not* the first sort). But the terms *Russians* and *Russian-speaking population* come in second and third. Since negations are no basis for an adopted identity, and *Russian* is not quite apt, *Russian-speaking* in Latvia, as in Estonia, has developed as an ethnic category *sine qua non*.

The range of negations to identify non-Latvians is great. They have been referred to as "people born in Latvia whose parents did not have Latvian citizenship" and "unwanted residents" in a single article (*Izvestiia*, November 16, 1993); "the alien mass of colonists" (by Janis Freimanis, a parliamentarian, reported in *Novoe vremia* [1992]); and the "denationalized group" (*Komersant*, December 3, 1990). A correspondent for *Izvestiia* (August 28, 1993) picked up on the Latvian attribution of negative terms to others. "Already twice this century," he wrote, "Latvia has lost its most entrepreneurial and hard-working citizens among the non-indigenous nationalities (*nekorennye natsional'nosti*): in 1939 50,000 Germans left who still haven't returned to Latvia; and during the German occupation a genocide of Latvian Jews took place. . . ." The author fears for the Russian speakers today, who are also referred to as nonindigenous. In a witty ideological spin, Nikolai Gudanets, in a letter to *SM—Segodnia* (December 28, 1993), pleads to be legally identified as a noncitizen (*negrazhdanin*), to take away the present "psychological pressure" that noncitizens now live under, and he promises to carry the title of "Latvian non-citizen with honor." Perhaps totally imbued in the spirit of Latvian discourse, a U.S. Department of State statement on the nationality situation acknowledged that in the Latvian constitution, all of its residents are equal before the law, and pointed out that "nonethnic Latvians" (*neetnicheskie latviisty*) cannot participate in civic life.

A source of the negativity in Latvian political discourse is its penchant for euphemisms, or refusal to call a spade a spade (preferable is "a not-diamond"). A Latvian law (reported in *Diena*, April 23, 1993) is entitled "On the temporary residence of those people finding themselves in Latvia due to the temporary dislocation of the Russian Armed Forces in Latvia." In a *Komsomol'skaia pravda* (February 10, 1994) report, the leader of one Latvian party invented the term *self-made foreigners* (*vol'nostrantsy*) to lay blame on people he could not name.

Avoidance of positively identifying the targeted population for national ire has led to a "roots" fetish. In this mode, Latvian nationalists try to differentiate the bad non-Latvians (newcomers) from the good ones (historical minorities). In *Diena* (November 1, 1993) an article contrasts Jews, Estonians, and Gypsies, who are "historical minorities," with a high percentage of Latvian citizens from Ukraine and Russia who are considered "occupiers" or "new arrivals" with correspondingly lower percentages of Latvian citizens. The notion of "rootedness" comes up constantly in articles concerning ethnic relations. An article in *Pravda* (November 5, 1993) recounts tales of woe for "non-Latvians" in Latvia. One group of retired women sought official help for housing repair. Seeing the application written in Russian, the official "rebuked the retirees for their nonindigenous origins and communist past." Another story is of a Russian journalist born in Latvia who was upbraided by the president-elect for referring to Latvia as his homeland (*rodina*). "Why do you think you have the right to call Latvia your homeland just because you were born here? For that, he says, you need to have deep hereditary roots (*korni*) in the country." In an article in *Rossiiskaia gazeta* (November 3, 1993), there is a report of the radical nationalist Movement for National Independence in Latvia and its new citizenship bill (wittily called by its opponents the "Law of Eternal Refusal," the title of the article). Here the newspaper refers to those affected by the law as the "non-indigenous residents" (and in another context, as the Russian-speakers). To a great extent accepting the Latvian nationalist view that Russians haven't sunk roots in Latvia, a repatriation group in Latvia has called itself "Roots" (*Korni*), with the intent of returning to Russia. In an interview with the *Baltiiskoe vremiia* (Riga) (September 1992), its leader Viacheslav Tikhomirov admits to enthusiasm (but no money) from the Latvian government, and some support from former Russian vice president Aleksandr Rutskoi.

Nonrooted is the explanation for the refusal by the government to grant automatic citizenship, and this negative takes on the properties of a group noun in Latvian discourse. Even though 39.1 percent of Russian nationals in Latvia were automatically granted citizenship in Latvia, the term *noncitizens* (*negrazhdane*) is often used as a generic reference to non-Latvians. A related term that is commonly used in the same context is *stateless* (*apatridy*). Many Latvians wish their world were indeed so simple, with Russians being wards of the international community. One reason it took so long for a naturalization law to be passed is that nationalist Latvian politicians saw the delay as working like a zero quota. In one sardonic article in *Emigratsiia* (January 3, 1994), noted earlier, there was an interview with Vladimir Steshenko, editor of *SM—Segodnia* and Director of the

Nationalities Question in the first Latvian Popular Front government, who related that in his newsroom, noncitizens (*negrazhdane*) are called by the first four letters, suggesting that among Latvians they are thought of as "niggers." The article's title refers to Latvia's "soft ethnic cleansing." This "joke" was so well-circulated that a serious jurisprudential column in *Panorama Latvii* (May 17, 1995) got the headline "Legalized Niggers" (*Negry v zakone*). Russians have organized politically around this issue. There is a Noncitizens' League (reported in *Diena*, March 9, 1994, and also by *Literaturnaia gazeta*, January 26, 1994) that works to remedy some of the inequalities that noncitizens face in Latvia (in taxation, in ownership of property, in rights to vote in local elections). The latter article suggested that this organization was taken as a security threat by Latvian nationalists.

More so than in Estonian ethnic labeling, in Latvia the term *Russian* is used without hesitation. An article in *Diena* (January 14, 1994) is called "Unemployed Russians in Latvia," and the author insists that unemployed Russians are all potential supporters of the leader of the Liberal Democratic party in the Russian Federation, V. Zhirinovskii, because they are newcomers (*priezzhie*), and can easily become tools of neoimperialist Russian chauvinists in Russia. As I point out, this notion of newcomers has an important role in helping Latvian nationalists differentiate Russians from "historical minorities"; here it is sufficient to point out that in this article there is no attempt to come to grips with the ambiguities of Ukrainians, Poles, and Belarusans being lumped together as Russians. In *Novoe vremia* (1992, no. 29) an article entitled "Russians without Russia" has a similar theme but from the opposite point of view. Russian people (*russkie liudi*) who are newcomers (*priezzhie*) and migrants (*migranty*) are suddenly treated by Latvians as second-class people. The irony is that those who are doing so once stood as democrats against Soviet power. In *SM—Segodnia* (September 22, 1992) the title of the article "Russian Exodus" is that of a film by Russian director Andrei Nikishin and deals with the situation of Russians facing Latvian nationalism. They take refuge in unrealizable escapist fantasies of flight abroad. And they drink! The movie therefore emphasizes Russian stereotypes as standard portrayals of those facing problems in regard to Latvianization of society. In these examples, especially in the headlines, we see how normal it remains to label the non-Latvian population merely as "Russians."

Negations (however prevalent) rarely stick as identity categories.[6] And, for reasons made clear in the Estonia section, reliance on "Russian" is not fully satisfactory in that it excludes people whom Russian political entrepreneurs want to include and because it marks them as "national chauvinists," something that they associate with the titulars and not themselves; thus the reliance, albeit less prominently than in Estonia, on the notion of "Russian-speakers," a term that can serve most interests. The first reference to this term I have found is in a sum-

---

[6] However, the word for *German* in Russian, *nemets*, is a negative—i.e., those who cannot speak. I do not believe, though, that Germans—even when speaking in Russian—refer to themselves in this way.

mary of the 1989 political scene in Latvia by Iu. G. Prichozhaev, where he writes, in reference to the Popular Front, "One of the sharpest and nerve wracking problems in Latvian political life appears to be the granting of citizenship to the Russian-speaking part of the population." Here, as in Estonia, "part" is used in early references, but is dropped when "Russian-speaking" becomes a noun, rather than an adjectival phrase. It becomes a noun through regular reference to this part of the population as a natural group.

In the sardonic article about "niggers" reported earlier, the newspaper *Emigratsiia* in a routine way tells the reader the article is about the "Russian-speaking residents" of the Baltics. In an article in *Moskovskie novosti* (October 4, 1992), Uldis Augstkalns, the deputy chair of the Latvian National Liberation Movement (LNNK), promises a fair (but implies an ominous) citizenship law. "Those Russian-speakers who wish to take Latvian citizenship and pass the language exam will become citizens," he assures. "The rest can expect a normal, civilized departure." In a touching letter to *Pravda* (March 2, 1994), a woman who describes herself as a "Russian-speaking citizen of Latvia" tells of her visa problems, because she has a sister in Belarus and another in Russia. Her anger is mostly against the Russian government; but her self-description demonstrates that the conglomerate identity "Russian-speaking" has become normalized in everyday speech. In an ominous political commentary "There Is No Time to Lose" (*Vremia ne terpit!*), Vladimir Lukashuk writes (*Diena*, February 20, 1991), "The number of convulsively created societies which supposedly could unite the Russians, are already close to ten. . . . They wouldn't be created if the Russian-speaking Latvians felt that they were common citizens of a common democratic republic." To be sure, as in Estonia, some Russians express doubts about the term. For example, Vladimir Sorochin, general secretary of the "Russian Citizens of Latvia Party" told an interviewer (*SM—Segodnia*, April 29, 1995) that his party is "currently emphasizing the word *Russian* in 'Russian-speaking' because for a Russian [in Latvia] to be [just] a Russian-*speaker* is no good at all." But, as with the case in all republics, Russians rarely criticize the notion of *Russian-speaking* as an identity category.

The situation for Latvians is quite different, although they too use the category as a normal referent. In *Vek* (December 17, 1993), the Latvian consul to Russia is quoted as saying that "Russian-speakers do not take seriously the law on languages and have not started to study Latvian." Somewhat more sympathetic, K. Bikshe, the director of Latvian language courses, told an interviewer from *SM—Segodnia* (November 10, 1993), "You cannot request that Russian-speakers immediately speak Latvian without any mistakes." Another Latvian, Visvaldis Latsis of the "Latvian Committee," wrote (in *SM—Segodnia*, September 11, 1991) that the "Russian people" should recognize that the Russian Empire subjugated many nations, and that is why all nations (for example, Tatars and Bashkirs) "try to separate from the Russians." The idea of a unified nontitular identity that is not dominated by Russians is looked upon with great skepticism. Indeed, the Riga-based correspondent for the RF newspaper *Trud* (November 3, 1993) understood clearly the pragmatics of "Russian-speakingness" for most

Latvians. "It is not rare for Russians to be identified with Communists," he reported. "The term 'Russian-speakers' is widely used as a designation of a mass hostile to the Latvian mass."

A major reason for the focus on the Russian-speaking aspect of their identity for Russians is that, in principle, a person's lack of fluency in Latvian (and very few Russians have such fluency) exposes him or her to severe material hardships, including the loss of job. While there are only a few examples of people claiming to have lost a job due to the activities of the so-called language police, what is taking place is the gradual destruction of the Russian-speaking milieu in which non-Latvians lived for fifty years. Fewer and fewer Latvians now study Russian; more now study English. Russian is gradually losing its position as the language of inter-nationality communication in Latvia (Kamenska 1995).

Meanwhile, Latvian is being systematically promoted and its use in a broad variety of settings is encouraged, or even required by law. To be a Russian speaker in today's Latvia marks one as the member of an out-group. In a fascinating sociological survey of readers of *SM* (November 3–5, 9–12, 1993), a team of sociologists (Natal'ia Sevidova, Larisa Persikova, and Iuliia Aleksandrova) tried to find out "why Russian-speakers (*russkogovoriashchie*) up to this time en masse have not become Latvian-speakers." Although the articles focus on many of the difficult administrative problems in learning Latvian, they capture a mood of Latvia's Russian-speaking population in regard to Latvian attitudes. The respondents intuit that Latvians feel that "if they [the Russian speakers] don't speak it [Latvian], they don't respect us." While individual Russian speakers have not suffered a status loss in Latvia (Laitin 1998, chap. 8), it is perfectly plausible to criticize publicly people who do not use Latvian and despise privately those who do.

A particularly good example of the power of status reversal is in the government's insistence that science teachers in Russian-medium schools must pass the Latvian language exam. Some teachers complained and asked why a biology teacher needs to know Latvian. The official answer was that "teachers represent the intelligentsia . . . they are not only specialists in their subject but educators in the broadest sense" (Kamenska 1995). No one is to be esteemed as an intellectual, or so goes the implicit reasoning, without fluency in Latvian.[7] With such justifications, it becomes clear how non-Latvians can coalesce around an identity that reflects their common linguistic plight.

Indeed, the categorization of Russian speakers already has practical implications. An article in *Izvestiia* (November 16, 1993) tells of the deportation of Igor Zaretskii to Russia from Latvia, a place he considered his homeland. He told a reporter, "My father is Belarusan, and my mother also has no connection with Russia. Are they sending me to Russia because I speak Russian?" The journalist remarks that the Latvian Department of Citizenship and Immigration, by performing these deportations in a routine way, makes Latvia "the only country in

---

[7] This reasoning hits hard for people brought up in a Russian tradition, where intellectuals are considered *chest' i sobest' nashego obshchestva* ("the honor and conscience of our society").

the former USSR which continues to recognize, in a fashion, the existence of the now-disappeared state." I add that the category *Russian-speaking* has taken on official meaning as an indicator that this particular resident of Latvia's real homeland is Russia.

In Latvia, the "Russian-speaking population" is commonly used among foreigners observing the ethnic scene, among nationalist Latvians (who see non-natives as a homologous mass) and Russians, Ukrainians, and Belarusans (who see the language law as one of the great threats to their future in Latvia and feel that they all suffer from this common fate). The term is far less frequently used than a set of garden-variety negations and explicatives, and less used than "Russian" as well. But negations and Russians won't serve in the long term, since Russian-speaking is a valued term by Russians and a useful epithet for Latvians. Despite some new evidence of declining frequency of use since 1991, the term has staying power. While it often has a purely labeling function in today's discourse, we can see some examples of people using the term to belittle others or to give coherence to their own identity. In Latvia, then, we can see the beginning of an identity category "in itself" becoming one "for itself."

Ukraine

The notion of a "Russian" ethnos whose members live as a new minority is, unlike in Estonia and even more so than in Latvia, a vibrant discourse in Ukraine. In his presidential inaugural address of 1991, newly elected President Leonid Kravchuk, a Ukrainophone who had been ideological secretary of the central committee of the Ukrainian Communist party, declared that "as President I see an independent Ukraine as a state of Ukrainians, Russians and people of all nationalities who live within its midst. It simply cannot be otherwise" (quoted in Arel 1995; from *Kievskii vestnik*, August 2, 1994). A well-known professor who teaches history at Kiev University told a newspaper reporter that Russians should either love Ukraine or leave it. He then revealed, "by blood, I'm Russian (*ia russkii*), and of course I wish good fortune to my native people (*rodnomu narodu*)" (*Ostrov Krym* interview with Igor Losev, no. 11, n.d.). In this example, the writer had a multiple identity, as both a Ukrainian citizen and a Russian national. He had no intention of giving up either. In an article in *Svobodnyi Krym* (July 1992), there is a report on a L'viv demonstration condemning Crimean "chauvinism," with the mayor reported as saying that these chauvinists seek to ruin Ukraine. The author of the article objects and says that the "simple Russian people (*prostye russkie liudi*) in Crimea consider that it is better to live in rich Ukraine than starving Russia." In Crimea, a "Russian Society" is quite active (see, for example, *Pravda Ukrainy*, September 16, 1992, and *Nezavisimaia gazeta*, January 12, 1993). Its goal is to "unite the Russian people (*russkikh liudei*) in a foundational social organization . . . reflecting the Russian idea (*russkaia ideia*)." Its leader, A. Los', was questioned by a reporter from *Nezavisimaia gazeta* about the role of the "non-Russian nationalities" in Ukraine. He answered that "We are all Russians, we all speak Russian freely . . . producing a new ethnos, the Rossians (*rossikhskii narod*)."[8]

A clear alternative to "Russian" as a category of identification (suggested by the use of Rossian in the previous paragraph), and one that would build a closer union between Russians and Ukrainians, is a "Slavic" identity. Indeed this rhetorical move is common in nationality discourse in Ukraine. In a typical article in the Russian-language press in Ukraine, the author reveals that he took Russian citizenship but plans to remain working in Ukraine. To resolve this apparent contradiction, he seeks the "integration of all Slavs" and perhaps other peoples as well (*Pravda Ukrainy*). In a similar tone, *Pravda Ukrainy* (May 26, 1993) printed a letter from Crimea in which the author emphasized the Slavic (*slavianskaia*) identity of the peninsula that unites Russians and Ukrainians. Indeed, the *Rossiskaia gazeta* (November 1993) reported a new Party of Slavic Unity, as a counter to the anti-Rossian (*anti-rossiskii*) propaganda in the western oblasts.

But the "Slavic" card faces constraints. For one, during the Soviet period, "Slavic" wasn't an official category, and it has no institutions that speak for its population. The Commonwealth of Independent States (CIS) was first intended as a union of Slavic states, that is, before President Nursultan Nazarbaev of Kazakhstan insisted on being included. There was hardly a way to exclude him, as neither Yeltsin nor his comrades were willing to reveal publicly the reality of a Slavic bond. Partly for this reason, the rhetorical space of Slavism has been occupied by extremists and even fascists. The leader of the Slavic Union in Kiev was arrested for selling newspapers in a metro underpass. In an interview with a correspondent from *Russkii vestnik* (no. 1, 1993), he could not hold himself back from gratuitous anti-Semitic remarks, such as pointing out that three of the members of the Slavic Union were mysteriously attacked on the Jewish holiday of Purim.

To be sure, the noted poet B. I. Oleinik (whose father is Russian and whose mother is Ukrainian) has been writing on the theme of a "Slavic core" (*Slavianskoe iadru*). He writes of a common basis of Russian identity in Ukraine's history, "up till now we called ourselves just Russian—children from a single pre-Mongolian Russian womb, with similar rights of inheritance," and is appalled that Russian is being "driven out" of the Parliament. This, he says, shows disregard for the Russian-speaking population. Here, we see that Oleinik moves to the less incendiary, more comfortable label—the Russian-speaking population—to give boundaries to the group that is suffering from what he considers to be an unnatural Ukrainian nationalism.

The notion of a Russian-speaking population as a social/cultural category in Ukraine has several distinct and somewhat contradictory bases. First, it is a common category for those who wish to unite the 11.4 million ethnic Russians with

---

[8] The notion of an eastern Slavic identity, going back to Kievan Rus', is the best gloss on this term "Rossians." For a discussion of the nuances of this term, and an appeal for its use as a wider national identity for the Russian Federation, see Tishkov (1995).

an even larger group of self-identifying Ukrainians who do not normally speak Ukrainian (but rather Russian) in the comfort of their homes, and they are concentrated in eastern and southern Ukraine. With such a united bloc, the major cultural division in Ukraine would suddenly be erased, and this would highlight the east/west divide in Ukraine. This set of Russian speakers is the electoral bloc that overwhelmingly supported presidential candidate Leonid Kuchma (a Russophone Ukrainian) over incumbent Kravchuk in the 1994 election. In that election, as Arel (1995) demonstrates, a Russian-speaking population voting bloc was clearly evident in the eastern and southern oblasts.

In Crimea, this notion of a Russian-speaking population consisting of Russians and Russophone Ukrainians is commonly used, in this case with the intent of creating a cultural/political alliance against the Tatars. The Tatars, returning to their home area after a generation of exile due to Stalin's massive deportations of dangerous nationalities from border regions, are still small in number. Yet in their claim to be the sole nationality that is rooted in Crimea, they represent a threat to the Russians and Ukrainians who constitute an overwhelming majority of the peninsula's residents. To be sure, the Russian press often refers to the non-Tatars merely as "Russians." The Institute of National Problems in Education, in a report summarized in *Rossiiskaia gazeta* (date obscured), refers to the Russian population of Crimea (*Russkoe naselenie Kryma*) that has been in formation for two centuries. And in *Literaturnaia Rosiia* (June 25, 1993), Sevastopol' is referred to as a Russian city (*russkii gorod*) within a Russian Crimea (*russkogo Kryma*).

But categories are in flux in Crimea. *Pravda* (January 28, 1993) routinely cited that among Crimeans "85 percent are Russian-speakers." In 1993, a Russian-speaking movement (*Russkoiazychnoe dvizhenie Kryma*) organized to push for closer ties with Russia. This strong potential alliance was not lost on the Tatars. In *Izvestiia Kryma* (September 9, 1992), a Tatar, complaining about the slow pace of restitution of property, wrote, "At this time, there are many who are called the Russian-speakers (by the way, I up till now did not know there was such a nationality), who have two, or even three, dwellings." In Crimea the term "Russian speakers" serves not only the interests of Russians who want a united Crimea, in the face of the Ukrainian nationalizing state; it also serves the interests of Tatars, to expose a united threat against their interests. The term, therefore, appears widely in discussions of nationality issues in Crimea.

In the rest of Ukraine, however, the "Russian-speaking population" is more often used to refer specifically to Russian-speaking Ukrainians in the east and south. In a letter from a Donetsk mining collective to a fascist paper in the Russian Federation (*Den'*, June 20–26, 1993), the writers complain that "In Ukraine live 12 million Russians (*russkikh*) and 2–3 million Russian-speaking people (*russkoiazychnykh narodov*), and in the government of Ukraine there isn't a single Russian (*russkogo*)." "Is this not discrimination?!" they ask. In a letter from the Odessa organization Rus, printed in *Vecherniaia Odessa* (September 18, 1992), officials complain of a "humiliating" division of the "people of Ukraine" (*na-*

roda Ukraini) into "natives" (*korennaia natsia*) and "national minorities" (*natsional'nye men'shinstva*). They agree that many in the south and east feel personal ties with the motherland (*Rodina-mat'*). Yet, they argue, half of the population in this zone are non-Russified Russian speakers (*russkoiazichnye ne russifitsirovanye*) who are still natives (*korennye zhiteli*). In the Russian weekly *Argumenty i fakty* (December 1991), there was a report on a survey of 5000 Kievans. More than 80 percent of the respondents had never met discrimination of Russians (*russkii*) or of the Russian-speaking population (*russkoiazychnoe naselenie*) at work or in everyday activities. In these examples, Russian speakers are that set of Ukrainians who normally speak Russian, and this is distinct from that set of ethnic Russians who live in Ukraine.

Ukrainian nationalists pick up on this notion of a Ukrainian Russian-speaking population, and speak about it constituting potential fifth columnists who haven't yet been weaned from imperial subjugation. As Arel points out (1995), "Ukrainian nationalists . . . treat Russophone Ukrainians as 'victims' of Russian-Soviet policy at best. Increasingly, however, the Russophone Ukrainians are being referred to as 'denationalized' beings who do not know who they are, or as 'Little Russians' (the prerevolutionary name for Ukrainians) who like to defer to and be dominated by the 'elder brother,' the Great Russians. Nationalists are convinced that their 'Russified' brethren will 're-acquire' their national consciousness only through the Ukrainian language . . ." In an incendiary article in *Iug* (January 1993), a pro-Ukrainian candidate in science accused the Russian speakers of Ukraine of intimidating the population at large and pushing them toward bloodshed, which would destroy Ukraine. These were the activities, he suggested, of fifth columnists. In an even more incendiary polemic in *Holos Ukrainy* (Kiev, date obscured), an eastern Ukrainian sarcastically describes a rally in Simferopol where protesters demanded "Stop the peasant-Ukrainians (*khokhly*) who deprive the Russian-speaking population of its native language." Here the colloquial epithet for untutored Ukrainians implies those from the west who are pushing a radical nationalist program. The writer sees this so-called Russian-speaking population as a threat to the continued ukrainization of Ukraine. For Ukrainian nationalists, especially from Galicia (and those from Galicia who serve in Kiev ministries), the threat of the Russian-speaking Ukrainians is the principal threat to the nationalizing project. "Russian speakers," for them, is a code word for denationalized, threatening yet potentially recoverable, conationals.

In Ukraine, the category of "Russian-speaking population" serves multifaceted interests. Authorities from the Russian Federation and Russian ethnics in Ukraine can refer to this population without obvious national chauvinist overtones. Russian ethnics, furthermore, can use the term to build an alliance with Russian-speaking Ukrainians, who themselves use the term because it suggests that they may speak Russian but they are still Ukrainians. Tatars and Ukrainian nationalists use the term to point to a potential threat to their national projects. Because it is an identity still in formation, which interest in Ukraine will capture the term as theirs remains uncertain.

Kazakhstan

The notion of a "Russian ethnos" is alive and well in Kazakhstan's nationalist discourse. This is in large part due to the massive in- and outmigration of Russians to and from northern Kazakhstan. In 1993, for instance, 250,000 Russians emigrated from Kazakhstan, whereas between 100,000 and 150,000 migrated to Kazakhstan. Figures in the press of some 450,000 migrants out of Kazakhstan in 1994 give the impression of mass exodus; but inmigration remains significant. There is no other way to refer to these migrants than as Russians (*russkie*). In fact, in one article (in *Emigratsiia*, March 1994), even the Ukrainians who were visiting, returning from, or leaving for their homeland were referred to as Russians! In a typical letter to the press, here to the newspaper *Sel'skaia zhizn'* (January 18, 1994), a forty-three-year-old farmer wrote that the "Russians (*russkie*) in Kazakhstan are at fault simply for not knowing Kazakh." From this, he concluded that there is no future here for our children as Kazakhstan doesn't want or need Russians.

As in the case of Ukraine, the notion of a Slav identity holds some rhetorical advantages over Russian. This category would include the 6,255,983 Russians as well as the 823,156 Ukrainians who resided in Kazakhstan at the time of the 1989 census, who face a common fate in regard to the nationalizing state policies. But unlike Ukraine, a Slav identity excludes those Russian speakers who are members of the titular nationality. Thus, Slavism in Kazakhstan has a civilizational—or perhaps racial—intonation missing from Ukrainian discourse. Nonetheless, Slavic self-identifications cross the political spectrum among non-Kazakhs. On the one hand are those who wish to create a permanent Slav presence. For example, Victor Mikhailov, as is reported in *Kazakhstanskaia pravda* (March 5, 1994), as a spokesman for a movement called *Lad* (Harmony), which by May 1993 had sixteen regional organizations and more than 8000 activists, told a reporter, "Unfortunately, the collapse of the USSR shook the confidence of Kazakhstani Slavs in living a life with full rights in this land. . . . We will try to open a Slavic university in Kazakhstan." On the other hand are those who see the handwriting on the wall for Slavs. A Russian living in Kazakhstan writes to *Vek* (January 28, 1994) that "we can confirm that the Slavic population (*slavianskoe nacelenie*) is leaving and the process is speeding up. All classes of society have," he wrote "'suitcase fever.' A survey reports that 3.2 million, or 33.4 percent of the Russian-speaking population" intend to leave. The majority of those leaving are Ukrainian and Belarusan.

This last reference mixes the Slavic imagery with the category of a Russian-speaking nationality, which is far more common than Slavic in Kazakhstan's political discourse. As with the case of "Slavic," the Russian-speaking category is most often used to unite Russians and Ukrainians against Kazakhs.[9] The alliance between Russians and Ukrainians is not now, and maybe never was, considered

---

[9] As of this writing, I have found only one reference to Russian-speaking population in which the referent was non-Kazakh and non-Russian. *Pravda* (March 1994) wrote, "The most important ques-

"natural," and needs to be forged. When Nazarbaev visited Moscow in March 1994, the Kazakhstani embassy, reported in *Moskovskii komsomolets* (March 29, 1994), was surrounded by pickets from a group calling itself "Russian Societies and Cossack Communes," which is a Cossack society organized to protect Russian interests, but its name raises two complementary identities, those of Russians and of Cossacks. That same month, in *Izvestiia* (n.d.), there was an announcement of a union of "Russia and Kazakhstan Siberian Cossacks" to defend the citizenship rights of the Russian-speaking population living in Kazakhstan. Russian-speaking was a convenient way to include Russians, Ukrainians, and Cossacks without making a long list. Within Kazakhstan as well, *Kazakhstanskaia pravda* (January 15, 1994) reports on a meeting of the "Conference of the Society for Agreement and Assistance" to discuss issues concerning the Russian-speaking population.

President Nazarbaev has sought to dampen the threat of a united Russian-speaking population standing against Kazakhs. In an interview with *Kazakhstanskaia pravda* (January 15, 1994), he was asked whether Kazakhstan would respect the rights of the Russian-speakers. He responded testily: "First of all, I don't use the term 'Russian-speaking nationality.' In Kazakhstan, practically all the residents are Russian-speaking, including, of course, Kazakhs. Only rarely do you find a person who does not command Russian. . . . Regarding nationality issues. . . . I think that before a politician . . . seizes upon this delicate theme, he should first carefully consider whether he possesses all of the necessary arguments. Even after this, he should consider seven times over whether such a theme will incite the formation of a people (*narod*), and bring tension to society . . ." This astute cup of vitriol had within it the insight that if people talked enough about people as being threatened as a population (*naselenie*), a real group (*narod*) might in fact form.[10]

Despite such efforts by the president, both the Kazakh and Russian governments collude in reifying this population category. In an article from *Novoe vremia* (March 1994), a correspondent wrote, "Moscow has conveyed the idea that the only republics of the former USSR that can count on economic support from Moscow are those which recognize the rights of the Russian-speaking population on an equal level with the indigenous population." The article goes on to quote a leader of a Russian society, who said "only fear, which is sitting in the genes of the Russian-speakers in Kazakhstan . . . is saving Nazarbaev from the enormous displeasure of the people in northern Kazakhstan." Correspondingly, an article in *Pravda* (March 1994) mentions that Nazarbaev in a speech to the Russian society of Petropavlovsk tried to allay fears of the Russian-speaking population that a massive outmigration from Kazakhstan is taking place.

Among the various strands of the Russian-speaking population in Kazakhstan, there is a clear sense of a civilizational divide between all of them versus the

---

tion for millions of Russians (*russkiye*) and Russian speakers (*russkoiazychnye*) in Kazakhstan is citizenship. . . ."

[10] In an October 1995 reshuffle of his Cabinet, Nazarbaev appointed a few Russians, in a clear attempt to signal to the Russian-speaking population that they are full-fledged citizens of Kazakhstan.

Kazakhs, in which they share a more civilized culture. For non-Kazakh Russian speakers, assimilation into Kazakh culture is seen as an absurdity. In 1995, one long-term and loyal Kazakh citizen of Jewish nationality told me that it was not only useless to learn Kazakh but impossible as well. This common view that Kazakh language is impossible to learn and represents a lesser culture induces Jews and especially Ukrainians to emphasize what they share with, rather than what separates them from, Russians. Lumping Russians, Ukrainians, and Belarusans into a simple Russian-speaking population is a standard postsoviet reference in Kazakhstan for both Kazakhs and the Russian-speakers themselves.

The principal challenge to the notion of a Russian-speaking population consisting of Russians and others against the titular Kazakhs is that of a Russian-speaking population that includes Russians, Ukrainians, Jews, and Russified Kazakhs. This last set is often referred to as the "*mankurty.*" This term derives from the famous novel by Kyrgyz writer Chingiz Aitmatov (written in Russian), "*I dol'she veka dlit'sia dyen'.*" In it, a *mankurt* is a zombie slave who has lost all memory of his past and culture. "*Mankurt,*" writes Bhavna Davé, "has become an apt metaphor for the 'modernized' members of uprooted nomadic cultures, forced to part with their cultural roots in the process of adaptation and survival" (1994: 2). Although in the 1989 census 97 percent of Kazakh nationals report that Kazakh is their native or first language—making the idea of forgetting your "own" language seem beside the point—it is widely believed that Kazakh respondents made such a claim to the enumerators as a symbolic gesture rather than as an accurate representation of their language history. The number of *mankurty* is surely higher than the 2.2 percent of urban Kazakhs who report Russian to be their first language (Kaiser 1994: Table 6.4). Indeed, referring to Silver's (1978, 1986) work, Kaiser admits this (1994: 283): "Clearly," Kaiser points out, "the designation of first language in the censuses was not necessarily a choice made on the basis of fluency level alone, and also reflected attitudes toward the native and Russian languages."

The widespread existence of *mankurtism* in Kazakhstan is palpable in everyday life in Kazakhstani cities, which were all initially populated as cities by Russians. Virtually all government meetings, public announcements, and directives throughout the Soviet era in Kazakhstan were in Russian. Popular stereotypes in central Asia further suggest that the Kazakhs have massively underreported their linguistic assimilation. Davé reports (1994: 18–19) an Uzbeki popular refrain: "if you want to become a Russian, first become a Kazakh." This view has some official recognition, as Kazakh ambassador to Russia, Tair Mansurov, told a *Pravda* (March 26, 1994) correspondent that "in Kazakhstan, the whole population is Russian-speaking." In 1989, 62.8 percent of Kazakhs reported speaking Russian as a second language, the second highest (next to Latvians) of reported Russian proficiency among titulars of the former union republics (Kaiser 1994: Table 6.8). The percentage of *mankurty* falls somewhere between 2.2 and 62.8 percent, but it is significantly higher than the former figure.

The key question for national identity formation in Kazakhstan is whether Kazakh nationalists will be able—as their Galician counterparts have already begun—to trump an identity category of Russian-speaking population that includes Russified titulars. In an article in *Delovoi mir* (February 17, 1995), there was reference to a letter written by ten famous Kazakh businessmen who encouraged Russians to remain in the country. The article reports on a Kazakh group called "Azat" that has organized a demonstration to "stigmatize" these "apostates." Apostasy and betrayal are the charges nationalists will make to those Kazakhs who see themselves as part of a Russian-speaking population. While "Russian" far outpaces "Russian speaking" in the nationalist discourse of Kazakhstan, the vague boundaries but attractiveness of "Russian-speakingness" keep that identity category alive and contested.

Ethnic Conflict in the Soviet Successor States

The underlying theme of the first section is that the elements of four of the postsoviet ethnically mixed states can recombine into a variety of compounds. To postulate conflict between two teams—Russians and titulars—as is so often done in the ethnic conflict literature, is to miss the possibilities of new compounds formed and reformed in the wild "frontier" opened up by the "Leninist extinction" (Jowitt 1992). To analyze the level of tension that exists between Russians and titulars, as a barometer of potential violence, is possibly to miss the sources of ethnic conflict that are brewing on the frontier. In this section, I outline the sources of ethnic conflict, taking into account new compounds of identity, in the same four postsoviet republics.

Consider a strategic conflict between the government of one of the postsoviet nationalizing states and a minority, or underrepresented, Russian-speaking population.[11] The conflict of interest between nationalizing governments and the Russian-speaking populations became readily apparent in the wake of the Soviet collapse. The leaders of the newly sovereign states had a vision of their nation "owning" the state (Brubaker 1995); in fact, because the former union republics were themselves states-in-formation, having policies in regard to membership and nationality was part of becoming a bona fide state. Thus titular leaders felt impelled to make decisions about the kind of national state they would lead, and the idea of ownership by the titular nation of the state was a deep-seated wish. But the large numbers of Russian speakers in those states made ownership (and the titular dominant language laws of 1988 to 1989 that reflected a goal of ownership) seem problematic. The question thus arises: What role will nontitulars play in the newly sovereign state?

Given the nature of the Soviet breakup, in which the leaders of the union republics were in the best position to assert control over the institutional apparatus of the state (for example, call referenda, make treaties with foreign countries, pass laws), these leaders had a strategic advantage in being able to make the first move to address this fundamental question. The Russian-speaking popula-

---

[11] This discussion around Figure A has been developed from an earlier formulation in Laitin (1994).

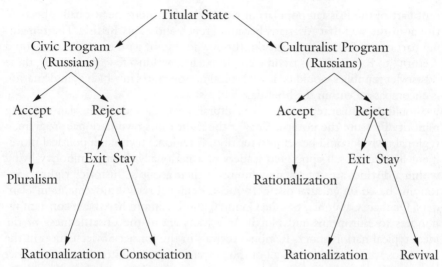

Figure A. Political Contexts and National Trends

tions, to the contrary, had no organizational resources to take any such initiatives, and they could only respond to the situations the republican leaders fashioned for them.

And so, in this strategic confrontation, the nationalizing government moves first. It can press a vigorous nationalist agenda in which membership in the nation will be carefully controlled by racial, linguistic, or religious criteria (a set of policies I loosely combine as "cultural"), or it can define national membership based primarily on "civic" (territory, work, loyalty) criteria. In response, members of the Russian-speaking population have a complementary choice. They can accept the régime as structuring their opportunities or they can seek to pressure the government to recognize the national distinctiveness of the group they purport to represent.

Each of the four end points—illustrated in Figure A—is the outcome of the choices by government and minority group. And each end point evokes a somewhat distinct political trajectory with its own strategic dynamics. The four outcomes should not then be considered final political results, but rather new fields in which the game of ethnic politics will be played. Here I give a capsule summary of the dynamics that are unleashed by the confluence of choices within Figure A.

Should the government press a culturalist agenda and the minority population accept the régime, rationalization will be set in motion. *Rationalization* is the process by which a ruler specifies a common set of practices that become standard for the entire population and make for the efficient enterprise of rule. Max Weber identified the process of legal and administrative rationalization (Weber 1968: 71, 1108, 655, 809–38); I have applied this notion to issues of language rationalization (Laitin 1992: 9–10); and here the concept is stretched to include criteria for national membership. Under conditions of rationalization, a significant part of the Russian population would slowly (intergenerationally) become titular in the way that Alsatians became French and Scots British. The remaining part of the Russian population, those who do not wish to assimilate, would "return" to Russia. If this trend were dominant, within a few generations, these postsoviet republics would be ideal-typical nation-states in which a single nation is encompassed within the boundaries of a state.

Should the titular republic press a culturalist agenda and the Russian-speaking minority pressure the government for the right to its own national program, a regional revival would be set into motion. A regional revival is a political movement headed by self-appointed leaders of a nationally distinct minority living within a distinct area of a state who assert their group's "historic" right to autonomy based on cultural distinctiveness. Regional revival movements in Flanders, Quebec, Catalonia, Basque Country, and Piedmont have been constant reminders to Europeans and North Americans about the unsettledness of the ideal-typical nation-states. Regional revivals in the former Soviet Union in the late 1980s were reminders to all of the power of cultural entrepreneurs to upset state domination through appeals to common national membership. Should this trend be dominant in any of the republics we have analyzed, we would observe a politics in which the state reluctantly grants minimal levels of autonomy to a quasi-autonomous Russian territory within the state and the leaders of the newly recognized Russian autonomous community pressure for ever higher levels of such autonomy.

Should the titular government downplay its national agenda while the Russian-speaking population organizes itself as a political community, a consociation would be in the making. A *consociation* is a form of government in which there are distinct cultural pillars. Each pillar has a considerable degree of autonomy on a range of political functions (especially in education and cultural affairs), and policy at the center is made through bargains among the leaders of the pillars. Each group has the right to a veto over any policy, and proportionality becomes the basis for political representation, bureaucratic position, and dispersal of government funds (Lijphart 1977: 25). Consociational systems have helped bring stable democracy to culturally (quasi) heterogeneous states such as Netherlands, Belgium, and Austria. Should this be the trend in any postsoviet state, there would be reserved positions for Russians in the parliament, in the cabinet, in the police force, in the army, and in the bureaucracy; and all central policy would be the result of intergroup bargains, with Russian leaders able to veto any policy they find anathema to their group's interests.

Should the titular government downplay its national agenda while the Russian-speaking population does not organize itself (as Russians) against the titular majority, pluralism would be the political trend. Pluralism, as defined by Dahl (1961: 86), is a political system "dominated by many different sets of leaders, each having access to a different combination of political resources." Under pluralism, political coalitions would be distinct for each policy domain, and the political elites in any issue domain would likely be non-elites in other issue domains. In the United States, the politics of Italian-, Irish-, Jewish-, German-, and

Japanese-Americans have a pluralist cross-cutting cleavages element. Each forms to a limited degree a voting bloc, but make cultural membership only a limited element of one's political identity. (For African Americans, the situation is quite different.) In a postsoviet republic, under conditions of pluralism, for some issues Russian speakers might coalesce against the interests of titular speakers (say, on educational policy), but on other issues, the population might be divided by class, by region, or by associations with the past régime. Should Russian and titular cleavages in a republic be noncumulative, we could say that the cultural divide in that republic was real, but had only limited salience, and in only a few issue domains. The former Soviet republic would then be considered to have a pluralist régime.

In regard to the possibilities laid out in Figure A, the four cases I have examined fall into two distinct patterns. In Estonia and Latvia, hegemony of the titulars in capturing the postsoviet state, explained in the introduction, has made it possible for the nationalizing governments to set a strong and unequivocal course for their states. Meanwhile, in both Ukraine and Kazakhstan, radical nationalists could not achieve hegemony and have had to play minor roles in the state apparatuses with leaders who have been setting civic courses for their states.

The differences in the policies of the nationalizing states have had broad implications for the way cultural reidentification has been taking place, and as well for the types of national tensions that can already be observed in these states. In Estonia and Latvia, with the states choosing a "culturalist" national program, the Russian-speaking population can either accept rationalization or seek revival. Pluralism and consociation have been ruled out, at least in the current state of play. On an individual level, Russian speakers in Estonia and Latvia who recognize the political costs of organizing for a revival are beginning to position themselves for potential intergenerational assimilation, or at least cultural integration into these republics. But on a group level, leaders of the Russian-speaking population see assimilation as undermining their representative legitimacy as monopoly spokesmen for an aggrieved minority. They are aided in their efforts by the nationalist leaders in the Baltics who claim that assimilation is necessary for citizenship but who deny resources to make assimilation feasible. Baltic nationalists hope for outmigration, but may be willing to settle for a permanent, culturally distinct lower caste. In any event, the leaders of the Russian-speaking populations in the Baltics have an interest in consolidating as large a constituency as possible to confront the policies of the nationalizing states. We can expect to see in these two cases great efforts to name and reify a Russian-speaking identity and attempts to encourage Russians, Ukrainians, Belarusans, Poles, and Jews, all residents of these republics, to identify themselves as sinking together in a common ship. To forestall this, the Estonian and Latvian governments will seek to divide this constituency, in part by providing funds to promote Ukrainian, Polish, and Belarusan cultural societies; they will also seek to forestall the consolidation of this identity through efforts at assimilation and subsidized outmigration. But the motor of ethnic/national politics will be attempts at boundary expansion (by leaders of the Russian-speaking population) and concomitant attempts at contraction (by government leaders) of an aggrieved Russian-speaking nationality-in-formation.

In Ukraine and Kazakhstan, because governments have taken the civic route toward national consolidation, ethnic/national politics will have a different dynamic. In these two republics, the leaders of the nontitular subset of the Russian-speaking nationality will seek to limit the move toward pluralism, which many Russian speakers will happily or grudgingly accept. Pluralism, after all, would delegitimate the representative monopoly these leaders would have in speaking for "their" people. If they pressed for consociation, they would get such a monopoly. However interesting this dynamic between pluralism and consociation, it is likely to remain a political sideshow. The main event in ethnic/national politics in Ukraine and Kazakhstan is likely to be within the titular group itself, between the aggrieved nationalists who will not give up the hope of rationalization and the Russified titulars who have an interest in pluralism. A well-known strategy for the aggrieved nationalists is to foment violence between Russians and titulars as a self-fulfilling prophesy, showing that an ethnically mixed state cannot be peaceful. Its purpose would be to win over the allegiance of the Russified titulars, and thereby to create a rigid Russian/titular divide. Those Russians who were fitting comfortably into a new Russian-speaking nationality would, under these conditions, be forced to reidentify as primordial Russians. While journalists would be reporting on the ancient Russian/titular antagonisms, the real source of such a conflict is that between radical nationals and their own—to use the Kazakh symbol—*mankurty*.

THE cultural elements in the Soviet successor states are multiple. There are Russians, titulars, Slavs, members of other official Soviet nationalities, and—still with fluid boundaries—Russian-speaking populations. Scholars who study nationalism are well aware of the "constructedness" of nationality and how, in the cauldron of postsoviet politics, a variety of recombinations is possible. If Palestinians could emerge out of the chaos of 1947–1948 as a real nationality, so could Slav or Orthodox or Russian speakers emerge after the extinction of Leninism. But scholars who study ethnic conflict have been less attuned to the possibilities of recombination and have treated groups as real, as countable, and as eternal. In this essay I sought to integrate the insights developed in the nationalism literature into a discussion of ethnic conflict. I have shown that an identity in formation in four postsoviet republics, one that had no role in national enumerations in the Soviet era, will likely play a crucial role in republican national politics. This identity formation is occurring at the level of popular discourse, in large part autonomous of the plans of state bureaucrats or nationalist entrepreneurs.

This paper has also shown that the Russian-speaking populations in formation have a variety of possible configurations. Such an identity category could exclude Russians and include only nontitulars and non-Russians whose primary language is Russian. It could exclude Russified titulars and include all nontitular Slavs. Or it could include Russians, titulars, and other Slavs who share a common situation of speaking Russian as a primary language and feeling threatened by the language policies of the nationalizing state.

For a perspective on the cultural turn in state theory, it is the dialectic between quasi-autonomous cultural discourses and the strategic interplay between the state and cultural formations that will set the boundaries of the emerging Russian-speaking populations. Under conditions of state-formation, the discourses by and about cultural groups who do not fit into the national frame help create new identity formations. Yet the elements of these formations are reconstituted into new compounds by those states. This is a dialectic that is missed in many theories of ethnic conflict that assume the existence of groups, and in traditional state theory as well, where cultural factors are often downplayed. Thus the need to take the "cultural turn."

References

Anderson, Barbara A., and Brian D. Silver. 1990. "Some Factors in the Linguistic and Ethnic Russification of Soviet Nationalities: Is Everyone Becoming Russian?" In *The Nationalities Factor in Soviet Politics and Society*, edited by Lubomyr Hajda and Mark Beissinger. Boulder: Westview.

Arel, Dominique. 1995. "Ukraine: The Temptation of the Nationalizing State." In *Political Culture and Civil Society in the Former Soviet Union*, edited by Vladimir Tismaneanu. Armonk, N.Y.: M. E. Sharpe.

Brubaker, Rogers. 1995. "National Minorities, Nationalizing States, and External National Homelands in the New Europe." *Daedalus* (Spring).

Dahl, Robert A. 1961. *Who Governs?* New Haven: Yale University Press.

Davé, Bhavna. 1994. "Becoming Mankurty: Russification, Progress, and Social Mobility among Urban Kazakhs." Paper prepared for the annual meeting of the American Political Science Association, New York.

Evans, Peter, Dietrich Rueschemeyer, and Theda Skocpol, eds. 1985. *Bringing the State Back In*. Cambridge: Cambridge University Press.

Hobsbawm, Eric, and Terence Ranger, eds. 1983. *The Invention of Tradition*. Cambridge: Cambridge University Press.

Jowitt, Ken. 1992. *New World Disorder: The Leninist Extinction*. Berkeley: University of California Press.

Kaiser, Robert J. 1994. *The Geography of Nationalism in Russia and the USSR*. Princeton: Princeton University Press.

Kamenska, Angelita. 1995. "The State Language in Latvia: Achievements, Problems, and Prospects." Riga: Latvian Center for Human Rights and Ethnic Studies.

Karklins, Rasma. 1986. *Ethnic Relations in the USSR*. Boston: Allen and Unwin.

Laitin, David. 1986. *Hegemony and Culture: Politics and Religious Change among the Yoruba*. Chicago: University of Chicago Press.

———. 1992. *Language Repertoires and State Construction in Africa*. Cambridge: Cambridge University Press.

——. 1994. "Russian Nationalism in Post-Soviet Estonia." In *Nationalism in Europe: Past and Present*, edited by Justo G. Beramendi, Ramón Máiz, and Xosé M. Nuñez, vol. 2, 522–544. Santiago de Compostela, Galicia: Universidade de Santiago de Compostela.

——. 1995. "Identity in Formation: The Russian-speaking Nationality in the Post-Soviet Diaspora." *Archives Européennes de Sociologie*, no. 2.

——. 1998. *Identity in Formation: The Russian-speaking Populations in the Near Abroad*. Ithaca: Cornell University Press.

Lijphart, Arend. 1977. *Democracy in Plural Societies*. New Haven: Yale University Press.

Silver, Brian. 1978. "Language Policy and the Linguistic Russification of Soviet Nationalities." In *Soviet Nationality Policies and Practices*, edited by Jeremy Azrael, 250–306. New York: Praeger.

——. 1986. "The Ethnic and Language Dimensions in Russian and Soviet Censuses." In *Research Guide to the Russian and Soviet Censuses*, edited by Ralph Clem, 70–97. Ithaca: Cornell University Press.

Skinner, Barbara. 1994. "Identity Formation in the Russian Cossack Revival." *Europe-Asia Studies* 46, no. 6: 1017–37.

Solchanyk, Roman. 1982. "Russian Language and Soviet Politics." *Soviet Studies* 34, no. 1: 23–42.

Suny, Ronald. 1993. *The Revenge of the Past*. Stanford: Stanford University Press.

Tishkov, V. A. 1995. "What is Russia: Prospects for Nation-Building." *Security Dialogue* 26, no. 1: 41–54.

Vallières, Pierre. 1968. *Nègres blancs d'Amérique*. Montréal: Editions Parti Pris.

Weber, Max. 1968. *Economy and Society*, 2 vols. Berkeley: University of California Press.

10

Motherhood, Work, and Welfare in the United States, Britain, Canada, and Australia

Ann Shola Orloff

Cultural understandings and ideological preferences about gender relations, particularly the inevitability, naturalness, and rightness of gender difference, have shaped welfare states since their origins in the late nineteenth and early twentieth centuries and through periods of expansion and consolidation in the 1940s through 1960s. The programs of social insurance, social assistance, universal citizenship entitlement, and public services that developed over the course of this period were built on assumptions about the gender division of labor in which women were to be mothers, wives, caregivers, and domestic workers (even if they also worked for pay), and men were to support families economically, most often through paid labor. This was reflected in gender-specific expectations imposed on all citizens making claims on welfare states and in a gendered dualism within all systems of social provision: some programs catered to the "failures" of the labor market (for example, unemployment, retirement, work injury), and others targeted family "failures" (for example, loss of a family breadwinner, widowhood). Moreover, the family-related programs used principally by women were in many ways inferior to programs targeted to paid workers, mainly men. Yet state welfare programs did provide some support for some women to sustain autonomous households. Provision for solo mothers has been a contested part of social welfare from the beginning. By conditioning support on women's performance of their traditional mothering and caregiving duties, these programs reinforced the gendered division of labor and helped to valorize a model of motherhood as full-time caregiving; but by offering women a certain autonomy they challenged aspects of women's economic dependency and the concomitant restriction of their choices relative to partnering and household formation.

As the movements for women's equality gained power within political organizations in the 1960s and 1970s, a range of reforms abolished de jure discrimination and made the provisions of welfare state programs formally gender-neutral. Programs supporting solo mothers' autonomous households no longer categorically exclude women of color or "unfit" mothers. New legislation regulating the labor market opened up employment opportunities for women; along with greater demand for women's labor, this helped to provide the basis for economic independence. Still, despite dramatic changes in the patterns of women's participation in the labor force, many other aspects of the division of labor have changed far less—most centrally the assignment of the lion's share of responsibility for unpaid caregiving and domestic labor to women, and men's continuing to avoid much of this work. Consequently, the gendered dualism of welfare states has been eroded only minimally. In addition, income support programs continue to institutionalize a model of traditional (that is, stay-at-home) motherhood. To some extent, different identities for women are promoted by different state agencies; the emphasis on gender neutrality in family law and equal treatment in the workplace promote a gender-neutral model of citizen-worker or private employee relying on the market for income and services, while various income support programs promote an identity based primarily on unpaid caregiving for women.

Cultural assumptions and ideological preferences about gender difference are challenged by some sectors of the feminist movement and by the realities of women working for pay, even if they remain predominant among both policymakers and other elites and the population at large. As gender difference enshrined in traditional conceptions of motherhood has been questioned in the wider society and undermined in practice, the model of motherhood institutionalized in programs that provide support to solo mothers has been challenged. This has resulted in various welfare reform efforts that are beginning to institutionalize a new model of motherhood—one closer to the citizen-worker or private employee reflected in employment-related policies—in the terms of state support for women's autonomous households. At best, this may signal new opportunities for women to combine waged work with caregiving labor; at worst, this may represent an undermining of material well-being and the conditions under which they provide care for children and others.

How are cultural assumptions and ideological preferences about gender institutionalized, then reproduced or challenged, in the realm of social policy? Is there significant cross-national and historical variation in the gender ideologies institutionalized in social policy? In this essay, I draw on my work on gender in the welfare states of four predominantly English-speaking countries, the United States, Canada, Australia, and Great Britain, which are often characterized as "liberal" policy regimes (O'Connor, Orloff, and Shaver 1999). All four share a liberal democratic political heritage and have experienced the resurgence of neoliberal political forces, particularly directed against welfare state spending and toward reinforcing "the whip of the market." Yet there are important differences in the gender ideologies and practices of the four, which are playing out in the course of reforms and cutbacks of their welfare systems, most notably in terms of whether mothers are to be subjected to market discipline and to what extent.

By examining the significant components of gender ideology—sameness/difference, equality/inequality, autonomy/dependency, and racial/ethnic differences in models of motherhood—and their articulation across dimensions of welfare states, I argue that we can specify the contours of that variation.

My project generally aims to uncover the mutually influential relationship between gender relations and systems of social provision. I focus on the ideological, discursive, and cultural aspects of this relationship as it is revealed in state support for women's capacities to form and maintain autonomous households. This dimension of the welfare state, like others, reflects the institutionalization of ideological premises and cultural assumptions about gender relations: the division of labor (gender differentiation), gender inequality, and relations of dependence, interdependence, or autonomy among women and men. I agree with Nancy Fraser (1996: 22; see also 1997) that culture and economy are "thoroughly imbricated with one another." Culture as much as political economy is necessary to understand welfare state programs: "Even our core economic practices have a constitutive, irreducible cultural dimension; shot through to the core with signification and norms, they affect not only the material well-being of social actors, but their identities and status as well." Social policy has symbolic significance in upholding or undermining the gender order. I assume as well that the state is critical to gender relations; ideological and cultural assumptions institutionalized in state programs shape gender and other social relations. As R. W. Connell (1987: 130) argues, "The state has a constitutive role in forming and re-forming social patterns. . . . In managing institutions and relations like marriage and motherhood the state is doing more than regulating them. It is playing a major part in the constitution of the social categories of the gender order . . . [and] the constitution of the interests at play in sexual politics."

Ideology, Culture, and Discourse in the Shaping of Social Provision

I begin with a discussion of how ideology, culture, and discourse have been conceptualized in the literature on welfare states, including the feminist strands of that literature, and where amendments to those conceptualizations are needed. During the period when pensions and social insurance were first being considered for adoption, participants in national and transnational debates analyzed certain characteristics of the new programs in terms of their relationship to national character. For example, the compulsory quality of social insurance contributions, a feature of the German system of social provision, was seen by many Britons and Americans as antithetical to the principles of liberal democracy and the national character of their peoples and as reflecting what they saw as the paternalism of German national political culture (Orloff 1993a: chap. 5). This view of social provision as shaped by national character or culture was also present in the early phases of our contemporary academic debates about the welfare state. In the 1960s and early 1970s, against the then-dominant consensus that welfare states were simply the more-or-less automatic result of economic development, a few analysts argued that national cultures influenced both the timing of individual countries' initiation of modern social protection and the character of programs adopted (see Orloff 1993a: chap. 2). Rimlinger's (1971) comparative study of the origins of welfare states, probably the most sophisticated of this genre, argued that the individualist liberalism of British and U.S. national culture slowed the development of modern welfare programs relative to Germany, the "pioneer" of modern welfare states, where elites could draw on statist, paternalist ideological, and cultural understandings to develop new social protections. Thus, early on there was a sense that ideologies and cultural understandings could facilitate certain types of action and policy while constraining others. Such analyses, however, assumed too much cultural and ideological uniformity within countries, and never considered the gendered components of ideologies and cultures.

Political economy–based explanations of differences among the rich capitalist countries took over the field in the 1970s. According to these analysts, there was no such thing as an undifferentiated national culture; rather, class-based political interests were expressed in different political demands, and policy reflected the demands of whichever group was in power. Thus, ideologies—meaning sets of beliefs and policy goals that reflected class interests—were implicated in policy development, and it was assumed that these were relatively invariant across national boundaries. Note that these analysts have utilized a "descriptive" rather than "critical" view of ideology, to use the terminology of Michele Barrett (1991): ideologies do not mystify social relations; rather, they simply *reflect* adherents' social position—ideology is not an autonomous causal factor. The focus was much more on organizational "power resources" of workers and capital, which did vary cross-nationally (Korpi 1978; Stephens 1979).

In the last decade or so, this view, too, has been challenged by the power resources camp itself, by feminists, and by institutionalist analyses. These newer trends—in contrast to the universalistic tendencies of political economy–based explanations—manifest a greater concern with nationally specific historical trajectories of policy development and/or with differences among citizens based on gender, race, and so on. Power resources analysts have investigated qualitatively differing policy regimes that are backed by distinctive class coalitions and shaped by their characteristic ideologies (see, for example, Esping-Andersen and Korpi 1987; Esping-Andersen 1990). Gone is the assumption that socialism or social-democratic organization is the "natural" outcome of working-class mobilization; rather, working classes may embrace various means of articulating their interests, including social Catholic doctrines (van Kersbergen 1995) as well as social democracy (note that these analysts assume that working classes will always be significant political actors).

Beginning in the 1970s, feminist historians and social scientists criticized dominant theoretical frameworks for ignoring gender in welfare states and challenged their assumptions of the universality of categories such as "citizen," "worker," and "class" and their focus on class conflict between workers' and employers' organizations (whose gendered character was analytically occluded).

They emphasized that common cultural assumptions and ideological preferences about gender—most often about the gender division of labor and women's economic dependency—have been embedded in all Western systems of social provision. At first, this followed radical functionalist lines—welfare states were upholding patriarchy along with capitalism (see, for example, McIntosh 1978). The male architects of the modern welfare states adhered to an *ideology* of separate spheres, gender difference, the family wage for men, and economic dependency as a condition for women's full-time mothering and domestic work—and institutionalized these precepts to the extent they could (Pascall 1986; Lewis and Piachaud 1992; Cass 1983; Kessler-Harris 1995). Recent work has given greater attention to women's activities as clients, reformers, and administrators of welfare programs, and to the contribution of their cultural assumptions and ideologies, and of the gendered discursive context more generally, to policy outcomes that vary over time and cross-nationally (see Orloff 1996). For example, American Progressive Era women reformers, touting full-time motherhood, opposed the expansion of child care services that would have allowed poor women, especially single mothers, to work for pay. Instead, they promoted mothers' pensions, which were supposed to allow mothers to stay at home, as the preferred policy for helping poor widows (Michel 1993).

Feminist work has made clear that nowhere have men and women been treated in equivalent ways; rather, cultural assumptions and ideological preferences about men's and women's distinctive roles and relationships were institutionalized in state policies. This was evidenced during the first part of the twentieth century, when mothers and married women were not usually subject to the same strictures of the work test, commodification, and proletarianization as were men because it was assumed they were occupied with childrearing and domestic work. (However, their sexual relations and housekeeping activities were policed.) Similarly, men, forced to sell their labor power and expected to earn a family wage and support a dependent wife and children, were not expected to be caregivers, nor, typically, were their intimate relations regulated (unless they departed from heterosexuality). Thus, state welfare systems reinforced women's private, unpaid responsibility for caregiving and domestic work, directly connected to women's economic dependency and a significant source of men's power (see, for example, Cass 1983; Sassoon 1987; Hobson 1990; Gordon 1988). Even in our now formally gender-neutral systems of social provision, feminist analysts have identified a "gender subtext" to welfare states and social citizenship in which expectations of men and women in regard to care work and paid work continue to differ, for example, as expressed in custody decisions (Fineman and Karpin 1995) and in which there are stark inequalities between men and women clients of the welfare state (for example, Fraser 1989; Gordon and Fraser 1994; on differing expectations, see, for example, Monson 1997).

Meanwhile, institutionalists have argued that social provision has been shaped not only by the "class balance of power" but by state administrative capacities and the strength and ideological perspectives of actors such as state bureaucrats and policy intellectuals. With greater attention to national and historical specificity, ideologies and cultural assumptions feature importantly in institutionalist accounts of social policy development—not as disembodied national cultures mysteriously shaping all political outcomes but as resources for and constraints on various political actors who operate within specific institutional and discursive contexts. Moreover, in a trend analogous to some strands of feminist analysis (for example, Pringle and Watson 1992; Jenson and Mahon 1993), institutionalists have eschewed attempts to discover the "real" or "objective" interests of classes or other groups to investigate how identities and interests are, or are not, politically constituted and linked over time. Thus, policy interests are not simply "given" in terms of social location but constituted in the course of politics, especially in reaction to existing policies—"policy feedback"—in which policymakers and others define problems and construct remedies in the context of earlier interventions (Weir, Orloff, and Skocpol 1988: 424). Institutionalists have assumed that these processes—along with distinctive political institutional configurations—may affect the salience of a number of potential political identities—class, racial/ethnic, national, religious, gender, and so on (for example, Skocpol and Ritter 1991; Sklar 1993; Katznelson 1981).

An institutionalist approach to ideology and culture focuses on how various beliefs, preferences, assumptions, and categories come to be embedded in social and political institutions, including specific policies, and how they play out in historically specific instances of political struggle. It is important to distinguish between culture and ideology. According to analysts from Weber to Geertz, culture, when not used in the most expansive sense of a community's "way of life," involves meaning. Griswold (1994: 11) defines culture as a community's "pattern of meanings, its enduring expressive aspects, its symbols that represent and guide the thinking, feeling and behavior of its members." National cultures may provide common vocabularies, symbolic elements, and assumptions from which political actors develop ideological arguments for particular purposes (Wuthnow 1987; Skocpol 1985). Wuthnow (1987: 145) sees ideologies as sets of ideas and symbols that "express or dramatize something about the moral order," including "definitions of the manner in which social relations should be constructed." (Again, this reflects the use of a descriptive conception of ideology.) Thus, ideologies inevitably are connected with struggles over and claims about power. They "are developed and deployed by particular groups or alliances engaged in temporally-specific political conflicts or attempts to justify the use of state power" (Skocpol 1985: 91). Cultures, by contrast, are not tied to specific groups and times. Cultural systems and the ideologies derived from them are implicated in the mobilization of political actors. As Wuthnow (1987) has suggested, ideology offers a way of dramatizing and maintaining the solidarity of groups mobilizing politically and identifies the sources of problems and solutions, suggesting a strategy for reform. If, as Therborn (1980) argues, ideologies are sets of beliefs about what is, what should be, and what is possible, they will be integral to different policy approaches to the welfare state, which has, for the last century, figured prominently in strategies to make "what is" come closer to "what should be" (greater equality, protection, and so on), as limited by what is considered possible. Thus, the recent political successes of various new right movements in the English-speaking countries have depended in part on constricting the range of what is considered possible by emphasizing state, rather than market, "failure." Similarly, to the extent that gender difference is naturalized through appeals to "selfish genes" or other biological mechanisms, it is difficult to mobilize support for policies that undermine such differences.

Ideologies, drawing on cultural systems, affect the scope and character of transformations attempted by political actors; the range of preferences, idioms, and other symbolic elements available within a given cultural system or discursive formation may structure ideological arguments and political debates in partially unintended ways, as is the case for any structure (Wuthnow 1987; Sewell 1985; Skocpol 1985). Yet ideologies—even of those elites involved in framing specific policies—do not operate in unmediated fashion to shape policy choices. Ideologies are never simply "blueprints" for action; given that complex political outcomes, like systems of social provision, result from the actions of many, we would be hard pressed to name a specific outcome that resulted from the ideology of a single group or individual, no matter how succinct and coherent its formulation. Rather, ideologies are produced and affect historically specific political, social, and discursive contexts.

How do we specify the discursive context? Jenson and Mahon (1993: 79) suggest using the concept of a "universe of political discourse," which "encodes an accepted set of meanings about who the legitimate actors are, the place they hold in politics, the appropriate sites of political struggle and the form social relations ought to take." For example, women were not initially considered legitimate actors in debates about social policy, and gender relations within families were not legitimate objects of intervention; women reformers had to challenge their exclusion from policy discussions, and they were often able to open at least some aspects of family relations to political intervention (see, for example, Gordon 1988 and Skocpol 1992). While many doubt the possibility of reconciling the concepts of ideology and discourse, given their disparate sources (e.g., Barrett 1991), it seems that both notions, or some approximations thereof, are needed (see also Purvis and Hunt 1993). Within specific discourses, competing ideological orientations and the cultural idioms and symbols on which they draw are developed by political actors in reactions to existing policy, political coalitions and enmities, and political and administrative institutions. Thus, discourses reflect what can be thought or imagined, in part reflecting our cultural assumptions; this use of the term *discourse* may then have a certain resemblance to the Gramscian concept of hegemony. Discourses also reflect what is likely to be thought, as prior ideological choices and reactions to existing policies—as well as the alliances and capacities these put in place—narrow the range of what are understood to be practical or feasible policy options. But within discursive contexts, different actors mobilize around different ideologies. To summarize, I argue that ideologies should be understood as resources for and constraints on collective action and state policy; cultural assumptions and discursive structures are elements of the political and institutional context within which the whole range of political activities occur. Different types of welfare states are in part the institutional expressions of different mixes of ideologies.

How does this view about the influence of culture, discourse, and ideology mesh with views about state autonomy? As Steinmetz notes in the introduction to this book, to the extent that one analyzes decision making in state organizations, the ideologies of those elites who participate in the actual drafting of laws, programs, and administrative regulations are going to matter, although they will be constrained by political, institutional, and economic factors as well as by cultural assumptions and discursive structures. Some analysts seem to have interpreted the claim of institutionalists that there is a *potential* for state autonomy to imply a denial of this last point, that is, a claim of state autonomy would mean that state elites are free from *any* influences outside the state, cultural or otherwise. State autonomy is always *relative* to specific social groups, although this does not necessarily imply that there are particular, known limits on what they can do (that, I argue, is a function of their specific relations with any given group and their various *capacities*). Rather, state autonomy refers to the independent formulation of views, interests, and goals by state actors—independent in the sense of not being determined by the views, interests, and goals of other social groups. This independence is different from the idea of not being formulated within the same overall cultural, political, and institutional context within which other actors operate—one of the points of institutional analysis is to highlight the ways in which different locations within those contexts shape distinctive viewpoints, interests, and goals.

Gender Ideologies in the Development of Welfare States

What are the substantive components of gender ideologies and cultural assumptions affecting social policies? To date, discussion of variation in the gendered ideologies or discourses has focused especially on the issue of whether women's—actually, mothers'—paid work is accepted and supported; this is then a question about how biological and social reproduction is articulated with the gender division of labor. Contemporary comparative analyses show that women's paid work is far more accepted and even promoted in Scandinavia and France than it has been in central and southern Europe (for example, Hernes 1987; Borchorst 1994; Ruggie 1984; Leira 1992; Roberts 1995; Jenson 1986). In Ireland, the Netherlands, Spain, Germany, Switzerland, and Austria, social provision has been shaped by social Catholicism and Christian Democratic parties, with their valorization of gender difference, full-time mothering rather than wage work for women, and family solidarity—implying women's economic dependency, but not (openly) gendered inequality of resources (Jackson 1993; Knijn 1994; Bussemaker and van Kersbergen 1994; Cousins 1995; Schmidt 1993; Ostner 1993).

Some understand the variable levels of support for women's paid labor as a by-product of larger institutional patterns of state-society relations, which in turn partly reflect ideological preferences about the role of the state (for example, liberalism versus statism or social democracy). Thus, political support for women's entrance to the labor force is linked to social-democratic policy and ideology, and most important the willingness to use governmental means to alter market outcomes and a generally egalitarian orientation (that is, social-democratic economic egalitarianism is understood to be unproblematic with respect to gender). A number of studies contrasting Scandinavian countries such as Sweden and Denmark with English-speaking, liberal countries such as the United States and Britain find that overall relationships between states and societies—determined by the character of governing coalitions—affected whether states provided services to alleviate women's domestic care burdens and thus facilitate their labor-force participation (see, for example, Siim 1990; Ruggie 1984; Esping-Andersen 1990). Most mainstream accounts of these relationships stress the importance of public versus private provision, but, unlike feminists, have not noted the role of families in the provision of welfare. Provision of welfare "services" everywhere has a large private and familial component, usually in the form of women's unpaid labor (Land 1983; Waerness 1984; Taylor-Gooby 1991). Yet analysts usually fail to note cross-national differences among countries with similar levels of reliance on "private" provision (for example, the liberal countries) in the relative roles of different private institutions: markets, voluntary or charity organizations, and families.

While general views about state intervention are implicated in the support given to women's paid work, one must also consider political actors' specifically gendered ideologies about motherhood and women's paid work. Many assume that women's political movements will be important—and certainly the different visions of gender equality held by different women's groups do influence outcomes—but it is essential to assess the gendered ideologies of *all* actors. Jenson (1986) and Pedersen (1993) compared British and French policy for the support of children and social reproduction in the first part of the twentieth century. Policy debates were situated within an international context that encouraged concerns about population, declining birthrates, and high rates of infant mortality, yet these "problems" were solved in dissimilar ways because of differences in discourses about motherhood and paid work, as well as in the capacities and gendered interests of organized workers, employers, and state elites and in the levels of demand for female labor.[1] France emerged from World War II with less

[1] Women wanted recognition as mothers or as equally paid and equal workers. British and French trade unionists—mainly men—defended a "family wage" and preferred that their wives be kept out of the labor market. Employers in both countries appreciated cheap female labor and saw merit in using family allowances to restrain men's wages. British unions had the capacity to keep most married women out of paid work and to block such use of family allowances. French employers had the capacity to block measures preventing married women's work and acceded to state-mandated allowances that promoted wage restraint while aiding families with children. Pedersen (1993) argues that in France, family allowances, carried into the policy debates by conservative and religious forces, were associated with pronatalism and national reconstruction and thus were attractive to employers looking to justify their economically motivated commitment to such programs. In Britain, fem-

institutionalized support for a male breadwinner wage than did Britain, where strong male-dominated unions succeeded in making it central to social provision; the French "parental welfare state," though initiated under patriarchal auspices, offers relatively generous support for two-earner families and children's welfare. Such ideologies can also vary among countries with similar levels of state intervention. For example, Leira (1992) argues that differing "models of motherhood" are associated with significant variation in the level of public child-care provision and women's labor-force participation among the Scandinavian countries; Denmark and Sweden offer greater support for combining motherhood with paid work, particularly for mothers of very young children, than does Norway. What I call the "social organization of welfare"—the ways countries organize the provision of cash and care through families, states, voluntary organizations, and markets (Orloff 1993b)—reflects, then, not only ideologies about the role of the state, but also cultural assumptions about gender difference, most important women's responsibility for caregiving work.

Among feminists, there has been disagreement about the extent to which women's economic dependency, lack of autonomy, and inequality are linked to the gender division of labor, including how it is reinforced by welfare states. Recent historical work on policy developments in the early years of the twentieth century in the English-speaking countries shows that these facets of gender relations are not always linked in ideology or in policy. Women reformers—like their male counterparts—almost all shared the view that the gendered division of labor was both natural and good, and supported the development of gender-specific legislation and programs. This did not, however, necessarily imply agreement about other aspects of gender relations, particularly the family wage for men and women's economic dependency, or the idea that women should not participate in the public sphere. In fact, women did enter the political sphere— indeed, they entered it largely on the basis of "difference," claiming that their work as mothers gave them unique capacities for developing state policies that would safeguard mothers and children (Skocpol 1992; Sklar 1993; Koven and Michel 1993; Lake 1992). These perspectives, recently called "maternalism," may be defined as "ideologies and discourses which exalted women's capacity to mother and applied to society as a whole the values they attached to that role: care, nurturance and morality" (Koven and Michel 1993: 4; see also Bock and

---

inists, the initial promoters of motherhood endowment (an independent state-supplied income for mothers) and then family allowances, associated such programs with women's emancipation; moreover, they argued that ending family wages would undercut gender discrimination in pay. These gendered connotations stimulated unionists' opposition; they accepted family allowances after they were scaled back and thus were less effective in terms of their potential to reduce wages. The lack of policy input from French feminists reflected their weakness, while British women's superior organization enabled them to open up questions of family dependency although they were not strong enough to enact their preferred policies. French women could work and were supported as mothers, but, not having the right to vote and legally subjugated to their husbands, were hardly emancipated.

Thane 1991; Skocpol 1992; Gordon 1994).[2] Thus, maternalist reformers' claims on the state were for a kind of "equality in difference," and constituted a challenge to patriarchal ideologies and practices that linked women's "difference" to their inequality and their exclusion from politics. In essence, women reformers took part in the discourse of gender difference but attempted to rearticulate gender difference to equal citizenship claims (with limited success).

The maternalist ideological orientation contrasts with the views of many second-wave feminists, especially those critical of welfare programs for promoting the traditional gender division of labor, and who made claims on the basis of "sameness" rather than "difference." Yet some of the maternalists—particularly those in Britain and Australia—shared with contemporary women activists a radical orientation toward women's autonomy. They challenged the family wage as the basis of support for mothering and called for state financial support of the motherwork of all women, or the "endowment of motherhood" (Pedersen 1993). This would have decreased women's economic dependency, thereby challenging a principal source of male power, an effect clearly understood by its proponents and detractors (see, for example, Lake 1992). State support for mothers was seen to recognize the socially valuable work of mothering, even if women had no access to a male breadwinner's wage—their mothering was understood as a service to the state parallel to men's soldiering or industrial work (Skocpol 1992; Orloff 1991; Ladd-Taylor 1994).

In the end, most states gave income support only to mothers without husbands (most often widows), blunting but not entirely eliminating the "independence effect" of such benefits. Yet women's heading households under any circumstances was a radical break with ideas of their inevitable dependency on men (sons, sons-in-law, or brothers if not fathers and husbands), as well as an important policy departure: Under the particularly harsh version of poor relief obtaining in England, the United States, and other countries in the late nineteenth

---

[2] Koven and Michel (1993) emphasize the ambiguous and competing meanings and uses of maternalist ideas. By their definition, maternalist thinking encompassed pronatalists who were more concerned with population increase than women's subordination, women who accepted the ideal of a family wage for men as the source of support for mothers, and feminists who called for the motherhood endowment. Other historians (for example, Ladd-Taylor 1994: 5) have preferred a more restricted definition that contrasts maternalism to feminism, particularly in terms of their positions on the desirability of the family wage and women's economic dependence (maternalists supported them; feminists opposed them). I agree with Ladd-Taylor that it is useful to distinguish among different gender ideologies, even if all operated within a common—in this case, maternalist—discursive framework. And however we classify maternalisms, scholars do not agree on their impact. While maternalism may have provided an ideological resource for reformers and their middle-class followers, some argue that it became a constraint on the choices of welfare clients when maternalist ideals were institutionalized in social programs. Mothers' pensions, which reformers had hoped would work to allow widowed mothers to remain at home caring for their children, were never implemented as reformers intended, suffering from inadequate funding and underdeveloped administrative capacities; many poor single mothers had to work to supplement their pensions, but could do only certain jobs (often work in the home) due to lack of child care services and the requirements of the pensions themselves (Orloff 1991; Goodwin 1992).

century, unmarried (that is, widowed, deserted, or never-married) women who were not taken in by kin usually had to give up their children to orphanages (given that women's wages at the time were not sufficient to support children) (Orloff 1991, 1993a: chap. 4; Vandepol 1982). Later calls for family allowances built on these understandings; feminists such as England's Eleanor Rathbone contended that family allowances would undermine the justification for men's family wages and wage discrimination against women—with children supported at least partially by the state, men and women workers could be treated more equally in the workplace (Pedersen 1993). Family allowances paid to women could alleviate their economic dependency at least to a limited extent. These issues continue to influence the politics of supporting families; some countries offer support for children through the wage packets of mainly male workers, bolstering the position of male breadwinners, whereas others channel children's support through their mothers, on the grounds of women's claim to an independent income (albeit a small one) and the efficacy of assisting children (Wennemo 1994).

Examining the debates over mothers' and family allowances makes clear that policymakers and other political actors considered the question of who was paid state benefits an important one, precisely because it had implications for women's economic dependency and men's capacities to support families and their "independence." Thus, these issues may be linked with recent discussions of "social citizenship rights," or institutionalized claims on the state for support that affect the relative balance of power across a range of social relationships, including class and gender. Analysts have distinguished among various types of such claims. Power resources analysts focus on rights relative to the market. Decommodification, according to Esping-Andersen (1990), is at the core of a social-democratic vision of the state's emancipatory potential, "rolling back the frontiers of capitalism"; decommodification "protects individuals, irrespective of gender, from total dependence on the labor market for survival. . . . [a] protection from forced participation, irrespective of age, health conditions, family status, availability of suitable employment, [that] is obviously of major importance to both men and women" (O'Connor 1993: 513). In my earlier work (Orloff 1993b), I argued that several other rights are also relevant for gender relations. Access to paid work refers to citizens' right to employment—the dominant mode of securing citizenship rights, economic independence, and political capacities, and thus of concern to feminist analysts as well, given that women have traditionally been denied full access to work and full citizenship (see, for example, Pateman 1988). The capacity to form and maintain an autonomous household identifies rights relative to family and household formation. Having the capacity to form a household without depending on the economic support of anyone else increases one's range of choice and enhances leverage within families or partnerships. Addressing a *capacity* to form an autonomous household does not indicate a preference for separation or a denial of interdependencies. Rather, it indicates a belief that equality and freedom of choice—including a choice to partner—require an absence of coercion, including the kind imposed for years on women to marry because of their own dismal economic prospects. Such autonomy is the embodiment of liberal individualism as extended to women and has been a central aspiration of women's movements in the four liberal welfare states. Just as it is important to consider both access to employment and one's level of dependence on paid labor, it makes sense to consider the right to have a family (Saraceno 1994) along with capacities to exit from family relationships. This right refers to who is allowed to have families, thus including some of the legal and policy issues around the heading of households, child custody, and sexuality; this issue is particularly important when considering support for families of different ethnic, racial, and nationality groups.

Notions about imagined communities of race, ethnicity, and nationality have also shaped policies for the support of mothers, parents, and children. In the United States, Australia, and Canada, maternalist programs—mothers' pensions, maternal health programs, and the like—were not consistently accessible to African Americans, other women of color, and aboriginal women (Bellingham and Mathis 1994; Lieberman 1995; Goodwin 1992; Gordon 1994; Roberts 1993; Boris 1995; Lake 1992, 1994; Little 1994). For example, legal frameworks determining who shall have the right to a family often incorporate race- or ethnicity-specific standards, as when Australian, Canadian, and American officials deemed the culturally specific family and household practices of indigenous peoples as prima facie evidence of "unfitness" and grounds for the removal of children from their parents (see, for example, Kline 1995; Burney 1994; Broome 1982; Shaver 1989). The motherhood (and infant life) to be supported was bounded in racial and ethnic terms, although there is disagreement about the extent to which this reflected the ideologies and interests of maternalist reformers or was simply a reflection of the power of racist forces in these states. In Europe, nationalism undoubtedly contributed to policies that gave support to women's reproductive activities (Bock and Thane 1991). And certainly, class constraints on support also have been common. Clearly the value to elites of the children of the poor, of the working classes, or of different populations must be considered when investigating support given to the mothers raising them.

The amount of support given to citizens and in what social roles they are supported—mothers, fathers, parents, members of specific nations or races, workers, citizens, poor people—is both symbolically and materially significant; I call this dimension *stratification*. Systems of state social provision, through the structure and character of social programs and the process of making claims on the state, shape social identities. They also undermine, reinforce, or alter patterns of social inequality via access to valued resources—including gender inequality reflected in the treatment of men versus women and of paid versus unpaid labor (for example, Hernes 1987; Fraser 1989). In turn, these processes affect political interests and alliances constituted in the context of existing policies.

I suggest that across these various elements of the welfare state we can distinguish at least four separate components of variation in ideologies and cultural assumptions about gender relations, the division of labor, motherhood, fatherhood, women's paid labor, and social policy:

1. *Sameness/differentiation*: the value attached to gender difference (that is, the gender division of labor), reflected in women's access—or lack of it—to paid work and related public supports (for example, day care) and in premises about women's activities, especially as mothers, as reflected in income maintenance programs; premises about men's activities, too, reflect this value, but generally are taken for granted

2. *Equality/inequality*: the position taken on women's inequality (that is, unequal treatment in terms of access to valued resources)

3. *Autonomy/dependency*: the choice made between women's economic dependence on men and their subordination to male authority, or women's decisional autonomy and their capacity to form autonomous households, the latter implying that women would have a choice as to which family, household, or marital arrangements to enter

4. *Which mothers (parents) are to be supported*: supports available to mothers or parents, offered to everyone or only to certain groups, defined on the basis of race, ethnicity, religion, class, or other categories

These components are articulated differently in different "models of motherhood"—full-time stay-at-home mothering, either supported by husbands or the state; mothering combined with paid work, implying a measure of economic independence for women but perhaps not much change in the overall division of labor; or a fully egalitarian vision of motherhood and fatherhood that implies equal involvement in caregiving and economic provision. Of course, different models may be applied to different groups. While a certain model may be institutionalized in any given state's policies, it is possible that more than one will be embedded in the state, perhaps in various policy arenas. And it is useful to emphasize that although some of these differences are between feminists and those defending the traditional gender order, feminists disagree in their visions of gender equality and the associated ideologies of motherhood as, for example, in Fraser's (1997: chap. 2) distinction between equality based on a "universal breadwinner" model and equality based on "caregiver parity" (and her own preferred alternative, "universal caregiver").

I use the cases of state support for the household autonomy of women in the United States, Britain, Canada, and Australia to illustrate how the different components of gender ideologies are reflected in the terms of support. (This material is drawn from *States, Markets, Families: Gender, Liberalism, and Social Policy in Australia, Canada, Great Britain, and the United States*, O'Connor, Orloff, and Shaver, 1999.) Does the state promote women's autonomy? How do such households sustain themselves: through state support of women's full-time caregiving or through employment with state-provided services and/or employment equity provisions? Access to paid work and to the services that facilitate employment for caregivers has been one of the dominant demands of women's movements vis-à-vis the welfare state, but it is not the only route for women to achieve independence from male breadwinners. Women have also pursued the equivalent of a citizen's wage for mothering (for example, motherhood endowments).

Some regimes have promoted women's employment through varying combinations of child-care services, wage subsidies, or improved-access policies (for example, affirmative action or employment equity); other regimes have offered support for solo mothers to stay at home to care for their children. (Policy may vary for different groups of women.) Finally, it is important to examine *who* is to be supported—are all mothers or parents to be supported, or are there racial, ethnic or other exclusions? I hope to establish that gendered ideologies are institutionalized in the social policies of these countries, that they have changed over time, and that they differ across the four countries.

I selected four liberal regimes (classified in terms of institutional characteristics) for comparison—a "most-similar nations" strategy (Lijphart 1975)—to highlight specifically gendered dimensions of state provision. Given the increasing importance of the liberal model (for example, in the European Union), it is also important to understand the relationship between liberalism(s) and gender relations, including gender ideologies and policies. The liberal countries share certain key institutional features that are significant for gender relations. The emphasis on private sources of welfare has left women more vulnerable to poverty than in countries where more universalistic social provision offers citizens at least some protections without regard for labor market participation (including those who fare least well in the market). But they do differ in terms of the ways in which women's households are supported, reflecting (among other things) significant variations in state-institutionalized gender ideologies.

The Policy Legacy

From their origins in the first part of the twentieth century through the 1960s and 1970s, welfare states in these four countries institutionalized the gender division of labor, underlined distinctive gender identities, and thereby helped to shape gender interests. Most reform, women's, and working-class organizations in Britain, the United States, Canada, and Australia accepted the goals of a family wage for men and stay-at-home, full-time motherhood for women, although at first this was limited in practice to members of the dominant racial/ethnic groups, reflecting also the ideological preferences of many reformers and administrators. Income security systems were marked by a paid work/family dualism, and inequality in the benefits available to wage-earners and caregivers was the concomitant of gender-differentiated programs, whether the explicit aim of policy or not. As in other parts of the West, maternalist discourses were important among women reformers in all four countries, but the radical notion of "motherhood endowments" (although never embraced by the majority of reformers) was discussed to a relatively greater extent—perhaps reflecting the political potential of individualist liberalism. These states offered support to some women's autonomous households. Widows—single mothers through no choice of their own—received support that allowed them to keep their children and to forgo full-time waged work; they were not forced to depend on other family members through subsidiarity, which requires reliance on kin before state support will be given, as was the policy in most European countries during the same time period. (It has been the fundamental inequality of such programs compared with labor-market related programs that has preoccupied contemporary feminist commentary, not the support to women's autonomy.) However, women of color in the United States were often expected to obtain paid work (Glenn 1994). And the cultural specificity of motherhood models meant that some women of color—particularly indigenous women in the United States, Canada, and Australia—as well as women who defied conventional sexual morality ("unwed mothers") would be declared "unfit" mothers and therefore ineligible for income support. Thus, state-institutionalized gender ideology articulated difference, inequality, and dependence, but a limited independence for white women was also a part of modern state social provision in these countries from the beginning. Women of color were to support themselves, yet this was still associated with inequality and difference.

The right to benefits that enabled a woman to form and maintain an autonomous household without working for pay—that is, to be a full-time mother—expanded from widowed women of the dominant racial group to almost all women over the course of the twentieth century, as de jure exclusions (for example, of Native women) and de facto discrimination have been challenged; moral criteria (for example, excluding unwed mothers) and residence requirements, too, have been abolished. Thus, women of color gained access to benefits allowing them to stay at home caring for children only in the 1960s and 1970s.

In the 1960s and 1970s, these four countries experienced fundamental shifts in gender relations in the polity, the family, and the workplace involving women's work, control of sexuality, and reproduction. Policy debates about public child care and parental leaves featured conflict among proponents of different motherhood models, with the first explicit, mass-based challenge to dominant cultural and ideological assumptions about motherhood. The four liberal countries were not alone in this, although the responses to these challenges differed cross-nationally. In Sweden and Denmark, policy was aimed at encouraging women to enter the labor force as public day care services and allied programs were initiated and expanded under social-democratic auspices, fueled by a new model of mothers as workers and caregivers. Even fatherhood models changed slightly, as men began to be encouraged to take on limited caregiving responsibilities albeit less strenuously than women are encouraged to work for pay.) By contrast, some continental European countries explicitly endorsed "traditional" models of motherhood, to be supported by generous state subsidies or through the principle of subsidiarity.

In the four liberal countries, most attention around women's rights focused on opening up women's employment opportunities by challenging discrimination in the workplace (and, in North America, by establishing reproductive rights [Shaver 1993], justified in part by the need to be able to compete equally in the workforce). Thus, the challenge to women's inequality and dependency was linked to undermining gender difference in women's responsibility for full-time, unpaid caregiving and domestic work. There have been only limited government efforts along Scandinavian lines to shift some of women's "private" domestic burden through public provision of services (although more in Canada and Australia than in the United States and Britain). Yet women in all four liberal countries have entered the labor force in increasing numbers, lured by new employment opportunities and by the fact that public and private benefits of so many kinds remain tied to employment, and impelled by declining male wages or loss of access to male wages as a result of marital breakdown and the constriction of state benefits. Increased labor force participation and employment-equity policies have also produced gains for the material well-being of some women (wage gaps have narrowed, occupational sex segregation has lessened, and women have moved into some positions of authority) (Reskin and Padavic 1994). Rising levels of paid work among women has also been associated with rising rates of single parenthood, divorce, and nontraditional living arrangements as well as with shifting responsibilities within heterosexual relationships (Gerson 1995). These trends are most notable in the United States, where individualism, preference for provision through the market, and a workplace-oriented feminism have been strongest.

These changes have created a situation in which both men and women are supposed to rely on the market, representing a greater degree of official endorsement of gender "sameness." Men's individual autonomy and capacity to support families in all four countries has from the initiation of modern state welfare been based principally on paid work or employment-based benefits such as occupational pensions, reinforced by state social provision such as unemployment benefits when employment is not possible. With existing gendered patterns of work, even as "good jobs" decline in number, men have far greater access both to favored employment opportunities and to the state benefits that act as a backup to the market. Yet it is worth noting both that some women have now gained access to work-based sources of support and related state programs and that not all men have access to them; labor-market standing is the key criterion.

Significant efforts were made to remove gender discrimination from social policy in the 1960s and 1970s and almost all social programs are now formally gender-neutral. Where provision in earlier periods was explicitly premised on the ideal and material reality of gender differentiation in roles, legislation and court decisions shifted social provision toward formal gender neutrality, as when the Australian sole parents' pension was made available to men for the first time in 1977 (Shaver 1993: 8), Britain discontinued the "married woman's option" under National Insurance in 1975 (Pascall 1986: 208), and most discriminatory provisions were eliminated from U.S. Social Security programs (Burkhauser and Holden 1982: 7–13).

I contend that this set of changes has helped open to women a formally gender-neutral identity of citizen-worker, what Fraser (1997: chap. 2) calls a "universal breadwinner" model, though one with strong associations with the traditionally male pattern of work; this identity provides competition for older models of motherhood. Access to this status depends on success in the market. Given that social and workplace arrangements still make women the most likely caregivers of children and others, most women's capacity to compete in the workforce remains constrained. But the expansion of opportunities for women has made it possible for those with the best education or training to do relatively well (by international standards) in the labor market, and, for the most advantaged, to use resources garnered there to pay for services. Thus, class differences among women may be reflected in different gendered political identities—citizen-worker versus citizen-mother (stay-at-home or part-time worker).

Despite these important shifts, however, a "gender subtext" of these countries' welfare states remains, reflecting the persistence of the gender division of labor and household forms that support it. Paid work is a key source of women's (including single mothers') independence and enhanced leverage within households; this is especially noticeable in North America, where women's patterns of labor-force participation (in terms of full-time versus part-time work and over the life course) are converging on men's. Yet among most married couples, even when women do work for pay, men contribute disproportionately to family income and women contribute disproportionately to family domestic labor (although both the proportion of housewives and the overall level of dependency are declining) (Hobson 1990, 1994). Even outside marriage, women tend to do more caregiving and domestic labor than do similarly situated men. The gendered dualism and symbolism of the welfare state also persists—programs still cater principally either to labor market or to family "failures," and the clientele of the respective programs remains predominantly male and female, respectively. (With the exception of Australia's, labor-market related programs are in most respects superior to family-related programs.) The vast majority of men make their claims for state assistance on the basis of their labor-market participation; only a minuscule number make claims based on their family status (that is, as spouses or single parents). While a minority of women have moved into "male" labor-market programs, the majority of women make claims on the basis of their marital ties to wage-earning men, as dependents or survivors (note that in the case of survivors, this amounts to support for women's household autonomy). Other women—those outside marriage—make claims as mothers. Sole parents' benefits—income-tested assistance for unmarried, divorced, or deserted parents—have given (non-aged) women with children a way to make claims on the state as individuals, thus freeing them from total dependence on men without being forced to have recourse to the market. In Canada, Britain, and Australia, a single mother can maintain a household without access to support from a male wage-earner and without working for pay. Eligibility requirements differ to some extent across the three countries, but basically, one must be very poor (income and work tests are stringent, to the extent of making most parents who work for pay ineligible); benefits continue until children reach adulthood (assuming the other criteria are met). This was true in the United States until 1996; assistance is now conditioned on working outside the home.

Clearly, these states continue to institutionalize ideologies of gender differ- ence even as gender sameness is increasingly supported. The model of mother- hood institutionalized in sole parents' programs in Australia, Britain, and most Canadian provinces—and until recently in the United States—is a full-time, stay-at-home mother who as a condition of program eligibility eschews paid work. This model reflects less and less the practices of women who are not rely- ing on state provision, and also is incongruent with the employment regime emerging in the post-Keynesian era, with the greater push for an "active soci- ety" (as the Organization for Economic Cooperation and Development terms it) and increasing pressures to restrict eligibility within the welfare system as working-class wages stagnate or fall. In this context, it is worth noting the com- patibility of women's waged work with many claims based on *spousal* status, the majority of which are for the elderly—having worked for pay, even if insufficient to bring work-based benefits, does not undermine one's entitlement to spousal benefits in old-age insurance.

Contemporary Welfare Debates, Gender Ideologies, and Policy Legacies

Contemporary politics increasingly features contestation of male dominance and the emergence of counterhegemonic ideologies, most important a variety of feminisms, along with fundamentalisms that call for a strengthening of or return to traditional patterns—and all these ideologies feature in policy debates about welfare "reform." Most political concern focuses on the social rights of work- ing-aged mothers who have in some sense chosen to be outside of marriage, that is, divorced or never-married mothers; in these cases, ideological contesta- tion around gender difference/sameness—whether women should be worker/ mothers or full-time mothers—and the extent to which women in these roles should be supported by the state—around dependency/autonomy—is very pronounced.[3]

These ideological issues are reflected in policy debates about whether single mothers can claim state support and avoid the strictures of the market: Should states support single mothers who are not working for pay? Conservatives are distressed by the costs of welfare and the flaunting of traditional morality—the fact of single mothers' autonomy—and propose reforms that make it harder to establish and maintain such households. Liberals, too, worry over costs, but, es- pecially in North America, are more likely to see the problem as one of treating

[3] Survivors' benefits in the social insurance systems of the United States, Britain, and Canada pro- vide widows with young children a non-means tested, relatively generous entitlement; this is politi- cally uncontested.

women receiving state support differently from other citizens, including other mothers. Most feminists agree that women's autonomy ought to be given state support and along with social-democratic forces are concerned about the level of poverty among women welfare recipients and their status relative to male beneficiaries of the welfare state (that is, gender inequality). But views among feminists and others sympathetic to the welfare-state project diverge about gender difference as it relates to paid and unpaid work. Some criticize policy-created "poverty traps" and lack of support services that prevent women from undertaking employment, but others put more emphasis on defending women's right to support for full-time caregiving or their right to choose whether to work in the home or for pay (for example, Mink 1995; Mandell 1995).

Modern sole-parent benefits were established with the aim of allowing white single mothers to pursue the distinctive, noncommodified life pattern deemed appropriate for white mothers. In the post–World War II period, public provision construed all single mothers as unemployable, full-time, stay-at-home mothers rather than as potential workers. This is being challenged ideologically and eroded in practice to some extent in all four countries. All of them have developed or are attempting to develop incentives for solo mothers to take paid work, such as wage supplements, subsidized services, and the like, along with disincentives for staying on public support. Yet there are some significant differences among the four, notably that the United States has moved away from giving any sort of support to poor women's full-time mothering, while the others continue to offer such support, albeit in modified form and manifesting differing levels of feminist influence.

Britain retains the most support for gender difference, even in a policy climate marked by increasing residualism and celebration of the market. The Thatcherite attack on the welfare state has pushed for greater reliance on private sources of support—and interestingly, collecting child support from fathers has featured more prominently than encouraging the labor-market participation of women on Income Support (the social assistance program that supports single mothers, the long-term unemployed, and other groups). While budget-cutters in the United States also have embarked on programs of enhanced child support collection, this has been pursued less strenuously than have efforts to force women into the labor market. Given the huge pool of unemployed male workers drawing on public support, this was not the highest priority of the Conservative government, which also professed concern for "the family," meaning the traditional gender division of labor. Strengthening child support enforcement allows for cuts in social assistance spending for single-mother families while not upsetting the traditional gender roles of men supporting their families financially and women being caregivers (see, for example, Jeffries 1996). The New Labour administration of Tony Blair uses less family values rhetoric and professes admiration for some of the Clinton administration's welfare reforms. Blair has called for greater efforts to move those on social assistance, including single mothers, into paid employment (*New York Times*, June 3, 1997, A3); yet there is little indication that Blair intends to remove entitlement to assistance or to make paid work or work activities a requirement for solo mothers to obtain public benefits.

Australia presents an important variation on the model of supporting difference in the context of a relatively strong public safety net. Mothers—and parents generally—get more public support than their U.S. counterparts, reflecting a pronatalist legacy and recent Labour commitments to reducing child poverty. As in Britain, solo mothers in particular can claim a longer period for staying at home with their children than can Americans. But the system no longer provides for the traditional woman's pattern of full-time caregiving and housewifery with the safety net of a widow's pension, which supported women whose children had left home but who were too young for old-age pensions (Shaver 1993). Australia is now pursuing a policy of encouraging sole parent pensioners to enter the labor force while their children are young and requiring work after children reach age sixteen (when entitlement for the pension ends, forcing parents to work or move to unemployment programs) (Cass 1994). This support for mothers in Australia until the election of a conservative government in 1996 was combined with relatively stronger antidiscrimination and affirmative action efforts in the employment sphere than in Britain. Whether these will be continued under the conservative Coalition government elected in 1996 remains to be seen; however, the Coalition's first attempt to impose work requirements on social assistance recipients has focused on young people without children.

The changes under way in Canada until the 1990s seemed fairly similar to those in Australia; that is, there were moves to encourage paid work among mothers receiving assistance. Solo mothers are inconsistently required to be workers—some provinces are like the United States in imposing strict work requirements on assistance beneficiaries, others do not (Evans 1992). Whatever the extent of formal requirements, Canadian policy in practice has been less draconian in forcing the commodification of women's labor, and work-for-welfare schemes ("workfare") were forbidden under the terms of the Canadian Assistance Program. In 1995, however, CAP was eliminated and replaced by the Canada Health and Social Transfer, a block grant to provinces to run their own welfare programs. This eliminated the guarantee of social assistance to any needy Canadian (Battle 1997) and allows provinces to institute tougher work requirements and workfare (Schragge 1997). Election victories by conservatives such as Premier Mike Harris in Ontario promise to change the policy direction that had obtained under CAP; indeed, Harris immediately cut benefit levels and imposed stronger work requirements but, interestingly from the point of view of ideologies about gender and caregiving, retained an exemption for mothers of young children (Lightman 1997).

Of the four countries the logic of U.S. social policy is based most strongly on gender sameness, with women, including mothers, to be treated principally as workers. Moreover, this is a sameness that largely ignores the issue of caregiving, which is understood principally as a barrier to labor-market participation. Even before recent changes, U.S. social assistance programs allowed the shortest period of support for full-time mothering of the four countries (three years, with states allowed to impose work requirements on mothers of children as young as one year old). In August 1996, welfare reform legislation was passed that ended Aid to Families with Dependent Children (AFDC), the federal program that had since 1935 given very poor single parents and their children an entitlement to assistance. In its place, the federal government gives block grants to states, which design and run their own welfare programs with almost no federal regulation or oversight. One federal mandate does stand out: there is to be a lifetime limit of five years on social assistance and a two-year limit for any given spell of welfare. Motherhood—after a maternity leave of twelve weeks—will no longer bring an exemption from commodification. Single mothers or other caretakers receiving welfare are required to enter the paid labor force or undertake work in exchange for welfare benefits, whatever the age or health of their children and without regard to the availability of quality child care or jobs. Here it seems a new gender ideology is at work—one that demands formal gender equality in the treatment of welfare clients in terms of requirements to work for pay (gender sameness). Yet this occludes remaining differences between men and women in terms of responsibilities for caregiving and access to jobs and simply assumes caregiving is not problematic (see, for example, White 1996). Autonomy is to be open only to those who work for pay. Of course, this is also the source of the attraction of employment, bringing out starkly the class differences among American women.

Welfare reforms—meaning increasing restrictions and work requirements, occasionally with enhanced child care services or training, or abolishing AFDC— have been politically popular proposals, backed by both Democrats and Republicans. Two main paths for reform were, and to some extent still are, in play, yet both are premised on the idea that mothers, even of very young children, should work for pay. Both operated within the dominant policy discourse, which valorizes paid work above caregiving and which pushes everyone toward a model of citizenship based on paid work. Here, a greater degree of gender sameness is seen as necessary for women to claim equal treatment and autonomy.

Democrat-sponsored reforms, most memorably put forward in then-candidate Bill Clinton's promise to "end welfare as we know it," would have required welfare recipients to work after two years of benefits but with a promise of public employment if no private employment were available, as well as continuation of various services. Although Clinton administration officials evidenced some concern about children's poverty, they did not focus on lessening poverty through raising benefits. Their approach has been to attach benefits to paid work, seeking to "make work pay" (Ellwood 1988) for women as well as for men through enhancing the Earned Income Tax Credit (EITC) and increasing the minimum wage. These efforts have been rather more successful than is usually recognized, and increases to the EITC enacted in the 1993 budget meant that the program reached far more families than did AFDC and that spending was considerably higher. Federal spending on EITC surpassed AFDC in 1992 ($12.4 versus $12.3 billion); for 1996, it was projected to be almost twice as much ($25.1 versus $13.2 billion) (Myles and Pierson 1997: Table 2). Significantly, the EITC is gender-neutral and tied to employment—it helps workers with children.

After the 1994 election of a Republican House, the political dynamics around welfare shifted and President Clinton signed a much more restrictive and less generous Republican welfare bill, despite it being clear that the legislation would increase children's poverty (Weaver 1998). In the immediate aftermath of the law's enactment, Democrats have focused even more on workplace-based strategies for dealing with poverty. Thus, the policy preferences of the Democrats look like a much less generous version of Sweden's or France's supports for single mothers, which also require paid work after a limited time period. Their approaches are all premised on the idea that most citizens are earners, some are caregivers, but state support is needed to combine work and caregiving, particularly for vulnerable populations such as poor single mothers. Yet the U.S. Democrats' preferences are distinctively liberal in the sense that state support is residual—most supports are limited to the welfare population and the working poor.

The Republicans' welfare bill ended the entitlement status of AFDC and federal oversight. At the state level, Republicans have promoted other provisions that would undercut the capacities of poor women to have and support children, for example, denying additional benefits for children born to a beneficiary on welfare (the so-called "family cap"), conditioning benefits on using contraception, and enacting a lifetime ban on aid to children born to unwed mothers under the age of eighteen. All these changes will further limit full-time caregiving—indeed, even the possibility of maintaining a home—as an option for poor mothers, already severely circumscribed by the only partially implemented reforms of 1988. This is gender sameness with a vengeance—requiring that mothers as well as fathers rely on the market results in great inequities, given mothers' disproportionate share of the caregiving burden. Making mothers do paid work may be viewed as a form of punishment, which may also explain why these "reformers" are so uninterested in making paid work a *viable* way for single mothers to support themselves and their children. Their goal is to make it impossible or extremely difficult to do so; in their view, poor single women should not have a right to bear children (Jencks and Edin 1995). This is the logic of the poor law, which attempted to use the mechanism of market discipline to curb childbearing by single women and the poor generally. However, market mechanisms alone do not work to prevent autonomy for better-off segments of the female population, who support themselves without men—as high rates of divorce and solo motherhood among middle-class and working-class women indicate. Here, different factions among conservatives divide; some "laissez-faire feminists" or social libertarians do not want state interference in family matters, but social conservatives invoke family values rhetoric, attempting to remake conditions under which single parenthood was shameful and divorce was difficult to obtain. One might construe this debate as premised on the idea that motherhood is a class privilege, but with differences of opinion about whether women should be able to claim the privilege based on their own economic standing or only on the basis of wifely ties to wage-earning men.

U.S. Democrats wanted to make AFDC more like unemployment insurance—a short-term benefit to help claimants "get on their feet" after the crisis of job loss, divorce, or birth of a child outside of marriage, but resolutely pushing them to commodification and the labor market with the threat of short benefit duration or benefit termination and the reward of job training, day care subsidies, and health insurance guarantees. Their Republican opponents, with a platform that attacks women's autonomy across a range of policy areas, simply aim to make welfare unbearable or unobtainable as a way of enforcing paid work on poor mothers. Some ultimately hope to prevent motherhood outside of marriage altogether (even for those who can afford to support themselves through employment). For most Republicans, autonomous women of any class and race, but especially poor black women, are a threat to good social order. Although favoring traditional gender roles they have been unwilling to use substantial state resources to supplement men's wages or support mothering and caretaking work directly (for example, as have Christian conservatives in Germany). They hope to curtail women's autonomy and prevent women from having children out of wedlock or deciding to divorce by promoting a traditional moral agenda and restricting access to abortion and to public services and benefits.

Both visions of reform are premised on imposing the *logic* of the market on all citizens. This reflects the residualism of liberal social policy in U.S. policy history; what is novel is its extension to women. Those segments of the nonelderly populace that do not receive any public assistance (whatever other government largesse they may enjoy) must depend on their capacities in the labor market to gain access to valued resources, including health benefits. There is widespread sentiment that mothers as well as fathers "must" work to have a decent lifestyle and to support children. It is this compulsion that is extended to welfare recipients, just as in the course of debates about family caps, proponents argued that wage-earners get no supplement when they have another child, so why should welfare recipients? It was difficult for critics to mount an effective response to this logic of the market. One suspects that their task would have been easier had family allowances or other explicit forms of government support of all citizens' reproduction ever been instituted in the United States. (Yet such supports usually reflect some commitment to the children of "imagined communities" of an ethnically homogeneous nation, among other things—a condition never in place in heterogeneous America.)

Even before the end of AFDC, that is, on the basis of the Family Support Act of 1988 (passed with bipartisan support during the Reagan administration), a strong push was made toward paid work for mothers. Single parents were required to be at work or in training after their youngest child reached three years of age, and states had the option of requiring work or training for parents of children as young as one year (U.S. Social Security Administration 1993: 83–97). Indeed, formal work requirements (though mild by today's standards) were introduced into AFDC in 1967—the earliest such requirement among these four countries. (It is interesting to note that proposed new supports for breadwinner families, such as the negative income tax, were rejected at the same time, as was the expansion of day care services [Quadagno 1994]; one might view these as U.S. analogues to the Christian-democratic and social-democratic policy approaches, respectively.) Yet AFDC regulations made it difficult to combine on-the-record work and welfare, although most women on welfare have depended on some outside income, from family, boyfriends, or unreported work (Edin and Lein 1996). Thus, the model of motherhood institutionalized in AFDC was sharply at odds with the predominant thrust of policy relevant for gender relations and with dominant patterns of women's work. (Indeed, the clamor for reform intensified despite U.S. single mothers exhibiting relatively high rates of labor-force participation; only about two-fifths of single mothers received AFDC—a much lower proportion than in the other liberal policy regimes, and many mothers cycled between paid work and welfare, in effect using AFDC as an unemployment benefit.)

Australia and Britain, and to a lesser extent Canada despite the changes of the mid-1990s, still offer single mothers the capacity to maintain an autonomous household without participation in the labor market for a certain period of their children's lives. The United States requires that all who want to maintain a household obtain the means of supporting that household through the market. For some women, the market—particularly since it has been subjected to equal opportunity regulation—does offer wages capable of sustaining independent households. Although the United States does not support women's capacity to form and maintain autonomous households through generous social provision, the market coupled with antidiscrimination and a residual system of social provision has allowed and forced a great many women to be independent of men. Among the four liberal countries, despite the lack of public support, the United States has the highest rates of solo motherhood (28 percent of all families with children as compared to 20 percent in Britain, 15 percent in Canada, and 14 percent in Australia) and divorce (21 divorces per 1000 married women per year, compared to between 11 and 13 in the other three countries). But for the poorest women, whose husbands are unable to support families and who themselves tend to have poor earning capacities, the market offers little and the state is offering less and less (see, for example, Jencks and Edin 1995); market-generated stratification is creating increased differentiation among women. This is a fairly significant difference in the character of social rights as it applies to gender relations. Certainly, there has been a shift from gender difference to gender sameness in all these social security systems, but the shift toward entitlement being based solely on worker status has been far more dramatic—and coercive—in the United States.

VARIATIONS in gender ideology, including those among feminists and other politically active women of the different countries, are helping to shape the di-

vergent policy developments of the liberal countries. A pattern of stronger traditional arrangements relative to the sexual division of labor, along with a stronger
enhancement of gender difference, obtains in Australia and Britain, evincing
higher rates of housewifery and of part-time versus full-time paid work for all
women—a model of motherhood based on full-time caretaking (or its nearest
equivalent, part-time, non-career-oriented work)—different from that in North
America, where combining full-time work and parenting for mothers is common and has gained widespread acceptance and backing from the state. Mothers with young children are still expected and allowed to stay at home to care for
them in Australia and Britain; this is also largely the case in Canada. By contrast,
in the United States mothers are increasingly treated as workers who must rely
on the same inadequate protection from unemployment and low wages as male
workers.

These patterns in gender relations are associated with the strength of organized labor (which is in turn related to racial and ethnic heterogeneity) and the
extent of state capacities, which have affected the level of support given to the
traditional male breadwinner–female caregiver family and the development of
social rights more generally. Historic differences in geopolitical pressures that
contributed to the perceived need to increase fertility are also reflected in the levels of public support given to families to care for children. Where social assistance
is available to all, there seems to be less obsession with getting solo mothers depending on public support into the paid labor force. This is reinforced by differences in the character of the low-skill labor market and unemployment levels—
the United States has more low-skill jobs and a lower unemployment rate than
the other three countries (although Canada is moving toward the U.S. pattern).
The absence of public support "encourages" participation in that low-wage,
low-skill labor market.

The policy divergences around support for women's ability to form and maintain autonomous households are related to the racial composition of the clientele of sole-parent programs in the four countries; this has been historically
created by the structures of social provision and immigration and settlement patterns. And models of motherhood have differed historically for white women
and women of color (Glenn 1994). Australian, Canadian, and British sole-parent
pensioners are overwhelmingly white. In the United States, single mothers on
benefits have been disproportionately minority. A majority of claimants are African American and Latino; white women have been a significant proportion of
AFDC recipients, but, not being concentrated in the ghettoes of major metropolitan areas, have less public visibility and have indeed been less likely than minority mothers to be on the program for long periods (Bane 1988). Differences
in the emerging models of motherhood expressed in U.S. policies versus those
of the other three countries may relate to the fact that U.S. women of color have
been held to requirements about combining motherhood and paid work that
have differed historically from those applying to whites. As the clientele of AFDC
becomes perceived as less white, the standards applied to women of color be-

come required of the entire program, a trend reinforced by the increasing proportions of all women entering the labor force.

Given the emphasis placed on women's workplace access and equality by feminist groups, one might well ask whether it is in the interests of women to be enabled by welfare payments to stay at home. Earlier feminist critics of the welfare state indeed focused on the negative aspects of reinforcing women's domesticity in this way. Certainly, there are drawbacks for women withdrawing from the labor force to care for their children full-time, even for a few years (accommodating caregiving by working part-time also "costs," though not as much; see, for example, Joshi 1992). It is hard, however, to champion paid work as reflecting the gender interests of women if that work is in substandard settings and brings no access to employment-related benefits or exists in the absence of sufficient support services, without a second adult helping out, and in dangerous neighborhoods. In the United States, feminist and other reformers may well disagree about the proper strategy for the short term, attempting instead to reinstate "welfare as we knew it" or campaigning for support services that would help poor and other parents, especially mothers, working for pay. One might consider the pragmatic political issues—AFDC was so unpopular with the American public that they preferred *anything* to the current system (Weaver 1998). And clearly elites were persuaded that there was no political return to supporting welfare. Yet I think we can go beyond pragmatic politics to consider the terrain in terms of gender ideologies.

My analysis emphasizes a model of citizenship based on paid work and on progress by women both in the workforce and in private relationships in the United States. This leads me to argue that the best option exists in supporting better treatment for single mothers by accepting that they will be workers and in campaigning for better supports for all workers (for a similar argument, see, for example, Hartmann and Bergmann 1995).

Women's access to benefits that might support an autonomous household outside the workplace remains hedged in with racial, gendered, and class-based restrictions—but to the extent that it has existed and been generalized to all single mothers, it is premised on women's—or at least mothers'—exclusion from the compulsion of proletarianization, a reflection of ideological preferences for gender difference. The sanctity of motherhood has shielded women from the sanctity of the market. This continues to be the case in Australia, Canada, and Britain, even if motherhood is no longer defined as a lifelong occupation. Only in America, then, are the demands of the market really stronger than "concerns of gender," meaning either the protection of mothers of young children from the compulsion to sell their labor power for survival or the defense of the traditional family and men's privileges within it, as Esping-Andersen (1990) claimed was the case for all liberal regimes. American models of motherhood have been transformed to incorporate paid work, reflecting a mix of women's own demands for access to paid work, capitalist labor-market demands, and policy preferences, and the transformation of race relations. This certainly suggests that gender ideologies, "concerns of gender"—and the ways these intersect with race and class—differ within the cluster of liberal policy regimes. And it also suggests that, for Americans at least, the way forward to greater gender equality will come through strategies premised on women's employment. The trick will be to redefine the terms of work to allow for caregiving, by both men and women.

References

Bane, Mary Jo. 1988. "Politics and Policies of the Feminization of Poverty." In *The Politics of Social Policy in the United States*, edited by Margaret Weir, Ann Shola Orloff, and Theda Skocpol, 381–96. Princeton: Princeton University Press.

Barrett, Michele. 1991. *The Politics of Truth*. Stanford: Stanford University Press.

Battle, Ken. 1997. "Transformations: Canadian Social Policy since 1985." Paper presented at the Annual Meeting of the American Sociological Association, Toronto.

Bellingham, Bruce, and Mary Pugh Mathis. 1994. "Race, Citizenship, and the Bio-politics of the Maternalist Welfare State: 'Traditional' Midwifery in the American South under the Sheppard-Towner Act, 1921–29." *Social Politics* 1: 157–89.

Bock, Gisela, and Pat Thane, eds. 1991. *Maternity and Gender Policies: Women and the Rise of the European Welfare States, 1880s–1950s*. New York: Routledge.

Borchorst, Anette. 1994. "The Scandinavian Welfare States—Patriarchal, Gender Neutral, or Woman-Friendly?" *International Journal of Contemporary Sociology* 31: 1–23.

Boris, Eileen. 1995. "The Racialized Gendered State: Constructions of Citizenship in the United States." *Social Politics* 2: 160–80.

Broome, Richard. 1982. *Aboriginal Australians*. Boston: Allen and Unwin.

Burkhauser, Richard, and Karen Holden, eds. 1982. *A Challenge to Social Security: The Changing Roles of Women and Men in American Society*. New York: Academic Press.

Burney, Linda. 1994. "An Aboriginal Way of Being Australian." *Australian Feminist Studies*, no. 19: 17–24.

Bussemaker, Jet, and Kees van Kersbergen. 1994. "Gender and Welfare States: Some Theoretical Reflections." In *Gendering Welfare States*, edited by Diane Sainsbury, 8–25. Thousand Oaks, Calif.: Sage.

Cass, Bettina. 1983. "Redistribution to Children and Mothers: A History of Child Endowment and Family Allowances." In *Women, Social Welfare and the State in Australia*, edited by Cora Baldock and Bettina Cass, 54–84. Sydney: Allen and Unwin.

——. 1994. "Citizenship, Work and Welfare: The Dilemma for Australian Women." *Social Politics* 1 (Spring): 106–24.

Connell, R. W. 1987. *Gender and Power*. Stanford: Stanford University Press.

Cousins, Christine. 1995. "Women and Social Policy in Spain: The Development of a Gendered Welfare Regime." *Journal of European Social Policy* 5: 175–97.

Edin, Kathryn, and Laura Lein. 1996. *Making Ends Meet*. New York: Russell Sage.

Ellwood David. 1988. *Poor Support: Poverty in the American Family*. New York: Basic Books.

Esping-Andersen, Gøsta. 1990. *The Three Worlds of Welfare Capitalism*. Princeton: Princeton University Press.

Esping-Andersen, Gøsta, and Walter Korpi. 1987. "From Poor Relief to Institutional Welfare States: The Development of Scandinavian Social Policy." In *The Scandinavian Model: Welfare States and Welfare Research*, edited by R. Erikson, E. Hansen, S. Ringen, and H. Uusitalo, 39–74. New York: M. E. Sharpe.

Evans, Patricia. 1992. "Targeting Single Mothers for Employment: Comparisons from the United States, Britain, and Canada." *Social Service Review* 66: 376–98.

Fineman, Martha, and Isabel Karpin, eds. 1995. *Mothers in Law: Feminist Theory and the Legal Regulation of Motherhood*. New York: Columbia University Press.

Fraser, Nancy. 1989. "Women, Welfare, and the Politics of Need." In *Unruly Practices*, 144–60. Minneapolis: University of Minnesota Press.

——. 1996. "Social Justice in the Age of Identity Politics: Redistribution, Recognition, and Participation." Tanner Lecture on Human Values.

——. 1997. *Justice Interruptus: Critical Reflections on the "Postsocialist" Condition*. New York: Routledge.

Gerson, Kathleen. 1995. *No Man's Land*. New York: Basic.

Glenn, Evelyn Nakano. 1994. "Social Constructions of Mothering." In *Mothering: Ideology, Experience, and Agency*, edited by E. Glenn, G. Chang, and L. Forcey, 1–32. New York: Routledge.

Goodwin, Joanne. 1992. "An American Experiment in Paid Motherhood: The Implementation of Mothers' Pensions in Early Twentieth Century Chicago." *Gender and History* 4: 323–42.

Gordon, Linda. 1988. "What Does Welfare Regulate?" *Social Research* 55: 609–30.

——. 1994. *Pitied but Not Entitled: Single Mothers and the History of Welfare*. New York: Free Press.

Gordon, Linda, and Nancy Fraser. 1994. "'Dependency' Demystified: Inscriptions of Power in a Keyword of the Welfare State." *Social Politics* 1: 14–31.

Griswold, Wendy. 1994. *Cultures and Societies in a Changing World*. Thousand Oaks, Calif.: Pine Forge.

Hartmann, Heidi, and Barbara Bergmann. 1995. "A Welfare Reform Based on Help for Working Parents" and "Get Real! Look to the Future, Not the Past." *Feminist Economics* 1 (2): 85–90, 109–19.

Hernes, Helga. 1987. *Welfare State and Woman Power*. Oslo: Norwegian University Press.

Hobson, Barbara. 1990. "No Exit, No Voice: Women's Economic Dependency and the Welfare State." *Acta Sociologica* 33: 235–50.

———. 1994. "Solo Mothers, Social Policy Regimes and the Logics of Gender." In *Gendering Welfare States*, edited by Diane Sainsbury, 170–87. Thousand Oaks, Calif.: Sage.

Jackson, Pauline Conroy. 1993. "Managing the Mothers: The Case of Ireland." In *Women and Social Policies in Europe: Work, Family, and the State*, edited by J. Lewis, 72–91. Hants, Eng.: Edward Elgar.

Jeffries, Alison. 1996. "British Conservatism: Individualism and Gender." *Journal of Political Ideologies* 1: 33–52.

Jencks, Christopher, and Kathryn Edin. 1995. "Do Poor Women Have the Right to Bear Children?" *American Prospect*, no. 20 (Winter): 43–52.

Jenson, Jane. 1986. "Gender and Reproduction: Or, Babies and the State." *Studies in Political Economy* 20: 9–45.

Jenson, Jane, and Rianne Mahon. 1993. "Representing Solidarity: Class, Gender, and Crisis in Social-Democratic Sweden." *New Left Review* 201: 76–100.

Joshi, Heather. 1992. "The Cost of Caring." In *Women and Poverty in Britain: The 1990s*, edited by Caroline Glendinning and Jane Millar, 110–125. New York: Harvester Wheatsheaf.

Katznelson, Ira. 1981. *City Trenches*. Chicago: University of Chicago Press.

Kessler-Harris, Alice. 1995. "Designing Women and Old Fools: The Construction of the Social Security Amendments." In *U.S. History as Women's History*, edited by Linda Kerber, Alice Kesler-Harris, and Kathryn Kish Sklar, 87–106. Chapel Hill: University of North Carolina Press.

Kline, Marlee. 1995. "Complicating the Ideology of Motherhood: Child Welfare Law and First Nation Women." In *Mothers in Law: Feminist Theory and the Legal Regulation of Motherhood*, edited by Martha Fineman and Isabel Karpin, 118–41. New York: Columbia University Press.

Knijn, Trudie. 1994. "Fish without Bikes: Revision of the Dutch Welfare State and Its Consequences for the (In)dependence of Single Mothers." *Social Politics* 1: 83–105.

Korpi, Walter. 1978. *The Working Class in Welfare Capitalism: Work, Unions, and Politics in Sweden*. Boston: Routledge and Kegan Paul.

Koven, Seth, and Sonya Michel. 1993. *Mothers of a New World: Maternalist Politics and the Origins of Welfare States*. New York: Routledge.

Ladd-Taylor, Molly. 1994. *Mother-Work: Women, Child Welfare and the State, 1890–1930*. Urbana: University of Illinois Press.

Lake, Marilyn. 1992. "Mission Impossible: How Men Gave Birth to the Australian Nation—Nationalism, Gender, and Other Seminal Acts." *Gender and History* 4: 305–22.

———. 1994. "Personality, Individuality, Nationality: Feminist Conceptions of Citizenship, 1902–1940." *Australian Feminist Studies* 19: 25–38.

Land, Hilary. 1983. "Poverty and Gender: The Distribution of Resources within the Family." In *The Structure of Disadvantage*, edited by M. Brown, 49–71. London: Heinemann.

Leira, Arnlaug. 1992. *Welfare States and Working Mothers: The Scandinavian Experience*. New York: Cambridge University Press.

Lewis, Jane, and David Piachaud. 1992. "Women and Poverty in the Twentieth Century." In *Women and Poverty in Britain: The 1990s*, edited by Caroline Glendinning and Jane Millar, 27–45. New York: Harvester Wheatsheaf.

Lieberman, Robert. 1995. "Race, Institutions, and the Administration of Social Policy." *Social Science History* 9: 511–42.

Lightman, Ernie S. 1997. "'It's Not a Walk in the Park': Workfare in Ontario." In *Workfare: Ideology for a New Under-Class*, edited by Eric Shragge, 85–108. Toronto: Garamond Press.

Lijphart, Arend. 1975. "Comparative Politics and the Comparative Method." *American Political Science Review* 65: 682–93.

Little, Margaret. 1994. "Ontario Mothers' Allowances." Ph.D. dissertation.

Mandell, Betty Reid. 1995. "Why Can't We Care for Our Own Children?" *Feminist Economics* 1 (2): 99–104.

McIntosh, Mary. 1978. "The State and the Oppression of Women." In *Feminism and Materialism*, edited by A. Kuhn and A. Wolpe, 254–89. London: Routledge and Kegan Paul.

Michel, Sonya. 1993. "The Limits of Maternalism: Policies toward American Wage-Earning Mothers during the Progressive Era." In *Mothers of a New World: Maternalist Politics and the Origins of Welfare States*, edited by Seth Koven and Sonya Michel, 227–320. New York: Routledge.

Mink, Gwendolyn. 1995. "Wage Work, Family Work, and Welfare Politics." *Feminist Economics* 1 (2): 95–98.

Monson, Renee. 1997. "State-ing Sex and Gender in Paternity Establishment and Child Support Policy." Ph.D. dissertation, University of Wisconsin–Madison.

Myles, John, and Paul Pierson. 1997. "Friedman's Revenge: The Reform of 'Liberal' Welfare States in Canada and the United States." *Politics and Society* 25, no. 4: 443–72.

O'Connor, Julia. 1993. "Gender, Class and Citizenship in the Comparative Analysis of Welfare State Regimes: Theoretical and Methodological Issues." *British Journal of Sociology* 44: 501–18.

O'Connor, Julia, Ann Shola Orloff, and Sheila Shaver. 1999. *States, Markets, Families: Gender, Liberalism, and Social Policy in Australia, Canada, Great Britain, and the United States*. New York: Cambridge University Press.

Orloff, Ann Shola. 1991. "Gender in Early U.S. Social Policy." *Journal of Policy History* 3: 249–81.

——. 1993a. *The Politics of Pensions: A Comparative Analysis of Britain, Canada, and the United States, 1880–1940*. Madison: University of Wisconsin Press.

——. 1993b. "Gender and the Social Rights of Citizenship: The Comparative

Analysis of Gender Relations and Welfare States." *American Sociological Review* 58: 303–28.

——. 1996. "Gender and Welfare States." *Annual Review of Sociology* 22: 51–78.

Ostner, Ilona. 1993. "Slow Motion: Women, Work, and the Family in Germany." In *Women and Social Policies in Europe: Work, Family, and the State*, edited by J. Lewis, 92–115. Hants, Eng.: Edward Elgar.

Ostner, Ilona, and Jane Lewis. 1995. "Gender and the Evolution of European Social Policies." In *European Social Policy*, edited by Stephan Liebfried and Paul Pierson, 159–93. Washington, D.C.: Brookings.

Pascall, Gillian. 1986. *Social Policy: A Feminist Analysis*. New York: Tavistock.

Pateman, Carole. 1988. "The Patriarchal Welfare State." In *Democracy and the Welfare State*, edited by Amy Gutman, 231–60. Princeton: Princeton University Press.

Pedersen, Susan. 1993. *Family, Dependence, and the Origins of the Welfare State: Britain and France, 1914–1945*. New York: Cambridge University Press.

Pringle, Rosemary, and Sophie Watson. 1992. "Women's Interests and the Post-Structuralist State." In *Destabilizing Theory*, edited by M. Barret and A. Phillips, 53–73. Stanford: Stanford University Press.

Purvis, Trevor, and Alan Hunt. 1993. "Discourse, Ideology, Discourse, Ideology, Discourse, Ideology . . . " *British Journal of Sociology* 44: 473–500.

Quadagno, Jill. 1994. *The Color of Welfare: How Racism Undermined the War on Poverty*. New York: Oxford University Press.

Reskin, Barbara, and Irene Padavic. 1994. *Women and Men at Work*. Thousand Oaks, Calif.: Pine Forge.

Rimlinger, Gaston. 1971. *Welfare Policy and Industrialization in Europe, America, and Russia*. New York: John Wiley and Sons.

Roberts, Dorothy. 1993. "Racism and Patriarchy in the Meaning of Motherhood." *Journal of Gender and the Law* 1: 1–38.

——. 1995. "Race, Gender, and the Value of Mothers' Work." *Social Politics* 2: 195–207.

Ruggie, Mary. 1984. *The State and Working Women*. Princeton: Princeton University Press.

Saraceno, Chiara. 1994. "The Ambivalent Familism of the Italian Welfare State." *Social Politics* 1: 60–82.

Sassoon, Ann Showstack, ed. 1987. *Women and the State: The Shifting Boundaries of Public and Private*. London: Hutchinson.

Schmidt, Manfred. 1993. "Gendered Labor Force Participation." In *Families of Nations*, edited by F. G. Castles, 179–237. Aldershot: Dartmouth.

Sewell, William Jr. 1985. "Ideologies and Social Revolution: Reflections on the French Case." *Journal of Modern History* 57: 57–85.

Shaver, Sheila. 1989. "Social Policy Regimes: Gender, Race and the Welfare State." Paper presented at the "Women in the Welfare State" conference, University of Wisconsin, Madison, Wisconsin.

———. 1993. "Women and the Australian Social Security System: From Difference towards Equality." Discussion Paper no. 41. University of New South Wales, Social Policy Research Centre.

Shragge, Eric, ed. 1997. *Workfare: Ideology for a New Under-Class*. Toronto: Garamond Press.

Siim, Birte. 1990. "Women and the Welfare State: Between Private and Public Dependence. A Comparative Approach to Care Work in Denmark and Britain." In *Gender and Caring*, edited by Clare Ungerson, 80–109. New York: Harvester Wheatsheaf.

Sklar, Katherine Kish. 1993. "The Historical Foundations of Women's Power in the Creation of the American Welfare State, 1830–1930." In *Mothers of a New World: Maternalist Politics and the Origins of Welfare States*, edited by S. Koven and S. Michel, 43–93. New York: Routledge.

Skocpol, Theda. 1985. "Cultural Idioms and Political Ideologies in the Revolutionary Reconstruction of State Power: A Rejoinder to Sewell." *Journal of Modern History* 57: 57–96.

———. 1992. *Protecting Soldiers and Mothers*. Cambridge: Harvard University Press.

Skocpol, Theda, and Gretchen Ritter. 1991. "Gender and the Origins of Modern Social Policies in Britain and the United States." *Studies in American Political Development* 5 (Spring): 36–93.

Stephens, John. 1979. *The Transition from Capitalism to Socialism*. Atlantic Highlands, N.J.: Humanities Press.

Taylor-Gooby, Peter. 1991. "Welfare State Regimes and Welfare Citizenship." *Journal of European Social Policy* 1: 93–105.

Therborn, Goran. 1980. *The Ideology of Power and the Power of Ideology*. London: Verso.

U.S. Social Security Administration. 1993. *Statistical Supplement to the Social Security Bulletin, 1992*. Washington, D.C.: U.S. Department of Health and Human Services.

van Kersbergen, Kees. 1995. *Social Capitalism: A Study of Christian Democracy and the Welfare State*. New York: Routledge.

Vandepol, Ann. 1982. "Dependent Children, Child Custody and Mothers' Pensions: The Transformation of State-Family Relations in the Early Twentieth Century." *Social Problems* 29: 221–35.

Waerness, Kari. 1984. "Caregiving as Women's Work in the Welfare State." In *Patriarchy in a Welfare Society*, edited by Harriet Holter, 67–87. Oslo: Universitetsforlaget.

Weaver, Kent R. 1998. "Ending Welfare as We Know It: Policymaking for Low-Income Families in the Clinton/Gingrich Era." In *The Social Divide: Political Parties and the Future of Activist Government*, edited by Margaret Weir, 361–416. Washington, D.C.: Brookings and Russell Sage.

Weir, Margaret, Ann Shola Orloff, and Theda Skocpol, eds. 1988. *The Politics of Social Policy in the United States*. Princeton: Princeton University Press.

Wennemo, Irene. 1994. *Sharing the Costs of Children: Studies in the Development of Family Support in the OECD Countries*. Dissertation Series No. 25. Stockholm: Swedish Institute for Social Research.

White, Lucie. 1996. "Searching for the Logic behind Welfare Reform." *UCLA Women's Law Journal* 6: 427–42.

Wuthnow, Robert. 1987. *Meaning and Moral Order*. Berkeley: University of California Press.

II

Political Belonging: Emotion, Nation, and Identity in Fascist Italy

Mabel Berezin

Peculiarities of the Italians

The March 1994 Italian elections produced a governing coalition that brought "post-fascists" into a legally constituted Italian government for the first time since 1945. A few weeks before this historic election *La Repubblica*, the national Italian daily, asked Umberto Eco to discuss the apparent drift to the right in Italian politics.[1] Eco, internationally known for his theory of semiotics and his allegorical fiction, has in recent years honed his interpretive skills on the Italian political scene.

According to Eco, the Italian right, in contrast to other European right-wing parties, is in revolt against the state. The contemporary right's rejection of the Italian state is neither new nor particularly characteristic of the right: "Italy never wanted a State, and it has always been a land of communes and corporations." Antistatism was, and is, deeply embedded in Italian political culture. Eco describes Italy from the Renaissance to the present as a country of "small family lobbies"—an understated, but nonetheless apt, characterization of the Medicis. Hegemonic Italian families believed that an Italian nation-state would attenuate the political power of family business, and whenever possible they mobilized against national unity.

Grants from the University of Pennsylvania Research Foundation, American Philosophical Society, Salvatori Research Fund, and National Endowment for the Humanities Travel to Collections Grant funded this research. I wrote this article while I was a Visiting Fellow in the Department of Social and Political Science at the European University Institute in Florence, Italy, supported by a grant from the German Marshall Fund of the United States. This essay benefited from the critical comments of the contributors to this book who participated in the Wilder House conference, September 22–23, 1995. Particular thanks to David Laitin for his careful reading and expansive comments, to Paul Lichterman for title discussion, to Luisa Passerini, and to Joseph La Palambara for providing more insights than I could ever possibly hope to incorporate.

[1] Umberto Eco. *La Repubblica*, March 3, 1994, 2–3.

Nineteenth-century Italian antipathy toward the state resulted in Italy's lagging "behind" its European neighbors where state-making was proceeding at a rapid pace. Italy, in contrast to France, Germany, and England, never found a "paternal image"—that is, a state—and instead remained, "a confederation of uncles. With an indulgent Mother, the Church." Occasionally, Italy has felt the need for a "strong man" to stabilize its family squabbles and to place it back on course. During such moments (and Italy may have experienced one in 1994), the desire for a father figure becomes intense.

Eco attributes the initial success of Mussolini to the fleeting Italian desire for stability. He describes the crowd's desecration of Mussolini's body in Piazza Loretto in Milan as a "ritual killing of the father." The fascist "experiment" with the "too virile father" sent Italians fleeing into the "maternal arms" of the Christian Democrats for fifty years. Eco concludes, "The father is the Law. Our country has never succeeded in identifying with the Law," and until Italy acknowledges the authority of the father/state/law, political scandal and instability will be "endemic."

A central paradox, which Eco only partially suggests, underlies Italian state-formation and political culture. Italy does not lack laws—the institutional buttresses of the modern state; she lacks feeling for the law. From Allum's (1973) "republic without government" to Putnam's (1993) "working" democracy, Italy, with over fifty governing coalitions since 1945, has been the prototype of a peculiar political stability resting on apparent institutional chaos. The source of Italian political resilience is not simply the product of microlevel political bargaining lying somewhere between Machiavelli and *commedia dell'arte*.

Eco's renarration of Italian state-making in terms of familial dysfunction articulates with new developments in the starker realm of political and social theory (for example, Hunt 1992). The metaphors of emotion—love, romance, family—are beginning to seep into cultural accounts of state-making and point in directions that suggest Italy might be less dysfunctional than standard state theorizing, collapsing governments, and omnipresent political scandals imply.

State theory, no matter what its analytic or empirical focus, is predicated on a Weberian ideal type of a modern nation/state. Nation/state is a dyadic concept. State theory tends to elide this distinction and undermines the cultural context of state-making and state-formation. Failure to uncouple the nation/state dyad leads in two directions: first, it establishes discussions of nationalism as independent of state theory; and second, it privileges the efficiency of institutions and neglects cultural process.[2] Recent discussions of nationalism suggest that scholars are beginning to pay more attention to the distinction between nation and state. For example, Brubaker (1996) in his institutionalist account of nationalism implicitly acknowledges the importance of drawing distinctions between state and nation when he argues that "the analytical task at hand . . . is to think about nationalism without nations" (ibid.: 21). Miller (1995: 18) argues that the "con-

---

[2] Steinmetz (this volume) reminds us that Weber did discuss the nation in terms of a "subjective sense of belonging," which Weberian-inspired state theory tends to overlook.

fusion of 'nation' and 'state' obfuscates discussions of nationality." Uncoupling the nation/state dyad expands the parameters of state theory by incorporating a concept of culture, and permits an alternative view of Italian political development to emerge.

Eco's family metaphors have salience that go beyond the Italian case. The nation, in contrast to the state, is, to borrow from Benedict Anderson (1991: 141), the locus of "political love." The process of making inhabitants of a bounded geographical space feel attachment to, or "fall in love" with, a larger territorial entity is a significant dimension of successful state-making. Citizenship and civic virtue are the more conventional formulations of collective commitment to the nation/state.[3] Identity is the analytic term that describes how individuals and groups understand various dimensions of the self as bound to external objects— in this case, the public entity of the nation.

This essay explores the peculiar Italian iteration of the relation between "political love" and state-formation during the fascist period. Its analytic task is to explore fascist state strategies of projecting religious, romantic, and familial love on a larger object: the nation/state. The essay has three parts: (1) it theorizes the relation between states and identities, paying particular attention to the idea of a totalitarian state; (2) it lays out the cultural contours of the Italian nation/state project as prolegomena to the fascist project; and (3) it explores the linguistic strategies and cultural narratives that served as vehicles of fascist identity.

The regime that controlled the Italian state from 1922 to 1943 was a political project that aimed to recreate the Italian self or to create new identities as citizens of Fascist Italy. The "fascist project," the actions and programs that the regime undertook to accomplish its desired cultural ends, was an exercise in "hyper" nationalization and "hyper" state-building.[4] The years between 1922 and 1943 represent Italy at the extremes and allow microscopic analysis of processes that appear more diffuse in later and earlier time periods.

States and Identity

Feeling Identity

In the broadest terms, identity is the process of feeling "at one" with another or others—the recognition of similarity. Identity and cultural meanings are intimately connected. Psychological theories of identity focus on individuals. So-

---

[3] Viroli (1995) explores these issues in terms of patriotism.

[4] The regime "fascistified" Italy's principal cultural and social institutions. It reorganized schools, took over popular and elite artistic institutions from cinema to theater to publishing, controlled the press, and created a web of voluntary organizations in the National Fascist party that mobilized men and women of all ages. It made peace with the Catholic Church in the *Concordat* of 1929 and instituted demographic policies that redefined the nature of the Italian family. Although many specialized studies have emerged, the best general introductions remain Cannistraro (1975); Tannenbaum (1972); De Grazia (1981). For a recent summary of regime demographic policies, somewhat overburdened by its theoretical apparatus, see Horn (1994).

cial theories of identity focus on the formal matrix of relations, or networks, in which individuals are enmeshed. Social identities are first steps to political identities and customarily are formed before political identities. Who we are, how we define and conceive of ourselves, how we recognize others who are one of us and determine who is not, is connected to how we construct ourselves in public and private space.

Identity is an inescapable dimension of social life. William Connolly (1991: 158) argues that ". . . each individual needs an identity; every stable way of life invokes claims to collective identity. . . ." Identity may be conceived in terms of similarities or of the communities of selves toward which individuals orient their actions. The social construction of identities involves the specification of a web of social relations or communities that envelop the self and through which individuals feel themselves as identical with others. Identity without community is incomplete.[5]

Social, political, and economic institutions, the organizational forms of modern community, serve as arenas of identity. Institutions organize identities.[6] Identity is an issue of modernity that is connected to an ideological conception of individualism. Liberalism, as ideal and political organization, institutionalized the central cultural chasm of modernity—the fractionalization of individual and collective identities into public and private selves.[7] Liberalism incorporates a multiplicity of identities—political, social, national, gender—the list is potentially endless and subject to ever greater refinements.

Public and private as a broad categorization schema captures all possible identities. As an analytic frame, it has an intellectual history that usually incorporates a discussion of the differences among the state, civil society, and the market. I advocate a slightly less conventional use of this distinction as a convenient shorthand for what we think of as private or "ordinary" life—family, gender, love, religion—arenas of deeply felt identities that are beyond the purview of the liberal democratic state.[8]

Public identities principally include citizenship and work identities that are institutionally buttressed by the legal organizations of the modern nation-state and the market. Private identities originate in their purest forms as biology or kinship relations. Whether or not we acknowledge the social ties of kinship, by virtue of our existence we are mothers, fathers, sons, daughters.

[5] Much of the current sociological discussion of identity has been carried out at the level of theory and not empirical analysis. For example, see the essays in Calhoun (1994). Philosopher Charles Taylor's (1989) nuanced definition of *identity*, framed in terms of community and not difference, is a useful starting point for an analysis of the political construction of identity. Theories of identity tend to share a focus on language and narrative as communicative vehicles of identity. Common language is the dimension of identity that provides the discursive cues that signal like-minded subjects to each other (for example, Somers 1994).

[6] For a discussion of how institutions create meaning, see March and Olsen (1989).

[7] Legal and feminist theory makes this point but not in quite the way I use it in this argument. For one example among many, see Elshtain (1981).

[8] The terms *public* and *private* are used with more frequency than with precision. For an overview of recent uses of these terms, see Weintraub (1997: 1–42).

Other forms of identities are more fluid and not as easily located on a public/ private continuum. Cultural identities—religious, national, regional, and ethnic—may be *either* public or private, depending on the political regime. Liberalism tends to legislate religious, regional, and ethnic identities out of the public sphere and to invoke selectively the affective dimensions of nationalism to support the nation/state.[9] What all these identities share is that they are based on meanings—religious practice, homeland, and race—and they are able to generate and have generated powerful public emotions and militancy.

Identities are neither essential nor purely constructed; they are multiple but they are not schizophrenic (Calhoun 1994: 9–36). Individuals relate to and derive meaning from many communities of similar selves. However, this does not imply that all identities carry equal meaning to those who participate in them. Many identities are, to borrow from Connolly (1991: 173), "contingent." These identities are circumstantial and more or less given at will. Some identities are more vulnerable to contingency than others. Identities belong to a category of objects that Taylor (1989) has described as "hypergoods," by which he means objects that are of relatively more value to us than others.

Identities are felt as hierarchies. There are some identities that we value more than others, ones we experience as "hypergoods"; and some we experience as essentially contingent. The felt force of some identities is so potent we might be willing to die for them. Those identities that generate powerful emotions carry political importance. Religious, national, and ethnic identities frequently fall into this category.

Fascism and Identity

Fascism, in contrast to liberalism, rejects the fractionalization of identities into public and private selves.[10] Democracy, the organizational vehicle of liberalism, upholds the integrity of individualism and multiple identities but sometimes has a political effect that diverges from its theoretical intent. Lefort (1986: 303), in his discussion of totalitarianism, suggests the alienating potential of democracy when he notes that "Number breaks down unity, destroys identity." Lefort's analysis suggests that the split between public and private self is the historical exception rather than the historical norm—a split that became structurally tenable in the caesura known as modernity. It is precisely this aspect of liberal democracy that fascism rejects, and it is the void that fascism attempts to fill when it rejects the liberal democratic state.[11]

Italian fascism's rejection of the liberal bifurcation of identity made it similar to other forms of pre-Enlightenment social and political organization. Where fascism departed from older organizational forms was that it sought to recreate

---

[9] There is a burgeoning literature on nationalism. Hobsbawm's (1990: 14–45) discussion linking nationalism to the development of the nation/state is most congruent to the issues I raise.

[10] The constraints of this essay do not permit full elaboration of this point. For extended analysis, see Berezin (1997: 11–27).

[11] On the relative novelty and cultural particularity of democracy, see Di Palma (1990: 16–26).

a public/private version of the self in the political arena, or the fascist community of the state. A. James Gregor (1969: 26) maintains that, "Fascism as an ideology was a far more complex and systematic intellectual product than many of it antagonists (and many of its protagonists as well) have been prepared to admit." According to Gregor, Giovanni Gentile, the Italian philosophy professor who was Mussolini's first Minister of Education and general cultural adviser, was the intellectual architect of the new "third way."

Gentile's collected works number in the volumes. But the salient point of Gentile's political analysis was that the fascist citizen found his or her self in the community of the state (Gregor 1969: 216). Gentile's (1991: 86) own words best capture the spirit of this argument: ". . . the State is itself a personality, it has a will, because it knows its aims, it has a consciousness of itself, a certain thought, a certain program, it has a concept which signifies history, tradition, the universal life of the Nation, which the State organizes, guarantees, and realizes." Gentile's argument blurs the boundaries between society and the state or between culture and the state. His formulation suggests that political identities are natural, whereas the historical evidence suggests that they are highly problematic and always constructed regardless of whether the state in which individuals live is nominally democratic or totalitarian.

Political Emotion

Political identities tread a difficult line because they require of their partisans a feeling that something exists outside the private self—the party, the state—that is worth dying for. War making, as Charles Tilly (1985: 169–87) has argued, may be a major activity of the modern state, but conscription alone does not make soldiers. The modern nation/state is the ideal type of modern political organization and a vehicle of mass political commitment. As I contended in the introduction, nation/state is a dual concept and a discussion of state- and identity-formation, in either liberal democratic or totalitarian states, requires that we uncouple this dyad. The state part of this dyad is in the "business of rule" (Poggi 1978) and focuses on bureaucratic efficiency and territorial claims; the nation part of the dyad is in the business of creating emotional attachment to the state or "noncontingent" identities.

To borrow Benedict Anderson's familiar formulation (1991: 7), the modern nation/state is an "imagined community" that creates a spirit of "fraternity" that "makes it possible . . . for so many millions of people, not so much to kill, as willingly to die for such limited imaginings." A principal goal of the nation side of the equation is to create a feeling of "attachment" to the state in the form of "love for the nation." The "nature" of "political love"

> . . . can be deciphered from the ways in which languages describe its object: either in the vocabulary of kinship (motherland, *Vaterland, patria*) or that of home (*heimat* . . .). Both idioms denote something to which one is naturally tied. As we have seen earlier, in everything "natural" there is always something unchosen. In this way, nation-ness is assimilated to skin-colour, gender, parentage and birth-era—all

those things one can not help. And in these "natural ties" one senses what one might call the 'beauty of *gemeinschaft*' (Anderson 1991: 141, 143).

The nation side of the nation/state dyad, although it appears as the product of natural emotions, is highly constructed. The success of individual nineteenth-century nation/state projects lies in the strength of constructed emotion, and some nation/state projects were more successful than others. France is the paradigmatic case to which analysts turn when exploring these issues. As Lynn Hunt (1984) has shown, a repertoire of political inventions, symbolic practices, and images constituted the culture of the French revolution; and it was not until the nineteenth century that "peasants" became "Frenchmen" (Weber 1976) and the process of a modern French political identity tied to a nation/state was completed.

Historical and theoretical accounts of nation/state demonstrate that nineteenth-century nation/states did not just come together as a result of the elective affinity of compatriots. They were forged from wars, the reorganization of cultural institutions, principally education, and the standardization of language. National cultures were made at the expense of local and regional cultures. While it is impossible to have any form of modern political organization without either a state or a nation, it is possible to have a nation without a state, or a state without a nation. The Arab-Israeli conflict may be construed as a problem of nations without states; the former Eastern European bloc countries and Soviet Union fall into the latter category of states without nations, which perhaps suggests why these states crumbled with the Berlin Wall.

The uncoupling of nation and state forces a reexamination of the concept of totalitarian states. If states are simply the organizational and technological side of the nation/state dyad, then states may be conceived of as relatively neutral formal entities akin to what Bourdieu (this volume) discusses as a "field." A nation, on the other hand, is a highly specific cultural construct tied to historical context. The nation side of the dyad introduces variance to the concept of state.

Standard definitions of totalitarian states do not make these distinctions. For example, Linz (1975: 191–92) summarizes the characteristics of a totalitarian state as: (1) having a monolithic center of power; (2) having an exclusive ideology to which all must subscribe; and (3) mandatory citizen participation in the form of active and continued mobilization. Linz distinguishes between totalitarian and authoritarian regimes based on the instrumental versus expressive character of the state. He places Nazi Germany in the former category and fascist Italy in the latter (1975: 275). Linz's formulation leads to an overly static conception of the totalitarian state form.

If we accept historical accounts that suggest nation/states are end products of a political process that bears greater resemblance to arranged marriage than to spontaneous coupling, we can think of totalitarian states as states without nations, or states in which the failure or weakness of the nation/state process has demanded a "hypernationalization" project. If we conceptualize fascism as a political ideal that denies the separation of the public and private self, then we can think of totalitarian states as the organizational form of that destroyed boundary. To the extent that all nation/states need to create citizens who will sacrifice some parts of their private selves to the state, whether their income in taxes or their bodies in war, then the terms *totalitarian* and *liberal-democratic* as demarcations of state forms start to appear as only differences of degree.

Imagined community was a novel concept when it first appeared in 1983. Its principal battle has been won and scholars generally accept the constructed dimension of "nation-ness." However, scholars have either glossed over or simply assumed "political love" without delving into what sociologist Robert W. Connell (1990: 526) has described as the "structure of cathexis" or the "patterning of emotional attachments" to the polity. This lacuna is problematic in all accounts of nation/state making, and particularly problematic in the case of totalitarian states where, as Linz's definition suggests, attachment is assumed to be a product of coercion. Recent theoretical and empirical work, such as Connell's, that weds notions of gender to concepts of state suggests approaches to the understanding of political emotion.[12]

Anthropologist Katherine Verdery (1994) has advocated that nation/state is an inherently gendered term.[13] She hypothesizes that "nation" represents the feminine, soft, cultural side of the equation, and that "state" represents the masculine, hard, bureaucratic, and military side of the equation. According to Verdery nation, that is, the imagined community of belonging, is always expressed in gendered terms in either the physical body of the woman (we have only to think of Marianne) as the image of the nation, or in the language of emotion and sexual longing through which love of the nation is expressed. John Borneman (1992: 39, 284–91) in a study of the former East and West Berlin notes that nineteenth-century nation/state builders deliberately separated "personal" history from state history and relegated the "personal" to the realm of folklore. With the breakup of Germany during the cold war, the state reclaimed the "personal" in terms of narrative tropes expressed in gendered terms and institutionalized in new codes of family law.

Lynn Hunt's (1992: 194) discussion of the "family romance" of the French Revolution, which owes its conceptualization to Freud, makes the case that images of "parricide, incest, sodomy, the disorderly woman, and the orphan" were inverse images of fraternity and revolutionary community. Hunt's concluding summary of her argument serves equally well to summarize the general trend that I have identified:

> The family romance was a kind of prepolitical category for organizing political experience. If kinship is the basis of most if not all organized social relations, then it is also an essential category for understanding political power. Traditionalists in Euro-

[12] For example, Orloff (this volume) and Adams (this volume) point to the importance of gender in social policy and emotional investment in the state, respectively. In a related vein, Goodwin (1997) suggests the relation between emotion and social movement commitment.

[13] Mosse (1985) was one of the first to point out the relation between nationalism and sexuality.

pean history had long pointed to the family as the first experience of power and consequently as a sure model of its working; just as the father was "naturally" the head of the family, so too the king was naturally the head of the body politic. I hope that it is clear by now that family romances, like kinship systems, could take many different forms and serve many different political ends. The family was indeed every individual's first experience of politics, but the family experience was not immutable, especially in revolutionary times. (1992: 196)

This new literature that reflects a gendered view of the state may suggest an overly textualized view of political process; it does serve, however, as a useful starting point to excavate the cultural cues that generate "political love." Attachment to the nation/state forms in the space between shared social meanings and formal organization. Culture (nation) and rationality (state) fuse to create the nation/state. Yet, as Hunt suggests, the shared experience of family and all that it implies is vacuous if it is not situated in a specific cultural and historical context. "Making" political love is a form of state action derived from the repertoire of available emotive cultural symbols and practices.

A State Without a Nation

Italy 1860: A Loveless Marriage

Nation/states may be "imagined" and "felt" as community, but the feelings and imaginings of national belonging are evanescent without an underlying structure of cultural institutions and symbolic practices. National languages and education systems as well as museums, monuments, and national anthems serve to keep the spirit of national belonging alive.

The Italy that came into being in 1860 had a weak hold on the imagination and consciousness of a people who were now forced to think of themselves as Italians. To say that Italy was culturally fragmented in 1860 is to attenuate the deeply felt regional identities and loyalties that divided the inhabitants of the new nation/state. Historians so frequently cite Massimo D'Azeglio's epigram on Italian culture, "having made Italy, we must now make Italians," that they rarely reference it.

The concept of a unified, democratic, and liberal Italy had limited popular appeal. Democracy and liberalism in Italy meant little more than a united territory and a parliament. This conception of nonaristocratic government was thin by contemporary standards of democratization, and even by nineteenth-century standards of bourgeois states, but nonetheless a considerable advance for an agricultural territory dominated by nobles, brigands, and bandits. In comparison to France in 1789 and Germany in 1850, Italy lacked a prominent commercial, let alone industrial, bourgeoisie. The principal partisans of the *Resorgimento* were a group of men belonging to the relatively small social category of what we would today describe as the educated middle classes, university graduates whose parents possessed neither land nor capital (Lovett 1982: 68).

In Italy, the work of "mass-producing" the "traditions" that were the glue of French, German, and even British nineteenth-century nation/state projects was beset with obstacles (Hobsbawm 1983: 263–307). Unification was as much a French as an "Italian" invention. The monarchy, the House of Savoy, was French and many Italians viewed it as foreign. Cavour orchestrated the unification of Italy from Piedmont in the northern corner of the new Italy. Piedmont and its capital, Turin, where the first parliament met, were culturally French. Cavour's first language was French and he spoke Italian only when necessary and with difficulty. Even the territory was contested. Advocates of unification found it difficult to determine where Italy began and ended. Italy's northern borders were in continual dispute, in part because Austria and France had spent the greater part of the eighteenth and first half of the nineteenth century invading.

In 1922, sixty years after the unification, Italy remained a state without a nation. "Feeling" Italian was a tenuous emotion. The standard institutional buttresses—education, common language, and print culture—of the nation side of the nation/state dyad were weak and ineffective. Scholars have frequently noted the widespread theatricality and emotionality of Italy and its citizens. This was not simply a biological or cultural trait. Italians could not speak to each other very easily. Lexicographers had been lobbying since the eighteenth century to promulgate the Tuscan dialect as the official language of Italy. They were joined by literary figures in the early nineteenth century (Migliorini and Griffith 1984: 310–11; Lyttelton 1993: 72–73). Yet, Italians by and large communicated in their local dialects. At the time of unification, scholars estimate that only 2.5 percent of the population spoke Italian (Hobsbawm 1990: 38). The standardization of the legal system with the passage of the civil code in 1865 and the penal code in 1889 forced members of the state bureaucracy to have a working knowledge of Italian.[14]

The education system did little to diffuse the language. King and Okey (1904: 233), two early twentieth-century Italian social observers, painted a portrait of schools in disrepair, schoolteachers on charity, and a general indifference to education among a poor and, for the most part, illiterate population chained to local dialect. In the late nineteenth century, theater schools, a middle-class phenomenon, did as much as the education system to promulgate spoken Italian (Migliorini and Griffith 1984: 404–5; Berezin 1994: 1256–59).

The problem with language made the Italian public sphere, the hallmark of political modernity, comparatively weak.[15] The normal channels of liberal political discourse, newspapers and literary circles, existed although they were inaccessible to many Italians. As late as 1921, Italy reported rates of illiteracy that ranged from a high of over 50 percent in the south to 25 percent in the center. Rates were in the single digits in the industrialized north (Klein 1986: 34).

[14] My analysis suggests that language may have solidified the bureaucratic apparatus of the state but did not create a nation. This departs from Laitin and colleagues' (1994) account of Spanish state-building.

[15] Habermas (1989) is the principal proponent of this argument. For a summary of the research directions that his argument has taken, see Calhoun (1993).

The Fascist Nation/State: Generating Political Passion

On this landscape of cultural, social, and economic fragmentation, the fascist regime, the group of political actors who commanded the Italian state from 1922, began its cultural project.[16] Italy may have lacked "Italians," but it did not lack fascists.

A central paradox of Italian political and cultural development was that the strength of its state was inversely proportional to the weakness of Italian national identity. Italy spent the postunification period building the state. A labyrinthine structure of bureaucratic offices was in place by 1922. The Italian state was a source of social mobility for large segments of the overeducated and underemployed Italian population. The further south one went in Italy, the more citizens distrusted the state and the more they depended on it for career advancement (Berezin 1991: 157–58). The Italian state that the fascist regime inherited was unwieldy, and the bureaucracy did not move quickly. The reconstruction of the Italian state, a large portion of the fascist political project that lasted well after the fall of the regime, was an ongoing task. The state as a formal bureaucratic mechanism was the principal vehicle that orchestrated the fascist cultural project. The Italian state was a resource at the regime's disposal to rewrite the rules of the cultural game and to create a new form of noncontingent identity.

The style in which Italian nineteenth-century nation/state builders imagined Italy was at sharp divergence from the style in which Italian citizens constructed their identities. Noncontingent Italian identities tended to be private and tied to family, local and tied to place, and religious and tied to the Catholic Church. Family, region, and religion were the cultural communities that provided the cultural repertoires, modes of thought and behavior, that were the sources of the Italian self—the loci of emotional attachment. The unification and the fascist project were attempts to supplant regional identities with national identities.

By 1927, "passion" became a central theme of regime propaganda. Arnaldo Mussolini, Mussolini's brother and the editor of the fascist daily *Il Popolo d'Italia*, narrated what he portrayed as the popular "passion" for the regime and fascist revolution in terms of a love affair turning into a stable marriage. He rhapsodized: "We affirm that the fascist demonstrations of this fifth anniversary of the March on Rome have shown clearly that the spirit that animates our faith has maintained itself intact with its original freshness. If in the past, it was the passion of tumult, today it is the same passion in a more serene, more solid, stronger ambiance forged by time."[17] If Italians were to feel the political passion that

---

[16]The fascist regime determined the political context in Italy until 1943. Scholars debate whether one can speak of a regime before the 1930s. From March 1929, the year of the plebiscite, Mussolini and the Fascist party were in complete control of the Italian state. This was a formal event, however, since Mussolini and the party were de facto in control of the state from 1922. Lyttelton (1966: 75–100) marks the beginning of the dictatorship, or "second wave" of fascism, as coincident with Mussolini's speech of January 3, 1925, in which he responded to the murder of the socialist deputy, Matteotti.

[17]Arnaldo Mussolini. *Il Popolo d'Italia*, November 1, 1927: 1.

would incorporate "love" of nation, the twin sources of identity, family, and religion had to bend to political exigencies. The fascist regime, just as the regimes that preceded and succeeded it, needed to channel emotion away from these powerful sources of the Italian private self and project it onto the nation/state. The Italian nation/state project, the *Risorgimento*, was a font of cultural and political memory from which the fascist regime crafted its political narratives. *Risorgimento* meant "rebirth" and the phrase was, as historian Clara Lovett (1982: 1) claims, carefully chosen instead of "revolution," which the fascists favored, to suggest a pact between Italy's past and future.

Giuseppe Mazzini was the *Risorgimento* cultural figure to whom the fascists turned to advance their own cultural project. Mazzini was particularly astute at appropriating the sources of Italian emotional life—church and family. In contrast to Cavour who advocated a free church in a free state and championed the liberal separation of church and state, Mazzini espoused a new political religion based on the motto "God and People." The "nation" was the arena where the "people" realized their noncontingent selves. Coupled with "God and People," Mazzini celebrated the cultural meaning of the Italian family. A fascist school textbook cited Mazzini's slogan, "The family is the Fatherland of the heart," to underscore the fascist regime's appropriation of the family (Biloni 1933: 143).[18] Mazzini was the voice of an "intransigent unitarianism" with a "Messianic streak" that seemed to speak to the 1840s (Lyttelton 1993: 82–83). He also spoke to the 1920s and 1930s. *God, Nation, Family*, and *People* were the keywords of Mazzini's political religion that the fascist regime borrowed to legitimate its own cultural project.

The Practice and Narrative of Fascist Political Love

The strategies the regime used to create fascists—citizens who submerged their private identities within the new fascist nation/state—focused on religion and family as vehicles of emotional attachment. Roman Catholicism was comprised of doctrine and institutions. The doctrine was functionally irrelevant to the popular practice of Roman Catholicism in a semiliterate country such as early-twentieth-century Italy where a battery of cyclical liturgical rituals obliterated whatever nuances of church doctrine seeped into popular consciousness. The popular practices of Roman Catholicism, engraved in the mental frames of even the fascists, provided an opportunity for cultural transposition. The central paradox in the relation between the Catholic Church and Italian politics in general is that, despite the Church's obvious power, there is a high degree of anti-Catholicism and anticlericalism in Italy.

Yet, Roman Catholicism was a form of popular culture—that is, everyone knew that some Catholic practices were independent of doctrine or belief and

---

[18] School textbooks required the state's sanction before they could be used, which then made them official fascist documents (Schneider and Clough 1929: 98–99).

were fonts of deeply felt attachment.[19] Family, as religion, was also a source of intense emotion. In Italian culture family is central to social identity, and the social processes that constitute the creation of new families are deeply resonant. In the next three sections, I provide illustrations of how fascism went about wedding religion and family to the nation by examining the appropriation of popular religious practice, the language of emotion that structured fascist public narrative, and the political use of the body of the mother.

The Popular Culture of Roman Catholicism

The Mass is central to Roman Catholic religious practice. The Mass celebrated in Piazza Siena in Rome that began the first anniversary commemorations of the March on Rome, which brought fascism to power, provides an example of the fascist appropriation of this popular form of Catholic ritual practice. The Mass represented the political union of church and state that the regime hoped to negotiate.[20] A Mass was celebrated at exactly the same time in every part of Italy and was a symbolic enactment of the new national unity that fascism had brought. It was also a concrete attempt to combine the familiar liturgy of Catholicism with the new ritual forms of fascism.[21]

The rite that exerted a "mystical fascination" on the crowd was an intricate blending of Catholic and fascist practice. The use of the term *rite* instead of *liturgy* (the more appropriate term for variations on the staging of a Roman Catholic Mass) is in itself a clue to the subtle shifts in consciousness that the newspaper representation was trying to encourage for those who could not attend.[22]

The elevation of the Eucharist, when the priest recites the words that change ordinary bread and wine into the body and blood of Christ, is the center of the Catholic Mass.[23] This action is such a central part of Catholic liturgy and doctrine that it would be a rare Italian Catholic who did not understand its significance.[24] The Mass inserted fascist ritual practice into the most sacred part of the liturgy. At the moment the priest raised the Eucharist and turned to the audi-

[19] What literature exists on the Italian practice of Roman Catholicism suggests that belief is low, more form than substance, but that its ritual practices are readily adopted to serve political ends. The majority of work on the popular practice of religion in Italy has focused on the premodern period. The most noted exemplar here is Ginzburg (1982). Scholars have noted the interaction between fascist and Christian symbolic practice, but there has been no deep textual analysis of how this actually worked. For an elaboration of the Italian Communist party's manipulation of Catholic practice, see Kertzer (1980: esp. 130–68).

[20] This Mass is remarkable given that the regime did not make the pact that finally drew the Catholic Church into the state of Italy until 1929. The Catholic Church had refused to recognize a unified Italy and forbade Catholics to participate in the Italian state. Jemolo (1960) is the standard account of church and state relations in Italy. Webster (1960) pays particular attention to the fascist period and its relation to the development of Christian democracy.

[21] I draw my account from *La Tribuna*, October 30, 1923: 4.

[22] For a historical account of the development of Catholic liturgy in Italy, see Dix (1946: 563–75).

[23] Although there is a general recognition that fascism borrowed religious rites (see, for example, Gentile 1990, 1993), no in-depth study explores how the regime took over Catholic symbolism.

[24] For a discussion of the significance of the Eucharist to Catholic liturgy, see Fitzpatrick (1993).

ence, a trombone sounded, the troops presented arms, and the fascists raised their arms in a Roman, fascist, salute.

As the priest consecrated the Eucharist, the fascists consecrated themselves and blurred the distinction between the sacred and the secular—the church and the state. This fascist imposition on Catholic ritual suggested that one could be both fascist and Catholic. This is an important point because the Socialist party was not the only threat to fascist domination. The Popular party, today known as the Christian Democrats, was competing for the same constituents as the fascists in 1923.[25] Although it was clear that one could not be socialist and Catholic, it was not so clear that one could not be fascist and Catholic. Of course, the Eucharistic transformation is also a miracle that one has to believe. The bread remains bread and every one knows that it is not the body of Christ. So too the fascist "revolution" in 1923 was more an object of belief among devoted adherents than of felt popular experience.

Fascism as Political Romance

The popular Italian cultural idiom was a language of sentimentality and emotion (Forgacs and Nowell-Smith 1985: 342–86). The love affair was the standard plot that enframed Italian social imaginings. The repertoire of characters in this Italian kitsch were frequently adulterous wives or mothers who, as deserted wives, had to deal with the problem of children. Juxtaposed against the language of sentimentality was the language of melodrama. Italian opera is suggestive of the underside of Italian sentimentality with its frequent focus on unruly passions and out-of-control emotions.

The Italian language of emotion became part of the political vernacular of a fascist regime that wished its citizens to literally fall in love with it. The language of sexuality and romance suffuses fascist public narrative. This language is frequently viewed as fascist, however, it was a cultural resource on which the regime drew to construct its own political discourses. The language of sentiment and emotion spoke to the status-deprived petite bourgeois who craved the cultural outpourings of the new regime and was a major constituency of fascism (De Grazia 1981: 127–50).

For example, the rhetorical structure of the newspaper accounts of the first anniversary commemoration of the March on Rome in Bologna suggests a courtship narrative. Bologna had been a socialist stronghold in the prefascist period, and for that reason it was doubly important to suggest that the fascists had conquered and won. *Il Resto del Carlino*'s accounts of Mussolini's visit anthropomorphized Bologna and employed all the cultural cues of romance and womanhood.

On the day of Mussolini's visit, the "splendid" autumn sunlight merged with flags and banners that "throbbed" with excitement in the breeze. The city as

---

[25] For a discussion of the struggle between popolari and fascists in the political arena, see De Rosa (1966: 277–418).

well as the crowds waited "expectantly" for Mussolini, who was scheduled to arrive at 9:30 on the morning of the celebration.[26] The wait was "fervid" and "wrenchingly full of jubilation and enthusiasm." "Vain words" were inadequate to convey the "heat and rhythm of the grand manifestation." Few times in its history had Bologna demonstrated such "a superb and fascinating spectacle of vitality."

The "anxious" city, as a woman awaiting a suitor, dressed itself in anticipation of Mussolini's arrival. Every corner, piazza, and road prepared "feverishly." Festoons of greenery and Italian flags were hung from all the balconies of the city. Even the shops that were closed on the day of the event took the opportunity to redesign their windows to demonstrate to passing foreigners that Italy was the land of "good taste and riches." Bologna would welcome Mussolini as an "apostle and conqueror," and he would "feel" in the "delirious greeting of the multitude" the "throbbing" and "maternal passion" rising from the "earth of his Emilia . . . the profound heart of Italy."[27]

Crowds lined the streets. Even the train station was painted for the occasion with an exterior mural of the March on Rome, and the piazza in front of the train station was decorated with flags, disks with the fascist *littorio*, ornamental plants, and laurel wreaths. At 9:25, the presidential train arrived; the band played *Giovinezza*, the fascist anthem; a guard of honor presented arms; and Mussolini, with an entourage of Fascist generals and high ranking Fascist party members, stepped off the train. Roman salutes and "resounding applause" greeted Mussolini, and a five-year-old girl presented him with a bouquet of flowers. Mussolini left the station and began the march down the Via Indipendenza which was "swarming with an anxious crowd." The fascist spectacle of commemoration began: "The imposing line-up of the Militia and the Sindacates offered an unforgettable spectacle. From the balconies an uninterrupted storm of flowers brought the gentle homage of the women of Bologna to the Duce."

The language of feeling dominated *Il Resto del Carlino*'s journalistic accounts to create an iconography of emotion. The editorial writers of *Il Resto del Carlino*, a newspaper with distinctly fascist sympathies, wanted their readers to feel excitement and anticipation. Their purple prose evoked the charged language of standard Italian melodrama. The words "throbbing" and "delirious" appeared repeatedly in the account. Antithetical images of women as mothers and mistresses dominated the text. The city assumed the feminine aspect of a woman waiting for a lover—a familiar and congenial image in Italian cultural discourse. The Emilian earth exuded "maternal passion." The text used language of sexuality to evoke the dual and contradictory aspects of fascism and its cadres of supporters. The fascists were men of tradition who beat back the "subversive" socialists and defended the established order—they saved the mother and family; they were also virile, romantic men of a ction who conquered women and cities, with the same élan with which they marched on Rome. The courtship rituals

[26] *Il Resto del Carlino*, October 30, 1923: 1.
[27] Mussolini was born in a small village, Varano di Costa in Emilia-Romagna.

that created the Italian family would create the new Italian family in the fascist state.

The rhetorical strategy of "falling in love" with the regime frequently focused on the figure of Mussolini.[28] In a visit to Verona fifteen years after the Bologna event, a fascist publicist employed the same language of emotion that was rote in all accounts of fascist spectacle. In the Roman amphitheater the Arena, Mussolini found a spectacle of "36,000 souls" waiting for him—"8000 fascist women, 8000 rural housewifes and laborers, 20,000 members of the G.I.L. [fascist youth groups]. . . ." (Manzini 1938: 86). To begin the performance in the Arena, the secretary of the party cried out to the crowd, presumably without sound amplification, "Fascist women, housewifes, workers, youth of the Littorio, salute the Duce the Founder of the Empire." Each group shouted the fascist chant "to us" as their names were called and then began a collective chorus of "Du-ce, Du-ce" that the singing of fascist anthems only briefly interrupted. The propagandist narrator invoked the emotion of the crowd as a blend of sexuality and romance.

> The *Arena* is throbbing totally with love and devotion towards him, 36,000 hearts are offered to Him as one heart, because they are at his disposal, because he consumes them, burns them at the fire of His genius. And the Duce does not know how to resist: he feels all the regret that he would leave behind him if he would not at least say some words to this crowd that cry out in the last spasm of love, and He shows himself yet another time, after having signalled, yet another time to leave. (83)

The words Mussolini left behind were, "I want [*voglio*] to tell you only that I will never forget the spectacle of faith and joy that you have offered me in this grand and sacred vestige of Rome." Mussolini's choice of the word *voglio*, the strongest expression of volition, reinforced the feeling of emotion and desire that the spectacle and the regime presumably invoked.

The Fascist "Family Romance" and the Mother's Body

The women who participated in events such as the Bologna and Verona ceremonies were the mothers and widows of the "fallen for the revolution"; their appearances at these events were in exchange for their widows' and family pensions and not necessarily due to an outpouring of fascist emotion. Their bodies were paraded often at fascist public rituals as the regime marched forward with its cultural project.

The union of family, motherhood, and nation was not unique to either Italy or fascism. But it does have a peculiarly Italian variant. A fascist school text reminded youth that according to Mazzini, "The first cell of the organism of the

---

[28] Spackman (1990) summarizes the relation between sexuality and fascism in terms of a "rhetoric of virility."

Patria is composed of the Family," and that the mother is the "angel of the family" (Biloni 1933: 243). The fascist "cult of the mother" that appropriated a visceral Italian feeling about the nature of motherhood did not need Mazzini for inspiration. Indeed, Mazzini's rhetoric and the regime's strategy sprang from the same cultural well. Motherhood has deep cultural meaning in Italy. The idea that motherhood is woman's most valuable role crosses class and educational boundaries.[29]

The obituary narrative of a twenty-six-year-old schoolteacher who died in a communist "terrorist attack" in the city of Fiume in 1942 illustrates both the appropriation of motherhood to the nation and the cultural importance of motherhood. The local Fascist party in Trieste constructed the "spinster" as a fascist heroine.[30]

The spinster was an active member of Fascist Women's Organizations and received a public funeral in Trieste that merited a page of reporting in the inside section of *Il Piccolo Di Trieste*, the local newspaper. The headlines read in bold print, "Trieste saluted the corpse of Letitia M. with a unanimous demonstration of fascist faith." The woman's death was used to dramatize the perfidy of the traditional fascist enemies, the communists. The funeral received national recognition because both the National Fascist party secretary and Giuseppe Bottai, the minister of education, attended. The newspaper representation of the funeral suggests that the woman is more of an icon than a person.

The funeral is described in the language of emotion that dominated fascist discourse. The funeral sparked a "wave of collective emotion" in Trieste where "Thousands of tears streamed down the faces of the crowd as the white coffin in which the ripped apart flesh of the Martyr was arranged." This is the only mention of the woman's body, and from the account it becomes clear that she is invisible except to the extent that she stands as a rallying point for the devotion of fascist mothers and a symbol of political strife on the frequently contested Austrian-Italian border.

The crowd that lined the street as the coffin was carried from the central train station to the cathedral, where the bishop officiated at a solemn High Mass, was composed of the "common faces" of "laborers, salesgirls, office workers and above all good mothers; faces of simple and pure creatures, who in the morning hour, have left their work and their hard and uncertain daily existence to create an act of solidarity in sorrow and in love of country as only a people and its most noble flowers, women, knows how to fulfill."

---

[29] No specific research supports my claim, and that is perhaps sufficient evidence for making it. The importance of motherhood is so taken for granted in Italian "local knowledge" that it has never occurred to anyone to study it.

[30] I use the term *spinster* to describe this unmarried woman as a convenient shorthand for how she would have been construed in 1940s Italy, as well as a device to protect her privacy. Where I have had to use a name, I have substituted Letitia M. for the name in the archival records. The data for the "story" of the spinster is found in Archivio Centrale dello Stato, Rome, Partito Nazionale Fascista, Mostra della Rivoluzione Fascista, busta 4 (Fiume).

If women have a special gift for emotion, they also have a special gift to serve as symbols of the nation.[31] This secular tradition, which is common to other European nations, has no counterpart in Italy but finds its sacred counterpart in the body of the Blessed Virgin Mary, the Mother of Christ who is a virtual cult figure in Italian Catholic culture.[32] In the representation of the funeral of the spinster, the mother and the nation merge.

The death of the woman at the hands of local terrorists was important because it firmly implanted Trieste in the Italian camp and created a symbolic bridge between the soldiers who gave their life in the war and the mothers of those soldiers.

> The mothers, the wives, the children that yesterday accompanied the corpse of Letitia M. with a Roman salute that formed a superb arch of force and human gentleness, are the mothers, wives, sisters of soldiers, of sailors, of pilots and of *Black Shirts* laboring in the hardest struggle ever recorded in the history of our Patria. In their salute vibrated the will to victory of their sons, of their husbands far away; vibrated a faith that the enemy will never be able to conquer or scorn.

Soldiers who give their lives in national war achieve importance by nature of their sacrifice. This is why the Tombs of the Unknown Soldiers achieved such prominence and also why it does not really matter who is in them. But even in a field where personality is secondary to membership in the community, the spinster is curiously invisible—in part, because as an unmarried woman she has no real place in either Italian or fascist culture.

The representations of the spinster render her invisible and her invisibility provides the link in the story between fascist political identities and longstanding cultural identities. The spinster has no voice, no body, and no family. She is completely a construction of others. Elaine Scarry (1985: 216) makes the point that, "To have a body is, finally, to permit oneself to be described." As a spinster, she is socially and culturally invisible. Her body is beyond description.

The spinster's death is passive—an accident of being in the wrong place at the wrong time. And with the exception of the one newspaper reference to her torn-apart body (she was killed by a terrorist bomb), she is pure spirit—her soul and her intelligence—intangible qualities are the only characteristics that are mentioned. Her body is sacred and excluded from the story with one exception—the mention of her "luminous eyes" that gazed on the heavens.

More strikingly, the spinster is portrayed as without family. She may have been an orphan but we do not know that; in fact, the public narratives reveal nothing of her family background. Yet, she is important because she merited a public fu-

---

[31] Although there is no woman who stands as a national symbol of Italy, it was quite common to use the woman's body to convey national solidarity; see, for example, Agulhon (1981: esp. 122–34) on the connection between Marianne and the Blessed Virgin Mary.

[32] The cult of the Virgin Mary is deeply engrained in Italian culture. The history of its significance for the modern period has not yet been written. For the premodern period, see Carroll (1986, 1992).

neral and numerous propaganda narratives of her role in the party. But she is not important for herself—the self in the spinster's case is denied.

The spinster was depicted in virginal terms and as such she evoked the Virgin Mary whose importance in Catholic doctrine is her role in giving birth to Christ the son of God. The spinster gave birth to nothing and thus she can serve only as an icon, but as an icon that reinforces the sacrifice of mothers—the purveyors of cultural power. Mothers were sacred in a culture where woman's sexuality was invisible until it resulted in fertility.[33] Yet there is a cultural paradox here because sexuality was quite visible in the language of virility and emotion that dominated the descriptions of fascist public narratives.

The spinster was important as a cultural cipher that forced the mothers into the streets to assert their solidarity with the regime. The spinster achieved her social importance by dying. Paradoxically, fascism actually provided women such as the spinster a measure of economic and political power as they worked at jobs in the public sphere (De Grazia 1992: 166–200). But social and cultural power was reserved for the mothers. The regime was somewhat schizophrenic in its position on women. On one hand it wished women to work as a feature of the modernization project, and on the other it initiated demographic policies that taxed bachelors and gave monetary rewards to mothers of large families. As fascist bodies lay in shambles on the battlefield, it was the mother as the producer of new fascist bodies that had power in this story. The offering by the mothers of their sons to the nation takes precedence over the death of the spinster.

The State and Cultural Context

The peculiarities of the Italian state underscore the cultural specificity of state-making and its attendant political romances. In Italy, the bureaucracy of the state has been overdeveloped; the affective, emotional claims of the nation, the feelings of belonging have been underdeveloped. Nation-ness has been historically weak in Italy, and, as I have argued, if we uncouple the terms *nation* and *state*, we can describe Italy as a state without a nation. It was not until 1922, with the advent of the fascist regime, that a deliberate nation/state project, albeit a peculiar one, was under way.

The fascist regime attempted to colonize the principal sources of Italian emotional attachment, the family and religion, and submerge them in the community of the state. It pursued this activity in the policy arena with demographic campaigns and reconciliation with the church as well as in the symbolic realm. The fascist regime was no more successful at "making fascists" than the *Risorgimento* intellectuals had been at "making Italians." Commitment to the fascist state crumbled as Allied army bombs fell.

[33] For a discussion of the price paid by Italian women who gave in to their sexuality without benefit of matrimony, see Kertzer (1993).

The relative failure of the fascist project raises the broader issue of state and culture. *Success* and *failure* are overly bounded terms to describe a process for which hard outcome measures do not exist. The Italian state, past and present, "does," in idiosyncratic fashion, what every modern state "does"—it taxes, builds infrastructure, runs elections and social welfare, and employs state bureaucrats. Where the Italian state continues to fall short is, as Eco suggested, in the production of a political community whose citizens can imagine goals and norms that transcend local interests. As any dysfunctional family, the Italian state has existed and continues to exist "in itself" but not "for itself." [34]

I have argued that *Risorgimento*, and then fascist political discourse, enlisted popular religious practice and gender imagery in the service of nation/state making. But a black box between discourse and political efficacy remains. Emptying the content of that box would explain why "feeling" for the nation never developed in Italy. Timothy Mitchell's (1991; this volume) analysis of the state as a series of more or less powerful effects is evocative in this respect and provides the basis of a speculative conclusion for this article. According to Mitchell, standard state theory posits a rigid and artificial boundary between state and society. He argues that the state is not simply a structure but a "structural effect" whose degree of efficacy is highly conditioned by the social context of which it is a part. Structure and context are inextricably connected and cannot be analyzed separately.

If Mitchell's argument is reversed, that is, if we look at the state as an outgrowth of social effects, then we can begin to retheorize in terms of culture the Italian difficulty with national commitment. In short, if as in the Italian case the social institutions that buttress the cultural norms (that is, family and church) are strong, then the cultural meanings that they generate are fairly resistant to political appropriation. It is possible to have a situation in which social "effects" are stronger than state "effects." The strength of social effects would greatly attenuate the state's ability to produce nation "effects"—or to project identity or emotion upward on the nation/state. Or to reframe within the Italian context, the more functional the family remains as a social institution, the more dysfunctional, to return to Eco, the Italian state. Social "effects" have, to date, produced an Italy in permanent flirtation with the nation/state.

References

Agulhon, Maurice. 1981. *Marianne into Battle: Republican Imagery and Symbolism in France, 1789–1890*, translated by Janet Lloyd. New York: Cambridge University Press.

Allum, Percy. 1973. *Italy—Republic without Government?* New York: W. W. Norton.

---

[34] I owe this formulation, which evokes the Marxist formulation of class "for" and "in" itself, to Bob Jessop.

Anderson, Benedict. 1991. *Imagined Communities: Reflections on the Origin and Spread of Nationalism*. London: Verso.

Berezin, Mabel. 1991. "Created Constituencies: The Italian Middle Classes and Fascism." In *Splintered Classes*, edited by Rudy Koshar, 157–58. New York: Holmes and Meier.

——. 1994. "Cultural Form and Political Meaning." *American Journal of Sociology* 99: 1237–86.

——. 1997. *Making the Fascist Self: The Political Culture of Interwar Italy*. Ithaca: Cornell University Press.

Biloni, Vincenzo. 1933. *Cultura Fascista: Secondo i programmi delle scuole secondarie d'avviamento professionale*. Brescia: Giulio Vannini.

Borneman, John. 1992. *Belonging in the Two Berlins: Kin, State, and Nation*. Cambridge: Cambridge University Press.

Brubaker, Rogers. 1996. *Nationalism Reframed: Nationhood and the National Question in the New Europe*. Cambridge: Cambridge University Press.

Calhoun, Craig, ed. 1993. *Habermas and the Public Sphere*. Cambridge: MIT Press.

——. 1994. "Social Theory and the Politics of Identity." In *Social Theory and the Politics of Identity*, edited by Craig Calhoun, 9–36. Cambridge, Mass.: Blackwell.

Cannistraro, Philip. 1975. *La Fabbrica del consenso*. Rome: Laterza.

Carroll, Michael. 1986. *The Cult of the Virgin Mary*. Princeton: Princeton University Press.

——. 1992. *Madonnas That Maim: Popular Catholicism in Italy since the Fifteenth Century*. Baltimore: Johns Hopkins University Press.

Connell, Robert W. 1990. "The State, Gender, and Sexual Politics." *Theory and Society* 19: 507–43.

Connolly, William. 1991. *Identity/Difference*. Ithaca: Cornell University Press.

De Grazia, Victoria. 1981. *The Culture of Consent: Mass Organization of Leisure in Fascist Italy*. New York: Cambridge University Press.

——. 1992. *How Fascism Ruled Women*. Berkeley: University of California Press.

De Rosa, Gabriele. 1966. *Il Partito popolare italiano*. Bari: Laterza.

Di Palma, Giuseppe. 1990. *To Craft Democracies: An Essay on Democratic Transitions*. Berkeley: University of California Press.

Dix, Gregory. 1946. *The Shape of the Liturgy*. Glasgow: The University Press.

Elshtain, Jean Bethke. 1981. *Public Man, Private Woman*. Princeton: Princeton University Press.

Fitzpatrick, P. J. 1993. *In Breaking of Bread: The Eucharist and Ritual*. Cambridge: Cambridge University Press.

Forgacs, David, and Geoffrey Nowell-Smith, eds. 1985. *Antonio Gramsci: Selections from the Cultural Writings*. Cambridge: Harvard University Press.

Gentile, Emilio. 1990. "Fascism as Political Religion." *Journal of Contemporary History* 25: 229–51.

——. 1993. *Il Culto del littorio*. Rome: Laterza.

Gentile, Giovanni. 1991. "L'Organizzazione scientifica dello stato e l'istuto di finanza." In *Giovanni Gentile Politica e Cultura*, edited by Herve A. Caval-lera, vol. 2, 86–95. Florence: Le Lettere.

Ginzburg, Carlo. 1982. *The Cheese and The Worms*, translated by John and Anne Tedeschi. England: Penguin.

Goodwin, Jeff. 1997. "Libidinal Ties and Solidarity: The Huk Rebellion, 1946 to 1954." *American Sociological Review* 62: 53–69.

Gregor, A. James. 1969. *The Ideology of Fascism*. New York: Free Press.

Habermas, Jurgen. 1989. *The Structural Transformation of the Public Sphere*, translated by Thomas Burger. Cambridge: MIT Press.

Hobsbawm, Eric J. 1983. "Mass Producing Traditions: Europe, 1870–1914." In *The Invention of Tradition*, edited by Eric J. Hobsbawm and Terence Ranger, 263–307. New York: Cambridge University Press.

——. 1990. *Nations and Nationalism since 1780*. New York: Cambridge University Press.

Horn, David G. 1994. *Social Bodies*. Princeton: Princeton University Press.

Hunt, Lynn. 1984. *Politics, Culture, and Class in the French Revolution*. Berkeley: University of California Press.

——. 1992. *The Family Romance of the French Revolution*. Berkeley: University of California Press.

Jemolo, Arturo C. 1960. *Church and State in Italy 1850–1950*, translated by David Moore. Oxford: Basil Blackwell.

Kertzer, David I. 1980. *Comrades and Christians*. New York: Cambridge University Press.

——. 1993. *Sacrificed for Honor: Italian Infant Abandonment and the Politics of Reproductive Control*. Boston: Beacon Press.

King, Bolton, and Thomas Okey. 1904. *Italy To-Day*. London: James Nisbet.

Klein, Gabriella. 1986. *La Politica linguistica del fascismo*. Bologna: Il Mulino.

Laitin, David, et al. 1994. "Language and the Construction of States: The Case of Catalonia in Spain." *Politics and Society* 22: 5–29.

Lefort, Claude. 1986. *The Political Forms of Modern Society*, translated by John B. Thompson. Cambridge: MIT Press.

Linz, Juan J. 1975. "Totalitarian and Authoritarian Regimes." In *Handbook of Political Science*, vol. 3, edited by Fred I. Greenstein and Nelson W. Polsby, 191–92. Boston: Addison-Wesley.

Lovett, Clara. 1982. *The Democratic Movement in Italy 1830–1876*. Cambridge: Harvard University Press.

Lyttelton, Adrian. 1966. "Fascism in Italy: The Second Wave." *Journal of Contemporary History* 1: 75–100.

——. 1993. "The National Question in Italy." In *The National Question in Europe in Historical Context*, edited by Mikulas Teich and Roy Porter. New York: Cambridge University Press.

Manzini, C[arlo]. 1938. *Il Duce a Verona*. Verona: C. E. Albarelli–Marchesetti.

March, James G., and Johan P. Olsen. 1989. *Rediscovering Institutions*. New York: Free Press.

Migliorini, Bruno, and T. Gwynfor Griffith. 1984. *The Italian Language*. London: Faber and Faber.

Miller, David. 1995. *On Nationality*. New York: Oxford at Clarendon Press.

Mitchell, Timothy. 1991. "The Limits of the State: Beyond Statist Approaches and Their Critics." *American Political Science Review* 85: 77–85.

Mosse, George L. 1985. *Nationalism and Sexuality*. Madison: University of Wisconsin Press.

Poggi, Gianfranco. 1978. *The Development of the Modern State: A Sociological Introduction*. Stanford: Stanford University Press.

Putnam, Robert. 1993. *Making Democracy Work*. Princeton: Princeton University Press.

Scarry, Elaine. 1985. *The Body in Pain: The Making and Unmaking of the World*. New York: Oxford University Press.

Schneider, Herbert W., and Shephard B. Clough. 1929. *Making Fascists*. Chicago: Chicago University Press.

Somers, Margaret R. 1994. "The Narrative Constitution of Identity: A Relational and Network Approach." *Theory and Society* 23: 605–49.

Spackman, Barbara. 1990. "The Fascist Rhetoric of Virility." *Stanford Italian Review* 8: 81–102.

Tannenbaum, Edward R. 1972. *The Fascist Experience*. New York: Basic.

Taylor, Charles. 1989. *Sources of the Self*. Cambridge: Harvard University Press.

Tilly, Charles. 1985. "War Making and State Making as Organized Crime." In *Bringing the State Back In*, edited by Peter B. Evans, Dietrich Reuschemeyer, and Theda Skocpol, 169–87. Cambridge: Cambridge University Press.

Verdery, Katherine. 1994. "From Parent-State to Family Patriarchs: Gender and Nation in Contemporary Eastern Europe." *East European Politics and Societies* 8: 225–55.

Viroli, Maurizio. 1995. *For Love of Country*. New York: Oxford at the Clarendon Press.

Weber, Eugen. 1976. *Peasants into Frenchmen*. Stanford: Stanford University Press.

Webster, Richard A. 1960. *The Cross and the Fasces*. Stanford: Stanford University Press.

Weintraub, Jeff. 1997. "The Theory and Politics of the Public/Private Distinction." In *Public and Private in Thought and Practice: Perspectives on a Grand Dichotomy*, edited by Jeff Weintraub and Krishan Kumar, 1–42. Chicago: University of Chicago Press.

12

Narrating the Future of the National Economy and the National State: Remarks on Remapping Regulation and Reinventing Governance

Bob Jessop

In this essay I consider the changing articulation of the economic and the political in contemporary capitalism. This topic is often reduced to the changing relationship between markets and the state. The following account broadens such analyses by examining the social and cultural embeddedness of market and state and the ways in which they are articulated both discursively and extradiscursively. To illustrate this claim I refer substantively to changes in the state form that has been centrally associated with Atlantic Fordism.

Theoretically, my account draws on three complementary approaches concerned in their different ways with the discursive as well as extradiscursive aspects of economic and political phenomena.[1] First, the regulation approach suggests that the role of market forces is merely one among several contributing factors to capitalist expansion. The economy in its broadest sense includes both economic and extraeconomic factors. It is an ensemble of socially embedded, socially

This paper draws heavily on my earlier work and my intellectual debts are correspondingly wide. I nonetheless acknowledge the special contribution of all participants in the Chicago workshop, especially George Steinmetz, together with earlier comments from Frank Deppe and Ngai-Ling Sum. I wrote this paper after receiving a grant from the Economic and Social Research Council (United Kingdom) (No. L311253032), and I revised it while I was Hallsworth Fellow in Political Economy at Manchester University.

[1] The distinction between social and cultural phenomena is analytical and based on their respective emergent properties. Whereas the "social" concerns configurations of social interaction, the "cultural" refers to properties of both narrative and non-narrative discursive formations. However, insofar as social relations are discursively constituted and meaningful, they have a cultural dimension; and, insofar as cultural phenomena are realized in and through social relations, they have a social dimension.

regularized, and strategically selective[2] institutions, organizations, social forces, and actions organized around (or at least involved in) the expanded reproduction of capital as a social relation. In this sense the regulation approach could be seen as providing (at least implicitly) a neo-Gramscian analysis of *l'economia integrale* (the economy in its inclusive sense) and could even be related to Gramsci's own reflections on Americanism, Fordism, markets, and economic agents as cultural phenomena (see Jessop 1997b). Second, neo-Gramscian political analysis treats *lo stato integrale* (the state in its inclusive sense) as an ensemble of socially embedded, socially regularized, and strategically selective institutions, organizations, social forces, and activities organized around (or at least involved in) making collectively binding decisions for an imagined political community. One way to interpret Gramsci's famous definition of the state as "political society + civil society" is to see it as highlighting the complex and variable articulation of government and governance in underwriting state power. Certainly this definition and Gramsci's related claim that state power involves "hegemony armored by coercion" both suggest that the state system embraces far more than juridicopolitical institutions and that there are important sociocultural aspects to the state (Gramsci 1971).

Third, drawing both on critical discourse analysis and more recent work on social narrativity,[3] I note the discursive constitution and regularization of both the capitalist economy and the national state as imagined entities and their cultural as well as social embeddedness. Thus, the economy is viewed as an imaginatively narrated system that is accorded specific boundaries, conditions of existence, typical economic agents, tendencies and countertendencies, and a distinctive overall dynamic (Daly 1994; Barnes and Ledubur 1991; Miller and Rose 1993). Among relevant phenomena here are technoeconomic paradigms, norms of production and consumption, specific models of development, accumulation strategies, societal paradigms, and the broader organizational and institutional narratives and/or meta-narratives that provide the general context (or "web of interlocution") in which these make sense (see Jessop 1982; Jenson 1990; Somers 1994; Jessop 1995a). The state system can likewise be treated as an imagined political community with its own specific boundaries, conditions of existence, political subjects, developmental tendencies, sources of legitimacy, and state projects (see Jessop 1990; Kratochwil 1986; Mitchell 1991).[4] Combining these three approaches enables me to analyze the discursive mapping of the economy as a

[2] In regulationist terms, strategic selectivity refers to the differential impact of the core structural (including spatiotemporal) features of a labor process, an accumulation regime, or a mode of regulation on the relative capacity of particular forces organized in particular ways to successfully pursue a specific economic strategy over a given time horizon and economic space, acting alone or in combination with other forces and in the face of competition, rivalry, or opposition from yet other forces. (With regard to the state, see Jessop, 1990: 260, and passim.)

[3] My use of the term *critical discourse analysis* subsumes this recent work on narrativity unless it is important to distinguish between them.

[4] Discourse analysis is a generic methodology rather than a substantive field of inquiry; it is therefore as relevant to political and economic investigation as to work on ideology or other forms of social relation.

distinctive object of regulation, to argue that the postwar national state is but one form of imagined political community, and, given the emerging barriers to continued accumulation and the paradigmatic crisis of Atlantic Fordism, to note some key changes in the overall articulation of the economic and political in contemporary capitalism.

The following comments are not a novel effort on my part to introduce culture into state analysis.[5] Instead I show how three theoretical perspectives already widely adopted in critical studies of political economy each share a strong, albeit often neglected, concern with the cultural as well as the social embeddedness of economic and political activities. Thus, I am not so much concerned to "bring culture back in" for the purposes of economic or political analysis as to make the cultural concerns of recent neo-Marxist theorizing more explicit and to highlight their compatibility with the more self-conscious constructivism found in critical discourse analysis. Some Marxist theorists see the distinction between the economic and the political as just an illusory, fetishized reflection of the so-called separation-in-unity of the capital relation (for example, Holloway and Picciotto 1978; Wood 1981). Although I reject this essentialist position, I do share its insight that the cultural and social construction of boundaries between the economic and political has major implications for the forms and effectiveness of the articulation of market forces and state intervention in the "reproduction-régulation" of capitalism. And, in offering an alternative interpretation of this insight, I combine arguments from the regulation approach, neo-Gramscian state theory, and critical discourse analysis to highlight the discursive (or sociocultural) construction of political economic realities.

Some Key Features of the Postwar National State

These arguments are developed in relation to the ongoing transformation of the Atlantic Fordist economy. This was defined primarily by its economic foundation in the postwar dominance, in North America and northwestern Europe, of a mode of growth based, at least paradigmatically, on a virtuous macroeconomic circle generated by mass production and mass consumption. This was linked to a distinctive social mode of economic regulation (involving specific norms, expectations, and forms of calculation as well as special structural forms) and a distinctive mode of societalization (or "societal paradigm") for the wider society (for a review of accounts of Fordism, see Jessop 1992a). Given the current book's concern with "state/culture," however, I focus on the state form that helped to sustain Atlantic Fordism.[6] This can be called the Keynesian welfare na-

---

[5] Although it must be admitted that earlier ideas have been reworked in the light of critical discourse analysis and theories of social narrativity.

[6] For a more extended and more rounded discussion of Fordism and post-Fordism in terms of labor process, accumulation regime, social mode of economic regulation, and mode of societalization, see Jessop (1992a).

tional state (hereafter KWNS). In tandem with the continued restructuring of the Fordist economy, this particular political configuration is also witnessing significant changes. These changes can be analyzed from a regulationist perspective in terms of the remapping of accumulation regimes and their "reproduction-régulation" on different spatial scales or from a neo-Gramscian, more state-centered, viewpoint in terms of the reinventing of "government-governance" relations. From the former perspective, these changes in the state have been characterized in terms of the development of a "competition state" (see Cerny 1989; Hirsch 1994) or Schumpeterian workfare regime (Jessop 1993). Here I consider these changes from a more state-theoretical perspective and so examine the restructuring of the state in its inclusive sense. In particular, I contend that, at least since the 1980s, the KWNS has seen major structural reorganization and strategic reorientation as evidenced in three general trends: denationalization, destatization, and internationalization. Before detailing these changes, however, I introduce the idea of "national state" (as opposed to nation-state) and identify the key features of an ideal-typical Keynesian welfare national state.

Not all advanced capitalist states can be characterized as "nation-states" in the sense of being ethnonational states based on a *Volksnation*. Some are based on a civic nation (*Staatsnation*), encompassing shared commitments to the constitution and representative government; and others incline more to cultural nationhood (*Kulturnation*) based on the active conforming by an ethical state of its citizens to a shared understanding of national culture and civilization.[7] Regardless of the nature of their corresponding form of nationhood, however, they can all be described as national states, that is, as formally sovereign territorial states presiding over "national" territories. Moreover, within the context of Atlantic Fordism, these states can also be characterized as Keynesian welfare national states. In this regard they are all subject to similar pressures for change due to the emerging dynamic of globalization and regionalization in different functional domains. In this essay I suggest how this particular variant of the national territorial state came to be constituted in and through particular metanarratives concerning economic and political realities in the postwar world and their implications for the institutional design of postwar capitalism. I also consider how the material pressures to change this state form have recently been constructed through particular metanarratives concerning economic and political realities in the postwar world.

The Keynesian Welfare National State

Although most national economies have long been organized around major urban economies and have been integrated into plurinational productive systems (such as colonial systems or trading blocs), the various urban and pluri-

[7] These three forms of nation are illustrated, respectively, by Germany, the United States, and France. I employ the terms *Staatsnation* and *Kulturnation* somewhat differently from Meinecke's more established usage (1928).

national economies associated with Atlantic Fordism were primarily managed in and through national states. Thus, as an object of political management, the complex field of economic relations was handled as though it was divided into a series of relatively closed national economies. One could perhaps argue here that separate "Keynesian welfare national states" never really existed as such but were just the imaginary, discursively constituted form in and through which an effectively plurinational Atlantic Fordism was organized under U.S. hegemony. However, this would involve ignoring how far national economies and Keynesian welfare national states were structurally coupled as well as strategically coordinated through the naturalization of these organizational principles; and thus ignoring the extent to which economic regulation through the KWNS itself contributed significantly to the material as well as discursive constitution of national economies as objects of regulation. This path-dependent national structural coupling and coevolution can in part explain the contrasts between different national variants of Fordism (see, for example, Boyer 1988; Boyer and Saillard 1995; Tickell and Peck 1992). These contrasts can by no means be explained by ignoring the specificities of the imaginary spatial constitution of economies as objects of regulation or neglecting the role of national political regimes in consolidating national economies.

International as well as urban and regional policies had supporting roles to play in this regard, of course; but they were mapped onto and organized around these "imagined" national economies and their national states. Thus international economic policy promoted cooperation to underwrite the smooth workings of national economies and, where possible, to secure and reinforce their complementarity rather than abolish them or integrate them into some superimperialist system. Likewise, urban and regional policies were mainly redistributive, pursued in a top-down manner orchestrated by the national state, and primarily concerned with equalizing economic and social conditions within such national economies. Hence they helped to secure the conditions for mass production, mass distribution, and mass consumption and to reduce inflationary pressures due to localized overheating in a largely autocentric economy.

These and other features of the KWNS can be summarized as follows:

- Among the various spatial scales of formal political organization, the sovereign state level was regarded as primary. Local and regional states served primarily as transmission belts for national economic and social politics. The key supranational institutions comprised various international and intergovernmental agencies—typically organized under U.S. hegemony—and were designed to promote cooperation among national states in securing certain key conditions for postwar economic and political regeneration in Europe[8] and continued economic expansion in North America.

[8] On this aspect, see Milward, Brennan, and Romero (1992). More generally, it should be noted here that I am far from claiming that all economic and political processes were confined within the borders of the power container formed by the national state: I argue that many economic and political processes organized on an international basis served to underpin the national state in the early stages of postwar reconstruction.

- State economic strategies and economic regulation assumed a relatively closed national economy. The international economy was understood mainly in terms of financial and trade flows among various national economies.
- Among the various spatial scales of economic organization, the national economy was accorded primacy for state action, defined and measured in terms of national aggregates, and managed primarily in terms of targeted variation in these aggregates (Barnes and Ledubur 1991: 130).[9] Local or regional economies were treated as subunits of the national economy and interregional differences regarded as unimportant.
- The primary object of welfare and social reproduction policies was seen as the resident national population and its constituent households and individual citizens. Many of these policies assumed the predominance of stable two-parent families in which men received a "family wage" and could also expect lifetime employment.[10]
- The primary units of the state's social basis were individual political subjects endowed, as citizens of the national state, with various legal, political, and social rights and organized as members of economic-corporate organizations (trade unions and business associations) and/or as supporters of responsible political parties.
- The axis of struggles over political hegemony at home was the "national-popular" and its realization in the development, expansion, and protection of such rights in an "economic-corporate" political process.

In short, there was a close and mutually reinforcing linkage between the national state form and Keynesian welfarism. It is tempting, therefore, to argue that the KWNS represented the apogee of the national state insofar as most of its key features were organized as if they were confined within the "power container" of the national state. The KWNS probably gave fullest expression to the organizational and societalizing possibilities of the national state with its retreat from formal empire and its limited commitment to integration into supranational economic blocs. This focus is not due to some teleological unfolding of this potential but to specific economic and political conditions associated with the organization of Atlantic Fordism under U.S. hegemony. Thus, to argue counterfactually, had Nazi Germany secured through economic and military imperialism the conditions for its projected "New Order," a much more strongly plurinational and far more polarized mode of economic regulation would have been established in Europe. Instead, the Allied defeat of the Axis powers created certain essential conditions for generalizing the American New Deal to Europe through the paradoxical reassertion of the organizational principle of the national state. It was through the national state that the national economy would be regulated as a distinctive imagined economic space and efforts made to secure a complementary expansion of national production and consumption as the basis for a politics of prosperity rather than right-wing or left-wing political extremism

---

[9] This also meant the exclusion of the informal economy and the sphere of domestic labor from direct economic management.

[10] Lifetime employment should not be confused with having the same job for life.

(see Siegel 1988; Maier 1978; Hall 1989; van der Pijl 1984; Milward, Brennan, and Romero 1992).

In this sense, the postwar national state can be distinguished from preceding forms, such as the mercantilist, liberal constitutional, or imperialist state—each of which occupied its own distinctive imaginary national space and had its own distinctive forms of insertion into the system of plurinational economic orders. It can also be distinguished from currently emerging "postnational" state forms that are oriented to the management of recently rediscovered or newly formed regional economies on various sub- and supranational scales, including localized cross-border linkages, as well as their articulation with the emerging global-regional dynamics. In short, the construction of the national economy and its associated national state in the postwar period was a specific historical moment in the overall mapping and organization of the "reproduction-régulation" of capitalism. This suggests, in turn, that the recent transformation of the national economy and its associated national state is related to changing spaces and forms of accumulation and their impact on the continued feasibility and/or plausibility of treating economic relations as primarily national in form.

In What Sense Is This National State Being Eroded?

KWNS development was marked by reformist optimism until the mid-1970s. Expert and public opinion then became more critical and the significance of the national state came to be narrated and debated in other ways. Thus, after initial assertions that the modern state was no longer functioning as expected, proposals emerged for managing or even resolving the crisis in the state: its functions should be shared with nonstate bodies to reduce overload on an overextended state apparatus and/or be reduced by returning to the liberal night-watchman state. The diagnosis and narration of failure and crisis and calls for some degree of intervention were important sites of struggle during this period; and, depending on the outcome of this struggle, different political solutions were essayed. Moreover, since the distinctiveness of the KWNS often went unrecognized, its failures and/or crisis-tendencies were often attributed to the "modern state" as such. After a period of conflictual (if not always crisis-driven) experimentation during the late 1970s and the 1980s, there came growing awareness that the resulting changes in the KWNS have not (and never could have) been restricted to simple redistribution or reduction of pregiven functions. Thus, attention turned to the emergence of a qualitatively new state form and how it might be inserted into the wider political system. Of more immediate interest here, however, are several analytically distinct, but empirically interrelated, crisis-tendencies of the KWNS:

- The centrality of the sovereign state itself was questioned due to the growth of allegedly overloaded "big government," to a legitimacy crisis as the state no longer seemed able to guarantee full employment and economic growth, and to an emerging fiscal crisis that threatened to undermine the welfare state. Growing conflicts between local states and central government aggravated these crisis-tendencies. The crisis of the international regimes organized under U.S. hegemony also undermined their ability to facilitate effective economic and political performance by national states. More generally, all three forms of the national state (based, respectively, on the *Volksnation, Kulturnation*, and *Staatsnation*) found in the space of Atlantic Fordism were challenged by growing internationalization or globalization. The latter trends have contributed to declining ethnic homogeneity due to migration, to declining cultural homogeneity with a plurality of ethnic and cultural groups and even an embrace of multiculturalism (especially in large cities), and to the declining legitimacy of the national state as internationalization makes it harder to meet the economic and social expectations generated by the growth dynamic of Atlantic Fordism and the political commitments of the KWNS.

- It became harder to achieve official national economic objectives such as full employment, stable prices, economic growth, and viable balance of payments, helping to undermine the national economy's taken-for-grantedness as the primary object of economic management. These issues led to protectionist calls to defend the national economy (or, at least, so-called "sunset" sectors and their associated jobs) and/or attempts to create a wider economic space within which "reproduction-régulation" could be renewed (often in a neoliberal policy context).
- Regional and local economies were increasingly recognized to have their own specific problems, which could be resolved neither through national macroeconomic policies nor uniformly imposed meso- or microeconomic policies. This situation prompted demands for specifically tailored and targeted urban and regional policies to be implemented from below.
- Internationalization led to a growing contradiction in the field of social reproduction. As the Atlantic Fordist accumulation regime developed, more advanced European economies began to import labor from their colonies, southern Europe, or North Africa (Kofman 1995). Initially intended to reconcile the need for cheap labor with the preservation of the Fordist class compromise for national citizens, such migration later became a source of tensions. These tensions were especially acute insofar as "the spatial distinction between the closed welfare state and the open movement of foreign labor across territorial borders was increasingly subverted by the tendency of foreign migrant workers to remain permanently in the receiving state and (legally or illegally) to be reunited with their families" (Klein-Beekman 1996: 451). This shift led to growing concern to police the boundaries of national citizenship and its associated Fordist capital-labor compromise and welfare rights.[11] By the mid-1970s, immigration was being constructed as a threat to national cohesion, full employment, and the welfare state. Further destabilizing factors for welfare states organized around citizenship rights were the decline of the stable two-parent family, the feminization of the paid labor force, and the rise of long-term unemployment. These factors began to transform the patriarchal nuclear family into an anachronism (Pringle 1995: 208).
- There was a crisis of political representation based on "governing parties," "business unionism," and capitalist associations, evident in growing electoral volatility and disaffection with parties and in sometimes militant rejection of postwar

[11] In the United States, migration from the Deep South and later from abroad (especially Mexico) served similar purposes. The struggle to include black Americans in the Fordist class compromise was especially acute because they were already nominally U.S. citizens.

capital-labor compromise. "New social movements" developed to challenge the industrial logic of Atlantic Fordism and the statist logic of Keynesian welfarism in favor of alternative forms of economic and political organization and an antibureaucratic, autonomous, politicized civil society (see Offe 1985; Hirsch and Roth 1985).

- The national-popular problematic of hegemonic struggles shifted from expanding prosperity and welfare rights toward a more nationalist, populist, and authoritarian discourse and/or toward a more cosmopolitan, neoliberal demand for "more market, less state" in a more open economy.

These various crisis-tendencies had their own dynamic but were often held to crystallize into an "organic crisis" of the KWNS as a whole. This theme was more resonant in some economies and political systems than others. But even those less susceptible to domestic discourses of crisis still encountered it secondhand through international agencies such as the OECD which, under the influence of U.S. and transnational financial capital, relayed the discourse of crisis and its neoliberal solution. These agencies thereby became major players in the internationalization of policy regimes (see below). Nonetheless, the KWNS was not immediately dismantled. Initially, efforts were made to intensify its features, by reinforcing and complementing them, to rescue it through corporatist concertation and/or top-down austerity measures. In this way, the KWNS underwent specific conjunctural transformations. In the wake of failure to restore postwar growth conditions, however, the problem was interpreted as a crisis *of* (and not merely *in*) the KWNS. Economic and political forces stepped up the search for a new state form (or forms) able to solve the deepening contradictions and crises of Atlantic Fordist accumulation and restabilize the state system. Now emerging stepwise from this search process is a basic structural transformation and strategic reorientation of the capitalist type of state, closely linked to the remapping and rearticulation of the territorial and functional bases of the postwar national state and to the reinvention of government-governance as it is reoriented in a more Schumpeterian workfare direction.

Three Trends in the Reorganization of the KWNS

This transformation is reflected in three major trends: denationalization, destatization, and internationalization. The first two affect basic structural features of national states; the third involves strategic reorientation and the changing nature of policy making. I discuss them briefly in general terms (for more details, see Jessop 1995a, 1997c), disregarding their individual and combined realization from case to case. Thus, my comments on denationalization ignore important differences between federal states, with clear constitutional powers allotted to national and regional levels of state organization, and unitary states, such as Britain, where local states exercise only such powers as are currently required or permitted by the central state. Similarly, in dealing with the phenomenon of destatization associated with the shift from government to governance, I neglect the extent to which some KWNS regimes had tripartite macroeconomic governance based on state, business, and unions and/or adopted forms of regulated self-regulation for delivering social welfare. Nonetheless I maintain that, here too, the role of governance has been strengthened at the same time as the range of partners has changed. Nor do I consider the differential importance of various governance mechanisms (for example, the contrast between a strengthened neocorporatist "negotiated economy" in Denmark and the rise of neoliberal parastatal organizations in Britain). Finally, in dealing with internationalization, I ignore differences among Schumpeterian workfare regimes (SWRs), the extent to which they can be described as postnational, and their articulation into specific "workfare-welfare" mixes (for a discussion of variant forms of SWR and their combination in specific cases, see Jessop 1992b, 1993). I also ignore the extent to which different states are more or less hegemonic in defining international policy regimes.

The Denationalization of the State

In part, the reorganization of the national state involves major changes in relations on the same organizational level. Thus, apart from shifts in the relative power of the executive, legislature, and judiciary, there are also shifts in the relative weight of financial, educational, technological, environmental, social security, and other organs (on Britain, see Jessop 1992b, 1994a). But reorganization also extends to the reordering of relations among different political tiers. Sometimes labeled "hollowing out," this trend is perhaps better discussed under the less metaphorical rubric of denationalization.

This process involves the active rearticulation of the various functions of the national state. Specifically, whereas the national state retains a large measure of formal national sovereignty rooted in continued mutual recognition among national states and remains an important site for political struggles, its actual capacities to project its power inside its borders (let alone beyond them) in the interests of accumulation have been decisively weakened both by movement toward more internationalized, flexible (but also regionalized) production systems and by the growing challenge posed by risks emanating from the global environment. Nonetheless this loss of autonomy does not lead to the simple "withering away" of the national state or the steady and unilinear erosion of its boundaries as a "power container."[12] Instead the loss of autonomy engenders both the need for supranational coordination and the space for subnational resurgence and extends thereby the scope for the national state itself to mediate between the supra- and subnational. Thus some state capacities are transferred to a growing number of panregional, plurinational, or international bodies with a widening range of powers; others are devolved to restructured local or regional

---

[12] On the divergent patterns of boundary rearticulation in this context, see Taylor (1994).

levels of governance in the national state; and yet others are being usurped by emerging horizontal networks of power—local and regional—that bypass central states and connect localities or regions in several nations.

The Growth of Supranational Regimes

First, supranational state apparatuses and international political regimes continue to expand both in number and in the scope of their responsibilities. This expansion is obvious in the European Union, with its widening and deepening field of operations and growing organizational complexity. It is also evident in the continuing proliferation and/or operational expansion of other supranational regional and transnational associations charged with regulating, guiding, and governing economic activities on territorial and/or functional lines. Some of these activities are considered in the next subsection. Here, I focus on a major area of expansion in the functional responsibilities of state apparatuses: concern with "structural competitiveness" in the various supranational economic spaces in which they have interests. These imagined spaces range from cross-border growth triangles through various plurinational productive spaces and so-called triad growth poles to hemispheric, intertriadic, and global economic relations. State concern with structural competitiveness goes well beyond managing international monetary relations, foreign investment, or trade to include a wide range of supply-side factors, both economic and extraeconomic in character. And these changes in turn are actively shaping the structure of the global economy, especially in its three major growth poles: Pacific Asia, European Economic Space, and North America.

The Resurgence of Regional and Local Governance

"Hollowing out" also involves a stronger role for regional or local states below the national level, which reflects the growing internationalization of economic flows and spaces as much as the economic retreat of the national state. Globalization of the world economy means that "the local economy can only be seen as a node within a global economic network [with] no meaningful existence outside this context" (Amin and Robins 1990: 28). Thus, at the same time as the triad regions are emerging, interest is renewed in promoting subnational regional and local economies rather than the national economy as such. This trend is occurring for many reasons, among them ecological, technological, economic, and political. Whereas some ecological problems need global, continental, or cross-border policy responses, others are best met locally or regionally (see Meinhardt 1992; Hay 1994). New technologies are also giving renewed importance to municipal as well as international policy. In more general economic terms, the supply side is increasingly seen as the key to national competitiveness. But this leads to mounting pressure for needed improvements in infrastructure, human resources, innovation systems, and so forth, to be identified at the appropriate level and implemented regionally, sectorally, or locally rather than through a uniform national policy.[13] And, in political terms, as national states lose effective powers internationally and prove less capable of delivering jobs and growth nationally, pressures mount for more effective local or regional government that might be able to satisfy economic demands. All these factors are closely linked, of course, to the rediscovery of cities, conurbations, and metropoles as crucial economic sites with major repercussions on the competitiveness and/or growth potential of surrounding economic spaces (see Jessop 1997a). Indeed, in certain respects, cities as much as (if not more than) firms are now being sponsored by the central state as "national champions."

An Emerging Trend toward Translocal Linkages

Growing links among local states extend beyond national boundaries to include foreign partners. These connections emerged in the 1970s and have expanded rapidly in the late 1980s and 1990s. In ever more cases in all three triad regions, there is increased cross-border cooperation among neighboring local or regional states from different national states. For example, there are growing links between cities in the growing number of transborder metropolitan regions between Mexico and the United States as well as along the U.S.-Canadian border. This is in addition to increased cooperation among individual states within the United States where they belong to the same imagined economic region or share common problems (see Fosler 1988: 312–26). Likewise, the European Union is now actively involved—especially with the collapse of communism in Central and Eastern Europe—in sponsoring translocal linkages among regions both within and beyond its borders. Thus, we find regional or local authorities engaged in vertical links with EU institutions, especially the European Commission, and/or direct links among nonpropinquitous local and regional authorities in member states.

The Destatization of Politics

The second general trend in the reinvention of the state in its inclusive sense is the shift from the centrality of govern*ment* to more decentralized forms of govern*ance*. This trend concerns not so much the territorial dispersion of the national state's activities as a reorganization of functions in the broader political system on whatever territorial scale the state operates. It involves movement from the taken-for-granted primacy of official (typically national) state apparatuses toward the taken-for-granted necessity of varied forms and levels of partnership between official, parastatal, and nongovernmental organizations in managing

[13] Boisot offers a telling critique of Porter's work on the competitive advantage of nations (Porter 1990) for its exaggerated concern with, and serious underestimation of, the capacities of the national state to promote the competitiveness of clusters. He notes that most clusters are regionally concentrated and that this indicates the relevance of proactive regional policies (Boisot 1993).

economic and social relations.[14] Hence it also involves a shift from the top-down hierarchical political organization typical of sovereign states to emphasis on promoting and/or steering the self-organization of interorganizational relations. In this expanding range of networks, partnerships, and other models of economic and political governance, official apparatuses would remain at best *primus inter pares*. Although public money and law would remain important in underpinning their operation, other resources (such as private money, knowledge, and expertise) are also critical to success. In this sense, the state's involvement tends to be less hierarchical, less centralized, and less dirigiste in nature. This movement is reflected in a change in organizational paradigm, which parallels other discursive shifts linked to the development of post-Fordism (without being reducible to this shift). In particular, we can note growing interest across a wide range of academic and professional disciplines and fields of social activity in governance itself as well as the new importance attached to network and/or partnership arrangements in corporate and regional governance (see Cooke and Morgan 1993) and the emergence of strategic thinking about the "governance of governance" (see Jessop 1995b).

This general trend is linked to the turn from imperative coordination imposed from above by the sovereign state to an emphasis on interdependence and the division of knowledge, on reflexive negotiation and mutual learning. It is variously reflected in conscious deployment of the principle of subsidiarity, in expansion of mechanisms such as "regulated self-regulation" and officially approved "private interest government" (see Streeck and Schmitter 1985), in increased importance of the informal sector (especially in the delivery of welfare and collective consumption), and in the role of national and supranational states in promoting decentralized context-steering and facilitating self-organization (see Matzner 1994; Willke 1992).[15]

Such shifts are evident on all territorial scales of state organization as well as in a wide range of functional areas. They are closely linked to the hollowing out of the national state and to the structural transformation and strategic reorientation of the key economic and social functions of the KWNS. The expansion of regional-local, supranational, and translocal or cross-border linkages has played a major role in promoting the growth of governance at the expense of national government. The enhanced role of the state's supply-side functions in increasingly open economies also points in this direction. For the moment, however, I

---

[14] Before the state's expansion this century, various forms of partnership existed between state and nonstate bodies. But there were probably two main differences with the post-Fordist situation: (a) the state was relatively hierarchical in form compared to the flatter and leaner post-Fordist state, and (b) there was less emphasis on partnership (certainly at the discursive level) and a greater tendency to take for granted a mutual indifference and division of labor between state and civil society.

[15] In the discussions at the conference from which this book derives, Julia Adams suggested that this amounts to a partial dedifferentiation of the economic and political. The plausibility of this suggestion depends on reducing their prior differentiation to a naturalized distinction between market and state. Both regulationists and neo-Gramscians would reject this.

focus on the multitiered nature rather than the variable functional geometry of governance mechanisms.

Although much of the debate (especially in Britain) about the future of the European Union is highly state-centered, it is actually on the European level that the general destatization trend is especially remarkable. These two phenomena are far from being unrelated, for it is difficulties in European state-building as much as changes in the European economy that have prompted the strategic reorientation from government to governance. Thus the current development of supranational European governance involves far more than the emergence of a federal, confederal, or intergovernmental apparatus. It also involves the active constitution of other supranationally organized and/or oriented economic and social partners—whether functional or territorial—and their integration into loosely coupled, flexible policymaking networks through specific communication, negotiation, and decision-making channels (see Tömmel 1994: 14).[16] Indeed, "the European Commission places a major emphasis on the formation of networks as a means of encouraging the achievement of the difficult goal of European integration and . . . cohesion" (Cooke and Morgan 1993: 554). Especially interesting in this regard is the commitment to multitiered networks involving both territorial and functional actors (for more details, see Jessop 1995a).

The same trend toward governance is found at national, regional-local, and the translocal levels. Having made the case in general terms and illustrated it from the supranational level, however, I simply refer to the large literature on regional and local governance and its role in promoting the "joint product" of endogenous economic development based on enhanced structural competitiveness. The strengthening of local and regional governance is linked with the reorganization of the local state as new forms of local partnership emerge to guide and promote the development of local resources. For example, local unions, local chambers of commerce, local venture capital, local education bodies, local research centers, and local states may enter into arrangements to regenerate the local economy. This trend is reinforced by the central state's inability to pursue sufficiently differentiated and sensitive programs to tackle the specific problems of particular localities. It therefore devolves such tasks to local states and provides the latter with general support and resources (see Dyson 1988: 118).

The Internationalization of Policy Regimes

This trend refers to the increased strategic significance of the international context of domestic state action and the latter's extension to a wide range of extraterritorial or transnational factors and processes. It involves both a change in

[16]The following argument draws heavily on Tömmel's path-breaking work on the European Community (1992, 1994); it has also been influenced by recent theoretical work by Schmitter (1992), Scharpf (1994), and Streeck and Schmitter (1991).

the balance of the state's strategic orientations to different scales of political action and a change in the relative importance of national and international sources of policy. This shift blurs the distinction between domestic and foreign policy and widens the territorial bases of actors who are either directly involved in decision making and/or whose opinions and likely reactions are taken into account. International agencies and international regime-building are especially significant in this regard. This trend applies to all territorial scales on which states are organized: it is not limited to the national state.

This trend is reflected in economic and social policy, for example, insofar as the prime object of economic and social intervention by national states in North America and the EU has been changing from the well-balanced domestic performance of the "national economy" to its overall "international competitiveness" understood in very broad terms. It can be seen in the tendential shift from the Keynesian welfare concerns of the postwar European national states to less state-centered Schumpeterian workfare concerns in an emerging postnational or "multiscalar" political regime. Economically, such concerns involve promoting product, process, organizational, and market innovation in open economies to strengthen as far as possible the structural competitiveness of the national economy by intervening on the supply side. Such concerns are reflected at local, regional, and supranational levels and in new forms of interlocal or interregional competition as well as at the level of the national state. Socially, they involve subordinating social policy to the needs of labor market flexibility and/or to the constraints of international competition. In both respects, these concerns involve an awareness of the international context of economic and social policy far greater than that which marked the heyday of the Keynesian welfare state.

In particular, the Schumpeterian workfare regime marks a clear break with the Keynesian welfare state insofar as (1) domestic full employment is deprioritized in favor of international competitiveness; (2) redistributive welfare rights take second place to a productivist reordering of social policy; and (3) the primary role of the national state is deprivileged in favor of governance mechanisms operating on various levels (see above). At the same time, a growing trend to the internationalization of policy regimes reflects a perceived need for coordination of policy and policy contexts across scales of economic and political action.

In mentioning the first break, I accept that full employment remains on the political agenda, but it is no longer regarded as an immediate objective of state intervention. Job creation is now seen to depend heavily on the active management of the supply side and on the flexibility of the labor force rather than to flow quasi-automatically from effective management of national demand (see, for example, the 1993 European Commission "White Paper" on growth, competitiveness, and employment). In certain respects, of course, small open economies already faced this problem in the period of Atlantic Fordism; and we can find prefigurative aspects of the Schumpeterian workfare regime, such as active labor market policies, in their operation. But even small open economies have been forced to adjust to the changed conditions of international competition and far wider and deeper range of factors considered to bear on international competitiveness. Likewise, in noting the second break, I highlight a change in the workfare-welfare mix, that is, an ongoing shift in the importance of welfare rights linked to tax- and/or contribution-based consumption of services as compared to workfare dependency in which reproduction is subject to "disciplinary normalization" overseen by (para)state agencies (see Fraser 1987; Rose 1993). Welfare rights are tending to become residualized and their provision subject to restrictions on demand and downward cost pressures, especially for those excluded from the labor market due to age or incapacity; and workfare is tending to become differentiated, subordinated to supply-side and market criteria, and more closely policed. In both cases, welfare and workfare policies are closely related to their impact on international competitiveness. Finally, it is the increased importance of governance mechanisms in the delivery of the changing workfare-welfare mix that prompts me now to talk of the Schumpeterian workfare regime rather than, as in my previous work, of the Schumpeterian workfare state. Whereas the KWNS, notwithstanding some crossnational and/or policy-specific variations in the welfare mix, was organized in crucial respects through the national state, Schumpeterian workfare is less state-centered even in its concern with the social reproduction of labor-power, let alone in its concern with the conditions for the valorization of capital. There is clearly some significant variation in the emerging welfare-workfare mix and the forms in which it is delivered from case to case. But the general trend is certainly evident and becoming stronger.

Is There Still a Role for the National State?

In addressing the possible erosion of the national state as a decisive factor in contemporary politics, two accounts of "erosion" must first be rejected. It should be confused neither with a gradual withering away of the national state, nor with its simple displacement through "more market, less state." Instead, erosion is best understood as a process of decomposition involving a progressive loss of effective state unity. This loss of unity need not mean that specific state apparatuses tend to disappear (although this may be a contributory factor); rather it entails a loss of their coherence in securing state functions tied to a specific state project. In the first instance, such an erosion can be discerned in the internal disarticulation (institutional crisis) of state apparatuses (in terms of their vertical coherence across different organizational levels and/or horizontal coordination of different domains of state activity) and in declining effectiveness (or, in Habermasian terms, "rationality" crisis) in securing declared state functions linked to the dominant state project. Linked phenomena might be failure in the state's strategic selectivity as evidenced in the disorganization and disorientation of the hegemonial bloc (if any) and its associated state managers and/or dissolution of the social basis of support for this state and its projects. This attenuated selectivity could be linked in turn with a representational crisis of the state (whether in its mass or national-popular social basis as reflected in growing volatility or absolute loss of support for governing parties and other "mass integrative apparatuses" or in growing instability or disintegration of institutionalized compromise in the power bloc) and/or a legitimation crisis (that is, loss of faith in the specific claims to political legitimacy of this state form such as, in the current case, its claim to be able to deliver economic growth and generalized prosperity).

Thus interpreted, one can talk of erosion of the national state. But this erosion applies to the Keynesian welfare national state: not to all possible forms of the national state. Most European national states experienced institutional crisis in the 1970s and major attempts were made to address this through internal reorganization and a redrawing of the state's boundaries. There was also a clear crisis in their capacity to deliver growth, jobs, balanced trade, and stable prices and to meet growing expectations for social welfare. In several European national states there was also a major institutional and hegemonic crisis accompanied by representational and/or legitimacy crises. Evidence for this can be found above all in the growth of new social movements, the rise of the "New Right," and the turn toward neoliberalism.[17] But erosion of one form of national state should not be mistaken for its general retreat. It may well be, indeed, that, as the frontiers of the KWNS (especially those extended during crisis management) are rolled back, the boundaries of the national state are rolling forward in other respects and/or other forms of politics are becoming more significant.

In this context, despite the three general trends noted above (denationalization, destatization, and internationalization), a key role remains for the national state. This suggestion can be clarified through Poulantzas's distinction between particular state functions and the state's generic (or "global") function. Poulantzas identified three particular sets of activities: technoeconomic functions regarding the forces and relations of production; political functions (for example, taxation, policing, defense, legislation, official audit) concerned with the self-maintenance of the state's core military, police, and administrative activities; and ideological functions (for example, education, patriotic and national rituals, mass communication). He also defined the generic function as securing the social cohesion of a society divided into classes (Poulantzas 1973). Thus, regarding reorganization of the national state, I refer mainly to the erosion of key particular functions associated with the KWNS state project and the displacement of key particular functions linked to an emerging SWR state project. But this reorganization does not mean the loss of the national state's key role in exercising its generic political function, for the national state remains the primary site for this crucial generic function and, indeed, national state managers jealously guard this role even as they concede more specific functions. Thus the national state is still the most significant site of struggle among competing global, triadic, supranational, national, regional, and local forces. And, just as the "hollow corpora-

---

[17] Minimally, this involved major neoliberal-inspired policy adjustments (as in the Scandinavian economies); elsewhere serious attempts were made to transform the whole political regime in a neoliberal direction (most notably, of course, in Thatcher's Britain).

tion" retains its core command, control, and communication functions within the home economy even as it transfers various production activities abroad, so the hollowed-out national state retains crucial general political functions despite the transfer of other activities to other levels of political organization. In particular it has a continuing role in managing the political linkages across different territorial scales, and its legitimacy depends precisely on doing so in the perceived interests of its social base (see Kazancigil 1993: 128). Moreover, just as multinational firms' command, communication, and control functions are continually transformed by the development of new information and communication possibilities and new forms of networking, bargaining, and negotiation, so, too, as new possibilities emerge, are there changes in how hollowed out states exercise and project their power (for example, Willke 1997).

Ziebura (1992) notes the continued importance of the generic political function of the national state. He argues that the tendencies toward globalization and transnational regionalization provoke a countertendency in a popular search for transparency, democratic accountability, and proximity. He adds that the desire for local, regional, or (at most) national identity reflects powerful drives, especially in small national states, to compensate for threats from powerful neighboring states and/or the rise of supranational institutions that lack any real democratic accountability. This point is reinforced when we consider that the national state is currently still best placed to deal with social conflicts and redistributive policies, social integration and cohesion. Although supranational bodies seem preoccupied with the internationalization of capital and promoting (or limiting) the structural competitiveness of triad regions and their various constituent national economies, they are less interested in social conflicts and redistributive policies. These concerns are still mainly confined within national frameworks and it is national states that have the potential fiscal base to change them significantly in this regard. Indeed, without central government support, it is hard for most local or regional states to achieve much here. This situation presents the national state with a dilemma. On the one hand, it must become actively engaged in managing the process of internationalization; on the other, it is the only political instance with much chance of halting a growing divergence between global market dynamics and conditions for institutional integration and social cohesion.[18]

In short, there remains a central political role for the national state. But this role is redefined due to the more general rearticulation of the local, regional, national, and supranational levels of economic and political organization. Unless or until supranational political organization acquires not only governmental powers but also some measure of popular-democratic legitimacy, the national state will remain a key political factor as the highest instance of democratic political accountability. How it fulfills this role depends on the changing institutional matrix and shifts in the balance of forces such as globalization, triadization, regionalization, and the resurgence of local governance proceed apace.

[18] The argument in this section derives in part from Jessop (1994b).

Making Culture More Visible

My analysis has drawn on categories from the regulation approach, neo-Gramscian state theory, and critical discourse analysis. Some readers may adjudge it economistic and/or politicistic and claim there is little "culture" in either the description or the explanation. Here my account is "re-presented" to show how deeply regulationist and neo-Gramscian categories rest on assumptions, concepts, and explanatory principles rooted in cultural analysis. In doing so, I also invoke insights from critical discourse analysis (and the "new" narrative theory) and stress their implicit complementarities and potential contributions to integral economic and political analyses.

A useful starting point is Jenson's extension of regulationism to include discourse theory as well as structure-agency dialectics (1989; 1990; 1995). She calls for concrete analyses of historically developed sets of practices and meanings that provide the actual regulatory mechanisms for a specific mode of growth and/or the specific "societal paradigms" that govern a wide range of social relations beyond the realm of production. Accordingly, economic crises involve more than a final encounter with pregiven structural limits. They are manifested and resolved in an interdiscursive field (or representational system) through which social forces assert their identities and interests. Thus, for Jenson, newly visible and active forces emerge in a crisis and participate in the expanding universe of political discourse. They present alternative modes of regulation and societal paradigms and enter political struggles over the terms of a new compromise. If a new "model of development" becomes hegemonic in the emerging universe of political discourse oriented to new structural relations, it sets new rules for recognizing actors and defining interests (see Jenson 1990: 666).

Such comments help us to interpret and extend the implicit constructivism in regulationist accounts of the economy as an object of regulation and in theories of governance. They reinforce arguments about the discursive constitution of objects of regulation and/or governance with their insights on how new paradigms may be constructed through the entry of new social subjects. Just as the national state can be seen as but one specific form of imagined political community, so the national economy is only one possible imagined space of economic activity. Accordingly, rather than seek objective criteria to identify the necessary boundaries of economic space (on whatever territorial or functional scale), it is more fruitful to pose this issue in terms of an imaginary mapping (and naturalization) of the economy. At the same time, the social modes of economic regulation help constitute and naturalize its objects in and through the very processes of regulation (see Jessop 1990: 310–11). Of course, naturalizing discursive formations and specific regularizing practices are contestable. Struggles to define specific economies as subjects, sites, and stakes of competition and/or as objects of regulation typically involve manipulation of power and knowledge. The effectiveness of these public narratives in naturalizing and regularizing specific conceptions of economic space depends in part on their links to wider cultural and institutional formations that provide "a web of interlocution" (Somers 1994: 614). But their resonance is also related to material contradictions and tensions in existing forms of economic regulation and/or governance as these impact on personal and organizational narratives. Their overall plausibility depends in turn on metanarratives that reveal links between a wide range of interactions, organizations, and institutions or help to make sense of whole epochs (see Somers 1994: 619). And, of course, the tendential, provisional, and unstable nature of regulation always threatens the continued plausibility of the currently hegemonic technoeconomic paradigms, bounded accumulation strategies, and societal paradigms (on this, see Jessop 1990).

From this perspective, the postwar "naturalization" of the relatively closed national economy as the taken-for-granted object of economic regulation can be seen as a product of convergent public narratives about the nature of key economic and political changes facing postwar Europe and North America. This approach involved acts of imagination and social mobilization as well as institutional innovation. It depended in part on the definition of an "imagined economic community" grounded both in an "imagined economic space" and an "imagined community of economic interest" among social forces with a joint interest in domestic prosperity and resistance to communism. This economic space became the site and stake in national accumulation strategies aimed at securing the economic and extraeconomic conditions for the successful insertion of the national economy into the Atlantic Fordist mode of growth. The development and consolidation of the latter also involved struggles to establish the economic hegemony of these accumulation strategies and to articulate them into different state projects and national-popular hegemonic projects (on accumulation strategies and hegemonic projects, see Jessop 1982 and 1990: 155–60). There were also major efforts on the part of economic, political, and intellectual forces to generalize new norms of production and consumption. Although this constitution of national economies and national modes of growth was mediated through national states, it was closely connected with the "making of an Atlantic ruling class" under U.S. hegemony (see van der Pijl 1984; Rupert 1995; Maier 1978). Moreover, once constituted, these imagined national economies coevolved in conjunction with the dynamic of national politics as shaped in and through struggles within individual national Keynesian welfare states (see, for example, Scharpf 1987; Keman, Paloheimo, and Whiteley 1987; Hall 1989).

Thus the emergence of a new accumulation regime and its mode of regulation involve a veritable "cultural revolution" as well as radical institutional innovation. Technoeconomic paradigms are transformed—witness the contrast between the discourses of economic and political planning and of productivity based on economies of scale in Atlantic Fordism and the emerging discourses of enterprise and market forces and of flexibility in the transition to post-Fordism. Changes are also occurring in organizational paradigms—witness the newfound economic and political emphasis on the role of networks, partnerships, stakeholding, and good governance. New norms and expectations must be defined to complement new structural forms and social practices—thus the transition to new accumulation regimes is typically associated with public campaigns to adopt new bodily, production, and consumption practices and to share new visions of economic, political, and social life (in addition to Gramsci's classic notes on Americanism and Fordism, see also the interesting case study by Banta [1993] and, from a more Foucauldian perspective, Miller and Rose [1993] on neoliberalism). Economic strategies and spatiotemporal horizons must be realigned with changes in the structurally inscribed strategic selectivity of modes of growth and their associated political regimes. This is reflected in the rhetoric of the enterprise culture, the learning region, and the information society.

Likewise, the Schumpeterian workfare postnational regime tendentially replacing the KWNS is also the product of a new consensus. Of central significance here is the emerging geoeconomic metanarrative concerning globalization and its translation into pressures to prioritize structural competitiveness on various territorial scales. This metanarrative has been linked to other narratives that have been persuasively (but not necessarily intentionally) combined to consolidate a limited but widely accepted set of diagnoses and prescriptions for the economic and political difficulties now confronting nations, regions, and cities and their various economic branches. Significant discourses in this context are those of the enterprise culture, enterprise society, innovative milieux, networks, strategic alliances, partnerships, governance, and so forth. A second major set of metanarratives are more geopolitical in character and concern the end of the cold war, the collapse of communism, and the economic threats to national survival from East Asia. These and other stories combined to reinforce the claim that the national state's borders have been undermined, thereby rendering it anachronistic, and that all national economies are now subject to greatly intensified global competition that is difficult to evade, thereby exerting downward pressure on "unproductive" public expenditure and prompting a "race to the bottom." The prime goals of postwar economic policy (full employment, stable prices, economic growth, and a sustainable balance of payments) can no longer be delivered in and through the national state. This in turn undermines the national state's capacity to deliver redistributive social welfare and limit the degree of social exclusion. In this sense, the postwar economic and political regime has failed and, if economic forces are to escape the consequences, it is essential to modify economic strategies, economic institutions, modes of governance, and the form of state. These must be redesigned to prioritize "wealth creation" in the face of international, interregional, and intraregional competition, since this is the prior condition of continued social redistribution and welfare. Such narratives lead, inter alia, to the discovery of triad regions, the "region state," the "transnational territory," "entrepreneurial cities," and so forth, as new phenomena and their naturalization on practical, if not normative, grounds (see Horsman and Marshall 1994; Kennedy 1993; Luttwak 1990; Ohmae 1991; Sassen 1994).

These recent paradigm shifts illustrate well the close, mutually constitutive links between academic discourse, political practice, and changing economic realities. Academic discovery of networks and governance has coincided with economic changes that make big business and big government ineffective means of economic and political organization. This confluence may help to explain the widespread fascination and experimentation with alternative forms of governance, whether rediscovered or newly invented. This point is surely reinforced to the extent that structural competitiveness is discursively constituted as a joint product requiring active cooperation across a wide range of economic, political, and social actors. For the stage is then set for the proliferation of governance arrangements committed to the pursuit of enhanced economic performance.

Such major changes neither bypass the state nor render it helpless. Thus, the state is actively involved in developing new accumulation strategies, state projects, and hegemonic projects based on the discourses of globalization and structural competitiveness. New governmental rationalities and subjects of governance are also required to sustain changed articulations of government and governance. States have become actively involved in generalizing new norms of production and consumption through such measures as privatization, fiscal incentives to investment and enterprise, flexibilization and market proxies in the public sector, workfare and learnfare rather than social citizenship entitlements, and promoting public-private partnerships. The imagined boundaries of political regimes and their social bases of support are also changing. On a supranational scale, for example, there are attempts to create European culture, to develop an ASEAN or East Asian identity as a basis for "saying no" to the West; and, on a regional scale, there is a new celebration of regional and "tribal" identities as the basis for place marketing and imaging.

Indeed, given the argument about the generic function of the state in securing social cohesion in a conflictual society, changes of this magnitude have profound implications for the state and its exercise of power. We see this reflected in the denationalization of the state and the destatization of politics: processes that are far from automatic but always mediated through paradigm shifts and social struggles. Moreover, as politics is not, *pace* Lenin, "concentrated economics," these changes reflect the relative autonomy of the state in its inclusive sense. Indeed, given the argument about the generic function of the state in securing social cohesion in a conflictual society, changes of this magnitude have profound implications for the state and its exercise of power. Thus each of the trends noted above is associated with a countertrend in which the generic role of the national state is reinforced. This change is seen in the increased importance of the national state in managing the relationship between different levels of state organization and the corresponding politics of scale in the interests of social cohesion (see Brenner 1997; Collinge 1996; Ziebura 1992); in the enhanced role of the state (on various territorial scales but especially the national) in metagovernance, that is, in managing the forms of governance and intervening in the case of governance failure (see Jessop 1995b); and in the struggle by states (especially national states) to shape emerging international regimes.

WE now return to the continuing restructuring and reorientation of the Keynesian welfare national state. Three trends have been identified. First, some of the particular technical-economic, political, and ideological functions of the national state are being relocated to other levels of state organization. Second, some of the particular technical-economic, political, and ideological functions previously or newly performed by the national state have been increasingly shared with, or wholly shifted to, other (that is, parastatal or private) political actors, institutional arrangements, or regimes. And, third, the international context of domestic state action has become of greater significance to national, regional, and local states and their fields of action because domestic purposes have been expanded to include an extensive range of extraterritorial or transnational factors and processes. All three of these trends are associated with partial redefinition of the particular functions of the state.

Many commentators have discussed one or more of these trends, sometimes in terms similar to those deployed here. Few have considered all three. Serious theoretical and empirical problems occur, however, if they are considered in isolation. This is especially true when they are extrapolated uncritically and unilinearly into the future—treating post-Fordism as something already achieved and consolidated or, worse still, as the telos of the current economic and political transformation of capitalism. An equally misleading extrapolation from current trends is the claim that increasing globalization requires a world state to organize the general conditions of a production on a world scale. This view ignores the complex global-regional-local dialectic and its implications for securing structural competitiveness and neglects various forms of subnational state and/ or cross-border restructuring of the state. Neoinstitutionalism offers another misleading perspective in the claim that the proliferation of functionally specific and nongovernmental international regimes is producing a postnational state system at the expense of territorially organized national states and intergovernmental arrangements (see Keohane 1984). Not only does this argument one-sidedly emphasize international governance at the expense of other scales of governance, it also gives the impression that the need for the state is somehow obviated. Yet the national state is not only a key player in many governance mechanisms but also has a major role in organizing the self-organization of interorganizational relations, regulating self-regulation, promoting the coherence of regimes in different areas, and dealing with the repercussions of governance failure (for a more extended comparison of alternative perspectives on the future of the national state, see Evers 1994 and Jessop 1995a).

My own conclusion from all three trends is that the articulation of the value- and nonvalue forms of "reproduction-régulation" in the former economic space of Atlantic Fordism is no longer associated politically with the KWNS complete with its local relays, corporatist bias, and international supports. It has been relocated in a postnational Schumpeterian workfare regime. The latter's particular functions have been dispersed among several tiers of territorial organization and are shared with an extended and institutionalized range of functionally relevant stakeholders. This change poses serious problems in managing the politics of scale since the primacy of the national level and domestic actors can no longer be taken for granted even in powerful states. Yet the generic political function of maintaining social cohesion is still exercised by the national state in this emerging politicoeconomic regime and its fundamentally altered strategic context. It will remain essential to the exercise of the generic functions of the capitalist state until such time as supranational regimes acquire the capacity to manage problems of social cohesion in a class-divided regional bloc or world system. Thus, despite tendencies toward crisis and erosion in its integral economic Keynesian welfare features, the postwar national state is acquiring new economic and social functions and remains significant as a general political force.

References

Amin, A., and Robins, K. 1990. "The Re-emergence of Regional Economies? The Mythical Geography of Flexible Accumulation." *Environment and Planning D: Society and Space* 8: 7–34.

Banta, Martha. 1993. *Taylored Lives: Narrative Productions in the Age of Taylor, Veblen, and Ford*. Chicago: University of Chicago Press.

Barnes, W. R., and L. C. Ledubur. 1991. "Toward a New Political Economy of Metropolitan Regions." *Environment and Planning C: Government and Policy* 9, mo. 2: 127–41.

Boisot, M. 1993. "Is a Diamond a Region's Best Friend? Towards an Analysis of Interregional Competition." In J. Child, M. Crozier, and R. Mayntz, eds., 163–85. *Societal Change between Market and Organization*. Aldershot: Avebury.

Boyer, R., ed. 1988. *The Search for Labour Market Flexibility: The European Economies in Transition*. Oxford: Clarendon Press.

Boyer, R., and Y. Saillard, eds. 1995. *Théorie de la régulation: L'état des savoirs*. Paris: La Découverte.

Brenner, N. 1997. "Trial by Space: Global City Formation, State Territorial Restructuring, and the Politics of Scale." Paper presented at the Cities in Transition conference, Humboldt University, Berlin.

Cerny, P. 1989. *The Changing Architecture of the State*. London: Sage.

Collinge, C. 1996. *Spatial Articulation of the State: Reworking Social Relations and Social Regulation Theory*. Birmingham: Centre for Urban and Regional Studies.

Cooke, P., and K. Morgan. 1993. "The Network Paradigm: New Departures in Corporate and Regional Development." *Environment and Planning D: Society and Space* 11, no. 4: 543–64.

Daly, G. 1994. "The Discursive Construction of Economic Space." *Economy and Society* 20, no. 1: 79–102.

Dyson, K., ed. 1988. *Local Authorities and New Technologies: The European Dimension*. London: Croom Helm.

European Commission. 1993. "Growth, Competitiveness, Employment—The Challenges and Ways Forward into the 21st Century" (White Paper). Luxemburg: Office for Official Publications of the European Communities.

Evers, T. 1994. "Supranationale Staatlichkeit am Beispiel der Europäischen Union: Civitas civitatum oder Monstrum?" *Leviathan* 1: 115–34.

Fosler, R. S., ed. 1988. *The New Economic Role of American States*. New York: Oxford University Press.

Fraser, N. 1987. "Women, Welfare, and the Politics of Need Interpretation." *Hypatia* 2, no. 1: 103–21.

Gramsci, A. 1971. *Selections from the Prison Notebooks*. London: Lawrence and Wishart.

Hall, P. A., ed. 1989. *The Political Power of Economic Ideas: Keynesianism across Nations*. Princeton: Princeton University Press.

Hay, C. 1994. "Environmental Security and State Legitimacy." In *Is Capitalism Sustainable? Political Economy and the Politics of Ecology*, edited by M. O'Connor. New York: Guilford Press.

Hirsch, J. 1994. "Vom 'Sicherheits-' zum 'nationalen Wettbewerbsstaat'." *Links* 287: 32–33.

Hirsch, J., and R. Roth. 1985. *Das neue Gesicht des Kapitalismus*. Frankfurt: EVA.

Holloway, J., and S. Picciotto, eds. 1978. *Capital and the State*. London: Edward Arnold.

Horsman, M., and A. Marshall. 1994. *After the Nation-State: Citizens, Tribalism, and the New World Disorder*. London: HarperCollins.

Jenson, Jane 1989. "'Different' but Not 'Exceptional': Canada's Permeable Fordism." *Canadian Review of Sociology and Anthropology* 26, no. 1: 69–94.

——. 1990. "Representations in Crisis: The Roots of Canada's Permeable Fordism." *Canadian Journal of Political Science* 24, no. 3: 653–83.

——. 1995. "Mapping, Naming, and Remembering: Globalisation at the End of the Twentieth Century." *Review of International Political Economy* 2, no. 1: 96–116.

Jessop, B. 1982. "Accumulation Strategies, State Forms, and Hegemonic Projects." *Kapitalistate* 10/11: 89–112.

——. 1990. *State Theory: Putting the Capitalist State in Its Place*. Cambridge: Polity.

——. 1992a. "Fordism and Post-Fordism: Critique and Reformulation." In *Pathways to Regionalism and Industrial Development*, edited by A. J. Scott and M. J. Storper, 43–65. London: Routledge.

——. 1992b. "Thatcherismus und die Neustrukturierung der Sozialpolitik—Neo-Liberalismus und die Zukunft des Wohlfahrtsstaates." *Zeitschrift für Sozialreform* 38, nos. 11–12: 709–33.

——. 1993. "Towards a Schumpeterian Workfare State? Preliminary Remarks on Post-Fordist Political Economy." *Studies in Political Economy* 40: 7–39.

——. 1994a. "Politik in der Ära Thatcher: Die defekte Wirtschaft und der schwache Staat." In *Staatsaufgaben*, edited by D. Grimm, 353–89. Baden: Nomos Verlag.

——. 1994b. "Post-Fordism and the State." In *Post-Fordism*, edited by A. Amin, 251–279. Oxford: Blackwell.

——. 1995a. "The Nation-State: Erosion or Reorganization?" Lancaster: Lancaster Regionalism Group Working Paper, no. 50.

——. 1995b. "The Regulation Approach and Governance Theory: Alternative

Perspectives on Economic and Political Change?" *Economy and Society* 24, no. 3: 307–33.

———. 1997a. "The Entrepreneurial City: Re-Imaging Localities, Redesigning Economic Governance, or Restructuring Capital?" In *Realising Cities: New Spatial Divisions and Social Transformation*, edited by N. Jewson and S. MacGregor, 28–41. London: Routledge.

———. 1997b. "A Neo-Gramscian Approach to the Regulation of Urban Regimes." In *Reconstructing Urban Regime Theory*, edited by M. Lauria, 51–73. London: Sage.

———. 1997c. "Capitalism and Its Future: Remarks on Regulation, Government, and Governance." *Review of International Political Economy* 4, no. 3: 561–80.

Kazancigil, Ali. 1993. "A Prospective View on the European Nation State." In *The Future of the Nation State in Europe*, edited by J. Iivonen, 117–29. Aldershot: Edward Elgar.

Keman, H., H. Paloheimo, and P. F. Whiteley, eds. 1987. *Coping with the Economic Crisis: Alternative Responses to Economic Recession in Advanced Industrial Societies*. London: Sage.

Kennedy, P. M. 1993. *Preparing for the Twenty-First Century*. New York: Random House.

Keohane, R. O. 1984. *After Hegemony: Cooperation and Discord in the World Political Economy*. Princeton: Princeton University Press.

Klein-Beekman, C. 1996. "International Migration and Spatiality in the World Economy: Remapping Economic Space in an Era of Expanding Transnational Flows." *Alternatives* 21, no. 4: 439–72.

Kofman, E. 1995. "Citizenship for Some but Not for Others: Spaces of Citizenship in Contemporary Europe." *Political Geography* 15, no. 2: 121–38.

Kratochwil, F. 1986. "Of Systems, Boundaries, and Territoriality: An Inquiry into the Formation of the State System." *World Politics* 39, no. 1: 27–52.

Luttwak, E. N. 1990. "From Geopolitics to Geo-economics: Logic of Conflict, Grammar of Commerce." *National Interest* 20: 17–23.

Maier, C. S. 1978. "The Politics of Productivity: Foundations of American Economic Policy after World War II." In *Between Power and Plenty*, edited by P. J. Katzenstein. Madison: University of Wisconsin Press.

Matzner, E. 1994. "Instrument-targeting or Context-making? A New Look at the Theory of Economic Policy." *Journal of Economic Issues* 28, no. 2: 461–76.

Meinecke, F. 1928. *Weltbürgertum und Nationalstaat: Studien zur Genesis des deutschen Nationalstaates*. München: Verlag R. Oldenbourg.

Meinhardt, U. 1992. "Wiedergeburt des Leviathan? Zu Uwe Kremers 'Entwicklungsagentur Staat.'" *Blätter für deutsche und internationale Politik* 10 (October), 1243–49.

Miller, P., and N. Rose. 1993. "Governing Economic Life." *Economy and Society* 19, no. 1: 1–31.

Milward, A. S., G. Brennan, and F. Romero. 1992. *The European Rescue of the Nation State*. London: Routledge.

Mitchell, T. 1991. "The Limits of the State: Beyond Statist Approaches and Their Critics." *American Political Science Review* 85, no. 1: 77–96.

Offe, C. 1985. "New Social Movements: Challenging the Boundaries of Institutional Politics." *Social Research* 54, no. 2: 817–68.

Ohmae, K. 1991. "The Rise of the Region State." *Foreign Affairs* 72 (Spring): 78–87.

Porter, M. 1990. *The Competitive Advantage of Nations.* London: Macmillan.

Poulantzas, N. 1973. *Political Power and Social Classes.* London: New Left Books.

Pringle, R. 1995. "Destabilising Patriarchy." In *Transitions: New Australian Feminisms,* edited by B. Caine and R. Pringle. St. Leonards, NSW: Allen and Unwin.

Rose, N. 1993. "Government, Authority and Expertise in Advanced Liberalism." *Economy and Society* 22, no. 3: 283–99.

Rupert, M. 1995. *Producing Hegemony: The Politics of Mass Production and American Global Power.* Cambridge: Cambridge University Press.

Sassen, S. 1994. *Global Cities.* New York: Oxford University Press.

Scharpf, F. W. 1987. *Sozialdemokratische Krisenpolitik in Europa.* Frankfurt: Campus Verlag.

Scharpf, Fritz W. 1994. "Community and Autonomy, Multilevel Policy-Making in the European Union." Working Paper. Florence: European University Institute.

Schmitter, P. C. 1992. "Representation and the Future Euro-Polity." *Staatswissenschaften und Staatspraxis* 3: 379–405.

Siegel, T. 1988. "Introduction (to Fordism and Fascism)." *International Journal of Political Economy* 18 (1): 2–9.

Somers, M. 1994. "The Narrative Constitution of Identity: A Relational and Network Approach." *Theory and Society* 23 (4): 605–49.

Streeck, W., and P. C. Schmitter. 1985. "Community, Market, State—and Associations? The Prospective Contribution of Interest Governance to Social Order." In *Private Interest Government,* edited by W. Streeck and P. C. Schmitter. London: Sage.

——. 1991. "From National Corporatism to Transnational Pluralism: Organized Interests in the Single European Market." *Politics and Society* 19, no. 1: 109–32.

Taylor, Peter J. 1994. "The State as Container: Territoriality in the Modern World-system." *Progress in Human Geography* 18, no. 2: 151–62.

Tickell, A., and J. Peck. 1992. "Accumulation Regimes and the Geographies of Post-Fordism: Missing Links in Regulationist Theory." *Progress in Human Geography* 16, no. 2: 190–218.

Tömmel, I. 1992. "System-Entwicklung und Politikgestaltung in der Europäischen Gemeinschaft am Beispiel der Regionalpolitik." In *Die Integration Europas,* edited by M. Kreile, 185–208. Opladen: Westdeutscher Verlag.

——. 1994. "Interessenartikulation und transnationale Politik-kooperation im Rahmen der EU." In *Europäische Integration und verbandliche Regulierung.* Marburg: Metropolis.

van der Pijl, K. 1984. *The Making of an Atlantic Ruling Class*. London: New Left
    Books.
Willke, H. 1992. *Die Ironie des Staates*. Frankfurt: Campus Verlag.
——. 1997. *Supervision des Staates*. Frankfurt: Campus Verlag.
Wood, Ellen Meiksin. 1981. "The Separation of the Economic and the Political
    in Capitalism." *New Left Review* no. 127: 66–93.
Ziebura, G. 1992. "Über den Nationalstaat." *Leviathan* 4: 467–89.

Epilogue:
Now Where?

Charles Tilly

As contributors to this book repeatedly declare, connections between culture and states present knotty problems. Rather than provide yet another critique of major traditions or review the many partial solutions proposed in previous pages, this closing statement untangles some strands, ties them together as neatly as possible, and says more generally how effective analytic binding of state and culture could occur. I confront George Steinmetz's challenge to take culture seriously without locating it inside, beneath, behind, or above every feature of states previous observers have attributed to interest, accident, individual will, or organizational inertia. I claim that a reasonable reply to the eternal book-ending query "Now where?" is not "Nowhere" but "Toward relational analyses of political processes." I eventually illustrate my arguments' applications to four culturally rich state-linked processes: citizenship, democracy, nationalism, and changes in contentious repertoires.

Among other essays in this book, John Meyer's "The Changing Cultural Content of the Nation-State" dramatizes what is at issue. His report provides extensive evidence of standardization in the organizational forms of states across the world and a plausible argument that widely recognized models of state organization promote that standardization. But what connects concrete organizations to international models? Meyer does not state a clear answer. His frequent resort to passive voice masks the critical agents and agency of the transformation.

Still, fragments of a causal account appear in Meyer's essay. Diffusion of rationalist culture throughout the world, his account suggests, predisposes decision makers to seek rational models for their organization-building. "Naturally," concludes Meyer, "the evolving codification of all this cultural theory has had enormous impact. All sorts of unlikely populations and areas are now at least

Thanks to Jeff Olick, George Steinmetz, and Viviana Zelizer for helping me correct confusions in this essay's earlier drafts.

nominally organized as nation-states. In so organizing, standard legitimated forms are employed. New nation-states copy them and gain strength and legitimacy by doing so; older ones adapt to the supply and constraints provided by highly legitimated exogenous rules." A powerful observation drives Meyer's observations: that people are incessantly creating and transforming social structures by incorporating elements of existing cultural models rather than inventing them anew or generating them as unintended byproducts of other activities. Sometimes, as in the case of blueprints for national states, people even borrow models for complete organizations.

More is happening, however, than Meyer says. Four very general classes of causal mechanisms produce the repetition of cultural patterns that Meyer detects in the organizational forms of states. We might call the crucial mechanisms invention, network ramification, emulation, and adaptation.

Within limits set by existing culture and social ties, people are constantly improvising social routines, often quite deliberately. Some of those improvisations work so well—whatever the criteria of "working well"—that their authors or observers preserve them; those routines count as inventions. Some organizational forms emerge without deliberate invention through network ramification, as when the sheer increase in number of persons within a communications network reduces the volume of information flowing between the average pair and augments the power of centrally located communicators, or as when the more or less fortuitous entry of a well-connected individual into an organization establishes a new set of relations to that individual's clientele. Much organization-building occurs through more or less intentional emulation, in which members or founders of organizations borrow elements of existing organizations. They import understandings, practices, models of relationships, and sometimes concrete sets of related persons from elsewhere; in the extreme case Meyer describes, organization-builders borrow complete models from authoritative sources. Adaptation has two main components: (1) improvisation of procedures that ease the effort of day-to-day interaction and (2) elaboration of valued social relations around existing structures. Adaptation simultaneously modifies invented, ramified, or emulated organizational forms in ways that accommodate the predispositions of organization members and reshapes members' routines in ways that attach them willy-nilly to the organization.

This view of organizational change counters strict efficiency accounts, in which managers search for the organizational structure—existing or new—that will maximize selected outputs and minimize selected costs for a given array of inputs, and competition destroys those who retain inefficient organizational forms. Efficiency accounts neglect the large and varied costs entailed by installation of new organizational forms, hence the relative short-run attractiveness of emulation as an organization-building strategy. They ignore strong indications that (1) organizations generally strike some balance among efficiency, quality, and power as criteria for their outputs, not to mention weighing both short-run and long-run estimates of possible organizational innovations' consequences for efficiency, quality, and power and (2) most organizations operate most of the time in partly protected niches that tolerate suboptimal performance.

Efficiency accounts of organizational design, furthermore, fail to consider a condition to which John Meyer's analysis calls attention: just as political opportunity structures shape the forms of social movements within their settings, what we might call organizational opportunity structures provide rewards and recognition for entrepreneurs who create structures that are visibly akin to others that already exist. Thus world financial institutions, great powers, international organizations, and their state-licensing agency (the United Nations) come to agree on what sorts of organizations they will recognize as states and hence what performances they will encourage on the part of aspirants to statehood. Need I point out the pivotal place of shared understandings and their representations—of culture—in any such process?

Organizational opportunity structures encourage emulation even where the basic relations and activities of a group of actors fit badly into the emulated organizational shell. Thus networks of political activists or money-launderers who do most of their business without resorting to formal organization create front associations to maintain legitimate presences in the public arena, and networks of financiers, filmmakers, or architects for whom bounded firms generally hold little interest extrude firms in efforts to hold intellectual property, bid on contracts, or coordinate some local activity. In all of these cases, as John Meyer's analysis suggests, structure and culture intertwine. What we need, obviously, is a better picture than Meyer's of how and why. My object here is to sketch such a picture.

That picture is relentlessly relational. To integrate culture into our analyses of state-linked processes, let us flee from methodological individualism, with its assumption that social processes center on and result from conscious decisions by maximizing individuals who operate within known constraints. We should also eschew phenomenological individualism, with its placement of individual experience at the center of all social processes or, at the limit, its reduction of all social processes to individual awareness. However plausible or implausible their accounts of individual consciousness, both individualisms lack specifications of (1) processes producing links among interacting states of consciousness, simultaneous or successive, in the same individual or connected individuals, (2) mechanisms by which states of consciousness produce their supposed effects in individual action, social interaction, social process, or social structure, and (3) mechanisms of change in relevant constraints and states of consciousness. Those deficits disqualify individualism as a basis for analyzing relations between state and culture.

My proposed strategy likewise rejects system realism, which posits the prior existence, self-maintaining logic, and lawful operation of social structures, including the grand social structures called societies, economies, cultures, civilizations, or modes of production. One might derive viable systems theories from individualistic or relational foundations. In principle, one might also treat large social aggregates as sites of ill-explained but powerful empirical regularities such as those that allow short-term weather forecasting. In practice, however, system realism has yielded neither well-validated empirical generalizations nor persuasive explanations of social processes.

Methodological individualism, phenomenological individualism, and system realism all have difficulty dealing with culture because they have no secure location for it. The two forms of individualism can pack bits of culture into particular human brains as preferences, cognitive filters, memories, or something of the sort, but they then lack any plausible account of culture's collective character, much less of its interdependence and systematic change. System realism faces the opposite problem: while locating culture in the aggregate as an organ of system-wide communication, control, or adaptation, it offers no credible account of cultural variability, multiplicity, conflict, and change, much less of how culture affects individual performance.

This relational approach to state and culture generates social structures and processes from culturally embedded interactions. Its causal mechanisms operate within social interaction. In the long run, of course, it leads back to the indispensable questions at which methodological individualism, phenomenological individualism, and systems theories have ordinarily aimed their fire: What motivates individual behavior? What cognitive processes shape individual behavior, and how? How does memory—individual or collective—work? What governs the survival, disappearance, and transformation of different kinds of organizations and cultural forms? Ultimately, any analysis of social processes that blinds itself to accumulating knowledge in neuroscience, cognitive psychology, linguistics, and evolutionary biology will commit intellectual suicide. In the short and medium runs, however, the approach I promote here relies on these as yet uncertain bets:

1. Human beings have a strong propensity to cast their social accounts in terms of deliberated actions by self-motivated actors, individual or collective.
2. That propensity encourages professional analysts of social processes, including historians, to favor individualistic and system-theoretical models, despite their difficulties.
3. Such models hide or misrepresent a wide variety of actually operating cause-effect relations in social life.
4. Relational accounts provide a welcome escape from difficulties inherent in models of self-motivated actors, individual or collective.
5. Whatever else is involved, large-scale social structures and processes emerge from regularities in social interaction.
6. Those regularities do not conform to invariant covering laws, but take the form of recurrent causal mechanisms that concatenate differently in various settings; some of those causal mechanisms, however, recur in a wide variety of settings.
7. Our great intellectual deficit lies in analysis of those regularities and hence of recurrent but variably concatenating causal mechanisms.
8. Relational accounts provide a way of overcoming the apparent opposition between culture and social structure that bedevils individualistic and system theories.

This bundle of ideas unpacks into relational explanations of political processes, explanations in which the crucial causal work occurs in social interaction.

It assumes intimate interdependence between shared understandings and social ties and hence between culture and states. It treats culture as congealed history, as the current residue of collective interaction. Ontologically and epistemologically, it rests on a sort of relational realism closest to the implicit philosophical positions of John Meyer and Bob Jessop in this book, positions most vigorously challenged here by Timothy Mitchell.

Although in this day of widespread idealism and skepticism such a position may seem naïve or retrograde, I claim for it at least these virtues: Its bald statement helps clarify which disputes addressing state and culture center on epistemology and ontology, and which of them center on questions of description or explanation within similar epistemological and ontological views. By rejecting the ontologies of methodological individualism, phenomenological individualism, and system realism in favor of social interaction as the starting point of analysis, it brings out the extent to which previous discussions of state and culture have built on one of those three ontologies and thereby challenges their advocates to state their ontological premises. By closing in on social interaction, it narrows the range of admissible causal mechanisms—neither universal instincts nor needs of the social system, for example, can figure as causes of social structures and processes—and similarly challenges advocates of rival positions to specify their causal mechanisms more carefully.

Additional virtues follow. This view identifies, then resolves, an important paradox of social analysis: that because collective experience congeals into shared understandings and their representations, large structures and sequences rarely or never repeat themselves, social processes are path-dependent, and social interaction takes place within strong cultural constraints, yet causal analogies among disparate situations abound; the resolution consists of recognizing the recurrence of the same causal mechanisms in highly variable settings and sequences, their exact order and conjunction being strongly conditioned by cultural context. Finally, it treats culture and identity, not to mention language and consciousness, as changing phenomena to be explained rather than as ultimate explanations of all other social phenomena. The broad explanatory model, indeed, brings out analogies between political processes and conversation, in which the very process of interaction modifies culture and social relations simultaneously. Thus it promises to lend insight into the state-culture nexus.

To stimulate discussion, let me state my position on culture and social relations more forcefully than prudence would dictate. Just as water binds hydrogen to oxygen, in concrete social life culture clings to social relations and vice versa; all we ordinarily see is culturally informed social interaction. For purposes of analysis, nevertheless, we can profitably abstract in either direction: toward culture or toward social ties.

Interaction's cultural component entails joint deployment, improvisation, construction, and modification of stories about what is going on. Some of those stories are extremely general, as in the recurrent grammars that separate agents, actions, and objects of action; one could hardly invent a more generic story than X does Y to Z. Others are narrowly particular, as in exchanges (verbal, tactile, or otherwise) that refer to immediately preceding exchanges; X challenges Y's explanation-cum-apology for arriving late.

Throughout the range we can usefully make a further distinction between shared understandings (those stories interacting parties are jointly adopting, adapting, or constructing but incessantly acting on as they go) and their representations (embodiment of those stories in objects, symbols, formulas, and rituals). Often representations provide our best available evidence of stories' structure and content. Of course, such stories have causes, effects, and counterparts in individual minds; I suspect, in fact, that genetically based features of human brains significantly limit the sorts of stories people tell. But as culture, stories reside in continuously negotiated social interaction. It is therefore no oxymoron to speak of culture's effects on minds or on social ties.

Seen as social ties, social interaction entails repeated exchanges of influence among persons. Influence includes information flows, provision of rewards or threats, physical contact, alterations of one person's environment by another, and much more. Influence is almost always asymmetrical, often markedly so; ties between leaders and followers, for example, are mutual, but by no means symmetrical. For analytical purposes, we may reasonably abstract such ties from the culture in which they are embedded, asking such questions as whether influence in dyads differs systematically from influence in triads or how much difference the variety of influences built into any particular tie makes to that tie's operation. That the answers to such questions will often be "It depends on the cultural context" poses no objection to the abstraction of ties—no more than noticing how preexisting ties shape the stories people construct poses an insuperable objection to studying the logics and permutations of those stories.

As applied to states and culture, this line of reasoning makes the analysis of interplay between social ties of state agents and citizens, on one side, and constructed stories of political processes, on the other, absolutely central. Although my formulations in this statement will surely prove inadequate, they offer a new map of difficult terrain in answer to the question "Now where?"

Rather than unveiling a grand set of laws in which citizenship, democracy, nationalism, and repertoire change appear as special cases, I concentrate on identifying causal analogies and connections among them. That means a good deal of my effort goes into conceptualization; effective social-science concepts assert causal resemblances among the phenomena they lump together. To reduce confusion and clarify what is at stake, let us therefore start with some simple (if eminently debatable) definitions:

Culture: shared understandings and their representations

Social tie: recurrent, culturally constrained interaction between occupants of two sites

Identity: actor's experience of any social tie for which the actor and at least one other party to the tie share a collective representation

Categorical pair: a socially significant boundary and at least one tie between sites on either side of it

Claim: collective assertion of fact, demand, or commitment concerning relations to others

Right: claim that third parties routinely act to support; thus an enforceable claim

Obligation: reciprocal of right; subjection of party to an enforceable claim

Contention: mutual claim-making across a categorical boundary that, if realized, would affect the well-being of persons on at least one side of the boundary

Contentious performances: recurrent forms of interaction by which agents make such claims

Repertoires of contention: interdependent sets of such performances

Organization: a special sort of categorical pair—a well-bounded set of social ties in which at least one site has the right to establish cross-boundary relations that bind members of internal ties

Government: an organization (1) that controls the principal concentrated means of coercion within a delimited territory and (2) whose agents exercise routine jurisdiction in some regard over all persons within that territory

State: a government (1) lacking rivals and superiors within its territory and (2) treated as an autonomous entity by agents of other governments

Citizenship: continuing series of transactions between persons and agents of a given state in which each one has enforceable rights and obligations uniquely by virtue of (1) the person's membership in an exclusive category, the native-born plus the naturalized, and (2) the agent's relation to the state rather than to any other authority the agent may enjoy

Democracy: the combination of relatively broad and equal citizenship with (1) binding consultation of citizens with respect to state policy and personnel and (2) protection of citizens from arbitrary action by state agents

Nation: categorical relation in which agents on one side of a boundary claim (1) common historical origins, culture, and destiny for all persons on their side of the boundary and (2) distinctness from others beyond the boundary, and in which those agents gain widespread acquiescence to their claims on both sides of the boundary

Nationalism: the collective claim that (1) nations should correspond to states, (2) states should correspond to nations, and (3) obligations to nations should supersede other obligations **or** (4) invocation of
claims 1, 2, and 3 on behalf of particular nations and/or states

State-led nationalism: demand by those who currently control a state that its subjects comply with a particular definition and implementation of the nation

State-seeking nationalism: demand by self-identified agents of a currently stateless nation that it acquire control of its own state

Each of these relational definitions creates an ideal type. Each one therefore requires qualifiers of the sort "to the extent that." We can call a claim "nationalist" and its collective assertion "nationalism," for example, *to the extent that* agents claim nations should correspond to states and obligations to nations should supersede other obligations. Explanations of nationalism in this vein therefore concern matters of degree, not necessary or sufficient conditions. Similarly, a government qualifies as a state *in so far as* (1) it lacks rivals and superiors within its territory and (2) agents of other governments treat it as autonomous; by such criteria, colonies, puppet regimes, and military-occupied territories have less stateness than their autonomous neighbors. We must also recognize that each element operates historically, for example, that previous experience of nationalist claims within a given setting affects the form and visible viability of current nationalist claims.

The definitions build from small-scale social transactions to large-scale structures and processes. They incorporate culture—seen as shared understandings and their representations—at each step along the way. They treat identities as crucial and omnipresent, but as embedded in social relations rather than formed in individual consciousness. The remainder of my essay simply illustrates the application of these relationally based concepts to four critical arenas of state-culture interaction: citizenship, democracy, nationalism, and contentious repertoires.

Citizenship

The relevant roads pass, among other places, through citizenship, democracy, nationalism, and changes in contentious repertoires. First, citizenship. How do culture and states intersect in citizenship? Recall the definition of citizenship as a kind of social tie: a continuing series of transactions between persons and agents of a given state in which each one has enforceable rights and obligations uniquely by virtue of (1) the person's membership in an exclusive category, the native-born plus the naturalized and (2) the agent's relation to the state rather than to any other authority the agent may enjoy. In the sense of shared understandings and their representations, culture pervades citizenship. While conceding that every state establishes at least a thin version of citizenship linking a ruler with his or her closest companions in rule, let us concentrate on relatively thick citizenship, where a substantial portion (say, one-tenth or more) of the population subject to a state's authority qualifies for some degree of categorically assigned rights and obligations.

Over the roughly ten thousand years that states have existed, very few have maintained relatively thick citizenship, and those chiefly since 1750. China may constitute the great exception; before we can decide that question, Chinese historians must reconstruct more of the routine relations between imperial agents and ordinary subjects of the empire before the Qing period, which began around 1650. In general, small states relied on dynastic, oligarchical and/or patrimonial rule excluding the great mass of subjects from categorical relations with state agents. Meanwhile large states implemented indirect rule, in which regional, confessional, or ethnic magnates enjoyed great autonomy within their jurisdictions in return for collaboration with the central authority in the extraction of resources and the maintenance of military control.

Within Europe, to be sure, smaller units such as municipalities often established the equivalent of citizenship well before 1750. Although few such institutions survived Europe's great nineteenth-century state centralization, they provided salient models for organization of citizenship at a national scale. Instruments of elite representation such as the English parliament and the French Estates General likewise served as models, and sometimes even means, for the creation of relatively thick citizenship in Europe. But citizenship in general emerged as a product of contention, often violent contention: revolution, conquest, and struggle over governmental demands for resources such as taxes, food, land, and military manpower.

As a consequence of its historical origins and continued negotiation, existing citizenship is always incomplete and uneven. All states, for example, exclude whole categories of persons who are subject to their authority from their fullest degree of citizenship on grounds of incompetence due to age, incarceration, or psychic condition. The larger categorical system to which citizenship belongs, further, typically includes further distinctions such as native-born citizen, naturalized citizen, legal resident, illegal resident, legal visitor, and excluded foreigner. Even in the immigrant-built United States, only native-born citizens are eligible to run for the national presidency.

Now where does culture enter this story? Everywhere. Note first the salience of boundaries in citizenship: boundaries among categories of citizens, boundaries between citizens and noncitizens. Those boundaries are social products whose locations, meanings, representations, and consequences are subject to continuous negotiation among parties to them.

Note next that citizenship entails enforceable rights and obligations, likewise subject to continuous negotiation. As Ann Orloff's contribution to this book shows most clearly, the rights in question always incorporate understandings concerning the character of the categorically defined parties to them as well as relations between them; among the four predominantly English-speaking countries Orloff compares, the United States most strongly attaches state-dispensed benefits for which citizens are eligible to their experiences as workers, whereas Great Britain imposes sharper gender distinctions in benefits than the others do. More generally (as Orloff does not say), in capitalist countries differential citizenship rights correspond to categorical differences in (1) relations with capital and (2) military service, modified by (3) political mobilization and struggle. All three involve the cultural construction of categories and relations among them.

Democracy

We touch on democracy. Consider a state's regime to be democratic insofar as it approaches four limits: (1) broad citizenship, (2) equal citizenship, (3) binding consultation of citizens with respect to state personnel and policy, and (4) protection of citizens from arbitrary action by state agents. If we think of each of these elements as a continuum from 0 to 1, positions of regimes along the four continua identify all the classic types: tyranny (0000), oligarchy (0011), totalitarianism (1100), and more; an ideal democracy scores as 1111. All real regimes occupy intermediate positions, with a plausible rating for the United States today being .80, .60, .75, .80 — as compared with regimes elsewhere and in earlier times, quite broad citizenship, less equal citizenship, substantial consultation of citizens, and widespread (but by no means universal) protection from arbitrary state action. (We can, of course, complicate the analysis indefinitely by introducing variable relations to the thousands of additional governments that operate within the limits of the United States, by examining fluctuations over time, and by concentrating on the relations of particular categories, such as African Americans or American Indians, to the state.)

Resting on culturally drenched citizenship and consisting of rights-filled relations between citizens and their state, democracy incorporates culture. Seen as current practice, broad citizenship, relatively equal citizenship, binding consultation, and protection all involve extensive shared understandings and representations of those understandings among citizens as well as between citizens and state agents. Seen as orientations to the future, these elements of democracy translate into experience-based understandings sufficiently strong and widespread to promote the persistence and commitment of contenders who lose the current round of contention.

Although some strictly defined structural conditions—notably deep poverty, extreme material inequality, and political autonomy of military forces—appear to create insuperable barriers against democracy, in general the conditions promoting effective democracy intertwine culture and social ties. They include especially (1) the incorporation into relations between citizens and states of externally generated networks in which trust and institutions supporting that trust have built up and (2) struggle-ending compacts between states and important segments of their citizenry that are backed by strong guarantees of third-party intervention in case of violations. Again the interconnection of culture and state structure is obvious.

Nationalism

Nationalism displays the interplay of culture and state structure even more clearly. Here I am not focusing (as Steven Pincus does) on elite ideas concerning the distinctness of one's own nation, but following John Breuilly in stressing nationalism as a form of politics. A nation is a categorical relation in which agents on one side of a socially constituted boundary claim (1) common historical origins, culture, and destiny for all persons on their side of the boundary and (2) distinctness from others beyond the boundary, and in which those agents gain widespread acquiescence to their claims on both sides of boundary. David Laitin's analysis of contemporary Eastern Europe shows us contestation, and variable outcomes, concerning just such claims. Nationalism consists of the collective claims that

1. nations, thus defined, should correspond to states;
2. states should correspond to nations;

3. obligations to nations should supersede other obligations;

OR

4. invocation of claims 1, 2, and 3 on behalf of particular nations and/or states.

Nationalism as politics therefore takes two main forms: state-led and state-seeking. State-led nationalism consists of demands by those who currently control a state that its subjects comply with a particular definition and implementation of the nation. Historically it has typically involved a combination of (1) suppression of nonnational cultural forms and, at the extreme, expulsion or massacre of nonconforming populations, (2) promotion of preferred versions of national languages, names, costumes, rituals, monuments, museums, histories, and educational programs. State-seeking nationalism entails demands by self-identified agents of a currently stateless nation that it acquire control of its own state, or at least distinct political standing within an existing state. Historically, it has typically involved its own versions of the suppression and promotion that characterize state-led nationalism, including struggles among rival leaders for recognition as authentic interlocutors for the stateless population. To those features it typically adds concerted resistance to state-led nationalism on the part of the state(s) within whose jurisdiction the stateless population currently resides and appeals to external parties for support of claims to recognition and autonomy.

Culturally informed political processes forged causal links from (1) transformations of states to (2) state-led nationalism to (3) state-seeking nationalism, and thence to (4) the international modeling of state structures on which John Meyer fixes our attention. To put it schematically, the same processes of extraction, conquest, centralization, bypassing of intermediaries, and bargaining with subject populations that yielded direct rule and citizenship also gave surviving rulers interests, incentives, and opportunities to impose their favored versions of national culture on their citizenry. But rulers' promotion of state-led nationalism stimulated state-seeking nationalism in three ways: by inciting mobilization and resistance on the part of culturally distinct minorities within their own territories; by justifying intervention across state boundaries by outsiders who claimed (often correctly) to be defending distinct nations from oppression or extinction; and by providing prestigious and exportable models of matching between state and nation.

Although no true large nation-state ever formed anywhere (even ostensibly homogeneous Sweden today contains substantial Sami- and Finnish-speaking territories, not to mention thousands of Asian immigrants), the organization of nationhood from top or bottom became a standard internationally supported form of politics. In composite newly independent states, indeed, the top-down and bottom-up forms of nationalism commonly accompanied and reinforced each other, as the faction that held power at independence forwarded its own version of the nation and organized segments of the population that would thereby lose their distinctness fought for political autonomy.

As in the cases of citizenship and democracy, nationalism exhibits the paradox of a general process characterized by path-dependent particularism. On one side, classic mechanisms of invention, ramification, emulation, and adaptation recur in the generation of nationalist claims. On the other side, each new assertion of nationalism responds to its immediate historical and cultural context, then modifies conditions for the next assertion of nationalism. Like all culturally constrained social processes, nationalism proceeds in cultural ruts that greatly limit the directions it can go, relies on collective learning, but by its very exercise alters relations—including shared understandings—among parties to its claims.

Repertoires of Contention

The paradox and its resolution appear even more clearly in changes of state-linked repertoires of contention. They bring together general causal mechanisms with particular, path-dependent arrays of action. As compared with the irrationalist portrayals of collective behavior that once dominated studies of popular contention or the strongly rationalist accounts that first displaced them, the last few decades' research has generally documented the narrow range of performances people employ repeatedly in contentious claim-making within any particular time, place, and social relation. That range is always far smaller than the set of performances of which members of the population are technically capable—at least as indicated by identification of logically possible but empty spaces between established performances, by interactions the same people carry out in other settings, and by comparison with similar populations elsewhere. Today's Western social-movement activists repeatedly create associations, hold public meetings, demonstrate, and organize petition drives, but they do not mount guerrilla warfare or assassinate heads of state as their counterparts in other times and places have often done. As the example indicates, claim-making performances covary in sets we can call "repertoires," one repertoire for each ensemble of actors who frequently make collective claims on each other. In the case of social movements, a common ensemble consists of movement activists, police, authorities, organized movement opponents, and various audiences.

On the whole, contentious repertoires evolve slowly and incrementally, chiefly through innovations at the edges of existing performances. Their patterns of change strikingly resemble those of language, of organizational form, and of prevailing artistic styles. They share with those phenomena:

- embeddedness in complex networks among multiple parties having partly competing interests
- engagement in communication among those parties and coordination of their interactions
- use of compressed codes whose comprehension depends heavily on prior experience and previous interaction with the same parties

- activation of previously negotiated agreements, implicit or explicit, concerning the conditions and limits of different sorts of interaction among the parties

In short, repertoires of contention are ineradicably cultural phenomena. They originate, survive, and change not in individual consciousness or in something abstract we might call "the Culture" but within concrete social relations among political actors. They differ from language, organizational form, and artistic style by always involving agents of governments as participants or monitors. Indeed, state agents intervene incessantly to promote, channel, contain, redirect, or repress particular kinds of contentious performances. In the process, their interaction with nongovernmental contenders produces a whole body of law and public practice concerning assembly, association, speech, petition, strike activity, policing, and arming. Much of the detailed legal and practical apparatus of democracy emerges from struggle over the proper forms of claim-making.

Although he draws explicit concepts chiefly from Pierre Bourdieu and James Scott rather than from theorists of social movements, democracy, or contentious politics, Nader Sohrabi's contribution to this book nicely analyzes mutations in contentious repertoires. As Sohrabi shows, the availability of coupled understandings and forms of action—in the instance, the House of Justice story and the routine of praising the shah while lambasting his advisers—channeled collective claim-making in the Iran of 1906, then facilitated a new synthesis of claim-making routines combining "traditional" and "constitutionalist" elements.

Contentious repertoires provide splendid illustrations of culture's general place in state-connected political processes. Existing repertoires incorporate collectively learned shared understandings concerning what forms of claim-making are possible, desirable, risky, expensive, or probable, as well as what consequences different possible forms of claim-making are likely to produce. They greatly constrain the contentious claims political actors make on each other and on agents of the state. They change incrementally through collective interaction. In telling and acting on established stories about feasible, desirable, and effective forms of claim-making, people transform both stories and collective action. Like citizenship, democracy, and nationalism, in short, contentious repertoires and their changes illustrate the value of relational approaches to the place of culture in state-linked social processes.

What claims, then, do I make for my hasty review of a complex subject? Certainly not that it provides handy solutions for all the problems raised by this book's rich studies of states, culture, and state-culture interaction. Let me insist only on these points: that uncertainty about culture's ontological standing is currently undermining strenuous efforts to integrate cultural analysis into studies of political processes; that a thoroughgoing relational ontology facilitates just such efforts; and that in a relational perspective such apparently disparate political phenomena as nationalism and democracy share significant causal mechanisms despite the very different concatenation of those mechanisms in particular cultural settings. Now where? Toward relational analyses of political processes.

Name Index

Subject Index

The Wilder House Series in Politics, History and Culture

A Series Edited by David Laitin and George Steinmetz